CHILD WELFARE CASE RECORDS

THE UNIVERSITY OF CHICAGO PRESS
CHICAGO, ILLINOIS

—

THE BAKER & TAYLOR COMPANY
NEW YORK

THE CAMBRIDGE UNIVERSITY PRESS
LONDON

THE MARUZEN-KABUSHIKI-KAISHA
TOKYO, OSAKA, KYOTO, FUKUOKA, SENDAI

THE COMMERCIAL PRESS, LIMITED
SHANGHAI

CHILD WELFARE CASE RECORDS

EDITED BY

WILMA WALKER

Associate Professor of Case Work
School of Social Service Administration, University of Chicago

THE UNIVERSITY OF CHICAGO PRESS
CHICAGO · ILLINOIS

PREFACE

Child welfare case records are continually in demand, not only by instructors in schools of social work for teaching purposes, but also by social workers who are constantly seeking new and better methods of work. The eighteen case records in this volume were selected from a number of records generously loaned from the files of the children's agencies in Chicago and the outlying community, and then edited and mimeographed for the use of classes in child welfare case work in the School of Social Service Administration, University of Chicago. During this period of classroom use, the records that proved to be most valuable for teaching purposes were selected and re-edited for publication in order that they might be made available to meet the wider demand for teaching material in this field.

Social workers know that the assembling of a collection of records is not a simple task. The perfect record has never been kept, and many social workers are reluctant to have their records so minutely scrutinized. Many of the limitations of case work arise out of the limitations of the social thinking of the period and also out of the limitations of the resources of the community. When records are published, they are almost inevitably soon out of date in many ways, and agency workers not infrequently are unwilling to have their work of several years ago used for criticism in the light of more recent theories and practice. However, the old record may still remain of value to the student, for the problems do not change so radically, and it is good practice for students to consider in their thinking the various possibilities in treatment in addition to the policies that were used in the cases selected.

Some workers also sincerely object to having such confidential material as case records published even after careful editing. Sharing every desire to preserve the confidential character of this material, every effort has been made to protect the anonymity of these records. All proper names have been carefully disguised, and, in some few cases, when the agency so requested, even the dates were changed to make any identification impossible. It is believed that the information in these materials, presented to meet the needs of professional workers and of professional students in professional schools, has been protected against any possible misuse.

These eighteen records were selected from the files of seven different child welfare agencies dealing with dependent children. In many of these

vii

records the student learns also of the work of the other agencies which co-operated with those especially organized for work with children, and such agencies as the United Charities, the Cook County Bureau of Public Welfare, the Jewish Social Service Bureau, and various medical agencies appear frequently in this material. The main function of these seven children's agencies (with the exception of the Mothers' Pension Division of the Cook County Juvenile Court) is the placement and supervision of children in foster-homes. In several of these cases, however, the children were kept in their own homes under supervision. In three cases it was possible to keep the children with their parents through the help of a housekeeper. In some cases the children were placed away from home.

One record was furnished by the Mothers' Pension Department of the Juvenile Court of Cook County. Five records were contributed by the child-placing division of the Joint Service Bureau for Children's Institutions, a private agency which has carried on the placing of dependent Negro children in foster-homes because there was no adequate institutional provision for this group.

Five records were selected from the files of the Chicago Orphan Asylum, the agency founded for the care of children orphaned in the great cholera epidemic of 1851. A large and very well-equipped institution for children was maintained for many years, but in the last decade the whole program of this agency has been brought in line with the best modern standards of boarding-home care, with the large congregate institution given up for a small receiving home where children may be kept for a short time, and two cottages for small groups of children.

The Chicago Home for the Friendless furnished three records. This is another of Chicago's earliest social agencies, and for many years this Home furnished only temporary institutional care for children. More recently, however, the agency added a Visiting Housekeeping Department to its services and thereby made it possible to leave children in their own homes instead of removing them when the mother became ill or for any other reason became unable to care for them. The agency has now entirely abandoned its institutional program, and housekeeping service and foster-home care are exclusively used for the children.

Two records were furnished by the Jewish Home Finding Society, an agency for the placement of children in foster-homes. This agency also furnishes a housekeeping service, making it possible in one of these cases for a father to keep his children with him when their mother died.

The record of a family with many children was furnished by the Illinois

Children's Home and Aid Society, a state-wide placement agency interested in dependent children throughout Illinois. This agency, which has a central office in Chicago, maintains a receiving home, two institutions for a small number of children, and places many children over the state in boarding-homes, free homes, and wage homes.

The Children's Service League of Sangamon County, with headquarters in Springfield, Illinois, an agency which places children in foster-homes throughout the county, contributed one case record on which they co-operated with the State Department of Public Welfare and the Illinois Children's Home and Aid Society.

On the whole, the material is presented as it appears in the original records; but there has been some deletion to avoid repetition, and some summary letters and reports have been omitted when the material has been included in the body of the record.

Finally, it should be said that these cases are not presented because they illustrate the best methods of work or because the records are especially satisfactory or well written. They were selected rather because of the variety of problems presented and because of the clearness and directness with which the situations, and in some cases the treatment, have been recorded. In many of these cases much more detail in process of treatment would have been desirable.

No attempt is made to interpret the case work in the records. It is believed that each teacher will prefer to analyze and interpret the work in her own way, that interpretations and lists of questions often interfere with the student's thinking and analyses. Only those explanations are made that seem necessary in order to give the reader an understanding of the local situation and resources. It must be constantly kept in mind, however, in all the discussions of these records, that the case work was carried on in the years between 1929 and 1936—a time of great unemployment, of very heavy "case loads" in many agencies, and of serious inadequacies in all services. These are children's agency records, but they were affected in many ways by the difficulties of the period.

Deep appreciation is expressed of the help of the executives of the agencies who so generously offered these records. Special acknowledgment should be made of the help given by Miss Ethel Verry, of the Chicago Orphan Asylum; Mr. Jacob Kepecs, of the Jewish Home Finding Society; Mr. Louis Evans, formerly of the Joint Service Bureau's Placement Division and now of the School of Social Work of the University of Indiana; Miss Ruth Burbridge, also of the Joint Service Bureau; Mr. C. V. Williams, of the Illinois Children's Home and Aid Society; Mrs.

Elizabeth Littler of the Chicago Home for the Friendless; Miss Mildred Arnold, formerly of the Children's Service League of Sangamon County and now director of the Children's Division of the Department of Public Welfare of the State of Indiana; and to Mr. Harry Hill, chief probation officer, and Mrs. Mary McPartlin, head of the Mothers' Pension Division, of the Cook County Juvenile Court. Warm appreciation must also be expressed to Dean Edith Abbott, of the School of Social Service Administration, for her encouragement and guidance in the publication of teaching material for the use of students; to Miss S. P. Breckinridge and Mr. Harrison A. Dobbs of the faculty of the School of Social Service for valuable counsel and advice at many points; and to Miss Eulah Belle Orr, formerly field-work instructor in Child Welfare in the School of Social Service Administration and now of the Omaha Child Welfare Association, and to Miss Gladys G. Fraser, formerly field-work assistant and now of the staff of the Indiana Children's Division, for their help in the reading of records during the early stages of this work. Finally, the financial assistance given by the Local Community Research Committee (now the Social Science Research Committee) of the University of Chicago and by the Samuel Deutsch Foundation of the School of Social Service Administration is gratefully acknowledged. Acknowledgment is also made of the assistance of Miss M. E. Lavery, who helped in many ways in the preparation of the material for the press, in proofreading, and in the preparation of the Index.

WILMA WALKER

SCHOOL OF SOCIAL SERVICE ADMINISTRATION
UNIVERSITY OF CHICAGO
April 9, 1937

TABLE OF CONTENTS

SECTION I

CASE RECORDS OF CHILDREN WHO WERE SUPERVISED IN THE HOMES OF THEIR PARENTS BY THE CHILDREN'S AGENCY

1. The Children of Antonio and Mary Morotto

(Two Children Whose Father Is Incapacitated Are Supported by a Mothers' Pension and Continue To Live with Their Parents)

April 2, 1929.—Mrs. Morotto came to the Juvenile Court to apply for Mothers' Pension for her three children. She had her husband's second papers, dated December 7, 1918, taken out in the United States District Court. He has been ill since May, 1928. He has been in the County Hospital for the past five weeks.

There are three Morotto children: Rose, eight years; Susie, five years; and Rocco, three years of age.

State of Illinois
County of Cook } ss.   Mary Morotto

Being first duly sworn, on oath doth depose and say that the written statement under the various printed headings on the opposite side of this application card were voluntarily made by this affiant and written thereon by direction of this affiant and that the statements thereon, both written and printed, are true in substance and in fact.

[*Signed*] MARY MOROTTO

(This applies to face sheet information)

Agencies and persons interested reported by Social Service Exchange:

Agency	Name	Date
County Welfare..............	Morotto, Antonio, Mary	November 14, 1928
Family Agency—Union District	Morotto, Antonio, Mary	October 29, 1928
Free Dispensary No. 82278.....	Morotto, Antonio, Mary	August 7, 1928
Children's Protective Agency No. 55354................	Morotto, Antonio, Mary	July 12, 1928
Infant Welfare Society No. 7785	Morotto, Antonio, Mary	December 6, 1927
Warner Dispensary No. 48302..	Morotto, Antonio, Mary	May 24, 1926

June 4, 1929.—Letter written to the medical social worker at Warner Hospital by Probation Officer of the Juvenile Court:

Mrs. Mary Morotto has made application to this court for assistance under the "Mother's Pension Act." Before this aid can be granted, it is necessary for this department to be informed concerning the mother's mental, physical, and moral fitness to care for her children.

Social Service Bureau shows that you registered on this family May 24, 1926.

Will you kindly send us a detailed report concerning your contact with the family so that we may be fully advised in making our recommendation to the Judge of this court.

Thanking you kindly for your co-operation in this matter, I remain

Later.—Report received from Warner Hospital:

Mary Morotto was treated in our Skin Clinic for a slight non-infectious rash in June, 1926. We have no social information on this family.

June 5, 1929.—Letter received by the Chief Probation Officer of the Juvenile Court from the County Welfare Bureau:

In compliance with your request of June 1, we are sending the following report of our contact with the Morotto family:

Mrs. Morotto applied to us for assistance on October 30, 1928, as Mr. Morotto was suffering with swollen legs and had been unemployed since May, 1928. He was then receiving treatment at the Free Dispensary. Since then we have been sending a Number 3 ration,[1] coal, and one quart of milk a day.

Mr. Morotto was sent to Veterans' Hospital in November and was discharged in December, 1928. It was suggested that work in damp places would aggravate his arthritic condition. He could do light work only; and on May 17, 1929, Mrs. Morotto informed us that he had found work as a watchman, but she could give no further information nor has Mr. Morotto called at our office since, as we requested, to give us further details.

June 11, 1929.—Letter received by the Chief Probation Officer of the Juvenile Court from the Children's Protective Agency:

In reply to your letter of June 1 requesting information regarding our contact with the Morotto family, we send the following report:

On July 6, 1928, Mrs. Morotto came to us saying that her husband had been sick for two months, was not working, and was drinking heavily.

Our worker visited, found Mr. Morotto at home, and had a talk with him. He claimed to be too sick to work, but had never had a physical examination. Our worker advised him to go to the Free Dispensary, which he did not do. We later found that the family was being assisted by the Family Agency, and when

[1] [Number 3 Ration at this time consisted of $5.29 worth of staple groceries delivered once every month.]

Mrs. Morotto came to us again for help we referred her to the Union District Office of the Family Agency.

We had no further contact.

June 12, 1929.—Letter received by the Probation Officer from the Social Service Department of Free Dispensary:

In answer to your letter of June 1 would say that Mr. Morotto reported at our General Medicine Clinic August 6, 1928, at which time he was referred to the Orthopedic Department because of flat feet. A Wassermann taken August 7, 1928, was negative. Patient was examined in our Dental Department November 8, 1929, at which time one tooth was extracted, and he was instructed to return to University Dental College for the necessary fillings and cleaning of teeth. On December 28 when he was seen in our Orthopedic Department he stated that his tonsils had recently been removed. Patient was last seen in our Orthopedic Department January 15, 1929, at which time his feet were somewhat improved.

This patient was referred to us by the Family Agency, Union District.

June 18, 1929.—Letter received by Probation Officer from the Infant Welfare Society:

We find Mrs. Morotto, living at 345 Farragut Street, a very good mother. The children are well cared for and co-operation with us has been very good.

August 22, 1929.—Called. Mrs. Morotto states that Mr. Morotto's health is much improved and that he is working regularly.

August 29, 1929.—Recommendation—dismissed. Man working.

September 16, 1930.—Reapplication. Mrs. Morotto in office to reapply for the pension, having been sent in by Miss Marony of the Charitable Society.[2] She states that Mr. Morotto has been in the Veterans' Hospital for four months. The Charitable Society and the County Welfare Bureau are assisting her.

Telephoned Miss Marony of the Charitable Society. She stated she had spoken to Miss Gibbons of the Juvenile Court over the telephone with regard to Mrs. Morotto's reapplication for a pension. She will send a report of Mr. Morotto's condition as soon as they get one.

September 27, 1930.—Letter received by Juvenile Court from Charitable Society:

Following your request of September 17, we are enclosing letters of June 13 and September 18 from the Veterans' Hospital regarding Mr. Morotto's condition.

Enclosure, dated June 13, 1930:

This will acknowledge receipt of your letter of June 3, 1930, requesting information regarding above-named veteran. Mr. Morotto was admitted to this

[2] [The Charitable Society is maintained by the Catholic Church.]

hospital on May 27, 1930, and has been given diagnosis of psychosis with other somatic disease (pellagra). It is believed that hospitalization will be required indefinitely.

Owing to Mr. Morotto's mental condition we are unable to secure information from him in regard to his compensation. However, the files here show that he has no service-connected disability so that he is not entitled to compensation.

Enclosure, dated September 18, 1930:

This will acknowledge receipt of your communication of recent date, making inquiry relative to above-named veteran. Please refer to communication sent you on June 15, 1930. This veteran has recovered from his psychosis, and his physical condition has improved somewhat, but he is considered to be totally and permanently incapacitated. The prognosis is, of course, guarded. It cannot be stated at this time just how much longer it will be necessary to hospitalize him, but it will undoubtedly be for a long period of time.

As you were previously informed, he is not entitled to compensation, neither is he entitled to disability allowance as he was not in service a sufficient length of time to make him eligible.

We shall appreciate hearing from you as to whether or not Mrs. Morotto is granted a pension.

October 24, 1930.—Letter received by Probation Officer from the Board of County Commissioners:

This will introduce Mrs. Mary Morotto, who resides at 320 Farragut Street, second floor, rear.

Mrs. Morotto's husband is a war veteran who was so badly gassed that he has been in the Veterans' Hospital for the past four or five years. She is not receiving relief from the government. I have just requested that she be assisted with County aid, and I would like to have you arrange to have her application taken for a mother's pension as soon as there is an available opening.

November 3, 1930.—Mrs. Morotto in the office. She showed her marriage certificate giving the date of marriage as February 12, 1921, but it was not signed. She said that later her marriage had been blessed at All Saints Church. She showed birth certificates from the Chicago Health Department for her three children:

Rose Morotto, born August 23, 1922, at 345 Farragut Street—C.H D. No. 98372
Susie Morotto, born May 22, 1925, at 345 Farragut Stree —C H.D. No. 22165
Antonio Morotto, born October 9, 1927, at 345 Farragut Street—C.H.D. No. 74932

Mrs. Morotto said that her mother had eight children, one of whom died. The others are listed on the face card. Mr. Morotto has only his father in Italy and one brother in Chicago. All other relatives are dead.

The County Bureau is supporting Mrs. Morotto and the children.

November 15, 1930.—Verified marriage of Antonio Morotto and Mary Simonelli, which took place February 12, 1921. License No. 42361, recorded in Volume A. Ceremony performed by Manus Donohoo. License returned February 21, 1921.

Later.—Read record of Mrs. Morotto's mother, Mrs. Marie Simonelli, who received a Mothers' Pension from December 21, 1922, to October 8, 1925. Mrs. Morotto's father, who was a laborer, died of pneumonia in 1921. Both her parents were born in Italy. Her mother attended citizenship classes at Neighborhood House faithfully and learned English. Other members of the family attended Neighborhood House classes and clubs. When Mrs. Morotto was interviewed in February, 1922, regarding assisting her mother, she said that she was unable to do so because her husband worked irregularly. She was afraid that if she went to work herself that he would not work at all. She said that her marriage was unhappy and if she had known her father would die she would never have married. Mrs. Morotto was a child of about two years when her father, who had previously come to the United States, sent for her and her mother. She seemed to take a real interest in her mother, brothers, and sisters, and frequently took them for medical care as suggested by the court officer.

November 17, 1930.—Called upon Mrs. Simonelli, mother of Mrs. Morotto. They live in a four-room flat and pay $18 per month rent. Mrs. Simonelli says that she is afraid to move into better rooms with times as uncertain as they now are. Her family consists of herself and six children, only one under working age. Joseph is employed in a candy factory but is getting only from two to four days' work a week. When he works full time he earns $25 per week. Carlotta is a file clerk and earns $14 per week. Frances earns $16 per week. John has stomach trouble and is not well enough to work. Andrew is an errand boy and earns $10 per week.

Later.—Called upon Mrs. Morotto. Checked Rocco's birth certificate, which is in the name of Antonio. Mrs. Morotto said she supposed the midwife made a mistake in sending in the registration. Rose attends All Saints School. She formerly attended Phillips School, but the County Bureau encouraged a change to parochial school, which Mrs. Morotto does not like as books and paper are not free. Mrs. Morotto could not give the names of any employers of Mr. Morotto, who worked for so many different companies for only short periods of time. He was a sewer-digger.

The Fourteenth Division of American War Mothers pays Mrs. Morotto's gas and electricity bills. Mrs. Morotto sends her bills each month to Mrs. Shane, 231 Campbell Avenue, telephone Blue Ridge 405, who is one of the officers in the Division. This aid was arranged through Miss Arthur, social worker at Veterans' Hospital.

Later.—Called upon Mrs. Pinelli, present landlady. Mrs. Morotto moved into her present rooms in June, 1930. Mrs. Pinelli understood that she had lived in Chicago since childhood though she did not know her until she moved to the present address.

Later.—Called upon Mrs. Fouletti, 345 Farragut Street, former landlady. Mrs. Morotto owed four months' rent when she moved out. Mrs. Fouletti realizes that Mrs. Morotto had no money to pay and could not help this. Mrs. Fouletti liked her and Mr. Morotto very well. They were good, dependable tenants, and Mrs. Fouletti would like to have them back. The Morottos were there for several years, Mrs. Fouletti said about ten years. They moved away last summer.

Later.—Called upon Mr. Felix Morotto, brother of Mr. Morotto. He said that he, too, is a sewer-digger but has been unemployed for six months. He has a wife and four children. He could not give the names of any of Mr. Morotto's employers except the last one, who he said was dead. Mr. Morotto never worked for any one concern more than six months because of the nature of his work. Both Mr. Felix Morotto and Mr. Antonio Morotto were born in France, their parents having emigrated there from Italy.[3] Both boys attended school in France and learned to read and write. Mr. Felix Morotto went to school three years. He does not know how much schooling his brother had. Mr. Antonio Morotto cannot read or write English.

Mr. Felix Morotto says that they have been unable to help the Morottos. Their own rent is $25 per month. There are no other relatives in the United States. An aged father is in Italy.

Later.—Telephoned Mrs. Shane of American War Mothers. They have given no assistance except to provide a coat for Rose. Mrs. Morotto has asked that they provide underwear for the children. She said that they need no other clothing at present. Mrs. Shane believes that Mrs. Morotto is very reasonable in her requests and a very intelligent mother. They have visited her in her home. The probation officer asked that they care for the family at Christmas. As the Division has a meeting November 21, 1930, Mrs. Shane will take up this matter and if they decide to take the family

[3] [The family lived in France for eighteen years and then moved back to Italy.]

will register with the Christmas Bureau.[4] They plan to provide the underwear needed for the children.

November 18, 1930.—The following report was received from the principal of All Saints School in response to a request from the Probation Officer:

TO THE JUDGES OF THE JUVENILE COURT:

The records of this school show the following in the case of the above-named child [Rose Morotto]:

Record of attendance for the term beginning Sept. 3, 1930. ABSENCES: Excused, 2—Unexcused, 0; DEPORTMENT, Excellent; GRADE, 3; SCHOLARSHIP, Good; DATE OF BIRTH: Aug. 23, 1922

SUMMARY

(Prepared November 17, 1930, by Probation Officer for the Judge of the Juvenile Court)

Morotto, Antonio and Mary, 320 Farragut Street

Citizenship.—Mr. Morotto has second papers taken out in the United States District Court December 7, 1918. Seen by Miss Huggins upon application.

Residence.—Verified by present landlady, Mrs. Pinelli, and by former landlady, Mrs. Fouletti. See dictation November 17, 1930.

Incapacity.—Mr. Morotto is diagnosed (Veterans' Bureau Report, June 16, 1930) as having psychosis and other somatic disease (pellagra). A later report (Veterans' Bureau, September 18, 1930) states that he has recovered from the psychosis but is permanently and totally incapacitated. He is now in the Veterans' Hospital.

Marriage.—Verified at County Clerk's office. See dictation November 15, 1930. Antonio Morotto and Mary Simonelli, February 12, 1921. License No. 42361, recorded in Volume A.

Births.—Rose Morotto, born August 23, 1922, City Health Department No. 98372; Susie Morotto, born May 22, 1925, City Health Department No. 22165; Antonio Morotto, born October 9, 1927, City Health Department No. 74932 (Rocco). See dictation November 3, 1930.

---

[4] [At Christmas time the Council of Social Agencies of the City of Chicago attempts to direct the indiscriminate giving of Christmas baskets. A clearing house, called the Christmas Bureau, is set up where the names of needy families may be sent and where those persons who wish to give may register and get the names of those in need. This service helps to avoid duplication and also to make sure that especially needy families are not forgotten.]

Resources.—County Bureau is paying rent of $16 and giving allowance of $4.00 per week and the Fourteenth Division Chapter of the American War Mothers pays gas and electric bills, which usually is under $2.00. See dictation November 17, 1930. Mr. Morotto is not entitled to any compensation from the United States government for his army service. See letter from Veterans' Bureau, September 18, 1930.

Property.—None.

History.—Mrs. Morotto was but two years old when her father, who had come to the United States previously, sent to Italy for her and her mother. Her father was a laborer and died in 1921 of pneumonia. Her mother received a Mothers' Pension from December 21, 1922, to October 8, 1925. Mr. Morotto was a sewer-digger and had somewhat irregular employment until about a year ago, when he became too ill to do any work. He is of Italian descent, though born in France, where his parents lived for about eighteen years.

Relatives.—Mrs. Simonelli, 432 Cambridge Avenue, mother of Mrs. Morotto. Joseph Simonelli, 432 Cambridge Avenue, brother of Mrs. Morotto. Carlotta Simonelli, 432 Cambridge Avenue, sister of Mrs. Morotto. Frances Simonelli, 432 Cambridge Avenue, sister of Mrs. Morotto. John Simonelli, 432 Cambridge Avenue, brother of Mrs. Morotto. Andrew Simonelli, 432 Cambridge Avenue, brother of Mrs. Morotto. Paul Simonelli, 432 Cambridge Avenue, brother of Mrs. Morotto.

As stated above, Mrs. Simonelli formerly received a Mothers' Pension, which was stayed October 8, 1925, because her family became self-supporting. None of the children except Mrs. Morotto is married. Joseph, the oldest of those at home, is twenty-five years old. Four of them are working though none earning much. For detailed report see dictation November 17, 1930. Felix Morotto, 2239 E. Kaster Street, brother of Mr. Morotto is a sewer-digger and has been unemployed for the past six months. He is married and has four children. He is unable to assist. See dictation November 17, 1930.

School.—Rose attends the All Saints School. Mrs. Morotto states that she is in third grade. School report sent for November 17, 1930.

November 20, 1930.—Recommendation. Grant $55.[5]

February 12, 1931.—Letter received by the Probation Officer from Mrs. Morotto:

Will you please call at the hospital and ask for social service, Miss Arthur, and ask her if the war mothers will keep up paying my gas bills. Please let me

[5] [This is still dependent on diagnosis of total and permanent incapacity of Mr. Morotto.]

know. I forgot to tell you the doctor's name the day you came to see me. When you call at the hospital ask for Dr. Fuller. That is the doctor that took care of him for ten months, and he will tell you all about his disability.

September 15, 1931.—Mrs. Morotto said that she has been looking for a flat farther west and asked officer's permission to move. They are paying $16 for a three-room flat with no bath. The rooms are small and dark. Mr. Morotto has been complaining of a tight feeling in his chest. He was advised to return to the Veterans' Hospital for an examination and treatment. Rose and Rocco are to have their tonsils removed at the County Hospital on November 29. Rose and Susie attend the All Saints School. Rose is in the fourth grade and Susie in the first. Mr. Morotto expressed his willingness to do some type of work in the home after the officer suggested that she would write to the Shut-in Society for work.

October 2, 1931.—Mrs. Morotto promised the worker to go to Neighborhood House and register in the cooking classes. She is unable to prepare the proper dishes for her husband, who is on a diet.

November 2, 1931.—Letter written by the Juvenile Court to the County Bureau:

May we refer the Morotto family (Antonio and Mary) 320 Farragut Street to you for supplementation. Mr. Morotto has been in the U.S. Veterans' Hospital because of psychosis and pellagra. He is unable to work. The children are attending the All Saints School and are good students. You will note in the attached budget, the family are $30 below.

We are asking that you supplement as much as you can. The children are attending the Barnard Dispensary and are underweight.

We would appreciate it if you will take care of this family at your earliest possible convenience.

November 18, 1931.—Mr. Morotto is planning to return to the Veterans' Hospital for treatment. Rose has gained two pounds. Family has been referred to the County Bureau for supplementation.

December 11, 1931.—Mrs. Morotto has taken Mr. Morotto to the Veterans' Hospital for an examination. She is to return during the week for further examinations. County Bureau has paid one month's rent for her. The children were running temperature at the time they reported to County Hospital for tonsillectomy and were unable to have their tonsils removed. They are to return in April. Mrs. Shane of the War Mothers will take care of the family for Christmas.

January 4, 1932.—Mrs. Morotto has not taken Mr. Morotto to the hospital for an examination because of lack of funds. Advised her that Mrs. Shane of War Mothers would reimburse her for the carfare, and asked her to call Mrs. Shane and tell her when she would go to the hospital. The War Mothers supplied family with clothing and a large basket of food. Mrs. Morotto has been borrowing money from a neighbor, in order that she may purchase food at the cheaper stores. Spoke to Mrs. Morotto of the necessity of keeping Rose in bed in the morning instead of sending her to early mass.

January 17, 1932.—Letter received by Juvenile Court from the Veterans' Hospital:

Replying to your letter of December 24, 1931, requesting information on Antonio Morotto, we submit the following.

He was admitted to the Veterans' Hospital May 27, 1930, for treatment of Pellagra and Neuritis. He was discharged February 6, 1931, with maximum hospital benefit. The diagnosis upon discharge was Pellagra, Psychosis, with other somatic diseases, in stage of remission, Polyneuritis, Tachycardia moderate. The claimant gained in weight and he gave no indication of mental abnormality at the time of discharge. No evidence of Tachycardia. His prognosis was favorable. Estimate of average impairment of earning capacity for present or pre-war occupation of laborer was moderate. Proper diet and general hygienic measures were recommended. A diet of beef juice, green vegetables, Brewers yeast, eggs, fruit, and food light in starches was recommended. There is no service connected with this disability, and the disability allowance was disallowed as the claimant did not aggregate a total of ninety days before the Armistice was signed which was necessary. He enlisted November 6, 1918, and was discharged December 31, 1918.

February 3, 1932.—Mrs. Morotto was not at home. Mr. Morotto was advised to return to the Veterans' Hospital for re-examination. He said that Rose is now attending mass only once a week. The worker cautioned him about making her go to early mass because of her weakened condition.

May 5, 1932.—Rose was to make her first Communion so she had a new white outfit which was made by a neighbor woman. She was very excited about it. All three children are attending Neighborhood House classes. Rose does drawing there in which she has a very great interest. All the children are attending Barnard Dispensary. Rose had an abscessed tooth removed at County Dental Clinic.

May 14, 1932.—Request sent by Juvenile Court to Barnard Hospital:

May we have a report as to the diagnosis, probability of recovery, and your plan of treatment for Mrs. Mary Morotto and her children at your dispensary, in order that we may co-operate with you?

If there is need of special diet, will you kindly state the kind and amount of food, in order that we may provide for it in the family budget.

May 19, 1932.—Following reply received from Barnard Hospital:

Rose and Rocco have not been in for six months. Mrs. Mary Morotto is not registered here. Rose has made one visit since our report of November 10, 1931. On March 26, 1932, she was examined and found ready for a tonsillectomy.

May 27, 1932.—Letter received by the Probation Officer from the Nutrition Center:

I am inclosing an application blank to Green Valley Farm for Rose Morotto, which I have partially filled out. I am unable to fill in a great deal of the information. Will you kindly complete this record and return it to Mrs. Allan Williams at 8970 Washington Boulevard?

Mrs. Morotto is very anxious to have Rose go to the Farm this summer. Miss Foster probably has talked with you about this.

Later.—Note received by Probation Officer from Mrs. Morotto:

Monday afternoon when I came back from the Juvenile, the lady next door told me she was going to Northwood to see her sister-in law. And they told me if I want to take a ride with the children, and I thought on my way I'd stop to Veterans' Hospital and tell Dr. Fuller that you wrote him two letters and he did not answer them cause they were not addressed to the manager of the hospital and I showed him your letter and he said, whenever you write to him, address it just as he's got it here in your letter.

He is very sorry that he did not receive your letters, he's willing to answer your letters any time you write to him. Please write to him soon cause he might leave for a vacation.

June 3, 1932.—Rose had not been very well. Her face was flushed and she had a hacking cough. Mrs. Morotto has her rest in the afternoon. The mother appears to be very intelligent. She is careful about the appearance of the children and also of her housekeeping. Mr. Morotto spends most of his time about the house but he is unable to assist very much. He will go back to the Veterans' Hospital for an examination as health reports must be secured for all incapacitated men every six months.

Veterans' Bureau of the County Bureau has sent supplies which include thirty quarts of milk and Number 3 rations.

June 13, 1932.—Mrs. Morotto took Rose to the Hospital for a tonsillectomy, but as she had a high temperature they would not perform it. She is anxious to get Rose cared for at Green Valley Farm.

June 14, 1932.—Miss Bell, nurse, was seen regarding the securing of a date for a tonsillectomy for Rose. She told Mrs. Morotto to have the child examined at the Tuberculosis Sanitarium as she had a bad cough.

Mrs. Morotto was seen in the office. She asked that a history of Rose's health condition be sent to Memorial Hospital. The attending physician at the Tuberculosis Sanitarium advised Mrs. Morotto to place the child in Memorial Hospital for observation care.

Later.—Tuberculosis Sanitarium was called. Doctor gave the same report that Mrs. Morotto had given.

Letter written to Memorial Hospital:

Rose Morotto, one of our pensioned children, was recommended for Green Valley Farm by Dr. Wynetti of the Nutrition Center on May 27, 1932. She had enlarged tonsils and slightly enlarged thyroid at that time. Rose was examined at Memorial Hospital for tonsillectomy June 6, 1932. At that time she had had a temperature for about two weeks. She was told to return June 16, 1932, for an examination and appointment for a tonsillectomy.

She was examined at the Tuberculosis Sanitarium on June 14, 1932. By telephone it was learned from the examining physician then that he found her tonsils to be enlarged. He recommended that Rose be placed under observation care at Memorial Hospital for a week in order to determine the cause of her continual temperature

If, in your judgment, Rose should be placed under observation care, we should appreciate it very much if you would arrange to care for her in your hospital.

June 15, 1932.—Mrs. Morotto was examined by Dr. Jones on May 31, 1932. She has tachycardia. Otherwise physical findings were negative. She is not physically able to do any work beside the care of her three children and her household work. Mr. Morotto was examined by Dr. Jones on May 31, 1932. He is not able to do laborious work but could do some light work.

Dr. Fuller of Veterans' Hospital stated through telephone conversations of June 13, 1932, that he had not seen Mr. Morotto since February 6, 1931, but according to the diagnosis of Mr. Morotto's condition at the time of discharge, which was pellagra, the doctor was under the impression that the man's condition would not have improved. Dr. Fuller would give a definite answer after he has re-examined Mr. Morotto.

Letter written to Veterans' Hospital by Juvenile Court:

May we have a written report as to the present condition of Antonio Morotto, who was re-examined at your hospital on June 8, 1932.

I am enclosing Mr. Morotto's consent for this information. We should appreciate it if you could give us an immediate reply, as this report will be used to facilitate the securing of additional assistance for the family.

June 17, 1932.—Letter received by Juvenile Court from Memorial Hospital:

Rose Morotto reported to Medical Clinic on June 15, where a diagnosis of upper respiratory infection and chronic hypertrophied tonsils was made. The doctor did not seem to think it advisable to admit this child to the hospital, as her record states her temperature varies between 99° and 100°. At the time of her examination here her temperature was 99°.2. The doctor thought that the temperature variations were due to the upper respiratory infection and the in-flamed throat.

As the child's pulse was 120, the physician thought that there was some indi-cation of thyroid disturbance and advised a Basal Metabolism test. She was given an appointment for June 25, to enter the hospital and have this test made.

June 22, 1932.—Talked with Dr. Jones, who said that he meant that Mr. Morotto could do full-time work at any occupation that was not too laborious (as laborer), as there is nothing seriously wrong with him.

July 1, 1932.—Letter received by Juvenile Court from Veterans' Hos-pital:

Acknowledgment is made of your recent letter in which you enclose a signed statement from Antonio Morotto authorizing us to give you information from his folder.

Please be advised that he did not report here on June 9, 1932, for an examina-tion and that the date of his last examination was on December 2, 1931, at which time he was found to be suffering from mild hypertension and carious teeth. Hospital care was not recommended, but he was advised to have his teeth looked after. As he was in service less than ninety days during the World War, he is not entitled to any remuneration from the government in the way of compensa-tion or disability allowance.

July 5, 1932.—It was impossible for Rose to receive a date for a tonsil-lectomy as she is having a continual temperature. Mrs. Morotto said that she had accompanied her husband to the Veterans' Hospital the week previously, where he had been examined.

July 9, 1932.—Letter received by the Juvenile Court from Memorial Hospital:

Rose Morotto reported for her Basal Metabolism test, but apparently was rather nervous that morning, and it was difficult to get an accurate accounting. She is to return on August 3, for further observation.

I regret that it is taking us so long to come to a decision in the case of this child. On her last visit to clinic her temperature was only slightly elevated. We will be glad to inform you as to the final outcome of this case when the patient has again been in clinic.

July 11, 1932.—Dr. Fuller of Veterans' Hospital, who formerly cared for Mr. Morotto, was seen at the hospital. He did not know about Mr. Morotto's examination there in June. From the hospital records and the Director of Social Service it was learned that no examination was made, or at least not recorded, as Mr. Morotto was not entitled to out-patient care. If a private physician recommended hospital care for Mr. Morotto, they would be glad to take him back. Veterans' Hospital recommended that Mr. Morotto receive an examination at Free Dispensary.

July 12, 1932.—Mrs. Morotto was in the office for extra assistance which she needs for her husband, who formerly received necessities for his special diet from the Veterans' Bureau. Mrs. Morotto felt certain that her husband had been examined the day she accompanied him to the Veterans' Hospital. She readily agreed to a psychiatric examination at Free Dispensary. Mr. Morotto is very anxious to go to work if the doctors find his condition favorable. Mrs. Morotto, however, is doubtful about this as he continually complains of pains. Mrs. Morotto planned to go to the American Legion regarding compensation rights of her husband.

The worker from Green Valley Farm called regarding Rose. If her tonsils are removed, they may be able to find a place for her this fall in a sanatorium.

July 14, 1932.—Letter to Free Dispensary regarding a psychiatric examination for Mr. Morotto.

August 4, 1932.—Rose has not yet received a date for tonsillectomy. Susie is now attending the Memorial Hospital, where she expects to have her tonsils removed but as yet a date has not been set. Mr. Morotto complained of pains in the abdomen but otherwise he said that he felt well. Mrs. Morotto said that she would be glad to have her husband examined at the Free Dispensary, regardless of the fact that she might lose her pension if he was found able to work.

August 8, 1932.—Mr. Morotto can be considered as totally incapacitated until after the mental examination in October at Free Dispensary.

August 8, 1932.—A letter was left with Mrs. Morotto referring Rocco to Memorial Hospital for a tonsillectomy date. Mrs. Morotto was particularly satisfied with the attention that Susie and Rose had received there.

The mother had been to the County Welfare Bureau that day to ask for assistance but this she was unable to get because of the new division of work between the Pension Department and that office. Mrs. Morotto was told that supplementation would be asked temporarily until some definite diagnosis was made at the Free Dispensary regarding Mr. Morotto.

The father speaks very vaguely about his experiences and about his physical condition. It was impossible to exact direct answers to questions presented to him regarding his physical condition from the time that he was discharged from the Army until his entrance into Veterans' Hospital.

He would give the name of one doctor who had treated him and then would follow this by saying, "That's all." When Mrs. Morotto would question him about physicians who she knew had examined him he would agree that they had done so. Mr. Morotto is glad that they are going to permit him to be examined at Free Dispensary. Dental work which was started at Veterans' Hospital was not finished when he left there. He has received no dental attention since he has been home from the hospital.

August 23, 1932.—Letter written to the County Bureau by the Juvenile Court Officer:

We are asking supplementary assistance for the Morotto family, who are now receiving the maximum pension of $55 per month. Mr. Morotto is an ex-service man. We are considering him as totally incapacitated until a psychiatric examination has been given in October at Free Dispensary. We shall inform you if there is any change in the status of this family.

The budget has been figured as $78.11. Deducting 10 per cent[6] and the pension of $55, there is a deficit of $15.30. Will you supply the following:

    1. Two quarts of milk $7.20
    2. Grocery order 8.10

Mrs. Morotto will trade with the Italian Grocery Store at 540 Farragut Street. Enclosed is a copy of the budget, face sheet, summary, health sheet and present status.

September 19, 1932.—A letter for dental care at the University Dental Clinic was sent to Mr. Morotto.

September 20, 1932.—Mrs. Morotto has not yet secured a tonsillectomy date for Rose. She feels certain that the child's condition must be serious or otherwise the doctors would not deliberate so long. Mr. Morotto walks every day, usually to the lake. He feels that the warm air and sunshine are beneficial. He continually complains of pains in the abdomen and is unable to sleep at night because of this. Mr. Morotto is hoping that the doctor will find his condition of such nature that it will not prevent him from going to work if work can be secured.

September 23, 1932.—Following is a history regarding Mr. Morotto sent to the Psychiatric Clinic of Free Dispensary by Probation Officer:

The patient is the father of one of our pensioned families. A report as to the physical condition and working ability of incapacitated men must be secured

---

[6] [At this time the fund for Mothers' Pensions was very much in arrears, and the families were being referred to the Cook County Bureau of Public Welfare for supplementation. As the budget used by the Mothers' Pension was higher than the budget used by the Cook County Bureau of Public Welfare, the County refused to supplement for the full amount of the deficit. It was agreed that they would supplement up to 10 per cent of the Pension budget rather than eliminate any specific items from the budget.]

every six months. Patient was in Veterans' Hospital for a year, but he is not entitled to out-patient care there as his disabilities were not service connected. Patient is suffering from pellagra. He is listless and scarcely ever talks.

Family history.—Patient was born in Paris, France. His parents who were of Italian nativity moved to France, where they lived for eighteen years and here the patient was born. Patient is the second oldest in a family of four children. He and his older brother attended school in France for three years where they learned to read and write. He is unable to read English, but can write his own name. He came to America to his brother when he was thirteen years of age. He has worked as a laborer until his health prevented him from working. Most of the time he worked on sewers. The aged father of the patient is still living in Italy with a married daughter. No communication has been had with them in recent years. Patient has another sister living in France, but he does not know where she is living. He has a brother living at 2239 E. Kaster Street, who is also a laborer. He is married and has four children.

Patient received citizenship papers in December, 1918. He was enlisted in the army November 6, 1918, and was discharged December 31, 1918.

Wife and children.—Patient's wife came to America when she was two years of age. Her father preceded his family to this country. His death occurred in 1921, resulting from pneumonia. Before her father's death in 1921, she was married to the patient. Her mother, six brothers and sisters were supported by a mothers' pension from 1922 until 1925.

Patient's mother-in-law attended English classes faithfully, as did the other members of her family who came to America. They all belonged to activities at Neighborhood House.

When the patient's wife was interviewed in 1922 in order to ascertain her ability to assist her mother financially, her husband was not working regularly. She was quoted as having expressed a deep regret for having married, and had she known her father would die so soon, she never would have left home. Her marriage was unhappy.

Patient's wife is a very careful housekeeper. There are always flowering plants in the kitchen and bright colored curtains and covers. The children are well cared for. They are always as attractively dressed as possible. They are members of the Nutrition Weighing Classes, which they attend regularly. All three children have been recently examined at Memorial Hospital. Rose has had a continual history of temperature which has prevented the removal of her tonsils. This has caused considerable concern to the mother.

Rose is in the fifth grade and Susie in the second grade of All Saints School. Rocco has not yet been enrolled in school. All are well mannered and attractive children.

Neighborhood.—The patient, his wife and the members of her family have all lived in the present neighborhood since they came to Chicago. It is populated chiefly by Italian families. Most of the houses are in need of repair, but the patient's home is in good condition.

History of patient's illness.—Patient was examined by Dr. Anton Scalo of 4000 Farragut Street several times during the year 1919. He reported at that time that he was suffering with pains in his toes. His blood pressure was then 190 systolic. His lungs were negative. Heart had a slight systolic murmur. He was advised to go to the hospital for future examination.

Patient was married in February, 1921. He never complained of any illness to his wife, and she did not know that he had been receiving treatments from Dr. Scalo.

On July 6, 1928, the patient's wife went to the Children's Protective Agency, where she told the worker that her husband had been ill for two months and had been drinking heavily.

Patient was referred by the Family Agency to the Free Dispensary for examination on August 6, 1928. He had flat feet at that time and was referred to the Orthopedic Clinic. A Wassermann was taken on August 7, 1928, and was negative. Patient was again seen on November 8, 1929, in the Dental Department. Patient's tonsils were removed at about this time. When the patient was last seen in the Orthopedic Department in January 15, 1929, his feet were somewhat improved.

Patient was sent to the Veterans' Hospital in November, 1928, and was discharged in December. It was suggested that work in damp places would aggravate his arthritic condition. He could do only light work.

In May, 1929, patient found work as a watchman.

Patient was examined by Dr. Jackson, a private physician with offices at 500 N. Washington Street, in the early part of 1930. He was given free care. Dr. Jackson referred him to Grace Hospital, where he was hospitalized from May 3, 1930, to May 27, 1930. (Dr. Jackson no longer has an office, so we were unable to get a report from him.) The nature of the patient's disease on discharge from Grace Hospital was pellagra, and his condition was unimproved at the time of discharge. He was put on a high protein diet, but refused to co-operate.

While in Grace Hospital patient was seen by the nurses and other patients throwing his food away. He seemed to be quite agitated and picked objects out of the air. The physicians' opinion was that the patient was obviously psychotic. His judgment was poor, and most of the time he showed a marked progressive mental dullness. There was no definite psychosis, but from his behavior it was quite evident that he was disoriented. Recommendation of Grace Hospital was that the patient should be removed to Psychopathic Hospital. However, as he had been enlisted in the army, he was transferred to Veterans' Hospital.

Story of patient's illness as told at Grace Hospital.—Two years ago the patient began to have pains in his legs and feet. The pain began in both feet and was sharp in character. He did not believe that anything exaggerated or relieved the pain. One year ago the pain extended to his knees and he was never free from it. Some days it would be worse, and perhaps for a week it would not hurt him so much, but for the last three weeks it has been very severe.

Patient was admitted to Veterans' Hospital on May 27, 1930. The diagnosis of his condition at that time was psychosis with other somatic disease (pellagra). It was believed that hospitalization would be required indefinitely. Owing to Mr. Morotto's mental condition, no information could be secured from him.

A letter from Veterans' Hospital on September 9, 1930, stated that the patient had recovered from his psychosis and his physical condition was somewhat improved. He was considered to be totally and permanently incapacitated. Patient was discharged from the Veterans' Hospital on February 6, 1931. The diagnosis upon discharge was pellagra, psychosis, with other somatic diseases, in state of remission, polyneuritis, tachycardia moderate. His prognosis was favorable. Estimate of average impairment of earning capacity for present or prior occupation of laborer was moderate. Proper diet and general hygienic measures were recommended.

Patient was examined by Dr. Jones of the Juvenile Court on June 3, 1932. He complained of pains in his feet and legs and constriction at upper part of the abdomen. He was found to have flat feet. Dental care was advised. The examining physician stated that the patient could do only light work.

Patient's behavior.—When questioned about the medical care he has had since he first became ill, the patient would finally recall the name of only one physician and then say, "That's all," until his wife reminded him of another examination, and he would say, "That is all," again. Patient sits in a chair in the kitchen with his hands folded. He very seldom talks. According to his wife, he conversed very infrequently before he became ill, but now he scarcely ever says anything. When spoken to, he usually smiles.

Patient sometimes walks to the lake where he sits for several hours in the sun. It is his habit to go out somewhere every day. His wife encourages this. Patient is willing and will try to do anything that his wife asks him to do, as putting up the clothes line or watching the children. He sometimes becomes angry, but his wife does not notice any greater display of anger now than before his illness. When he does become angry, he never abuses her or the children.

Present complaints.—Patient complains of continual pain in the abdomen. The pain hinders him from sleeping at night. His appetite is very poor. He has chronic constipation and must take enemas continually.

His wife never noticed psychotic tendencies in him before he was placed in Grace Hospital.

To the patient's knowledge, no one in his family has ever been affected by a mental disease.

Very truly yours,
CHIEF PROBATION OFFICER

October 19, 1932.—Mr. Morotto was examined at Free Dispensary on October 4, and was told to return October 22, for additional examination —the doctor gave him medicine. Mrs. Morotto was told there that her husband was still suffering from pellagra. He answered questions very slowly so the doctor questioned his mental ability somewhat.

Rose is to have her tonsils removed October 20. She has another cold, so Mrs. Morotto is not certain whether the tonsillectomy can be performed or not. All the children have joined Neighborhood House play classes. Rose has rejoined the art class in which she has a great deal of interest. Although it was only one o'clock, Rocco was insisting that his mother get him ready for play classes which would begin at 3:30. This small boy tries to wash himself. His mother does not stop him although he does succeed in making a great deal of mess in the kitchen. Rocco dresses and undresses himself and puts on his own shoes. According to the mother he has improved greatly in his behavior. When he was at play class this last year, he would hide away in a corner or if his mother was there would hide behind her skirt. Now he will join in the circle and ask to be picked out. He helps himself to things about the house while the visitor is present. He would not do this before. Mrs. Morotto believes that all the children are much too shy. The girls are always being asked to be in plays at school but they worry a great deal about being asked to appear first or to lead the line. Mrs. Morotto will talk to the Sister about Rose, especially to ask her to encourage her to take responsibilities with less fear. Mrs. Morotto herself does not take the children on many excursions, but they do attend picture shows at Field Museum and make trips to interesting spots with Neighborhood House groups. The mother sees the advantage of having the children meet new situations and contacts in order to make them feel more self-confident.

October 22, 1932.—Report received from Free Dispensary:

At your request Antonio Morotto was examined in our psychiatric clinic October 5, 1932, by Dr. Slater, who makes the following statement:

At the time of examination this man shows no actual psychotic symptoms, but there is evidence of a definite deterioration (from pellagra), also some trophic changes, a slowing down on the mental side, and in moving and thinking. We do not think that the patient is fit at this time to do any type of physical or mental work sufficient to care for his family, and all possible aid should be given the family.

Patient was referred to general medicine for treatment. It is not necessary that he return to this clinic unless definite psychotic factors develop. Patient was seen October 12 and 15, in the General Medicine Clinic. He was placed on a low residue diet and prescription.

Hoping that this will be of service to you, I am,

November 23, 1932.—Rose went to the Memorial Hospital on November 22, 1932, but as she had a temperature of 100 they would not remove her tonsils. She was told to return again. The worker from Green Valley Farm called at the home and told Mrs. Morotto that they would accept Rose for convalescent care after her tonsils were removed. Rose and Susie both enjoy the clay-modeling classes which they attend at Neighborhood House. They have made bright colored cups for their mother. Rocco still starts to get ready for the play class several hours before time as he is so anxious to get there. Arrangements were made to accompany Mrs. Morotto to the Red Cross, to ask them to investigate Mr. Morotto's claim for government compensation.

November 26, 1932.—Letter written to Gas Company by Probation Officer:

Mrs. Mary Morotto is being cared for by the Mothers' Pension, which is now five months in arrears.[7] We should appreciate it if you could continue to give her service until her check is received. She has told us that she would pay on this account immediately upon receipt of the pension money.

November 30, 1932.—The worker at the Red Cross believes that Mr. Morotto might be eligible for compensation. Dr. Scalo's letter, stating that he had treated Mr. Morotto in 1919 for disabilities which still seemed to be present, might be of great value in proving that his illness was service connected. Red Cross would like to interview Mr. Morotto on Thursday.

December 23, 1932.—Mr. Morotto has gone back to the Free Dispensary. Both Mr. and Mrs. Morotto have been to the Red Cross but they do not feel that Mr. Morotto's claim for government compensation will be very strong as he is unable to locate any friends who were with him during service. Two of his best friends are dead and another cannot be located.

Rose is to have her tonsils removed on December 27, 1932. The children are having their teeth cared for at the County Dental Clinic. Rocco does not mind when his teeth are pulled and never cries.

The children attended several Neighborhood House Christmas parties. A neighbor woman gave Mrs. Morotto a coat which one of her friends remade for Susie.

December 24, 1932.—Letter received by the Juvenile Court Officer from the Red Cross:

Several weeks ago you referred Antonio Morotto, an ex-service man, to our office for assistance in reopening his claim for Government compensation.

[7] [The delay in the payment of Mothers' Pension checks in 1932 was due to the financial breakdown in the County finances.]

We are in receipt of information from our Red Cross Liaison Representative informing us that the veteran's claim was disallowed as insufficient evidence had been submitted to prove his present condition the result of his World War service. We talked with the veteran a couple of weeks ago at which time he could give us very little information regarding the names and addresses of his employers, as well as medical treatment he has had since the date of his service.

We are wondering if your record might give us this information and if so, may we ask you to give us a detailed report at your first opportunity so we may secure the necessary evidence in support of the claim.

Appreciating any information you may be able to give us, we are

January 9, 1933.—Letter written to Red Cross, telling of medical history of Mr. Morotto.

January 18, 1933.—Mrs. Morotto and her husband had gone to the Red Cross office with two witnesses as was requested by that organization in order to prove Mr. Morotto's incapacity at the close of the war. Mrs. Morotto feels hopeful that her husband will receive some compensation from the government. Mr. Morotto has not yet received any dental care at the Free Dispensary, although they told him that they would make arrangements. Mrs. Morotto will go there this week in order to ascertain whether dental care will be given. Mr. Morotto is to return to Free Dispensary for another examination the latter part of January.

Mrs. Morotto owes four months' rent to the present landlady. She has borrowed about $50 from Mrs. Panzinco, a neighbor. There is a bill at the court amounting to $20 against Mrs. Morotto.

Mrs. Simonelli, mother of Mrs. Morotto, came to visit. Her family is being cared for by the Unemployment Relief.[8] She seemed to be very pleasant and intelligent. She speaks English fairly well.

Mrs. Morotto received three kitchen chairs and a radio cabinet from Neighborhood House when one of the boys' clubs broke up. She is hoping that she some day may be able to have the radio fixed. At Christmas time the Veterans' Bureau through Veterans' Hospital took care of the family very generously, even providing new uniforms for Susie and Rose and also new shoes for all members of the family. The children received many toys and a Christmas tree from that organization.

Rocco is becoming more friendly. He asked assistance in constructing a tunnel for his train which he was pulling. He does not say very much to anyone coming into the house but smiles very readily. He is still much interested in the play classes at Neighborhood House.

[8] [The Unemployment Relief Service was public relief—an agency caring for the unemployed person and his dependents.]

Mrs. Morotto allows him to do anything about the house which he may feel is a great help to her. For instance, he was cleaning all the woodwork with water. He enjoyed any comments which were made about his ability to assist his mother.

Mr. Morotto goes for a walk every day because he becomes very restless in the house and finds enjoyment in walking around the neighborhood and in talking with his friends.

February 16, 1933.—Mrs. Morotto had gone to the Free Dispensary with her husband, who was to receive another treatment. Mrs. Donatti, neighbor, was in the house caring for Rocco. During the visit Rocco had nothing to say but busied himself with a small set of tools which he had received at Christmas time. Rocco is able to lose himself in his toys and make-believe games. He, however, plays outdoors every day with small children in the neighborhood.

February 17, 1933.—Mrs. Morotto was in the office and was very much upset over the fact that she had gotten into difficulty at Barnard Dispensary, where she had gone at the advice of Dr. Wynetti to make arrangements for Rose's tonsillectomy.

Later.—Social worker from Barnard Dispensary said that they could not give Rose an immediate date for a tonsillectomy; and, since Mrs. Morotto had accepted advice regarding Rose's care from Memorial Hospital and Barnard Dispensary which conflicted, they had told her that she must make up her mind which she wished to attend.

February 22, 1933.—Mrs. Mossman, Nutrition Center, advised Mrs. Morotto that Dr. Wynetti would make arrangements for Rose's tonsillectomy so that she could be placed in Green Valley Farm.

March 14, 1933.—Mr. Morotto was given dental care by a neighborhood dentist who has known the Morotto family for a great many years. His charges will be nominal. The three children are attending the County Dental Clinic and are to return there in June. Mrs. Morotto has decided that she will not worry any more about Rose and will leave the matter with Dr. Wynetti.

Rocco was still enthusiastic about play classes at Neighborhood House. Mrs. Morotto explained that since the school is inconvenient and since Rocco seems to be responding to the teachers and children at Neighborhood House kindergarten placement would not be so necessary.

Rose rests every afternoon on returning from school. She does not complain of being ill. She is anticipating Green Valley Farm. The worker from there has called at the home and has told her about it as has the

Nutrition Worker from the Center. Mr. Morotto has not been called to the Red Cross recently. Mrs. Morotto said that they had promised notification when they wished him to come. Mrs. Morotto is very patient with her husband. At times she is pathetically kind to him, lowering her voice when addressing him. Mr. Morotto is very kind to the children and allows the discipline matters of the family to rest with his wife. The rent for the flat is now $14 per month. Mrs. Morotto would like to move into a larger place, but hesitates to move away from the present flat, as she knows everyone in the building. Her next-door neighbor is particularly good at sewing and often assists Mrs. Morotto in remodeling clothes for the children which, when finished, are usually very attractive. Both Rose and Susie have spring coats made from old ones given to Mrs. Morotto.

Later.—Sister Superior of the All Saints School, which the Morottos attend, said that they have found Susie and Rose to be very likable children. They always appear at school well dressed and apparently well fed. There were no outstanding problems in connection with their school work.

[Several special sheets are used in the Mothers' Pension Records. We are including here the Court Order, the Budget, and the School Record. There are also detailed Health Record Sheets, which are not included.]

COURT ORDER

Surname: MOROTTO   *Father:* ANTONIO   *Mother:* MARY

Name of Child:	*Docket Number*	*Date*	*Court Order*
SUSIE	234517	Dec. 5, 1930	County Commissioners to pay $15 per month December 1, 1930

Name of Child:	*Docket Number*	*Date*	*Court Order*
ROSE	234518	Dec. 5, 1930	County Commissioners to pay $15 per month December 1, 1930

Name of Child:	*Docket Number*	*Date*	*Court Order*
ROCCO	234519	Dec. 5, 1930	County Commissioners to pay $25 per month December 1, 1930

BUDGET

Surname: MOROTTO   *Father:* ANTONIO   *Mother:* MARY

MONTHLY BUDGET			MONTHLY INCOME		
Items	11–19–30	8–15–32	Source	11–19–30	8–15–32
Rent............	$16.00	$16.00			
Upkeep of house..	....	....	Father.......	Incap' ed. Vet-	....
Food............	32.20	31.70		erans' Hos-	
Special diet.......	....	....		pital	
Clothing and toilet				9–18–30*	
articles.........	18.30	13.56	Mother......	Has two young	Probably could
Fuel and light....	8.50	8.20		children	do light wk.†
Household inciden-					$11.20
tals............	5.00	3.85	Amer. War		
Education........	1.00	1.30	Mothers‡..	$ 2.00	2.00
Recreation.......	1.25	1.25	Mothers' Pen-		
Carfare.........	1.00	1.00	sion........	55.00	55.00
Care of health....	1.25	1.25			
Total........	$84.50	$78.11	Total....	....	$68.20

* Considered totally incapacitated until October. (Mental examination at Free Dispensary.)
† Examined by Dr. Jones 6–3–32.
‡ Pay gas and light bills. Mrs. Morotto says $2.00 month average.

ITEMIZED BUDGET

NAME OF PERSON	DATE, 11–19–30			DATE, 8–15–32		
	Age	Food	Clothing	Age	Food	Clothing
Mother........	....	$10.00	$ 4.45	....	$ 6.95	$ 3.00
Rose..........	8	8.00	3.65	10	6.30	3.00
Susie.........	5	7.60	{ −10 per cent	7	5.85	{ −10 per cent
			3.65			2.40
Rocco.........	3	6.60	2.45	5	5.85	2.40
Father (incap.).	....	....	4.45	....	6.75	3.00
Total.....	....	$32.20	$18.65	....	$31.70	$13.80
			− .35			− .24
			$18.30			$13.56

SCHOOL RECORD

Name of Child: SUSIE MOROTTO   *School:* ALL SAINTS   *Room 1*

| | 1931 | | 1932 | |
	Oct.	Dec.	Feb.–Mar.	May–June
1. Grade	1	....	1	1
2. Scholarship	B	F	A	A
3. Deportment	B	G	A	A
4. Personal appearance	B	F	A	A
5. Absences excused	0	....	5	3
Absences unexcused	0	....	0	0

Name of Child: ROSE MOROTTO   *School:* ALL SAINTS   *Room 4*

| | 1931 | |
	Oct.	Dec.
1. Grade	4	....
2. Scholarship	B	A
3. Deportment	A	A
4. Personal appearance	A	A
5. Absences excused	0	....
Absences unexcused	0	....

SUMMARY OF THE RECORD TO JANUARY 27, 1936

During this period the family has continued under the active supervision of the Mothers' Pension Division. There have been no significant changes in the family situation.

The use of community recreational facilities has been important in the life of the Morotto family. The mother and children have been actively interested in the activities of a neighborhood settlement. The mother has attended knitting and cooking classes. The family has attended outdoor movies and concerts in the city park. Rose became an enthusiastic member of the Girl Scouts and the family has made use of library facilities.

The worker has helped the mother to get health care for the children. She has also kept in touch with the school and has showed interest in the good records which the children were making.

The condition of the father has remained about the same. He usually sits in the corner of the kitchen quietly, but rarely speaks. He has continued under medical supervision, but the doctors do not believe they can help him.

The family situation is pictured as being a happy wholesome one. The effect of the father's condition is minimized by the mother's adequate handling of him and her acceptance of his care. There are pets—a white rabbit, gold fish, and a puppy—in the home.

2. Paul and Molly Gray

(A Negro Mother and Her Two Children Are Supported and Supervised by Social Agencies until the Deserting Father Is Gradually Brought Back into the Household)

[This case opened with a letter, dated January 22, 1931, from the Chief Probation Officer of the Juvenile Court to the secretary of the Children's Agency as follows:]

The committee on dependent cases, at this court, discussed the cases of Paul Gray, age four years, and Molly Gray, age two years, at their meeting of January 20, and suggested that the Children's Agency be asked to provide boarding-home care for them. We have secured a date of hearing for February 4 and hope to hear before that time whether or not you can accept the children. The committee suggested that an order be placed on the parents for the children's support. Both of them are apparently physically able to care for the children, and both are working.

Our attention was called to the case about December 12. The children were placed in the Juvenile Detention Home by the police, when Mrs. W. G. Haney, of 406 Mt. Pleasant Street, 1st floor, who had been the caretaker of the children since September, 1930, complained that the parents had deserted, that they were in arrears with the board, and that she was unable because of her financial circumstances to care for the children longer.

Mrs. Haney stated that she had agreed to board the children, and that the father, Paul Gray, Sr., was to pay $7.00 a week for their care. We found that the father works as a houseman for various families in Wynot, Illinois, and that his earnings vary. His employers all live in the immediate vicinity of the place where he lives, at 416 Lane Avenue, Wynot. Mr. Gray's telephone number is Wynot 723.

The mother, Molly Gray, lives with relatives at 4624 Lincoln Avenue, Chicago, and works as a maid at 2234 Ames Avenue, Chicago. She earns $8.00 a week, and out of this sum pays $3.50 room rent.

Mr. and Mrs. Gray have had considerable domestic difficulty and have been to the Court of Domestic Relations. We recently had Mrs. Gray go back to the Court of Domestic Relations and complain of her husband's non-support; and as a result, on January 7, 1931, Judge Bain of that court heard their grievances and ordered Mr. Gray to pay $8.00 a week to the Clerk of the Court for the support of his children. That day the children were taken by the mother to the place where she lives at 4624 Lincoln Avenue, and there during the mother's absence they are now cared for by the maternal aunt, Mrs. Cora Carey. Mrs. Carey claims that she is unable to continue the care and has insisted upon being relieved of the responsibility. At one time Susie Roberts, the paternal aunt of the children, and her husband had expressed a desire to take Paul, Jr. in their home, but they were not willing to do so unless they were given the right to adopt him. The father hesitated to give his consent. The Roberts live in a kitchenette apartment at 1508 Vernon Street, which is probably not suitable for the child. Mrs. Roberts works irregularly and would leave the child while she is employed.

Mrs. Emma Gale at 625 Bell Avenue, who was interviewed by our Probation Officer, is a cousin of Mr. Gray. She claims that at one time the family lived with her and that the children were neglected by the parents.

The paternal grandmother, Mrs. Lorraine Dole, aged forty-eight, who resides in Milwaukee, is in Chicago visiting, and can be found at 16 E. 45th Street, 2nd floor, at the home of a paternal uncle, Oliver Gray. She knows of the domestic difficulty of her son and his wife, and has done all she could to assist them financially while they lived together.

There seems little hope of this couple's living together and establishing a home where the children would get good care. It seems best that they should be placed, and the parents forced to contribute toward their support; therefore, we are asking the Children's Agency to provide this boarding home care. We will do our utmost to have the order entered in the Court of Domestic Relations against Mr. Gray enforced, although to date he has paid nothing.

The family.—The family consists of the father, Paul Gray, twenty-five years; the mother, Molly Gray, twenty-five years; and Paul, Jr., and Molly, four and two years respectively.

Father's early history.—The father, Paul Gray, was born in Louis, Mississippi, in 1905, the third child in a family of seven children. His father deserted while he was quite young, leaving his mother with the responsibility of supporting this large group of children. The paternal grandfather remained away five years, during which time he was neither seen nor heard from. In his absence the family went through quite a struggle. Two of the seven children died. Father was only able to complete the fourth grade in school before his help was enlisted to increase the family income. Soon after he left school the race relations grew so bad and the feeling so intense against Negroes in Louis that paternal grandmother feared for the safety of her children. One by one, as she secured the money for transportation, they were sent North to relatives and friends.

Former employment.—Upon arriving in Chicago, father immediately sought employment in the only field in which he was trained, that of housework. He secured work on the North Side as houseman. It was during his trips to and from work on the elevated railway that he met mother, who was also employed on the North Side.

Mother's early history —The mother, Molly Gray, was born November 2, 1905, in Genoa, Kentucky. She was the youngest child in a family of nine children—four brothers, three sisters, and one half-sister. Her mother died in 1915 of cancer of the breast. Her father and two sisters are still living in Genoa; two sisters are in Chicago. Mother does not know where her brothers are.

Education.—Mother was about nine years of age before she started to school. The school was quite a distance from the home, and no one attended regularly. Her mother could read and write, so that some tutoring was done at home. She does not know exactly how far she went in school. She went to night school for several terms while living in York, Pennsylvania. She has had to work so hard since coming to Chicago that she hasn't had a chance to attend school here.

Mother says her memory has been very poor since she was quite small. She feels that an accident which occurred when she was about four years of age affected her brain. One of her brothers was chopping wood while she was playing. Her sister was chasing her and in an effort to get away she ran under the falling ax. No one could understand why she was not seriously injured. She was, of course, dazed, and had a very painful, throbbing head but was soon running around and playing as though nothing had happened. Mother was about fifteen years of age before the soreness entirely disappeared.

When mother was sixteen years of age she went to York to live with an aunt and a cousin. She remained in York until the spring of 1924, when she came to Chicago. Up until the time of her marriage in 1926 she was employed as a maid in a private home in Wynot, Illinois. Since her marriage she has been working at 2234 Ames Avenue, Chicago, in a small apartment hotel, earning $8.00 a week.

She and the children have been living at 4624 Lincoln Avenue, in a kitchenette apartment building, operated by her sister, Mrs. Cora Carey. She was paying $3.50 per week for her room. Out of the remainder of her wages came carfare and her other expenses. Father contributed nothing toward her support.

Marital life.—Father and mother married August 10, 1926, after a brief courtship. Two children were born to them. Except for a very short period immediately after their marriage father has failed to support his family adequately. His earnings have been supplemented from time to time by his mother, who remarried and has been living in Milwaukee. Mother states father was "all right" until he began associating with "fast people"—people who operated "buffet flats" where they sell liquor and gamble. He would reproach mother because she did not sanction such places and refused to accompany him. He grew spiteful and began "running around" and throwing his money away. If mother mentioned that the children needed "this or that" he would tell her to get it the best way she could—he didn't have any money. Mother would sometimes look through his pockets while he was asleep and if he was confronted with the fact that he did have money he would turn it off by saying he had some bills to pay. At other times father would leave a dollar and expect it to last two weeks or more. When father learned that a second child was to be born he accused mother of having "run around" to get it. He put her out of the house and refused to re-admit her. Mother went to her sister's home, and father disappeared.

Situation leading to Juvenile Court action.—The baby was born in County Hospital during the separation. Information was later secured to the effect that father was living and working in Wynot. Mother secured his telephone number but each time she called he would hang up the receiver. Finally in August, 1930, she took the two children to his home. She remained all day and a part of that night, but stole out early the next morning—shoes in hand—leaving the children with their father. Father sent for one of his sisters to come to Wynot and care for the children, but this arrangement was soon broken up by the Department of Health. They condemned the place as unfit for the rearing of children—there were no modern improvements of any kind—not even running water. In September, 1930, father then brought the children into Chicago and arranged with a Mrs. W. G. Haney, 406 Mt. Pleasant Street, to care for them. He was to pay $7.00 per week. He paid this amount up until about the latter part of November. After three weeks of silence the caretaker attempted to get in touch with the parents. Father's address was unknown. She tried to reach him by telephone only to be told that it was disconnected. Mrs. Haney then took the children to the Police Station, stating that she could care for them no longer. The Juvenile Officer placed them in the Juvenile Detention Home on December 12, 1930.

Efforts to effect an adjustment.—On December 31, 1930, after much difficulty in getting in touch with the parents, including a visit to mother's supposed place of employment, where the landlord denied having employed anyone by the name of Gray, the Probation Officer was able to arrange a family conference. Those present were father, mother, maternal aunt, and paternal aunt. There was a great deal of bickering. Paternal relatives accused mother of the neglect of the children, while the maternal relatives accused father of non-support and cruelty. Father gave many conflicting statements as to his income. The outcome of the conference was that mother was to go to the Court of Domestic Relations January 2, 1931, and file a complaint. Father was to pay mother's sister, Mrs. Carey, $4.00 per week for the care of Molly, age two years. Father's sister, Mrs. Susie Roberts, and her husband were to care for Paul until some definite plan could be made. All the relatives seemed satisfied with the temporary plan.

Court of Domestic Relations decision.—When the case came up January 7, 1931, before Judge Bain, an order of $8.00 per week was entered against father. Payments were to begin January 10, 1931, and were to be paid to the Clerk of the Court. Father insisted that he could not pay this amount, but the judge would not consent to a smaller order.

Father's previous work record.—For the past few years father has been employed as houseman for various families in Wynot. His work is seasonal, his services being in greater demand during the summer. Because of the irregularity of employment it is difficult to know how much he earns, but it may be estimated as approximately $5 per day.

Attitude of employers.—Mrs. J. B. Thomas, 416 Lane Avenue, Wynot, thinks that father is quite a reliable person. She has known him for some time and recently he has been living in a small apartment over her garage doing odd jobs for her and for other people in the neighborhood. His work is rather slack in the winter. Mrs. Thomas was under the impression that father visited his children regularly—once a week. From time to time she gives him toys for them and was sure that he delivered them.

A Mrs. R. B. Garner, 8 Mount Curve, Wynot (Wynot 445) has known father at least three years but did not know that he was married. He has been employed at her home regularly during the summer as houseman, irregularly during the winter. She has found him to be honest and reliable.

Mrs. W. B. Dix, 702 Tenth Street, Wynot (Wynot 105) states that father worked for her several years irregularly. She has advanced his wage from time to time, but owes him a small sum ($7.50) now.

Another employer is a Mrs. Gemel, 45 Cecil, Wynot.

Relatives.—Mrs. Lorraine Dole, paternal grandmother, has been visiting in Chicago since Christmas, 1930. For the past few years she has been living in Milwaukee, working as a maid. At the time she was preparing to come North after having sent her children, Paul Gray, paternal grandfather, returned home after an absence of five years. She refused to live with him again. She divorced him and came to Chicago, where she married a Mr. Dole. Shortly after this they moved to Milwaukee, where she has remained even after Mr. Dole's death. Paternal grandmother believes that paternal grandfather is still in Louis; that he is ill and has some sort of "spells" which she cannot describe—which he did not have when she lived with him.

Paternal grandmother has always felt that father was the most conscientious of all her children. She says father's marriage to mother was "forced"; that they had little or nothing to go on at first and that every other week she sent them $10. She did this for several months until she learned of their domestic difficulty and felt that they did not appreciate what she was trying to do for them. Paternal grandmother never has known father to have the habits she understands he has now. She attributes his change to bad associates who influence him. If father and mother were let alone they probably would get along. Relatives are possibly to blame for a lot of the trouble—too much interference and expressing of opinions. If it would help matters any, paternal grandmother would be willing to remain in Chicago to help father and mother establish and maintain a home. At any rate she intends to influence father to return to mother and assume the proper responsibility for his children.

Mrs. Anna Sharron, maternal aunt, is a widow and the mother of a seventeen-year-old son. She lives in one of her sister's kitchenette apartments at 4624 Lincoln Avenue. She is financially unable to assist mother in any way.

Mrs. Cora Carey, maternal aunt, 4624 Lincoln Avenue, occupies a very large house which has been converted into kitchenette apartments. She has assisted mother in caring for the children occasionally since her marriage. She would like to see mother and father together if father would "do right"—but he won't. He will make all kinds of statements and promises to the Judge and then when he is with mother he will abuse her and say he didn't mean to do a thing; "go on over to your sister's and let her help you take care of the children," etc. This makes the fourth week maternal aunt has cared for the children without any money and she does not feel that she can do so much longer.

Mrs. Susie Roberts, paternal aunt, 1508 Vernon Street, first apartment, is greatly interested in Paul, Jr. She has had him in her home for two or three days' visits on several occasions. She and her husband would be willing to adopt Paul, Jr. "if matters come to that." They would prefer, however, to see father and mother go back together and assume their own responsibility. "Father is no more responsible for their difficulties than mother."

Mr. Roberts is a porter in a hotel, earning between $18 and $20 per month. Mrs. Roberts does an occasional day's work. The couple occupy one room in a building remodeled into kitchenette apartments. Paul, Jr., if taken by the Roberts, would have to sleep in the same room with them. Mrs. Roberts would employ someone to look after him on the days she works. Mr. Roberts did not feel that he could contribute anything toward the child's support outside his home.

Mrs. Emma Gale, paternal cousin, 625 Bell Avenue, seems interested in the children. For one year the Grays lived in Mrs. Gale's home. "They fussed and fought continually" and for days either or both would desert, leaving the children "on her hands." From November, 1929, to August, 1930, Mrs. Gale kept them and they paid her only $44 during the entire period for the children's care.

Mrs. Anna Stevens, paternal grandaunt, 415 Valley Avenue, states that she hopes some agreement between mother and father can be reached whereby they can go together and care for their own children. They are both healthy, strong, and working and should assume their own responsibility. If one or the other were ill or dead she would be glad to take one or even both of the children free. As it is she would not think of taking either one into her home. If the parents do not "iron out" their difficulties she would like to see the paternal aunt, Mrs. Roberts, adopt the little boy. Paternal aunt feels that there is a possibility that both parents have been influenced too greatly by other people.

Children.—Paul, Jr., was born January 26, 1927, in Chicago. He was a full-term, breast-fed baby. He has always been a healthy child. He walked during his fourteenth month; teethed late—in the sixteenth or seventeenth month. He has had none of the diseases common to childhood. His only illness was a slight attack of the "flu" about a year ago. Paul is a sound sleeper. He goes to bed about eight o'clock—never later than nine—and is awake at seven o'clock. He is inclined to be a trifle stubborn. "If you get right down to business though he'll mind anyone." He has a remarkable memory but doesn't hold malice. He makes friends easily.

Molly was born July 27, 1928, in Chicago. She was a full-term, breast-fed baby. She was rachitic and was fifteen months old when she started walking alone. "Even now she does not walk straight." Molly, like her brother, Paul, teethed late. One tooth is still developing. There is some evidence of weak kidneys. Molly has been sleeping in the room with a maternal aunt and though put to bed early has found it difficult to go to sleep until late at night. She sleeps soundly and has to be awakened in the morning.

Home and neighborhood.—There has been little family unity in this group. The father and mother have moved from place to place and have been separated for longer intervals than they have been together.

Treatment by other agencies and interested persons.—Family Welfare, Union District, knew the family under date of July 21, 1928. They have only a blue card record which shows that mother applied July 21, 1928, and at that time was twenty-three years of age; husband twenty-four. Her father's name was Andrew Black, Genoa, Kentucky. According to mother, father deserted July 10, 1928. She was expecting confinement in a few weeks. Mother applied again July 31, 1930. She then had the information that father had been working in Wynot, Illinois, since May, 1930. He had sent her only $9.00 during this period. He had paid no room rent or board for the family since November, 1929. Mother intimated that father drank.

The report received from the Social Service Exchange showed registrations by the Juvenile Court on December 17, 1930; Court of Domestic Relations August 20, 1930, and January 7, 1931; Infant Welfare Society, September 14, 1928; County Hospital, September 1, 1928; and Family Welfare, July 21, 1928.

A letter of inquiry, dated January 29, 1931, was sent to each of these agencies as follows:

The Social Service Exchange reports that your organization knew the above-named family. May we have a brief report of your contact? We have been asked to place the Gray children in a foster home so would appreciate any family history or other information you may have been able to secure that would aid us in effecting a satisfactory adjustment for these children.

January 29, 1931.—Mrs. Molly Gray, mother, on telephone, states that she lost her job yesterday because of shortage of work. The proprietor promised to call should he need someone in the future. Mother is "up a tree." Father has not paid any money for the children's support, and she has been able to pay only her rent and buy a little food. Mother's sister, Mrs. Carey, is very impatient and says she cannot keep them much longer without money. Mother cannot see the advantage of going back to father since he is not working regularly. Sometimes he doesn't make more than $3.00 or $4.00 a week. Then, too, in winter he has little or no work.

Plan.—(1) Bring father into Court of Domestic Relations because of his failure to comply with order given on January 7, 1931, by Judge Bain. (2) Recommend that the Juvenile Court refer the case to Family Welfare. It is felt that, were foster-home placement the final plan, the Children's Agency would gladly accept the Gray children but that placement is not the step to be taken at this time. Not enough effort has been expended to cope with the situation as a family problem (Case Committee, January 29, 1931).

February 4, 1931.—Juvenile Court hearing. Gray case continued for six months, during which period the case is to be under the supervision of the Family Welfare Society.

February 5, 1931.—Court of Domestic Relations telephoned that the Gray case is on call for this morning.

Case hearing deferred until February 6, 1931, because of the failure of the police to bring the father to Court. A capias had been issued, and father was taken into custody when he appeared at Juvenile Court, February 4, 1931.

February 6, 1931.—Court of Domestic Relations, Judge Bain presiding; case reviewed. The order of $8.00 per week previously imposed was sustained. The case was continued generally. It was explained that the father had a letter to the Governor's Commission entitling him to three days' work a week ($16.50).[1] The Judge intimated that if the father failed to comply with the order this time there was no alternative but the House of Correction. Case rehearing was put on schedule for February 27, 1931.

Letter received at Children's Agency from County Hospital:

Mrs. Molly Gray, 406 Mt. Pleasant Street, was a patient in Wards 20 and 21, January 26, 1927, and July 27, 1928, respectively. Mrs. Gray said she was married to Paul Gray, June 1, 1926, in Chicago. Their first child, Paul, was born about six months later—and the second child was admitted as a feeder—born before reaching the ward, July, 1928.

We have knowledge of Court of Domestic Relations being on the case for non-support, although Mr. Gray was working as a cleaner in Wynot in 1927 and as a laborer at 75 cents an hour in 1928.

[1] [The Governor's Commission on Unemployment and Relief was organized October, 1930, and functioned until March 31, 1931. The purpose of the Commission was to subsidize deficits of local charitable organizations by the raising of voluntary funds. Much of the relief was given in the form of work relief.]

Mr. Gray's sisters, Susie Roberts and Anna Sharron, helped patient. We have no further knowledge of this family.

Report received from Infant Welfare:

Gray—Paul and Molly

Address—3708 Madison Street, 2nd floor rear

Father—cleaner. Day work

Total income—$15 per week, irregular

Rent—$5 per week

Home hygiene—fair

Paul, Jr., was registered 3-17-27 at the age of one and one-half months

The case was discharged 10-31-28 because the family moved

Conferences attended—20

Visits made—16

Co-operation of mother—fair

Condition of child—fair

Worker reports on 9-11-28:

    Father deserted and took baby with him

    Mother did not know his address, so could not get aid through court

    Molly was registered 9-16-28 at the age of six weeks

Family lived with mother's sister at that time

The case was discharged 10-30-30 because family moved

Conferences attended—13

Visits made—23

Co-operation of mother—fair

Condition of child—fair

February 7, 1931.—Letter received at Children's Agency from the Municipal Court of Chicago:

August 14, 1930, a capias was issued charging non-support of wife and children for Paul Gray.

Case continued to August 21, 1930.

Case again continued August 28, 1930, at which time it was continued generally.

January 7, 1931, case again brought before the Court at which time a temporary order was entered for $8.00 a week, first payment due January 10, 1931. Case continued generally.

January 27, 1931, a capias again issued charging non-support of wife and children for Paul Gray.

February 10, 1931.—Mrs. Samuels, Superintendent, Family Welfare, on telephone was given a verbal report of Court of Domestic Relations hearing. She will assign the case as soon as possible and have the worker get in touch with mother.

Later.—Mrs. Samuels telephoned, asking that Children's Agency assume the case-work responsibility of this case. Because of the increasing demands coming in on account of the depression, their work has taken primarily the form of relief; very little intensive case work can be done.[2]

Mrs. Samuels was informed that Children's Agency would be glad to co-operate in this way; a budget would be worked out and forwarded to her office within a few days.

February 11, 1931.—Mrs. Cora Carey, maternal aunt, at home, 4624 Lincoln Avenue, states that she has only two rooms available which would be suitable for mother's use. One will be out of the question because of the price; the other is a large back room on the second floor. It has only a folding cot in it now, but she will add a full-sized bed if it should be decided that it is to be used. She will make a concession in the price of this room for her sister. The price will be $6.50 a week. There is a gas plate, room for provisions, etc., in a closet across the hall. This part of the house would give mother the privacy of an apartment.

Since this was the most reasonable offer which had been received, it was decided that mother should move here as soon as it could be prepared for her use.

February 16, 1931.—Clerk of Alimony, Municipal Court, on telephone states that nothing has been paid by Paul Gray.

February 17, 1931.—Letter written to Family Welfare by Children's Agency:

According to our telephone conversation on Tuesday, February 10, 1931, we have worked out a budget for the Gray family and are sending it to you.

At the time of Mr. Gray's appearance in the Court of Domestic Relations on February 6, 1931, the order of $8.00 per week, previously imposed, was sustained. At that time Mr. Gray had a letter from the Governor's Commission which entitled him to three days' work per week. He had had the letter two days but because of his arrest had not been able to report to work. Up until the present time we have been unable to learn whether he finally reported or not. However, we do have information to the effect that nothing has been paid through the clerk's office for the support of the children. We have been unable to communicate with Mr. Gray, and his relatives say that they do not know where he

---

[2] [In 1931 the private family agencies were attempting to care for the large number of families whose breadwinners were out of employment. The case loads were very large, and there was little time to give to any problem except relief needs. The family agency in this case is agreeing to supply the relief, but asking the Children's Agency to continue carrying all case-work responsibility. After the public relief agencies were developed such a co-operative plan for many cases was carried on between the public and the private agencies. In these cases the public agency gave the relief and the private agency (family or children's) did much of the case work. Some difficulties develop from such a plan, and many questions regarding the wisdom of it may be raised.]

is. His case is due in the Court of Domestic Relations on February 27, 1931, on rehearing. If he has worked and has failed to pay, the presiding Judge, Judge Bain, intimates that there is no alternative but the House of Correction.

This is the beginning of the seventh week Mrs. Gray's sister, Mrs. Carey, has cared for the children without pay, and she is growing rather impatient. We would appreciate it if you would give this matter your earliest consideration.

BUDGET

ESTIMATE FOR FAMILY CONSISTING OF MOTHER AND CHILDREN—
TWO AND FOUR YEARS OF AGE (WEEKLY BASIS)

Rent (kitchenette)	$ 6.50
Food (bread bought)—mother	2.30
Food—child four years	1.75
Food—child two years	1.75
Clothing and toilet articles—mother and children	2.89
Recreation	0.30
Miscellaneous	0.25
Total	$15.74
Father's court order	8.00
Amount to be paid by Family Welfare	$ 7.74

P.S. Until Mr. Gray pays it will be necessary to include the $8.00 which will make the weekly check $15.74.

February 19, 1931.—Letter received at Children's Agency from the Family Welfare:

I have your very clear letter about the situation in the Gray family. I am sending a check for $21.15, which will take care of the budget from February 20 through March 6; that is two weeks. I am altering your figures with the following explanation:

First of all, the food budget is now being revised because, as you know, prices are very much lower than last year. We have been estimating $1.50 apiece in a family. In this instance, I am allowing the mother $2.00 and the two children $1.50 apiece. As for the clothing, I am enclosing three sheets from the Governor's Commission which are self-explanatory. One sheet should be attached to the record. I would suggest that you be modest in your demands as the Commission has complained. Whatever cannot be met by this can be met by relatives and what we call "invisible relief."[3] The Family Welfare has never been able to meet a complete clothing budget, but must make use of relatives, the

---

[3] ["Invisible relief": a very indefinite something on which some relief-giving agencies depended a great deal in the early days of the great unemployment. This relief was supposed to be furnished by odd jobs, unknown relatives, and hidden resources. It was many times non-existent as well as invisible.]

Bureau of Public Welfare, School Children's Aid, etc.[4] In the need of a very immediate and special article, we give money.

I am sending, beginning tomorrow, one quart of milk, which is $4.20 a month. Hence, I have deducted $1.10 from the cash allowance. I am appending also a white sheet which is supposed to be filled out with a typewritten request on the back, asking for supplies from the Bureau of Public Welfare. If you have a doctor's statement as to the need of any member of the family for milk, they will also give that. I understand that Mrs. Gray does not need coal, or they would give that too.

If it were not for the fact that the father's wages are in question, I would put a memorandum on my calendar to send this amount on March 6. However, I will await your word at that time.

Thanking you so much for your kind service, I am,

February 21, 1931.—Mrs. Molly Gray, mother, in office received a check for $21.15 to cover the period from February 20, 1931, to March 6, 1931. The second quart of milk came this morning. Mother does not feel that she will have to use the requisition orders at the present time because she is fairly well taken care of as far as clothing is concerned. The children have been given some summer clothing by a former employer.

Late in the evening of February 16, 1931, mother received a call from paternal grandmother stating that father had some money for mother but that he did not want to bring it to her; in fact, he didn't want to have anything to do with mother or her people. Mother explained that father was not supposed to bring the money but was to pay it through the Clerk of the Court. Paternal grandmother added that father had not gotten the work at the Governor's Commission. On February 18, 1931, an envelope containing $4.00 was received.

February 27, 1931.—Mother at the Court of Domestic Relations states that she received another $4.00 last night. There was no message attached. Court of Domestic Relations hearing, Judge Bain, presiding: case review postponed until March 6, 1931, because of father's absence. A letter is to be sent telling him to come in March 6, 1931. Another capias was not issued for fear his employment might have interfered with his appearance. A continued effort is to be made to check up on the actual dates of employment and the amount earned.

March 2, 1931.—Mother, at home, is just about settled in her new apartment. The room is light and airy and she is sure they will enjoy it.

Mother is very anxious that an appointment be made for Molly at the

---

[4] [The "School Children's Aid Society": a private agency which provides new clothing for needy public-school children. It is supported by the annual Thanksgiving collection of school children and by interested individuals.]

Dispensary, for it is necessary for mother to "get up" with her three or four times during a night.

She is afraid Paul will mar some of maternal aunt's furniture. "He is into everything." A day or so ago he slipped into maternal aunt's room and picked some of the molding off a bed and tore a silk spread "as quick as you could say jack rabbit." It was explained that a child must have some outlet for his energy; that to buy him ample play toys might solve the problem since he is only into mischief when he is inside. His toys have been left at various places.

March 3, 1931.—Letter written to Family Welfare by Children's Agency:

Enclosed please find signed receipt for the check for $21.15. Mrs. Gray was very happy to receive it.

We think that it will not be imperative to use the requisition blanks immediately because the Gray children have necessary summer clothing. Mother, too, is fairly well provided for as far as clothing is concerned. We will, however, retain the blanks, in preparedness. Thank you. The milk has been delivered. We are asking for an appointment for examinations of the children at Harper Hospital Dispensary and will request, at that time, the statement as to the milk needs of the family.

The Gray case was in the Court of Domestic Relations on February 27, 1931, for review. Mr. Gray was absent, and the hearing was postponed until March 6, 1931. In the meantime a letter is to be sent to the father informing him of the new date. A capias was not issued because it was felt that employment might have interfered with the father's appearance. Father did not secure the work at the Governor's Commission. We are attempting to find out why through Headquarters. We feel that he either did not report or did not want to do the kind of work assigned to him; probably the former. It seems that it will be necessary to go to Wynot to check up on his work and earnings there, as there have been no responses to letters to employers. Mr. Gray has paid only $8.00, half of which arrived late on the evening of February 26, 1931.

We wish to thank you for your prompt action. The delayed return of the receipt was made necessary because of the illness of the visitor on the case. We hope that it has not inconvenienced you. We shall keep you informed of any further developments.

June 26, 1931.—Visits have been made to the Gray home on the average of once every two weeks, since March, 1931.

Physical.—Both children, Paul, Jr., and Molly have been attending Harper Hospital Dispensary regularly. Both were considerably underweight at the time of registration at the clinic, and a diet consisting of such vegetables as spinach, white potatoes, carrots, rice with milk, etc., was recommended; a prescription for cod-liver oil was given. Recently, decided improvement in their physical condition has been noted, and Molly's weight is now given as 25 pounds; Paul, Jr.'s, as 33 pounds. Both of the children have normal appetites for their ages, and neither is particularly choosy about foods.

Home adjustment.—Outside of the ordinary "tilts" which occur between brothers and sisters, Molly and Paul get along "beautifully" together— playing more peaceably by themselves than when with other children. Any disciplinary problem which might arise may be attributed to the interference of other relatives who will give counter orders and who, in the children's presence, will make such remarks to mother as "you know he [or she] won't mind you" or "they can run all over you," etc. Mother feels that this tends to make the children feel that she has no real authority and that the others are the ones they should actually obey.

Mother has become somewhat dissatisfied with her surroundings because of the difficulty in disciplining the children, as well as other difficulties such as the free use of mother's provisions by others who seemingly have no idea of replacing them; the constant questioning as to where she is going or has been and why she has remained away so long; the insistence that she perform certain household tasks outside of her own apartment— run errands, etc. Her plans are constantly upset, and there is a "big row" if she raises the least objection. By the time she has finished her own work and that assigned to her by her sister, she does not feel like taking the children out for walks and if she does so, will only go around the block and back. She has not been able to take them to the park this summer.

Contact with father.—The father telephones occasionally and asks to talk to his son but never mentions Molly. He has been sending on the average of $5.00 per week for their care but never bothers or inquires as to how the family gets along on this amount. Whenever the children's needs in the way of clothing, etc., are mentioned, he makes such remarks as "That's too bad" or "I can't help you any because I've got myself to look after and I don't have very much work." During May his payments fell off considerably—no payment being made during the last week. During June he paid $11 and gave no explanation as to why he did not send more. Mother has reason to know that he has plenty of work; that this is his busiest season. Through paternal grandmother she learned that he is purchasing a radio—yet "he cannot afford to send much money." Mother has tried to conceal from the father the amount of money which the Family Welfare is giving her for fear he will not continue such assistance as he has sent in the past. Efforts are being made to see that father fulfils the full court order of $8.00 per week, and it is felt that if the money is paid through the Alimony Clerk, as had been designated, he might take his obligation more seriously. A change of residence for mother and children is under consideration.

August 6, 1931.—Letter written to father by Children's Agency:

I have some information for you which I think you will consider very good news. Since I first talked with you and learned how much better off you felt your wife and children would be if they were away from relatives, I have tried to find a little flat at a reasonable rent where they would live independently and where you could come to see the children when you wish without being bothered by unfriendly relatives. I have after much searching found a three-room rear flat on the second floor at 610 Ash Street, which seems quite suitable and which your wife likes very much. It is light and airy and has a rear porch. It is reached by a private stairway at the rear of the building. The rent is $15 a month, only about half of what your wife's sister, Mrs. Carey, charged.

The Family Welfare, realizing that it takes most of your money to help support the family and that it would be very hard for you to pay for the furniture, donated to Mrs. Gray furniture to use for the present.

Although there are a few small repairs to be made, the flat has for several days been in readiness for your family. However, your wife owes her sister some rent and until it is paid Mrs. Carey will not allow her to move her trunk and their clothing. I am trying in every way to convince Mrs. Carey that she should let your wife take her things, but I have had no luck so far. If it is at all possible for you to send a little extra money to pay toward this back rent, I hope you will do so immediately, because otherwise there may be quite a delay in the moving.

Last week Tuesday I received $5.00 from you. It came in just the right time, for Mrs. Gray and the children were almost out of funds. I was a little disappointed at not hearing from you early this week, but I imagine that by this time you have sent the money and that I will receive it tomorrow or Saturday. When your family is in their own home, it will of course be more important than ever that you send money each week, for if they run out of food there will be no one to give them any. However, I know you realize that. Your wife seems to understand very well that things are not easy for you now, and I am sure she appreciates all you can do for her.

I'll try to get out to Wynot again in two or three weeks. Perhaps by that time you will have seen the children. If so, we can talk things over. I shall let you know when your family has moved. They could have been in the new flat last Monday if Mrs. Carey had not held back their clothes.

I hope I shall hear from you very soon.

August 12, 1931.—Letter written to father by Children's Agency:

In the letter which I wrote you last week I promised that I would let you know when your wife and children had moved. I am glad to say that they are now in their new flat. Mrs. Gray's sister is still holding some of her clothes because she was unable to pay the back rent, but she gave up most of the things.

You are falling behind in your payments again, Mr. Gray. Your wife and children are almost out of food so *please* do your very best to send something right away. Probably the best plan is for you to continue sending the payments in my care, as it is necessary for me to keep a record of everything received from you.

Now that your children are away from the relatives I am sure you will want to see them very soon. They live in the rear flat on the second floor at 610 Ash Street. They are very eager to see you, and I know you have been waiting a long time for a chance to see them. If you take the elevated line you should get off at either 6th or 7th Street.

August 22, 1931. Reasons for change.—Several circumstances combined to necessitate the removal of Mrs. Gray, and the children, Paul and Molly, from the home of Mrs. Carey.

Mother was continually imposed upon by other relatives in the home and especially by Mrs. Carey, maternal aunt. Although being charged a weekly rental of $6.50, mother was nevertheless expected to perform the work of a domestic servant. She was allowed no personal freedom, being forced to account for her every movement to maternal aunt, as would a strictly disciplined child. Maternal aunt took upon herself the management and control of the children whenever mother's methods did not suit her. The children were forced to confine their play activities to the back yard because their aunt did not want mother to take them for walks or to Washington Park. Maternal aunt exerted every effort to prejudice mother against Mr. Gray, continually denouncing him in the presence of the children. Relatives did not hesitate to take any food which mother might have on hand as a result of economical buying in quantity lots. Maternal aunt could not understand why mother objected to giving her the cream from each bottle of the children's milk.

Maternal aunt did not carry out an agreement which she had made to improve the condition of the room used by mother and children. She was accustomed to refuse father the privilege of talking over the telephone with his wife or son. (His feeling toward the aunt and other relatives kept him from attempting to visit personally.)

The small amount and irregularity of father's payments were a large factor in mother's inability to pay the rent. On July 30, 1931, she was four weeks in arrears, with no means of making immediate payment, inasmuch as the Family Welfare do not pay back debts.

Change of residence.—After considerable searching, a suitable three-room flat was found on the second floor at 610 Ash Street. It is very light and airy, has gas, electricity, and a complete bathroom, and is in good repair. The landlord has promised to redecorate within a month. The apartment is reached by a private rear stairway which leads to a porch, also private. Although the district is residential, stores and street-car transportation are less than a block away. The distance to the nearest school is three blocks. The monthly rental is $15. The flat was selected by the mother after she had inspected two others which the visitor also had in mind.

Arrangements were made with the Salvage Bureau to allow mother to choose essential pieces of furniture (including a full-sized bed, with spring and mattress, a cot with mattress, a dresser, a center table, a large parlor chair, three kitchen chairs, an icebox, and a kitchen table) and necessary household articles. A gas plate was obtained by visitor. The total cost of the purchases, met by Family Welfare, was $22.71.

The furniture was delivered August 3, 1931. As mother was ill, she could not move on that day. Her nephew, Ed Sharron, superintended the moving of the furniture. Moving was completed on August 7, 1931, after Mrs. Carey was persuaded to release everything with the exception of three of mother's dresses.

Reaction to new environment.—Mother appears more happy than at any other period of our contact with her. She said it is a great relief to have some responsibilities, to be free from interference, and to "be her own boss." Several times she expressed appreciation of all that the Family Welfare and the Children's Agency had done for her. Mother has made the home fairly presentable. She finds it difficult to keep things in order with two active children around. The children immediately became acclimated to the change. They have established fast friendships with other children in the building and spend most of the day playing in the front yards. Mother takes them for walks nearly every day.

Revision of budget.—The change of residence has reduced the monthly budget, which does not provide for clothing or incidentals, from $45.47 to $35.47. County food rations are now being received.

Physical condition.—Junior has been in perfect health throughout the summer. Molly had a slight cold during July but speedily recovered. No special clinic visits have been necessary. Both children eat heartily and sleep well. Mother says she attempts to provide a properly balanced diet with plenty of milk, fruit, and green vegetables. By holding back liquids at bedtime, Molly's enuresis has practically ceased.

Father's situation.—Mr. Gray, father, has been very irregular in his payments. During June and July he sent only $11 each month, and during August $10 was received. Since July 1, payments have been made through the Children's Agency. Three visits were made during the summer months to father's home and two letters were written him.

Father insists that his failure to keep up in payments has not been due to lack of effort. There is evidence that his work has been infrequent and that he is often forced to wait a long time for money due him. He hesitates to press employers for payment as he fears that such action might result in his dismissal. Wynot is filled with men who have come out from Chicago willing to work for almost nothing.

Father has a radio. He stated that it was practically given to him by a generous employer who is in the radio business. He pays $1.00 a month if he is able. During July he made no payment. Father's telephone which is quite necessary for his work, was disconnected during July for non-payment, but has since been reinstated.

He expressed great pleasure on hearing of his family's change of residence. He felt that the home of Mrs. Carey, maternal aunt, was a "dissipated house," and no environment for his children. He said he feels more interested in the situation now that he will be able to see the children once in a while and to know that they are away from the influence of relatives. He promised to try harder than before to send at least $5.00 each week, the original order of $8.00 having been lowered by "some lady at the court," because of his "utter inability to pay such a sum."

Father visited mother and children twice during the month of August. Mother said unpleasant subjects were avoided, and all enjoyed his calls. Father told mother that he has some clothes for the children and a rug given him by an employer which will be suitable for the living-room. He persistently gives the impression that he feels he should be a kind of "good fellow" whose duty is to help when he can, but whose burden must be automatically shifted to someone else when times are hard for him.

Mother's attitude toward father.—Mother is very patient and tolerant in her attitude toward father. She mentions his former neglect, but apparently does not hold it against him. She feels that he is now having a hard time, and appreciates the money he has sent. She refuses to allow her relatives to prejudice her against him, and attempts to build up in the children a feeling of love for him.

Grandmother's viewpoint.—Mrs. Dole, paternal grandmother, is the one relative who has influence with both mother and father. Both care deeply for her, and she does her best to help them. She has been troubled with rheumatism which has made her inactive, but she is now well enough to look for work, and her first desire seems to be to do something for the children.

Early in August, mother and children spent a pleasant Sunday at the home of the grandmother. She has later visited them at their new home. The grandmother promised to co-operate fully in attempting to offset the influence of other relatives which has been such a large factor in causing friction between mother and father.

September 24, 1931.—Letter written to father by the Children's Agency:

The seven dollars which you sent finally arrived this morning. If you mailed it on Monday, I believe the reason for the delay was that when you addressed the envelope you did not include the name of the city. The safest way is to use the full address. You should also remember that the only perfectly safe way to send money through the mail is by postal money order.

So far this month you have sent $11 to your family. Next Thursday will be October 1, and if you make another payment before that time, which I hope you will try hard to do, you will have made a better showing during September than in any month since May. The Family Welfare is anxious to know how much you send, because if they see that you are doing all you possibly can to support your family they are more willing to aid until you can manage things by yourself.

Colder weather will soon be here, which means that your wife will need a stove and some coal. I think that if you are able to make your payments of $5.00 each week, the Family Welfare will in return help you by furnishing both stove and coal. That would be a "break," wouldn't it? So do your best! Your wife has not been able to find anyone with a car to call for the rug and the box of clothing. I hope that you will be able to find someone soon, because it is cooler now and very unhealthy for the children to walk barefooted on a bare floor.

Mrs. Gray has the house looking nicer than ever. You will notice the difference on your next visit. Junior likes kindergarten and never misses a day. He certainly is a fine-looking boy when he is all dressed up for school. I suppose you will be seeing them soon. They were disappointed that you were not able to come last week end.

September 25, 1931. Home condition.—On September 2 and 3, Mrs. Gray's landlord had her apartment completely redecorated and the necessary repairs made. A series of donations from relatives and friends followed, so that Mrs. Gray now has a complete set of dishes and cooking utensils, curtains for every window and drapes for two, a bedspread, a scarf for the center table, and several books, in addition to the furniture and household articles purchased by Family Welfare. The decorating and the donations proved a great stimulus to Mrs. Gray. She now tries hard to keep the house clean and neat. She has painted her old kitchen table green and has bought orange oilcloth for it.

Mrs. Gray's next-door neighbor, a kind and friendly lady, allows her to make and receive necessary telephone calls from her husband and occasionally cares for the children while their mother does her shopping and other errands.

Inasmuch as Mrs. Gray is practically illiterate, it is very difficult for her to keep a running account of her expenditures. However, the fact that she is operating satisfactorily on a small budget is proof of her economy.

Father's part in situation.—As yet the changed conditions have not resulted in increased payments by the father, who continues to send about $11 per month. Nevertheless, his visits, which occur about every ten days, give evidence of more interest. On one occasion he brought a heavy box of toys given him by an employer for the children, a difficult task because of the long ride on the elevated, with a walk of several blocks at each end of the trip. He also has a rug for the living-room and some clothing for the children. He has not yet succeeded in finding a friend with a car, who will deliver them.

Mrs. Gray through fear of pregnancy has avoided sexual relations with her husband, causing some resentment on his part. She has, however, agreed to visit a center for birth-control information in the near future and Mr. Gray has promised to be more considerate of her.

Health.—On September 9, 1931, the children were examined at Harper Hospital Clinic. Paul, Jr.'s, condition was reported satisfactory. His weight, 35 pounds, is only 1 pound under the average. Molly remains underweight, though her weight of 28 pounds indicates a gain. She is slightly rachitic, and is given cod-liver oil. Mrs. Gray strained a muscle in her side while opening a window, but after a visit to the County Hospital she soon recovered.

Home duties.—Junior at times helps with the dusting and sweeping, though rather ineffectively. This is a part of Mrs. Gray's disciplinary program, to which she is devoting much time and patience. The children's general behavior is improving and their willingness to obey their mother has increased markedly since she has had sole responsibility for them.

Junior attends an afternoon kindergarten class at Washington School. He was afraid when first left by his mother with so many strange children, but he now seems to enjoy himself. A ten-year-old neighbor girl often accompanies him to and from school.

September 26, 1931.—Letter written to the Family Welfare by the Children's Agency:

During the month of September, Mrs. Gray received $11.00 from her husband, leaving $24.50 of her budget to be included in her October check from the Family Welfare. Thank you kindly for arranging with the Bureau of Public Welfare to supply a pair of shoes for Paul, Jr. He has the shoes and they are very satisfactory.

Mrs. Gray now tells me—and I have observed—that the shoes which she uses for everyday wear are completely worn out. She has dress shoes, which she says would soon be ruined if she wore them for her work. I told her that I would refer the matter to you, and should you decide that her request is reasonable, will you please give her the necessary note to the Bureau of Public Welfare when she calls for her check?

I should like to say for Mrs. Gray that since June 25, at which time I was assigned this case, the two requests for shoes are the only clothing requests she has made for herself.

October 8, 1931.—Letter written to the Family Welfare by the Children's Agency:

I have just purchased from Bailey and Son, 704 S. Ash Street, a heating stove for Mrs. Gray. It is an iron stove which is in good condition and perfectly safe. I am enclosing the bill. Will you please have the check sent directly to Mr. Bailey rather than to the Children's Agency?

May I also ask that at your convenience you arrange to have the Bureau of Public Welfare furnish coal? I wish I might spare you this trouble, but on a previous occasion, when I first referred Mrs. Gray to the County Bureau of Public Welfare for food supplies, they indicated that they preferred a direct reference from you.

October 28, 1931.—Letter written to father by the Children's Agency:

I am much disappointed that you did not visit your wife as you promised last week, Wednesday. Your family was at that time completely out of food and money. Since then, they have had a great deal of difficulty, and I don't know what they would have done had it not been for the generosity of Mrs. Bales, who let them take fifty cents and some food. I am sure you will be glad to know that they have been helped in this way. Mrs. Bales, however, is hard pressed herself, and will not be able to do anything more.

I certainly hope you are planning to send or bring something to your wife today or tomorrow. You have sent only $4.00 so far this month. On Friday I must send to the Family Welfare a report of what you have done, and a report showing only $4.00 received from you certainly would not please them. That is why I ask that you do everything possible to send something right away.

I would be glad to hear from you at any time, by mail or telephone.

October 30, 1931.—Letter written to the Family Welfare by the Children's Agency:

Mr. Gray, I am sorry to say, during the month of October contributed only four dollars ($4.00) toward the support of his family. I feel, however, that his attitude toward the situation is not fairly represented by this sorry showing.

I have tried to maintain frequent contacts with Mr. Gray, and while I have learned that he is careless, stubborn, irresponsible, and a poor manager, he certainly does not at present and has not since I have known him seemed totally indifferent to the needs of his wife and children as our records report him to have been in the past. On the contrary, since his family has been living in the apartment on Ash street, away from relatives, several incidents have at least partially borne out his statement that he is interested and doing all he can.

There is also good reason to believe that his income is now very small. As you may recall, he does general housework, which is one of the many services for which the demand has greatly decreased during this period of depression. Several of his former employers are now performing themselves tasks for which he would ordinarily be hired; others have released him in favor of unemployed workers from Chicago who are willing to work for almost nothing in Wynot; still others continue to employ him occasionally, but as he says, "They expect me to accomplish in one day what I used to do in four days." He also is forced to wait for his money until his employers are inclined to settle with him.

Under the circumstances I feel strongly that I should continue my policy of attempting patiently but firmly to gain his co-operation and to stimulate his apparently reviving interest in his family, rather than to resort to the coercive attitude which would necessarily be involved in threats of further court action.

Because Mrs. Gray, in view of the small amount of money received from her husband, was unable to carry on for the entire month, we have advanced five dollars ($5.00) for her use.

Mrs. Gray's budget calls for thirty-five dollars and fifty cents ($35.50), which indicates that her November check from the Family Welfare should be drawn for this amount, less four dollars ($4.00) (supplied during October by Mr. Gray), and less five dollars ($5.00) (due this agency), or for twenty-six dollars and fifty cents ($26.50).

It appears that the children have one or two clothing needs, in regard to which Mrs. Gray will ask your advice when she visits your office next week.

November 28, 1931.—Letter written to Family Welfare by Children's Agency:

During the month of November Mr. Gray, due to the fact that he obtained only two or three days' work, was able to contribute only six dollars ($6.00) toward the support of his family. The monthly budget calls for $34.50, leaving $28.50 to be supplied by the Family Welfare in the December check to Mrs. Gray. (I am assuming that the change in budget, whereby the family will receive a larger food ration from the Bureau of Public Welfare and a proportionately smaller check from the Family Welfare, is not yet in effect, inasmuch as I have received no notice of the revision and have observed that in November Mrs. Gray received the usual rations from the Bureau of Public Welfare.)

Mrs. Gray thinks since she does not have a private mailbox, it will be much safer for her to continue to call personally at your office for her check. Therefore, unless you feel that the procedure causes too much confusion, you may expect the usual visit from her about the first of the month.

Mrs. Gray tells me that Paul, Jr., needs a pair of overalls as his only pair has been completely worn out. Molly needs underwear and stockings. These articles, she stated, were not obtainable at the County Bureau. I wonder if you can suggest a plan whereby these necessities may be supplied. The budget, of course, does not provide for clothing requirements.

May I call your attention to a sentence in my last letter which mentioned that in October this agency advanced $5.00 to help Mrs. Gray carry on until the first of the month? This was necessary because Mr. Gray had been able to send only $4.00 during October. I understand we have not been reimbursed for this amount.

December 7, 1931. Home situation.—Mrs. Gray, Paul, Jr., and Molly have become thoroughly accustomed to the changed living conditions. In the administration of her household duties and the care of the children Mrs. Gray seems much more interested and efficient than while living under the control of her sister. She is adept at cooking and is very economical in the purchase of her food. She makes a sincere effort to keep her living-room in perfect order, although the kitchen, where the children do most of their playing, at times presents an untidy appearance.

An iron heating stove, which has been installed in the kitchen, affords sufficient warmth for both rooms. Coal is being furnished by the County Bureau of Public Welfare which also continues to send monthly food rations.

Contact with father.—Mr. and Mrs. Gray are now on friendly terms. He visits approximately once a week. He is able to contribute very little to her support, as he obtains practically no work. His change of attitude, however, is plain. He has brought several articles donated by various employers, including a large rug and a heavy box of clothing, each of which was very difficult to deliver, the elevated line being his only means of transportation. He managed it nicely and without complaint, despite the long walk involved at each end of the trip. He appears genuinely to regret his inability to help his family financially. He states that he is "not a kid any more" and that he realizes his responsibilities. This is probably true, at least to a certain extent. His own situation is very disheartening.

His living quarters are cold, he is forced to depend for food upon a kind employer, and his telephone has again been disconnected for non-payment. He once mentioned that when conditions improve he hopes to obtain a larger dwelling and have his wife, children, and possibly his mother, move to Wynot, thereby ending the long period of separation.

Contact with relatives.—Mrs. Dole, paternal grandmother, is incapacitated by rheumatism most of the time and has of late been unable to visit the family as frequently as she would like.

Mrs. Bales, maternal grandaunt, has shown a very helpful attitude. She has given Mrs. Gray valuable advice regarding the care of her house and has donated several useful and attractive household articles. She is now making a dress for Mrs. Gray and often aids in mending and repairing the children's clothes. She recently advanced fifty cents and considerable food to Mrs. Gray, who left her purse, containing two dollars, in a telephone booth. Mrs. Bales herself has a difficult time financially.

Mrs. Carey, maternal aunt, has evidenced no interest in the family. Mrs. Gray, showing surprising initiative and remarkable firmness, has with the assistance of the Legal Aid recovered the three dresses which Mrs. Carey had been holding.

Mrs. Gray is very positive in disciplining the children. She rightly feels that such an attitude is necessary, as the former interference of relatives had led the children to believe that their mother had little authority. Her occasional threats are so effective that it is rarely necessary for her to whip them. She is gradually developing in the children the characteristics of respect and politeness though they are very active and still tend to be rather unruly.

Health.—Paul, Jr.'s, physical condition has continued to be satisfactory. He was last examined at Harper Hospital Clinic on September 9, 1931. On October 7, 1931, Molly was examined. Her weight had increased to $29\frac{3}{4}$ pounds, 2 pounds under the average. Rickets continue, for which she is being given cod-liver oil and an especially regulated diet. Her general condition was pronounced satisfactory.

School.—Junior attends the kindergarten class at Washington School. Miss Balland, his teacher, states that she finds difficulty in gaining his attention, and that he is very sensitive to criticism, crying upon slight provocation. She has promised to take especial interest in him. She is acquainted with Mrs. Gray, who frequently inquires about Junior's progress. The visiting teacher will establish contact with the home.

Religion.—Each week Mrs. Gray takes Molly and Junior to Sunday School at the Second Baptist Church, 41st and Mt. Pleasant.

December 30, 1931.—Letter written to the Family Welfare Agency by the Children's Agency:

During December Mr. Gray contributed three dollars ($3.00) toward the support of his family. As you know, he experiences great difficulty in finding work. Inasmuch as the budget calls for $35.50 in addition to the food ration furnished by the County Bureau, it seems necessary that the Family Welfare supply thirty-two dollars and fifty cents ($32.50) toward the January expenses.

Thanking you very kindly for the attention you may give this matter, I am

January 29, 1932.—Letter written to the Family Welfare Agency by the Children's Agency:

Early in January I conferred with your worker on the matter of revising Mrs. Gray's monthly budget. For the sake of clarity I am including a summary of the budget before and after the change.

REVISED MONTHLY BUDGET IN EFFECT FROM AUGUST, 1931, THROUGH JANUARY, 1932

Food...................	$21.67	($2.00 per week for Mrs. Gray, and $1.50 for each child)
Rent....................	15.00	
Gas and electricity........	3.00	
	$39.67	
Less...............	4.20	(for one quart of milk daily from Family Welfare)
	$35.47	

From County Bureau: Ration No. 3, coal, and milk.

REVISED MONTHLY BUDGET TO BECOME EFFECTIVE FEBRUARY, 1932

Food.........................	$12.60
Gas and electricity............	3.00
Rent.........................	12.00
	$27.60

From County Bureau: Ration No. 4, coal, and one quart of milk daily.[5]

The item for gas was retained in the new budget because Mrs. Gray has only a gas plate on which to depend for cooking. The electric bill amounts to about 60 cents per month.

[5] [Ration No. 3 was worth $4.32 and Ration No. 4, $5.53.]

The item for rent was also retained, realizing that it might not be paid in February. You asked that I attempt to obtain a reduction from the landlord, which I was able to do through the agents. When the flat was first rented, last August, a reduction from $18 to $15 was allowed, on the condition that the Children's Agency give assurance that the rent would be paid regularly. I obtained the further decrease as a temporary measure in view of the recent situation. If Mr. Gray were working he would be able to pay the rent, and I know he would be willing. (His attitude apparently has changed completely, and he is doing his best to co-operate by visiting regularly.) However, he has had no work this month, and probably will be able to send little or nothing before March or April. As usual, Mrs. Gray will call for her check. She will probably also bring to your attention the fact that Paul, Jr., needs shoes badly. I hope you will find it possible either to have a new pair supplied or to have the old ones repaired.

SUMMARY TO APRIL, 1935

November 30, 1932.—The Children's Agency closed the case as the Family Agency agreed to assume the entire supervision and relief. Mr. Gray returned to the home, and for a period of several months the Family Agency worker reported that Mrs. Gray was managing the household and children very well and that the relationship between Mr. and Mrs. Gray seemed quite satisfactory.

April 7, 1933.—The family was transferred to the Unemployment[6] Relief Service. Mr. Gray was put on work relief, but his money was not always spent as budgeted by the agency. Mrs. Gray seemed to assume most of the responsibility and managed the family very well, but although Mr. Gray remained in the family it appears more and more doubtful that he could ever be counted upon as a real help.

3. The Children of Mary Heilman

(The Illegitimate Children of Mary Heilman Are Kept with Her)

September 16, 1930.—The Juvenile Court referred the five Heilman children (illegitimate) to the Children's Agency for placement.

September 18, 1930.—The following letter, dated September 17, 1930,

[6] [By February 1, 1932, the fund which had been raised by private subscription to care for the families of unemployed men and women was exhausted. The first week of February the Governor created the Illinois Emergency Relief Commission and appropriated funds for its use. The agency operated in Cook County as the Unemployment Relief Service and became a division of the Cook County Bureau of Public Welfare. To the Unemployment Relief Service were referred all those clients whose problem was chiefly unemployment.]

was received by the superintendent of the Children's Agency, from the Chief Probation Officer of the Juvenile Court:

At a meeting of our Dependent Committee, which you attended, it was decided that the Heilman children should be referred to you for consideration with regard to placement. These children are at the present time in the Children's Shelter; they are the illegitimate children of Mary Heilman. Philip Miller, a colored man, who is legally married, living with his wife at 205 East 20th Street, is the father of the children. Miss Heilman is of German descent; she has lived in Chicago since she was nine years old. Her father came to the United States from Germany at the age of five. The Heilman family lived in Cicero for twelve years. Mary attended the Adams School until the age of twelve, when she was in the fourth grade.

Mary admits relations with Mr. Miller regularly over a period of years. She met him when she lived with her parents; he was a janitor in the building where they lived. She claims that after her father died Mr. Miller helped her mother manage the property, which she was trying to buy. Mr. Miller is twenty-four years older than Mary.

At the time that Mary became interested in Mr. Miller he was separated from his wife. Mary's mother died in 1925, and the record of the Family Welfare shows that both Mary and her mother had intimate relations with Mr. Miller. Mrs. Heilman is said to have left $2,000 insurance, which Mary gave to Mr. Miller to invest, but she has been unwilling to press him for an accounting of the money.

Mary has worked irregularly since her relationship with Philip Miller. Since the Family Welfare Society has known the family, Mr. Miller has neglected his own home to help Mary. The Family Welfare Society has attempted several plans. They have considered the possibility of Mr. Miller securing a divorce from his wife and marrying Mary, thus making the children legitimate. Mr. Miller, however, has no grounds for divorce, and his wife is unwilling to divorce him. They have also considered the possibility of establishing Mary in a home with a promise that she give up her relationship with Mr. Miller, but she has not agreed to do this.

Mary states that she is anxious to have her children with her and will make any sacrifice for them; she says she would give up the man temporarily, but will not discuss the possibility of giving him up permanently. She will not consider taking out bastardy warrants for him, as she knows that he will have to go to jail, and does not think his imprisonment will help the situation.

Our officer has interviewed Mrs. Flossie Miller, the legal wife of Philip Miller. She refused to discuss the matter with any patience whatever. She was absolutely unwilling to consent to securing a divorce from her husband, inasmuch as she did not care to remarry. She frankly stated that Mr. Miller lives with Mary and has not slept at home since the first day or so after Mary returned from the hospital, after the birth of the last baby.

The house in which the Millers live is now in the hands of the receivers. Mrs. Miller states that this has happened because Mr. Miller has spent so much money on Mary and her children. Mr. Miller admits living with Mary and states that he intends to secure a divorce.

The case will be heard in this court on September 29, at which time the matter of the possibility of giving these children in adoption will be considered. If they are to be given in adoption, we will ask the Illinois Children's Service to place them. If not, we are asking that you consider these children for placement in foster homes.

Later.—From Social Service Exchange it was learned that this family was known to the Juvenile Court August 4, 1930; County Hospital No. 41, July 15, 1930; Children's Shelter No. 1543, June 11, 1930; and Family Welfare, Union District, December 9, 1929.

October 16, 1930. Social history.—The family consists of the mother, Mary Heilman, age thirty-two years; Bernice, age eight years; Mabel, five years; Phyllis, three years; Philip, two years; and a baby girl yet unnamed, born July 6, 1930.

Philip Miller, alleged and admitted father of the children, is fifty-six years old.

Father.—Philip Miller, alleged father, was born in Baton Rouge, Louisiana, in 1874. He had two brothers, both of whom are dead. Hiram, one of these brothers, died of acute bulbar palsy in County Hospital March 15, 1928 (verified).

Nothing is known of Mr. Miller's childhood or family history.

Work history.—Mr. Miller says that when he worked as a janitor in Cicero he took care of fifteen buildings and had three or four men working under him. He earned $200 and $300 a month. He states that he gave up this work to go into the barber business, which later failed. His wife says that he lost the job in Cicero because of his affair with mother and maternal grandmother, and that he went into business because of the necessity for earning a living. Mr. Miller was for a time precinct representative in the fourteenth precinct of the Second Ward, National Republican organization. He also claims that he held a clerical position in the Industrial Commission for a short period prior to December, 1928 (not verified).

During the early part of 1930 he worked as a laborer at the Rock Island Freight Station. He was laid off because of slack work (verified by Family Welfare). For the past few months he has worked irregularly as a janitor because he owes the union some $200 back dues, and they will not allow him to take a regular job until he pays this.

Marital relations.—Mr. Miller was married to Flossie Ewers in Chicago, February 28, 1906 (verified). It seems that they have never gotten along very well. Mr. Miller claims he overheard a conversation between his wife and cousin of his which led him to believe that Mrs. Miller had had relations with another man before their marriage. He says this has ruined his life. Mrs. Miller denied that this was true, and Mr. Miller stated that from the way they talked he thought it might have been so but at any rate he knows that she has never "misbehaved" since their marriage and he respects her for this. About the year 1918 Mrs. Miller, according to Mr. Miller, refused to cohabit with him and they separated.

Contact with Heilman family.—Mr. Miller was janitor in the building where the Heilmans lived. He had held this job for some years and knew the family quite well. According to employees of the Manton Lithographing Company, Mr. Miller was intimate with mother and maternal grandmother before maternal grandfather's death. He said it began when maternal grandmother wanted some interior decorating done and did not have the money to pay for it. He also helped grandmother in straightening out her property after the death of her husband, and it was at this time that mother began to take an interest in him because of his apparent kindness to them (Family Welfare record).

Mr. Miller did not want to place the blame for this affair on mother but he did not wish to accept the blame himself. He said that mother made the first advances. She had sexual relations for a year before the first child was born, and since then there have been four more children; the last child was born July 6, 1930.

Mr. Miller until recently refused to divorce his wife because he said he respected her and had no grounds for a divorce. Mrs. Miller states that he has told her on many occasions that he does not love mother and that he hated to divorce her although he feels he should devote the rest of his life to his children.

Mrs. Miller frankly admits that Mr. Miller spends nearly every night with mother. He came home after mother went to the hospital last time because he had no place to sleep.

Attitude toward children.—Mr. Miller claims that he stays with mother at night because she sleeps so soundly that she does not know when the children get uncovered or cry. He insists that he is quite devoted to the children and has visited them regularly since they have been in the Children's Shelter, where they were placed before mother went into County Hospital at the time of her last delivery. The worker at Children's Shelter states that when father visits he talks at great length about what he has done for the children and of what he is going to do. He is very demonstrative with them and seems to make a conscious effort to impress people with the fact that he is a devoted father. However, when he is asked to do anything definite for them he agrees, but always fails to keep his agreement. When approached, he has many excuses. Neighbors and former landlords say that Mr. Miller mistreated the children and used vile language before them. Mr. Miller states that he is willing to go to court and declare himself the father of the children provided it does not necessitate his imprisonment, but since he has no money for a bond he does not want to go in court at the present time.

Contemplated divorce.—Since it has become apparent that the children may be taken away from their mother and he knows that the Family Welfare at one time suggested that he get a divorce and marry mother, Mr. Miller has gone to John Slaughter, attorney, to file for a divorce. Mr. Slaughter, however, knowing that the Juvenile Court is interested and also knowing father's record, had not done anything about it.

Police record.—Father has been arrested nine times, according to the police record, although the record of only four arrests have been seen by the Family Welfare worker. They are as follows:

1. For carrying a weapon with intent to assault, April 15, 1924
2. For violation of prohibition act, February 21, 1925
3. Contributing to the delinquency of a child, June 4, 1927
4. For keeping a house of ill fame, June 23, 1929

Personality.—Mrs. Miller says that Mr. Miller has a terrible temper and is always getting into fights. She states that he has always "run after other women," although Mr. Miller told Family Welfare worker that he had only been intimate with Mrs. Miller and mother. Former landlords of mother state that for months during the time that Family Welfare and neighbors were assisting mother Mr. Miller came for his meals there but he did not pay rent for the family. They say that he took advantage of the fact that people would not put mother and the children out because they were sorry for them.

Since mother has been out of the hospital this last time Mr. Miller has moved her and the baby into the basement apartment at 4260 Pleasant Avenue, where he is to do janitor work in return for the use of this apartment.

Mother.—Mary Heilman, mother, born in York, Pennsylvania, 1898, is of German descent. She was an only child.

Family history.—Maternal grandfather was born in Germany and came to the United States with his parents when he was five years old. He went to grade school during the day and night school in the evenings, studying to be an artist. When he was thirteen or fourteen years old he went to work and almost immediately had an accident while cleaning some machinery, which caused him to lose his arm.

Maternal grandmother was born and reared in Wilmington, Delaware. She was unhappy in her home and married maternal grandfather in order to get away and because maternal grandfather was able to make a good living. Mother states that her parents were never happy together; that maternal grandfather was almost repulsive to maternal grandmother because of his physical handicap and because he drank heavily, had a dreadful disposition, and spent his money on other women. A foreman at the Manton Lithographing Company where grandfather worked for six years stated, however, that maternal grandfather was a fairly decent person but that it was well known by other employees that maternal grandmother was a drug addict and heavy drinker. It was felt that she neglected mother when she was a child and people who knew mother felt sorry for her because she looked so anaemic and seemed so "silly." They also knew that maternal grandmother and maternal grandfather fought so that it sometimes amounted to physical combat. Shortly before maternal grandfather's death, which occurred in 1918 from asphyxiation, it was rumored that maternal grandmother and mother were living with Mr. Miller. Those who knew the situation in the family were inclined to believe that Mr. Miller was the cause of maternal grandfather's death as they understood he died in Mr. Miller's house.

Education.—Mother states that she attended the Adams School in Cicero until she was fourteen years old at which time she had finished the seventh grade. The Family Welfare worker visited the Adams School and they could find a record of mother's having been there in the fifth grade at the age of twelve but nothing more, although they had no record of a transfer. Mother says that she was regarded as an apt pupil.

Early work history.—Mother went to work first at a Woolworth's store and later at the Middle Electric Company. It is not certain at what age she started to work at Woolworth's or exactly how long she remained, but she was seventeen when she became ill while working at the Middle Electric Company.

Early medical history.—Mother at this time had an attack of pneumonia which was later followed by a lung infection. She spent one year recovering from this condition.

Disappointment in love.—Shortly after her recovery, mother fell in love with a Paul Kent, who was living with them at the time. She believed that he loved her also, but had not yet let him know how much she cared for him when he told her that he had to marry another girl because he was to be the father of her child. Mother "stood for him" when he was married but she became very depressed and even contemplated suicide. It was at this time that her father died.

Later employment.—She worked for one and a half years in the Middle Electric Company, earning $10 a week. Then for one and a half years as multigraph operator for Hamilton Packing Company, making from $18 to $20 a week (County Hospital record). Then from March to October of 1927 she worked in a candy factory at nights (mother's statement to Family Welfare, December 9, 1929).

Later medical report.—According to a recent report from County Hospital (July 15, 1930) mother has a double mitral murmur and has been referred to the cardiac clinic of the Women's Dispensary. A Wassermann taken then was negative. The delivery of the baby girl, born July 6, 1930, was normal.

Appearance.—Mother is a very tired, worn-looking person who looks much older than her age.

Attitude toward marriage.—She states that Mr. Miller has always planned to marry her but Mrs. Miller will not give him a divorce. Mother believes that he has not pushed it because of their property. She says that sometimes she is inclined to think it would be better if he lost the property and then be in a position to marry her and recognize his children.

Attitude toward the present situation.—Mother states that she will not give up Mr. Miller permanently. She may do so temporarily for the good of the children but not for always. Mother regards her love for Mr. Miller as something divine (according to her statement to Juvenile Court worker). She feels that she is being Christian-like in giving up "the dearest thing in her life," which she thinks she has done in allowing Mr. Miller to remain with his wife. Neighbors feel that mother loves Mr. Miller more than she does the children and would give them up rather than lose him. An attempt was made to get mother to swear out a bastardy charge against Mr. Miller but she refuses to do so because she says she knows he would be put into jail since he has no job at present and no money to pay bond. She states that she is as much to blame for this affair as Mr. Miller and even if he is unable to marry her she does not worry about it except in so far as it affects the children. She says that she has passed the age when marriage makes a difference to her.

Mrs. Flossie Miller, formerly Flossie Ewers, was married to Philip Miller, alleged father, February 28, 1906. For a while Mrs. Miller allowed Mr. Miller to help the Heilman family without objecting. When she was approached on the matter of giving Mr. Miller a divorce, however, she became very antagonistic. She stated that she does not love Mr. Miller but intends to remain his wife until she is certain she has some way to care for herself; that she has spent her life with him and does not intend to be "thrown-out" now. She is willing to give him a divorce if she can have the property, which they are buying together, in such shape that she does not need to worry about the mortgage being foreclosed on it. If the mortgage is foreclosed she will expect to remain with him so that he can work and take care of her. She sees no reason why she should give Mr. Miller a divorce for his convenience.

Children.—Bernice was born in Chicago, November 15, 1921. She is a very attractive and bright child and takes a motherly interest in the younger ones. She is quite attached to her mother and looks forward to the time when she will be able to go home to her. Mabel was born in Chicago, June 29, 1925. Phyllis was born in Chicago, March 5, 1927. Philip was born in Chicago, April 9, 1928. He has tonsils which are enlarged to the extent that they obstruct his breathing. Margaret was born in Chicago, July 6, 1930, is a bright and active baby, and seems to be in fair physical condition.

Home and neighborhood.—Very little is known about the homes that the family has occupied in the past although they have lived for some years in the neighborhood where they are at present. Mother and Margaret are at present living in the basement apartment at 4260 Pleasant Avenue. Mr. Miller stays there part of the time. The apartment consists of three rooms and bath and usually rents for $30 per month but Mr. Jim White, politician, who is a friend of Mr. Miller, allows him to have the apartment without charge in return for keeping the furnace fired. The apartment is very clean and well ventilated. There is not much furniture because the landlord of the last place where they lived seized their furniture because they were unable to pay rent. There were no sheets on the bed but the place was very neat and well kept. The floors are cement, but it is well heated and does not seem to be damp. There are sanitary wash tubs which are inclosed in a little room in the rear. The block that the home is in seems to be a very quiet one of well-kept residences.

Treatment by other agencies.—Juvenile Court has known this family since August 4, 1930, when Family Welfare referred the case to them asking that some plan be made for the children. After taking up the case with their Dependent Committee it was decided that the children should be referred to the Children's Agency for consideration with regard to placement.

Cook County Hospital delivered mother at the time of Margaret's birth, July 6, 1930.

Children's Shelter first knew the family June 11, 1930, when Bernice, Mabel, Phyllis, and Philip were placed there by Family Welfare.

Family Welfare, Union District, first knew the family December 9, 1929, when mother came to them for assistance as Mr. Miller was out of work and they were threatened with eviction. Mother's story at that time was that she was the widow of Hiram Miller who had died in County Hospital in 1927. She stated that her brother-in-law, Philip Miller, had been assisting her with the support of the children since the death of his brother; that she had worked part of the time but since she and Mr. Miller were both out of work she had to ask for assistance. Mrs. Miller when visited stated that Mr. Miller did help the family but was unable to do so now. She would not consider taking the children into her home. The Worker could not understand the reason for this last statement until in verifying the births of the children she found that Philip Miller was the father of the children. The Family Welfare Society gave some assistance to the family for a while, then offered two plans: one that Mr. Miller secure a divorce from his wife and marry mother, and the other of establishing mother in a home with a promise that she give up relationship with Mr. Miller. The first could not be carried out because Mrs. Miller refused to give Mr. Miller a divorce and mother refused the second. Family Welfare then referred the case to the Juvenile Court.

Plan.—Case Committee, October 16, 1930, could not come to any definite decision with regard to whether the children should be placed or given in adoption. It was decided that the court be asked to continue the case for a month during which time mother be examined thoroughly both physically and mentally. It was decided that she should be taken to Harper Hospital for a period of observation following which she might be placed in a convalescent boarding-home for a short period. Meanwhile the children will be kept in the Children's Shelter, the baby being placed also.

October 21, 1930.—The Judge of the Juvenile Court heard the statements of the probation officer, mother, and Mr. Miller and agreed to the suggestion offered by the Case Committee as stated by the Superintendent of the Children's Agency. The case was continued until December 2, during which time the recommendations of the Committee are to be carried out.

Medical history.—Miss Sammons, Social Worker at County Hospital, reported that their record showed that mother had been referred to them by the Women's Dispensary. She entered County Hospital and a baby girl was born. County Hospital accepted the findings of Women's Dispensary and did not make an additional examination. The information contained in the report from the Women's Dispensary showed: edema of the right ankle and varicose veins. Wassermann and other findings were negative. At the time of mother's discharge from the hospital, July 17, 1930, they referred her to the Cardiac Clinic of the Women's Dispensary.

Clerk at Women's Dispensary stated that mother had never reported to their Cardiac Clinic and consented to have her examined at Harper Clinic.

October 24, 1930.—Mother at Harper Clinic was given a thorough physical examination.

October 30, 1930.—Following letter was sent to mother from the Children's Agency:

I have talked to Miss Mason at Harper Hospital and she tells me that the doctor does not find it necessary for you to go into the hospital although he felt a rest period would be very helpful. I shall come to talk to you about this either Saturday of this week or Monday of next week.

The children are still in the infirmary but are getting along nicely. I hope the baby is well.

November 1, 1930.—Following letter was sent to mother from the Children's Agency:

Will you please telephone me on Monday? Any time on Monday will be convenient except between the hours of 12 and 2. I want to tell you of a plan for the next four weeks. We should like you to start on the rest period on Tuesday, and I shall come out then and go with you if you will get ready. Will you call me on Monday?

Later.—Mother reached by telephone was told of recommendations of the doctor and when told that the baby would go with her to a boarding-home in Dover, Illinois, where she might have the rest period, agreed to go. She would like to wait until Tuesday in order that the visitor might go with her.

November 4, 1930.—Mother and Margaret placed in the home of Mrs. Jane Clayton, 8745 W. 46th Street, Dover, Illinois, rate of board $15 per week.

November 18, 1930.—Mother and baby are getting along very well. Mother found it a little lonely in Dover and missed seeing Mr. Miller but she had written him and talked over the telephone to him. The baby is getting along very well. She is gaining weight and has kept in good health.

December 3, 1930.—Visitor of Children's Agency at the office of Miss Parsons, supervisor Union District of Family Welfare, for conference. Miss Parsons listened to the suggestions that the Family Welfare support the mother and children away from Mr. Miller in an apartment where she could get some supervision and agreed to discuss the matter with Miss Smithson of Park District as it would be handled by them. She felt, however, that the Family Welfare Society would want mother to take out a bastardy warrant before they would accept the case as this would assure them of support from Mr. Miller if he did get work.

December 9, 1930.—Case before Judge Martin, Juvenile Court. At this hearing mother agreed to give up all relations with Mr. Miller in order that the children be returned to her. She expressed her willingness to swear out a bastardy warrant against Mr. Miller if she was sure that he would not be put in jail.

At the Court of Domestic Relations it was learned that if mother filed a bastardy warrant against Mr. Miller he would be sent to jail if he could not put up his bond.

December 13, 1930.—Miss Smithson, Park District, Family Welfare, on telephone stated that she had taken up the matter of supporting the Heilman family with the Assistant Superintendent of the Family Welfare Society and she felt that they could not accept the case before getting an estimate of the mother's intelligence.

December 16, 1930.—Mother was reached by telephone and told of the necessity for the mental examination. She was quite discouraged with having to have another examination of any kind but agreed to go when the situation was explained to her.

December 17, 1930.—Mr. Miller in the office of the Children's Agency to learn just what is being done for his family. The necessity of the mental examination was explained to his satisfaction, and he was asked if he would be willing to have his share of the property used as his bond. He said he would be quite willing to do this provided they would accept it. He gave the following information about the property: This property located at 205 East 20th Street is valued at $8,000. It is an apartment house consisting of three floors and basement and is located on two lots. It is at present under a $4,000 mortgage. There was a foreclosure about three months ago, and the amount of $500 has to be paid in twelve months in order to renew it and get a new contract. Dr. M. L. Good of 5030 Ellis Avenue took the mortgage. He died recently and his daughter has inherited his property.

Later.—Letter written to the Social Worker of Barnard Hospital Mental Clinic by the Children's Agency:

Inclosed you will find the Social History of Miss Mary Heilman. If you wish any additional information, will you write Miss Nelson, worker, who will accompany Miss Heilman to the clinic.

We have asked the Family Welfare Society to re-establish this family on a three months trial basis under our supervision. Miss Heilman is willing to take out a bastardy warrant for Mr. Miller, but we have not asked her to do it as we have not arranged the matter of bond yet.

December 29, 1930.—Mary Heilman, mother, in office of Children's Agency for conference with Superintendent and visitor. She was quite distressed because of the treatment she had received at the clinic. The doctor who examined her had her come into a room and called in a number of doctors. One of the doctors stood with his back to the door and frightened her a great deal. They read over some papers and looking at her the doctor said, "What do you think of a woman who has had five illegitimate children by a colored man? She must be crazy." He also read several statements from the Social History. Mother was quite humiliated by the whole affair and felt that it was unfair to ask her to return and be embarrassed further. She wept a great deal and said she realized she had made a mistake but that there was nothing to do now but make the best of it. She insisted that Mr. Miller had not taken advantage of her but that she had felt he was the only friend that she and her mother had. None of these difficulties would have arisen if Mr. Miller had not been out of work. He had always supported his family up to this time. She does want her children back, however, and is willing to go through the rest of the examination if this is necessary in order to get them. The Superintendent led the conversation away from personal matters and very soon she was laughing and talking in a friendly manner and seemed to feel much better. She showed the Superintendent pictures of her mother and father, of which she seemed quite proud.

Miss Hanley, Social Worker at Barnard Hospital, was told of the disagreeable episode which the mother had described. She said that she would take the matter up with Dr. Hayes, psychiatrist.

Later.—Miss Hanley, Social Worker at Barnard Hospital, called to postpone the appointment because of illness in the family of the psychologist.

January 13, 1931.—The mother and visitor at clinic. Mother was in a fairly cheerful frame of mind although she was still a little fearful that there might be some disagreeableness attached to it. She pointed out the "doctor" who had examined her before. It proved to be Dr. Hayes, psychiatrist.

Dr. Hayes, psychiatrist, called visitor in for a conference and stated that he was not deciding this case on a basis of prejudice but that he felt that mother's attitude toward the whole situation was such that he could recommend nothing other than commitment.

January 15, 1931.—The following letter, dated January 14, 1931, from Barnard Hospital Mental Clinic, received at Children's Agency:

The psychologist's report on Mary Heilman is as follows:

"The patient is co-operative and non-resistive. She is hard of hearing, which somewhat handicaps her comprehension. She underestimates her own ability, which is higher than was evident at first. Her ability is consistent and without scatter. Her mental age is twelve years, I.Q. .75."

The psychiatrist's report dated January 13, 1931, is as follows:

"The patient has no insight into her problem. She thinks God will forgive her faults as he has forgiven them before. She is just on the verge of being feeble-minded (Binet Simon test) and because of her lack of adjustment would seem to be definitely in this class. The diagnosis is high-grade moron. Advise commitment to an institution for the feeble-minded. A letter for commitment has been signed. If you wish to carry out this recommendation will you let me know and I will take care of the interrogatory."

Later.—Case Committee chairman felt that the recommendations of the mental clinic were absurd, that the whole situation should be laid before the Family Welfare Society, and that they be asked to consider supporting the family in spite of the recommendations of the psychiatrist.

It was also recommended that another psychiatric examination be had a little later on when mother was better adjusted.

January 16, 1931.—The Superintendent and visitor of the Children's Agency called at the office of the Park District of Family Welfare to discuss with Miss Smithson, District Superintendent, the matter of supporting this family over a trial period of three months, the Children's Agency to be responsible for the case work if this is satisfactory to Family Welfare.[1] At the end of this time, the Family Welfare was to be asked to accept the family as a permanent case if the plan proved successful. Miss Smithson asked for a written statement of the situation as viewed by the Children's Agency, together with a statement of the unpleasant experiences mother had at Barnard Hospital Mental Clinic. The Superintendent dictated such a statement, addressing it to the Assistant Superintendent of Family Welfare.

January 21, 1931.—Miss Grimes, Assistant Superintendent of Family Welfare, at her office discussed the case with the Superintendent of the Children's Agency. She was hesitant about accepting the support of this

[1] [See n. 2, p. 35 (Gray case).]

family for even a short period of time. After a long discussion she said they would try it but that she did not feel that it would be successful. The case would be carried by the Lawn District of Family Welfare.

January 23, 1931.—Mrs. Pearl Haney, boarding mother for Children's Agency since April 10, 1929, was asked if she would rent her second floor to this family. The situation was explained to her briefly without giving any names, and after considering it she felt that she would take the family. Her daughter has occupied this apartment until recently. She will rent it for $25 per month.

January 27, 1931.—Mrs. Grayson, District Superintendent of Lawn District of Family Welfare, went over the facts in the Heilman case with the visitor and was willing to accept the second floor of the Haney home for placement of this family. It was agreed that mother should have $10 per week in cash for food and that two quarts of milk be sent in daily. The County was to be asked to provide the staples once a month, and to send in the necessary coal. Clothing and furniture would be supplied from the donations of secondhand articles sent to the Family Welfare. Mother was not to go into the Family Welfare office. All contacts with the Family Welfare were to be made by visitor.

January 29, 1931.—Letter written to Family Welfare by Children's Agency:

You will find inclosed the budget for the Heilman-Miller family. The 5 per cent discount was made because of the difference in prices due to the present depression. We have also used the minimum budget. I want also to tell you that Mrs. Haney will accept eight dollars ($8.00) for the stove.

BUDGET FOR THE HEILMAN-MILLER FAMILY
Based on the Chicago Standard Budget[2]

Food		Clothing	
Mother	$ 9.10	Mother	$ 4.25
Bernice, nine years	8.65	Bernice	3.10
Mabel, five years	7.15	Mabel	3.10
Phyllis, three years	7.15	Phyllis	2.25
Philip, two years	7.15	Philip	2.25
Margaret, seven months	7.15	Margaret	1.70
	$46.35		$16.65

[2] ["The Chicago Standard Budget" is issued by the Council of Agencies of Chicago. The material was collected and compiled by Florence Nesbitt of the United Charities of Chicago. From time to time, when necessary, revisions of this budget are made to meet fluctuations in the cost of living. The "budget" provides a common basis for determining an allowance for dependent families under the care of Chicago agencies.]

BUDGET FOR THE HEILMAN-MILLER FAMILY—*Continued*

```
Food...................  $46.35
Clothing................   16.65
Light and fuel...........    9.75
                         _____
                          $72.75
5 per cent discount........   3.63
                         _____
                          $69.12
Rent...................   25.00
                         _____
                          $94.12
```

N.B. When I figured the budget before, I figured the baby as being under six months which is not correct. That accounts for the budget being $94 rather than $93 as I told you when I talked to you.

February 2, 1931.—Mother, Bernice, Phyllis, Philip, and Margaret moved to the second floor of the Haney home. (Mabel was in the Contagious Hospital with scarlet fever and was not yet ready to be discharged.)

February 3, 1931.—Mother was delighted with her new home. Things were still quite upset, and Philip had been sick all night; but she was sure everything would work out all right. She likes Mrs. Haney very much already. She has been so kind to her; helping her when Philip was ill last night, etc.

February 11, 1931.—Mother assisted by Mrs. Pearl Haney took Phyllis and Bernice to the clinic for complete physical examinations and Philip on a return appointment. The baby, Margaret, was left with Mrs. Haney's mother. Mother was given some medicine for Philip's nostrils, which was intended to help make his breathing less difficult. She was also told to give him cod-liver oil and more nourishing food.

Phyllis was examined and found to have a temperature of 101° and was sent home to bed.

Bernice was also given a thorough physical examination. The examination revealed that she was of good nutrition and development. She was found to have hypertrophied tonsils and was given an appointment to the throat clinic.

February 12, 1931.—Mabel taken from the Contagious Hospital.

February 16, 1931.—Letter received at the Children's Agency from the Social Worker at Harper Clinic:

Phyllis Miller was examined in the Pediatrics Clinic on February 11, 1931. Her weight is 29 pounds and height 38½ inches. She appeared listless and has a cough. She had a temperature of 101°. She was given a prescription and the mother was advised to take her home and put her to bed and not to return her to the Clinics for the present.

February 17, 1931.—Mother at home. She had the house in order and was becoming more accustomed to caring for the children again. She had found it quite difficult at first after so long a time away from them and she had to be up so much at night with Philip when he had the choking spells. Now Philip is better and she is getting more rest.

Mabel was ill the evening after coming home from the hospital. She could not keep any food on her stomach. Mother was a little worried, but Mabel is quite well now. The weather is so bad mother thinks she had better not send her to school for another week or so. She still has coughing spells, which seem to be the result of the whooping cough which she had before she had the scarlet fever. Mother finds Mabel quite disobedient since she returned from the hospital. She has to speak to her several times before she will move and occasionally has to be quite severe with her.

Bernice is very helpful at home and obeys without any trouble. She is working hard in school also. Her teacher found that she was interested in her school work and has given her some extra help. Mother is quite pleased with the interest the teacher is taking.

Mr. Miller has been to visit twice since the family has been moved.

Later.—Mr. Miller, father, on telephone, was asked to call in office to talk with worker.

Later.—Mr. Miller, in the office, was willing to do whatever is asked of him regarding visiting mother and the children. He agreed to visit on Sundays for about two hours during the day every other week.

February 18, 1931.—Miss Blackmar, of the Children's Shelter, gave visitor a set of dishes, some spreads, and a dress for mother to be taken to this family.

February 19, 1931.—Letter received at Children's Agency from the Social Worker at Harper Clinic:

Bernice Miller received her first physical examination here on February 11, 1931. Her weight was 56 pounds and height 50 inches. The examination revealed that she has very good nutrition and development. She has hypertrophied tonsils and was given an appointment to the Throat Clinic for February 14, for further advice. She failed to keep the appointment. Will you please have her return on February 20 or 21 at 9:00 A.M. to the Throat Clinic?

Later.—Letter written to Family Welfare:

I am inclosing the lists of necessary clothing and furniture which Mrs. Miller made herself. We should be very glad if you can supply the things she asks for, or as many of them as possible.

Will you please let me know whether or not you want me to call for the shoes and the other things when you get them? The children really need the shoes badly. Mabel cannot go to school until she gets shoes.

February 24, 1931.—Mother, at home, was quite happy. Philip is getting along fairly well; Mabel is improving rapidly and mother thinks she will be able to go to school soon now. Bernice has had a promotion. She did so well in 3B grade that the teacher promoted her to 3A. Mother is quite proud of this progress.

Mother states that she likes it so much here that she feels she never wants to move away even if some other arrangement is made for the family later. Mr. and Mrs. Haney are so pleasant and friendly; they have made her feel quite at home.

The only needs of the family now are shoes for the children and another bed or cot. Margaret has grown so her bassinet is too small; if another cot could be secured for Philip she could use his crib. They also need more bedding as mother has only four sheets.

February 27, 1931.—Mrs. Grayson, District Superintendent of Lawn District of Family Welfare, stated that the Family Welfare could secure shoes and bedding for the family from the County Bureau. She asked that the visitor trace a picture of the feet of the children who need shoes and she would send to the County for them. She will also try to get another cot for the family.

March 5, 1931.—Mother, at home, was a little disturbed by the fact that Philip had caught more cold. He has a bad head cold which has caused his breathing to be very difficult again. The moment he is exposed in the least he catches cold and becomes worse.

March 9, 1931.—Miss Adams, Social Worker at Harper Children's Clinic, was told of the great difficulty Philip had in breathing, especially at night. She was asked to take up the matter with Dr. Benton to see if something could not be done to relieve his condition.

March 12, 1931.—Mother, at home, discussed the matter of diet with visitor. She was asked to keep a record of all expenditures as well as a record of her menus for a week. Mother expressed her willingness to do this.

March 16, 1931.—Miss Adams, Social Worker at Harper Clinic, telephoned that Dr. Benton had discussed Philip's condition with the throat specialist and they both felt that a tonsillectomy and adenoidectomy would help him. Miss Adams had arranged the operation for this week.

March 17, 1931.—Mother, at home, was anxious to talk over the matter of Philip's operation with visitor. She wants to have his condition improved, but she wanted to be quite sure that he would not be injured rather than helped by the operation. She was assured that as long as Dr. Benton had agreed that it was the best thing to do she need have no fear of the results.

Mother told visitor that Margaret had outgrown her sweater. She wanted to know if the visitor would give it to some baby. As mother was wrapping up the suit she said, "Some other baby may as well use it because I won't need it again. I'm not going to have any more babies." Visitor did not answer at once as one of the children was talking to her at the time. Mother came over and said, "You know I'm not going to have any more babies, don't you?" Visitor could feel that she was quite in earnest about it so answered emphatically that she was quite sure mother would have no other children.

March 21, 1931.—Philip was given a tonsillectomy and adenoidectomy at Harper Hospital. Letter received at Children's Agency from Family Welfare:

May I please have a report of your contact with the family of Mary Heilman since she and her children moved into the Lawn District of Family Welfare? I should be very glad to know something about the health situation of the children. If milk is recommended by Harper Hospital for Margaret I think this can be secured from the County Bureau. Any information that you would like to give me as to Miss Heilman's housekeeping, behavior, etc., would be appreciated.

Family Welfare spent $105.75 on the family in February, in addition to the milk bill which was paid in March. This was over the budget; I presume because of the $8.00 for the stove and $7.00 moving expense.

I am sending a requisition today to the Governor's Commission,[3] asking for whatever they can give of Miss Heilman's needs in clothing, bedding, etc.

March 24, 1931.—Mother, at home, was exceedingly gratified for the improvement which has followed Philip's operation. He had a slight hemorrhage yesterday but it had been easily checked. Today he is feeling very well. He is active, bright, and has no head cold.

Mother has not yet received shoes from the County, but she had received food and coal from them. This leaves her some surplus cash. She

[3] [See n. 1, p. 33 (Gray case).]

wondered if she might use this for shoes for the children and also a dress for each of them.

March 30, 1931.—Letters sent to Superintendent of Lawn District and to the Assistant Superintendent of Family Welfare from Children's Agency, giving a detailed report of the Heilman family.

April 1, 1931.—Mother went shopping and bought a dress and pair of shoes for each of the girls. She plans to clean up some old coats for Phyllis and Mabel for spring, but she has nothing for Bernice. They all need hats.

April 3, 1931.—Mother at Children's Agency office. She was given orders for hats for three girls and a coat for Bernice.

May 3, 1931.—During the past month regular visits have been made to the home. The home conditions are steadily improving. Mother manages to save a small amount of cash each week from her food allowance. With this she buys small things needed for the home and small articles for the children which are not provided by Family Welfare.

Mother has co-operated in every way possible. She takes the children to the clinic willingly whenever asked and never leaves any of them alone. Either Mrs. Haney keeps some of the children while mother goes to the clinic with the others or Mrs. Haney goes along in order that all the children may go. Occasionally mother has left Bernice to look after the younger children when she has gone to the store, but this does not happen often.

Visitor went over with mother the menus she used, and it was found that she was using too many starchy foods and not enough vegetables and fruits. Visitor helped mother plan menus for the week explaining just what foods the children needed. She listened attentively and was very eager to try them.

Mother took Margaret to Harper Children's Clinic on April 29. She was found to be in perfect health and was referred to the Infant Welfare Station for occasional check-up. (See letter from Harper Clinic filed.)

Mabel had to attend clinic quite regularly after her return home from the Contagious Hospital. She is now in very good physical condition except for hypertrophied tonsils. Mabel is now attending kindergarten at the Madison School.

The relationship between the Miller family and Mrs. Haney's family is very good. Whenever the Haneys have anything nice to eat they usually share it with the Miller children. The Miller children go to Sunday School with the children boarding with Mrs. Haney, and all the children leave for school together. If any of the Miller children are ill, Mrs. Haney helps out as much as she can. Since Mrs. Haney is a trained nurse she can be of great help.

Mother occasionally asks visitor anxiously if she is carrying out her side of the agreement sufficiently well to keep the children. She also wants to know what will happen if the Family Welfare does not feel that this plan is a success. She is told that the children will be taken away if the plan is unsuccessful, but is assured that she is doing all she can to co-operate and that as long as everything goes on as it has been going there is nothing to fear.

Mother is always very cheerful and uncomplaining no matter what is asked of her. She adores the children and will do anything for them. When she had a small amount of money to spend, she spent it all on the children in spite of the fact that there were many things she needed. She feels that her children are unequaled as to attractiveness and training. She states that Mabel was inclined to be impudent when she returned from the hospital but is sure that she will get back to normal very soon.

May 4, 1931.—The matter of support for this family was taken up again with Miss Grimes. It was pointed out to her that the three months' experiment had been successful. A report was sent to Miss Grimes and she agreed to carry the cases for two months longer (until July 1, 1931), the budget, etc., to go on as before. Case heard before Judge Martin. The case was continued indefinitely.

May 6, 1931.—Letter received at Children's Agency from Miss Adams, Social Worker at Harper Clinic:

The following are reports on the Miller children. Bernice received her initial examination on February 11, 1931, at which time her chief complaint was a skin condition (crusted sores on left elbow). She weighed 56 pounds and measured 50 inches. The only physical defect was hypertrophied tonsils. She was referred to the Throat Clinic and, as the appointment was not kept, I am asking that she come to the Throat Clinic at an early date. Clinic days are Monday, Wednesday, Friday, and Saturday at 9:00 A.M. Please telephone and let me know what date to expect her. The Wassermann and Kahn reactions were negative. A vaginal smear was negative.

Mabel was examined first on March 11, 1931, and found to be well developed and well nourished. Her weight was $36\frac{3}{4}$ pounds and height $39\frac{1}{4}$ inches. Although she has hypertrophied tonsils, no recommendations have been made regarding them. No other physical defects were revealed. The Wassermann and Kahn reactions were negative. A vaginal smear was negative. On April 1, 1931, she was given a prescription and recommendations for acute bronchitis, which had cleared up on her last visit on April 7, 1931. She was given an appointment to return to Pediatrics Clinic on July 14, 1931.

Phyllis was examined on February 11, 1931. She was found to have good nutrition and development. She weighed 29 pounds and measured 38¼ inches. Except for moderately enlarged tonsils no physical defects were revealed. As she had a temperature of 101°, was listless, and had a cough, a prescription was given; she was sent home to be put to bed. She was advised to return to Clinic when she recovered. No blood for a Wassermann was drawn and no vaginal smear was made. These tests will be made when she returns. She may return to Pediatrics Clinic when Philip returns on May 27.

Philip, who was registered December 17, 1930, was found to be a poorly nourished, moderately well-developed child. He has made five subsequent visits. On March 22, 1931, his tonsils and adenoids were removed here. They were quite enlarged and obstructed his breathing greatly. There is a noted improvement in nutrition and weight since the operation. However, he is still 4¼ pounds under the average weight. Philip is rachitic, and cod-liver oil and orange juice were recommended. He should be exposed to the sunlight as much as possible. A circumcision had been recommended and his name placed on the waiting list for operation. The Wassermann and Kahn reactions were negative.

Margaret was examined on April 29, 1931. She is a well-nourished and well-developed infant, weighing 19 pounds, 5½ ounces and measuring 26 inches. As she is in excellent condition it was advised that her observation be continued at the Infant Welfare Station.

May 14, 1931.—Mother was seen downstairs in Mrs. Haney's apartment. Philip and Bernice both have the mumps but are getting along very well.

Mother brought down a cretonne bedcover which she had bought and which she wanted visitor to see. She was so proud of it and pleased that she had been able to get it.

After talking about fifteen minutes, she said she felt she'd better be going back up and see what was going on. She is afraid to leave the children too long.

May 19, 1931.—Letter received by Superintendent of Children's Agency from Assistant Superintendent of Family Welfare:

Since agreeing to continue until July 1 the present arrangement for the Miller family, I have gone over the record carefully and have talked with Mr. Laird (Superintendent of Family Welfare) about it.

It seems to me a very fine piece of case work in making and carrying out the present plan. I believe that it is the only practicable arrangement which would keep mother and children together. It is one which our organization would not have been able to make. It seems to me a combination of boarding and home care for the children and that it has more of the characteristics of a boarding home than of an independent one. Certainly, Mrs. Miller is not a mother for whom any organization would care to assume support and responsibility under living conditions which would leave her with complete responsibility for the maintenance of the home and the care of the children.

For the months February, March and April, the Family Welfare Society spent $318.51. I think that we would all agree that it is not good practice for one social service organization to finance the work of another. Mr. Laird and I both feel that you should try to work out some plan for the support of this family—independent of the Family Welfare Society—after July 1.

Later.—A conference was held with Mr. George Laird, General Superintendent of Family Welfare, at which Miss Grimes, Assistant Superintendent of Family Welfare; Mrs. Norton, Head of the Family Division of the Juvenile Court; Mr. Willard, Superintendent of the Children's Agency; and visitor were present. Mr. Laird listened to the facts in the case very carefully but stated that he felt that the responsibility for this family was the job of a children's agency and that as such it should be handled entirely by a children's agency; that is, as far as financing it and doing the case work are concerned. Since the Children's Agency did not have funds for such cases he agreed to finance the case a while longer but felt that the Children's Agency should make an effort to raise funds from some source to finance it.

PERIODIC SUMMARY FROM JULY 1 TO DECEMBER 1, 1931

During the next month and a half the Children's Agency made every effort to secure funds from persons who might be interested in helping a family. It was also taken before our Case Committee, and the members were asked to approach certain people on the subject. This was unsuccessful so the Family Welfare Society agreed to finance the family a while longer.

As to the family: Since a tonsillectomy had been recommended for Bernice and the clinic set a date for her to have her tonsils taken out the middle of June, she was sent in for the throat culture which always precedes such operations. The throat culture was positive for diphtheria which of course made the tonsillectomy impossible for the time and made it necessary to put the house in quarantine. All the children who had been in the Children's Shelter had been immunized while there so it was arranged for the baby to go in to Harper Hospital for diphtheria antitoxin. Meantime the doctor from the Board of Health went in regularly and treated Bernice's throat. All the children were kept away from other children but were allowed to play together in the yard. Bernice was kept in the house, which was trying for her. Finally after eight weeks the throat culture was negative and the sign was taken down.

In August it was planned that as many of the Children's Agency girls as possible would go to the Y.W.C.A. Camp. Bernice was interested in the fact that two of the girls with Mrs. Haney were going and was so disappointed because she could not go that the visitor took her to the camp the day the other children went and spent the evening there, then took her home over night. Bernice was elated over this trip. She enjoyed everything. In the morning she got up very early, dressed herself, and when the visitor left the room for a short time made up her bed and attempted to straighten up the room. Before going to bed she had carefully folded each garment that she wore and laid them neatly on a chair.

Bernice is a very bright and active child of pleasant disposition. She is extremely courteous and never fails to beg your pardon if she accidentally strikes you or passes in front of you. She and all the children express their thanks when any small thing is done for them. If one of the younger ones accidentally bumps into the visitor and does not say "Excuse me" Bernice calls out "Say, excuse me, Phyllis" or whichever child it happens to be. Bernice seems to feel that she is partly responsible for the discipline and training of the other children, and they seem to accept this attitude as a matter of course. All the children are quite fond of each other and, when Bernice spent the night away, upon her return the whole family greeted her as though she had been gone for months.

During the summer months the children played out of doors nearly the whole day and acquired quite a sun tan. They all seemed to be quite well and happy. Mother is very anxious to have a radio. She thinks that it will be company for all of them. The children, she thinks, would enjoy the children's programs, and she could get news and talks over the radio which might be educational for her. She is going to try to save $5.00 for a first deposit.

The children do not have as much clothing as they need, but mother has bought articles from time to time, and occasionally the Children's Agency has made a contribution so that they are fairly well clothed.

On July 29 a circumcision was done on Philip, and he had a very difficult time for a while, as there was a great deal of bleeding.

Visits of alleged father.—On the night of July 26, 1931, visitor called at the home of Mrs. Haney, landlady, about 8:30 P.M. and found that Mr. Miller was there although this was not his visiting time. Visitor did not go upstairs but had Mrs. Haney call mother. Mother did not mention that Mr. Miller was there. The next day, however, she was asked to come to the office and then she admitted that Mr. Miller had made several visits at times other than those agreed upon between him and the Children's Agency. She had first telephoned him the night Philip had the circumcision because he was bleeding so and was so miserable. Several times since then Mr. Miller had come on Saturdays and helped her scrub the floors, wash the clothes, and bathe the children. Mother said she knew this was wrong and that she should have told the worker. She did not know why she allowed him to come except that the job of washing and caring for five small children is such a heavy one for her, and Mr. Miller helps her a great deal. She was terrified lest something happen to Mr. Miller and wept bitterly at the suggestion that he was as much to blame as she. She said that the judge had told her that she must have no more children or Mr. Miller would be dealt with harshly and she would not think of taking any such risk. Mr. Miller had come to help her out. It was explained to her that the Family Welfare was furnishing the money for them and that they had been told that Mr. Miller would visit only once every two weeks and on Sunday afternoon. For that reason it would only be fair to ask that he refrain from visiting altogether for a while, perhaps for six months. Mother wept aloud and said she felt Mr. Miller should be allowed to see his family, but she said she would agree to this if it were a means of keeping her children. Visitor tried to explain to her that it was necessary to keep faith with the Family Welfare; that they had believed the plan would fail and so we had to try doubly hard to make it a success. She finally agreed that it might be best this way for a while.

Mr. Miller was called into the office the next day and was told of the new arrangement. He promised to co-operate. He still has no work and has a very difficult time getting food. As usual, however, he knew of a job that he was almost sure to get.

Since this time Mr. Miller has not been to the home and mother has not seen him as far as visitor knows. Mother and Mr. Miller do call each other on the telephone and write to each other.

Medical care for mother.—Because mother complained that a lump on her back was quite painful and made washing difficult, a clinic appointment was made and mother went to the general medical clinic where the lump was diagnosed as a skin tumor and she was referred to the surgical clinic. The doctor in the medical clinic told her that the tumor was not serious and that she would probably have to stay in the hospital only two or three days. When mother went to the surgical clinic, the doctor came in, picked up her chart, read a bit, then turned to her and said, "What are you here for anyway?" This confused mother so she did not know what to answer. Finally someone seemed to explain to him and then he examined her and told her an operation was necessary and she would have to remain in the hospital from three to seven days. She went home quite upset.

Mother telephoned visitor next day that she did not think she would like to have the operation now. They did not seem to know much about it at the hospital, and she is feeling very well and does not think that she wants to run the risk of making her condition worse. Visitor went to talk over the matter with her but her treatment at the clinic had made such an impression upon her that the visitor thought it would be wise to drop the matter for the time. Visitor explained to Miss Bentley, Social Worker, at clinic just what had happened, and she promised to talk to mother the next time she brought the children to the clinic to see if she could regain her confidence and get her to consider the operation.

A week later Miss Bentley reported that she had talked to mother and that mother said she might consider the operation after Christmas. She does not want to be away from her children right now. Mother was told that whenever she consents to have the operation a housekeeper can be placed in the home while she is in the hospital.

Philip's breathing has gotten bad again. They seem to think at the clinic that another operation is necessary. The clinic has also asked that Bernice have her tonsils out as soon as possible. Mother is hesitating as she has not regained her faith in the clinic. She did, however, promise to think it over. She wants to co-operate but she finds it difficult to make up her mind to have the children operated upon.

Margaret is growing rapidly now. She is walking and has nearly all her teeth which she has been cutting for the past six or seven months. She has had only one bad spell during teething. At that time she had a high fever and a bad case of diarrhea. She is in very good condition now. Mother adores her and will sit and watch her happily, murmuring, "Sweet thing." The other children are very protective of Margaret too. That is, all except Philip, who still seems to resent the fact that Margaret has taken his place as the baby of the family. He will occasionally strike or push her. Margaret takes it quite good-naturedly and rises up after every bump with a smile.

Mabel is the most attractive of the children. She has black curls. She is the least communicative. It was a long time before she accepted visitor and even now there are times when she will have nothing to do with her. At other times she will stay around trying to talk to visitor during the whole visit. She is in the first grade at Madison School.

Phyllis is very affectionate and playful. She will remain at visitor's side during the whole of the visit unless she is asked to leave the room.

During this time she either leans against visitor, plays with her gloves and purse, or sits on her lap. At times she insists upon kissing the visitor. She began attending kindergarten this fall, and mother has a difficult time keeping Phyllis at home when the weather is too bad for her to go out.

Philip seems to feel that his position as the only boy in the family is important. He is somewhat spoiled and likes to have his way. He, too, is a little slow in making friends, but once he has formed a liking for someone, he is very faithful.

Mother had some trouble getting the children, and especially Bernice and Mabel, to take care of their teeth. It was suggested that they keep a chart and now Mabel and Bernice compete for the best chart, and their teeth have regained their natural color.

Mother visits the Holmans, a family in Lawn, whom they knew formerly. The Holmans have a car and take the Miller children out quite often. There are two children in the Holman family, and they make a "great fuss" over these children. Mother enjoys the visits to Mrs. Holman, also.

Visitor took mother to the theater not so long ago and she was elated. It was the first time she had seen a talkie and she had not been to any theaters for several years. She talked about it for weeks afterward.

See School Reports on Mabel and Bernice:

SCHOOL REPORT

Name: Bernice Miller   School: Madison
Address: 5420 W. Vincennes Road   Present grade: 3-B
                                     Probable grade: 3-A

Scholarship:

Arithmetic	G	Spelling	G
Drawing	G	Writing	G
English	G	Citizenship	G
Music	E	Effort	E plus
Reading	P		

Recreation under school supervision: Excellent
Character traits and habits—attitudes: Excellent

SCHOOL REPORT

Name: Mabel Miller   School: Madison
Address: 5420 W. Vincennes Road   Present grade: Kindergarten

Attendance record (if truancy, note) absences, tardiness:

School month of May—absent 12 days; School month of June—absent 4 days.

Recreation under school supervision: Good

November 30, 1931.—Letter sent to Family Welfare from Children's Agency:

We are mailing, in the next few days, a report on the Heilman-Miller case which will cover our contact with the family from the time of the last report up to date. We are sorry that we have not been able to give you this report sooner.

May we ask that coal be sent in to the family as they are again in need of it.

December 10, 1931.—Letter sent to Family Welfare from Children's Agency:

In accordance with our agreement we are sending you an interim report on this family.

As you know, Mr. Laird and Miss Grimes asked in May that we make an effort to finance this family ourselves. Since we have no funds except board actually ordered on children removed from their parents and made our wards by legal procedure in the Juvenile Court it was necessary to secure this money from other sources.

For a month and a half we made a serious effort to secure funds from persons who might be interested in helping a family. The matter was also brought to the attention of our Case Committee and they agreed to approach certain individuals on this matter. All attempts were unsuccessful and we were deeply appreciative of Mr. Laird's decision to continue his assistance to this family.

We wish to thank you for the co-operation you have given us in this case for we know that without your financial aid we could have done nothing. If there is any further information which we can give we shall be glad to do so.

SUMMARY OF RECORD FROM DECEMBER, 1931, TO APRIL, 1934

For six months' period Mr. Miller faithfully kept his promise of staying away from the family, but after this time he began visiting regularly, helping the mother with the washing and the cleaning and caring for the children while the mother took some of them to the clinic. In the fall of 1932 the mother again became pregnant. The worker had discussed the possibility of sterilization with the mother, but she was never willing to agree to it. Mrs. Miller, the father's wife, came to visit the mother when she learned of her condition. She decided that she would no longer oppose a divorce.

The Agency Case Committee agreed that the restrictions which had been placed on the mother had been unreasonable and that an attempt should be made to legalize the relationship. The parents of the children were married and the County Agency then accepted the family for relief. The record of the County Agency shows the father to be a real stabilizing influence in the family. The difficulties are very much those of any family on relief—off and on work relief, relief being stopped because of general policy, etc. It is interesting that the first Mrs. Miller was not resentful. She gave the family her piano and music lessons were arranged for the children. The children on the whole seemed to get along well in school; at one time the record reports that one child told her mother that some child at school had asked if her mother were white. The child had not seemed especially disturbed; in fact they seemed to have no feeling regarding color and were well accepted in the community.

The case was closed by the Children's Agency, April, 1934, and was continued as the responsibility of the County Agency.

4. Genevieve DeLand and Her Children

(A Young Mother Who Is Anxious and Afraid Is Helped To Keep Her Two Young Children in Spite of Many Difficulties)

Date of application (at Children's Agency).—August 16, 1929.
Applicant.—Mrs. Genevieve DeLand, 3201 Pine Street, Chicago.
Child.—Georgiana DeLand, born June 11, 1925, in Chicago, Illinois.
Reason for application.—Husband deserted four months ago. Mrs. DeLand would like to find a place where she and her little girl may be together if possible. She intends to get work so cannot look after Georgiana.

Family history.—Genevieve Bach DeLand was born in Chicago, January 9, 1901. Her father died when she was eleven days old. She had one sister ten years older than herself and two who died in infancy. Her mother supported the children by taking in washing. Mrs. DeLand says she remembers picking up coal on the railroad tracks and carrying home large washings in a little cart. As a baby she was well but when she was about seven years of age her spine began to grow crooked. She attributes this to the fact that her mother fell when she was carrying her. She attended school but went through fourth grade only, as it hurt her back to sit in school.

Mrs. DeLand's mother died when she was fourteen years old. At this time her sister Betty was married but she didn't want to bother with Genevieve. She went to friends of her mother's Mr. and Mrs. Andrew Miller, who lived on Pleasant Avenue. She stayed there for two years. They were unkind to her and made her work very hard. She was made to do housework and then had to give them every cent she made so she had nothing left for clothes. Mrs. Miller kept a large rooming-house. When Mrs. DeLand was sixteen years old, she ran away and has not seen the Millers since.

She secured her first position at the Haines Candy Factory at Tenth and Pine and rented a room near by. Later she moved to Forty-first and Drury. While living there she met George DeLand and after a two months' friendship she married him. At the time of their marriage Mr. DeLand told her he had worked at one place for seven years. After their marriage he never worked steadily. He was bothered with heart trouble and couldn't walk upstairs or lift heavy things. Mrs. DeLand worked as a punch-press operator most of the time; even after the baby came, she continued to work. Part of the time Mr. DeLand stayed at home and took care of the baby and part of the time Mrs. DeLand worked at night and cared for Georgiana during the day.

Mr. and Mrs. DeLand always lived in furnished rooms. Mr. DeLand deserted four months ago while they were living at 1102 College Avenue. At this time Mrs. DeLand went to stay with her friend, Mrs. Simons, whom she met while living at this address. Mrs. DeLand does not wish to return to her husband because he was more hindrance than help. She believes she can work and take care of herself and Georgiana much better without his assistance. Mrs. DeLand seems devoted to the child and is most anxious to keep Georgiana with her.

Maternal relatives.—Aunt, Mrs. Betty Anderson, Grant, Iowa. Mrs. DeLand has not seen her sister for fourteen years.

Paternal relatives.—Grandmother, Mrs. DeLand, 5400 South Pine Street. Mrs. DeLand is an old lady who lives alone. She supports herself by house cleaning. Her husband has been dead for several years. Mrs. Genevieve DeLand said George cared nothing about his mother and she thought it doubtful if she had any idea of his whereabouts.

Friends.—Mrs. Simons, with whom Mrs. DeLand is living at the present time, is her only close friend. Mrs. DeLand said she was always shy and never mixed with people because they "took exception to her looks."

August 17, 1929.—Looked through marriage register but was unable to verify marriage of Genevieve Bach to George DeLand.

August 19, 1929.—Attempted to locate Mrs. DeLand at 5400 South Pine Street. There is no such number on Pine. Spoke with mailman who happened to be near. He could recall no one by the name of DeLand.

Called on Mrs. Simons. She has known Mrs. DeLand for about one and one-half years. She became acquainted with her when they lived in the same apartment building at 1102 College Avenue. Mrs. Simons took care of Georgiana during the day while Mrs. DeLand worked. Mrs. Simons believes that Mrs. DeLand is very much better off away from her husband since he never supported her. Mrs. Simons allowed Mrs. DeLand

and Georgiana to come to her home after Mr. DeLand's desertion. She said she had had some pretty hard knocks herself and knew how difficult it was for Mrs. DeLand. Mr. Simons is working out of town for a time but will soon be back in Chicago, and then Mrs. Simons will not have room for Mrs. DeLand and Georgiana. She is also anxious to find work as there is no reason for her staying at home because she has no children. Mrs. Simons is willing to have Mrs. DeLand stay until she can secure a position. Mrs. Simons lives in a small rear flat and has very few pieces of furniture.

August 19, 1929.—Called at 1102 College Avenue. The present land-lady has been there only two months so did not know Mr. and Mrs. DeLand. She said the name sounded familiar and she thought she had heard some of the tenants mention it.

Called at Harriett House for Women to see if they had a vacancy. Miss Macklin, Superintendent, said they could make room for Mrs. DeLand and could admit her at any time. Her expenses will amount to about seventy-five cents a day.

August 20, 1929.—Visited Mrs. DeLand and accompanied her to Har-riett House. She was pleased with the place and delighted because she could keep Georgiana with her. She has been looking for work but so far has been unsuccessful in finding anything but night work. She would not be able to take this job and live at Harriett House. Gave Mrs. DeLand a letter (letter follows) explaining her need for day work. Mrs. DeLand is devoted to Georgiana. She talks about her almost constantly and then will say, "I know I shouldn't talk this way but I do think she is awful cute."

This will introduce Mrs. DeLand. Mrs. DeLand came to the Children's Agency in regard to placing her little girl Georgiana, age four years, because it is necessary for her to get work.

We were able to make arrangements for Mrs. DeLand to stay at Harriett House, where she will be able to keep her little girl with her. It will be necessary for her to get day work as she has to get the child from the nursery at night. We are particularly anxious to make it possible for Mrs. DeLand and Georgiana to stay together as there is a very close bond of affection between them.

Mrs. DeLand has had considerable experience in punch press work. Anything you can do for Mrs. DeLand will be greatly appreciated.

August 22, 1929.—Visited. Mrs. DeLand has been promised work as soon as there is an opening at the National Radio Factory. She said she thought the letter helped considerably because they turned away most of the girls without an interview. Mrs. Simons has offered to let her stay there until she gets work so her expenses won't be accumulating at Harriett House. She will go there just as soon as she gets a position. Advised her not to wait too long as there might not be a vacancy.

October 14, 1929.—Called at 3201 Pine Street but found no one at home. Talked with lady who lives in the rear. She said Mrs. DeLand is working days. She has sent Georgiana to her husband, who is living with his brother. Mr. DeLand is not able to work. This lady said Mrs. DeLand grieves to have Georgiana away from her so much. Mr. DeLand brings her over on Sunday only. The worker left a message asking Mrs. DeLand to get in touch with her if she were not satisfied with the present arrangement.

October 30, 1929.—Mrs. Masters of the *Evening News* telephoned to ask if Mrs. DeLand was known to the Children's Agency. She received a letter from Mrs. DeLand, asking for assistance. She said her husband was ill and that she expected to be confined at Christmas time. She said she would not be able to work very much longer. They have no coal and need assistance. Social worker agreed to call on Mrs. DeLand again and report conditions to Mrs. Masters.

November 2, 1929.—Visited. Mrs. DeLand was at home alone. The house smelled very strongly of spoiled fish as Mrs. DeLand burns old fish crates which are discarded by the market close to her house. She said Georgiana was with her grandmother. Mrs. Simons has gone to Duluth to join her husband; she allows Mrs. DeLand to use her rooms and furniture so long as she pays the rent. Worker spoke to Mrs. DeLand about the letter to the *Evening News*. She insists that she knew nothing about the letter; she did not write it and had no idea who might have done so. She said she didn't think anyone knew about her condition. She has tried to keep it a secret and because she is naturally so misshapen, it is not evident. Even Mrs. Simons does not know but is suspicious. About a month ago she offered Mrs. DeLand $10 to have an abortion, but Mrs. DeLand denied she was pregnant. She said she remembered how very ill Mrs. Simons was the last time she had an abortion and would take no chances for Georgiana's sake.

Mrs. DeLand is very much afraid of doctors. She is pathetically ignorant concerning medical matters. She has not been to a doctor, but believes her baby will arrive in January. One reason why she distrusts doctors is because of her experience when she was pregnant with Georgiana. The doctor demanded his money in advance and was very rough with her when he examined her. The doctor did not make it clear to her when she should go to the hospital and as a result the baby came unexpectedly when Mrs. DeLand was alone.

Mrs. DeLand went to the Medical Research Hospital recently, which was recommended by a fellow-worker, to receive attention for a sprained ankle. While there, she made known her condition and was waiting for an examination, but when a woman sitting beside her enlarged upon the dangers of a Wassermann test, she became frightened and left.

Mrs. DeLand says the information which she gave at Children's Agency was all true except that she didn't mention her physical condition. She has not seen her husband. When the worker told of her conference with the lady next door, Mrs. DeLand said she was afraid people would think it queer that she was there alone and so talked about leaving Georgiana with her father. Mrs. DeLand insists that she has not seen him since spring. She said again that she didn't want to return because it would only mean giving him part of her wages. The worker mentioned a mother's pension as a possibility if he remained away. She couldn't believe such a thing possible and said, "Why that can't be true, no one is going to pay you for doing nothing." She said Mrs. Simons told her the aldermen take children away from parents who are poor and send the parents to the poor farm to work for nothing. Her whole life seems to be wrapped up in Georgiana, and she is terrified at the thought of losing her. Therefore she has always managed to pay her board somehow without asking a social agency for help. When Georgiana was ten months old, she placed her in the Day Nursery which she thought was an Infant Welfare Station. The woman in charge asked $10 a week for her care. Mrs. DeLand said, "Of course I didn't mind if she was getting good care, because it was worth it." Georgiana was very poorly cared for here and became very ill. When Mrs. DeLand went to take her away, the matron said she must give a week's notice. This made Mrs. DeLand suspicious and since that time she has never been to a social agency. Mrs. DeLand was amazed when worker told her this wasn't an Infant Welfare Station. She said she couldn't understand this because the woman in charge had told her that she started the first one in Chicago. Mrs. DeLand does not like to leave Georgiana with her mother-in-law, but thinks it preferable to having her with strangers because she knows her mother-in-law does not want to keep her so won't try to take her away from her.

Mrs. DeLand (grandmother) has one room on Pine Street near Madison. She insisted that the number was 5400 which she had given worker before. At this time Mrs. DeLand is working at the University Radio Company on piece work. She showed worker an account book of which she is very proud. She has the amount she makes each day carefully marked down. She likes piece work because she can always make her carfare extra if nothing more. She is working only four days a week and averages about $3.50 a day. She is trying hard to save something toward her confinement. She has no plans. In order to make extra money, she is thinking of trying to make some organdy flowers in the evening. The workers are paid $1.10 a gross. She was amazed when she learned how many there were in a gross for she had thought a gross was less than a dozen.

Mrs. DeLand thinks she will be able to work up until her confinement, she feels very well and thinks her condition won't be evident. She does not know where she can stay if Mrs. Simons returns. She said she did not go to Harriett House because she was afraid she would be put out when they learned she was pregnant and it was also impossible to arrange her working hours in accordance with their schedule. The worker stayed with Mrs. DeLand nearly two hours before she could gain her confidence in the least. She would not give her consent for worker to see her mother-in-law because she was afraid she would tell her about her pregnancy. She finally agreed to let worker accompany her to a clinic and make arrangements for her confinement. When worker left, Mrs. DeLand called down the stairs and said, "Oh, I'm glad you came. Now you know my secret, but I do wish the examination was over."

November 4, 1929.—Reported situation to *Evening News*. Children's Agency will attend to case work, but Mrs. Masters will try to secure a layette for Mrs. DeLand.

November 5, 1929.—Case discussed by Application Committee. Committee agreed to allow Children's Agency worker to take the DeLands since it would be difficult to transfer them to a family agency when Mrs. DeLand is so suspicious of everyone. Committee will admit Georgiana to Orphanage of Children's Agency if it becomes necessary.

November 8, 1929.—Visited. Mrs. DeLand had Georgiana at home. All the girls in Mrs. DeLand's department were laid off when they reported for work on November 4. The "boss" said it might be for two weeks and it might be for two months. She received her pay check of $14. Mrs. DeLand was chopping fish crates. She had already chopped eight that day. She agreed to go with worker to the clinic the following day.

November 9, 1929.—Called to take Mrs. DeLand to the prenatal clinic. The back porch was filled with wood which she had chopped. The kitchen was very clean but had a very disagreeable odor due to burning the fish-crate wood. Mrs. DeLand wore her smock to the clinic. Worker asked her if she needed clothing, and she said she had one dress and wouldn't need anything for she could keep her one dress cleaned and pressed by wearing her smock most of the time. Mrs. DeLand told more today about the homes where she had placed Georgiana. She has paid all the way from $5.00 to $9.00 a week for her. Mrs. DeLand was most disturbed because Georgiana was never kept clean when she was away from her. Even her grandmother allowed her to get very dirty. The more one sees of Mrs. DeLand, the more evident is her devotion to the child. She is very proud of her and thinks she is so sweet that someone will surely try to take her away. Mrs. DeLand said, "I am just crazy about her looks. I can hardly wait to have her grow up so I can see how she will look then."

In spite of her devotion, she is very sensible in her treatment of the child. She said, "I always do exactly as I promise even if it's bad. I have even had to spank her because I told her I would. Isn't that terrible?" Mrs. DeLand told worker more about Mrs. Simons. She does not approve of her behavior. She said Mrs. Simons makes all kinds of fun of her and calls her old-fashioned and an old hag but if to be modern it is necessary to be "hard boiled" like she is, Mrs. DeLand prefers to be considered old-fashioned. She feels very bad because Mrs. Simons cut her hair. Mrs. Simons told her she would never get a job if she didn't try to look more up to date. Mrs. Simons is apparently trying to get out of her all she can. She had a better hat than she was wearing today but Mrs. Simons took it to Duluth with her. What hurts Mrs. DeLand more is that she took a string of red beads given her by a girl who worked beside her. Mrs. DeLand said she had never worn them because they were too nice for her and she was afraid people would think they did not belong to her. She enjoyed having them in her possession. Mrs. Simons bought herself a new dress trimmed in red and said the beads were just what she needed.

Mrs. DeLand pays $18 a month rent but doubts if she could live more cheaply anywhere else. The landlady locks the gate at twelve o'clock every night so Mrs. Simons was unable to get in after that time. When Mrs. Simons lived there, she used to go out with men every night and Mrs DeLand would have to sit up until 2:00 or 3:00 A.M. to let her in. Mrs. DeLand seemed much more cheerful today and chatted all the afternoon. She seemed almost starved for someone on whom she could unburden her troubles. Before worker left, she agreed to bring Georgiana to the Orphanage if it became necessary to place her again rather than to place her in a private home.

November 15, 1929.—Accompanied Mrs. DeLand to the clinic at St. Martin's Hospital. She was quite cheerful after her examination and said this doctor didn't hurt her as the doctor did who examined her before Georgiana's birth. She overheard one of the doctors speaking with a social worker about two babies for adoption. This alarmed her very much and she began to cry, saying she didn't want to stay there. Asked worker at St. Martin's to tell Mrs. DeLand about the circumstances under which they allowed mothers to give their babies for adoption. This reassured Mrs. DeLand and she was quite contented.

Mrs. DeLand told worker how "thrilled" she was when Georgiana was born and began to cry. She said, "She was crying for me only, and no one ever cried for me before. I don't see how any mother can give up a baby after hearing it cry." The doctor said Mrs. DeLand seemed in good condition. Her blood pressure was normal and there were only slight traces of albumin. She does not need to return to the clinic until December 14.

On the way home worker stopped at the Orphanage of Children's Agency to let Mrs. DeLand see the nursery. Her eyes fairly stuck out of her head, and she said, "Oh, it doesn't seem real. Isn't it wonderful! There are people who are good to children, aren't there?" She said, "Why this is so much better than the nursery where I paid $10 a week for Georgiana." Mrs. DeLand seemed almost convinced that we would not try to take Georgiana away from her.

November 20, 1929.—Called to see Mrs. DeLand but did not find her at home.

December 2, 1929.—Visited. Found the flat empty. Talked with Mrs. Morton, landlady. Mrs. DeLand told her she was going to put her furniture in storage and go to live with a friend on the North Side. Mrs. Morton asked if her husband and mother-in-law knew that she was moving and she said no. She had formerly told Mrs. Morton that her husband was living with his brother in Aurora.

Called at several houses in the 5400 block on Madison Street but could not locate Mrs. DeLand, Senior.

Called at a grocery store in the neighborhood but could not get any trace of her there. The proprietor suggested that worker go to Center Street as most of the white people in that neighborhood live in this block. Worker was not able to get any trace of Mrs. DeLand, Senior, in the 5400 block on Center Street. Mrs. DeLand had said that her mother-in-law lived on Pine near Madison but these streets do not meet.

December 3, 1929.—Mrs. DeLand telephoned the Children's Agency today and gave her new address as 3100 South Ash Street. She said she had meant to telephone worker before but had neglected to do so. She has been staying with her mother-in-law because she has had a severe cold. Mrs. DeLand asked the worker not to visit her until she had had a chance to clean her new flat.

December 6, 1929.—Visited Mrs. DeLand at her new address. She is living in a basement flat at the rear of 3100 South Ash Street. She has four rooms—a kitchen, bedroom, pantry, and bath—for which she pays $15 a month. She is very much pleased with her new location. Mrs. DeLand said Mrs. Simons had loaned her $6.00 and her mother-in-law had loaned her $10.00 so she is able to get along for a time.

Talked with Mrs. DeLand again about applying for a mother's pension and explained the need for verifying her marriage and the birth of Georgiana. Mrs. DeLand said her mother-in-law has both certificates. She does not know her mother-in-law's exact address but will find out so worker can visit her. She is sure she lives on Madison Street in a large wooden house.

Mrs. DeLand mentioned of her own accord our taking Georgiana during her confinement. She does seem to be gradually getting confidence and when worker mentioned her clinic appointment for the following week, she made no objection to going.

December 14, 1929.—Visited to take Mrs. DeLand to clinic. On the way home worker drove west on Fifty-fourth Street in the neighborhood of her mother-in-law's. Worker asked Mrs. DeLand to show her the house since she could not give her the address. Mrs. DeLand began to cry and said she didn't want worker to see her mother-in-law because she was afraid she would stop helping altogether. Mrs. DeLand, Senior, had promised to pay the December rent for her. Worker agreed not to visit until she gave her consent but she could not be prevailed upon to show worker the house. She said she had mentioned worker to her mother-in-law and she told her to have nothing to do with the Agency. She refused to give her the marriage certificate. Mrs DeLand said she had decided to tell her mother-in-law of her condition and then worker could see her. She said her mother-in-law suspected she might be pregnant and she is angry because she has not worked for a long time. Mrs. DeLand was quite upset about the whole situation. She was afraid to anger her mother-in-law because she is the only one to whom she can go and she isn't quite well enough acquainted with the social worker to trust her completely.

December 16, 1929.—Letter received from County Clerk:

In reply to yours of the 13 inst. beg to advise that I fail to find record of marriage of George DeLand upon investigation of our marriage records for the months of August and September, 1923.

December 18, 1929.—Social worker took Mrs. DeLand and Georgiana through the toylands in several of the loop department stores. Mrs. DeLand evidently enjoyed the trip just as thoroughly as Georgiana. She said she had been downtown only a few times.

December 20, 1929.—Looked through marriage records from March, 1923, to November, 1926, under the names of Genevieve Bach and of George DeLand but was unable to verify their marriage.

Accompanied Mrs. DeLand to St. Martin's. Worker had to leave before she had her examination. The doctor thought her condition serious enough to ask her to stay at the hospital for observation. Mrs. DeLand did not want to stay and told them she had no place to leave Georgiana. Miss Harrison, social worker at St. Martin's, telephoned the Children's Agency and reported Mrs. DeLand's condition. She said Mrs. DeLand ought to enter the hospital at once.

December 21, 1929.—Visited in the morning to try to persuade Mrs. DeLand to go to the hospital and place Georgiana in the Orphanage. She was afraid to go but finally agreed to do so. She seemed to feel very badly at the thought of being away from Georgiana at Christmas time. Worker suggested she plan to have Georgiana's Christmas the following day and enter the hospital on Monday morning.

Worker called again in the afternoon and took several articles for Mrs. DeLand's and Georgiana's Christmas.

December 23, 1929.—Visited. Mrs. DeLand was delighted with her Christmas celebration yesterday and told in detail how they had spent the day. She said she had not felt at all well last night. She can keep practically nothing on her stomach except black coffee and tea. She made no objection to going to the hospital today. She has her rent paid to January 21 and the landlord has offered to keep a small fire in order to keep the pipes from freezing.

Asked Mrs. DeLand to give the worker her mother-in-law's address before entering the hospital. Mrs. DeLand said, "I don't suppose you will believe me if I tell you the truth now. She isn't there any more, and I don't know where she is. She told me she was going to move and wouldn't say where she was going because she didn't want me to keep bothering her." Mrs. DeLand said she took her new address and said she might send her some money some time. Asked Mrs. DeLand to tell worker where she used to live. Mrs. DeLand said she always got off the car at Sampson and Pine Streets and walked about two blocks east. She said she thinks her mother-in-law must have lived in the 5400 block on the east side of the street in a wooden house.

Mrs. DeLand was admitted to the hospital on the clinic doctor's diagnosis, which was high blood pressure and vomiting blood. The doctor who admitted her today said he could find nothing wrong.

Georgiana admitted in Orphanage today. Rate free.

Georgiana made no objection to leaving her mother and going with worker.

December 24, 1929.—Mrs. DeLand telephoned in the morning and said she had been discharged from the hospital. She came to the Orphanage and worker gave her a lunch of vegetables, bread, and tea. She was not able to retain it and shortly afterward vomited both food and blood. Worker showed Mrs. DeLand about the Orphanage and the children in the nursery gave part of their Christmas program for her. Mrs. DeLand was simply amazed and delighted. She asked if she might take Georgiana home and worker told her she could but thought it would be wise to leave her here until the doctor examined her.

Nurse had weighed Georgiana and she weighed just twenty-five pounds which is very much underweight for her age and height. Mrs. DeLand said she had never realized how thin Georgiana was until she had seen the children here. She was quite contented to leave Georgiana until she could be examined.

December 25, 1929.—Mrs DeLand came and visited with Georgiana during the afternoon.

December 26, 1929.—Dr. Cook examined Georgiana today and found nothing wrong except that she is so very much underweight. Dr. Cook talked with Mrs. DeLand about Georgiana's condition. Social worker talked with her about leaving Georgiana until she had another examination at St. Martin's.

December 27, 1929.—Accompanied Mrs. DeLand to the clinic. There was apparently some misunderstanding at the hospital for Mrs. DeLand's doctor thought she had retained three regular meals during her stay, whereas she had been given only one cup of tea during the time she stayed there. She was examined this morning and the doctor advised her to eat small amounts five times a day. For two days he wants her to eat nothing but tea, toast, crackers, and boiled milk. If she cannot retain this, she should return to the hospital.

December 28, 1929.—Mrs. DeLand telephoned this morning to ask if she could take Georgiana home. Worker told her if she thought it best, she could, but asked her to come and talk things over.

Mrs. DeLand came and said she had not slept and had not been able to eat anything today because she felt so lonesome without Georgiana. Georgiana has been quite unhappy also although she is eating quite well now. Mrs. DeLand said she would try very hard to see that Georgiana had sufficient food at home. Told her we would bring Georgiana in and weigh her again in a few days.

Georgiana dismissed from the Orphanage of Children's Agency.

December 31, 1929.—Case discussed by Application Committee. Georgiana's admission was approved. Committee agreed that Children's Agency should continue with the case work until Mrs. DeLand should be admitted to the hospital for confinement. Worker will then arrange for conference with Family Agency in an attempt to work out the best plan for the family. Members of the Committee contributed $16 which worker will give Mrs. DeLand in small amounts. This money will enable Mrs. DeLand to take care of her expenses until she goes to the hospital.

Visited Mrs. DeLand. She said Georgiana was eating very well since she came home. Took a bottle of cod-liver oil and talked with Mrs. DeLand about the kind of food to give her. Left $2.00 for wood as she was almost entirely out of fuel. Asked Mrs. DeLand to come to the Orphanage in the morning on January 3 and social worker would accompany her to clinic.

January 3, 1930.—Mrs. DeLand did not come this morning.

Visited in the afternoon. Mrs. DeLand did not look at all well. She said she has had severe pains for the past two days. It hurts her to walk and she is very sore.

January 4, 1930.—Accompanied Mrs. DeLand to St. Martin's. She was examined and admitted to the hospital as she was "in term." It took nearly one and one-half hours to persuade Mrs. DeLand to remain at the hospital. She cried and said she wanted to see her home again before she left and was worried for fear the landlord would burn all her new wood. She did not want to be separated from Georgiana again. Mrs. DeLand made all sorts of excuses but finally was prevailed upon to remain.

Georgiana was readmitted to the Orphanage of Children's Agency. She was placed in the nursery. The worker sent a special-delivery letter to Mrs. DeLand, telling her that Georgiana had no temperature and was placed with the nursery group. Mrs. DeLand had been afraid we would keep Georgiana in the hospital as she had a slight cold.

January 5, 1930.—Nursery was placed under quarantine for chicken pox today.

January 6, 1930.—Visited Mrs. DeLand at the hospital. She looked rested and said she felt better and is having less pain. She has been able to keep most of her food down. Told Mrs. DeLand that Georgiana seemed much happier at the Orphanage this time and that she understood she was going to stay only until her mother was out of the hospital. Mrs. DeLand cried when worker left and said she wished she could go home.

January 7, 1930.—Visited the hospital. Mrs. DeLand was very happy today because the doctor told her she could leave this afternoon as it was uncertain whether the baby would be born within a day or two weeks. Mrs. DeLand looks very much better than she did when she entered the hospital. She did not ask to take Georgiana home. Worker told her today about the quarantine and explained to her that chicken pox is a very mild disease. She received this information surprisingly well and, when worker was leaving, she said, "I think you are awfully nice to tell me about the chicken pox. Some people wouldn't even tell a child's mother if her child got sick at their house."

January 8, 1930.—Visited. Mrs. DeLand was very tired from her trip home from the hospital. She asked if she might come and see Georgiana. Worker told her she was afraid it would upset Georgiana if she saw her mother as she had been told that when her mother came back from the hospital this time she was going home to stay. Mrs. DeLand was quite understanding and said she would be satisfied if she could just peek at her, without Georgiana's knowing she was present.

January 9, 1930.—Mrs. DeLand came to Orphanage and worker arranged for her to look at Georgiana. Georgiana was playing quite contentedly and her mother was simply delighted. Talked with Mrs. DeLand today about her childhood and she gave more information which in many respects does not quite coincide with the information previously given.

Mrs. DeLand's parents were both born in Europe. Her mother was of French and Belgian descent; she married Mr. Bach when she was fourteen years of age, and he was thirty-eight years older than she. One child was born in Europe and later died. Alice, the oldest child who lived, was born in the United States and there were four other girls—Hazel, Mary, Genevieve, Catherine—and a baby who died.

Mary was Mrs. DeLand's favorite sister. Her father died when Mrs. DeLand was a baby. Mrs. Bach supported the family by taking in washings. When Mrs. DeLand was about three years old, Mrs. Bach had an opportunity to work as housekeeper for an old man in Marion, Illinois. He was very stingy and would give the children very little to eat except mush and milk. Mrs. DeLand said she wasn't sure whether she really remembered this man or whether she remembered him only because she had heard her mother and sisters talk about him. Mrs. Bach did not stay there very long but took in washing in Marion as she had done in Chicago.

Mrs. DeLand's life at home was very unhappy. Her oldest sister was very mean to her, and her mother always took Alice's part. Mrs. DeLand said she had heard her mother say she wished she had wrung all their necks when they were born, and again she had said she would like to leave them and go back to the old country. When Mrs. DeLand was about twelve years old, her sister Mary, who was the only one she cared about, ran away. Mrs. DeLand said, "I thought she must have found it swell because she never came back. That's what gave me the idea to go." When Mrs. DeLand was fourteen, she ran away to Chicago. She returned to Marion once about a year and a half after she left. She found that her mother had died in her absence so she left again and never returned.

The last Mrs. DeLand knew, both Hazel and Alice were living in Marion. Mrs. DeLand's memories of the town are very pleasant. She said the air smelled good, and the town was full of apple and pear trees. There was no opportunity for work for girls, however. She said she ran away to Chicago because she had lived there before.

Worker accompanied Mrs. DeLand home because she had come in a very severe snowstorm and the walking was very hard. Mrs. DeLand showed worker the clothes she had prepared for her new baby. She has made bands by sewing together the legs of Georgiana's old woolen stockings. The little shirts were peppered with holes and Mrs. DeLand has mended them all very carefully. She has put new pink ribbon in the little worn crocheted jacket and cap. The blankets which cost only twenty-five cents in the first place were thin and worn. Mrs. DeLand is very proud of these articles and has carefully made them into a neat bundle to take with her to the hospital. While showing them to worker, she fondled them and kept saying, "Ain't they cute?"

January 10, 1930.—Visited and took Mrs. DeLand several articles, such as baby clothes, pieces of sheets, and towels which could no longer be used at the Orphanage. She was very much pleased with them. She is lonesome without Georgiana and has sewed on her dresses and a few clothes which she has at home until there is nothing left to do on them. She has apparently worked on them more because she enjoyed handling Georgiana's things than because they needed sewing.

January 11, 1930.—Visited to make sure that Mrs. DeLand would be all right over the week end. She said she was feeling quite well. She showed worker a picture of Georgiana which she had had enlarged from a snapshot, and also some snapshots of herself. She looked stouter and was much better dressed than she is now. Most of these were taken when Georgiana was a few months old but there was one picture of Mrs. DeLand taken on the beach before her marriage. She gave worker the name of her sister in Grant, as Mrs. Frank Myers, but would not give the name of her oldest sister; when urged, she just cried and said when the baby came, she thought she would run away.

Mrs. DeLand is a very sensitive person, yet apparently many people who know her say things to hurt her. She asked social worker if she thought Georgiana would still like her after she was grown up. She said her mother-in-law told her that she wouldn't have any respect for her then, and a neighbor once told her that unless she dressed better and straightened the hump on her back, Georgiana would be ashamed of her. Mrs. DeLand mentioned the meager schooling she has had. She attended a Catholic school in Chicago for about three weeks, and was a short time in the public school. She said she could add but could not subtract or divide or multiply, except by two. However, she does understand how to count money and can do simple problems worker asked her involving the buying of articles from the store. She is also able to figure out the amount of pay she should receive when working by the hour but does this by the process of addition.

January 13, 1930.—Visited and took Mrs. DeLand a basket of wood. She had no fire and was lying in bed to keep warm. When she does have fuel, she doesn't build a fire unless she can see her breath in the room. She was quite confidential and talked in more detail about her life and her meeting with Mr. DeLand.

Worker felt she was telling the truth today in so far as she went but was leaving out some things. Mrs. DeLand admitted this and cried when worker asked her to give her sisters' correct names. She kept repeating, "I don't want to go back to Marion. If I tell you, you will make me go back to them and they will 'lick' me again and take all my money."

Worker could not make her realize that she was an adult and that they could not treat her that way now. She kept saying, "You don't know how mean they are; they could do anything," and "I am not going to have Georgiana brought up the way I was. Every night when I went to bed, I used to wonder how I could die." Mrs. DeLand said her sister Mary was the only one who ever played with her. When she was about three years old, she and her sister Mary were playing on the porch where the railing was insecure and she fell over backward on the ground below. Her mother took her to the doctor, but he could find nothing wrong although she had severe pains for several days. It was after this accident that her back began to grow crooked.

She said that at one time she was almost completely turned around. Her mother took her to a harness-maker and had a brace made for fifty dollars. Mrs. DeLand said wistfully, "She must have liked me a little bit to pay out so much for me." However, her mother was always partial to her sisters when she was at home. Alice once bought her a pair of shoes which were too short for her. After she froze her heels, it was torture to wear these shoes but her sister insisted that she wear them and when she complained, told her mother that she ought to be given only one meal a day and a whipping for the other two meals. She always called her "Hunchback."

Mrs. DeLand said she secured a job in a bedspring factory when she was so short she had to stand on a box to work. She had thought if she brought money home every week that her family might treat her better. When she ran away from home, she first worked in Marion for a short time on the other side of the town. She washed dishes in a restaurant and then did housework. After she had a little money saved, she took a train as far as her money would take her and then got off and worked until she had earned enough to get a little farther. She has no conception of time. When asked how long it took her to reach Chicago, she said, "Oh! It was long. It was warm when I left Marion, and it was cold by the time I got to Chicago."

She had only two dollars when she reached here, and it was a long time before she could get any kind of work. She said she had nothing to eat but bread and milk for several days and she used to stand and look in the windows of the butcher shops and long for some of the sausages hanging there. Mrs. DeLand's first job was cutting threads in a tailor shop. Later, she worked in a candy factory, packing marshmallows, and at one time worked for the Cracker Jack Company. Business was seasonal, and she was laid off frequently. At one time she worked sand-papering furniture which was very hard. She said she preferred the hard work because she got more money.

She met Mr. DeLand when she was working at Hamilton Packing Company. Her work was to turn hogs' stomachs inside out and wash them in preparation for filling with head cheese. She said she thought Mr. DeLand was a very handsome man, and added with tears in her eyes, "I think he is now, too." It was a long time before she had an opportunity to talk with him but finally they happened to be in the twine room at the same time and he asked her where something was. After that he invited her to go out with him. When asked if she went many places with him, she said, "I went to two shows and an ice-cream parlor."

She knew Mr. DeLand about six weeks before they were married. Her affair with Mr. DeLand was her only experience with men, and she apparently lives his proposal over and over. She was afraid the worker would consider her "very silly" to like him so well and she was surprised at herself because she had told the worker so much about him and her family.

She said she had never told anyone so much before and had never told her husband about her family. She said, "It was so bad, I don't like to talk about it."

After Mr. and Mrs. DeLand were married, they lived in furnished rooms and moved frequently. They lived at Forty-seventh and Elm for the longest period. Mr. DeLand stayed away from home a great deal of the time and never said where he had been. Mrs. DeLand said she asked him once but he didn't tell her and this hurt her feelings; she never asked him again. She said he always seemed very fond of Georgiana and she could hardly believe that he has left them for good. She would like very much to find him. She is afraid something has happened to him because he was never gone so long before. She looks through the papers for notices of people found dead who are unidentified and always thinks one of them may be Mr. DeLand.

January 14, 1930.—Letter written to Central Charities:

We should like to know whether or not you have had any contact with the family of John and Mabel Bach. The children are Alice, Hazel, Catherine, Mary, and Genevieve.

Genevieve is now Mrs. George DeLand and she has a little girl, Georgiana, aged three years for whom we are caring at the Orphanage. Genevieve is now thirty years old. I am not able to give you the ages of her sisters but know that they are older than she.

If you had any contact with this family, it was probably during the years previous to 1914. Mrs. DeLand happened to mention that she had attended a parochial school for a short time. It is very difficult to get any authentic information from Mrs. DeLand and it is quite evident that she is withholding a great deal of information about her family.

Letter written to Hamilton Packing Company:

Do you have any record of the employment of George DeLand at Hamilton & Company between 1923 and the present time? I believe Mr. DeLand was employed in the pickle department.

We are anxious to locate Mr. DeLand because he is the father of a child for whom we are caring at the Children's Orphanage. We shall appreciate having Mr. DeLand's work record and any other information about him which you may have.

Letter written to Vital Statistics Bureau at Marion, Illinois:

We should like to verify the death of Mabel Bach, who is supposed to have died in Marion sometime between 1910 and 1920.

We should appreciate having the cause of her death, the name of the doctor who attended her, and the names and addresses of any relatives.

We are very anxious to secure some information which will aid us in locating her relatives.

Thank you very much for this information.

January 15, 1930 —Letter received from Vital Statistics Bureau, Marion:

No record of the death of Mabel Bach since 1900. Mary Bach, of Maryville, died at the Peoples Hospital, Camby, Illinois, Jan. 16, 1926. Mrs. Mary Bach was born in Pennsylvania.

Visited. Mrs. DeLand feels about the same. She didn't tell worker any more about her sisters except to say she knew they would come to Chicago and find her if they knew where she was. She said if they knew how much money she could earn they would want to take it from her. Mrs. DeLand wrote her sisters when she first saw Mr. DeLand and told them she might get married. She wrote again after she was married but never received an answer. The worker tried to make Mrs. DeLand see that this was a pretty good indication that they wouldn't bother her but she could not understand it.

January 16, 1930.—Looked through the records at County Building but was unable to verify the birth of Genevieve Bach or the death of John Bach in January 1899, 1900, or 1901. Mrs. DeLand seems quite sure of her age for she told worker that she was always the age of the year. (Records were not kept very accurately before 1916.)

Social Service Exchange has no record of the Bach family.

January 17, 1930.—Mrs. DeLand telephoned today to ask if she could come to see Georgiana. It was a very cold day and worker told her she would drive her to the Orphanage tomorrow. Mrs. DeLand said she had no fire and the coal company told her they wouldn't promise to deliver her wood before morning. In the evening, worker took her a basket of wood and coke as the temperature was 15° below zero. She said she had been thinking about the wood she had seen in an alley near the Orphanage and how she would have picked it up if she had lived near. There are several stores which throw their empty boxes there, and it was these Mrs. DeLand had noticed. Mrs. DeLand told worker about picking up three pieces of coal which had dropped from a wagon. She thought she was very lucky to get them.

January 18, 1930.—Letter received from Central Charities:

Replying to your letter of January 14, asking information about the Bach children, wish to advise you that we have made a thorough search of our records several years prior to 1914 and since that time but find no record of these children. We have also cleared the case with the Dependent Child Commission and they can find no record.

If you have not already done so, may we suggest that you clear with the Juvenile Court as it is possible they had some contact with the family.

Regretting that we have been unable to assist you, we are

Drove Mrs. DeLand to the Orphanage to see Georgiana. She watched from a position where Georgiana would not be able to see her. Mrs. De-Land was very much pleased because Georgiana seemed contented.

January 19, 1930.—Drove Mrs. DeLand to St. Martin's Hospital, where she was admitted today. The doctor said he thought the baby would be born very soon.

January 21, 1930.—One of the members of the Application Committee gave worker $25 for Mrs. DeLand. Fifteen of this was to be used for the rent. Called to see landlord, and paid $15 which pays Mrs. DeLand's rent to February 22. Told him Mrs. DeLand would be away about two weeks. He will build a fire occasionally so the water will not freeze and burst the pipes.

January 22, 1930.—Letter received from Hamilton Packing Company:

Answering your inquiry of January 14: From the information furnished we are unable to locate record of Mr. DeLand's employment with us.

We regret our inability to be of service to you.

January 22, 23, and 24, 1930.—Visited Mrs. DeLand at St. Martin's. It was necessary to visit often in order to keep Mrs. DeLand contented. Each time she cried and begged worker to take her home.

Letter written to Board of Health, City Hall, Chicago:

Will you kindly look again for the birth record of Georgiana DeLand, born June 11, 1926, in Chicago, registered No. 64512–11?

We would like to have the address at which she was born, the name of the doctor attending, mother's maiden name, and any other information which the record may contain.

We are very anxious to secure as much information as possible on this case and will appreciate your assistance.

January 25, 1930.—Visited. Mrs. DeLand was discouraged today. She is worried about her condition since she thinks there must be something wrong because the baby is so slow coming. She has been to the delivery room three times but they were not able to induce labor. She is so worried because she has had to stay at the hospital so long and has been such an expense to them. She said at every meal they asked her whether she would like tea or milk and she has always asked for tea because she thought it was cheaper. The last two days she has been asking for milk because she is afraid so much tea has made her nervous. She wanted to be sure worker thought it was all right for her to take milk. Talked with Mrs. DeLand about a bed for the baby. She had a crib for Georgiana but never had a mattress. She said she used to wind the springs with cheese-cloth.

January 26, 1930.—Visited. Mrs. DeLand was very happy because her baby boy was born last evening. The doctor told worker she had had a rather hard time and was very much frightened which made it seem worse to her. The baby is very well formed and weighs seven pounds, one ounce. Mrs. DeLand is trying to think of a name which begins with *G* so she and her husband and Georgiana and the baby will all have the same initials. She plans to have the baby christened. She said Georgiana was christened at a Lutheran church in Glen Ridge.

January 28, 1930.—Letter written to County Welfare Worker in Grant, Iowa:

Is it possible for you to find out for us whether or not there is such a person in Grant as Mrs. Frank Myers? Is there a Reverend Saylor living there at present or do you happen to know whether there was ever such a person living in Grant? I am sorry I cannot be more explicit but I have very meager information.

Mrs. Genevieve DeLand, sister of Mrs. Myers, came to the Children's Agency for assistance. Mrs. DeLand's husband deserted in May, 1929, leaving her to care for her little three-year-old girl, Georgiana. Mrs. DeLand worked as long as she was able and is now in the hospital for confinement. Georgiana is being cared for at the Orphanage during this period.

The story of Mrs. DeLand's life is that of a hunchbacked, very ignorant, superstitious, probably subnormal, little girl thrown on her own resources to earn her own living at a very early age. Her life at home was made miserable by the ill treatment she received from her sisters. She ran away from home in Marion, Illinois, when she was about fourteen years of age and came to Chicago. She has worked very hard to obtain enough for a mere existence. Her husband, who suffered from heart trouble, was more of a hindrance than help so she is no worse off financially since his desertion.

Mrs. DeLand is devoted to Georgiana, who is an exceptionally well-mannered attractive little girl. She is the only bright spot in Mrs. DeLand's existence and she lives in constant fear that someone will try to take Georgiana away. Mrs. DeLand distrusts everyone and it is very difficult to get from her any information about her family. She refuses to give social worker the name of her sister in Marion but she gave Mrs. Myers as the name of her sister in Grant. Mrs. DeLand seems afraid that she will be forced to return to Marion and work for her sister again.

I am not sure that Mrs. Myers knows of her sister's marriage. Her maiden name was Genevieve Bach, and Mrs. Myers' name was Catherine Bach. Mrs. DeLand said her sister was married in Grant by Reverend Saylor. Mrs. DeLand has no conception of time so I cannot give you even the approximate year. Mrs. DeLand is thirty years of age and is the youngest of a family of five girls. She speaks of her sisters as being "awful old."

We are very anxious to make a plan whereby Mrs. DeLand can be helped to stay at home and care for her two children. She has done remarkably well on the meager income she has had and with a little help ought to be able to make a good home for her children. She has shown a great deal of ability in handling Georgiana. If her story is true, she will be eligible for a mother's pension shortly. We shall appreciate very much your attempt to locate her sister. If you are successful in interviewing her, please do not give any more information about Mrs. DeLand than you feel is absolutely necessary. We should like to have her story of Mrs. DeLand's early life and the names and addresses of all relatives. Mrs. DeLand has two sisters in Marion, Illinois, but will not give worker their last names. The names of the Bach girls are: Alice, Hazel, Catherine, Mary, and Genevieve.

Thank you very much for your help in this case.

Visited Mrs. DeLand and took her a long list of names beginning with *G.* She seems quite contented at the hospital now that she has the baby.

January 30, 1930.—Called at the house to leave several articles for Mrs. DeLand. There were several gas bills under the door. These were addressed to G. Bachman and Genevieve Bachman. There was also a letter from the Curtis Publishing Company, addressed to Mrs. DeLand.

Later.—Visited Mrs. DeLand at the hospital. Mrs. DeLand feels well except for having trouble with her breasts because of a large supply of milk. The baby is getting along nicely and is already gaining.

February 1, 1930.—Ordered one-fourth ton of coal to be delivered for Mrs. DeLand today. Located Mrs. Smith at 7421 East Thirty-first Street. The house is very shabby but Mrs. Smith's kitchen was very clean. She said she had taken care of Georgiana during the fall of 1928 and the winter of 1929. At this time, Mrs. DeLand was living at 6577 South Center Street. She was working at night as a punch-press operator in a factory on the northwest side. Mrs. Smith kept Georgiana at night for five dollars a week. Mr. DeLand used to call for her frequently. He was tall and had light hair. He seemed to be fond of Georgiana. Mrs. Smith said he did not work steadily, and his wife told her he had heart trouble. Mrs. DeLand never mentioned her people except to say that her mother was dead. She sometimes mentioned Mr. DeLand's mother and brother. At one time, Georgiana stayed with her father's people in Aurora. Mrs. Smith said she thought Mrs. DeLand was very queer because she once said to her that she would take Georgiana and jump in the lake if she thought she couldn't take care of her. Mrs. DeLand told Mrs. Smith she had to give Mr. DeLand money because he wasn't able to work. Called at 6577 South Center Street and talked with the landlord. He remembered Mrs. DeLand and said she worked very hard. Sometimes he would hear her washing at two o'clock in the morning. Then, part of the time, she worked at night. He said Mr. DeLand was a tall heavy-set man. He had heart trouble and Mrs. DeLand used to spend a great deal for his medicine. He lived there off and on, but spent a great deal of time in Aurora. The landlord was under the impression that he had people in Glen Ridge. He said Mrs. DeLand used to call a Glen Ridge telephone number. He suggested worker call on Mrs. Fagan at 6342 South Center Street, as she used to live in his house when Mrs. DeLand was there.

The worker talked with Mrs. Fagan. She said Mrs. DeLand had very little to say to her. She seemed to feel that Mrs. DeLand was inclined to be unfriendly and wanted nothing to do with other people in the house. Asked her if she had ever heard Mrs. DeLand telephone. She said she called Riverside frequently but had never called Glen Ridge. Mrs. Fagan said Mr. DeLand was a fine-looking man. He was away a great deal of the time and she understood he was in Aurora. Mrs. Fagan suggested that the worker talk with the Italian family who live on Forty-fifth Street as Mrs. DeLand used to visit them frequently.

Located the Italian family at 400 West Forty-fifth Street and talked with a young girl with whom Mrs. DeLand worked at the National Radio Factory. She said her mother had taken care of Georgiana while Mrs. DeLand worked. Mrs. DeLand never talked with her very much about her personal affairs except on one day when she seemed to feel especially blue. She told her the same story she had told the worker about running away from home. This Italian girl has seen Mr. DeLand and has seen his mother. She is under the impression that Mrs. DeLand, Senior, lives on Eighty-seventh Street but has never been to her house. Mrs. DeLand, Senior, is a very selfish woman and resents her son's marriage for she wants him all for herself. She said Mr. DeLand spent a great deal of his time in Aurora. She has asked Mrs. DeLand about her sister's names several times but Mrs. DeLand would always reply, "What possible difference could it make to anyone?" She has told her that she saw them on the streetcar two or three times and when they said, "Oh, there goes Genevieve!" she just ignored them. They had always made fun of her and said she would never marry because of her crooked back. The Italian girl said she thought Mrs. DeLand's mother had died about two years ago.

Called on Mrs. Morton. She said she had asked Mrs. DeLand to move because she didn't approve of a woman in her condition living alone. She said she told her not to call on her if she became ill. Mrs. Morton said Mr. DeLand and his mother had visited Mrs. DeLand there. She was under the impression that they were quite well-to-do. Mr. DeLand was well dressed and drove a car. She understood that he drove up from Aurora. He was a very good-looking man, heavy set, and of medium height.

February 3, 1930.—Drove Mrs. DeLand home from the hospital. She asked if she might stop at the Orphanage to show the baby to the ladies. She said she thought he was so cute she wanted someone to see him. She said she did wish Mr. DeLand could see him. She was delighted with the way her rooms had been arranged while she was away. Worker had taken a bed for the baby and a few pieces of old furniture from the Orphanage. Mrs. DeLand looked around in amazement and kept repeating, "I don't believe it!" She was very much disappointed because Georgiana couldn't go home today but accepted the fact that she had German measles very well.

February 4, 1930.—Case discussed by Application Committee. Although it was recognized as a case for a family agency, it did not seem that the case worker could be changed satisfactorily at this point, since it has taken months of frequent visiting to gain Mrs. DeLand's confidence in the least. The committee feel that we might make an exception of this case and carry on with it at least for the present.

Georgiana's birth certificate:

This is to advise you that there is preserved under File No. 64512 in the Department of Health of Chicago, Illinois, a Record of Birth of Georgiana DeLand.

Georgiana DeLand.   *Sex:* Female

Born on June 11, 1926, at 4701 Elm Avenue

Name of father: George DeLand

Name of mother: Genevieve Skogland

Birth attended by M. G. Neyman

Mother's name was given as Genevieve Skogland. Called on Dr. M. G. Neyman who remembered Mrs. DeLand and the circumstances of Georgiana's birth. He has seen Mr. DeLand only once or twice. The bill for Mrs. DeLand's care was paid in full. Dr. Neyman knows nothing about the family. He has not seen Mrs. DeLand since last July when he sent her to the Municipal Contagious Hospital with diphtheria. Dr. Neyman had not known that Mr. DeLand had left her. He said he wouldn't have kept sending her a statement each month had he known the circumstances.

Talked with Mrs. Geyt who rented rooms to Mr. and Mrs. DeLand at 4701 Elm Avenue. Mrs. Geyt said they lived there between one and a half and two years. They paid $8.00 a week for their rooms. They always seemed to get along well together and never quarreled. Mr. and Mrs. De-Land used to drive off together early in the morning and return at night.

Mr. DeLand drove an old Moon car. He used to take trips to Aurora frequently to visit friends. Mrs. DeLand went only once. She said his friends tried to use her as a maid and she wouldn't stand it. Mr. DeLand was a very fine-looking man, and Georgiana favored him. People in the house knew nothing about Mrs. DeLand's condition until Georgiana was born. After her birth, Mrs. DeLand continued to work and placed Georgiana out by the day. Mrs. Geyt said she asked them to move because they used an electric heater at night. She was quite sure of it, although Mrs. DeLand denied it and became very angry at her when she accused her of this. Mrs. Geyt said Mrs. DeLand had a terrible temper when she got started. (Mrs. DeLand had previously told worker about the trouble she had with Mrs. Geyt. She said Mr. Geyt used to look into their room with a flashlight at night to see if he would find a heater on. Mrs. DeLand said Mrs. Geyt didn't like her because she would not allow a friend of hers to board Georgiana. Mrs. DeLand had thought this woman took very poor care of her own children.) Mrs. Geyt suggested that the worker call on Mrs. Dyckman, who lived in the house when Mrs. DeLand lived there. She said they always seemed to have some secret. She said to be sure not to tell Mrs. Dyckman that she had sent her.

Called on Mrs. Dyckman. She helped Mrs. DeLand with Georgiana several times. She gave worker no more information about friends and relatives than she received from Mrs. Geyt. Mrs. Dyckman said she had considered Mrs. DeLand a very nice person but she didn't call on Mrs. DeLand often because she didn't like Mr. DeLand. She didn't think he was very good to his wife. He frequently went to Aurora and took Georgiana with him, but Mrs. DeLand never went along. Mrs. DeLand always worked very hard.

Visited Mrs. DeLand. Asked her about the name Genevieve Skogland. The name apparently meant nothing to Mrs. DeLand. She said she had never heard the name and was quite sure her husband had not. She said he gave the information to the doctor. Asked her how she happened to have her gas bills come addressed to Genevieve Bachman. She said one day she just got to thinking she wouldn't use Mr. DeLand's name any more if he wasn't coming back to her, so gave her maiden name to the gas company. She said she told them Bach rather than Bachman.

Telephoned to the only Skogland in the telephone directory. The woman was quite surprised, said she thought her family was the only one by the name in Chicago, and she knows of no one by the name of Genevieve. Skogland is a Swedish name.

February 5, 1930.—Located Lutheran church on Grove Avenue in Glen Ridge. Rev. Schnider has been pastor there for many years. He was not at home, so left message with his daughter-in-law. She said he would write worker any information he had about the DeLands. She said she had never heard of the family.

Visited Mrs. DeLand. She seems to be getting along very well with the baby. She is trying to do too much but she is so happy to be at home again, she can't seem to help working around the house. Mentioned to her the possibility of Mr. DeLand's being in Aurora. She said she was sure he wasn't there; as far as she knows he was never in Aurora but she tells everyone this as "people would think it was funny for a wife not to know where her husband is."

February 7, 1930.—Called on Mrs. Wilson at 421 Prairie Avenue. Mrs. Wilson took care of Georgiana for a short period in the fall of 1928. She said she considered Mrs. DeLand a very peculiar person because she seemed so suspicious about everyone who had anything to do with Georgiana. She said Mr. DeLand used to drive them over about four o'clock in the afternoon. Frequently Mrs. DeLand would return with the excuse that she had forgotten something, when Mrs. Wilson was certain she only wanted to see if she was mistreating Georgiana. Mrs. Wilson said Mrs. DeLand told her that her own folks were ashamed of her and once, when Mr. DeLand left her for a time, she said her folks had conspired against her to take Mr. DeLand away. Mrs. DeLand took Georgiana from Mrs. Wilson because she found a black-and-blue mark on her spine. Mrs. Wilson said she wrote her a very insolent letter about this. Mrs. Wilson explained to worker that Georgiana had received the mark by sliding downstairs. She said she thought Mrs. DeLand was a very quarrelsome person. (Mrs. DeLand had previously told worker about Mrs. Wilson. She said when she went for Georgiana one morning, she was crying very hard and clung to her. She wouldn't even allow Mrs. Wilson to dress her. Always before this, she had called Mrs. Wilson "nice lady" and "pretty lady." Mrs. DeLand said she couldn't understand what was the trouble but when she undressed her found a black-and-blue mark on her back. She said she thought Mrs. Wilson might have whipped her so never took her back but wrote Mrs. Wilson a letter telling her about it and saying she didn't know whether or not she had done it but if she had, God would punish her for mistreating a little child.)

Visited Mrs. DeLand and took her a blue woolen dress. Mrs. DeLand thought it was much too good for her to wear but said with her eyes just shining, "Maybe I could get a good job with a dress like this. Perhaps I could be a waitress instead of working in a factory." Mrs. DeLand mentioned today that the people at the Orphanage had treated her better than anyone had treated her during her whole life. She is still a little bit worried about Georgiana because it has been so long since she has seen her. She said she sometimes wondered if she were still at the Orphanage.

Letter received from Rev. Schnider:

This is to inform you that Georgiana DeLand was not baptized in the First Lutheran Church of Glen Ridge. I remember nothing of it and the records show nothing.

Possibly she was baptized by Rev. Stoll or Rev. Kremm, the other two Lutheran ministers here.

February 10, 1930.—Called at County Bureau district office, and talked with worker regarding county supplies for Mrs. DeLand. Asked if it would be possible for supervision to remain with the Children's Agency.

Later.—Letter written to Contagious Disease Hospital:

Do you have a record of the hospitalization of Genevieve DeLand in June or July, 1929?

Mrs. DeLand is the mother of Georgiana DeLand, for whom we are caring at the Children's Orphanage. If the story of Mrs. DeLand, as told us by her, is true, she will be eligible for a mother's pension shortly.

However, in order to get this, there are many facts that will have to be verified. We are anxious to have as much information as possible and will appreciate it if you can send us that contained in your records. We should like to have her maiden name, birth date, birth place, and the names and addresses of any friends and relatives which you may have.

Thank you very much for your help in this case.

The following letter sent to Rev. Stoll and Rev. Kremm of Glen Ridge:

We are caring for Georgiana DeLand at the Children's Orphanage during her mother's confinement at St. Martin's Hospital. We are anxious to make a plan whereby Mrs. DeLand can keep her children at home with her. If her story is true, she will be eligible for a mother's pension shortly. However, in order to obtain this, it will be necessary to verify certain facts.

Mrs. DeLand tells us that Georgiana was born June 11, 1926, and was christened at a Lutheran church in Glen Ridge. She said her husband and mother-in-law took the baby to the church. We have not been able to locate Mr. DeLand or his mother and are very anxious to do so.

Would you be willing to see if you have a record of Georgiana DeLand's being christened at your church? We would like to have the names and addresses of any relatives and any other information you might have.

Mrs. DeLand tells us that her husband went to Glen Ridge to have the baby christened because his brother's children were christened in this church. I believe John DeLand is the brother's name. His children are older and possibly were christened as far back as 1915. We are not absolutely sure of the given names, so would appreciate having information about any DeLand family on which you may have a record.

Thank you very much for your help in this case.

February 11, 1930.—Georgiana was dismissed from the Orphanage.

Mrs. DeLand was delighted to see how well Georgiana looked. The five pounds which she gained made her seem ever so much heavier to Mrs. DeLand. Took the baby to St. Martin's for an examination. The doctor said he had made a marvelous gain, thirteen ounces since he had left the hospital. Mrs. DeLand was very much pleased because so many people at the hospital and Orphanage admired the baby. She said, "I don't believe I could be any happier. I think I would burst if I were." Mrs. DeLand said to worker, "I wish you had come to see me later in the afternoon yesterday for my mother-in-law was here." She said she had been there three times before and brought the $5.00 for Georgiana's Christmas. She scolded Mrs. DeLand for not being at home and accused her of gadding around. Mrs. DeLand felt very bad because she took very little notice of the baby and did not ask to hold him. She asked Mrs. DeLand where she had secured the new furniture, and when told she had received it from the Children's Agency, told her she ought to send it back as she was depriving someone who needed it. She said when she had her babies, no one helped her except the neighbors who gave her only rags. She told Mrs. DeLand she ought to give the baby away and get work and give everything she had received from the Children's Agency back again. Mrs. DeLand said to worker, "You know I really don't need so many things and if I am taking them away from someone else I want to give them back to you." She tried to make worker take the $5.00 as part payment for what had been given her. She would keep it only when it was explained to her that she could use it to buy supplies and we would not furnish her with anything so long as her own money lasted. Mrs. DeLand said she asked her mother-in-law about her husband and she said, "If I didn't think you knew where he was, I would comb the city for him." Mrs. DeLand said her mother-in-law is cross with her because she thinks that she is keeping Mr. DeLand's whereabouts hidden. Worker talked with Mrs. DeLand again about Mr. DeLand's friends. She said she doesn't know the name or address of any of his friends. He used to borrow a blue Moon car from a Polish fellow whom he called "Con" but she doesn't know where this man lives.

Worker talked with her about the proper kind and amount of food for Georgiana. Mrs. DeLand has no knowledge of even the most elementary cooking. When worker asked her what she had cooked, she said sometimes they had frankfurters, potatoes, and onions cooked together and a stew made of a soup bone and vegetables. When she was a girl at home they lived mainly on cabbage and stew made from the neck bone of a pig. She said they had never had puddings and she believed she liked chocolate pudding better than anything in the world. She tried to make one once but the egg became all lumpy. Today worker showed her how to make a chocolate cornstarch pudding and potato soup and described how to make other kinds of cream soups. Mrs. DeLand thought worker quite extravagant in using so much milk and asked if she couldn't have used water. She had been under the impression that flour and water took the place of milk because it looked white.

Later.—Letter received from Contagious Disease Hospital:

Your recent inquiry concerning Genevieve DeLand has been received. According to our records the patient referred to was admitted to the Municipal Contagious Disease Hospital on July 14, 1929, suffering from tonsillar diphtheria from which she recovered and was discharged on July 25.

At the time Genevieve DeLand was a patient in this hospital her age was given as twenty-six, and her date of birth, January 9, 1903, Chicago being her native city. Our records indicate that her parents' names were John and Mary.

We are unable to give you Mrs. DeLand's maiden name. Her address is shown as 3201 Pine Street.

February 12, 1930.—Letters received from Rev. Stoll and Rev. Kremm, saying they have no record of baptism of Georgiana DeLand.

Visited before breakfast. Georgiana had a good substantial breakfast this morning. Worker showed Mrs. DeLand how to prepare tomato and brown rice and orange custard pudding. Mrs. DeLand had one orange and she asked if she couldn't make something out of it as it seemed too bad just to eat it. When worker separated the egg, Mrs. DeLand said, "Why, I wouldn't have believed it could have been done." Gave Mrs. DeLand instructions of what to feed Georgiana for two days and promised to visit again at the end of that time and help her prepare other foods.

She is very anxious to learn but has many mistaken ideas about foods. She has no conception of the value of foods either. She bought some bouillon cubes a long time ago which she has been saving. She understood that they were a substitute for meat and had expected to give them to Georgiana instead of meat. She is very economical and asked worker what she could make out of the water in which the rice was boiled. Worker described how it might be made into a soup by adding vegetables, etc. Mrs. DeLand looked at it and said, "I think it would be good, now it looks so rich." Mrs. DeLand showed worker the stove poker she had improvised. She said she bought a basket of grapes last summer and she thought the handle too pretty to throw away so saved it, thinking she would have a use for it some time, and now she has a fine poker. Mrs. DeLand is most anxious for Georgiana to keep the weight she has gained and will try very hard to feed her correctly if she only knows what to give her.

February 13, 1930.—Letter written to County Bureau of Public Welfare, giving a very full summary of the information known to the worker regarding the DeLand family.

February 14, 1930.—Visited. Drove Mrs. DeLand to the Gas Company office to pay her bill as she had received an overdue notice saying that the gas would be shut off unless paid at once. Left $3.00 for coal. Yesterday Mrs. DeLand and Georgiana visited her friend, Mrs. Elam, who lives on Long Avenue. She said Mrs. Elam gave her $2.00 and she wanted the worker to help her write an advertisement asking for work to do at home. She felt badly when advised against this and said she had been so happy since she received this money because she thought she would surely be able to get plenty of work by advertising.

February 17, 1930.—The Supervisor at the County Bureau of Public Welfare telephoned about the DeLand case and said that after reading the report they had decided to make an exception to this case and grant supplies without supervision. She suggested that the worker place Mrs. DeLand's name on the waiting list for a mother's pension and if possible persuade her to take out a warrant for Mr. DeLand at the Court of Domestic Relations.

Visited Mrs. DeLand and showed her how to prepare several new dishes. She said that she believed that, if she knew how to cook better, she would get fat because she enjoys eating so much now. Mrs. DeLand is worried because she isn't earning anything. She asked if worker thought she could earn by offering to wash windows at ten cents apiece, or she thinks she might be able to do scrubbing and take the children with her. Another idea of hers is to hire someone to stay at night while she works;

then she will take care of Georgiana and the baby during the day. She doesn't seem to realize that there is any limit to her strength and said she used to do this when Georgiana was small. Mrs. DeLand said she had a good plan so worker could see her mother-in-law. She frequently goes to Stein's Department Store on Saturday morning to look for bargains. Mrs. DeLand went last Saturday and waited but did not see her. She said she had put a note on the door for the worker to stay until she returned and she had planned to bring her mother-in-law back and find the worker waiting for her. She said, "Then she wouldn't have blamed me for she wouldn't know I had planned it." Mrs. DeLand wouldn't give the worker the names of her sisters but said just as soon as she was working, she would, for she knew then the children could not be taken away from her. She is perfectly certain that children can be taken away from poor parents. She said she had read about this in the newspaper and had seen their pictures so knew it was true.

February 18, 1930.—Visited in the evening. Mrs. DeLand said Georgiana had eaten well all day. She showed the worker a chocolate pudding which she had made. It was just fair.

February 20, 1930.—Called at the County Bureau and decided upon No. 2[1] ration for Mrs. DeLand. Before it can be arranged to have milk delivered daily, it will be necessary to have a doctor's statement of Georgiana's condition.

February 21, 1930.—Visited Mrs. DeLand to tell her about the grocery order which would be delivered today. She doesn't quite comprehend the fact that she won't be deeply in debt later on for all the supplies she receives now. She said, "Won't I have to pay more for them afterward than I would have to pay in the stores now?" Worker showed Mrs. DeLand how to prepare three new dishes today.

Attempted to find home work for Mrs. DeLand. The Woman's Exchange seemed to offer the only possibility. If Mrs. DeLand can hemstitch and miter corners on lace, they will be able to give her work.

February 23, 1930.—Letter received from County Welfare Worker, Grant, Iowa:

We have made inquiry for relatives by the name of Myers, as requested in your letter of Jan. 28, but our investigation has not revealed anything that would be of any help so far as we can see. Furthermore, we find no one having known a minister in this community by the name of Rev. Saylor. We find a

[1] [Rations No. 2 issued by the Cook County Bureau of Public Welfare at this time cost $2.78. The variety of food was very limited—the box included dry beans, soap, rice, rolled oats, coffee, tea, flour, sugar, lard, syrup, bacon, prunes.]

Frank Myers here but he is not the relative of Mrs. DeLand. We appreciate the difficulty under which you labor but have no clue or suggestion to make.

Should you find more definite information on which to work and would like us to try further in regard to this problem, we will be glad to do so. We might add that we will try to do so more promptly than we have done in this instance. We regret that we are unable to serve you more effectively. Again let us suggest that you write us if it seems desirable.

Later.—Visited but did not find Mrs. DeLand at home. (Note which was left pinned to door addressed to social worker.)

I have gone away to-night Saterday and may be if I can stay a day or two will save for me. I try to call you up but I can't get you. I won't stay longer than monday.

February 24, 1930.—Letter written to Mothers' Pension Division of Juvenile Court:

May I have the name of Mrs. Genevieve DeLand, 3100 South Ash Street, placed upon the waiting list for a mother's pension?

Mrs. DeLand has two children, Georgiana aged three and one-half years, and Gerald, four weeks, and was deserted by her husband last year. May I know how long it will be before Mrs. DeLand's case can be considered?

Answer.—"Number C-4842. Possibly year. There are about 1300 ahead of her."

Later.—Visited in the early part of the afternoon. Mrs. DeLand had not yet returned; left note asking her to be ready to take the baby to clinic in the morning.

February 25, 1930.—Worker drove Mrs. DeLand to the Children's Agency so she could get a bus which passed the hospital. She took the baby to the clinic alone and apparently got along all right. The baby is gaining nicely. Mrs. DeLand returned to the Children's Agency, and worker showed her how to hemstitch and miter corners on lace. She caught on rather quickly and is very anxious to learn to do it well so she can get work at home. Mrs. DeLand said her mother-in-law called again on February 22. She gave Georgiana five cents but gave Mrs. DeLand nothing toward the rent. Mrs. DeLand said her mother-in-law told her she did not think Mr. DeLand was dead but that he was probably working out of the city and earning only enough to support himself. She asked Mrs. DeLand for a ring which George had left with her but she did not give it up. She said when he was packing his things, he handed her the ring and said, "You can keep this," so she thinks it belongs to her. Worker gave Mrs. DeLand a small notebook containing several simple recipes incorporating the foods which she will receive from the county. Several suggestions about meal planning were included and several sample menus. Mrs. DeLand was very much pleased with this and expressed the desire that she hoped she could learn to make everything in the book.

February 28, 1930.—Visited and demonstrated one of the recipes. Mrs. DeLand had finished the hemstitched sample but made a slight mistake. She is anxious to have a perfect sample and will try again.

Letter written to Superintendent of Schools, Marion, Illinois:

Would the school records show whether or not Genevieve Bach was enrolled in the Marion schools between 1910 and 1914 or thereabouts? Was there a teacher, by the name of Alice Freeman, teaching in the public schools at that time? And if so, do you know whether or not she is living now?

Genevieve Bach is now Mrs. DeLand. She was deserted by her husband and was left with a little girl, three and a half years of age, and a new-born baby. We are taking charge of the family at this time but hope to be able to secure a mother's pension for Mrs. DeLand.

In order to secure this, it is necessary to get more definite information than we have at this time. Mrs. DeLand lives in constant fear that someone will try to take her children away from her and for this reason is very hesitant in giving any information about herself. We are anxious to locate her sisters, who are supposed to be living in Marion at this time. We do not know their married names.

The Bach family consisted of the mother, Mabel, and five girls—Alice, Hazel, Mary, Catherine, and Genevieve. Genevieve has curvature of the spine and has quite a large hump on her right shoulder. She tells us that she ran away from home when she was fourteen years of age. She is now thirty.

Is there a Reverend Saylor in Marion? Mrs. DeLand tells us that her sisters were married by Reverend Saylor. Her mother is supposed to have died about fourteen years ago in Marion, but I have been unable to verify her death.

I will appreciate any information you can give me. Can you offer any suggestions as to whom I might write in Marion to get information regarding the Bach family? Do you happen to know of any old residents? Mrs. Bach used to take in washing and do day work so it might be possible that someone would know about her.

Thank you very much for your assistance.

March 3, 1930.—Letter received from Superintendent of Schools, Marion, Illinois:

I have looked over our school files and find we have no school record of the attendance of the five girls mentioned. I talked with our truant officer, Miss Price, and she has no recollection of such a family living in Marion. She knows more about the people of Marion than anyone else living here and if she does not know them, I doubt if they have lived in Marion.

I never heard of Rev. Saylor in Marion. I was told that there was a minister by that name in Streator. It is just possible that that may have been this young woman's home.

The County Clerk went over his death records and did not find the death of Mabel Bach. There was an Elizabeth Bach who died in 1909.

March 3, 1930.—Took a sample of Mrs. DeLand's work to the Woman's Exchange. Miss Coleman said the sample showed that Mrs. DeLand would be able to do satisfactory work and they will give her something the end of the week.

March 5, 1930.—Visited. Showed Mrs. DeLand how to prepare Cream of Wheat pudding, plain muffins, and Junket. She tried a couple of the recipes and was very much pleased with her success.

March 8, 1930.—Called but did not find Mrs. DeLand at home. Shortly after worker got back to the Orphanage, Mrs. DeLand telephoned. She said she had just come from Warner Hospital, where she had gone to answer an advertisement for a wet nurse. They took a blood test and will let her know if she is acceptable. They pay $10 a week and maintenance. Mrs. DeLand was most enthusiastic about going and she kept repeating, "Just think, $10 a week and it won't cost me anything to live. Pretty soon I can pay you back for everything you have given me."

March 9, 1930.—Visited today. Mrs. DeLand was busy cooking. She apologized for the appearance of the house and said, "You know I have been cooking so much I haven't had time to clean." She had made muffins, rice pudding, and vegetable soup this morning, all of which looked very good. She seems to be capable of following directions quite well but can do nothing without explicit instructions. Mrs. DeLand said Georgiana has been eating very well since she heard worker tell Mrs. DeLand to put her in bed if she didn't eat because she wouldn't be strong enough to run and play without plenty of food. There is a little girl about ten years old with whom Georgiana enjoys playing very much so she is spending quite a bit of time out of doors.

March 11, 1930.—Mrs. DeLand telephoned and asked worker to come over as she had a lot of things to tell her. She had just returned from her friend, Mrs. Elam's. She gave her $2.00 and a tricycle for Georgiana which her child no longer used. Mrs. DeLand said her mother-in-law came to her house at eleven o'clock at night and left at five thirty in the morning. She said she wanted to sleep with the children and insisted that Mrs. DeLand put Gerald in the large bed. Mrs. DeLand, Senior, said she had to go to the hospital for an operation for rupture and she was afraid she might die. Mrs. DeLand seemed rather frightened because her mother-in-law had acted so queerly. She has never before wanted to stay overnight. Mrs. DeLand doesn't know who her doctor is or to what hospital she might be going and she is afraid she will lose all chance of finding Mr. DeLand if his mother dies. Mrs. DeLand really seemed quite upset about this.

March 14, 1930.—Accompanied Mrs. DeLand to St. Martin's Clinic today for a final check-up of her condition. Drove Mrs. DeLand to Warner Hospital to see Miss Mayby who had asked her to come in today to start work as a wet nurse. After talking with two of the doctors at Warner Hospital, Miss Mayby said she would not be able to use Mrs. DeLand because of the hump on her back which probably indicated that she had had tuberculosis at some time. Although she is apparently all right now, they cannot afford to take any risks. Mrs. DeLand was very disappointed. She believes that she must be very well to have been able to work so hard. She will gladly go to one of the Municipal Dispensaries to see if there is any question of tuberculosis. Worker had asked Miss Mayby if she would take Mrs. DeLand if we could get a statement that she was all right from a doctor at the Dispensary. Miss Mayby said she didn't believe they could use her anyway, because of her appearance. If the babies became ill, no matter what the cause, people would be apt to believe they were not getting milk from healthy mothers.

March 18, 1930.—Visited but did not find Mrs. DeLand home. She telephoned later in the day and said she had been doing washing and ironing for a woman on the North Side. She received $1.75 and was able to take the children with her. She was quite delighted to be earning. The milk from the county is being delivered daily now.

March 20, 1930.—Visited and took Mrs. DeLand a pair of shoes. She had been wearing a pair for best which were so much too short that they were making her joints protrude. Her everyday shoes were worn through to the ground. Apparently she has always worn shoes too small. She usually gets them on sale for $1.50 or $2.00 a pair. Her foot measures *8AA* so it probably is difficult for her to be fitted in cheap shoes. Worker was able to get a pair of shoes of an expensive make for $3.95 at a sale. Mrs. DeLand was perfectly delighted with them and said they were the nicest shoes she had ever had. Mrs. DeLand had twenty pairs of stockings to mend for a friend of Mrs. Elam. She couldn't quite understand this woman, because she said she didn't like to do ugly work like darning. Mrs. DeLand said, "You know, I think darns are pretty if they are made nice and woven like a carpet."

March 28, 1930.—Took Mrs. DeLand material from the Woman's Exchange to be made up into towels. She was very much pleased to get the work. She has finished part of the darning and has delivered it but will not be paid until she has completed it. Her mother-in-law has not been back to see her. Paid Mrs. DeLand's rent with money furnished by one of the committee members. Georgiana seems to be slipping back into her old habits of sleeping late in the morning and not eating as much as she should. Impressed upon Mrs. DeLand again her need of plenty of food. Mrs. DeLand has tried several of the recipes in the book which worker gave her and seems to be doing quite well with her cooking.

April 1, 1930.—Mrs. DeLand came to the Children's Agency today to show worker her progress on the towels. She was anxious to have Georgiana weighed because she has been worried for fear she has lost weight. Found Georgiana had not lost but she has gained only one pound since she was dismissed from the Orphanage.

April 8, 1930.—Drove Mrs. DeLand and Gerald to the clinic. Gerald is getting along remarkably well. The doctor ordered fifteen drops of cod-liver oil and three teaspoons of orange juice daily. Gerald was referred to the surgical clinic for circumcision which is quite urgent. The social worker at St. Martin's gave Mrs. DeLand a generous supply of cod-liver oil. On the way to the clinic Mrs. DeLand said, "Sometimes I wish I weren't living" and began to cry. She wouldn't admit that there was any special thing worrying her but she again mentioned her mother-in-law's advice about going to work and letting her take care of Gerald. Mrs. DeLand said she would be afraid to do this because she might lose the baby since she doesn't know where her mother-in-law is living now. Mrs. DeLand agreed today to go to the mother-in-law's old address and if she were there, she would tell her that she was going to tell the social worker where she was living; if not there, she would give worker the address. Mrs. DeLand also said she is afraid that when the children grow up they will blame her for taking so much help now, and asked if she couldn't get a job to work nights. In talking about the possibility of her working and placing the children in a day nursery when Gerald is older, Mrs. DeLand mentioned that she had gone to Sunshine Kindergarten when she was a child. Mrs. DeLand earned $1.50 yesterday, washing for Mrs. Elam.

April 11, 1930.—Took Gerald to a surgical clinic today. He can be admitted to the hospital for circumcision on April 14. Mrs. DeLand was quite disturbed because Gerald will have to stay in the hospital two or three days. Mrs. DeLand still worries about the possibility of her husband's being dead. Yesterday she went to one of the undertaking parlors where she had seen a notice in the paper about an unidentified man. The undertaker said possibly she might find her husband in the morgue at

County Hospital and she says she can't be satisfied until she goes there. Mrs. DeLand said she didn't know whether she was glad or sorry that the body wasn't that of Mr. DeLand. She said, "If it had been, then I would have found him, and now that I found that it wasn't he, I think maybe he is alive."

April 14, 1930.—Called to get Mrs. DeLand and Gerald to go to St. Martin's. Mrs. DeLand was not at home. Telephoned Mrs. Elam to see if she were there. Mrs. Elam said she had not seen Mrs. DeLand for a long time. When worker reached the Children's Agency Mrs. DeLand was waiting for her there. She had understood that she was supposed to be at the Children's Agency. Gerald was admitted to St. Martin's to-night.

Mrs. DeLand became very angry at the nurse who hurried her about leaving Gerald. Mrs. DeLand showed a considerable amount of spirit and spoke very sharply to her. It was quite difficult to persuade her to leave Gerald. After she left she cried because she had made such a scene. She said she was so angry because the nurse told her to get out when she turned to kiss Gerald that she didn't know what she was saying.

April 16, 1930.—Gerald returned home today. His mother was delighted to find he was not ill and was very much relieved at getting him back again. She said she had thought she might never see him again.

Talked with the mailman on Madison Street. There is no one by the name of DeLand living on Madison Street near Fifty-fourth Street.

Called at *Evening News* office and read letter supposed to be written by Mrs. DeLand (see entry of October 30, 1929). This letter was not in Mrs. DeLand's handwriting.

April 22, 1930.—Mrs. DeLand came in and brought her hemstitching. The worker helped her press it and get it ready to take to the Exchange. The work was done only fairly well; in some cases the thread was fastened on the right side and was not noticed by Mrs. DeLand until worker called her attention to it.

Georgiana was weighed and she had lost one pound. When worker took Georgiana to the hospital to be weighed, she talked on the way and told about how she had spent Easter with Aunt Hazel and Uncle James. She said they lived at Forty-first and Pine Streets.

April 29, 1930.—Visited Mrs. Elam in the evening. Worker had tried to see her several times before but had never found her at home. She has not seen Mrs. DeLand for a year. She came to her house only once with two other girls from the National Radio Company. She knows very little about Mrs. DeLand. She said her husband suffered with heart trouble and had been under care at the Post Graduate Hospital. She has heard her say that Mr. DeLand frequently stayed with his people in Aurora. Mrs. Elam said she always liked Mrs. DeLand and had wondered why she never returned. She left Mrs. Elam's home late in the evening and remarked that she was afraid she had outstayed her welcome. Mrs. Elam assured her she had not and invited her to return, but has never heard from her again.

April 30, 1930.—Letter written to Children's Aid Society:

Will it be possible for your worker in Aurora to see if she can get any trace of the DeLand family? Mr. DeLand deserted his family and is supposed to be living with relatives in Aurora. His mother's name is Mary and his brother's name is John. Are there any people of this name listed in the city directory?

Mrs. DeLand tells us that she knows very little about her husband or his people. He deserted frequently during their married life, but has never stayed away so long before. He left several months before the birth of the last baby.

Mrs. DeLand is very anxious to get some trace of her husband. She halfway believes he is dead since he has remained away so long. She is a very pathetic figure, hunchbacked, very ignorant, and very much afraid of social workers for she believes that they are able to take children away from their parents. Because of this fear she is withholding some information, but she has mentioned to several people that her husband frequently went to relatives in Aurora.

We shall appreciate your attempt to locate these relatives of Mr. DeLand.

Letter written to Post Graduate Hospital:

Do you have a record of George DeLand having been a patient in the Post Graduate Hospital within the past five years? Mr. DeLand was probably in the hospital because of heart trouble. If you do have a record we should appreciate your giving us any information you may have regarding names and addresses of relatives.

We have been maintaining his wife and two children since last November. Mr. DeLand is supposed to have deserted his family last June. If the information Mrs. DeLand has given us is true she will be eligible for a mother's pension soon, but it will be necessary to attempt to prove certain facts.

Mr. DeLand has told his wife very little about himself or his people and we have very little information which will aid us in locating him. We shall appreciate whatever help you can give us.

May 1, 1930.—Visited Mrs. DeLand. When worker told her she had known for some time that she had not been staying with Mrs. Elam, she began to cry. She said she had told worker this because she didn't want her to know where she had been staying. When asked if she were with her sister Hazel, she denied this and said Georgiana called the woman aunt. Mrs. DeLand has been going out with the children attempting to get day work. Occasionally, the people for whom she works let her stay overnight. She thinks if she gave up her rooms she could get enough work to keep her busy and could probably sleep where she works. Worker talked with her about a mother's pension and the Family Welfare Society, but she couldn't understand the kind of aid which they can give. Worker told her she would have to ask the County Bureau to discontinue supplies and she was very grateful. She said she would rather this were done for she doesn't feel right in accepting charity because she is able to work. She sincerely believes she is going to be able to pay back everything she has had from the County Bureau and Children's Agency.

May 2, 1930.—Letter written to the County Bureau:

I want to express our appreciation for the help you have given us on the DeLand case.

Now that Mrs. DeLand is feeling stronger she is able to do quite a bit of day work so is earning small amounts. She gets many of her meals when she works, so I believe she will be able to get along without county supplies.

Although I believe it would be best for Mrs. DeLand to stay at home with the children for a few months longer instead of trying to go out by the day, dragging the children around with her, I have not been able to convince her of this. She is still under the impression that she is under a great obligation to anyone for material assistance, even to the extent of their being able to take her children away from her. While she works she feels independent and even though the children can't get proper care under this arrangement, I see no way of bringing her to any other viewpoint.

Under the circumstances I believe the supplies which you have sent her could be used more advantageously by someone else.

Again I thank you for your assistance.

Later.—Letter written to the Municipal Tuberculosis Dispensary:

Will you be so kind as to examine Mrs. DeLand and Georgiana? Mrs. De-Land is not aware of ever having had tuberculosis but when she applies for a position this possibility is often considered. Arrangements were made recently for her to enter Warner Hospital as a wet nurse, but due to the possibility of tuberculosis she was denied the work, although her own baby has developed wonderfully well.

Mrs. DeLand would appreciate knowing about her condition, and we would also like very much to have a report.

May 6, 1930.—Reported to the committee the present status of case. They agreed that we could do nothing further at present with Mrs. De-Land's attitude as it is.

May 7, 1930.—Called at County Hospital. Could find no record of George DeLand at County Hospital in years from 1926 to 1930.

May 9, 1930.—Letter received from Children's Aid Society, saying they were unable to locate DeLands in Aurora.

Mrs. DeLand telephoned tonight saying she wanted to talk over something important with worker. The connection was very poor and it was almost impossible to understand anything she said. She said she would call again on another telephone. Worker asked her to leave her number but she said she would rather not.

May 10, 1930.—Called at 3100 South Ash Street and found Mrs. De-Land's flat empty. The girl in the second-floor flat front said that she had left Saturday and said she was going to live around Seventy-fifth and Audubon streets. She told the landlord she did not have money for the rent, but would bring it to him as soon as she had it.

Later in the afternoon Mrs. DeLand came in to the Orphanage. She said she had seen Mr. DeLand about two weeks after Easter. He was sitting on a fire plug on Fifty-first Street and she saw him out of the car window. She went over to him and asked if he were going to run away again. She said he just laughed. He told her he had been in New York and was going to return there. She told him about Gerald and he asked when he was born but didn't say he wanted to see him. He gave Mrs DeLand ten cents for Georgiana. He said he couldn't give her any more for he had only enough to get back to New York. Mr. DeLand told her he had written his mother at Easter time, but had not seen her. Mrs. DeLand saw her mother-in-law once after she talked to Mr. DeLand. She showed her the letter postmarked New York City, in which he said he was writing just to let her know he was on top of the ground and not in it. He said he wanted to get away from everyone and that is why he left.

Mrs. DeLand is now determined to go to New York. She feels perfectly sure she can find her husband there, because she happened to run into him here. She said, "I feel that I am supposed to find him and I will." The woman for whom she is keeping house has offered to give her $25 to go to New York. She is an old Irish woman who believes in hunches, judging from what Mrs. DeLand said about her, and she is urging her to go. Mrs. DeLand has inquired about the fare to New York and is determined to go just as soon as she has enough for railroad fare. Worker talked to her about the size of New York, the difficulty in getting work, the uncertainty of finding Mr. DeLand, etc. but she could not be dissuaded. Her determination to find Mr. DeLand outweighs everything else. She wouldn't give worker her present address because "she wouldn't let her go to New York." Neither would she leave her telephone number even though worker promised not to try to locate her. When she refused, worker offered her

$1.00 to keep for telephoning but she refused it and said with tears in her eyes, "No, I'll always have money to call you." Worker gave Mrs. De-Land some stationery and stamps so she could write if she got into difficulties. She said, "I'll write because you have treated me better than anyone ever has in all my life."

June 14, 1930.—Letter dated June 12, 1930, received from Mrs. De-Land in New York:

Please ask for Mrs. Skogland, 122 Lane Street.

I am in New York and have both children with me. I am staying at the St. Cecilia's Home, 122 Lane Street. I have found that my husband is staying at the Washington Heights section of the City and is in charge of a small sausage room and he is using the name of Skogland and to make things easier for us I am too. please can you help me he is using that name too to get a passport. and I don't know if he has got one yet, please help me find out for me if he has got it yet and maybe they will tell you the exact address of his. I got here Wednesday afternoon, please, please let me hear from you, I am so nervous and afraid I can hardly write. I can only stay here a few days they said. Thank you so Long.

Later.—Worker answered letter and advised Mrs. DeLand to talk to social worker at St. Cecilia's Home or if there was not one there to go to the Charities. She asked specific questions about the name Skogland and asked Mrs. DeLand to write her more definite information.

June 18, 1930.—Cleared with Central Charities under Skogland. No record.

June 23, 1930.—Verification of Gerald's birth with parents' names De-Land and Bach. See Georgiana's birth certificate, under February 4, 1930, giving mother's name as Genevieve Skogland.

July 11, 1930.—Received information from a friend of worker's in New York City that she telephoned St. Cecilia's Home and learned that Mrs. Skogland had been sent back to Chicago.

July 17, 1930.—A check from Woman's Exchange for $2.70 came to Children's Agency for Mrs. DeLand today.

Letter written to Superintendent of St. Cecilia's Home:

May I have a report of your contact with the Skogland family? Mrs. Skogland wrote me from New York on June 12 saying that she was staying at St. Cecilia's Home for a few days. She asked my help in locating Mr. Skogland and in preventing him from securing a passport. I advised her to get in touch with the social worker at the home. At this time I was in Massachusetts on my vacation, and since I have returned to Chicago I have not heard from Mrs. Skogland.

The family is known to us under the name of DeLand. I have interviewed several people who knew both Mr. and Mrs. DeLand but no one was able to give me any information which was helpful in locating relatives, so I know very little about the family situation.

Mrs. DeLand came to the Children's Agency for the first time in August, 1929. She was looking for work and was anxious to find a place where she could keep Georgiana with her. Arrangements were made for her to go to Harriett House for Women but she never went there as a friend offered to take her in. When worker learned she was pregnant arrangements were made for her confinement and Georgiana was cared for at the Orphanage during this period. After she left the hospital the Bureau of Public Welfare gave groceries. The Children's Agency paid the rent until Mrs. DeLand felt she could manage alone. She always seemed very much afraid of losing her children and she was convinced that children could be taken away from poor parents who accepted help. Mrs. DeLand would have tried to work just as soon as she returned from the hospital if worker hadn't insisted that she wait until she were stronger. Meanwhile she was able to get some mending and embroidering to do at home so she didn't feel entirely dependent.

Mr. DeLand had deserted eight months before Gerald's birth. Worker was never able to locate him although she found several people who had known him slightly. Next to the children, Mr. DeLand was uppermost in Mrs. DeLand's mind and she was determined to find him. She insisted upon looking up any unidentified man found dead in the hope of finding her husband. She couldn't believe he would stay away so long unless he were dead. Although he had left her frequently during their married life he never stayed away longer than a few weeks until his desertion in May, 1929.

In May, 1930, Mrs. DeLand came to the Children's Agency very much excited. She said she had seen her husband out of the car window and immediately got out to talk with him. He told her he had been in New York and intended to go back at once. She talked to him only a short time and he promised to see her in the evening, but did not keep his promise. Mrs. DeLand was determined to save money enough to go to New York to look for him. Worker tried to show her the uselessness of the trip but she couldn't be convinced. She kept repeating, "I feel that I am supposed to find him and I will. I felt that way before and I found him in Chicago, so I will in New York." Mrs. DeLand had just moved and wouldn't give worker her address for she said, "You will stop me from going to New York and I've got to go."

I shall appreciate very much having a report from your agency. Do you know whether she is known to any other social agency in New York? How did she happen to find St. Cecilia's Home? Would you be willing to clear with the exchange under DeLand also? I can't understand how she happened to use the name Skogland. She always told me her maiden name was Bach, although on Georgiana's birth certificate Genevieve Skogland is given as the mother's maiden name, and George DeLand as the father's.

In Mrs. DeLand's letter of June 12 to me, she said she was using the name of Skogland because her husband was going by that name.

I am anxious to locate Mrs. DeLand because I believe she is well worth helping. Her devotion to the children is very strong and she has cared for them to the best of her ability. When Georgiana was a baby she worked in a factory nights and cared for her during the day. Mr. DeLand did not work steadily because of heart trouble. Mrs. DeLand would be eligible for a mother's pension if her story is true. I have been able to verify many points but I know she has left out a great deal, and she certainly knows more about her husband than she is willing to tell. At the present time, I have a check here from the Woman's Exchange for which she had done some embroidering and I should like for her to receive it.

July 24, 1930.—Returned check to Woman's Exchange.

July 30, 1930.—Letter dated July 28, 1930, received from St. Cecilia's Home:

Your letter of July 17, re Mrs. Genevieve Skogland, was received. I am afraid that we know very little about the family that will be of any aid to you in trying to help her. She was referred to us by the Police Department on June 11, and stayed here until June 17, when she left saying that she was going to Chicago. We cleared her through the Social Service Exchange and found that she was unknown to them. Mrs. Skogland gave as her Chicago address, 3100 Ash Street.

I feel also that she is a very worth-while little woman. Here at the house she made friends with the other women, and everyone seemed anxious to help her. She was quite cheerful and brave in spite of her troubles.

I hope that you will be able to help her.

August 1, 1930.—Letter received from Mrs. DeLand in Chicago:

I have been sick so please forgive me for not letting you hear from me sooner. Georgiana is getting heavier and has a nice coat of tan. Gerald is a little tan and is doing fine. he is a big boy now he has 2 teeth. they came thru on the 13—and 14 of this month. they look so beautiful. I am staying with my sister. I have such a lot of trouble that I don't know if I am married or not and I couldn't ever have her know about that, so I told her a lie. I've got to. for Georgiana and Gerald, for myself I don't care. I guess you are awful angry about the things I did tell you and it is asking you too much to ask you to understand why, I am coming to see you soon and bring the children so you may see how pretty they are both growing, my sister and her husband like them a whole lot. I wish I could ask you to come see us here but I am too afraid she has a good and pretty home and when she asked me to come and stay with her she said I could stay until I am done nursing Gerald. my mother-in-law don't know where I am at, she knew I was by my sister. but I made her think I have left there. I got a letter from the U.S. Passport Dept. and they said no passport was issued to my husband they looked up the records six yr's back and I have heard he is back in Chicago. I dont want them to know where I am, cause I mean to catch up with him, and know I will some time soon. and everything will be made right or Ill bet he wont do the same to any one else. He was married befor. cause my mother in law said so. when I came back and said to her (when she was accusin me of knowing where he was). I told her Ill find him some day so he can tell you I never knew where he was, then she told me he was married and never divorced, and I've looked it up and she is telling me a lie, he is divorced. but, I am sorry to say to late for to suit me. he is only divorced a yr. or so, and I couldn't be married then so when I last saw you do you remember what I was saying I would do? I am waiting my time I dont want to do any thing that will make either one of my babies suffer any, but just for them I am going to make him sorry. I know that you can hardly read this, but I've wrote it so many times and I can't write pretty any more, please excuse my mistakes and bad writing. and I dont know if you will, let me come so, before I do, 'I will come see, you.' I will first telephone to you. thank you more times than I can tell, for your help and kindness, which I hope to try to repay to you if I can.

August 5, 1930.—Read Mr. Skogland's divorce record. Divorce record: Divorce No. C947687 was filed July 29, 1928, in the Circuit Court. George Skogland was married to Mrs. Mary Lyons in September, 1924 (later verified), No. 634621. The marriage was performed by Clergyman M. E. Master. Mr. Skogland gave as his address 5810 South May; Mrs. Lyons gave hers as 6387 Portland Avenue.

Mr. Skogland said he lived with his wife until December 31, 1925. They had one child, George, Jr., born prior to their marriage. (He was four years old in August, 1928.) The charge against Mrs. Skogland was adultery. Dan McMann and Dave Miles were named. Mrs. Skogland filed an answer denying charges August 2, 1928. There was a temporary order on Mr. Skogland for $20 a week.

At the hearing May 15, 1929, Mrs. Skogland was in default. Mr. Skogland gave his address as 361 West Fiftieth Street. He said he had lived in Cook County six and one-half years previous to the filing of the bill. He said he had not seen his wife since April, 1929. At that time she was living at 549 West Sixtieth Street and previous to that at 899 West Fifty-ninth Street. Mr. Skogland cited evidences of infidelity. He left her December 31, 1925, because he found his wife in the room of a roomer. He decided to "start the New Year right and get away."

The only witness was Ben Geiger who gave his address as 5749 South Green Avenue. The divorce was granted May 29, 1929, by Judge Ball. The worker looked through the marriage register to see if there was a record of Mr. Skogland's marriage after May 29, 1929. No record was found.

August 15, 1930.—Mrs. DeLand telephoned today. She seemed very much pleased because worker was glad to hear from her. She couldn't quite believe that she would want to see her after reading her last letter. She said she had been wishing she could send the children without coming herself. After reassuring her that she would be very welcome also, she promised to come the following day, August 16.

August 16, 1930.—Mrs. DeLand and the two children came in today. They came at 3:30 and stayed until 9:30, when worker offered to drive them home. Georgiana was very prettily dressed in a brown-and-tan coat and brown beret which her grandmother gave her last year for her birthday. Georgiana was weighed dressed except for shoes and weighed only twenty-five pounds. Gerald weighed twenty pounds. He is very strong and seems advanced for his age. Mrs. DeLand was thin but looked less worried and tired than usual.

The trip to New York was a very hard one. She went both ways by bus and stayed in New York just six days. After she arrived she realized that it would be very hard to find a person there. She went to New York expecting to find her husband in Washington Heights because that postmark was on the letter to his mother. She inquired about him at the police station but got no satisfaction. She wrote to Washington and learned that he hadn't been issued a passport.

Mrs. DeLand gave worker the names and addresses of all her relatives of her own free will today. She has always known her husband's correct name was Skogland. He used this name at their marriage ceremony. Mrs. DeLand has since been "to the place where people get married" and this wasn't where George took her. They went in a high building. She remembers distinctly because he scolded her for losing her breath and acting like a two-year-old when the elevator stopped suddenly. After the ceremony he told her they would use her name DeLand and assured her this made no difference about their marriage. Mrs. DeLand now thinks that George and his brother Joe (Red) were in some kind of crooked business. They made sausage in a basement and had no license. Her husband told her the electric company would arrest him if they found it out because he was using electricity for big pulleys and other machinery. He delivered the goods in his brother's car. Sometimes they took something they called "Moono" to places where people dance. Mr. DeLand had two revolvers, a 38 and a 22. He left one at home and she intends to use it to kill him. Mr. DeLand and his brother went to his brother's place in Granger every week end. Joe Skogland works for the Rock Island railroad. He has two dilapidated old houses in Granger. George Skogland is not on good terms with his brother Ivan Skogland, who lives on May Street. Mrs. DeLand has never seen Ivan. One of his sisters, Mrs. Mantle, came to their house two or three times. Mrs. DeLand does not know where she lives. His sister, Mrs. Stevens, lives at 361 West Fiftieth Street, and runs a grocery store and butcher shop about one-half block away from the house. Her mother lives there also. She works every day at a punch-board factory on Racine Avenue near State Street. Mrs. DeLand could not give the name of the factory but gave her mother-in-law's telephone number and the place of employment. Mr. DeLand's father died this past spring at County Hospital. His name was also Ivan Skogland. In the hope of locating George, Mrs. DeLand went to the Engle Undertaking Establishment on Belden Avenue and procured her father-in-law's address, and the address where his body was taken—231 Park Street. Mrs. DeLand thinks this may be the address of his daughter. She has heard her husband speak of a sister on the North Side. Mrs. DeLand never saw her father-in-law, but learned of his death through Mrs. Skogland.

Mrs. DeLand went to her sister Hazel's home when she left Ash Street. Until February or March of this year she had been completely out of touch with her own people since she left home the last time over six years ago. Mrs. DeLand's real name is Dalcour, but her mother never let any of the children use their father's name. She herself is using the name of Dalcour again. Mr. and Mrs. Dalcour separated when the children were very young. Mr. Dalcour drank, but Mrs. DeLand said she doesn't blame him so much now she is older for she thinks her mother may have driven him to it. Mrs. DeLand's mother and her oldest sister were very mean to the other girls. Angelina, her favorite sister, ran away. When Hazel, or Catherine as she prefers to call her, left home and was married at a very young age, her mother tried to have the marriage annulled. She went to some "social workers" downtown and it was the memory of this that made Mrs. DeLand fearful of a social worker. Catherine married Mr. James Payson, a government meat inspector at Hamilton's, about eleven years ago. Catherine is two years older than Mrs. DeLand. Mrs. DeLand continued to live at home. She worked hard for eight years in the casing department at Hampton's and was given an allowance of twenty-five cents a week. She said the only good thing she could ever remember that her mother had done for her was to buy her a brace and now she thinks that this was done so she could work harder. Mrs. De-Land went through the third grade in school, and she did not tell the truth about her age so she could start working earlier. At one time she saved enough from her twenty-five cents a week allowance to attend a night class in shorthand. She can still remember how to write a few words. She always hoped for a better job because the work in the casing department was too heavy. She had to squeeze the casings filled with water and this hard work made the veins in her hands prominent. Many nights she walked to the theater where she could go for ten cents, and sat until the show was over for she had no home to go to. Her mother frequently told her to leave and then one night when Mrs. DeLand got up courage to go her mother forbade her to leave the house. She accused her of having relations with men on the street.

She didn't want them to leave, however, because she missed their pay checks. Mrs. DeLand said the things her mother said about her and her two sisters were not true and added half-ashamed, "But that's what my oldest sister Alice is." When Mrs. DeLand left home for the last time she went to an old lady's house, Mrs. Bach, who lived at Twentieth and Green. Mrs. DeLand took her name because she was better to her than her mother had been. She met Mr. Skogland at Hampton's. After she married him she had no contact with her own people. When Gerald was about two months old her mother met her on Forty-first and Pine and Mrs. DeLand took her to the flat on Ash Street. She said her mother was very stylishly dressed and she hardly knew her. Since Mrs. DeLand left home her mother has married twice. She divorced her first husband after nine months, then married John Thomas, an old man who was janitor for one of the Commonwealth Edison buildings. Her mother had been house-keeper for the two men. She is very "crooked" and married them only to get their money. She fixed things so Mr. Thomas signed over his property to her. At the present time Mrs. DeLand's mother is living in the building with her oldest daughter, Mrs. Brinker, at 122 West Twenty-third Street. Mrs. DeLand's mother told her that her father had died last fall in the Rogers Park Old People's Home. Hazel came to visit Mrs. DeLand as soon as her mother told her where she was. Mrs. DeLand has been espe-cially careful to stay away from Hazel because Mr. Skogland didn't want Hazel's husband, who is a meat inspector, to know anything about his business. Mr. and Mrs. Payson, Mrs. DeLand's sister, have been very good to Mrs. DeLand and the children. They do not know Mrs. DeLand's husband's name, but think it is Kuhlman. Mrs. DeLand chose this name because she noticed it when she went to the Tribune Building to see if she could locate her husband. He occasionally worked there wrapping bun-dles of paper on Saturday night. Mrs. DeLand said she wished worker could see her mother and sister and her mother-in-law, but she doesn't want her to tell them who she is. Last winter she told her mother-in-law that the social worker had said she would locate her husband if she would tell her something about him, and her mother-in-law then said it would cause an awful racket if worker attempted to find George and she would kill herself before she would allow it. Mrs. DeLand asked worker if she would visit her at her sister's. Her sister has heard about the worker but thinks she is connected with a nursery and took care of Georgiana while Mrs. DeLand was in the hospital. She is afraid if she knows worker was connected with an orphanage she would think Mrs. DeLand had tried to give up Gerald.

Mrs. DeLand is willing to have worker call on Mr. Skogland's first wife, but does not want her to try to locate George until she has first gone to Granger. If she takes out a warrant at the Court of Domestic Relations she is afraid he will learn that a warrant is out for him, and will run away. The worker tried to show her the seriousness of her shooting him. She is very anxious to do something so he can't treat anyone else as he has treated her. The worker explained in detail what could be accomplished at the Court of Domestic Relations. (See picture of Mr. DeLand in envelope on back of record. See second face sheet for accurate information.)

August 18, 1930.—Read record at County Hospital for information regarding Mr. Skogland and relatives.

No. 1160879 admitted January 20, 1930. Address: 105 West 40th Street
    Name of friend or relative:
        Son—George, Granger, Illinois
        Nativity—Sweden. Age 61. Diagnosis: Organic Heart Disease
Discharged March 7, 1930

No. 1167000 readmitted March 22, 1930
    Name of relative, wife, Hilda
    Address: 231 Park Street (for self and wife)
Died March 26, 1930

August 19, 1930.—Letter written to Hampton Packing Company:

May we have the work record of George Skogland and Genevieve DeLand, Skogland, or Bach? They are the parents of Georgiana for whom we have been caring at the Orphanage. Mrs. Skogland said she worked in the casing department several years before her marriage. I believe Mr. Skogland also worked in this department.

We are anxious to locate Mr. Skogland and shall appreciate having any information about either of the children's parents.

Letter written to the Social Service Exchange:

Would you be willing to look through your files to see if there are any registrations under the following names?

Parents	Children
Skogland—Huldah or Hilda	George, age 29
Ivan, age 61, deceased	Joe ?
Addresses	Ivan E. ?
5310 S. May	Alma ?
105 W. 40th	Girl ?
361 W. 50th	(No record)

Parents	
DeLand—or Dalcour	Alice, age 48
Mabel, age 68	Angelina ?
Gus, age 84, deceased	Hazel, age 31
Addresses	Genevieve, age 29
122 West 23d Street	(See second face sheet)

Letter written to the Woman's Exchange:

Will you be so kind as to send Mrs. Genevieve DeLand's check here again? You will remember that I returned it to you on July 23 because I did not know where she was at that time.

I am in touch with Mrs. DeLand again and will see that she receives the check as soon as it arrives

Letter written to City Department of Health:

We should like to verify the death of Gus Dalcour which is supposed to have occurred in 1929. We should like to have the cause of his death, the place where his death occurred, the names of relatives, and any other information you may have.

The reason we are anxious to secure all possible facts is because we have been caring for his grandchildren here at the Orphanage. Mr. Dalcour's daughter has been out of touch with her family and we are anxious to locate her relatives.

August 21, 1930.—Check received from Woman's Exchange.

Letter received from City Department of Health that there was no record of death of Gus Dalcour under the spelling and date submitted.

Registrations received from Social Service Exchange were recorded on second face sheet. No record on Skogland.

August 23, 1930.—Called to see Mrs. DeLand at her sister's home. Mrs. Payson has a very comfortably furnished home, and a good-sized back yard. She was very cordial to the worker and took her out to see the yard and her garden. Gerald's bed which worker took from the Orphanage was in the yard airing. She seems to be very fond of Georgiana and Gerald. Mr. Payson was at home. He was holding Gerald on his lap and seemed to think him just about perfect. Mrs. DeLand was very happy to be able to have worker visit her there and she served her homemade root beer in a most gracious manner. Mrs. DeLand showed worker her shorthand book and notebook. The lessons were done very neatly and each symbol painstakingly made. Mrs. DeLand said she has been studying again and spoke about this hook and that curve quite intelligently. Worker took Mrs. DeLand and the children for a short drive. She gave worker the letter (letter follows) she had written on the 19th and hadn't mailed and asked her if she had time to read it then. While worker was reading the letter, tears rolled down Mrs. DeLand's cheeks. Now that worker knew the truth of the situation and was still her friend, Mrs. DeLand felt very much relieved. When worker marveled at the way she had expressed herself in the letter Mrs. DeLand said if she had plenty of time and no one bothered her she could write just what she wanted to say and this is why she wrote worker rather than came to see her. She said when she talks, she gets excited and cannot express herself clearly for she wonders what the person is thinking about her.

When worker left she gave her a beautiful picture of herself and Gerald which her sister had taken for her to send in to the *Tribune* contest. Mrs. DeLand looked very pretty and the baby was lovely. She invited the worker to come again and said she hoped she could stay longer next time so she could show her the basement for her sister has a machine to wash her clothes. She is using Mrs. DeLand's gas stove. Mrs. DeLand uses the cookbook which worker prepared for her and she has taught her sister to make pancakes without using prepared flour. She is so pleased that she has been able to do even these little things for Mrs. Payson.

Letter written by Mrs. DeLand, August 19, 1930, to worker:

Thank you very much for telling me all the nice things you did say to me. I believe you, and I only wish I had told you everything when I first saw you and the first time you asked. but I couldn't believe that he could be as I now know him to be. and I believed he loved me truly. and I, surrly did, or I would not have tried to keep his secrets with him. I have told you a little bit of my home life, of my people and I have given you the right addresses too so you can find out for your self if you want to but I have not told you all. I did tell you that him and I worked in Hampton and Co. together. I started to work there in 1917. July the first, and worked there for almost 8 yrs. and I believe 'but I am not positive to the exact time' that he started to work there in the sausage room as assistant foreman, while I had been working in the next room the casing dept. he was then about 23 yrs. old. and, I cant say how old I was then on the companys record cause I had put up my age to get work there. and after he came to work there I thought he was a very good looking young man but that is all, it was months before we ever enven spoke, then it was in regard to the twine and muslin bags that I had been put in charge of, belonging to his dept. and his immediate superior was Mr. W. McBain who was planning to leave so every one heard, and the Inspectors of the Gov't. and the bosses used to eat in the string and bag room, and I was made to sew and patch the bosse's frock coats and keep track of them as they went to the laundry and came back. They tried to steal them from each other all the time and from him the most and he asked me about some lost one's and one or two I recovered and he was as gentlemanly as any one could be, but the boss on the summer sausage side of the casing room, 'I worked for two Depts' didnt like it that I would return the frock's to the right parties especially to George Skogland cause he had become foreman of the sausage room. that is the other half of the sausage room called Domestic Saus. or fresh saus. such as frankfurts, pork saus. head cheese, liver saus. meat loaf and sausage stuffed in bag's and they later were dipped in parrafin. Of course to aggravate Mr. Skogland more 'I imagine' every one kidded the fellow a little about how well I watched things for the Domestic Saus. and I am telling you the truth I was just as careful about the things belonging to Summer Saus. but, again I must remind you I was being paid by the two Depts. they were charged with my pay the same amount of which was paid by each dept. and the boss who is in charge of Summer Saus. side yet. wanted me to let the girls or any one working for *him* or *his* Dept. take the bags that were used by the *other* Dept. and tear them up for wrapping around their fingers and as little bibs and aprons to keep their cover-all apron clean. and every time that, that happened. they would get them I dont know who would way before starting time and Mr. Skogland came to bawl me out and I told him the truth cause both bosses could fire me or I should say discharge me, and I didn't dare to lose my job. I don't know how it was but we used to come to work about the same time and try to catch some of them taking his bags and twine, and he started to tell me of how they were against him getting and keeping his job cause he was so young and he was not married. he said that from the Supt. down, every one seemed to think a person had to be married to be able to hold a steady position. so he told me he was going to get it circulating that he was married for the purpose of holding down that job and he was going to make them give him more money than they ever paid a foreman on that job befor, and I told him it was a good idea if it would work, so he told them, and it worked. he at one time told me he was getting $65.00 per wk. and some how he found out where I lived and he said the Supt. told him I must come to work at 6:30 tho' I only got paid starting at 7 A.M. on account of the loss of bags, the women would drop them all over the floor on the rush going home. they were all dirty and torn and would lay all over, so to keep him from bawling me out or firing me as he could if I didn't come to work so early. I come at 6:30 and then he said, it was a shame for them to make me do that, and he was going to call for me he had a car then too he said his mother paid for it, a present to him from her. he called in the morning and would blow his horn some times I was allready gone My mother knew all about him trying to keep his job, and finding it hard to on account of how young he was and she knew he came for me in the morning and knew how it came about and it was all right we didn't mean no harm by that. either one of us I was sure. My Mother and I had been having trouble was forever fighting and moving over to my sister Alices hows and trying to make me move with her. but I wouldn't so the last time she moved out on me. I was crying about it. I had nothing but empty rooms to stay in for over a wk. and only a meal every other day she had all my money except what I was paying on that furniture I bought at Jacob Stein on 64th and Ashland St. I think it is. He asked me what was wrong and I told him how I was trying to get along and couldn't. she was against me educating my-self but I was going to any way I was part way done with my shorthand course then and he even tried to help me, as he had taken up short hand. Munsons, too, and he told me to let her coax me back even after I had my furniture bought, so I went back home, and soon after he told me he cared a lot. in fact loved me he said and as I thought he was *it* too. he said he was going to save up first tho. and I didn't care I'd wait I thought. so not long after being at home, the fight-ing started and I was going to run away and he told me not to. I didn't then, I went and bought her, my mother an orthophonic victrola, and even put it in her name. to try to keep her from fighting with me, her and my sister at the same time and every morning and night and every day was finally to much and I left. wel to try and get even with me she went down to Hampton and Co. with my sister Alice and told them that I was running around with men and with George Skogland every night and it was a lie and she said he made me leave home and she said he was married and she never knew any more than I if he was, he said he wasn't but was going to tell every one that to keep his job. all though he must have been, for really, and lying about it to me, but she said I was the lowest thing possible to become. which I am not what she said.

Mr. H. Jones told me, he was Supt. yet is, and I didn't see Mr. Skogland for a long time when I went back to get my check, I had quit Hampton's found out what was said. and I had gone to visit my mother and I asked her if she went and said that at Hampton and Co. and she said. she only told the Supt. to fire George Skogland cause she had talked to Mr. Skogland and Mr. Skogland was supposed to have told her at the time she went to see him (which was shortly after I left home that he and a lot of others had me out in his car doing every thing to me.) so I asked him the Supt. to bring Mr. Skogland befor me and make him tell both of us what he told my mother and *he* came and said my mother only asked him if he knew where I could be, and he said he didn't, I only stayed home and no one knew if I had quit or why I dind't come to work as I had worked there so long then. I asked my mother to come face the Supt. and Mr. Skogland and she wouldnt do it. You can look up the record of the Central Electric Com-pany and find out she done the same with my two sisters the one that I am now staying with and the one that is gone since 1916 I think or 1915. their names were Hazel and Angelina DeLand. and they worked for a man named DuMont. My big sister Alice going along that time too. So after having been to your house Saterday I cam back and asked my brother-in-law if he ever was stationed at Hampton & Co. in the yrs I was gone and he said yes. everyone was asking him where I was and he couldnt tell them so in the course of talking about the different people there he said there was a man that took the job of assistant foreman at Hamptons after Mr. Skogland his name was Ben. and he said that it was funny but when my Mother raised that big row, she hit the nail on the head. for Mr. Skogland was married and the awful scenes that went on when him Ben and Mr. Skogland were getting grounds for divorce he said he was awful sorry for Mr. Skogland and so when I asked my brother in law what had become of Mr. Skogland, he said I asked Ben and he said George was staying with a brother in Granger and was down on account of his heart, both physicaly and financially. and he told my brother in law that he had been giving Mr. Skogland money time and again, that does not sound plausible to me, for him a stranger to give Mr. Skogland money. (He may have found out Mr. Payson was my brother in law from Mr. Skogland, he may not have told this Ben who I was or anything like that, he may have told him not to give any information as I try to figure it out. but any way since I need help from my sister and her husband I am kind of glad that Georgiana insisted on being called Anna instead of Georgiana for I wouldn't want them to know that the name is Georgiana or that I had ever thought my self married to Mr. Skogland, it is a shame to be in such a mix up and I am sorry that two innocent children are the real sufferes and the biggest losers, but I am responsible for their being in the world and I am going to give them everything I can and try to make up to them what they are sure to find out some day. but please call her Anna when you come to see us as mine is a family that would make it unbearable I dont care about myself. but God helping me I am protecting them as much as I can and am praying as hard as I know how, and please you wont forget not to call her Georgiana but Anna. I have wrote a long letter to you trying to have you know that if I had not been in love I would never have believed him or be in such a mess, and the children should not suffer, and they wont, that shall be the only bit of happiness in my life caring for them and giving them a good education and a good home and Ill love them hard enough for Mother and Father both.

I am still in love but it is only with my babies. and that is the truth. I know that they love me truly and there never was anything for me in life until they came. Please dont forget if you do come to see us, will you call her Anna. My sister is buying a pint of milk a day for Anna I dont know how long she will do that but she is doing that now, I wish I could find something that I could work at. I look the paper thru every day—may be some time Ill be lucky and see some thing. I am sending you the Address and name of the Masonic Lodge that sent him that big paper. and if you want to have me tell you any thing else no matter what it is I will gladly tell you, tho I am afraid I have woke up too late.

I shall call you and keep in touch with you. but I forgot to say I would like to get a warrant for his arrest as you say if they wont tell him or let any one know we are trying to find him. my Mother in law started to go to the address on May street about the time you must have telephoned there, as I remember since you told me you called, there on the phone. I hope I have not bored you with such a big letter but I want you to believe me that I am not a bad woman. please do, I care more for what *you* think than what any one else thinks. I get so discouraged I dont know what to do some times. but. if it were not that my babies were in the world I wouldnt care to go on for them Ill go thru with every thing and if you want me to do any thing Ill do it too. I would have taken too much of your time if I had come over. I am glad you let me write to you. I have told my sister our names are Mrs. Genevieve Kulhman, Anna, and Gerald.

Please let me call you now and then? So Long.

August 25, 1930.—Called at Court of Domestic Relations and found that Mr. Skogland can be brought back from Granger for about $10. Money not used will be refunded.

The Dalcour record No. 132997 could not be located.

Called at Protective Association and found that Dalcour and DeLand records had been destroyed.

August 27, 1930.—Mrs. DeLand came in this evening. Before taking out the warrant she wants to be absolutely sure that Mr. Skogland is in Granger. She is planning to go down there on a train that arrives about nine in the evening and stay and watch until the early morning train goes out. She finally agreed not to do this after worker said they would drive down together some time next week to locate the house, and then would go to Court of Domestic Relations and take out a warrant.

Mrs. DeLand is very sure that it was in September, 1924, when Mr. Skogland pretended to marry her. She said she thought so much of him that she believed everything he told and to illustrate how strongly she believed in him she said even if she knew it were Tuesday and he told her it was Thursday, she would believe him. She said perhaps if she had had more education she wouldn't have been so foolish. She spoke again of how well they had always gotten along together. "Why, he even cut my meat for me, and he brought me a valentine and an Easter basket just like I was a little kid. I guess he didn't mean that either. I liked him so much and now it's just that much that I don't like him now."

Mrs. DeLand mentioned other ways in which Mr. Skogland might be located. Ray Gillman and Frank Ashby who worked at Hampton's were friends of his. His physician is Dr. Phillips, 4358 Ashland Avenue. He had his tonsils out at Post Graduate Hospital when Georgiana was a baby. He joined the Masonic lodge at Central Falls, and Mrs. DeLand will send worker a paper which he left.

Mrs. DeLand isn't very happy at Mrs. Payson's home. She will be so glad to get back to work so she can be independent again. Although Mr. and Mrs. Payson are kind, they say things which hurt Mrs. DeLand very much. They have told her that if they can offer the children a better home than she can, they can have the children. Mr. Payson suggested that he could get her work at Morrison's in the sausage room, but Mrs. DeLand doesn't want full-time work until she has nursed Gerald for ten months. She doesn't want to go back to the Stock Yards because the people there know so much about her. When she gets work she doesn't want to stay with her sister. She said, "I don't like my own people even though they are my relatives." Her mother and sister question her about Mr. Kuhlman. Mr. Payson became a little provoked when Georgiana told him she had a nice daddy and he had a prettier face than Uncle James. Mrs. DeLand asked worker if she would get mad if she told her what Mrs. Payson had said about her. She told Mrs. DeLand that worker was young so she guessed she wasn't so smart as Mrs. DeLand thought and said if she were a friend of Mrs. DeLand's she couldn't be a friend of hers for she (Mrs. Payson) was just as smart as worker. She said worker only came to see the children and was just watching for something to go wrong so she could take them away from her, but as long as she kept the children with her then Mrs. DeLand needn't worry. Mrs. DeLand said, "I know better now, I know you're not like my mother-in-law and sister say and I believe you." Worker advised Mrs. DeLand to say just as little about her as possible as there was no use in antagonizing her sister. Mrs. DeLand believes that Mrs. Payson is jealous of worker.

Mrs. DeLand's mother has visited often since she learned she was with Mrs. Payson. She is trying to persuade her to return home to her, but her memories of home are too unpleasant for her to do that. She offered her some money to go to the dentist but she refused to take it. When she lived at home and turned over all her pay check for years, her mother told everyone after she left that Genevieve had never given her a cent. Now she is not going to give her the chance to "brag about" what she is doing for her. Mrs. Payson upholds Mrs. DeLand in this attitude. Mrs. DeLand mentioned her brother Harry today. He is just a "bum" and never held a job more than two weeks at a time. He always begged money from his mother, and she gave him money which the girls worked so hard to earn. He has been in jail several times for holding up stores. Mrs. DeLand is very much ashamed of him and never wants her children to see him.

Angelina married Frank Myers and lived in Grant, Iowa, and Marion, Illinois. The Rev. Saylor she mentioned previously apparently runs a kind of matrimonial bureau, for it cost Mr. Myers a dollar to meet Angelina. Mr. Myers was a farmer, several years older than Angelina. The family last heard from her from Marion, Illinois, many years ago.

Mrs. DeLand's family lived at one time at Twenty-sixth and Ashland Streets in a house which was supposed to be haunted and so the rent was only $4.00 a month. This was near a small park where there was playground equipment. The doctor had said that if Mrs. DeLand hung on rings she might help straighten her back. So every time she went to the store for her mother she stopped and hung on the rings even though her mother told her to hurry back. She said it would seem only like five minutes because she kept thinking about her back becoming straight but she would notice that it was getting dark and she would run home and receive a terrible beating. In spite of this she said she couldn't help stopping every time she passed the park.

Another instance of her mother's cruelty is her scheming to get the children to work early. Before they could get a working certificate at the Board of Education they had to be weighed. Mrs. DeLand's mother tied horseshoes around the girls' waists so they would weigh heavy.

She said her own mother has said such terrible things to her that whatever is thought of her from now on can't hurt her any more than she has been hurt. Mrs. DeLand condemns herself just as much as she does the rest of the family. She knows they are bad and thinks she must be too, and it is her only concern now to protect her children.

Mrs. DeLand is anxious to have worker see all her family so she can know she is telling her the truth now. She said, "When I am telling the truth and then people tell me I am not, I get awful mad, but when I am lying and they call me a liar then I don't get mad because I know it is the truth." Mrs. DeLand will never make accusations against a person unless she is sure they are true. She said her sister has been saying her mother only came there to make trouble for them, but Mrs. DeLand said she would wait until there was trouble before she said anything. She thinks a mother should stand up for her children even when they are in the wrong and she can't understand her own mother's attitude in talking against her girls when they did nothing to warrant it.

August 28, 1930.—Following letter sent to Rev. Stoll and Rev. Kremm:

Perhaps you will remember that I communicated with you last February in regard to the baptismal record of Georgiana DeLand born June 11, 1926. I have since learned that her correct name is Georgiana Skogland. Mr. Skogland deserted his family last year, and I am very anxious to locate him.

Would you be willing to look through your records again and notify me if you do have any information about this family?

August 29, 1930.—Called at Family Welfare Society—Lower North District. Found only a blue card. There was a notation which said the record had been sent to Stockyards District October 29, 1912. Information on blue card was as follows.

Earliest date case was known to Family Welfare Society—March 27, 1898
Addresses: June 1, 1905—70 Dante Street
            October 20, 1912—879 East 24th Street
Parents: Mable and Gus Dalcour
Children: Alice 1888
         Harry 1894
         Angelina 1896
         Hanna 1900 (probably Hazel)
         Genevieve 1903

August 31, 1930.—Letter received from Mrs. DeLand.

Dont be angry because I am late in sending to you the name of that lodge. but things didn't go so good over here and I didn't get a chance to write to you. I am feeling awfully nervous yet. I am going to go over to my mothers house this afternoon. I didn't realize that I told you I had mailed your letter to you until I thought about it afters I was going to write it right away when I got back. My mother asked me to come over yesterday and I don't care to go but I will any how for today I guess she will try to have me stay there for Labor Day but I dont know if I should or not. the name of that lodge is Occidental Consistory No. 2, Central Falls, Montana.

He used to send money for his dues to a Mr. Brown I think he was the recorder. and I think his address to Mr. Brown was Granger, Illinois. Do you know what you said. that you feel like you was my friend? my I wonder did you know you said it for realy. and you even touched my hand. I hope I will hear from you some time soon.

September 5, 1930.—Drove Mrs. DeLand to Granger in the evening. Found that Mr. Skogland's house was located on the northwest corner of Front and Neithammer Streets. It is a two-story white house and compares very favorably with the rest of the homes in the neighborhood. Mr. Skogland was listed in the directory as John H. Skogland, Front Street. The house was dark. There was one car in the back yard. Mrs. DeLand said Mr. Skogland used to have a smaller car and it was her guess that the Skoglands had probably driven it in to Chicago to get Mr. Skogland's mother. She usually spends her week ends in Granger.

Letter received from Hampton Packing Company:

Mr. Skogland left our employ some few years back, and I was rather at a loss to know how I could be helpful to you in this situation. Just recently I have been able to get a trace of Mr. Skogland and I informed him of the contents of your letter and asked that he personally answer it and take whatever action was necessary in order to relieve this condition.

We trust that Mr. Skogland has, or very shortly will, get in touch with you and work this situation out. It is our understanding that he is working and doing fairly well by himself and there is no apparent reason why he cannot take care of those things which are his responsibilities.

October 13, 1930.—Worker has seen and talked with Mrs. DeLand several times since the last entry. She and the children are looking better all the time although Mrs. DeLand has suffered a great deal with her teeth. She is very much afraid of having them extracted. During this past month, Mrs. DeLand has been worried by her mother and sister. She telephoned late one evening in great distress to ask if it would really be her fault if her mother died. She had been sick, and Mrs. DeLand went to see her but did not take the children. She asked Mrs. DeLand to stay herself or send Georgiana to care for her. When Mrs. DeLand refused, she was scolded very abusively by her mother and sister Alice. A few days later Alice called and said her mother was dying. Mrs. DeLand was quite alarmed because she was afraid Alice would not get a doctor as she would like to have her mother die so she could collect the insurance. The worker suggested to Mrs. DeLand that she ask the visiting nurse to call with her. Mrs. DeLand did this but they were refused admittance. She then went to the police station and a policeman accompanied her. He went in and saw her mother and he said she wasn't nearly so sick as her sister had tried to make her believe and that she said she didn't want to see Mrs. DeLand.

On October 5, Mrs. Reinbeck of the Protective League called at Mrs. Payson's home and asked for *Miss* DeLand. It hurt her very much to be called Miss. She said they had received an anonymous letter which said that her two children were beaten black and blue and that the Paysons made and sold liquor. Both Mrs. DeLand and Mrs. Payson believe that their mother and Alice were responsible for the letter.

On October 9, worker took Mrs. DeLand to the laboratory to have her teeth X-rayed.

October 14, 1930.—Talked with Mrs. Reinbeck at the Protective League. After explaining the situation she said she would close the case, and mark it "Complaint unfounded." She had been very favorably impressed by Mrs. DeLand and the Payson home. The letter of complaint was sent to the Juvenile Court and was signed "A Citizen of the United States."

Letter written to Board of Health:

Do you have a record of the death of Hilda or Huldah Skogland who is supposed to have died during September or October of this year? Mrs. Skogland was the grandmother of Georgiana Skogland for whom we have been caring at the Children's Agency. We are very anxious to get in touch with Mrs. Skogland's son, George, the father of this child.

We shall greatly appreciate any information you can give us, including the cause of Mrs. Skogland's death, the place where she died, the doctor attending her, the name of the undertaker, and the names and addresses of any relatives.

Thank you very much for this information.

October 16, 1930.—Called at 122 West Twenty-third Street. After vigorous rapping for several minutes still no one came to the door. Worker went immediately and telephoned. Mrs. Brinker answered. When worker asked for Mrs. Dalcour, she said she was very ill, in fact on her death bed, and that the slightest excitement was likely to kill her. She wouldn't give worker permission to call even on a day the following week. However, just as soon as worker said she was investigating a complaint regarding Georgiana, she said at once, "Oh, wait a minute. I'll ask Ma. That will be all right; you can come this afternoon, any time at all, dear."

Worker called in the afternoon. They live in a small wooden cottage, Mr. and Mrs. Brinker on the first floor and Mrs. Dalcour in the basement. Harry, Alice, and Mrs. Dalcour were at home. Mrs. Dalcour speaks broken English and has no teeth so it was difficult to understand her. She began right away to describe the cruel beatings the children receive at the hands of Genevieve and Hazel. She said Anna is covered with black-and-blue marks. She has seen blood dripping from her ears as a result of being slapped. The children on the street know Genevieve as the mother who tries to kill her children. Harry said he tried to do a painting job for Mr. Payson, but had to leave it because he couldn't bear to see the children abused. Mrs. Dalcour said Anna is treated worse than any dog and on the hot summer days she was not allowed a drop of water. Hazel is no kinder than Genevieve in her treatment of the children.

Mrs. Dalcour described a time this spring when Mrs. DeLand and the children stayed with her two weeks. Anna and Gerald were badly mistreated, and, when she interfered, Genevieve would swear at her and say if she couldn't beat her own kids there she would take them where she could beat them.

Alice said she and her husband were awakened one night by Anna's screaming. Mr. Brinker was very much alarmed and went down to investigate because he was afraid Genevieve was killing Anna. Alice said she guessed she was too sensitive for she couldn't bear to hear the children scream day and night.

It is Mrs. Dalcour's wish to have the children brought to her, for then they will be raised properly. She said she had raised five children and never had to "lick" them. She explained how kind she had been to Genevieve when she was a little girl after she fell off the porch and injured her back. At one time her hip was turned to the back and her abdomen turned around with the center line where her hip should be. She said, "I took her down and bought her a brace, but what has Genevieve ever done for her babies?"

She explained how Genevieve had stayed out late at night, going to dances and cafés, sometimes not returning until four or five in the morning. James Payson told her that George Skogland used to meet her on the corner and drive her to work every day. In her estimation "George Skogland is lower than the deepest ditch." Genevieve left home for good just before Anna was born. They suspected she was pregnant because she was nauseated in the morning and Harry accused her which made her very angry. They lost complete trace of Genevieve until last spring.

They were all interested in having the husband produced. Mrs. Dalcour said, "That baby looks just like George Skogland and when I go to court, if he is there to claim the baby, I'll say, 'Who is the father of the little girl?" (Worker had not mentioned court so it seems fairly clear that Mrs. Dalcour was the source of the anonymous letter.) Harry said he knows there was crooked work somewhere because the two children can't have the same father as they don't look alike.

Alice said Hazel and Genevieve weren't raised up to be rich and she doesn't see why they think things at her home and her mother's home aren't good enough for them. Mrs. Dalcour took worker around to see her bedding. A soiled feather mattress was used as a comforter. The sheets and pillow cases were not clean. All the rooms were untidy though not actually dirty. However they were a great contrast to Mrs. Payson's or Mrs. DeLand's housekeeping. Mrs. Dalcour told of the awful shack in which she had found Mrs. DeLand living last spring.

She is very much provoked with Hazel because she bought her piano for $200 because she intended to have Anna live with her and take music lessons. She wants the worker to force Genevieve to live with her, and then the worker will be welcome to visit every week to see that the children are being properly cared for.

Mrs. Dalcour, Harry, and Alice were agreed that the children should be taken away from Genevieve. Worker explained the difficulty with which this could be done—the necessary proof. They had thought the three of them would be enough to bear witness of the abuse. Harry asked how to get in touch with the worker if they had anything more to tell her.

October 17, 1930.—See letter from Health Department verifying Mrs. Hilda Skogland's death, which had been reported to Mrs. DeLand by one of Mrs. Skogland's fellow-workers when Mrs. DeLand recently telephoned the factory where she worked.

The worker mentioned her visit to Mrs. DeLand's mother's home, and advised her to face the situation and tell her people the truth about the children. She agreed to go there with the worker upon her return and tell them the truth about Mr. Skogland. Mrs. DeLand gave worker permission to visit any members of the family she wished.

Accompanied Mrs. DeLand to the dentist for an examination of her teeth.

The X-ray showed seven abscessed teeth. There is no chance of saving the upper set. Dr. Hay took a slide of the infection in the lower gum.

Mrs. DeLand and the children left for Wabash, Indiana, with a social worker at Children's Agency, to spend two weeks at the worker's home. They were very happy to go.

October 20, 1930.—Dr. Hay telephoned to say that the slide showed the infection due to a type of organism causing trench mouth. The organisms were of the most virulent type. With precautions the infection can be checked until her return to Chicago.

October 27, 1930.—Harry DeLand came to Children's Agency today, referred here after calling Protective League. His attitude was very different from that of the other day, and his accusations mild. Mrs. De-Land's family will never be satisfied until they learn who is the father of Genevieve's children and whether or not she was married. Harry kept repeating, "That was no way to do, just go off and say nothing. Ma has been looking for her ever since she left home. Then for several months before she left home in 1925 she would come in at four or five o'clock in the morning and wouldn't tell where she had been. We asked her then if she were married and she wouldn't tell us." Harry spoke of the hard life his mother has always led. Mr. Dalcour used to drink heavily and three or four days after Genevieve was born he put the whole family out in the snow. He was arrested and remained away from home for seven years. He left again and remained away from home for fifteen years. Mrs. Dalcour refused to take him back when he appeared again and later divorced him. He died last year in the Old People's Home.

Harry said he left home at the age of thirteen. He went to St. Louis, where he remained four years. Since that time he has been over the whole country. He said Genevieve thinks he is a "bum" but he isn't for he has always worked hard. Genevieve blames her mother too much for the fact that none of them ever had an education but he thinks they are fortunate that they had enough to eat, considering the kind of father they had. Mrs. Dalcour used to take in washing to support her family.

Harry admitted today that he didn't know how much truth there was in the reports that Anna and Gerald were beaten. He said Hazel has been to the house when Genevieve didn't know about it and has told her mother that Genevieve beat the children. Genevieve also told her mother that Hazel slapped the children. Harry said he didn't doubt it because everyone in the family has a quick temper. They are a family of fighters and they are all jealous of one another. There is considerable ill feeling between Alice and Hazel. Hazel wants her mother to sell all her furniture and go to live with her, and Alice wants her mother to stay with her. Harry thinks it would be the best plan for his mother to rent a flat on the North Side and have Genevieve and her husband and children live with her. He said it wouldn't be necessary for her husband to go to work right away if he is sick. This arrangement would be fine because Hazel and Alice both own their own home so wouldn't be apt to move into the neighborhood selected by Genevieve and her mother.

Harry and the family suspect very strongly that George Skogland is Genevieve's husband. He said he had talked to James Payson a few days ago and he told him he believed this also. Harry asked worker if this were true and she told him she would give him no information but that she had advised Genevieve to tell her family about the whole situation as there is no reason for her to be ashamed of anything she has done. Harry said he knew she couldn't help it if some man had played a trick on her, but the family did want to be told about it. Worker mentioned Genevieve's sensitiveness, and Harry said he knew she was sensitive and he knew they had all said many things to her which they didn't mean. However they get angry with her because she always either cries about things or else gets provoked and "fights" with them. The members of the family do not get along well together.

Harry mentioned that Genevieve had asked him to drive her to New York this past spring, and he had agreed to do it until the Paysons decided to go along. When he refused, Genevieve took the bus. They would never have found Genevieve last winter if Mr. Brinker hadn't happened to see her walking with Anna around Thirty-third and Pine streets. He told Mrs. DeLand's mother and she made Harry drive around that neighborhood and inquire about her until she was located. It was in this way that they knew Genevieve was using her maiden name. If she is married the family can't understand why she is using her maiden name and if she isn't married they think she should live at home. Harry seemed satisfied when told that his sister was visiting friends of the worker's in Indiana to give her a chance to forget her worries for a time, then when she returned she would call on her mother and tell her about her husband. Harry said his mother just doted on Anna and was very much worried because she couldn't see her. He told about Genevieve's coming with the nurse and policeman and when it was explained why this was done and that the reason Genevieve had not brought Anna to see her grandmother was because she didn't know the cause of her illness and was afraid Anna might catch some disease, he said, "Well, why didn't she say so? Then everything would have been all right." His mother had been very angry because Genevieve didn't bring Anna and for that reason told her she never wanted to see her again unless she brought Anna with her.

Harry said he would do more for Genevieve than any of his sisters because of her deformity. He seemed anxious to impress worker with the good intentions of the family and in no way spoke as he did the other day.

October 29, 1930.—Letter received from Mrs. DeLand:

I hope you will excuse me for not writing to you sooner. but, really, I am having such a good time, I have never enjoyed myself so much before. everyday is Sunday out here and no one is ever angry at anyone, and gee I can't explain but I dont think I could believe people were so nice to each other and even me. Mrs. Adams and everyone here is so nice, They have all been. and Anna acts lots different than she used to, she seems lots happier, and They think so much of her and Gerald. and Mrs. Adams has the nicest funnyest names, pet names for them both. Oh just wait till I see you Ill tell you some of them. and she bathed Gerald and she liked him so she gave him a little love spank on his bareness. and he hasent got any bald spot any more, cause he can sit up by himself, nearly all the time he is awake. and he can get up on his knees and he has got a whole lot heavy but I wont tell you till you see him so you can get surprised and Anna got heavyer too. and she got real red cheeks and golly you should see all the pretty things Mrs. Adams has given her. Ill never be able to tell any one all about how good they are to us. they just are too good for any words to tell. maybe they will be so much better looking that you wont know them. Someday may be Gerald and Anna will be lucky enough to have some one like Mrs. Adams watching them when I am at work. I hope I have not made my letter too long. I will see you soon I guess. Anna said when are you coming to see her and her Aunt Blanche. she said she likes Aunt

Blanche's house better than Aunt Hazel's but she said dont tell Aunt Hazel cause she is liable to get angry at her. I will say Bye by till we see you. Thank you for your letter I was glad to get it and hear from you.

GENEVIEVE, ANNA, & GERALD

I forgot to tell you but we went to Sunday School and Anna wanted to go the next day again. and may be we will go again next Sunday. gee everything is so nice.

October 30, 1930.—Letter to social worker of Children's Agency received from Mrs. DeLand:

Thank you so much for having brought me to see your home and your folks. I am having just the time of my life. if this were my own home I never in the world would leave it. I hope you will come here again before I leave. Im hoping so hard you will all of us are. your Mother especially she will feel just so disappointed. Anna and Gerald have got heavy but I wont tell you how much so you can get a surprise and what do you think Gerald has 2 new teeth and they are just as cute he seems to be growing faster here than he did in Chicago. I wouldnt be surprise if he could walk before we get back. he likes everybody but he likes your Dad & Mother best. next to me. And your Mother said she loves him just like he was heres. honest she did. I think she holds him like that too. gee I like her. my goodness I feel so different out here, its not a small place at all your Mother and Dad have taken us on the loveliest rides into the woods and seeing different places and gosh I think she likes me a little tiny bit to cause she gave me a kiss. 2 of them. and I love her for that I never got a kiss from my own mother, and gee I was so happy to think your mother could do that. and she said just the sweetest words to me. and she meant it too. Your Folks have been just wonderful to us they have taken us just about all over we went visiting and we were at Carl and Lib's house and we were at Uncle George and Aunt Nell's and Anna is just too tickled at the thought of going visiting at those two places and every one thinks Gerald is the cutest baby and your Dad took Anna to his work place and she came home and she had a payenvelope and her name was on it and some money they put in too, aint it funny it was pay-day that day? Your Mother said people lose weight when they have a cold. and then she got surprized. when the baby and Anna got heavy. She gave Gerald a bath and she said he was so cute she gave him a love spank on his bareness. and he tried to pull his toe out of the water. He did look nice cause he was pink and white and the little tub was blue. and he just made all kinds of noises to her when she was washing him I wish you could have saw it. My goodness, but I must be a big expense to her cause she makes just the best things to eat I used to read about them but I never dreamed of ever eating them baked cake and muffins and green vegetables, creamed and buttered, and just the fluffiest pancakes and milk and lots and lots of different things and ever so many times you got to take more at the table and gee I bet I get fat too, I bet you will be surprised to see all the little dresses that Anna got. well I dont want to make you tired reading a letter that is too long so I will close now. I *Hope* real hard to have you come home here before I leave.

P.S. Anna said she wants to see you, you should come to *her* house she thinks it is hers now.

October 31, 1930.—Called at 541 West Forty-third. (Mistake in address given by Health Department.) Talked with Mr. Johnson who lives at this address. Hilda Skogland was his wife's sister. Her health had been failing for some time, but she was able to be up and around until a short time before her death which occurred in his home.

Mr. Johnson last saw George at his mother's funeral. He was with his wife whom he married two or three months ago. He thinks she was a nurse who took care of George one time when he was ill. George is working in Moravia; he occasionally spends week ends with his brother in Granger.

November 1, 1930.—Met Mrs. DeLand at the train. She was most enthusiastic about her visit. Georgiana had very little to say and looked very little and very sad. Her mother said she didn't want to go back to Aunt Hazel's home. After she was told that she was going to the worker's house first she brightened up a little.

The worker talked with Mrs. DeLand about going back to her sister's home, and she told more in detail about the situation there. Hazel has spells when she just shrieks at everyone. Hazel says it is because she is nervous. Georgiana is always greatly upset when she does this. When she won't eat, Hazel screams at her, and calls her "Monkey-face," telling her if she were her "kid" she would "lick" her. She doesn't talk this way to be mean, but it is just her rough manner. Hazel favors Gerald, and pays very little attention to Georgiana.

Mrs. DeLand is never allowed in the front part of the house. When Hazel has company she takes the children in to show them off, but never allows Genevieve to meet anyone.

Mrs. DeLand said, "I didn't tell you before, because I didn't know what you might think of me. Hazel hasn't been giving me any money, she has even borrowed from me, and I have been paying for all the milk. I used to get a quart, but then she would use some; now I get only a pint because I can make Georgiana drink all that; I have to save my money for I have just $20 left." She said she had almost $300 saved. When she was earning good wages she always saved a little unknown to anyone and she lived on this when she was out of work and expecting Gerald. She said her money would never have lasted if she hadn't accepted help from the Children's Agency, and she didn't feel right about accepting help when she had a little of her own. This worried her a great deal.

When worker mentioned that her brother had been to the Children's Agency, and suggested they go together to her home and tell them about Mr. Skogland, she agreed to go. However she was terribly upset, became very tense, and cried hard. She said she thought she would run away where no one could find her. She was a little afraid that worker might believe Harry because "he talks good but doesn't mean it." She said, "I know you won't believe how bad he really is, but he tried to get in bed with me when I lived home." He has several children by a woman in the West, whose husband is paralyzed. She feels very much humiliated because he named one of them Genevieve.

She was finally reassured after worker told her that she didn't believe Harry and that she wouldn't want her to go back home to live, and said that she intended to tell her people this if Mrs. DeLand would allow her to do so.

She was so upset about going back to Hazel's home that arrangements were made for her to stay at the Orphanage for a few days. Georgiana was very much pleased to stay there with her mother.

Mrs. DeLand, during the course of the conversation when she was telling about the wonderful time she had in Wabash, had said, "I didn't know if you had told Mrs. Adams anything about me and I got to thinking, maybe if she knew what kind of person I was she wouldn't want me and I just couldn't think of staying on and taking so much from her if maybe she wouldn't like me if she knew about me, so I told her anyhow. For a long time she didn't say anything and I thought maybe she was mad, so I said, 'Do you want me to go home?' and she didn't say anything but she kissed me so then I knew she wasn't mad."

While Mrs. DeLand was in Wabash, Mrs. Adams mentioned several incidents in her letter to her daughter. They had an insight into her very limited experiences. One night they popped corn and she was quite surprised to find how it was done. She was highly entertained by Mrs. Adams' twin daughters and son who amused them in various ways. She was particularly intrigued by the juggling and though it was getting late she wouldn't send Georgiana to bed because she didn't think she would ever see anything like that again.

For three or four days Georgiana would start to cry when Mr. Adams left for work. She asked him if he would come back and when he assured her that he would, said, "Once my daddy went away to work, and he never came back."

Mrs. Adams said Mrs. DeLand had told her all about herself after she had been there about five days. "She said she felt it was wrong for her to climb into our nice soft warm bed and accept our kindness and for me not to know what she was."

She kept asking for work and insisted on scrubbing the kitchen floor on her hands and knees.

Mrs. Adams inclosed in one of her letters the note Mrs. DeLand slipped into her hand just as the train was pulling out. The following is a copy of the note:

MRS. ADAMS:

Just a little while and then we will be leaving for Chicago and I don't know if you would want me to tell you in talking, so I will tell you in writing. you are just so sweet, I love you and I will hope we are lucky so fate will let us 3 meet you all again. You were just wonderful to us and we enjoyed our self to the limit. thank you a million times for your goodness and kindness.

Until we see each other again.

GENEVIEVE, ANNA, AND GERALD

November 2, 1930.—The worker accompanied Mrs. DeLand to her mother's home. Alice and Mr. Brinker were there. Worker did practically all the talking. Mrs. DeLand was pale and shaking from fear. They were merely assured that the children were well cared for, that they need have no fears about them, that Genevieve was a fine mother, respectable in every sense, and that worker had been in constant touch with her for over a year, and that no one could take the children away from her. They were told that regardless of any complaints made anywhere the complainant would be referred to the Children's Agency, as any agency would know we were interested in the family. They were also told that Genevieve was a grown woman, capable of making her own decisions, and that she had decided it was best for all concerned for her to keep away from home. Worker said Genevieve would be glad to tell them about the children's father if they were at all interested. Mrs. Dalcour grunted and said she didn't care if he were a "nigger from Arabia" so was informed then that since she wasn't interested there would be no point in telling her.

Alice tried to make a good impression on the worker by telling how she had nothing against any of her sisters, but she couldn't help it if they didn't like her. She talked very loud and used rough language, frequently swearing at the dog which barked and got in the way, or telling her husband to "shut up."

Worker left with the remark that if they were really worried about the children they would always be able to get reports on their development from her but that it would be impossible for them to see the children. When we reached the sidewalk, Mrs. DeLand breathed a sigh of relief and said, "You mean I don't ever have to go there again?" She said she never saw her mother and Alice keep still and listen before, and it was quite apparent that she had expected quite a scene.

Worker called on Mr. and Mrs. Payson in the evening. They were very cordial. Mrs. Payson told a great deal about her family but added very little to what Mrs. DeLand had already said. Conditions at home were evidently just as sordid as had been described. It was quite clear that Mrs. Payson has very little understanding of Genevieve, though she is not intentionally unkind. She told about one occasion when she came up from the basement unexpectedly and found Genevieve crying. She said, "I just said to her, 'Well, what is the matter with you? Are you so badly treated here that you have to cry about it?' " Mrs. Payson said, "You just have to talk up to her like that to make her snap out of it."

After Mrs. DeLand and the children came to her house, Mrs. Dalcour began to visit frequently, begging Genevieve to return home. Mrs. Payson told her that if she could get along with her mother it was, of course, the best place for her. However, after Mrs. DeLand and her mother lived together two weeks, they came to call on Hazel and she could see there was something wrong. Mrs. Dalcour kept telling what a mean child Anna was, how she wouldn't mind, and was in her opinion the meanest and worst child ever born. She kept asking Genevieve to tell about her husband and would wake her in the middle of the night thinking she might divulge something which she wouldn't tell when fully awake. Mrs. Payson told Genevieve she might come back to her house so she left the children and went back home to pack her things. She returned at one o'clock in the morning wheeling all her belongings in Gerald's baby buggy, walking all the way.

Mr. and Mrs. Payson have known all along that George Skogland was the children's father. Anna is the picture of him in profile. One day Mrs. Hilda Skogland telephoned. She always had said, "This is the little girl's grandmother calling," but on this day she forgot and said, "This is Mrs. Skogland." Mr. Payson used to live across the street from the Skoglands and has known George since he was a child. He has nothing good to say for him.

Since Genevieve has been away, Mrs. Payson said she had been doing a little investigating. She telephoned Mrs. Ivan Skogland on the pretext of wanting to know about Mrs. Skogland's death. She didn't ask about George because she didn't want to make her suspicious. She and Mr.

Payson plan to locate George and see that he is punished. When worker mentioned the possibility of his being in Moravia, Mr. Payson said if that is where he is he suspects he is working at a new packing house which opened up there recently. He will get the name and address of the packing house and will notify worker. They agreed to leave the matter of locating George to worker.

November 4, 1930.—The case was discussed by the Application Committee. It was decided to attempt to find a home where we can board Mrs. DeLand with the children. We will pay her board until the dental work is completed and she can secure a position. At that time she will contribute all she can to the support of herself and children and we will supplement as is necessary.

Problem

Mrs. Payson telephoned today and said that there was a Storey Packing Company in Moravia.

November 5, 1930.—The worker talked with Mrs. DeLand again about the exact time she had lived with George Skogland. She thought she married him in 1924, but finally decided it was in the fall of 1925. She lived at the American Hotel at Fortieth and Pine Streets for two or three months before she married him. She and George lived together "steady" until December, 1928. After that he came home only week ends until May, 1929, at which time he left permanently. She is quite sure this information is accurate.

Called at the Court of Domestic Relations to see what steps could be taken to bring Mr. Skogland into court. It is not possible to extradite on a bastardy warrant. However, since Mrs. DeLand believed she was legally married, he can be brought back for non-support, and if he claims he is not married, can then be held on the other charge. The worker was advised to return the following week as the judges were away on account of the election yesterday.

November 6, 1930.—Accompanied Mrs. DeLand to the dentist. She finally agreed to have one tooth pulled after much persuasion. She was very much frightened and shook for several minutes afterward.

See note which she wrote and handed to worker in the evening just before she left her room:

Might you be able to find time to read this. Thank you. Good night. No matter what you think Please dont get angry.

I am going to be making you awfully angry by writing this to you. But I cant make up my mind to getting my teeth all out and even if I shall look more better, I dont want them out. and I promise you I will get a job where I will get a lot of money and in the Stock Yards no body can make much money I have made the most when I was there and I never made as much as I need to make now, I want to make as much again as I done when I worked as a press operator and please dont get angry but this is what I want to do I want to stay at my sister's house and take care of Anna and Gerald myself to see that he is started the right way in habits and with stopping nursing him altogether by 10 or 10½ mo. old and I cant give him the best care if my teeth come out I dont think cause I get so wiggly. I love them and I want the pleasure of training them in those things myself cause other people will have them to teach in other things when they get older and go to school. and then Ill be working for them and wont have the chance to be with them to teach them. as soon as Gerald is weaned I will have me a job, I dont want to waste a whole week working for 14 or 15 dollars, cause I will have two of them to pay for and myself and I am planning to earn enough to have a home of our own and not give up our furniture, I made me a home everytime my mother moved away with the furniture and I kept our furniture ✓ for Anna and me and I made a good home for her and things only went awful when I was expecting Gerald and couldn't work for so long, please let me do things again for us and Ill show you, I am not so weak as I guess I look. and I want to go back to my sisters house this week cause I feel like I am in jaile, I am going to want to keep my teeth until things have got settled for Anna, Gerald, and me, and by that time I will not care if even all would come out. You know they should come out and its a great big thing to you, but forgive me for saying this, I cant let anything upset me like my teeth, ever since I got Gerald I have been making plans to get on my feet again, and in another couple of weeks Ill try some of them. I simply will not get fixed up until I have got them sitting pretty.

And I don't want to waste your Dentists and your time until then, and I am happy you said I could pay you back. I realize you are the only *real* friend I have and no matter what happens or what I do Ill tell you everything first, wont you have confidence in me doing things for us a little bit? please, I wish I could tell you how much I mean it when I say please. after thinking about every thing you are the only one who has ever cared about me in all my life and I hope I keep on knowing you always so Anna and Gerald will know you, you are so good I wish I could be like you. but I guess I can't and I want Anna to be like you. I dont want you to think I am telling you lies any more now, cause I believe you, I told them lies cause I couldn't be truthful for others sake. First I done it for him and then for Anna, I wish I need never lie for them but I didn't lie cause I only wanted to. but you are one person, in a whole world, who understands me.

November 7, 1930.—Talked with Mrs. DeLand about the note, and explained more carefully about the home we had in mind for her and the children, and about the need for dental work. She said she wouldn't mind having her gums treated, or fillings put in, but extractions are too upsetting for her while she has to care for Gerald.

She said she had wanted to stay at the Orphanage for two or three days, but not so long. She had thought she "dassen't" leave, and didn't quite know why. Because she had been afraid of frightening her, worker had not told her that the nurse was afraid Gerald might contract pneumonia if he was not watched carefully as he had a severe cold.

Dr. Cook examined Gerald today. He is anemic, otherwise in good condition. He should be given vegetables and fruit juice and cod-liver oil everyday, else there is danger of his developing rickets.

Drove Mrs. DeLand to her sister's house later in the afternoon. On the way Georgiana said several times, "Mamma, don't you think I should have stayed in the hospital until I was all over my cold?" When we reached the house she began to cry saying, "I don't want to stay here, let's go back to Mrs. Adams' house." She finally dried her tears and said, "I will look as if I was glad to see Aunt Hazel, but I won't be glad to see her." She put on a brave front and spoke to Aunt Hazel, but when the worker left she began to cry. Mrs. Payson took her in her lap and roughly bounced her up and down in an attempt to comfort her. Her voice was loud and shrill and the things she said, though not unkind, would hurt a sensitive child very much.

November 8, 1930.—The worker visited in the morning and took Mrs. DeLand to the dentist. Georgiana was crying and had just thrown up her breakfast. Mrs. DeLand was quite distressed and was not so averse to leaving Hazel's home sooner than she had planned.

Mrs. DeLand was very brave at the dentist's today and though the pain must have been very much worse than anything she felt when her tooth was extracted, she made no fuss and agreed willingly to return on the twelfth.

CHILD'S RECORD

Child.—Georgiana DeLand.
Birth date.—June 11, 1925.
Birthplace.—Chicago, Illinois.
Date of admission.—December 23, 1929.

Chronological history to time of admission.—Georgiana was born in Chicago. She lived with her father and mother until May, 1929. However, during this period she was placed out in private homes during the day or during the night depending upon which time her mother was away at work. She changed homes very frequently and in some of these homes she received very poor care. Since May, 1929, Georgiana has been with her mother or grandmother most of the time.

Health history.—Georgiana was born full-term normal birth and weighed six and three-fourths pounds. She was breast fed for ten months and then given cereal, vegetables, and soups. She had no diseases previous to admission to Orphanage.

December 28, 1929.—Georgiana dismissed from Orphanage because her mother was discharged from the hospital.

January 4, 1930.—Georgiana readmitted to Orphanage.

February 11, 1930.—Georgiana dismissed from Orphanage.

SUMMARY FROM NOVEMBER, 1930, UNTIL AUGUST, 1935

In 1932 arrangements were made for the Public Agency to supplement the mother's earnings with milk and a ration box. The Children's Agency was to continue doing the case work. However, in about two years, in conference with the worker of the Public Agency, it seemed to be the opinion of this worker that the case had been handled in an unprofessional way, that the intercession of the Children's Agency worker had made it impossible for the Public Agency to gain co-operation and had caused duplication of relief and service. The Public Agency felt that the frequent change of workers would not be an important factor, if the relationship were a professional one rather than a personal one. They wished to carry this case entirely or give up responsibility for both relief and service. The Children's Agency Committee agreed to accept the case for relief and case work on the basis that the very size and impersonal character of the Public Agency prevented the mother from feeling a sense of security, and that she needed a substitute for her own family which place the Children's Agency had filled for her. She has been earning eight or ten dollars a month depending on the number of Saturdays in the month. The Children's Agency has put in full budget, making the allowance for Mrs. De-Land's earnings. There were interesting developments during this period, some of which will be summarized here.

Mother's relationships with the father.—The mother gradually talked more about the father and his relatives, finally tracing him through his relatives. In May, 1931, the mother and the worker visited him in Wisconsin. The interview was unproductive since the father would not talk freely in the presence of the mother. The worker kept in touch with him, with the knowledge of the mother, and finally later persuaded the mother to allow her to talk with the father alone at the Orphanage.

The father said that when he first met the mother at their place of work, he felt sorry for her. She used to sit in his car until three o'clock in the morning. When he knew she was pregnant, he decided to live with her a few years though he had never intended a true marriage. He had been married previously, never divorced, and has only recently remarried. The mother had thought she was married to the father, but when she found she was not, took her maiden name, DeLand. She wanted to keep in touch with him, however, so that there would never be a question about the paternity of the children, as she could not have them called "that awful name."

In conference with the worker from the Court of Domestic Relations, the Children's Agency worker was advised not to try to settle the matter out of court. At the hearing the relatives were anxious for a settlement, but the father's lawyer insisted on a continuance to see how much money the father could raise. The case was continued and the father died of a heart attack November 8, 1931. At the hearing, after the father's death, it was decided that because there was no legal marriage, there was no possibility of claim on the father's estate and no possibility of establishing the paternity of the children.

The mother was very much grieved over the father's death, forgetting all her hatred for him.

Attitude of the mother toward the agency.—The mother gradually modified her extreme anxiety over the Agency's power to take away her children. While she was still overly apprehensive, the worker had felt that as a representative of the Agency she could never establish a confidential relationship because the mother reiterated the need for having the children forget their connection with the Orphanage so that as they grew up people could not tell them they had had no one to care for them.

In matters of health, particularly, the mother had felt the Agency would harm the children. She changed from refusal to have physical check-ups, however, to asking for them and later asked for a vaccination for Gerald because she would rather have him get sick from that than die from smallpox.

The mother wrote very long letters to the worker, describing her reactions to medical care, her husband, her relatives, or to plans which she and the worker had discussed, always imploring the worker many times not to "get mad at" her and reiterating how she appreciated what the worker had done and the fact that she could never have another friend who could mean so much. Gradually this humility and gratefulness have changed to self-reliance so that now she does not bring every minute problem and emotional reaction to the worker.

Living arrangements.—Up until 1932 the mother with the children continued to live with her sister. She was very unhappy there. Her sister and brother-in-law teased her about the way her husband had treated her, and because she had believed she was married when she had not been. When she went out on the street with her sister the sister always walked ahead of mother as she was ashamed of her. However, the mother could not decide to move where she would have to live with strangers.

Problem Solved

In the summer of 1932 the worker placed the family in an apartment where the landlady was extremely kind to the children and interested in initiating the mother into community activities by birthday parties for the children to which she would invite her friends, by sewing groups, and Parent-Teachers meetings. The family is living there still and has gained a sense of adequacy through community recognition.

Personality of the mother.—The mother has gradually grown from her feeling that no one should be interested in her to a feeling that she should have a happy life for herself as well as for the children. She remarked when moving away from her relatives to a home of her own that she did not see what she had done to be the happiest person alive. Her delight when some neighbors came to call on her was almost pathetic as she could not believe people would waste their time on her. She has finally accepted "social workers being nice" to her, but her acceptance of the recognition given her by the members of the Parent-Teachers group and other community gatherings has been slower.

The mother greatly desired to feel useful to someone. She repeatedly asked if the worker knew someone to whom she could teach what she knew of typing and shorthand. She wanted to earn her living by work that would help other people, not merely satisfy her own needs. She felt that the care of her children was her expected duty so that this could not be her only good. She makes patchwork quilts and other bright furnishings for her home, delighting in telling the worker about them. She is not so easily upset over minor incidents and she doesn't keep things to herself for long periods of time without talking them over.

Development of children from 1931 to June, 1935.—The children have both developed physically. In 1933 the mother agreed to a tonsillectomy for Gerald after which he gained well in height and weight. He has completed the kindergarten and has enjoyed it very much. Georgiana has also grown a great deal. She completed the fourth grade with a good record. Both children were extremely well liked by their teachers because they are so attractive, bright, and eager to be helpful.

SECTION II

CASE RECORDS OF CHILDREN WHO WERE KEPT IN THEIR OWN HOMES WITH THE HELP OF A VISITING HOUSEKEEPER

1. The Fennell Family

(The Housekeeper Teaches a Very Ineffective Mother How To Care for Her Children)

July 2, 1930.—The Fennell Family, 640 West Eighteenth Street, was referred to the Children's Shelter by the Family Agency, Union District, worker—Miss Howells. Children: Clarence (March 8, 1920); John (April 5, 1922); Frank (August 16, 1925); Jimmie (September 3, 1928).

REASON FOR REQUESTING CARE

(Including Agency's plan and time necessary to complete plan)

Mrs. Fennell is expecting confinement at any time, and John, Frank, and Jimmie must be cared for until she is discharged from Grace Hospital. Clarence left for Camp Wabash on June 30 and will remain there during the summer as he is underweight and undernourished.

SUMMARY OF FAMILY HISTORY

The Fennell family has been forced to seek shelter at the Children's Shelter in previous years, at times when Mr. Fennell deserted. He has been away from his family this last time since March, 1930. Our earlier history shows that Mr. Fennell is inclined to desert during Mrs. Fennell's pregnancies.

Since the Fennell family has been known to the Family Agency in Chicago and to the Associated Charities in Dunlap, Indiana, as well as to other charitable organizations in these cities and others, they have not established themselves in a home but have lived in rooming-houses, or stayed with relatives in Dunlap. When Mr. Fennell deserts, it is necessary for Mrs. Fennell to be assisted, and this the Family Agency has done throughout this spring.

EARLY CHILDREN'S SHELTER RECORD

July 27, 1925.—Clarence and John were admitted at the request of the father. Mother is to be confined at Women's Hospital.

September 25, 1925.—Children released to father.

April 8, 1926.—The boys were readmitted at the request of their father. He asked for care until he is paid and can re-establish the home. He has been ill since February 5. He now has temporary work, driving for the city. He expects to take Civil Service examinations Saturday. Mother and baby are staying with a friend.

April 15, 1926.—Union District of the Family Agency visited and record read:

1. *Record of care by other agencies.*—American Red Cross (Wayland County, Missouri) knew family from May, 1919, to June, 1921. They provided $100 at various times for transportation from Rapids City, Wisconsin, Pittsburgh, and Chicago. American Red Cross (Dunlap) knew the family from January, 1920, to March, 1923. They provided hospital care for the father; made small loans to him; assisted the mother during illness and father's desertion. War Bureau (Chicago) employed father December, 1923, collecting funds; also offered food supplies. Father applied at Family Agency, Union District, for help January, 1924. United Charities provided care for the children during the mother's confinement and secured transportation to Missouri in June following the father's desertion. Case reopened February, 1926, by County Agent on account of father's illness.

2. *Marital status.*—Father deserts frequently. The mother believes that he is interested in a lodger, Mrs. Close (February, 1926), whose picture he carries.

3. *Father.*—Entire family "irresponsible" (A.R.C.). Elder brother and father owe A.R.C. for loan. Youngest brother is "mentally incompetent" (A.R.C.). The father wanders from place to place, depending on social organizations for return transportation. He has applied to A.R.C. eight times for this. For four years he traveled with carnivals as contortionist, singer, chalk-talker. Also traveled with his half-brother, Mike Scotti, enlarging pictures. He worked for a few months as coffee mixer at Winters Brothers and as elevator man at the Desk Lamp Company. He worked two weeks in the Hampton Packing Company and several weeks as claim chaser for Minor Stores. He refused a new offer to collect funds for the War Bureau. He was indignant with the Family Agency for refusing him money. The United States Veterans' Bureau reported (February 20, 1926) that the father had a 10 per cent disability rating because of flat feet. He has not been able to prove present chest condition existed before January, 1922. Father was treated at Hills Sanitarium (Indiana), January, 1922. "Diagnosis: pulmonary tuberculosis; early, incipient; apparently quiescent. Prognosis: good. No vocational handicap." In June, 1922, he asked the American Red Cross for information about a venereal clinic. February, 1926, he left the County Hospital against advice. Diagnosis: pleurisy. In 1926, neighbors reported that he beat the children until interfered with.

4. *Mother.*—Her parents died in her infancy and she was reared by friends. She is reported to have been discharged from a position at housework because

of questionable character. She is a poor housekeeper. Prefers to live in furnished rooms. She has no control over the children.

5. *Relatives.*—Paternal grandmother has been married four times and had children by each marriage (Fennell, Scotti, Nanning, Murrow). Her present husband "goes off when he feels like it." She has helped the family with food, etc.; in 1923 she sent $10.50 for the mother's transportation to Missouri. She shields the father and continually takes his part.

6. *Home life and conditions.*—The family is usually found living in one furnished room. At one time when they had two rooms they took another family (also Family Agency case) in on condition that they pay the rent for both rooms. Mother says that the children "worship" their father, who has excellent control over them, and that they "pay no attention" to her because she "loves" them. She says they "drive her frantic."

May 2, 1926.—Children released to father.

July 23, 1929.—Clarence, John, and Frank were admitted July 10, 1929, at the request of the Family Agency, Union District. Care was requested during the hospitalization of Mrs. Fennell. There was a miscarriage. Clarence was dismissed to his father on July 20, 1929, while John and Frank were dismissed July 23, 1929.

July 24, 1930.—While the mother was confined, the boys made splendid adjustment in the Shelter. They were alert, active, happy children. At the request of the Family Agency, Union District, John was dismissed on July 14, 1930, to go to Camp, while Frank and James were dismissed on July 24, 1930, for Camp.

May 6, 1931.—Mr. Fennell makes a personal appeal, asking that Frank and James be admitted, as Mrs. Fennell is to be confined at any time. Mr. Fennell is a large, hardy-looking person, who is dressed neatly in old clothing. He is well groomed. He seems especially proud of the fact that he has been able to keep his family without assistance for five months. Mr. Fennell has sold apples on the street corners and has earned an average amount of $18 a week. He did not purchase his apples from the Veterans' Bureau because they charged $2.50 a box. Instead, he went to the Wholesale Fruit Dealers and bought them for $1.25 a box. When questioned regarding the last steady employment he had, he stated that he worked for the Webster Printing Company in December, 1929. This "steady job" lasted two months. Mr. and Mrs. Fennell have had no major domestic difficulties since he started selling apples. "You can't blame anybody for getting disgusted when your husband can't give you anything," he explained. "But now that I am doing a little she seems satisfied." Mr. Fennell is proud of the fact that he has remained with his family during his wife's coming confinement, as heretofore he has always deserted. He explained that he was trying to face difficulties and not run away from them. He became extremely serious when he mentioned the fact that his mother died in September and that also made him look upon life more seriously.

The Fennell family is living in a one-room kitchenette apartment for which they pay $7.00 a week. Mr. Fennell seems to feel that such an arrangement is satisfactory. Three beds are crowded in the one room.

Mr. Fennell's father died when he was twelve years old, and he went to work on a farm. He finished the fourth grade but explained proudly that he had learned a great deal during his travels from town to town. His mother remarried four years after her husband's death. Her second husband was a day laborer who earned sufficient wage to keep them comfortably. Mr. Fennell was never on good terms with his stepfather. He had no brothers or sisters. Mrs. Fennell's mother and father died when she was a baby and she was adopted. The foster-parents are dead. Mr. Fennell stated in a sad tone that they would always have to make it alone.

Mr. Fennell thinks that it would be possible for Clarence and John to attend school and remain at home. John, however, attends school on a half-day session schedule, so it was decided that he should enter the Children's Shelter, inasmuch as he would have no supervision after school. When Mr. Fennell was questioned as to the reason for his waiting until the last minute to make the arrangements, he replied that he thought neighbors would take the children. He had not, however, asked them to do so and when questioned regarding the names of the neighbors he was unable to give any information. Mr. Fennell escorted the three boys to the Shelter. The children were immaculate and were dressed in warm clothing.

Called the Union District of the Family Agency and talked with Miss Sampson. Their contact with the family closed in November, 1930. The Fennells have become very dependent and would be quite willing for the Family Agency to support them indefinitely. The Family Agency has known the family since 1924 and has assisted periodically. Mr. Fennell was never able to face difficulties and always deserted when there was any hardship. He did not tell the truth and would become furious when the Family Agency refused to carry out his demands. (They have suspected his morality.) Mrs. Fennell is completely under his power and does what he tells her to do.

December 28, 1931.—Mr. Fennell telephoned on an average of once a week regarding the children. The County Hospital reported on July 24, 1931, that Mrs. Fennell had not returned to the post-natal clinic. The doctor had advised at least a six weeks' rest after her dismissal from the hospital. Mrs. Fennell did not gain in strength and was not able to assume the household duties. She visited the children on September 4, 1931, appeared to be extremely sick, and explained that it was her first trip away from home. She had little to say as Mr. Fennell did all the talking. He seemed to glory in telling about his wife's serious operation. Mrs. Fennell expressed regret because she felt physically unable to care for her family and agreed to return to the County Hospital for a re-examination so that a definite report could be obtained. Checking back with County Hospital it had been impossible to secure a report on the post-natal examination.

Repeated efforts were made to have Mrs. Fennell returned to the hospital. On October 6, 1931, the case was assigned to Miss Norton.

Housing conditions.—The Fennell family live in three rooms on the basement floor of a two-story brick apartment house about a half block from a main thoroughfare. The apartment is furnished with the bare necessities. It is barren-appearing. During the visits the home is always upset and dirty. Mrs. Fennell explains each time that she does not feel strong enough to do the work.

Mrs. Fennell.—Mrs. Fennell returned to the hospital for the removal of a kidney on June 17, 1931. A visiting nurse dressed the wound until the last of September. She reported on September 30, 1931, that Mrs. Fennell seemed well enough to assume the responsibility for the care of her children. However, it was agreed that she should return to the County Hospital for another check-up. On November 2, 1931, she returned to the County Hospital. Dr. McCoy diagnosed her illness as a suspect renal stone. (See report.) Arrangements were made repeatedly for her to return to the Hospital for a thorough examination as requested. It was understood that the children in the Children's Shelter would return to their own home as soon as the doctors in the County Hospital reported that the mother's physical condition warranted her assuming the added responsibility. On November 22, 1931, a report was received from the County Hospital stating that Mrs. Fennell was able to care for the two children who were still in the Shelter.

Mrs. Fennell is a quiet, friendly person. She tries to hold her own against Mr. Fennell who "lords it over" his whole family. Whenever he is present during a visit it is impossible for Mrs. Fennell to say anything, as he always contradicts her. She questions the worker concerning the children's adjustment in the Shelter and at school. She is proud of their school reports. During one visit the boys came home from school and went immediately to their mother with their papers. Mrs. Fennell told with pride that the boys had gone out for dinner to the home of a neighbor and the neighbor had reported that she had never seen such well-mannered children. It was evident that Mrs. Fennell worries about not giving the children the attention and understanding that they need. The children are always neatly dressed in old clothing.

Mr. Fennell.—Mr. Fennell is a verbose, dictatorial person who domineers over his wife and his family. He seems to be shiftless and not overly concerned about assuming responsibility. He rarely questions the worker in regard to the children in the Shelter, but immediately begins to talk in a loud voice concerning his relationship with the Family Agency or concerning his poor physical condition. Several times when the worker called, Mr. Fennell was lying on the bed. He explained that he had to rest because he had walked around looking for work. Mr. Fennell threatens to desert if the children are returned. He seems to feel that his desertion would make it impossible for his family to get along. He never displays any kindness or consideration to his wife or family. He is always excited and ready to start an argument in regard to the treatment he has received from social agencies.

He was employed from January to August, 1931, at the Clayton Paint Company and made an average of $24 a week. The employer cut the amount to $20, and when Mr. Fennell objected he was discharged. He expounded at great length regarding the unfairness of the whole procedure. He does not seem to think it would have been wise for him to keep the job on a $20-a-week basis. He does not feel that he should have been cut even when most of the other men were. He feels that he is superior and should, therefore, not be considered on the same basis with the other employees. He continues to sell apples. He tried to sell an oil preparation for a few days but he made only $4.80 in three days and so decided that that was not worth while. He stated in no uncertain terms that he had certainly done all that anyone could do to support his family. Mrs. Fennell never talks during Mr. Fennell's long speeches.

Financial conditions.—The Fennells pay $6.00 a week for rent. They were unable to pay the October and November rent. They bought a radio in January, 1931, for $65.85 and still owe $10.85 for it. Mr. Fennell was on the defensive in regard to the purchase of the radio. He receives a monthly compensation of $35 from the Veterans' Bureau for disability of flat feet. The family received No. 4[1] rations from the County Bureau and one quart of milk from the Veterans' Bureau Division of the County Bureau.

When a definite statement was received from the County Hospital sanctioning the return of the children to their own home, a conference was held December 4, 1931, at Union District, Family Agency. Mrs. Anna Bilger, case worker for the Family Agency, and the two workers from the Children's Shelter considered the future plans for the Fennell family. It was agreed that Mrs. Fennell would be notified that the boys could be dismissed on December 23, 1931. It was assumed that Mr. Fennell would get in touch with the Family Agency as soon as he was informed that the children were to go home. When he applied, he was to be told that he would be given assistance when he saw a psychiatrist. This request was based on the long experience that the Family Agency has had with the Fennell family and the inability of any worker to maintain a co-operative, working relationship with Mr. Fennell, who exhibited serious temper displays and complete inability to get along with any adult for any length of time. It was thought that the request was justified because Mr. Fennell had never been able to hold a job although several good ones had been found for him. Because the social worker was unable to carry out any constructive program, it was thought that the psychiatrist might be of assistance. Mr. Fennell always deserted in the face of difficulties and has never felt that he should assume difficult responsibilities. It was agreed that the family should be moved to a new neighborhood and be established with furniture. The Fennells have lived in furnished rooms practically all the time. In one instance the Family Agency established the family and supplied furniture which Mr. Fennell sold. He used the funds to pay traveling expenses. It was agreed that the Children's Shelter would furnish a housekeeper for a two-month period, during which time an effort would be made to teach Mrs. Fennell household management. Mrs. Fennell was to have psychiatric and psychological examinations. The fact that she has had one baby after another was taken into consideration as a probable reason for slow reactions. (See letter to Mr.

[1] [Staples included for No. 4 ration intended for a family of six persons for a period of about twelve days, costing $5.69, were as follows: 5 lb. soap, 1 lb. lima beans, 1 lb. navy beans, 5 lb. rice, 3 lb. rolled oats, 3 lb. macaroni, 2 lb. coffee, 5 lb. flour, 10 lb. sugar, 1 24-oz. preserves, 4 lb. lard, 9 cans tomatoes, 8 cans milk (large), 4 lb. prunes, 4 lb. bacon, 1 lb. split peas, 2 lb. corn meal, 2 lb. dried peaches, 1 lb. raisins, 1 lb. American cheese, 1 lb. wheat cereal.

This ration could be varied somewhat to meet the dietary needs of the ill client and of Italian and Jewish clients.]

and Mrs. Fennell stating that the boys could be dismissed when the quarantine for whooping cough was lifted.)

Mrs. Bilger reported that Mr. Fennell had consulted the Family Agency as soon as he had received the letter. He agreed to see a psychiatrist and seemed to feel that he needed vocational guidance. He felt that he needed to talk to someone. He also suggested that Mrs. Fennell see a psychiatrist. Mr. Fennell was seen by Dr. Campbell of the City Department of Health on December 14, 1931. The examination was not completed.

January 14, 1932.—Frank was dismissed to go home on January 9, 1932. Mr. Fennell was extremely congenial. He stated that he was going to look for a flat immediately and that he hoped he would have James home shortly. He was thoroughly in accord with the housekeeping plan as Mrs. Fennell had spells when she was unable to do the work. Mr. Fennell stated rather proudly that he had learned to become quite handy. He had worked for the Forest Preserve for eight days, earning $5.00 a day. He had hopes of getting on the police force as a patrolman for school children. He showed the worker the write-up in the paper and stated that he was going to look into the matter. He stated in a grand manner that he was going to co-operate with the Family Agency and the Children's Shelter as he had never done before. This was voluntary information.

January 21, 1932.—Mr. Fennell finally selected a four-room basement flat in a brick building in a good neighborhood. The building had just been recently painted a bright red and it was obvious that this might have been one of the attractions, as otherwise the place was quite ordinary. Mr. Fennell was quite elated about the home and kept talking about how much he had to do and how hard it was. He produced an itemized list of the necessary household goods.

On January 12, 1932, the family moved to the new home, where the furniture provided by the Children's Shelter had been delivered. When the worker visited in the afternoon, she found Mrs. Fennell sitting in the living-room with the baby on her lap, while all about her in hopeless confusion was piled bedding, chairs, etc., just as set down by the delivery man. Mr. Fennell was out "on business." Mrs. Fennell had a slight infection in her finger and was unable to do much.

A woman was provided to go in by the day to help the family get settled; it took several days as Mrs. Fennell seemed to have no idea of how to begin. Whenever Mr. Fennell was seen, he talked about how hard he was working to establish his family. "You have no idea what hard work it is." It was impossible for him to agree that everyone with a household had these responsibilities. He continued to report frequently at the employment office, hunting work. When relief funds became more limited, he made a great speech about how carelessly the money had been spent. He, himself, had no qualms about asking for additional help, although the rent had been paid by the Family Society, despite a ruling due to limitation of funds which was to stop paying rent.

When worker visited January 20, 1932, at ten-thirty, Mr. Fennell was still in bed. There was no fire because the ashes had not been removed and Mr. Fennell had told the family to wait until he got up and he would take care of it. When the worker asked him about it, he said he had a headache; and when medical care was suggested he said, "Oh, it wasn't that bad." Worker finally waited until he was up and dressed. Then he said, "I don't feel like fighting with you this morning." Throughout the visit, Mrs. Fennell had little to say.

February 5, 1932.—The home has been visited twice weekly since Mrs. Swanson, the housekeeper, was placed January 26, 1932. Mr. Fennell had complained that they were hungry because the county sent flour, and they did not know how to make bread. Hence, the first thing the housekeeper did was to bake the bread for them. At first it was impossible for the housekeeper to do the washing, and so Mrs. Fennell did some of it alone. Frequently when the home was visited the fire was out, and it was necessary for the family to sit in the kitchen to get warm from the gas stove, which burned with a low flame. Mr. Fennell came to the office February 5, 1932. He was in a most expansive mood and kept repeating how he had respect for "old age" but "that woman" at his house was "too old." He claimed that the housekeeper used too much gas; whereupon it was pointed out to him that he had been advised to buy a coal stove for the kitchen which would cook and heat at the same time. Then Mr. Fennell attempted to show that the housekeeper could not get along with his wife and that they "had had words." One afternoon the housekeeper had taken a nap, and he complained that she slept too much.

Mr. Fennell presented a list of things for which he had spent most of his compensation. (See record.) It had been previously understood that the Family Agency would supplement the food. The worker had advised him to economize on household furnishings so that the family would not run short on food, as it was known that the Family Agency funds were nearly exhausted. Despite this, he had but $1.50 left for food for the month. He complained because the Family Agency was now sending rations. He refused to believe that it was cheaper for the Family Agency to buy foods wholesale and distribute them than for Mr. Fennell to buy from "Sol" on the corner.

In conclusion, Mr. Fennell became quite confidential and said that he believed that his wife should have an examination like he had had. He said that she had some insane relatives and that sometimes he wondered whether she was "all right."

The following day Mrs. Fennell and the housekeeper were seen apart from the rest of the family. Mrs. Fennell seemed disgruntled and believed that the housekeeper had not done enough work. She could not understand why the Children's Shelter would not continue sending the colored woman, although it was explained that Mrs. Swanson could be more of a companion to Mrs. Fennell. It was agreed that the housekeeper should continue for another week and if no adjustment could be made then a new woman would be placed.

February 15, 1932.—This letter was received by the social worker from the housekeeper:

When I came home Mrs. Fennell was so worried that I might have told you about him selling apples and I was afraid to tell her I had because she would be very angry with me, so I thought I would write and ask you not to let her know I told you. I don't think she would ever forgive me. She asked if I told you about their quarrels, and I said most likely you knew about them already. She said you couldn't have been out there all this time, so I told her how I had to go to the Library about the library card. It doesn't take much before she gets nervous and upset. So help me out, will you?

February 22, 1932.—The housekeeper remained in the Fennell home, although there continued to be friction and trouble. Mr. Fennell still believed that she was not doing her share of the work. Apparently he deliberately pushed his standard of cleanliness up to the point where practically no housekeeper could attain it. For several days he was in a pugnacious mood. He grumbled about the way in which relief funds were being administered, he claimed that women were holding jobs that men should have, and finally he concluded by saying that he "didn't have to stand for it, and he wouldn't." He was usually at home in the morning when the worker called. He was neatly dressed and carefully shaved. On one day when seen he was sulking by the stove like a little boy. At intervals he would interrupt the general conversation to say, "How can I find work without any carefare?" and then again several minutes later, "They only give us five pounds of flour; can't expect that to last." At times he was almost crying with self-pity.

Mrs. Fennell was seen alone on two occasions. It was apparent that she was most fearful of her husband, followed the line of least resistance, and agreed with him. She stated that he often went out about noon and did not return until one in the morning. She believed that he spent his time in pool halls. They had always quarreled, but since the housekeeper's coming it had been less frequent. It is apparent that Mrs. Fennell is most suggestible and agrees with whoever is talking with her at the time. On one occasion she spoke somewhat romantically of her meeting with Mr. Fennell and their marriage just four weeks later. She stated that he "was always a good talker." Arrangements were made for Mrs. Fennell to be invited to attend the mother's club at Neighborhood House. Numerous events have been scheduled, and Mrs. Fennell has been clearly stimulated by the new contacts. Mr. Fennell was sulky and jealous. He seemed to feel that it was unfair for him to take care of the children when she went out in the evening. The housekeeper when seen alone stated that Mrs. Fennell is nervous and excitable but that she is trying to make a good home for her children. (Mrs. Fennell is proud of the nice neighborhood in which they now live.) The housekeeper feels that Mrs. Fennell is inclined to be too particular and to take too much time with a single duty instead of working out a routine which would get everything done. It was agreed with Mrs. Bilger of the Family Agency that Mrs. Fennell should have a psychiatric examination as soon as possible.

Whenever the children are seen they seem to be clean and fairly well dressed. The housekeeper says that they are "naturally clean children." They like rough-and-tumble play and are usually scrambling about the floor when the worker calls. Clarence is a pale, less hearty-looking youngster than the other children. At times he is most loyal to his father and will have nothing to do with anyone else.

John was said to be having difficulty in school. He had been unable to learn to read, and his teacher had asked Clarence to help him with his work. John simply "made up" when he was asked to read. He seems to be a friendly child but has seemingly unreasonable outbursts of temper at which times he flies at the other children. Mrs. Fennell stated that she feels that he is not normal.

Frank is perhaps the most attractive of the boys. His cheeks are always shiny red, and he seems to be alert to everything going on about him. When excited about something he talks rapidly, but a speech defect makes him rather unintelligible.

James bears a marked resemblance to his father, with an untidy mop of brown hair, soft brown eyes, and a large, somewhat weak chin. He likes to fight with the other children and seeks, or makes opportunities, for doing so.

March 2, 1932.—Letter received by the social worker from the house-keeper:

Mr. and Mrs. Fennell came back from the hospital, and they were so nice to me. I have won out, Miss Norton. The only thing that worries me now is what I said about those apples. Please, Miss Norton, don't say anything about them. I am sorry I said anything about them. They went out tonight to visit some friends. I asked him especially to treat his wife with consideration during this great strain, and I think it will bring them closer together. She bore up bravely under the strain. I will feel so contented if they can be convinced that I mean them both well in all things. If he has faults that he is born with, it is quite hard to overcome. If they can stóp quarreling, it will be quite a happy change. They are such good friends tonight. We will miss the baby so much. Will you please help us pray for his recovery. I told Mr. Fennell I would give him a little help and he was not to bother you. He said he would be thankful for a couple of dollars. So I think if we work it out as you say there will not be any more fuss, and I won't have to be under the strain of him thinking I am putting them out so much in the line of food.

March 19, 1932.—Work was arranged for Mr. Fennell at Neighborhood House by the Family Agency. In this way he was enabled to work for cash. Mr. Fennell seemed to be much happier doing this but seemed to feel that he was working very hard for the amount that he earned. He continued to have the arrogant "know-it-all" attitude toward social workers and his wife. Frequently he would say to his wife, "I know you just want me to get out. All right, I'll go, but that compensation is paid to me, and not to my wife or children." He seems to feel that this is a good whip to use on his family. Miss Mayer at Neighborhood House reported that he is one of their best workers; he arrives early and works without ceasing.

On March 8, 1932, Mrs. Swanson, the housekeeper, became ill and was threatened with bronchitis. She was obliged to leave while Mrs. Fennell was at clinic with the baby; although Mr. Fennell was at home and able to take care of the children, Mrs. Fennell felt that the housekeeper had been disloyal in leaving. Neither Mr. nor Mrs. Fennell showed any sympathy for the housekeeper's condition. They were told that they would be expected to manage for a while just to see what they could do. The home was visited at intervals of two or three days. Each time it was found to be dirtier than the time before. Mrs. Fennell cut her hand and was able to do little. The beds were unmade; clothing was scattered about; dishes stood on the table and food on the stove. Mr. Fennell declared vehemently that he was working outside and that he should not have to do a woman's work. His wife stated that he had said, "If they want the mopping done, they can pay me as they would a housekeeper." Mr. Fennell continued to suggest that he might desert, or that it might be better if he and his wife lived apart. He offered to contribute half of his income to the support of his wife and the children, but would want to come and visit them and have something to say about the management of the household.

A conference was held at the Family Agency office on March 19, 1932. Miss Adams, Mrs. Bilger of the Family Agency, worker from the Children's Shelter, and Mr. and Mrs. Fennell were present. It was proposed to the Fennells that the Children's Shelter did not feel sufficient progress had been made during the housekeeper's stay, due largely to the uncooperative attitude of Mr. and Mrs. Fennell. It was pointed out that much of their energy went into quarreling and that this made a most undesirable home for the children. Mr. Fennell attempted to put all the blame on his wife. He charged her with being quarrelsome, profane, and unfaithful. Mrs. Fennell had little to say, but after prolonged questioning stated that Mr. Fennell slept late in the mornings, struck her occasionally, stayed out late at night at pool halls, and refused to help her about the house. Mrs. Fennell stated that he kept trying to provoke her to tell him to go ahead and desert. Instead, she just retorted, "Do as you wish." It seemed that Mrs. Fennell was fearful about being left alone with the children, although she could not get along with her husband. It was wholly impossible to get Mr. Fennell to assume any of his obligations in the home. The Fennells were finally told that they would be expected to take care of themselves from now on, as they felt competent to do so.

The Children's Shelter agreed that, should Mr. Fennell desert, placement of a housekeeper might be reconsidered for the purpose of determining what Mrs. Fennell was capable of doing while her husband was out of the picture.

April 2, 1932.—Mrs. Fennell called to report that her husband had left the day before after receiving his compensation. He had left her $5.00 with which to buy food and said he was going to look for work. The rent was due that day, and Mrs. Fennell was very much distressed. She stated that her husband had cut out all his pictures so that it would be impossible to advertise for him. Mr. Fennell's great fear had been of arrest and return to jail. Previously, Mr. Fennell had broken his parole from a penitentiary and had enlisted in the Army to avoid returning to jail. He had adopted an alias under which he was married to Mrs. Fennell. In some way he convinced her that this alias might be used to prove their marriage illegal. The Family Agency was advised of Mr. Fennell's desertion and suggested that before any action could be taken Mrs. Fennell should swear out a warrant for her husband.

May 26, 1932.—A housekeeper was again placed in the Fennell home on May 16, 1932, to work with Mrs. Fennell and determine if possible how capable she is of making a home for her children while her husband is away. At this same time the family was evicted and so moved to a more pleasant five-room flat.

Although situated on a car line the flat is more desirable with high ceilings, many windows, and two light bedrooms. The rooms seem barely furnished, but nevertheless it is possible to keep them cleaner and more orderly.

At first Mrs. Fennell seemed completely overwhelmed by the problem of moving. Gradually, with the housekeeper's assistance, the family became settled and some routine established. When the home was visited, Mrs. Fennell seemed to be in much better physical condition than at any previous time. She frequently referred somewhat wistfully to Mr. Fennell. She showed the worker a picture of Mr. Fennell with another woman. Mrs. Fennell somewhat unconvincingly said, "Isn't it terrible?" She seemed to have little idea of the seriousness of Mr. Fennell having left her completely dependent upon outside relief. She was busy as usual wiping the children's faces and combing their hair. All the children seemed well except the baby, who had a severe cold.

When visited at noon, the children were usually seated at table with Mrs. Fennell serving each one in his turn. They sat fairly quietly and seemed to enjoy their food. Clarence stated that he drank as much milk as he could get and knew that it was good for him. He was inclined to take a somewhat "grown-up" attitude toward the behavior of the younger children and would tell on them. For instance, he eagerly told the worker of the trouble into which John had gotten at school and then went on to say how well he himself was doing in school. In the past five weeks Frankie has showed a marked improvement in his speech and is fairly intelligible now. He recently had his tonsils removed and was advised not to return to school for the balance of the term. Jimmie is still rough and noisy in his play, but less so than when his father was in the home.

Because of the poor progress John was making, the worker visited the Washington School where John is in 2 A. The teacher reported that John is older than any of the other children in the room and will probably be passed because of this. She stated that occasionally he would fight with the other children but that his behavior is not really a serious problem. For the past two months he had been getting special remedial help. The teacher felt that he has made good progress with this added assistance. His attendance record has been good, and the teacher stated that he usually came to school cleanly and adequately clothed.

It was agreed with the worker from the Family Agency on May 26, 1932, that the Children's Shelter should be responsible for obtaining a child study examination of John and that the Family Agency would arrange for psychiatric examination of Mrs. Fennell at Warner Hospital.

June 20, 1932.—With Mr. Fennell out of the home, the family life seems happier and more stable, although Mrs. Fennell has difficulty in controlling the children and usually resorts to shouting at them. Mrs. Fennell rarely jokes and seems to have no real sense of humor. The children have discovered this. They like to tease her in various ways, knowing that she will become angry. There is usually a certain amount of rough-and-tumble scrapping in the house, but at times the children show an affection and gentleness for one another.

Mrs. Fennell has become more proud of her home and is delighted with the large and airy rooms. She does most of the shopping, and seems to manage well. She cooks fairly well, but has few ideas about planning meals in advance. She knows nothing about baking. It seems difficult for her to get things done.

The housekeeper reported on June 6, 1932, that Frankie is the only stubborn member of the family. He is finicky about his eating and just sits at the table rather than eating what is served. He is inclined to be rough with the younger children. Johnnie is said to be most forgetful and cannot be depended upon to remember even simple things for a short time. He is easily controlled by praise.

On June 20, 1932, Mrs. Fennell was taken to Warner Hospital for a psychiatric examination. She was deeply upset by the prospect and kept reiterating that she had had little education, so could not do arithmetic problems, etc. With some difficulty her mind was distracted to conversation about her neighbors, with whom she had become quite friendly. Some of them have taken her and the children riding, and she, in turn, has had them in for coffee in the afternoon. She was planning a picnic in a local park with one of the other mothers.

August 20, 1932.—Letter received from Warner Hospital:

Mrs. Fennell has, as you know, been under care in the Gynecological Clinic since June 20. At that time the question of the advisability of a therapeutic abortion was brought up. Mrs. Fennell gave history of having had a kidney removed, and it was at first thought that it might be advisable to abort her. She was at that time between three and four months pregnant. A careful study was made of her in both the Gynecological and Medical Clinics, and it was felt that the presence of only one kidney was not in itself an indication for terminating the pregnancy, particularly since the remaining kidney was functioning well. When Mrs. Fennell was seen on August 15, her condition was again found to be good and the kidney function normal.

Mrs. Fennell was also seen at your request in the Mental Hygiene Clinic, where she impressed the psychiatrist as being of rather limited intelligence. She showed absolutely no evidence of mental disease so that it was not felt, from the standpoint of mental hygiene, that an abortion could be recommended. She was considered socially inadequate, this being based on the social history sent us by social agencies; however, it was not felt that her intelligence was sufficiently low to warrant advising an abortion simply on that ground.

Further study of Mrs. Fennell is desired after our psychologist returns from abroad. We have no one at present equipped to give the type of psychological examination required for adults. We have made an appointment for Mrs. Fennell to come to see the psychologist on September 20, and we are enclosing a slip to be given to the patient for that date. Before this examination is made we cannot advise you as to how much you can expect of the patient. We shall very much appreciate a report of the observations of your housekeeper as to the patient's responsiveness and ability to learn.

August 22, 1932.—Mrs. Fennell does not "holler at" the children as much as she did when the housekeeper (Mrs. Miller) first went there. Mrs. Fennell saw that the children minded Mrs. Miller, who did not shout at them. Mrs. Fennell is calmer and happier. She mends and sews and tries to carry out a schedule in her household duties. Mrs. Miller has attempted to show her that washing, ironing, mending, cleaning, and cooking are done with much more ease when a routine is established. Mrs. Fennell, however, has been inclined to wash when all clothes were dirty, iron by degrees, and cook spasmodically. Mrs. Fennell has become more interested in planning a balanced menu and likes to learn to make new dishes. The family all sit down and eat together.

At first Mrs. Fennell cried and fretted like a child whenever there was a difficulty. As she regained her strength, she ceased this infantile behavior. She was inclined to dwell on her troubles. The children did irritate her, and she was inclined to nag at them. She did not reason with them or appeal to them. They all took advantage of her and knew that if they teased her long enough she would give in. Mrs. Fennell was inclined to let matters slide; it was so much easier.

She enjoys a clean house. She is happy when she sees her children washed and clean. She, however, makes no consistent effort to have her home in order and her children well cared for. There is no doubt but that Mrs. Fennell is genuinely fond of her children.

Frankie has temper tantrums. If he cannot have his own way he cries and screams. His mother always lets him have his way if he screams long enough. The housekeeper tries to tell Mrs. Fennell to ignore him and not give in to him. Mrs. Fennell does try and succeeds spasmodically.

Jimmie is a lovable, aggressive little boy who has been spoiled by too much attention. He is a "show off" and says "cute" things to make people laugh. He is not difficult and obeys. However, it is felt that as he grows older he will attempt to take advantage of his mother, as there is a tendency in that direction already.

John is a responsible, more likable, wholesome boy. He looks out for the younger children very well. He is an even-dispositioned, kind-hearted child.

The housekeeper remained until July 22, 1932. The Family Agency agreed to maintain the family.

December 29, 1932.—Mrs. Williams was placed as resident housekeeper when Mrs. Fennell went to Warner Hospital for confinement.

SUMMARY OF CASE RECORD TO FEBRUARY, 1937

Mr. Fennell returned to his family after the confinement of Mrs. Fennell. The Family Agency carried the Fennell family until April, 1934, when it was decided that the Veterans' Service of the Bureau of Public Welfare should take full responsibility for relief and supervision. The history over the whole period showed repeated desertion of Mr. Fennell. The agency tried to persuade Mrs. Fennell to take him into court and to refuse to allow him to return, but she was never willing to do this.

Mrs. Fennell had several illnesses, and there was much discussion regarding sterilization. She was anxious to be sterilized, but the hospital did not find sufficient grounds, mental, social, or physical, for sterilization. The children were sent to camp; the agency worker was interested in the health problems of the children and in their school records, which were always satisfactory.

After 1933 a permanent housekeeper was considered no longer necessary; but the agency made it possible for Mrs. Fennell to send the laundry out and to have someone come in once a week for cleaning. The record shows that Mrs. Fennell adjusted remarkably well to each new opportunity given her. The children seemed healthy and very normal in every way. There was evidence of a great deal of affection, especially between the mother and the children, although the children also seemed fond of their father and quite proud of him. Mrs. Fennell retained the standards of cleanliness and ideals of housekeeping which were taught to her.

At the time of the last entry the family was receiving full relief from the public relief agency.

2. The Davidson Family

(Through the Help of a Housekeeper an Attempt Is Made To Build Up a Feeling of Responsibility on the Part of an Escaping Father)

May 11, 1931.—Mrs. Amos, Family Agency, telephoned the Children's Shelter, asking that a housekeeper be placed in the home of Robert and Florence Davidson at 3220 Buchanan Street, pending a report of an examination of the mother at the Psychopathic Hospital. The examination will be postponed until arrangements for care of the children can be made. The children with birth dates are: Glenn, October 14, 1923; Sara Mae, September 18, 1924; Helen, October 27, 1925; Barbara, November 24, 1926; Paul, February 5, 1928; Sylvia, July 15, 1929; and James, October 12, 1930. The family is Protestant.

May 12, 1931.—Read record at the Family Agency. Summary follows:

The family was first known to the Family Agency on August 22, 1930, when the landlord found that Mr. Davidson, who had been unemployed for several weeks, had deserted. Mrs. Davidson was expecting to be confined very soon. After being gone three days Mr. Davidson returned bringing what was left of his pay check to his wife. The case was then closed August 28, 1930, but reopened March 11, 1931, when the Visiting Nurse Association thought Mrs. Davidson was a mental case. On May 5, 1931, Mr. Davidson reported that he believed his wife was going insane. She had tried to commit suicide twice, but never when she was home alone. She nagged him constantly and neglected the children. Their private doctor made a diagnosis of dementia praecox with paranoid tendency.

Investigation revealed that Mrs. Davidson, who was Florence Blair before her marriage, was a very retiring girl, whose own family life had been unhappy. She was born in Birmingham, England, August 18, 1901, the eldest of five children, and was her father's favorite. She had attended school until she was sixteen and then worked for two years as a cashier. She was engaged to Mr. Davidson for three years before their marriage.

Mr. Davidson, who was born in Chicago, was the youngest of six children. He left school when he was fifteen and after that was employed in a variety of ways. His last employer gave him a good work record. In August, 1930, Mrs. Davidson complained that her husband gambled; however, she said he did not drink. He had left home before during the past year but had never stayed away all night. The landlady said that Mr. Davidson made a very good impression, that he was polite and very kind to the children.

Mrs. Davidson's parents have been divorced for several years and her father has remarried. Mrs. Elizabeth Blair, Mrs. Davidson's mother, lives with her children, who quarrel because they are obliged to support her. Mr. J. D. Blair will have nothing to do with any of his children except Mrs. Davidson. He is living comfortably in the home of his second wife's relatives. His second wife does not wish him to have anything to do with his family.

Mr. Davidson's parents are dead. He has one brother, Walter, who is a streetcar motorman, but Mr. Davidson has little to do with him. Miss Williams, school nurse, is much interested in the children.

The family is known to the following agencies:

Infant Welfare Station, August 25, 1925

Legal Aid, April 12, 1930

Visiting Nurse Association, June 24, 1930

Family Agency, August 22, 1930

Court of Domestic Relations, May 12, 1931

Later.—Visited. The family live in a mediocre neighborhood. They occupy the second floor of a three-story frame building, which is generally in good repair. The Davidson flat is conspicuous because of the irregular shades and lack of window curtains. When the worker arrived, Glenn and Sara Mae were playing in the street. They seem to be attractive, friendly youngsters, but are obviously neglected. Their clothing was scanty and in need of mending. Inside, the home was in utter confusion. There are five light, rather pleasant rooms, but clothing was scattered all about and the air was foul. In the living-room, which has three large windows, there is a good overstuffed davenport, a plain rocking chair, and a bright cedar chest. A torn dirty rug partly covers the floor. Adjoining this room is the dining-room, crowded with a large stove, a broken square dining-room table, three straight chairs, and a china cabinet. The latter shows evidence of having once been carefully arranged. Off of the dining-room is a small dark bedroom occupied by the girls. Dirty bedding lay in confusion on the one double bed in it. Beyond the dining-room is the kitchen, also crowded with a good gas stove, a kitchen cabinet, and a breakfast table with four chairs to match. Adjoining this is the other bedroom with a double bed and a small dresser. The bathroom seems to have adequate plumbing, but the floor is in poor repair. There is a large back porch and a grass-grown yard.

Helen, a pretty child with black hair, blue eyes, and fair skin, was holding the baby when the worker arrived. She knew practically nothing of her mother's whereabouts. She said that her Grandfather Blair had taken her mother to the hospital that day and that her father had gone out to work and had not returned.

Later.—Talked with Mrs. Blair, Mrs. Davidson's stepmother. She refused to have anything to do with her husband's grandchildren. She stated that her husband was interested only in getting Mrs. Davidson out of the home so that she could get well.

Mrs. Amos arranged for a neighbor to care for the children overnight until Mrs. Davidson could be located.

May 15, 1931.—Visited, placing Mrs. Sawyer, housekeeper. Mr. Davidson had returned two days before, and had been taking care of the children. He was at home when the worker arrived. He is a thin, colorless man with a prominent nose and little chin. He explained "sheepishly" that things had just been so bad at home that he had gone on a spree and had been drunk for about twenty-four hours. He assured the housekeeper that this will not happen again and that he is only anxious for his children to be given a good home until he can find out what is to happen to his wife.

May 20, 1931.—Letter written to the housekeeper, from Children's Shelter:

Enclosed you will find your check for the past week's work in the Davidson home.

I would suggest that you encourage Mr. Davidson to feel that until some reasonable permanent plan can be made for his children he should provide the best care possible in their home. Please help him to understand that until such a plan is made the services of a housekeeper will be provided. I trust that the help of a cleaning woman this Friday will give you a little better chance with the housekeeping. Of course it should be easier all the time as the children and the home are cleaned up. You have already given a fine service to this family.

June 1, 1931.—Visits have been made at frequent intervals since the placement of the housekeeper. The children's heads, as well as everything else in the house, have been cleaned. The housekeeper has given special attention to Mr. Davidson as he was very discouraged about his family and frequently would say that the only thing to do was to have them all placed. He has difficulty with his finances, and, although he has been given an allowance each week for car fare, etc., he always has to borrow toward the end of the week. He likes to buy candy for the children but fails to recognize the practical needs in the home. At first he gave the housekeeper little help, but more lately he has been willing to work about whenever he is there. The housekeeper doubts whether he is really capable or willing to carry on for his family. The housekeeper has had some difficulty with Glenn. On May 29, 1931, he was sent home from school but lied to the housekeeper and said he had been in a fight with a boy. He has little to do with the other children in the family and likes to go off and play in the alley. On June 1, 1931, the housekeeper took James to the Infant Welfare Society, where he was found to be in good condition but in need of sunlight and special food.

June 4, 1931.—Mrs. Amos of the Family Agency telephoned. She stated that Mrs. Davidson had been committed to the State Hospital on June 3, 1931; diagnosis, dementia praecox; prognosis, poor. The case was at once referred to the Juvenile Court for a permanent plan for the care of the children.

It was agreed that if possible the housekeeping arrangement should continue until such plan was made, inasmuch as two placements would seem most undesirable. If, however, unusual difficulties arise and Mr. Davidson fails to co-operate in the plan, the children may be admitted to the Children's Shelter at once. The Family Agency will continue on the present budget basis. Assistance will also be given the housekeeper one day a week.

Later.—Visited. The home was cleaner, and the housekeeper stated that the burden was much lighter. Mr. Davidson was upset over his wife's commitment as he did not understand what the outcome might be. One of his friends came to the home to visit him night before last. At first Mr. Davidson wished to go out, but the housekeeper succeeded in getting his interest in taking care of the children. He has returned from work at a reasonable hour and has not shown any signs of drinking since the housekeeper's arrival. Despite this, the housekeeper doubts whether he really wishes to maintain his family, as at times, although less frequently now, he suggests placement.

June 11, 1931.—Visited. The house was neat and clean. Sylvia has been ill with an infection, so she has taken a large part of Mrs. Sawyer's time. The county doctor called, and the visiting nurse comes daily. Mrs. Sawyer believes that Glenn needs more supervision than she is able to give him. He stays out until nine and ten o'clock at night and is also truant from school. He pays no attention to his father, although Mr. Davidson has attempted to talk to him and has also punished him. Glenn is a leader, and the other children try to do the things that he does. He has attempted sexual relations with Sara Mae, stating that he didn't see why he couldn't do that as well as his mother and father. Mrs. Sawyer tried to talk with him about it. It was agreed that Glenn should enter the Children's Shelter, providing Mr. Davidson approves. The other children have presented no problems and only need attention for their physical needs.

A woman has been sent in every Friday to clean, beginning June 4, 1931. Mrs. Sawyer found that this made it possible for her to spend more time with the children. Mr. Davidson has shown much more interest in the children and no longer goes out with his men friends; instead he seems to enjoy coming home to a clean house and to children who are well cared for. He has expressed his desire to keep his family together, if they can be maintained on a decent scale of living.

Mrs. Sawyer has not received help from the Family Agency at regular periods and has been worried because she was unable to buy food that the children needed. She had taken money from her own purse to buy milk.

Later.—Telephoned the Family Agency and talked with Mrs. Amos. She agreed that she would send $4.00 for a grocery order every Monday.

June 13, 1931.—Mr. Davidson brought Glenn to the Children's Shelter, where he was admitted for care.

June 20, 1931.—Mrs. Sawyer reported that Sylvia had been taken to Warner Hospital following a diagnosis of mastoid.

June 22, 1931.—Visited. The house was immaculate. Mrs. Sawyer was fanning the baby, who was lying in the crib in the front room. The children, who were all dressed in clean clothing, were playing house on the back porch. They were laughing and having a glorious time. Mrs. Sawyer reported that the children have been easier to manage since Glenn left.

Arrangements have been made for a neighbor, a Mrs. Jake Brown of 2915 Buchanan Street, to iron every Friday, as Mrs. Sawyer expressed her desire to have the ironing done rather than the cleaning. The order from the Family Agency still has not come regularly, so Mrs. Sawyer has again had to take money from her own purse to buy the groceries. She also gave Mr. Davidson a dollar for train fare so that he might visit his wife at the State Hospital. Mr. Davidson is considerate and seems most grateful to Mrs. Sawyer for the care given his children.

Later.—Telephoned Mrs. Amos. Requested again that the grocery order be sent regularly. Mrs. Amos reported that on June 20, 1931, Miss Warren of the Juvenile Court read the Davidson record and consulted with the Family Agency with regard to continuing housekeeping service in the Davidson home, inasmuch as Mr. Davidson has informed both Mrs. Amos and Miss Warren that he wishes to keep the children with him.

June 27, 1931.—Visited. The rooms were neat and clean. Mrs. Sawyer still spends much time with the baby. The children seem quite self-sufficient and need very little attention considering their ages. Mrs. Sawyer has had no difficulty with any of them. Paul is inclined to be mischievous and "get into things." Sara Mae assumes a maternal attitude toward Paul and tries to look out for him. The children play well together.

June 28, 1931.—Talked with Mr. Davidson at the Shelter. He had come to see Glenn, whom he visits every Sunday. Mr. Davidson was neatly dressed and had on a freshly ironed shirt. He was glad to hear that Glenn was getting along nicely in the department and had presented no problems whatsoever. Glenn is a chubby-faced, active little boy who gets along well with the other children. When Mr. Davidson asked Glenn if he wanted to return home, Glenn replied that he wanted to stay in the Children's Shelter. Mr. Davidson has a calm manner. He spoke highly of Mrs. Sawyer and said he is pleased with the care she gives the children as she is patient and understanding. Mr. Davidson never enjoyed his home more. He used to come home tired after a hard day's work only to find the children crying and dirty and his wife irritable. He does not blame his wife as he realizes she had more than she could handle. Mr. Davidson does not wish to consider any plan other than the one which will make it possible for him to keep his children with him.

Mr. Davidson visited Mrs. Davidson on June 21, 1931, and at that time she believed that the whole world was against her. When she was talking she asked Mr. Davidson why he made signs to the people in the hall and seemed to feel that he was trying to make plans with the people to jeopardize her welfare.

She interpreted every move anyone made as a gesture against her. She did not inquire regarding the children; her whole interest was centered on her ideas of persecution.

June 30, 1931.—Letter received by the Children's Shelter from the Juvenile Court:

We have just received a letter from the State Hospital concerning Mrs. Davidson, whose name is given as Mabel instead of Florence, but whom we believe is our client, having been admitted to the State Hospital on June 5.

This letter states that Mrs. Davidson's examination has not been completed but that she is in the observation ward doing well, and that her case will be staffed within the next two weeks. After we have a definite report we will communicate with you again, and hope that meanwhile you will continue working with the family along the present lines.

Thanking you for your co-operation in continuing your interest in the Davidson children.

July 2, 1931.—Visited. Sylvia returned home from the hospital on June 29, 1931. The visiting nurse comes in every day. Mr. Davidson seems most interested in his family, and his whole attention is now centered in his children. On July 1, 1931, Mr. Davidson sent Helen to the drug store to get some ice cream as the children had been asking for it. On the way she was run down by an automobile and suffered a fractured leg. She was taken to the County Hospital. Witnesses stated that she had run directly in front of the car.

Mrs. Sawyer said that the longer she remains in the Davidson home, the more encouraged she becomes as Mr. Davidson is co-operative and interested.

July 12, 1931.—Letter received by the Children's Shelter from the Juvenile Court:

We are enclosing a copy of the letter which we have just received from the State Hospital concerning Mrs. Davidson. We hope that the present arrangement may be continued until after we have received a diagnosis, especially as the report shows that Mrs. Davidson is improving.

We will be very glad to hear whether or not you are willing to continue with the present situation.

Copy of letter to Juvenile Court from State Hospital:

We have your letter of June 30 regarding the admission of patient by the name of Florence Davidson; wish to advise that she is committed here under the name of Mabel Florence Davidson.

This woman was presented to Staff this morning, and she was left in the Undiagnosed Grouping.

She has many physical findings of exhaustion, has very low blood pressure, and she has lost considerable weight. Since her stay here she has shown some improvement, in that she has gained in weight.

We are keeping her under observation, and will be glad to report to you of our findings in the next month or so.

July 15, 1931.—Visits have been made twice weekly. Sara Mae and Barbara have suffered slight stomach upsets, and Mr. Davidson was most anxious that they be given proper care. The housekeeper stated that he is still hopeful that his wife may return to them but he believes Jimmie should be placed for adoption. His chief difficulty lies in managing his finances. He stated that he is now working five days a week, earning $4.95 a day, at the Johnson Spring Company. Of this amount $8.00 is paid on the rent; $2.00 on a loan from his employer; $2.00 to the Stein Furniture Company; and about thirty-five cents for group insurance. This does not leave him enough for food and personal expenses. The Family Agency agreed to maintain an adequate budget, but for various reasons the amounts given have been irregular and uneven.

On July 14, 1931, the case was discussed with Mrs. Amos, the worker at the Family Agency, who agreed to compute a budget and give relief on that basis until a permanent plan could be devised in conference with a representative of the Juvenile Court. It was decided that since a definite diagnosis from the State Hospital should be forthcoming within two weeks, a conference would be called at that time to determine whether the housekeeping plan should be continued under the auspices of the Family Agency or placement of the children arranged by the Juvenile Court. A letter to that effect was sent to the Juvenile Court July 15, 1931.

On July 15, 1931, Helen was visited at the County Hospital, Ward 32. The diagnosis was fractured tibia. No statement was made as to the length of time she would have to remain there. She lay quietly in bed, smiled faintly, and said little. Her father had gone to see her the day before and had taken her some fruit. She did not appear to be in actual pain but was weary from being in bed so long. She said she had been in the hospital "a long time." As there seemed to be very few toys about, the worker arranged for some toys to be sent.

July 23, 1931.—Visits have been made about every two or three days. Helen was released from the hospital on July 21, 1931, a bed being provided by the Family Agency. It was apparent that all the children enjoyed having her home, and the housekeeper stated that Mr. Davidson was delighted to have her back. Sylvia is to go to Miss Williams' (school nurse) home within a few days as she requires care and Miss Williams has offered to take her. All the children have improved physically. Sara Mae is like Glenn in that she enjoys being on the streets. Barbara, on the other hand, is a pale, thin, restless child who prefers to play in the house. Both she and Helen bite their fingernails. It was suggested to them that they have a race to see whose nails would be longer at the end of two weeks.

Mr. Davidson continues to believe that his wife may be released to him very shortly, though a report from the State Hospital was received by the Family Agency which stated that Mrs. Davidson would have to be there for at least five or six months longer. No diagnosis can be made as yet, and the possibility of parole is quite remote. In view of this it was decided that the Juvenile Court should proceed at once with permanent plans for this family. Miss Warren of the Juvenile Court arranged to present the case to the Dependent Committee on July 28, 1931, inasmuch as disposition of the case would involve a question of general policy.

July 31, 1931.—A conference of the Dependent Committee of the

Juvenile Court was held, attended by Miss Williams, school nurse, Mrs. Amos of the Family Agency, and the worker from the Children's Shelter. The Family Agency volunteered to maintain the family with a housekeeper as long as Mr. Davidson should prove his stability. It was noted how his interest in the children had increased during the preceding two months, and the decision reached that maintaining the home would not only benefit the children but would also help to steady Mr. Davidson and develop his responsibility for the children. It was recognized that the situation during the past two months has been of a rather temporary, emergency nature and that Mr. Davidson has perhaps not assumed as complete responsibility in his home as might be expected in the future, since the housekeeper has exercised considerable authority. At first the plan of placing the two younger children was discussed, as some believed that Mr. Davidson should not be expected to keep all the children. Miss Williams reported that Mr. Davidson would like to have the baby placed as he took so much of the housekeeper's time and was generally a disturbing factor in the family. The committee agreed to the placement of Jimmie and decided that if possible this should be arranged at Vincent Nursery by Miss Warren of the Juvenile Court. This placement would be made only until Mrs. Davidson returns or until the baby is older and does not require so much attention. Glenn is to be returned to his home as soon as the baby is placed, as it was believed his problems had arisen because of the lack of adequate supervision. It was particularly noted that a constructive recreational program for Mr. Davidson should be arranged and suggested that should Mrs. Sawyer continue, her husband might prove to be a good companion for Mr. Davidson.

The Family Agency asked that the Children's Shelter carry on for two weeks longer so that details of their plan, which included moving the family, might be worked out. The Children's Shelter volunteered to assist in securing a new housekeeper should a change be necessary. Miss Williams will give special attention to the medical program and the diet for the children. It was recognized that such close supervision as had been given by the Shelter could not be afforded by the Family Agency and that co-operation of the school nurse was essential. The Juvenile Court agreed to reopen the case at any time that Mr. Davidson should prove himself unfit or in case special problems should arise.

July 31, 1931.—Visited. All the children were up and dressed when the worker called at nine-thirty. Sara Mae and Barbara were playing out of doors. Sylvia returned from Miss Williams' home the day before and was sitting in bed with Helen. Sylvia appeared to be more friendly and alert.

She was proud of her new accomplishments which included saying "bye-bye" and "mama." During the visit Mr. Davidson took Sylvia on his knee and showed an interest in her and affection for her which had not been observed before. He was troubled because he had not worked during the last week but found satisfaction in the home conditions. The house-keeper's husband was present, and Mr. Davidson volunteered that he found him a very companionable person. Mr. Davidson was anxious to know when Glenn would be coming home and explained that when last visited, Glenn for the first time expressed a wish to go home. Apparently the novelty of the institution has worn off. Mr. Davidson said quietly how pleased he was that the children are to be kept together but agreed that the placement of the baby was wholly desirable.

August 3, 1931.—The following report was sent to the Family Agency:

Confirming our telephone conversation of today, I am sending this report of our contact with the Davidson family. Many of these facts are probably already known to you. The housekeeper was placed there May 15, 1931; since that time we have assisted by paying her wages and the laundry bill, and more recently providing a woman to do the cleaning a few hours each week. As agreed with Mrs. Amos we will continue until August 13, 1931, so that your plans may be completed.

When first visited, this home was found to be in utter chaos. The children were neglected and in need of proper food, clothing, and supervision. When Mr. Davidson deserted at the time his wife was taken to the Psychopathic Hospital, the children were left to shift for themselves. Due to Mrs. Davidson's illness, the home was dirty and poorly kept, although it showed a few evidences of having once been maintained at a good standard; for example, the china cupboard was still neatly arranged. Gradually the physical condition in the home was improved, and the more regular regime was reflected in the children's behavior. It has been interesting to note that the children rarely ask for their mother.

Mr. Davidson at first gave the impression of being a rather weak type of person. When seen on May 15, 1931, he was thin, colorless, and depressed looking. He explained that things had just been so bad at home that he had gone on a spree and been "drunk with the rest of the fellows." At the time of his wife's commitment he seemed utterly lost. Things had happened so quickly that he seemed confused and unable to assume the responsibility for his family. His one thought was to have his children placed. Gradually this attitude changed, and recently Mr. Davidson has displayed a more devoted, tender interest in his children. On June 28, 1931, he told the worker from the Children's Shelter that he had never enjoyed his home more. He used to come home tired from a day's work only to find the children crying and dirty and his wife irritable. He did not blame his wife as he realized that she was not responsible. He seems to be fond of his wife and looks forward to the time when she will be home and well. He has visited her as often as he could afford to go and always reports any slight improvement. At first he did little about the house but recently showed himself to be most helpful. Earlier Mrs.Sawyer had used him about the house to keep him from going out, but now it seems that Mr. Davidson is most dependable. Mrs. Sawyer should be responsible for the physical care of the children, and Mr. Davidson might take care of the discipline and recreation. As discussed at the conference he himself needs a constructive recreational program. It was suggested at that time that Mr. Sawyer might be a good companion for him. On July 31, 1931, Mr. Davidson volunteered that he liked Mr. Sawyer, who is a quiet man, perhaps fifteen years older than Mr. Davidson.

Early in the housekeeper's stay, Glenn presented some behavior problems. He was truant from school, played in the alleys, and returned home at nine or ten o'clock at night. Once he attempted to have sex relations with Sara Mae. Being the eldest, he had been accustomed to being the leader and setting the pace for the other children. It was apparent that Glenn could not get proper supervision in the home where so many demands were being made on the housekeeper. He was admitted to the Children's Shelter on June 13, 1931. Here he adjusted very well in a group where the boys were older as well as younger than he. It would seem that if given closer supervision and companionship at home Glenn could make a good adjustment there. Mr. Davidson said on July 31, 1931, that he was most anxious to have Glenn at home. Mr. Davidson would undoubtedly respond to an appeal to be a closer companion to the boy. As agreed at the conference Glenn will be released from here as soon as the baby can be placed.

Sara Mae is very much like Glenn in that she likes to play out of doors and be free of supervision. She rarely stays at home and is not accustomed to helping much there. She seems to be a bright, friendly, wholesome, confident child who usually is found playing in the midst of a throng of children. She is less neat in her personal appearance than the other children as she runs and plays so hard and wears out her shoes and rips her clothes. Sara Mae might be expected to have certain regular tasks about the house, for which she would be exclusively responsible.

Helen is the favorite in the family. During the housekeeper's stay she has assumed the most responsibility about the house and seems pathetically mature for her years. When the home was first visited on May 12, 1931, she was walking the floor with the baby in her arms. Since being in bed after the accident she has been most patient and uncomplaining. She seems to be a self-contained, undemonstrative child, but one who is highly sensitive. One feels an underlying tension. She had always bitten her fingernails but recently has refrained from doing so, after being appealed to on the basis of having them longer, like a "grown-up lady's." She likes to play with dolls, and usually plays with but one or two children at a time.

Barbara is a quiet child who occupies a very small place in the family. She does not like to play out of doors or engage in active games, and gives the impression of being very frail physically. She also bit her fingernails formerly but not so much as Helen and has succeeded in stopping this habit.

The picture of Paul is not so clear. He has been with his maternal relatives part of the time and seems to have been spoiled during his stay with them. Being with adults has kept him a baby. He frequently wets his bed at night.

Sylvia like Barbara seems to have but a small place in the family group. At first she always appeared to be a pathetic youngster standing just in the doorway or around the corner with her diaper and few clothes trailing about her. She was always a spectator and rarely participated in the usual activities of the home. She demanded little attention and had been neglected in favor of the baby. During her stay with Miss Williams after the mastoid operation she developed remarkably. She learned to say a few words and took pride in this means of getting attention. Physically she was much improved. Mr. Davidson and the housekeeper are now giving Sylvia more attention. Miss Williams recommended an abundance of sunlight and a diet which included fresh fruits and vegetables.

James is quite well now but has been a sick baby in need of a great deal of care and has been spoiled. All the children seem to be fond of him. He is the only child Mr. Davidson wants to place as he recognizes that the care of this baby by the housekeeper is given at the expense of the other children's welfare. The baby's crying also has kept him awake at night and generally seems to be the one disturbing element in the present situation. For these reasons it was agreed at the conference that the baby should be placed. Miss Warren had said that she is arranging for James' admission to Vincent Nursery just as soon as possible. From the foregoing it is apparent that all these children are in need of careful, individualized treatment. Such a family as this constitutes almost an institution and has similar problems. Mr. Davidson is now ready to give each child the affection he needs but has not done so until recently. Placement of Sylvia and Glenn has helped in this regard somewhat, but it would seem better for the children to secure these things in their own family group. As for the housekeeper it is only fair to recognize that Mrs. Sawyer did a fine service during what was clearly an emergency period. This time is past, and the housekeeper's role will be a different one in the future. Mrs. Sawyer is an intelligent person and should, it seems, be given an opportunity to understand this change and try to make an adjustment to it. Miss Williams believes Mrs. Sawyer needs special supervision in matters of diet, and Miss Williams would be glad to provide this. If Mrs. Sawyer cannot make this adjustment, we shall be very glad to assist by helping to secure a new housekeeper. We have learned that changing a housekeeper is not so drastic a step as might be supposed. The children adapt themselves readily to the change and so, if the need arises, a change can be made.

I am inclined to believe that much of the difficulty remaining in the home is due to the unstable financial basis. As part of the new plan Mr. Davidson will certainly assume complete responsibility for the family finances. Given a workable budget with a definite amount assigned to Mrs. Sawyer for food, I am sure that she would make a conscientious effort to provide the best possible diet. We should be very glad to co-operate with you again in the future in any way that we can.

August 6, 1931.—Took James to the Vincent Nursery, accompanied by Miss Warren of the Juvenile Court, Sara Mae, and Barbara. The baby was quiet throughout the ride. Barbara and Sara Mae, on the other hand, scrambled about and exclaimed loudly over all they saw. Apparently they had ridden about very little before, for even the small canal excited them. Barbara, in contrast with her previous conduct, was noisy, talkative, and even impertinent. She would repeat Sara Mae's sentences in high, nasal tones. She has a marked speech defect and changes "t" to "sh" and "sh" to "s." Even at the Nursery amid strangers she seemed unrepressed and scampered about the hall. Not until they were nearly home did they even mention the baby's absence.

Later.—Mr. Davidson called at the Shelter for Glenn. He was neatly dressed and was plainly delighted to take the boy home. He spoke in a quiet, intelligent manner about his responsibility for the children and how he planned to take them to the park, etc. As for himself, he stated wryly that there wasn't much a man could do without money. It was suggested to him that with a housekeeper he would be given a great opportunity to enjoy the children and that their pleasure would always be his. It was also proposed that he and Mr. Sawyer might have much in common as they were both "broke." While Mr. Davidson recognized the weight of his responsibility for the children and his financial difficulties, he was, nevertheless, determined to do his best to make a good home for the children. His last visit to his wife was discouraging, but he believes that she may come home to them in a year. For the first time he volunteered that it would be wiser for her to remain until she is really well and until the children are a little older. He stated that he expects to visit the baby every two or three weeks and believes that it will be possible for the other children to get better care now. He recognized that Glenn's difficulties have largely been due to inadequate supervision and that he himself will best be able to give this to Glenn. He decided to appeal to Glenn on the basis that, being the eldest, he should set an example for the other children. Glenn was beaming when he greeted his father and clung tightly to his hand. Glenn then took his father to meet the housemother, who was interested in talking with Mr. Davidson.

August 11, 1931.—Took Helen to the County Hospital accompanied by Barbara and Sara Mae. Barbara seemed less excitable, although her father said that her appetite is not very good, probably because she plays so hard. Sara Mae was more quiet and expressed herself in a manner better suited to a child two or three years older than she. She said in a matter-of-fact tone that she expects to go to grammar school and then to high school. She will be in 1 A this fall and inquired how old she would be when she finished grammar school and when she finished high school. Sara Mae reported that Glenn is taking his responsibility very seriously and sees that the children do not cross the street without permission. He does not go out to play without asking the housekeeper. Mr. Davidson stated previously that Mrs. Sawyer's place in the home has recently become more satisfactory. She shows a greater respect for Mr. Davidson and does not try to take over undue authority or responsibility. Barbara and Sara Mae were anxious about Helen and were delighted when she returned without the cast on her leg. Recently the children have displayed greater affection for each other. Barbara asked repeatedly about the baby and wondered when he would be coming home. They also spoke of their mother more often than formerly. It was explained to them that she is ill and that until she is better Mrs. Sawyer will try to take care of them and that they will be helping their mother by obeying Mrs. Sawyer. All the children are especially fond of Helen. Sara Mae seemed even a little jealous of her reputation for helpfulness in the household.

August 13, 1931.—Case closed. Family referred to Family Agency.

SUMMARY OF THE FAMILY AGENCY RECORD

From August, 1931, to February, 1932, the Family Agency assumed the entire responsibility for the family keeping Mrs. Sawyer as housekeeper. She became extremely interested in training the children and was quite successful with them. The father seemed to want to keep the children, but would not accept any responsibility for them. He would not give Mrs. Sawyer sufficient money to meet grocery bills and other expenses.

In January, 1932, without consulting the Family Agency, Mr. Davidson placed Paul and Sylvia and later Barbara with three different cousins. The children at this time were referred to the Juvenile Court for placement since it seemed unlikely that Mrs. Davidson could ever return and that there would be sufficient improvement in the home conditions under the housekeeping plan to justify further expense by the Family Agency. The reasons for removing the children were carefully explained to the father.

The Dependent Committee of the Juvenile Court decided that James should be placed permanently in the Vincent Nursery; that Paul, Sylvia, and Barbara should remain in the homes of the relatives which seemed quite satisfactory and where the children all seemed happy.

Sara Mae, Helen, and Glenn were committed to the St. Olaf's Orphanage, and Mr. Davidson was ordered to pay $15 a month in all for their care and to supply clothing.

The Juvenile Court corresponded with the father regarding the payment of the children's board frequently. He was most polite and co-operative in reply-ing, always asking for an extension of his promise to pay. On June 30, 1933, he was brought into court for contempt, but little was accomplished. Barbara was later also committed to the Orphanage since the family with whom she lived could not afford to keep her unless the father supplied clothing as he had agreed to do, but did not do, though earning about $18 a week.

3. Herman Stern and His Children

(A Father Is Encouraged To Maintain His Home with the Help of a Housekeeper Instead of Placing His Children in an Institution until He Is Ready To Remarry)

August 28, 1930—Letter received by the Children's Agency from the Welfare Council:[1]

We are referring the Stern family to you for permanent housekeeping service. Inclosed you will find a copy of our investigation.

INVESTIGATION BY WELFARE COMMITTEE

Re: Stern, Herman (Sophia)
Former Address: 2241 S. Hemlock Ave.
Present Address: 2405 S. Oak St.

Samuel	14½ years
Alfred	8½ years
Julia	6½ years
Viola	2 years 11 mos.

Application.—Mr. Stern applied to the Jewish Orphanage for the admission of the three older children on August 7,1930. He said his wife had died about six weeks previously; and the maternal aunt, at whose home the children are now living, is unable to care for the children permanently.

After discussing the situation with Mr. Stern it was learned that he intended placing the baby in a nursery until she was old enough to join the other children. He was not particularly satisfied with the plan but could think of no alternative. When the housekeeping plan was outlined, Mr. Stern believed that this would be much more satisfactory and desirable.

[1] [The Welfare Council was established to co-ordinate the work of Jewish child-caring agencies in Chicago. Its workers carry on investigations with reference to placement and discharges of children; intercity correspondence involving the care of children; and social research in child welfare problems.]

Information sources.—Mr. Stern, the father; Mr. and Mrs. Isaac Isenberg, sister-in-law and brother-in-law; Mrs. M. Stein, aunt.

Family situation.—Before the death of the mother the family occupied a four-room apartment in a fairly good residential section. The home was comfortably furnished, and the members of the family were all adjusted in the community.

After the death of Mrs. Stern, Mr. Stern considered the possibility of a house-keeping plan but because of past experiences during the periods of his wife's illness he decided against it. He formerly was unable to find an adequate house-keeper and did not know about the organization. He, therefore, decided to store his furniture, and the children temporarily went to live with a maternal aunt, Mrs. Isenberg. The latter, however, has three children of her own who are cared for by a colored maid, as Mrs. Isenberg assists her husband in their business. Mr. Stern roomed at the home of a cousin. Inasmuch as the children could not continue living at the home of the aunt, he applied for their admission to the Jewish Orphanage.

Mrs. Stern had not kept a kosher home; that is, she had one set of dishes and gave the children bacon for breakfast daily. She had, however, bought her meat in the Jewish market, but cooked it without the traditional preparations.

Financial situation.—For the last twelve years Mr. Stern has been employed as a milkman for the Monarch Dairy Company. His earnings are $50 a week. He is a member of the Milk Drivers' Union, where his dues are $18 for every three months. Mr. Stern carries a $4,000 insurance policy with the New York Life Insurance Company, the premium being $37 a year.

We are attaching a budget for the family which includes food allowance for the housekeeper.

Personal history of Herman Stern.—The father was born in Odessa, Russia, in 1887. His father was a baker and died at the age of about sixty-five, cause unknown. The mother is still living and is seventy years old. She is in Russia. Mr. Stern has no relatives in the United States. Two brothers are living in Europe, and his only sister died when she was a young woman; cause unknown.

Mr. Stern is a tall, well-built man, makes a good impression, and seems intelligent and very much interested in his family. He gives the impression of being rather cautious and foresighted as these qualities were brought out in his discussion of the housekeeping plan during which he raised various valid objections, and when an explanation was given him he apparently considered carefully before making his decision.

Mr. Stern says he received the equivalent of a public-school education in Europe. He is a tailor by trade and before coming to the United States lived and worked for a time in Paris and in London. He has been in Chicago since 1913 and received his naturalization papers from the Federal Court in 1926.

Because of the irregularity of tailoring Mr. Stern decided to make a change and twelve years ago became a milk driver. He has worked steadily at this job since. He works from about 12:30 midnight until 10 or 11 o'clock in the morning. He does not work on Monday.

As far as can be ascertained, Mr. and Mrs. Stern were very fond of each other and their marital life was congenial. They had known each other since childhood, and it was Mr. Stern who assisted in having his wife come to the United States.

Mr. Stern gives the impression of being greatly interested in his children and of being fully aware of his responsibilities for them. One of his reasons for being somewhat dubious about the housekeeping plan was the fact that he feared that a housekeeper would not be able to carry the full responsibility and because of his working hours he could not easily supplement her work. He is now, however, very agreeable to this plan and is pleased with the prospect of keeping the family together, particularly since they can be with him.

Personal history of Sophia Stern.—The mother was born in the same town as her husband and was about thirty-nine years old at the time of her death, which occurred on June 20, 1930 (verified) as the result of post-operative shock after amputation of the left breast upon which a carcinoma had developed.

Mrs. Stern is described as having been a fine-looking, healthy-appearing woman, very intelligent, and an excellent housekeeper and mother. According to her husband she had the equivalent of a high-school education in Europe and learned to read and write English after coming to the United States.

Both of Mrs. Stern's parents are dead; causes unknown. The father is said to have worked in a factory. One brother and two sisters are still in Europe. Another brother and sister live in Chicago.

Mrs. Stern was never considered a very strong woman. After the birth of Samuel she had two miscarriages; and because of her condition, Mr. Stern states, the doctor advised her to have another child. At the time of Julia's birth Mrs. Stern had a very difficult pregnancy followed by hemorrhages, as was the case also when her second child was born. She did not recuperate well after Julia's birth, however, and had been sickly since. Several months ago she complained of discomfort in her breast and was advised by a physician that there was no serious condition. A few days before her death she was in great pain, and when she went to her physician again it was found that a cancer had developed and immediate amputation was advised. She died on the operating table.

Children.—Samuel was born in Chicago on September 27, 1915. He is a tall, well-developed boy. According to the father he had a tonsillectomy performed when he was four years old and was ill with pneumonia about seven years ago. Other than that he is said to be in good health. He was examined in the Children's Examining Clinic of Warner Clinic on August 26. A report will be given to the child-caring agency.

Samuel attends the Roosevelt High School, where he is taking a four-year commercial course as he is interested in becoming a certified public accountant. Last summer he attended summer school so that he is in grade 2A at the present time. He states that he has a good school record. A report is not available at this time. The boy is interested in sports and enjoys baseball particularly. He has also taken an active part in school activities.

For the last six or seven years Samuel says that he has assisted his aunt and uncle in their grocery and meat market. He was very glad to learn of the plan to set the family up in housekeeping again. He states that although he does not play very much with his younger sister and brother he enjoys being with them and was sorry because of the possibility of the family being separated.

Alfred was born in Chicago on April 15, 1922. He is a plump, blond, attractive child. The father states that he has never been ill. A report of his recent examination will be given to the child-caring agency.

Julia is in 2B at the Drake School.

Viola was born in Chicago on October 1, 1927. She is a very attractive child, round face with blonde curly hair. She seems shy. She also was recently examined in the clinic, and the report will be given to the child-caring agency.

According to Mr. Stern his children are well trained and have excellent food habits. They always retire between 8 and 8:30 in the evening and sleep well. None of them presents any problems. The maid who has been caring for them in the aunt's home characterized the children as being "very good."

Family interrelationship.—It will be seen from foregoing information that the Stern family is apparently a closely knit and congenial one. From all sources consulted the same information was given, namely, that Mr. Stern and his wife were very fond of each other and both were devoted to the children. Mr. Stern maintains this attitude at the present time, and there is evidence that the children are very closely attached to him. He advised that whenever he went to visit his children while they were with his sister-in-law he had great difficulty in tearing himself away as they, particularly the baby, clung to him. All members of the family are happy in that they are to be reunited.

Relatives.—The only relatives which Mr. Stern has in the United States are two second cousins, Mr. Solomon Lawrence, 1025 Water Street, and Mr. Meyer, whose address is not known. Several efforts have been made to interview the Lawrence family, but they have never been found at home.

On the maternal side there is an aunt, a sister, and a brother as follows:

Mrs. M. Stein, aunt, 4720 Coyne Avenue

Mr. Jacob Lowenstein, brother, 308 W. 20th Street

Mrs. Isaac (Dora) Isenberg, sister, 759 W. 46th Street

CHILDREN'S AGENCY'S REPORT

Prior to the placement of the housekeeper, Mr. Stern was interviewed in the office. While he showed little desire to re-establish his home and care for the children under the housekeeping plan, he realized that there was no alternative, since the Orphanage refused to accept the oldest and youngest child, owing to their ages. A maximum budget was figured with Mr. Stern, and it was found that he should be able to pay a minimum of $5.00 weekly toward the housekeeper. He agreed to this although he didn't see how he would be able to manage.

Mr. Stern selected a four-room front flat, steam-heated and modern, in a good Jewish neighborhood, rental $52 monthly. While the rental was thought too high, he couldn't find anything under $50 and, since he considers this the most desirable flat seen, he rented it. He engaged a colored lady to clean the flat and had it in perfect readiness before the children returned from the home of their aunt.

The flat is located close to the Franklin School, about four blocks from Neighborhood House, and is especially convenient for Mr. Stern, as he works in this district and will be able to come home for all his meals.

On August 23, 1930, the worker called with Mrs. Rachel Weinberg, middle-aged Jewish housekeeper, being used for the second time; she came very well recommended, having cared for motherless children previously and was reported as a good housekeeper, capable and reliable. She hasn't a very appealing personality, is very businesslike, and seems to be worrying constantly about her own affairs, so that she didn't make a very good impression on Mr. Stern and his cousin, who were present when the visit was made. However, when the visitor explained that she was quite experienced, well known to the office, and one whom Mr. Stern could intrust with the care of his children, they readily accepted her. It was arranged that Mrs. Weinberg would have a bedroom for herself, that Mr. Stern would sleep with the three younger children in one bedroom, and the older boy would sleep on the day bed in the living-room.

The housekeeper was placed; the organization will pay $12 per week for her services; the father will contribute $5.00 of this amount to the organization weekly.

August 30, 1930.—Mrs. Weinberg put the house in immaculate order; she speaks highly of the children, and seems to be getting along quite satisfactorily. At the time of the call made during the week, the visitor found a number of children playing on the front porch, which is all fenced in and therefore a safe and desirable place for them. The oldest boy, Samuel, seemed to take a paternal interest in the younger children and apparently has been accustomed to taking care of them. He has been putting the baby to sleep, helping in her feeding, and taking her out-of-doors.

Mr. Stern called at the office and paid $5.00, as agreed, toward the housekeeper's pay.

September 2, 1930.—Mr. Stern called at the office; he stated that, while he could offer no complaints of Mrs. Weinberg, he considers her more of a housekeeper than a mother to the children, and intimated that he would prefer a woman who would devote herself more to the children than to the house. He insisted, however, that there could be no criticism of her management of the home. The only specific complaint he could make was that the housekeeper had refused to take the younger children out for a walk, saying that she was known in the neighborhood and didn't want to advertise the fact that she was working there. He was told that the matter would be reconsidered and, if it were thought necessary, that a change of housekeepers could be made.

September 8, 1930.—Mr. Stern was in office. He reported that Viola had been ill and that he had taken her to see Dr. Thomas, at 4205 West Twenty-first Street, who had attended the baby previously. The doctor had prescribed a mouth wash and douche for the baby's ears, but Mr. Stern has been unsuccessful in carrying out the recommendations because the baby cries when approached. Mr. Stern reports that the housekeeper is making no headway in preventing the baby's crying; she continues to cry just as much as before.

Telephoned Dr. Thomas, who reported that the baby had stomatitis and stressed the importance of carrying out the prescription given, as he was afraid the condition might spread if not cared for. He also stated that he had examined the child a year ago and at that time had recommended a tonsillectomy.

Later—Visited. Mrs. Weinberg, housekeeper, reported that she is somewhat discouraged with the situation as she does all in her power to make friends with the baby. She reported that she takes the child out for a few hours each afternoon and plays with her as much as she can. She also stated that, although Mr. Stern says he wants the baby to be cared for first, he complained one evening when he came home and found that supper was not ready. Mrs. Weinberg reported that when she is home alone with the baby the child plays around all day and talks to her without any great disturbance, but as soon as Mr. Stern comes into the house she clings to him and cries, not permitting him to leave her.

Mr. Stern returned home while the visitor was present, discussed the situation with her, and asked that she accompany him to his relatives, the Lawrences—his cousins. Mr. and Mrs. Lawrence both appeared to be quite intelligent. Mr. Lawrence also works for the Monarch Dairy Company. Mrs. Lawrence stated that she was certain the housekeeper was doing all she could in the management of the household, but did not feel that she was devoting enough time to the baby. She did not believe that the housekeeper takes the child out each day except when she takes her with her across the street to the grocery store. She knows that the baby is spoiled but felt that she had adjusted so nicely in the relatives' homes that it would be possible, if the right person were in the home, to have her adjust in her own home. She felt it would be a good thing to make a change in housekeepers.

September 9, 1930.—Worker called to see Viola. The housekeeper reported that no directions had been left with her as to the application of the medicine and therefore she was unable to show how the drops were to be applied.

Mrs. Weinberg reported that this day the child had been no trouble. She did not cry during the whole day or when her father came home. Both she and Mr. Stern were more encouraged by this.

September 10, 1930.—While passing near the Stern home, the visitor noted that Mr. Stern was standing near by watching the children as they returned from school. When approached, he reported that he had been standing there for approximately three-quarters of an hour and had seen Alfred return to school. Alfred had reported that he had left while Julia was still at home, and Mr. Stern was quite concerned at Julia's delay in returning to school. Visitor told him that she would investigate her delay. Julia was not home when the visitor arrived, and Mrs. Weinberg reported that she had been gone for some time. Mrs. Weinberg reported that Viola had gone back to her old ways and that she has wakened the whole family during the night by her intensive crying. She awakes each night and cries for the remainder of the night. Neither Mr. Stern nor anyone else is able to do anything with her. Mr. Stern was asked not to return home for breakfast or for lunch, as he had been in the habit of doing, as this tends to upset the baby. Although he promised to stay away previously, he has not kept his word and continues to return home several times each day.

September 15, 1930.—Accompanied Samuel, Alfred, and Julia to the Dispensary for dental work.

Later.—Visited. Both Mr. Stern and the housekeeper remain discouraged about the situation. The baby awakens in the middle of the night and cries for a long time, arousing the entire family. It was suggested that if the baby did not see Mr. Stern at night she perhaps would not cry. It was therefore suggested that the housekeeper assume the responsibility for the child at night and sleep in the same room with her, the baby occupying the crib, and Mr. Stern would take the other bedroom, sleeping with Julia. Mrs. Weinberg, however, felt that she gives up her entire day to the management of the child and of the household and is not going to be deprived of her regular night's sleep; the baby also has a nocturnal enuresis, and when Mrs. Weinberg suggested to Mr. Stern that he discontinue giving her water after she goes to bed, he refused to comply with her request. Mrs. Weinberg had prepared an appetizing meal for the family, consisting of a milk soup, cheese blintzes, and vegetables.

September 17, 1930.—Mr. Stern telephoned to report that Mrs. Weinberg had left that morning when he returned to have his breakfast. She left without bidding the children goodbye and without preparing breakfast for them.

Mrs. Sarah Kahn, known to the organization for some time, was placed in the household this date.

September 23, 1930.—Visited. Several telephone conversations have been had with Mrs. Kahn, housekeeper, since her placement in the Stern home, and during visits she corroborated her statements about the difficulties in the household. She reported that the baby does not sleep during the night, that she awakens every hour. The baby will not sleep in her own crib, according to her father and the housekeeper, but insists on sleeping in the large bed with the housekeeper. She always takes her afternoon nap in her own bed, without any complaint, and sleeps for about two hours each afternoon.

The management of the next two children is also somewhat difficult because of their food habits. They have not been trained to eat vegetables and have refused to eat the meals which Mrs. Kahn has been preparing. She usually consults the children about what they would like to have for lunch; and when this is prepared for them, they push it away and state that they do not care to eat it. They drink cold milk for breakfast and refuse to eat any kind of cooked cereal. For lunch they insist upon having bananas and cream and a glass of milk, refusing all else. Mrs. Kahn has no complaint to make about Samuel and says that he tries to please her by eating everything which she prepares and, when he is in the house, he is absolutely no annoyance to her. She also considers Mr. Stern a "perfect gentleman" but feels that he is "too easy" with the children. He does not discipline them when they fail to carry out his requests and will not make them eat.

Mrs. Kahn stated that when the father is not at home she has no difficulty in controlling the baby. The child will sing and dance and converse with Mrs. Kahn. Just as soon as the father comes into the home, however, the baby will not permit him to leave her and clings to him and annoys him constantly.

September 26, 1930.—Visited. The situation in the Stern home seems to be getting worse rather than better, and the second housekeeper does not feel that her health will permit her to stay very much longer. She has not had one night's sleep since she has come into the home and she has also reported that when she went away on Sunday she did not leave until late in the afternoon; Mr. Stern reported to her later that during the time she was gone the baby was so disturbed and was so annoying that he could not get any rest (Mr. Stern arises at 12:00 midnight Sunday mornings and returns about 10:00). He feels that he should be allowed some rest after this time.

Mr. Stern came home during the visit and also seemed quite discouraged. He too feels that the situation is not improving. He spoke of his difficulties with the baby on the previous Sunday and stated that he would like to have the housekeeper take two other afternoons during the week rather than to leave on Sundays. A relative had visited them on that day, and no one could do anything to quiet the baby. Mr. Stern is not anxious to make a change in the present arrangement but feels that something must be done as his health will not permit him to continue under the present strain. While the children were at the home of their aunt, Mrs. Isenberg, she had difficulty with the baby during the first few weeks but later on the child adjusted so well that she presented no problems. Mr. Stern reported that he would speak with his sister-in-law and see if she could send her maid to him to assist in training the child.

September 27, 1930.—Visited Mrs. Isenberg, sister-in-law of Mr. Stern, at her place of business, 4901 Evergreen Street. Mrs. Isenberg is the sister of Mrs. Stern and is very much interested in the Stern children. She regards them as her own. She is quite concerned because the housekeeping situation has not proved satisfactory and believes that the housekeepers were more to blame than the children. She stated that when the children were in her home she had absolutely no difficulty in feeding them, that she would have to bring "bushels of supplies" to the home each day, and, although it took her seven weeks in which to train Viola, she felt that she had succeeded after that time, that the child did create a great deal of disturbance during the night and was stubborn, but the maid who was caring for them disciplined them according to her own desire. The children were being cared for by a Negro maid, who is very young but who is well liked by them. Mrs. Isenberg has to spend a great deal of her time in her business and therefore did not have much to do with the management of the children. She does not feel that Mr. Stern is strong enough to continue under the present arrangements unless some change takes place. She reported that on the previous Sunday when they had visited the Sterns, the baby was so great a disturbance that Mr. Stern "almost fainted." She too stressed the point that Mr. Stern should be relieved of the care of the children on Sundays as this is his most strenuous day, and felt that the housekeeper should be willing to take another day. She would be willing to take Viola into her home but does not think that this would solve the problem, as sometime or other the child would have to be returned to her own home and the same situation would recur.

Mrs. Isenberg has three children and lives in a deteriorated neighborhood on the South Side. After the death of Mrs. Stern the two families had planned to rent a home together and employ two housekeepers to care for the children, but they felt that this would be too expensive and that Mr. Stern would have to sacrifice a great deal in order to travel from the South Side to his place of employment at his very inconvenient hours. Mrs. Isenberg and her husband still believe that this would have been the best plan.

Mrs. Isenberg also believes that another change in housekeepers would be detrimental to the child as with each change she seems to become worse.

September 29, 1930.—Mr. Stern accompanied Viola to the Ear, Nose, and Throat Clinic.

Letter received from the Welfare Committee approving continuation of housekeeping service.

September 30, 1930.—Visited. As Mrs. Kahn, housekeeper, decided that she could remain no longer, a gentile housekeeper known to the organization for several years was placed. The baby began to cry when Mrs. Kahn prepared to leave, but soon quieted down and took her nap under Mrs. James's (new housekeeper) direction.

October 3, 1930.—Visited. Mr. Isenberg, brother-in-law, his maid and baby, and Mrs. Lawrence, a cousin of Mr. Stern, were in the Stern home. Mr. Isenberg had come to take the baby to his home, where he plans to keep her through the winter. He thinks the situation is not at all improved with the change of housekeepers and says that Mr. Stern has requested that they take the baby for a while. Mrs. Lawrence stated that she has been doing all she can to assist Mrs. James with planning the meals, but feels that Mrs. James is not a good cook and therefore does not please the family.

When speaking with Mrs. James, the visitor learned that she feels she has had little difficulty with the baby. She sleeps most of the night, although the night before she was quite restless as she had had a party that day and had spent the day with the relatives at the Isenberg home. The restless night was evidently due to the fact that she had had a great deal of excitement.

Mr. Stern returned during this visit but did not permit Viola to see him as he felt that she would cling to him and would not go with Mr. Isenberg. He told the visitor that he did not believe that Samuel was very happy at home. He goes to Mrs. Isenberg's home as soon as he returns from school on Friday, remaining there until late Sunday. He is happiest at this time.

October 6, 1930.—Worker met Mrs. Isenberg at Warner Hospital with Viola. Viola was seen in Pediatrics Clinic. Mrs. Isenberg stated that she had had no difficulty with Viola. She sleeps through the whole night and eats well.

October 9, 1930.—Another change of housekeepers had to be made. Mrs. Rachel Becker, new to the organization, was selected. She is a sister of a foster-mother boarding an infant, has raised several families besides her own, and was therefore considered competent enough for this particular case, since so much difficulty was encountered by previous housekeepers. It was agreed, however, that the baby remain with the aunt, at least temporarily, possibly until she has a tonsillectomy and until the present housekeeper gets accustomed to the household and the older children.

Mrs. Rachel Becker, housekeeper, placed. She will live at the home, will receive $12 per week for her services. Mr. Stern will pay the office $5.00 weekly.

October 21, 1930.—Daily visits were made for a period of ten days in an effort to help Mrs. Becker in the home and straighten out previous difficulties. Although the housekeeper when seen in the office was most enthusiastic about entering this type of service, she seems to have lost her enthusiasm as soon as she walked into the Stern home, for numerous reasons. Mr. Stern is quite exacting and overcritical. He considers that the housekeeper is well paid and wants to see "real service" in exchange. He walks about the house and into the corners looking for dust. One day, after the housekeeper had prepared the wash for the laundry, counted, and sorted it, he took it upon himself to go through the laundry bag. She considers herself very competent and has had considerable experience in household management; this incident added to her general discouragement. The only help that the Sterns ever had was colored. The visitor had occasion to meet a colored girl who worked for Mrs. Stern a day a week for some time; since she knew Mrs. Stern, the visitor questioned her regarding the general run of the household when the mother was living. She said that the mother paid her about $2.00 or a little more for a day's work and she usually did most of their washing, ironing, and all the cleaning in the one day. She reported that Mrs. Stern had never been well since the birth of Alfred. She permitted the children to have their own way as she wasn't strong enough to handle them, and the colored girl characterized her as having been "soft." As for Mr. Stern, she knows that he is very hard to please, and Mrs. Stern considered him "temperamental." She said that sometimes he would not talk to his wife for days. This girl took entire charge of the household immediately after the mother's death and she found that a week after the death of the mother, the children, particularly the baby, showed some improvement in daily habits of eating and sleeping.

In the conversation with Mrs. Isenberg it was learned that Mr. Stern was considered a most devoted husband and father; that he never interfered in the least in the management of the home; and she therefore asked the visitor to discount the various housekeepers' reports that he is inclined to be interfering in the management of the home and children. The visitor had numerous talks with Mr. Stern, pointing out to him that he must not expect perfection and, unless he will learn to overlook minor deficiencies that any housekeeper may have, it will probably be useless to carry on this form of care for the children. The present housekeeper is an excellent disciplinarian, fine cook, and very economical; on the other hand, she is not so good as the former housekeeper, particularly Mrs. Weinberg, about whose leaving he expressed considerable regret. He had praise for each of the housekeepers, but none of them apparently attained the perfection he is looking for. The visitor on one occasion discussed with him the advisability of getting a colored housekeeper should the present one fail; he expressed no objection, feeling that a colored woman would do more of the heavy work, but asked the visitor to continue with Mrs. Becker at least for the present. Since the Sterns and the aunt, Mrs. Isenberg, have had very fortunate experiences with colored help, this may be the final solution for the Stern home. Mrs. Isenberg, whose business is located in the heart of the colored district, offered to assist in finding a suitable colored housekeeper when the need for one arises.

In addition to the differences with Mr. Stern the housekeeper finds the children most trying, particularly Julia, whom she and the other housekeepers considered the outstanding difficulty. The housekeeper believes that the child is "spoiled," has been pampered too much, and allowed to have her own way; she was the only girl in the home for four years, is very bright and attractive, and "papa's pet." She behaves fairly well in Mr. Stern's absence but when he is around she is described as "a little tyrant," constantly making demands on him for money, toys, and anything that comes into her mind. When the housekeeper or the father takes her out on the street she wants everything that she sees in the shop windows and creates scenes when her wishes are not fulfilled. She is considered a temperamental child, and the housekeeper cited the following instances: When she takes her to a movie she suddenly gets an idea that she is uninterested and insists upon going home, thus spoiling the housekeeper's good time as well as her own; at the table one day she will eat applesauce, or whatever it might be, and the next day or week she will not touch such a dish. The only time she is on her best behavior is when Mrs. Isenberg visits at the home; several times the latter gave Julia a hard slap on the face, and the housekeeper noticed that she responded well to this type of punishment. The housekeeper believes in firm discipline and, although Julia is only occasionally impudent to her, she continues to be severe with her. The other day, for example, when the housekeeper was sending her girl friends home at 8:30, Julia intervened, saying that she could not turn her friends out of her house at such an early hour. The housekeeper told her that she was very glad that they were her friends but it was time to go to bed, and led the friends to the door. Julia then compromised by asking for ten minutes more play, which the housekeeper allowed them, and without further argument, Julia retired. On one occasion Julia told her to "shut up," and the housekeeper very severely advised her that she should never speak in such a way to her again.

Samuel seems to be very companionable with the housekeeper; the visitor frequently found them conversing together at the table about school work and other matters; Alfred, though also somewhat spoiled, she considers herself well able to manage; the baby will continue to live with Mrs. Isenberg as the latter is anxious to keep her at least through the winter. Plans were made for a tonsillectomy for the baby but when she was brought to the hospital on October 27, although she was found to have a normal temperature at the time of admission, later in the day she developed a fever. The hospital therefore did not wish to operate that day; and the aunt, in her anxiety about the child, took her home, saying that she would let the tonsillectomy go until spring.

Mr. Stern has been paying $5.00 weekly toward the housekeeper, regularly; it was necessary to write him a letter when he was one week in arrears but he is now up to date. He has been complaining to the housekeeper about his expenses and seemed to feel that he is having difficulties in meeting his bills.

School reports for the children received:

JULIA, FRANKLIN SCHOOL, GRADE 2B, ROOM 104

Reading, English, Spelling, Deportment, Personal Appearance—E
Penmanship, Arithmetic—G

SAMUEL, ROOSEVELT HIGH SCHOOL, GRADE 2A, ROOM 337

Geography—G plus	English—G minus	French—P
Typewriting—F	Bookkeeping—E	Art—G
Deportment—G	Personal Appearance—G	

ALFRED, FRANKLIN SCHOOL, GRADE 3B

Reading, Arithmetic, Spelling, Deportment—E
Penmanship, Personal Appearance—G

October 30, 1930.—Semi-weekly visits were continued, one being made
on the housekeeper's day off (Monday) and the other with the housekeeper privately, extending to the after-school period so that all the
children were seen at least once a week. Mr. Stern continues to be somewhat dissatisfied with the housekeeper, although he doesn't openly express
himself. He is, first of all, somewhat prejudiced because she is a German
Jew and he is Russian (it seems to be somewhat traditional for German
and Russian Jews to look upon each other with suspicion); while the
Sterns do not keep a kosher home, Mr. Stern thinks that he should be able
to get a woman who can prepare the old-fashioned type of Jewish food,
such as "gefilte fish," etc., which Mrs. Becker cannot do. On the other
hand, the type of Jewish woman that he wants wouldn't go to his home,
as he insists upon serving bacon and does not adhere to the Dietary Laws.
He considers this housekeeper "Reformed" and therefore not in his class,
so to speak, although he is himself, in a sense of the word, a "Reformed"
Jew. The housekeeper, on the other hand, retaliates by saying that he
should have a "Litvach"[2] for a housekeeper, so that their differences would
seem to be mutual. She finds Mr. Stern a most unusually devoted parent
and cited numerous examples of this; on Halloween night he sat up all
hours of the night to prepare the pumpkins and other things for the
children's sport. He is, she says, too good to them and considers that he
often makes discipline impossible. She also talked about the children's
bad table manners, refusal to wash their hands before eating, and other
such matters. Julia, whom she still calls a "little tyrant," is beginning to
conform somewhat. The housekeeper hesitates very much about having

[2] [A Lithuanian Jew.]

the baby returned home, as she doesn't think that she can manage, considering the demands that Mr. Stern makes of her. He comes home for his meals three times a day; in fact, he is always around. He works in the neighborhood, and she never knows when he will drop in. As a result of this, the children are constantly under tension about "Daddy's coming home," are always looking for him at the window, and awaiting him. Although the children have some friends, they consider that "nobody counts" except their "Daddy."

November 11, 1930—Visits twice weekly reveal no changes; Mr. Stern is very anxious to bring the baby home—first of all, because he finds himself lonesome without her and, in the second place, because his sister-in-law is demanding that she be paid for her care. He visits her every Sunday and finds the child no longer cries when he leaves her. He believes that she has improved and may get along better at home now than she formerly did. On the other hand, according to him and his sister-in-law, she is receiving unusually good care at the hands of the colored maid in the Isenberg home, and it is very likely that the present housekeeper's handling of the baby will be criticized by him. He claims that the colored maid takes the baby out twice daily, bathes her daily, gives her the best foods and care possible, and in addition to this, finds plenty of time to sit on the floor and play with her. However, it was decided between Mr. Stern, the housekeeper, and the visitor that he bring the baby home for a visit, on trial, and should Mrs. Becker be able to manage her, he will be satisfied; otherwise, she will either return to her aunt or the agency will place another housekeeper. Mr. Stern was encouraged to accept a colored housekeeper, since he has already tried three Jewish women and has been dissatisfied. The visitor had numerous telephone conversations with the aunt, and she agreed that it might be a good plan to try a colored housekeeper next, since Mr. Stern is about the home so much and shares the supervisory responsibilities for the children with the housekeeper. Mrs. Isenberg and Mr. Stern both asked the visitor to have Mrs. Weinberg, the first housekeeper, return; she was approached on the question, and, while she expressed her willingness to return, visitor prefers to try out a colored housekeeper first, should Mrs. Becker be unable to manage with the baby.

November 24, 1930—Owing to the continued dissatisfaction on the part of Mr. Stern and the housekeeper, a change was made. Mrs. Belle Hollister, colored housekeeper, aged about forty, who has been known to the organization for one and one-half years, was placed. Visitor told Mr.

Stern, also the aunt, about the colored housekeeper in question, and they agreed to give her a trial, owing to her extensive experience with small children, ability to prepare Jewish-type meals, etc. She was, therefore, taken to the home, and the other housekeeper withdrawn from service. Mrs. Hollister will live in the home and receive $12 per week for her services.

The new housekeeper was told about the cause of the baby's absence from home, and, as she has had considerable experience with small children, she was not afraid of the additional responsibility. However, it was decided that she should remain at the home for about a week, see whether or not Mr. Stern will like her type of cooking, see whether or not she will be able to manage the older children, and at the end of that time to try the baby under her care. She was asked to visit the baby in the aunt's home, to see how the colored maid there handled the baby so satisfactorily, then try to continue to care for the child under the same type of regime.

November 28, 1930.—Daily visits were made; Thanksgiving Day the aunt came to the home with her entire family and the Stern baby for dinner, and left the baby there, as she has gained sufficient confidence in the new housekeeper to intrust the baby to her care. The aunt and Mr. Stern commented on the "wonderful" Thanksgiving dinner that Mrs. Hollister had prepared and reported her an excellent cook.

December 2, 1930.—Daily visits continued; while the baby was restless the first few nights she is now sleeping well, in her own bed, in her father's room, and Mrs. Hollister has thus far managed her satisfactorily. Mr. Stern was likewise seen several times and he expressed satisfaction with Mrs. Hollister's services. He was, throughout, insistent upon getting a Jewish woman in the home. Mrs. Hollister has worked in Jewish homes for so many years (even keeps a kosher kitchen) and knows how to make a good many Jewish dishes, so that she can be regarded almost as a Jewish housekeeper, as far as the kitchen and household are concerned. She is also good at mending and darning, and has good standards of cleanliness. On the other hand, she is not the type of housekeeper who would impose her supervision too much on the family, and this is probably the most important factor in this case. Mrs. Hollister has so far encountered no difficulty with any of the children; she finds that they eat all the food that she prepares and are considerate and helpful to her. Mr. Stern continues to do most of the shopping.

In a telephone conversation with the aunt it was learned that, while she was satisfied with the care the baby is now receiving, she really preferred to have the baby with her. She seems to be rather emotionally attached to her; calls her "my baby." However, she promised not to disturb the present arrangements.

December 24, 1930.—Semi-weekly visits were made, one visit with the housekeeper alone, and one with Mr. Stern in the late afternoon. The three younger children had chicken pox during the past few weeks. Mr. Stern obtained his own medical care, he claims that the doctor has been known to the family for some time and is not particular about being paid promptly.

The family was short of blankets, and the visitor offered to excuse Mr. Stern from a week's payment toward the housekeeper provided he purchase two blankets and warm nightgowns for all the children. The visitor also arranged for the housekeeper to use her own blankets which she had at her own home. Mr. Stern depends upon the visitor for every detail; and, when he complained that the children would probably catch cold because of the shortage of blankets, these details were carefully gone into. He had given the housekeeper the best blanket in the house and apparently did not have the courage to take it away from her when it turned colder, nor did he think of asking her to get her own blankets as the family needed all they had. Mr. Stern is very easily upset, and the children's illness disturbed him greatly. He talked about all the sacrifices he is making for them, how he has to stay up at night and administer the medicine, etc. When visitor asked him whether he would not be expected to do the same were his wife living, he responded by shrugging his shoulders. He is fond enough of his family but feels himself somewhat of a martyr in having accepted the present plan of caring for his children.

The housekeeper is giving very good service, and, according to a conversation with Mr. Stern and telephone conversations with the aunt and a cousin who lives in the neighborhood, she is doing her very best. Mrs. Isenberg has been ill with a severe cold, but has visited at the home two or three times, and telephoned the visitor to express her satisfaction with the present housekeeper and the way the children are now being cared for. On one occasion she asked the visitor to furnish some clothing for the children and when the visitor showed surprise at her request, she apologized and said that she thought such a thing might be possible. She seems to feel that her brother-in-law is in financial straits and pointed out several clothing needs of the children. She was informed that he was expected to contribute toward the housekeeper as well as carry the entire household responsibility himself. Mr. Stern has been regular about paying, except for one week when he was out of work two days owing to his own illness (a severe cold).

The children are not inclined to be friendly or talkative and only answer questions put to them. The visitor gave them Chanukah presents of games and toys. Samuel spends much of his time at his uncle's grocery store on the South Side, particularly since Mrs. Isenberg has been ill. His uncle pays him, but the visitor could not find out the amount.

Alfred was out of school for two weeks prior to the vacation and Julia one week. They are now out of bed. The visitor spoke with Mr. Stern about the advisability of giving his children toxin-antitoxin and he promised to discuss the matter with his family doctor. It seems that he prefers private medical care; when the baby was at the hospital for a tonsillectomy, he took her home primarily because he couldn't have his choice of a doctor for the operation.

January 21, 1931.—Twice-weekly visits continued, except during the past two weeks, when the visitor was able to call only once during the week. Mr. Stern complains that the visitor "neglects" him and thinks that she should have time to be there even more often than twice a week. While he is very well satisfied with Mrs. Hollister as far as her actual service is concerned, he claims to be extremely lonely, says that he misses his wife at every turn, not so much because he was so much in love with her but because he had a companion, someone to confide in. He enjoys discussing every little detail of his own life and the household with the visitor. He is inclined to brood, is very worrisome, and takes his responsibility much too seriously. The visitor had made arrangements to have the two girls sleep on a day bed in the living-room, primarily to separate them from the father at night, so that their dependency on him wouldn't be so great. After numerous talks with him, he appreciated the value of this point, and after several weeks of difficulties encountered by the housekeeper in connection with this arrangement, the two girls sleep on a day bed in the living-room. Viola was formerly in the habit of crying during the night and wanting to sleep with her father, and he, of course, would take her into his bed. Then, too, the visitor opposed the arrangement of Julia sleeping in the room with Alfred. The sleeping arrangements, therefore, seem to be more satisfactory at least for the present. The children have recovered from their colds, and the older ones all returned to school.

The question of diet is also one which gives Mr. Stern much concern. He thinks Mrs. Hollister can prepare a good meal but is very much aggravated when he sits down at the table with the children and finds that they often reject the food. After going into great detail with the housekeeper and Mr. Stern on menus for each day, diet, etc., the visitor learned that the children still refuse any cooked vegetable. Visitor therefore urged the housekeeper to use all the vegetables in the soup, and, if necessary, strain them; also asked her to let them eat raw carrots, cabbage, plenty of lettuce and tomatoes, and during the past few weeks, this has been followed out. Mr. Stern is appreciative of all the supervision and advice given and tries to co-operate, although he is himself the great drawback in the disciplining of the children. Mrs. Hollister pointed out, for example, that as soon as the baby cries at night, if she picks her up, the child stops crying and returns to bed, but if Mr. Stern runs to take her, she creates a scene. Mr. Stern was therefore asked to refrain from giving the children too much attention, and the visitor even suggested that the housekeeper feed the children before he eats as he is most aggravated at mealtime. He considers himself very "nervous" and attributes his condition to the irritability brought on by the children when they refuse to eat and nag him too much. Mr. Stern has been going out very little of late and, according to the housekeeper, this may be another factor in his "nervous" condition. The visitor tried to persuade him to go through the Warner Clinic for a general examination, but he stated that he has had good doctors, one of whom is a relative of his, and that all the doctors have told him that he is simply nervous and that his digestion is being affected by his nervousness. He realizes that he eats too fast, is inclined to be worried and hyperactive. However, since the children's health has improved and their habits to some degree are better, he has been complaining less.

Mr. Stern is a great "home" man and went into details with the visitor, telling her how helpful he used to be to his wife and how on his day off he works about the house. The visitor usually finds him doing something, such as straightening out the pantry, the medicine chest, etc. He is the one who applies the antiroach powder. He says he doesn't like to bother the landlord for this. He still does some of the shopping, although the visitor has insisted that the housekeeper take most of this responsibility and she has done so.

In further discussion with Mr. Stern about his personal life, he seemed to be rather apprehensive about a second marriage; he intimated that he has already considered some women and found that they weren't sincere and he thought they wouldn't "do the right thing by his family." He is, as previously stated, overanxious about his children and carries his anxiety to a degree of affecting his own physical condition. He said that people dissuaded him from entering into the housekeeping plan, pointing out the responsibility, and he often thinks this was a mistake; yet, on the other hand, he pointed to the fact that when the children were not with him, he was just as nervous and even more concerned about their well-being, and could hardly rest until the family was reunited.

Mr. Stern gave the visitor permission to have the three children given toxin-antitoxin and arrangements were made at the Central Dispensary, according to his request. He was rather opposed to the long trip to the Warner Clinic, saying that the children would be worn out by the time they got there. He also discussed recreational activities for the children and stated that Samuel at one time had had a membership at Neighborhood House for about a year, but that he could not afford to pay $6.00 now. The visitor suggested that he join activities at the Recreational Center located very close to the Stern home; also discussed Hebrew education for Alfred and Julia. Julia was very anxious to go, but Alfred didn't like the idea. However, Mr. Stern was quite enthusiastic and even offered to take the children along with him to Neighborhood House if it could be arranged. The visitor gave him a letter to Neighborhood House, asking that classes for them be arranged for the early afternoon so that they would not have to travel the distance at night.

In numerous private discussions with the housekeeper, she feels that the children are well fed and cared for, but that Mr. Stern simply expects too much and that his own irritability reflects in the behavior of the children. He is, she feels, too good to them and they take advantage of him.

Mr. Stern is apparently worried with his financial difficulties. He claims that he was heavily in debt at the time of the death of his wife and cannot pay up all his bills; that he lost a good many days' work, as the visitor knows, owing to his own illness and the illness of the children, in the last few months; and in addition to this, he reported that he engages a helper occasionally as he doesn't feel able to do all the stair climbing. He pays the helper $1.25 a day. Mr. Stern has been paying his $5.00 weekly at the office fairly regularly but complains that this additional expense is too much for him. The visitor spent a great deal of time pointing out to him that owing to the general economic depression, there are men in considerably more straitened circumstances than his and that he must appreciate the fact that he has a job.

February 5, 1931.—Visits twice weekly continued; Mr. Stern has co-operated in taking the children to Central Clinic for toxin-antitoxin. Since he himself continues to complain about his health, the visitor obtained his consent to have an examination at Warner Clinic.

He continues to take himself and his family too seriously; is overcritical of Mrs. Hollister; keeps comparing her with the young colored girl his sister-in-law has, about whom mention was previously made in the record. The visitor learned from Mrs. Hollister that the sister-in-law's maid is very attractive, a habitual smoker, and of the "flapper" type. Mrs. Hollister, on the other hand, is very mature and settled, considerably older than the girl mentioned. Mr. Stern is a great "busybody"; he knows at least half of the housekeeping families known to worker in the present and past and explains this by virtue of being a milkman, as he is out a great deal and comes in contact with so many people. He likes to discuss other situations similar to his own, and in one case, where a man remarried, he knew the details about the second marriage. He repeats over and over again that the responsibility of the home and children is too great for any man, says that, in anticipation of the future, his anxieties are great, as he feels that the older the children will get, the greater the responsibility will be. He is at present particularly concerned about Samuel, who he thinks may be brooding about the death of the mother, as he talks very little and is much more quiet than he was when the mother was alive. It has been very difficult for the visitor to get Samuel, or in fact, any of the children, to become friendly, as they talk very little to her. Their interest was aroused, however, when the question of recreational activity was discussed; Julia is very much interested in music and stated that since she was living at the home of her aunt, where there is a piano, she is able to compose little pieces and enjoys practicing at the piano. Alfred is interested in Neighborhood House activities, as is Samuel. The latter wants to be a C. P. A., and it will be noted on the school reports that he excels in bookkeeping. He failed, however, in French, and the visitor, in discussing recreational activity with him, told him that she didn't see how she could consider him for a scholarship at Neighborhood House as long as he was failing in one subject. He explained this by saying that he was taking five major studies and naturally dislikes languages.

Mr. Stern claims that Samuel was very confidential with his mother; that she visited at school frequently about all the children and particularly Samuel, and held out great hopes for him. Mr. Stern, therefore, feels that Samuel may miss his mother more than he admits. Mr. Stern claims that he purchased the radio solely for Samuel, as he thought, first of all, that it would keep him at home, and secondly to cheer him up. Mr. Stern, although full of anxieties and worries about his family, is on the other hand very proud of them. He spoke of the fact that although the younger children were out of school for many weeks owing to illness, they passed, and with excellent marks. He watches every move that the baby makes and comments on her brightness and cunning ways.

The visitor was able to obtain a piano for Mr. Stern through a former housekeeping case, where a piano was donated and the home later broken up. Mr. Stern went to see the piano and thought that it wasn't worth the moving charge, although the visitor looked at it and felt that it was in excellent condition. The visitor then suggested to Mr. Stern that he pay the organization something toward the piano, as he may appreciate it more if he does pay something for it, and is given the feeling of purchasing it.

Mr. Stern states that he has no relatives, except two distant cousins by the names of Lawrence and Meyer. He is very disappointed that these cousins do not visit and "advise" (he is always looking for advice). The housekeeper reports that he is so devoted to his wife's relatives that "they could make him jump in the lake if they wanted to." He is always at their "beck and call," serving them in one way or another. The housekeeper reports him as extremely nervous and as giving in to the children in every way. She reports that she has no difficulty in their management when he is away. The chief difficulty seems to be that the children nag him for candy, etc., and at the table, if they dislike anything that the housekeeper has served, Mr. Stern does not hesitate to find something else for them to eat. He states that this was a custom his wife always adhered to and he believes in it. The visitor spoke to him of this a number of times and tried to change his point of view.

Prior to sending the letter to Warner Clinic about Mr. Stern, the visitor tried to get a medical history from him and found it very difficult, as he apparently wants to make it seem that his illness must be attributed to his present responsibility. However, he admitted that he has had stomach trouble for the past two years and that numerous doctors have told him that he has a "nervous" stomach. He says he is troubled with pains on the right side, particularly during the day if he works hard, and at night if he has overstrained himself during the day. He claims that during the past two months the pains have been more severe, and that some days he is hardly able to walk and keeps on his feet mostly "on his nerve." He claims that when lying down he can lie only on the left side.

The worker asked for a scholarship for Samuel at Neighborhood House. The younger children went there to enroll in Hebrew School and were told that there was no room for the present.

School reports for the semester were received:

SAMUEL, ROOSEVELT HIGH, 2A

Bookkeeping—E   Geography—E   Art—E
Typewriting—F   Deportment—G   English—G
Personal Appearance—G   French—P   Physical Education—E

ALFRED, FRANKLIN SCHOOL, 3B

Reading—G   Penmanship—G   Arithmetic—E
Personal Appearance—G   Deportment—G   Spelling—G

JULIA, FRANKLIN SCHOOL, 2B

Reading—G   Penmanship—G   English—G
Spelling—E   Deportment—G   Arithmetic—G
                    Personal Appearance—G

February 18, 1931.—Semi-weekly visits continued. Mr. Stern continues to be irritable and has been steered through Warner Clinic, where he is being observed.

A visit was made to Mrs. M. Meyer, cousin of Mr. Stern; she showed a rather indifferent attitude toward Mr. Stern and his family and spoke about the remoteness of the relationship as an excuse for her indifference. However, she seemed to know Mr. Stern and particularly his wife's family for many years back and stated that Mr. Stern knew his wife in Europe; that she came to this country a good many years before he did and lived with her family here; and that he, although having no family in the country, came here for the purpose of marrying her. They both worked in the tailoring business and for a time were in business for themselves. Mrs. Meyer stated that Mr. Stern had only one sister, who died many years ago; that he has two brothers and a mother in Europe and no relatives in this country. She characterized Mr. Stern as being very "kind-hearted" and said that his father was "just like him." She stated that he always showed a great interest in the household and children, and she noticed, during the time she visited at the home, that it was Mr. Stern rather than his wife who purchased the delicacies, set the table, and did most of the work in connection with the entertainment. He was always a "home man," rarely went out, and both he and his wife devoted themselves entirely to their children. Shortly after the death of Mrs. Stern, she had Julia in her home and found her so cranky and finicky about her food that she had to return her to the father after a few weeks' time. Alfred, she reported, was always a great trial to his mother and was regarded as somewhat of a "bad" boy. Samuel was always the favorite.

Alfred did not begin to talk until he was about four years old, and in an interview later with Mr. Stern, he confirmed this fact.

Shortly after the visitor called on this cousin, she paid a visit to the Sterns.

Mr. Stern, in addition to attending Warner Clinic for study and observation, has been going to a private doctor once more, this time through the influence of his sister-in-law, who pays the bill. The visitor pointed out the dangers of going about from doctor to doctor and urged him to complete the tests and study at the Clinic. He has already received a diet list, which he is following.

Mr. Stern confided to the visitor that his one hope is to remarry and that his wife's family, with whom he is very close, oppose such a step for the present. He told the visitor of a woman in the neighborhood, about whom neighbors have been talking to him as a prospective wife, and asked her to make an effort to get acquainted with the woman and find out about her character. He states that she is childless, was formerly married, and has a good reputation in the neighborhood. He gave the visitor her name and address and suggested that visitor call on her and possibly suggest housekeeping work to her, as he knows that she is at the present time unemployed and would be willing to do housework. He realized, however, that it would be inadvisable to have her act as housekeeper in his home.

Mr. Stern is about as well satisfied with the present housekeeper as he probably could be with anyone. He says that he is just "marking time, waiting for something to happen," meaning matrimony. He believes that the longer he waits to be married, the more difficult it will be for the children to adjust to a stepmother, and he considers himself a young man and doesn't wish to continue to live without a wife. He looks as far ahead as the time when the children will marry, and says that at such a time he will have to live alone; therefore, he feels the need of remarrying. The visitor encouraged him in this, provided he will take the proper precautions in selecting a second wife. He proved to be well aware of the importance of this; as he has a fair understanding of people, associating with them in his work, he can probably be relied upon.

Samuel commenced activities at the Neighborhood House and will do some work in return for his scholarship; the younger children have not as yet enrolled in Hebrew School as there have been no vacancies. Julia is still very anxious about getting piano lessons. Mr. Stern says his sister-in-law has offered to give him her piano, and he will, therefore, wait for the present.

March 10, 1931.—Mr. Stern has been in a much more cheerful mood lately. His health, too, has slightly improved, and he has gained a little weight and is following the diet recommended at Warner Clinic, where he has received a complete examination. The clinic report stated that he seemed to be a little nervous and that his condition was aggravated by worry and strain, due to the death of his wife. He was given a diet and is to return within a month for further study.

The visitor had a lengthy interview with the neighbor in whom Mr. Stern is interested as a prospective wife. Her name is Mrs. Weinstein; she lives with her parents, Mr. and Mrs. Kohn, at 4212 West Twenty-first Street. Her father is a Hebrew teacher, and the family is highly regarded in the neighborhood. Mrs. Weinstein, who is separated but not divorced, is very attractive, apparently quite intelligent, and slightly crippled. She claims that she was born with one leg shorter than the other and has only a very slight limp. She was married about ten years and for the last three years has been separated from her husband. She says she is very friendly with her husband's family and gave them as references to her character and any information pertaining to her married life. The visitor referred her to the Legal Service Department as she was anxious to get a divorce and claims to be unable to pay a lawyer; it was thought in this way that more information could be gotten regarding her difficulties with her husband, cause of separation, etc. The Legal Service Department is now handling the matter.[3] In the meantime, Mr. Stern is quite impatient as he is becoming more and more interested in her. His sister-in-law, Mrs. Isenberg, who opposed the second marriage, left for California several weeks ago and, particularly since she left, he is anxious to remarry. He also told the housekeeper that he intended to surprise her and the visitor some day in the near future. Mr. Stern has not informed any of the children of his plans, nor has the woman in question visited at the home, although she lives only a few blocks away, and according to the housekeeper, he has been in constant touch or communication with her during the evenings. She telephones him frequently and he her, and he has admittedly been visiting with her until quite late at night.

Visitor asked the nurse to go in and see Viola, as she has been running a temperature, and Mr. Stern was quite anxious about her; the nurse reported that it was probably due to her markedly bad tonsils. The visi-

[3] [The Legal Aid Department of the Jewish agencies assists families and individuals in dealing with their legal problems. Service is given to the individuals and to the courts and public agencies in the interest of persons who come before the courts and who cannot pay for legal counsel.]

tor relayed this information to Mr. Stern and urged him to have a tonsillectomy performed without delay.

Samuel spends his week ends with his uncle on the South Side, since his aunt went to California, and works in the grocery store. He stated that he gets his expenses for the week, but would not give the amount. Samuel has recently become a little more friendly with the visitor, perhaps since Neighborhood House privileges were given him. He has been talking about his school work and future plans; he says that he will take a summer course to make up the subjects in which he failed during the last semester.

June 30, 1931.—Regular weekly visits continued; no new developments. Mr. Stern continues to act somewhat disgruntled at times, but, on the whole, things seem to be getting along rather smoothly. Arrangements were made to have the younger children attend the Neighborhood House Recreation School during the summer. Mr. Stern was very anxious to have all the children and the housekeeper sent to camp so that he could, at the same time, take his vacation. However, since the housekeeper is colored, it would not be possible to send her to camp with the children. He was advised that the baby is too young for camp and that the older ones are registered for the last period at Mark Camp, when Samuel will be finished with his summer school. Mr. Stern is planning to take his vacation July 15 to August 1. The visitor encouraged him to take a vacation by himself, as he would then be able to get a complete rest and change, which he apparently needs very much. He finds his work very trying, is always tired and irritable, and the least little annoyance on the part of the children seems to be too much for him.

July 15, 1931.—The previous week all the children were re-examined; all are up to weight, in fact overweight, with the exception of Viola, who is two pounds underweight but considered normal. Julia and Alfred were referred for tonsillectomy recommendations to the Ear, Nose, and Throat Clinic. All the children were referred to Dental Clinic, with the exception of Samuel.

Mr. Stern left for his vacation, taking with him Viola and Julia. He took a cottage at Carroll Lake together with his sister-in-law and her family. When the visitor learned about this arrangement, she tried to dissuade Mr. Stern from taking the children, but he insisted, saying that since our organization could not send them to camp, he wanted them to have some country life. The housekeeper will remain at home with the two boys.

August 15, 1931.—Mr. Stern did not seem to have profited very much by his vacation, as he came back as irritable as ever and very much discouraged about the girls, saying that Julia in particular made a nuisance of herself to him. She would not let him out of her sight, was constantly asking for things, and he was sorry he took her along. He did not complain so much about Viola. The children have been very difficult since their return, as they were very spoiled and pampered. Mr. Stern at first refused to have the children return to the Neighborhood House Recreation School, where they had attended before they left for the country, saying it was too warm and too far for them to go, but the visitor insisted that they go, particularly since they need the group discipline away from home and their father. The housekeeper has therefore been taking them regularly. In addition to this she takes them to the park in the afternoons and one afternoon took them to the circus.

Mr. Stern recently bought a monument for his wife at a cost of $155 and owing to this expenditure, he has been in arrears in his payment of $5.00 weekly toward the housekeeper. Visitor had to ask him several times before he finally brought in $20 today. He is constantly complaining about finances, although he works steadily, was paid for his vacation, and should be able to make ends meet. He is always paying back bills, and the present expense in connection with the monument will, of course, increase his indebtedness, as he is going to pay at the rate of $15 monthly.

The two boys are very enthusiastic about going to camp, and each time they are seen they inquire about the details of examination for camp, means of transportation, etc.

Mr. Stern was given the details of the recent examination of the children, and the visitor learned that they have some dentist in the family (a cousin). Mr. Stern was urged to take the children to him, as the clinic is so crowded it is difficult to get appointments. He was also informed about possible tonsillectomies for Julia and Samuel, and appointments were made in Ear, Nose, and Throat Clinic for further observation.

August 31, 1931.—Several evening visits were made to see Mr. Stern, as he was again thinking of having the children admitted to the Jewish Orphanage. He stated that, while his family is entirely opposed to any such plan, his friends have been telling him how much easier and cheaper it would be for him to give up the home and place the children at the Orphanage. Then, too, Mr. Stern thought of moving as he was paying too much rent and the conveniences for the children in his present neighborhood are not so good, as the school is a long way off, Neighborhood House too far from the home, etc. It appears that every time the worker lays stress on the need of his contributing toward the housekeeper he begins to consider breaking up his home. He claims that in spite of his wage of $50 weekly he cannot make ends meet; that there are constant deductions from his pay, such as $1.00 a week toward an unemployment fund, $1.50 weekly for union dues; and very frequently he pays several dollars weekly toward a helper.

The worker went into great detail with Mr. Stern in trying to help him understand the situation; it was pointed out to him that, as he has held this job for many years and although his wife has been dead only a little over a year, he evidently did not save in the past, since he was very much in debt at the time of her death. Furthermore, it was stressed that, should the children go to the Orphanage, he will be expected to pay to the fullest extent of his ability; and, since Samuel is ineligible for the Orphanage, he would have considerable expense in boarding himself and Samuel; so that from the economic standpoint, he need not feel that it will be any cheaper, should he break up the home and place the children. The worker made him feel that he was privileged to make application for the admission of his children to the Orphanage, but merely wanted to dispel any illusions to the effect that he wouldn't need to pay for their care, could save up money, etc. Aside from the economic angle, Mr. Stern was still complaining that the children annoy him to a great extent, although he admits that there was a great improvement up to the time that he took the two girls to the country for a vacation and that there is already some improvement since their return home. According to the housekeeper, it is entirely his fault, as he is constantly indulging them in one way or another. At this time he is not complaining about the housekeeper; he feels that she is doing all that can be expected of her, although he is constantly saying, "She is not the same as a mother." The worker also told him that she had learned from relatives and from him that when his wife was living he took a very active part in the household, and therefore she wondered why he was resenting responsibility in the absence of his wife. After a long interview it developed that Mr. Stern is very much discouraged about the prospect of finding a second wife. He admits that he has been very busy in trying to find "the right party," and now is beginning to wonder whether there is such a person. Of course, his requirements are many: he will not marry a woman with children, wants her to be intelligent, educated, and even to have some resources of her own. He wants to make sure that the children will be acceptable to her, and the first thing he does is to invite any "prospect" to the home, to get acquainted with the children. He claims to stress this in particular. The worker complimented him for trying to be careful in his selection, gave him several examples of hasty second marriages which proved a failure, and urged him to continue to be cautious in selecting a wife and mother for his children.

The boys left for camp the previous week; they carried out all instructions and were happy to go. Julia and Alfred were seen at the Ear, Nose, and Throat Clinic just before the latter left for camp, and both were recommended for tonsillectomy. Julia was also taken to the clinic for dental care.

September 15, 1931.—Visits at the home revealed that things have been considerably smoother during the past few weeks; Mr. Stern no longer talks about breaking up the home. He signed a new lease at a reduction of rental to $43.

The boys returned from camp, where they were reported as good campers, clean and neat in their appearance. Prior to going to camp the entire family was given a treat to the circus, and throughout the summer they were taken regularly to the parks by the housekeeper. Their attendance at Neighborhood House was fairly regular; the younger children took part in a performance given at the end of the school course, and they spoke a great deal about their activities there.

Mr. Stern was interviewed regarding tonsillectomies for both children and he gave permission to have them done; an appointment was made for Julia the following week.

October 15, 1931.—Both Alfred and Julia had tonsillectomies performed during the last month and both are getting along very satisfactorily. They were out of school about a week and have had no complaint. Julia was kept at the hospital one day longer than was expected, owing to a slight hemorrhage, but there were no recurrences upon her return home. She was, however, much slower in recuperating than Alfred. Mr. Stern, as usual, was quite panicky about the operation and upon their return about their recovery, particularly in the case of Julia. The housekeeper carried out all instructions regarding their after-care.

The housekeeper reports that Mr. Stern has been in much better spirits of late; has been less irritable and complaining. For some weeks he was not on speaking terms with his sister-in-law, owing to an indebtedness to him of about $100 which she claimed inability to pay; but since the children's tonsillectomies, the aunt has been visiting at the home, and the children, in turn, have been taken to her home. The housekeeper further reports that he has apparently, for the present, curtailed his activities in search of a wife; in fact, he tells the housekeeper that he is not in a hurry to remarry, "is not looking for trouble," etc.

Julia was again a little troublesome, particularly in the sleeping arrangements, for a while after her operation; the two girls sleep on a day bed in the living-room, while Mr. Stern and the boys sleep in the bedroom. When Julia becomes annoying, she insists upon sleeping with her father, gets Viola to do likewise, and thus disturbs the entire arrangement of sleeping.

Mr. Stern was seen regarding the question of finances; he has not been contributing his $5 weekly as agreed in the beginning toward the payment of the housekeeper; he has the habit of waiting several months, then sending in a check for $20 or $25. Worker therefore arranged that he pay the housekeeper directly $5.00 weekly and the organization will give her the difference. Owing to the general reduction in wages, particularly in household help, the worker reduced the housekeeper's pay from $12 to $10, so that the future financial obligation of the organization will be $5.00 weekly.

School reports received on Julia, Alfred, and Samuel:

ALFRED, FRANKLIN SCHOOL, 4B

Reading—G	Geography—A	Excused Absences—11
Spelling—G	Deportment—G	Arithmetic—G
Music—A	English—A	Physical Education—G
Penmanship—A	History—A	Appearance—G

JULIA, FRANKLIN SCHOOL, 2A

Reading—G	Penmanship—G	Music—A
Spelling—G	Deportment—E	Arithmetic—G
Excused Absences—7	English—G	Appearance—E

SAMUEL, ROOSEVELT HIGH, 3B, ROOM 152

English 4B—G	Industrial History—G	Bookkeeping 2B—G
	History 4B—G	

Passed in summer school work; "This boy is commendable in every way."

November 30, 1931.—Weekly visits were made at the home. Mr. Stern is working regularly and is still complaining of nervousness and of hard work, but, as a whole, the household is more peaceful than previously. He continually complains that his expenses are too high, but, as far as the housekeeping angle is concerned, there doesn't seem to be any extravagance. The worker had the housekeeper keep a budget for several weeks, and she is economical. He is constantly worrying because he cannot save, and this is uppermost in his complaints. He is no doubt comparing the expense of running a house with a housekeeper as contrasted with the expense of keeping the children in an orphanage, where he originally wished to place them, and in this comparison, of course, his expenses are higher. However, he is able to meet them, as he works regularly and frequently works on his day off, getting extra pay in addition.

The worker has been talking for some time of the need of enrolling the children in Hebrew or Sunday School. The younger children have refused to go to Hebrew School daily, and since Mr. Stern is not religiously inclined, the worker did not want to force this issue. However, it was finally agreed that the two younger ones should attend Sunday School. Samuel was encouraged to join the Neighborhood House Jewish cultural group for high-school boys and was given a letter of introduction to the Rabbi there. He has never had any kind of Jewish background and was interested when worker explained to him the advantages of getting a Jewish cultural background. Samuel belongs to several clubs, one at the Recreational Center located near the home, and another unorganized group with whom he plays football, in which he is very much interested. According to the housekeeper, he is a quiet, well-mannered lad, takes an interest in the younger children, and is agreeable about the house. The school report indicated that he is doing satisfactory work there. Samuel is planning to go to Washburne College and continue with the commercial course he is finishing at high school. He likes bookkeeping and accounting. He expects to graduate next June and will then be under seventeen.

The children have all been troubled with colds during the change of weather; Viola was taken to Central Pediatrics Clinic, where findings were reported as negative. The housekeeper was worried about diurnal enuresis, and a mild tonic was prescribed. Viola is to return for further observation for this condition.

The housekeeper seems to be well suited to Mr. Stern and his family. She is a very quiet, unemotional individual who does not take things too seriously. The children, too, have benefited by her disposition. The worker noticed, for example, on numerous visits, that the younger children are extremely active. During one visit, Viola completely turned over on a chair; the housekeeper, instead of becoming alarmed, laughed and joked about it, and the child got up as if nothing had happened. She has given them complete freedom in their play, and the entire house is filled with their toys and playthings. She caters to Mr. Stern in his food preferences, keeps the house in good order, and has taken almost all the responsibility away from him. His only comment is to the effect that no one could take the place of a wife, and of course, in this respect, the worker always agrees with him.

The worker remembered the children with small gifts of games and toys for Chanukah, about which they were very enthusiastic.

January 26, 1932.—Regular visits reveal that things continue to run peaceably in the home; on one occasion, the worker had supper with the family, Mr. Stern and the children insisting, and found a great improvement in the table manners of the children. The table was set very nicely; the entire family ate together. Mr. Stern is not so anxious about the children. The housekeeper reports that Mr. Stern goes out several evenings a week, is not concentrating on remarriage at this time, and is accepting the situation. The housekeeper said that he no longer talks about the question of breaking up the home and is more agreeable and satisfied.

The worker received a report from the Hebrew School that Samuel is not continuing with his studies there; neither are the younger children attending Sunday School. Worker had numerous talks with Mr. Stern on the necessity of Jewish education, and he reported to her that, since he is a member of the Workmen's Circle, he is planning to take the children to a new school about three or four blocks from the Stern home.

School reports received for semester ending January 31, 1932.

March 9, 1932.—Samuel's school report for some reason was not returned, but the worker learned from the father that the boy was promoted and expects to graduate in June.

The worker had several lengthy interviews with Samuel, in the evening at home, and in the office. Mr. Stern for some reason was anxious about Samuel; the worker went into this matter very closely. Mr. Stern claims that before his wife's death Samuel presented a contrasting picture to his present behavior, characterizing him as having been a regular tomboy, full of life and energy, even boisterous at times, and in the house constantly, making demands upon the mother and father. Now Samuel is very quiet and settled; sits reservedly in the house doing his homework or taking care of other personal matters, paying little attention to the younger children or anything going on about him, talks very little, and makes no demands. The worker, in talking to Samuel and seeing several of his friends, believes that he is quite a normal boy with wholesome interests and activities. He is very active in the Recreational Center Club and aspires to be a good football player. He is unusually tall and well built for a boy of his age and looks very much like an athlete. He is anxious to finish high school, hopes to make the grade, and to go on to Washburne College.

Mr. Stern feels that Samuel is getting to the age where he should be companionable with him; he wants the boy to talk to him, to discuss his own life, the activities of the younger children, and even to reminisce about the mother. The worker tried to explain to Mr. Stern some of the general psychology of adolescence. Mr. Stern has apparently not abandoned the idea of a second marriage but is still cautious about making his selection.

Mr. Stern enjoys his children; in the many visits at the home, the worker has observed that he likes to sit round the radio, listening to the children's favorite programs; the younger children climb up on him, play "horsey" and other games with him, and he never seems to tire of their sport. He is very proud of them and very much concerned about how any woman whom he might marry will treat them. No matter what the discussion might be, he always reverts to this subject.

Mr. Stern has not been complaining about his health. According to the housekeeper, he seems well, and things in general have been going better.

March 25, 1932.—The housekeeper reports that the household runs very smoothly; she is particularly high in her praise of Samuel, whom she considers entirely respectful toward her, well mannered, and a "perfect gentleman." She complains about Alfred, who is somewhat rough and can be impudent at times; also because he refuses to keep himself as clean as do the other children.

The housekeeper seems to take quite a motherly interest in the family. Recently the worker found her getting ready to go to school, because Julia was taking part in a play and the child insisted that she come and see her perform. She therefore dressed Viola up in her best clothes and took her to the performance.

The housekeeper reports that Mr. Stern again had some difficulty with his brother-in-law, Mr. Isenberg, for whom he signed a $300 note with another guarantor, and the brother-in-law now refuses to pay up his debt, so that he and the other guarantor may have to pay it. This in addition to the personal loan of about $100, which his brother-in-law refuses to pay, has made the relationship between them somewhat strained. However, the housekeeper reports that she visits them with the children, as the aunt is very anxious to see them. The aunt also visits at the house frequently, without her husband. The housekeeper takes the children to relatives living in the neighborhood, with whom she is very friendly. They help her improve her Jewish style of cooking, and she boasts about the fact that she now considers herself as good a Jewish cook as anyone wants to be. She makes "gefilte" fish and all other such complicated dishes, and the Jewish neighbors and relatives compliment her.

April 27, 1932.—Saw Mr. Stern and the children several times since the last report. Mr. Stern seems to be more calm, better poised, and less complaining than usual. He has recently had a cut in pay and is frequently laid off for a day or two, but, since his rent and other expenses have decreased, he is able to meet his obligations.

The housekeeper finds that the two girls are improving in their conduct as they get older; they do not nag their father so much as they did when she first came to the house, they eat better, sleep by themselves, and are generally less troublesome. She speaks in the very highest terms about Samuel, although Alfred she does find troublesome. He is impudent at times, is a great fighter, and neighbors frequently complain that he has hurt their children. The only one who can manage Alfred well is Samuel; when he's around, Alfred is on his best behavior. Viola is unusually bright and already wants to go to school. She attended the Neighborhood House Kindergarten last summer and has asked worker numerous times if she can go there this summer, too.

During the Passover Festivals, the Sterns observed the occasion. Although they do not keep kosher, there was no bread in the house during the holiday, and the housekeeper learned to make the special holiday dishes. She likes to learn different styles of cooking, and is proud of the fact that she can prepare special cakes, puddings, etc., made out of matzoth.

June 25, 1932.—There are no new developments in the home situation. Mr. Stern is still looking about for a prospective second mate but has not made his final choice as yet. The housekeeper reports that he is very particular and frightens most of the "prospects." He is working very hard at his job, is now on night service, and according to the housekeeper comes home from work completely exhausted. He has had several wage reductions. He is continuing to pay the housekeeper $5.00 per week, while the organization pays the difference.

School.—Samuel graduated from high school and there was a family celebration; the aunt, Mrs. Isenberg, gave a party for all the relatives. He received some gifts. Mr. Stern and the aunt were the only ones present at the graduation exercises. Samuel is planning to continue at Washburne College in the fall. He is interested in accounting.

Samuel graduated from high school with an E in Industrial History, and G in all other subjects.

Julia (Franklin) received E or G in all subjects, and S in Deportment and Personal Appearance; she was promoted to 4B.

Alfred (Harrison) received an E or G in all subjects; promoted to 5B.

Summer plans.—Mr. Stern was anxious to have the worker send all the children to camp at the same time that he will have his vacation, some time in July. The younger children are too young to go to camp by themselves, and, since the housekeeper is colored, it will be difficult to send her with the children to any camp. Samuel is now too old for Mark Camp, and Mr. Stern refuses to let Alfred go to camp without his brother. No definite plans, therefore, were made, except to ask for scholarships to the Neighborhood House city camp for Alfred and Julia. Last year Viola also attended summer school, but she is not eligible this year, as they are not taking children under six. Julia enjoyed the summer recreation school last year, was active in dramatics and dancing, and wanted to go again. Alfred, however, did not enjoy the activities, and it probably will be difficult for the housekeeper to get him to go. Worker suggested that Mr. Stern take his vacation by himself and allow the housekeeper to take care of the children in the city She could go to the various parks and beaches, and, not having Mr. Stern to worry about, would have full freedom to take the children around about the city for their recreation. He promised to follow this plan.

Mrs. Hollister, the housekeeper, is planning to go out of town for several weeks. The worker thought this would be an opportunity to try out a Jewish housekeeper, since in the many talks with Mr. Stern he frequently stated that, although Mrs. Hollister does cook Jewish style, it is not the same type of cooking as a Jewish woman would do. The worker selected an excellent cook, an elderly Jewish housekeeper, and took her to the home. Mr. Stern, immediately upon sizing her up, said that she was too old. He was formerly told, and this time as well, that it is against the policy of the organization to engage young housekeepers and that, unless he will accept this woman, the worker would again give him a colored housekeeper. Mrs. Hollister has a friend who frequently visits at the Stern home, and it was suggested that she might take her place in her absence. Mr. Stern was satisfied with any woman whom Mrs. Hollister knew personally and recommended. Worker learned from the housekeeper that Mr. Stern has some "modern" ideas about a housekeeper. He told her that he knew of some Jewish men who had Jewish housekeepers who acted not only as housekeepers but with whom they could have sexual relations. He told her that since he finds it so difficult to find the right kind of woman to marry, this would be a good solution for him. However, he has apparently taken no steps to find this type of housekeeper. The worker feels confident that there are no immoral relations between him and Mrs. Hollister, as she seems to have good standards and has always confided in the worker to the fullest extent. She told her, for example, on one occasion, Mr. Stern said jokingly that he could sleep with Mrs. Hollister when one of the children was ill and there was a shortage of beds. She responded, "What an idea!" and laughed it off, and has always reported that Mr. Stern never made any such statements or referrals again.

The housekeeper reports that Alfred is extremely wild and fights with all the boys in the neighborhood, so that the neighbors frequently have to complain. Samuel, she added, can manage the boy better than the father can, as Alfred has a lot of respect for Samuel.

Summary to August 11, 1932.—Mrs. Parker, the substitute housekeeper, appears to be very satisfactory. However, Mr. Stern was unwilling to let the children remain with her and took them to Carroll Lake with him July 19 and returned July 30. Before he left he arranged with his cousin to get in touch with Mrs. Hollister to make sure that she would be home when he returned with the children. Mrs. Hollister returned as housekeeper on July 30, 1932.

Mrs. Hollister stated that she gets along well with the children, particularly when the father is not at home. The visitor saw the children several times, and they appeared to be well cared for.

September 1, 1932.—The most important recent development is that Mr. Stern thinks he has the "right woman" and expects to remarry shortly. He met her about a month ago and seems to have full confidence in her; states that she became a widow about the same time that his wife died; that she is the owner of a delicatessen store in the neighborhood and has been highly recommended to him by friends and neighbors. The woman's name is Mrs. Sadie Wolfson. The worker was unable to get the information necessary for clearing when Mr. Stern introduced her, and worker was not in a position to question her. Mr. Stern can be depended upon to make a good selection, as he has the welfare of his children uppermost in his mind. He states that this woman is regarded very well by everyone in the neighborhood, where she is well known. Mrs. Hollister, the housekeeper, reported that she had seen Mrs. Wolfson frequently at the house; that she has a nice way with the children and they seem to like her.

October 1, 1932.—Mr. Stern was married on September 17, 1932. The worker verified the marriage in Book 2, Reg. No. 860, married by Rabbi Rosen. Worker felt the need of verifying the marriage, particularly since Mr. Stern expressed free-love ideas at one time or another, as the record indicates.

Mr. Stern's wife has two children, a boy of about fifteen and one of nine. While she had no money at the time of the marriage, she came to

Mr. Stern with an excellent supply of furniture, linens, etc. They rented a new flat with a sleeping porch which can be used as a summer kitchen and where two of the children sleep. Mr. Stern purchased twin beds for Samuel and his wife's boy, as he didn't want the two big boys to share one bed. The two smaller boys, Alfred and Mrs. Stern's boy, share a day bed on the sleeping porch. The two girls sleep in one bed in another room, and Mr. and Mrs. Stern have a bedroom for themselves. The new home is nicely furnished; Mr. and Mrs. Stern's furniture fill up the flat. The rental of the flat is $40 per month.

The worker called at the home after the family was settled in the present quarters, and things seemed to be running along ideally. The younger children call Mrs. Stern "Mother"; Samuel is apparently satisfied and accepted his father's remarriage; and Mr. and Mrs. Stern feel that they have made no mistake. Samuel is going to night school at Washburne College and works for his uncle during the day.

Mr. Stern is confident that his marriage is a substantial one. He points to the fact that he was very particular and cautious in his choice of a second wife and that he was seeking a practical marriage rather than a romantic one; that his wife was even a better choice as a mother for his children than as a wife for himself, although he says he is happy, too.

October 15, 1932.—Case closed. Housekeeper withdrawn from service.

SECTION III

CASE RECORDS OF DEPENDENT CHILDREN
NEEDING FOSTER-HOME CARE

1. Nancy and Jane Ambler

(Two Little Girls Are Placed with Their Father in a Boarding-Home)

Date of application to Children's Agency.—June 12, 1935.

Applicant.—John Ambler, referred by Mrs. Gemmill, probation officer, Juvenile Court.

Address.—460 Hamlin Avenue.

Children.—Jane Ambler, February 2, 1926, Chicago; Nancy Ambler, January 7, 1927, Chicago.

Present situation.—Children are at St. Cecilia's Orphanage.

Reason for application.—Father wants a private home where he can board with his children. He is earning $35 a week and can pay full cost for this kind of care.

FAMILY HISTORY [TAKEN FROM JUVENILE COURT RECORD]

Mother.—Marie Lamont was born in Chicago in 1907. She was the youngest member of her family and was badly spoiled. Her mother died when she was ten years old. After her death, Mr. Lamont found it very difficult to manage Marie. She refused to go to school and left before finishing eighth grade. She was placed in Christopher Training School in 1919 by private arrangement. In 1924 she was brought before the Juvenile Court on a delinquent petition. The truant officer of the Board of Education reported that she was living under improper conditions. She was said to be sleeping with her father, who was a drunkard. St. Theresa's, the school which Marie was attending at the time, reported her as impudent and boisterous. She was in the seventh grade at the age of fifteen. In July, 1924, she was picked up by the police with three intoxicated men. She was placed in a private home by the Child Placing Department of the Juvenile Court. She made a satisfactory adjustment and was released from supervision when eighteen.

Father.—John Ambler was born in Racine, Wisconsin, in 1896. His parents were divorced when he was two years of age, and his father died soon afterward. At the age of ten, he was placed in St. George's School for Boys and remained there for four years. He is bitter about his experience there and says, "Plenty can go on in institutions that people don't know anything about." When he left St. George's, he went to his mother, who supported herself by working as a dressmaker. Mrs. Ambler is said to have wandered about the streets, complained about headaches, worried about her son, and felt that everyone was abusing her. She was committed to the State Hospital on March 20, 1924, but was said to have been mentally ill ten years before her commitment.

Mr. Ambler married Marie Lamont on June 3, 1925. They were divorced March 12, 1928. Mrs. Ambler obtained the divorce on grounds of repeated cruelty. Mrs. Ambler married Jim Borders on March 23, 1928, and he divorced her September 30, 1928. Grounds were extreme and repeated cruelty. Mrs. Ambler remarried Mr. Ambler in April, 1931. The day after the marriage Mrs. Ambler got intoxicated and was away from home one and a half days. Mr. and Mrs. Ambler fought almost constantly. She drank and neglected the children, and he "beat her up" and frankly admitted that he would "do so again." The children were placed for short periods in private boarding-homes, at St. Anne's School, and the Protestant Service. After Mrs. Ambler's desertion after the second marriage, Mr. Ambler kept the children with him with the help of a young neighbor girl until they were accepted at the Children's Refuge on September 21, 1931.

SUMMARY OF JUVENILE COURT RECORD

Complaint, September, 1931.

Complainant.—Father. He said his wife had deserted and he had no way of caring for the children, who had been temporarily placed at the Children's Refuge.

Investigation.—Officer talked to Mrs. Bailey, landlady, 460 Hamlin Avenue. She said Mr. Ambler had lived in one of her rooms for many years. She considered him thoroughly reliable and honest. He owed back rent, but she wasn't worried because she knew he would pay when he could. Mrs. Bailey said that Mrs. Ambler had been seen in the neighborhood with strange men. She had come home "half drunk more than once."

Officer discussed with Mr. Ambler the possibility of placing his children at the State Home for Children, but he was anxious to have them with him. He said after the divorce, when Mrs. Ambler was given custody of the children, she put them in the Protestant Service instead of keeping them with her and he didn't know where they were for several months. Mr. Ambler said in all sincerity, "It was just like Hell not to know where my babies were."

A few days later, Mrs. Ambler came to court wildly excited. She said she had been trying for months to find her children. She finally met her husband on the street, and he told her to ask at the Juvenile Court.

Officer found old record on mother, Marie Lamont, No. 54775, a delinquent petition, filed in 1924. A visit to the Lamont home was made in 1924. Officer found Mr. Lamont to be a very interesting man and a good talker. Neighbors told her that Mrs. Lamont had been a cultured, intelligent woman. She had complained of her husband's drinking (see family history for other details).

When officer told Mr. Ambler of this record, he wasn't surprised that his wife "had a past."

Mrs. Ambler wanted support from her husband, and officer advised her to go to the Court of Domestic Relations. Court worker interviewed both Mr. and Mrs. Ambler and concluded it was a case for Juvenile Court.

Mr. and Mrs. Ambler went together for a conference at the Juvenile Court on December 18, 1931. Mr. Ambler seemed sorry for his many accusations. He said minor difficulties often led to serious quarrels and he became abusive. Both parents said they didn't want the children in an institution if there was any alternative.

Mrs. Ambler went back to court a few days later and said she had tried going back to her husband but couldn't stand it because he was too demanding sexually and they quarreled constantly. She said she was willing to have the children placed at the State Home for Children but thought Mr. Ambler would want them nearer.

Mr. Ambler asked if he could take the children home January 13, 1932. Officer pointed out that he couldn't afford to care for them. Officer felt he was "difficult and stubborn because he wouldn't give his consent to place the children in the State Home even though he had heard it was a good place. He didn't deny he was stubborn about refusing when he had nothing better to say than 'I want them near me where I can see them.' Mr. Ambler was asked to think over the whole situation and at the same time was told that the officer could send the children away if it should be expedient."

Officer visited Mr. and Mrs. James Lamont, Mrs. Ambler's brother and his wife, January 14, 1932. They were living in a comfortably furnished apartment at 7240 South Lane Avenue. They had two girls, nine and seven years of age. Mr. Lamont said none of the family approved of Marie's marriage to Mr. Ambler. He thought everything might have been all right had she married the right man. Only recently she had confided to them her aversion to Mr. Ambler. He was excessive in his sexual demands, and she was afraid of him because he was cruel. Mrs. Lamont said once she had been telephoned by people living in the building with the Amblers because they heard Mrs. Ambler scream. Mrs. Lamont found out that Mr. Ambler had bent his wife's fingers backward because she hadn't taken the right kind of bath. Mrs. Ambler was afraid Mr. Ambler would "railroad" her to a hospital for the insane as he had his mother. Mr. Ambler's mother had worked hard to support him; but, when she became ill, he had her committed to the hospital for the insane, where she committed suicide because of his cruel treatment of her. Once he is said to have beaten his mother and called her a "woman of the streets" because she had gone to church against his wishes. He never provided for his family. When Jane was a baby he refused to buy milk. She had dizzy spells due to improper care. He never paid his children's board at the Protestant Service and once was told to leave because he found fault with the clothes the children were wearing. Mr. Lamont said his sister has been anxious to have the children with her but hadn't said anything to the court about it because she didn't think the court would place them with either of the parents. Mr. Lamont heartily approved of the plan to place the children in the State Home for Children and felt the court would be justified in placing them without Mr. Ambler's consent.

Officer talked with Mrs. Ambler January 19, 1932, and she agreed with all her brother had said. She told of Mrs. Palmer, of 642 West Center Avenue, who had Jane six weeks and was willing to keep her but because Mr. Ambler was so offensive and interfered so much she sent Jane back to the Protestant Service.

Officer visited Mrs. Palmer and found she had wanted to adopt Jane. Mrs. Ambler would have given her consent, but Mr. Ambler wouldn't. He kept coming to the house and interfering and acted as though he were not mentally normal.

Mrs. Wright, 230 Kimball Avenue, said Mr. and Mrs. Ambler had roomed there. Mr. Ambler was queer, and she sometimes thought he should be in an institution. He was mean to his wife but never to his children. She thought he might have been cruel because he was shell shocked in the war. Mrs. Wright advised placing the children away from both parents.

Mrs. Grimes, superintendent of the Protestant Service, told officer that the Ambler children were there from September, 1930, to April, 1931, and that Mr. Ambler paid $5.00 during that period. Mrs. Ambler paid when she could. She did some work around the institution. She worked well there but wasn't entirely dependable when they sent her out to work in private homes. Mrs. Grimes said Jane Ambler occasionally told lies, and when only five years old preferred the company of boys to girls. She said the cook had seen Mr. Ambler put his hand under Jane's dress.

Case was discussed by dependent committee on April 19, 1932. It was decided to let the application for the State Home for Children stand and file for supervision under the care of the mother.

Officer visited Mrs. Forsyth, Mrs. Ambler's cousin and godmother of Jane. She had four children. She worked in the laundry at the Cook Hospital at night and wasn't able to care for more than her own family.

Mr. Ambler went to see the probation officer on May 8, 1932. "As usual" he was opposed to every suggestion. He said he would send in witnesses to prove Mrs. Ambler's unfitness.

Conference at Family Agency with court worker and worker for the Children's Refuge. The consensus of opinion was that Mrs. Ambler had never had an opportunity to see what she could do with the children and that she should be given a trial. Psychiatric examinations for both parents were recommended.

May 20, 1932.—Mrs. Ray, Mrs. Ambler's sister, was interviewed by probation officer at her place of employment, the Center Cafe at 125 North Gable Street. Mrs. Ray said she couldn't help her sister more than to give her a place to sleep free. She said Mrs. Ambler had never had a chance to show how she could get along with her children. Mrs. Ray said she thought Mr. Ambler wasn't "right." Once when he saw a war film, he "completely passed out."

August 20, 1932.—Mrs. Ambler stopped in to see officer. She was wearing a new dress and new shoes and had a new permanent wave. She said she had been unable to find a flat for the price the agency allowed. Officer felt she wasn't willing to make much effort.

August 24, 1932.—Mr. Ambler called at the court. He said he couldn't see why the court "keeps harping on sending my children away." He went to the American Legion and protested against the commitment of his children to an institution.

October 24, 1932.—Mr. Ambler came to the office, protesting because his children had been moved from the home where they were placed by the Children's Refuge. He said he was working at a garage at 425 Evans Avenue and wanted to board the children with Mrs. Anderson.

January 20, 1933.—Officer visited Mrs. Anderson. Mr. Ambler and the two children were boarding with her. She said that now the father was there she wasn't able to discipline Jane, as he showed favoritism for Jane. Mrs. Anderson found Mr. Ambler hard to get along with and he monopolized the house. He paid $45 a month for board, room, and laundry for the three.

The teacher at Adams School, grade 1B, told the officer that Jane was one of the most difficult children she had ever had. She didn't believe she was subnormal and was going to pass her to 1A. She said Jane was impudent and would talk out loud in the classroom. She would run around the room and crawl over the desk tops. The teacher said she had never seen any "immorality" in her conduct.

February 9, 1933.—Mr. Ambler called at court to report that he had lost his job.

March 6, 1933.—The children were committed to St. Cecelia's Orphanage.

December 20, 1933.—Mr. Ambler asked to have his children released for two days at Christmas time. Request was refused.

March 12, 1934.—Mr. Ambler's employer, Mr. Barnes, at the Distributing Branch for Prize Beer, 43 West Seventy-ninth Street, was interviewed. He said Mr. Ambler was a faithful employee. He thought he was peculiar and that he had very little mental ability. He was earning $20 a week. Mr. Barnes said they were going to move the office and didn't know how long they could keep Mr. Ambler.

March 14, 1934.—Mrs. Ambler called to see the officer by request. She said she was entirely dependent upon her sister. She had been visiting the children regularly. She was opposed to the idea of her husband's taking the children. She said she would like to have relief and keep them with her.

May 1, 1934.—Mr. Ambler went to the court to ask them to let him have his children with him and he gave the officer the name of a prospective foster-mother, Mrs. Garnes, 742 Everett Avenue. Mr. Ambler had been asking for his girls at intervals all winter.

The Juvenile Court officer said she would not release the children except under the supervision of the Catholic Children's Agency.

May 29, 1935.—Mr. Ambler asked again for his girls. He said he was earning $35 a week at the Prize Beer Company. Officer talked with his employer, who said the work would be permanent so far as he could tell.

Court recommended the release of the girls to their father. He was allowed to take them June 21, 1935, for a vacation in Michigan.

Reports from other agencies and employers obtained by court worker.

Divorces.—Circuit Court. Mrs. Ambler alleged repeated cruelty. She said Mr. Ambler had a violent temper and had beaten her on several occasions. Mrs. Ambler's brother, James Lamont, was a witness. Divorce was granted by default on March 12, 1928.

Superior Court. Jim Borders secured a divorce September 30, 1928. He accused Marie Lamont Ambler Borders of extreme and repeated cruelty. He said she attacked him with a kitchen knife, threw a milk bottle at him, and scalded him with hot chocolate. Mr. Borders married Mrs. Ambler March 23, 1928.

Reports of mental examinations made at Warner Hospital.—Mother. Warner Hospital, July 23, 1932. Marie Ambler:

Psychometric Finding
Stanford Binet
C.A. 25 years 2 months
M.A. 12 years 6 months
I.Q. 68, scatter 10 to 16 year level

Possible that I.Q. underestimates patient's mental ability but could hardly be rated above dull average. She was co-operative during test. On Ferguson Form Boards she made score 32 reaching sixth decile to be interpreted as average.

No psychotic factors were brought out.

Patient might be tried with children under close supervision.

Father. Warner Hospital, September 9, 1932. John Ambler:

After several broken appointments, Mr. Ambler finally came to see the psychologist and psychiatrist.

On August 29, 1932, on the Stanford Binet test he earned an I.Q. of 76; chronological age 35 years, mental age 12 years 2 months. The basal year was taken at 10. In year 12 he passed all but one test at which point he refused to go on, saying that he had been working all night for twelve hours and was too tired to listen. It cannot be determined to what extent this affected the I.Q., but in view of this the I.Q. should not be taken too literally. On the Ferguson Performance Test he scored 38 places which is to be interpreted as high average.

On August 12, 1932, he was seen by the psychiatrist. No psychotic symptoms were noted. Neurologically he was negative. The psychiatrist considered him an inadequate, undersexed, homosexual type. In attitude he was prevailing rather apathetic and indifferent showing some bitterness in relation to points concerning his wife and her family, blaming his wife for all the difficulty of the children. There was no bizarre or disturbed behavior, however. His responses were prompt, relevant and coherent, but intellectually inadequate. He denies chronic or intermittent alcoholism. He denies venereal infection, and a Wassermann given is negative.

From a social standpoint the situation was discussed in conference with the two psychiatrists who examined Mr. and Mrs. Ambler. Their opinion is that the children should be placed in an institution rather than re-established in a home with either parent. This opinion is given in view of the low I.Q's of the parents; the reaction of seeming disinterest in the welfare of the children by the mother; the father's inadequacy in personality and in sense of responsibility to give adequate care for the children; and the reaction of the parents on each other. Regarding the parents, there is no psychotic behavior and no other evidence at the present time for their commitment.

[*Signed*] GEORGIA CALLEN *Social Service Dept.*

Investigation made by Juvenile Court of Racine, Wisconsin, at home of Mr. Ambler's aunt.—Probation officer asked for information concerning the relation ship between Mr. Ambler and his mother, and Mr. Ambler and his wife.

Mrs. Kent lived at 405 West Salem Street. Her husband was earning $25 a week as a machinist, and a daughter was earning $13 a week in a candy shop. Mr. and Mrs. Kent had five children, ranging in age from seven to twenty-two years. The family occupied an eight-room house, which was immaculately kept. Mrs. Kent said there had been six major operations in the family during the past year so she couldn't do anything for Mr. Ambler. She said she couldn't take the children unless assured $5.00 a week.

She said as far as she knew John had always been very good to his mother. He impressed her as being exceptionally good. John's mother told Mrs. Kent many times that she never treated John very well, that she had placed him in institutions or homes when she could have cared for him.

In July, 1931, John told Mrs. Kent that his wife had left him. He asked her to take Nancy and she did so for two weeks. John paid her $12.

Mrs. Kent said John had relatives in Portland, Oregon. She hadn't heard from them for eighteen years. Mrs. Kent gave the officer a letter from Mr. Ambler dated October 13, 1931. The letter was just an ordinary chatty letter asking about all the members of the Kent family. Mr. Ambler said:

Jane and Nancy are not with me any more. I had to put them in a home as I could not do anything any more. I was sure in a bad fix, no work and no money, just could not make a go of it, but they are well and happy. It is a very nice place so I am glad of that. Well, they have been there three weeks yesterday. I go and see them two times a week. Everytime I leave them they cry for me, you know four months with them all the time and then for me not to see the kids makes me lonesome. Nancy talks about going to Racine lots of times so I know you must have been good to her.

Report from Veterans' Administration.—John Ambler. Probation officer in her letter said she understood Mr. Ambler left the hospital without permission. Reply said there was no record of Mr. Ambler's leaving the hospital without permission. He was admitted to the Soldiers' Hospital June 10, 1930, and was under observation for a gastric condition. He was discharged June 21, 1930, with maximum benefit. He refused an operation recommended for circumcision.

He was not entitled to disability allowance because his condition was not permanent.

State Hospital.—Mrs. Nancy Ambler was admitted to the State Hospital on March 20, 1924. Diagnosis—catatonic type Dementia Praecox. Wassermann, 3+Spinal Fluid. She was discharged as improved September 3, 1924.

She was readmitted July 3, 1926. Committed suicide July 16, 1926. No diagnosis had been made.

Record stated that Mrs. Ambler had had little education. She divorced her husband because he drank. She always had many friends. For seventeen years before her commitment, she was very religious, and was interested in Spiritualism and Christian Science.

Work record of Mr. Ambler.—Chicago Surface Lines. Mr. Ambler worked as conductor for the Surface Lines from September 24, 1923, to July 23, 1925. He was discharged. They are not permitted to give the reason because of an agreement with the Union. A man is always given three warnings before he is discharged.

Grant Club. Mr. Ambler was employed as floorman in their garage from April 3, 1931, to June 1, 1931, at a salary of $120 a month. He was entirely satisfactory.

Sims Garage, 302 Evans Avenue. Mr. Ambler worked one and a half days a week. He was given the job "for the sake of his children."

Private chauffeur for E. L. Haines for two years.

St. George's School for Boys.—John Ambler was admitted April 26, 1906, and discharged in July, 1910. His mother was supposed to pay, but the bill got beyond her control so she took him out.

John's academic grades were very good. His deportment in the schoolroom was always 90 to 100. There was not a very clear record as to his behavior outside of school, except that he was in several average boy fights and occasional disobedience was reported.

Society for the Protection of Children.—Mrs. Ambler was reported by the Court of Domestic Relations on July 15, 1931. Mrs. Ambler asked to have her children taken away from their father. She said they weren't receiving good care. The worker from the Society for Protection of Children visited at 460 Hamlin Avenue and thought that they were getting exceptional care from a father trying to work. The house was clean and comfortable, and the landlady was interested in the children.

Mrs. Ambler was not found living with her sister as she had said but came and went.

Mr. Ambler worked as a chauffer for the Grimes Cafe. He talked so much, drove the car so crooked, and behaved so peculiarly he was let go. Mr. Ambler was angry and hit his employer on the head with a club.

When called in to the Society for Protection of Children office, he wouldn't talk and said it was "none of our business."

Society for Protection of Children recommended Juvenile Court action.

Jane and Nancy Ambler were admitted September 21, 1931. They were isolated at once because of scabies. Mr. Ambler took them to the institution. He appeared to be a tired-out, restless individual. He said his main interest in life was his children. He was deeply moved at leaving the children.

Mr. Ambler said Jane was a thin, nervous child. She had a kind of fit while at the Protestant Service, which was diagnosed as epilepsy. The superintendent thought it was due largely to the excitement of group life. Mr. Ambler said Jane had no fits after his wife left and he was sure she would be all right.

Mrs. Ambler didn't visit until November 11, 1931. She told the social worker it might be best to have the children adopted. In one breath she said Mr. Ambler was a very cruel man and in the next said she thought of going back to him.

Jane's adjustment in Central Building at the Children's Refuge.—Housemother reported that she was an aggressive, domineering child who wanted to be the center of attention. She was rough with other children. She was very talkative and enjoyed telling stories. She would tell about her mother's bringing her a carload of candy, about a little boy who peeked under her skirt, about men who chased her down the street, about staying out all night, and her father's and mother's quarrels. Jane was affectionate and demonstrative. She sulked when crossed. She was enthusiastic over new projects and new people. She talked freely with strangers. Her response to praise was negative. The best way of dealing with her was found to be depriving her of pleasures. Jane's school teacher said she could be an apt pupil but she was inclined to give up easily and her interest span was short. She was original. Her special ability was singing.

Nancy's adjustment in Central Building.—Nancy was said to be a retiring, sweet-dispositioned child. She was stubborn when crossed. She was affectionate and wholesome. She would stand back and watch the others rather than enter into the play. She talked very little. Mr. and Mrs. Ambler both favored her. Nancy was rarely enthusiastic. She was a fair pupil in kindergarten.

Placement in foster-home, April 30, 1932.—Jane and Nancy were placed with Mrs. Frank Anderson, 795 South Templin Street. Mr. Ambler was greatly upset over the placement. Although he had complained continually at the Children's Refuge, he would rather have them remain there than go to a place "where no one knew what was happening." He acted like a sulky child. Mr. Ambler felt Jane was such a bad girl she needed constant supervision. Sometimes he said he thought she was "crazy." She was "like her mother." He said she was old for her age and knew everything the wrong way. Worker told him that Jane had had improper training but that she responded to attention. When first placed Mr. Ambler acted like a spy and would question the children and appear at the the home at all hours. After worker went over things with Mr. Ambler, he was less troublesome and when he saw the girls were gaining he seemed to have more faith in the foster-home.

Jane's adjustment in foster-home.—The foster-mother found Jane to be agressive, cheerful, and to dislike to submit to authority. She was polite in the presence of strangers. She was selfish and rarely shared. She was impatient and quarrelsome but improved in those respects. She was very affectionate. At times she was self-absorbed and unaware of what was going on around her. She was inclined to complain about trifles.

Jane lied protectively. She could always tell a plausible story to shield herself. When caught in the wrong, she would tell the foster-mother to "beat me and beat me as long as you want to."

Her habit of masturbation lessened while in the foster home but never entirely stopped. Jane's mother knew of this habit and told her she would stop growing.

Jane told neighbors that a boy at the Children's Refuge tried to have sexual relations with her. She was always able to get attention with this story because people were usually shocked. She said she showed herself to boys because they asked her to do so. She did so "loads of times."

Jane had no temper spells. She deliberately did what she wanted to do and was sulky if anyone interfered. Once she ran her wagon into a lady who was carrying a bundle because "the lady was walking where I wanted to run my wagon." Jane talked back. She was provoked if children didn't obey her. She wouldn't fight but would call names, threaten, swear and make faces in an attempt to make children submit.

Jane was careless about her personal appearance. She would get very dirty and tear her clothes. She had enuresis day and night when first placed but toward the end of her placement it occurred very infrequently and only after an exciting day.

Interests and recreation.—Jane enjoyed playing house, cutting pictures, using crayolas. She liked to be read to and especially enjoyed stories of adventure. She said she liked to talk to the monkeys at Lincoln Park and pretend to understand them. Jane learned to swim. She wanted to be helpful around the house.

Associates.—Jane had no lasting friends. She always wanted to be boss. At heart she was a coward, but she talked big and had a bold manner.

School.—Jane did fairly well in school. Her effort was only fair. She passed to 2B. There was no report of behavior difficulties.

Nancy's adjustment in foster-home.—Mrs. Anderson found Nancy to be a placid, rather serious little girl. She became less retiring after living in the foster-home for a time. She wanted to be treated as a baby. She was definitely a follower. Nancy was talkative when she became acquainted. Nancy rarely became excited. She didn't copy Jane's behavior. She was always neat.

Interests.—Nancy liked to play with dolls and liked to be read to. Her interest was of a longer span than Jane's. Nancy got along well with all children.

School.—Nancy was a fair pupil. She was persistent. She did not have a good imagination nor was she original.

June 12, 1935.—Mr. Ambler came to the Children's Agency to make application for a home in which he could board with his children. He has been very dissatisfied having the children away from him and now that he earns enough to support them he is determined to have them with him. He is very resentful toward his first Juvenile Court worker because he feels she was prejudiced in favor of his wife. The present worker he feels understands that he wasn't wholly in the wrong and thinks he should have a chance to have his children with him. Mr. Ambler seems to be sincerely devoted to his children and to want to take care of them. He said he has paid St. Cecilia's Orphanage $15 a month as ordered by the court. His wife has visited the children about every two weeks but hasn't paid the $5.00 as ordered. Mr. Ambler stressed the point that he has no bad habits and doesn't "spend his money foolish." He couldn't estimate his expenses but said he paid no attention for he always comes out all right. He pays $3.00 for room rent and $1.00 on back rent. He didn't know how much back rent he owed. Mr. Ambler is going to send his girls to Michigan for two weeks or more for a vacation, beginning June 21. They will board with Mrs. Cantor, who was recommended by friends. He will have to pay $12 a week for their board.

Mr. Ambler wants a home found as soon as possible. He was anxious to help and thought it might hurry things if he put an advertisement in the paper. It was hard for him to understand how the agency works, the matter of supervision, etc. Mr. Ambler will probably be difficult to work with because he is so vitally interested in his children that he will want to take over many of the things we expect a foster-mother to do. He kept stressing the point that he was reasonable and that he could get along with anybody if they did right. He wanted to be sure the children were going to be treated right and didn't think there was any way of telling unless one lived right in the house with the family.

Children's Agency Staff discussed the Ambler case.—It was questioned whether Mr. Ambler is as psychopathic as he appears from the record. How much of his desire to have the children is to give them a better life than he had? This kind of desire can often be used constructively. If we doubt the evidence it might be wise to try the plan of boarding him with the children.

What do the children mean to Mr. Ambler? They may be of value as evidence of his virility if it is true that he is a homosexual type as one psychiatrist thought. Mr. Ambler presents a typical projecting picture of a man with paranoid tendencies. He will assume no responsibility but blame the other fellow if things don't work. He is nervous, sensitive and hypercritical, insecure, restless and inadequate and he compensates by being demanding and domineering. It was decided to ask the court to release the children to their father. It might be irritating to him to have the agency in authority. If he isn't satisfied with the care the agency gives, let him go back to the court. Make sure he definitely understands the services he can and cannot have. Stick to the routine care given all children under care and give no extras, else there will be endless demands. If we select a good home and the plan of boarding Mr. Ambler with the children doesn't work, drop it rather than try to get other homes. The prognosis is poor but it is worth a trial.

Jane and Nancy Ambler admitted to the Children's Agency.

SUMMARY JULY 7–OCTOBER 1, 1935

Court hearings.—July 9, 1935, case was heard in Juvenile Court. Children were released to father under court supervision.

Conference with father regarding foster-home.—On July 11, worker talked with Mr. Ambler about the Norbeck foster-home. Worker told him very definitely some of the things we expected in the way of co-operation from him if we placed the children. Worker told him that he was not to talk about the children in their presence. The Agency nurse had said that he described all their ailments and habits when he brought them for examination. Asked him not to countermand any orders given by the foster-parents but if he disagreed to take up the matter later. Asked him not to question the children about things that had happened during the day, for if they think he is going to listen to every little complaint they will exaggerate every incident in order to gain attention. Told Mr. Ambler he could tell very easily whether or not the girls were happy and, if he felt they weren't, he should come to the worker. Told Mr. Ambler we must be responsible for medical care and for setting the standards regarding food, bedtimes, etc. Asked him to be careful about giving the foster-parents some privacy so that they could have some time alone. Told Mr. Ambler the rate we had decided on after discussing this with the Norbecks was $22 a month for each child and $1.00 a day for himself. This would amount to $75 a month. Asked Mr. Ambler to pay the children's board to us and we would send a check to the foster-family, but to pay his own board directly.

Mr. Ambler didn't protest in the least about the rate, and he took worker's suggestions in good spirit. He said, "What's right is right and what's wrong is wrong. I'm not one to kick." He said he didn't approve of the care the children received at the Children's Refuge and he told them it was no way to treat scabies to keep children cooped up in one little room but they should get lots of air and sunshine. Mr. Ambler said he guesses they thought he was complaining but he wasn't; he was just telling them wherein they were wrong.

Placement.—Jane and Nancy Ambler were placed in the home of Mr. and Mrs. Philip Norbeck, 920 South Morris Avenue, on July 17, 1935.[1]

Visited the foster-home July 24, August 15, September 7 and 25. Saw foster-father in office August 7 and 14. Saw foster-mother in office August 21. Talked with Mr. Ambler in office August 20 and September 17.

Adjustment in foster-home.—The children have seemed to enjoy their new home, and Mr. Ambler has seemed entirely satisfied. On August 20, he said to worker, "That's a good place." He said on another occasion, "That's the best home they ever had." Mr. Ambler seems to realize the children are happy and are treated well, and he isn't looking for something to criticize. He seems to trust the foster-mother more all the time. When he first came he said no woman was going to tell him how to dress his children, for he had bought his girls' clothes all their lives and he was going to continue, but a few weeks later he asked Mrs. Norbeck if she would have time to take the girls shopping for dresses and shoes.

Mr. Ambler has backed up the foster-mother in everything. One evening he even carried this too far. Mrs. Norbeck had dressed the girls in their best to go out with their father to a concert; and, after Nancy was dressed, she went out in the yard and deliberately stamped in a mud puddle. Mrs. Norbeck was provoked and spanked Nancy. When Mr. Ambler came home he spanked her again. When Mrs. Norbeck insists that the children eat some of everything, Mr. Ambler doesn't object al-

---

[1] [The foster-home study is not given here as it is not especially significant. Mr. Norbeck, fifty years old, is of German descent; Mrs. Norbeck, forty years old, is of Bohemian descent.

The house is a six-room, brick bungalow on a lot 35 by 165 feet. It is valued at $13,000, but there is a $4,500 mortgage. There are three bedrooms downstairs and the attic has been finished off to make a fourth bedroom. The house is very comfortably furnished.

The final evaluation is as follows:

Mr. and Mrs. Norbeck give the impression of being good-natured, kind, patient people who would make splendid parents for boys or girls. They seem equally interested in taking children to board and both would take an active part in the household. Although they have never had children of their own, they have had experience in caring for other people's children. They want children to board because they like children but also would welcome the added income.

The main drawback is Mr. Norbeck's unemployment and the family's inadequate income which make it impossible to place just one or two children.]

though he has very queer notions about food. At first when Nancy would not eat vegetables, Mr. Ambler made the suggestion that they dispense with desserts for a week until Nancy learned to eat.

At first Nancy gave more trouble than Jane. Nancy can be very stubborn. One day she demanded butter on her fried potatoes. Mrs. Norbeck explained that they were greasy already. Then Nancy said she would not eat them at all because they were "too greasy." After she is naughty she seems sorry and asks to be forgiven. Nancy is sweet and lovable at times. When Nancy was being naughty, Jane was being very good. She said she thought it served people right because everybody used to think Nancy was so cute. She said, "This proves I'm the best one, doesn't it, Uncle Phil?"

Jane began acting naughtier than Nancy about the middle of August. Nancy's behavior improved very much. She learned to eat everything and was much easier to manage in every way. The children are not loyal to each other, and when one is in disfavor the other will bring up everything bad she can think of about her. Jane was particularly hard to manage after her mother's visit early in September. Jane became very angry with her mother because she didn't bring the skates she had promised. She talked terribly to her and told her she never had been a mother to them. On her next visit Mrs. Ambler took Jane aside and whispered to her for a long time. Nancy kept following trying to hear. Finally Mrs. Ambler threatened to take a branch off of the bush and whip Nancy. She said, "I have a secret to tell Jane and she has one to tell me." When Mrs. Ambler first visited she used to play with the children and they seemed to have good times.

After this visit when Mrs. Ambler whispered so long to Jane, Mr. Ambler questioned Jane when he came home. Finally Jane told him her mother had asked if she would rather live with Daddy or with her. Mr. Ambler told Jane she must tell him the truth. Finally Jane said she told her mother she would rather live with her. Mr. Ambler gave Jane's chair a shove, got up, and began packing her suitcase. Jane cried and cried and told Mr. Ambler she didn't mean it. Several times Jane had said, "I don't want to stay here." Nancy reported Jane had said, "Youse are mean." Mrs. Norbeck said, "Who is mean; who are 'youse'?" and Nancy said surprised, "I don't know." Mrs. Norbeck talked to Jane alone one day and asked her why she said she didn't want to stay. Jane cried and said, "I do want to stay."

Mrs. Norbeck said Mr. Ambler is a very good father. He is very fond of his girls and is willing to get them anything they need or desire. He is very proud of them and likes to show them off. He took them to visit his sister-in-law recently and asked Mrs. Norbeck to put on their hair ribbons.

Mr. Ambler's only fault is his attitude at the dinner table. He doesn't interfere with the children but makes remarks about his own likes and dislikes. He has very peculiar tastes and notions. Sometimes he will take a small taste of something he has said he didn't like and then take another larger helping. He never says anything is good.

Mother and grandfather.—Mrs. Ambler and her father came to the Children's Agency on August 15. Mr. Lamont was very angry because the children had been moved from St. Cecilia's Orphanage. He said the father was no good and should be put into an institution. Mrs. Ambler was not so excited and tried to calm her father. She kept saying, "Never mind, let them find out for themselves." Mr. Lamont asked if the children were attending mass. He quieted down after worker told him neither our agency nor the foster parents had any objection to the children's attending mass.

Drove Mr. Lamont and Mrs. Ambler to the foster-home. They seemed favorably impressed with the home. Mr. Lamont said he had worked in that neighborhoud at one time and knew that fine people lived there. The children looked lovely. They did not show any special pleasure or excitement at seeing their mother.

Mrs. Ambler said she would like to visit the children every week, and arrangements were made for her to visit on Thursday afternoons. She said she didn't ever want to run into Mr. Ambler because he becomes "hysterical" when he sees her. Worker told Mrs. Ambler we expected to have Nancy's tonsils out before school started, and she said that would be fine.

Conference with Mr. Ambler about the Catholic church.—Worker talked with Mr. Ambler in the office on August 20 and told him what his wife had said about the children going to Catholic church. Mr. Ambler said he wouldn't send them to the Catholic church, that he believed the mother had no right to say anything if he supported the children and they go to some church. Worker told him it might be the part of wisdom to give in just on that one point, for when the children were older they could make up their own minds about church and that it didn't make so much difference what church they went to now. Said it seemed a pity to spoil a good home just for this, and it might be possible for Mrs. Ambler to make so much trouble the case would go back to court and the children would be committed to a Catholic institution if he wouldn't yield. Mr. Ambler said, "Let them take it to court." He said when Nancy was baptized,

Mrs. Ambler took another man along and said he was the child's father. He said Mrs. Ambler is just jealous because the children have a good home. If it wasn't church it would be something else she was fussing about. He thinks she is just spiteful. Her father is a troublemaker and isn't even interested in the children.

Children's health.—Admission examination of Jane on July 11, 1935, by Dr. Meek: General condition good. Slight cold now.

Admission examination of Nancy on July 11 by Dr. Meek. General condition good. Needs tonsillectomy. Slight squeaky systolic murmur at the base of the apex.

Father explained in great detail about their sunburn and mosquito bites. He asked to have Nancy's tonsils out and said he would pay for the operation. He seemed greatly concerned about the children's health and repeatedly said they were extremely nervous.

Jane received dental care July 11 and August 2.

Nancy received dental care August 2, 7, and 14.

Nancy had a tonsillectomy on September 10. Mr. Ambler paid $10.

SUMMARY OCTOBER 1, 1935–JANUARY 1, 1936

Difficulties connected with Mrs. Ambler's visits.—Visited foster-home November 23 and December 14. Probation officer visited once during worker's vacation.

On October 11, Mrs. Norbeck telephoned to say that Mrs. Ambler was making a great deal of trouble because she wouldn't permit her to take the children out. Mrs. Norbeck was apprehensive because she came in a car and was insisting upon Jane wearing a coat. Mrs. Ambler was angry at being refused and pushed Mrs. Norbeck. Mrs. Ambler's father talked very roughly to her and threatened her with court. Mrs. Norbeck was so upset she telephoned Mr. Ambler, but he didn't arrive until after his wife had left.

Worker reported this incident to the court, and Mrs. Matson, Probation Officer, agreed to visit because Children's Agency worker was leaving on her vacation. Mrs. Matson said Mrs. Ambler had secured an attorney and had attempted to have the case reopened, but so far the judge had refused. Their chief complaint is that Mr. Ambler refuses to send the children to the Catholic church. Mrs. Matson believes he should make this concession and she plans to talk with him though they have gone over the matter many times.

October 16.—Mrs. Norbeck called to know if she had to let Mrs. Ambler in this Thursday when she visited in view of all the trouble they had the last time. Told her to call Mrs. Matson directly and ask her opinion. Mrs. Matson told her that she would send Mrs. Ambler a telegram asking her not to visit.

October 17.—Mr. Ambler in to pay. He said as soon as Mrs. Ambler got Mrs. Matson's telegram yesterday she came right over to the home and caused another scene. Mrs. Norbeck called Mr. Ambler at work, and he came home in a cab but she had just gone. He was very indignant that she had ridden over the court's wishes and said Mrs. Matson still hadn't come out to see them.

October 23.—Mrs. Norbeck called to know if Mrs. Matson had gotten in touch with the office about visiting her home. She has not come out yet, and they are having so much trouble with Jane because the mother goes to the school and talks to her and then she won't mind at all.

October 24.—Mrs. Ambler called in her usual much agitated manner. She talked in a loud voice and said she wanted to know "right here and now" why she wasn't allowed to take the children to the corner. They were her children, and she didn't think a child should be turned against a mother or sisters against each other. She raved on in that manner for ten straight minutes and when the worker said she had no authority to give her permission for anything, she said that everyone was working for Mr. Ambler and against her. Worker told her to call Mrs. Matson and she said Mrs. Matson was just her husband's case worker and didn't know anything anyway. She also said Mrs. Matson lives just five blocks from her and knows all about the case because she has told her. She said her lawyer was looking up something about the divorce, and Mrs. Matson told him to stop meddling and wouldn't let him see any of the records. However, she finally said she would call Mrs. Matson and see if she could take Jane to the corner.

Controversy regarding church attendance.—Mr. Ambler will not carry out the court's request to send his girls to the Catholic church, although Mrs. Matson thought the matter was settled after her conference with him. He seems to feel very strongly on the subject and cried bitterly when told he must let his girls go to Catholic church. He said his life had been ruined. Just a few times he allowed them to go to eleven o'clock mass with Mrs. Norbeck but never permitted them to go to the children's service at nine. The children continue to attend a small Protestant mission.

When worker talked with Mr. Ambler, he said he was going to send the children to Protestant church at ten o'clock and Catholic church at eleven o'clock, and if that didn't suit the court they could take him before the judge. He feels that he is supporting the children and should be the one to decide where they will attend church. Mr. Ambler said he doesn't believe the judge would order the children placed in a Catholic institution even if he said in court that he wouldn't send his girls to Catholic church. He said, "How would that benefit the county?"

Mr. Ambler is convinced that his wife doesn't care whether or not the children attend Catholic church but that she wants something to fuss about. She does not attend church herself so he feels that she isn't sincere. She can't care much or she wouldn't have placed the children in two different Protestant institutions, the Children's Refuge and the Protestant Service.

Adjustment in foster-home.—The children have improved a great deal, and there have been no special problems. Mr. Ambler is very trying. First he worries because the children are too fat and then because they look peaked. He says Jane's mouth is crooked. At every meal he warns the children to chew their food so they don't get a weak stomach like his. One night just from force of habit he reminded the girls to chew when the main dish was soup. Nancy said in a disgusted tone, "How can you chew soup?" and even Mr. Ambler had to laugh. Regardless of what is on the table, Mr. Ambler always knows of a better kind. Whenever prunes are served, he tells them that Oregon prunes are the only good kind.

Just before Christmas Mr. Ambler decided that the girls were too old for presents and said he wasn't going to get them any presents but that they could consider their dancing lessons their Christmas present. However, the day before Christmas he bought them a great many gifts including dolls.

At times Mr. Ambler is very sociable and agreeable.

November 16.—Jane and her father came to say that Dr. Davis had missed several cavities in the front teeth; these are not cavities but spots on the teeth that do not mean anything.

Mr. Ambler talked with worker about Jane's teeth on December 4, 1935. He asked if she thought her diet could be faulty. He said, "Now I'm not complaining; I know what the children get at night but I don't know what they get morning and noon." He said he buys oranges in order to be sure they get enough.

School.—Both girls do poor work in school. Jane was put back to the third grade and Nancy to the second grade.

Visited foster-home February 7 and March 23. Saw foster-father in office January 11. Saw Mr. Ambler in office February 5 and March 17. Saw Mrs. Ambler in office March 27.

Adjustment in foster-home.—The children have seemed to be very contented in the Norbeck home. They are attached to both Mr. and Mrs. Norbeck. They seem to want to please them. When Mrs. Norbeck was ill with a severe cold, Nancy said she wanted to die if Aunt Maude died. Mr. and Mrs. Norbeck have no trouble whatever with the children unless Mr. Ambler has done something to upset them.

Children's attitude toward parents.—Jane is the favorite of both Mr. and Mrs. Ambler. Both Mr. and Mrs. Norbeck say she plays up to whichever parent is present. The minute her father comes in the house it is "daddy this and daddy that" the whole evening long and the same way when her mother visits. Jane will say things to please even though they are not true. Nancy, on the other hand, answers questions truthfully even though the answer won't please her parents. For example, when Mrs. Ambler asked Jane with whom she wanted to live, Jane said she wanted to live with her mother but Nancy said she wanted to live with Aunt Maude. Later Jane said to Mrs. Norbeck, "You know I told Mother I wanted to live with her but I don't. I want to stay with you."

Mr. and Mrs. Norbeck feel sure that Nancy notices the fact that Jane gets all the attention from her parents and that she resents it. Mr. Ambler will brush Jane's hair for half an hour and will say to Nancy, "Hurry up now, get your hair brushed." He will scrub Jane's knees when dirty and will brush her teeth but will scold Nancy for not getting cleaned up. He waits on Jane in many little personal ways but has no time for Nancy. Nancy never fails to come into the house at five o'clock, but Jane is usually late. When Mr. Ambler comes in he says "Where's Jane? Nancy, why didn't you tell Jane it was time to come home?" When Nancy says she did, he will say, "Well, why didn't you make her come?" He will make fun of Nancy because she likes to work around the kitchen and tells her she will be a kitchen mechanic all her life but Jane will be a dancer and a lady. Mrs. Ambler directs her conversation to Jane for the most part.

Mr. and Mrs. Norbeck believe that Nancy's attitude toward her parents is simply a result of their treatment of her. Nancy has to be urged to stay in the room when her mother visits and she will keep going out to find Aunt Maude. In February Mr. Ambler gave Nancy a whipping because she refused to sit on his lap, and since then she has drawn away more than ever. This has angered him very much. After the whipping, Nancy was stubborn for four or five weeks, and her behavior was similar to when she first went to the Norbeck home. Nancy likes to set the table and she looks over every dish carefully. She always puts the plate with a chip or crack at her father's place. If someone else has set the table, they have seen Nancy go in and shift the plates.

Mr. Ambler.—Mr. Ambler has improved a great deal except in his treatment of the children. He no longer complains about the food and does not take mints after every meal. He hasn't mentioned getting up in the night to take a pill in weeks. Mrs. Ambler told Mrs. Norbeck that all Mr. Ambler's friends have been talking about the change in him. Mr. Norbeck said he thinks Mr. Ambler probably never had a good home before and he didn't know how to act. They treat him like a member of the family, and he eats with them when they have company. They believe this "makes him feel good." Mr. Ambler is much more considerate than he used to be. Formerly when he heard someone call by telephone and invite them out for Saturday evening, he would get his hat and coat and hurry away so they would have to stay at home. Now he always asks them if they are going out before he ever makes plans to be away on Saturday evening. Mr. Ambler bought a secondhand Ford and offered to let Mr. Norbeck use it to attend a funeral in South Chicago.

Mrs. Norbeck said she thought there would be no living with Mr. Ambler if he could use the house just as he pleased. He recognizes a limit and so they manage to get along with a minimum amount of friction. Without asking Mrs. Norbeck's permission he invited all the relatives over to a birthday party for Jane and then told Mrs. Norbeck. She told him she would do the same for Jane as she had done for Nancy, that is, bake a cake and decorate it and have ice cream for dinner. Mr. Ambler wouldn't speak for two evenings afterward.

Mrs. Norbeck said she didn't mind having a party for the children but didn't think it fair to treat one better than the other and she didn't approve of Mr. Ambler's highhanded manner of arranging the party.

Mr. Ambler is just as unreasonable in his treatment of the children as ever. He does everything for them in a material way but when angry is always throwing it up to them. He will say, "Who buys your clothes, does your mother? Who pays your board? Does your mother ever do anything for you?" If she brings them anything he will say, "Who left this junk? Your mother is no good. She walks down the street half drunk. She's rotten." One day the children said to him, "You're always talking about mother, but she never talks about you." Mrs. Norbeck said she expected him to hit the children, but he flushed and didn't say a word. Mr. Ambler is very quick tempered. He hits the children on the head, and they have a habit of dodging when he goes near them. Mr. Ambler laughs about this. He has put his hand over their mouth and hit them and then will laugh and say that is the way he beat their mother. He says all women need their faces slapped. On Ash Wednesday he gave both children a whipping because they asked if they could go to the Catholic church with Mrs. Norbeck's sister.

Mr. Ambler asked Mrs. Norbeck's help in buying clothes for the girls. She and the girls met him downtown, and after they finished shopping he took them to supper and to the Chicago Theatre.

Mr. Ambler came to the office February 5 and March 17. He always pays the children's board regularly. He said on February 7 that everything was going just fine. (This was just a few days after he had been angry about Jane's birthday party.) On March 17, Mr. Ambler asked worker if the children were on probation for a definite length of time. He said he had thought it was a six-month period and he had not expected the Children's Society to be interested for longer than that period. He asked if he would be called back to court. Worker told him she thought the arrangement was for an indefinite period and that the case would not go back to court unless someone were dissatisfied and asked for a change. Mr. Ambler asked if he could make another plan if he had a chance to better himself. He said he had been considering going to housekeeping, but the present arrangement would be all right for a year or two. He said he wanted worker to understand he had no definite plans but had just been thinking and wondering if he could make a change if he wished. He thought he might want to make a change for the summer. He said, "I'm not complaining; everything is all right. It's only that I want a change if I can better myself." Worker felt he was troubled because Nancy was becoming attached to the foster-family. He said, "Jane is all right, she is different, but I don't want Nancy to get too attached." He said he didn't approve of the Dixon School because they have too much entertainment.

Mrs. Ambler.—Mrs. Ambler has visited the children every week. Her attitude is much more friendly than at first. She has stopped telling Jane things which upset her and no longer talks against the father in the children's presence. Mrs. Ambler told Mrs. Norbeck she had just learned that the Children's Agency selected this home for Jane and Nancy. She had thought they were friends of Mr. Ambler's and that they were going to try to make as much trouble as possible for her. (This misunderstanding hardly seems possible because worker explained agency's relationship to Mrs. Ambler and her father, September 15, 1935, but she may have been too upset and angry to comprehend it.)

Mrs. Ambler came to the office at worker's request and gave additional health history on the children. She talked continuously for an hour, and one statement reminded her of something else. She gave a very disconnected story. The main points seemed to be that she was satisfied with the home the children are in but "things aren't always going to be this way," apparently meaning that she would have them with her some day. She thought they should be allowed to go to the Catholic church since they want to. She doesn't think it is right for Mr. Ambler to talk against her. Jane tells her the things he says. Mrs. Ambler said it isn't safe to antagonize Mr. Ambler. He will never have a chance to beat her up again as he had done in the past.

Children's health.—On January 11 Jane had her annual examination. Her general condition was good; she had gained eight pounds in six months. Dr. Davis gave dental care.

On January 11 Nancy had her annual examination by Dr. Meek. Her general condition was good. She had gained fourteen pounds in six months. She also received dental care.

2. Joe and Veronica Tomchek

(Two Children Are Supported in the Chicago Children's Home and in the Home of Relatives until Their Father Is Ready To Take Them)

Date of application to Chicago Children's Home.—June 26, 1928.

Applicant.—Sava Tomchek. Address: 1853 West Lawrence Avenue.

Children.—Joe, October 7, 1921, Chicago, Illinois; Veronica, April 16, 1923, Chicago, Illinois.

Reason for application.—Mr. Tomchek's wife died, March 8, 1927. He is not able to keep the children with him.

Present situation.—Mr. Tomchek has a housekeeper, Frances West. She is very satisfactory, but he is not able to pay her sufficient wages to keep her. Mr. Tomchek is a tailor and has a shop on the first floor of his house. He and the two children occupy three rooms in the attic. His plan is to rent the second floor, but he has not been very successful.

Financial situation.—Mr. Tomchek's house is mortgaged for $10,000. He also owes $2,000, which he has borrowed from friends and relatives. Business is very poor as two other tailor shops are operating in the same block. He averages from $30 to $35 a week. He has been paying Miss West $9.00 a week.

Plan.—His plan is to place the children until he can get caught up on his debts.

Family history.—Mr. Tomchek was born in Hungary in 1885. He came to the United States nineteen years ago with his brother, who is his only relative. His parents are dead; his father died in an accident, and his mother died of blood poisoning. Mr. Tomchek and his brother came directly to Chicago from Hungary. He has always lived in his present neighborhood. He opened up a tailor shop, and his brother a shoe store and repair shop.

Mr. Tomchek married Veronica Krayes, also Hungarian, in 1919, in Chicago. She was always sickly and had frequent heart attacks. For two years before her death she was confined to her bed. She was pregnant at the time she died.

Mr. Tomchek is under observation at the Municipal Tuberculosis Dispensary. Neither his wife nor children contracted tuberculosis from him.

Mr. Tomchek is greatly in debt, owing to doctors' bills for himself and his wife. Since his wife's death in March, 1927, he has kept the children with him. He says he worries about them a great deal and feels that caring for two children is too great a responsibility for a man. He is not able to manage his tailor shop and attend to the children properly. The customers give the children pennies, and they go to the store and buy candy. They play in the streets all day. He says he knows he gives them too much freedom, but he is not able to work and watch them.

For a time, a neighbor came in to do the cooking, but she moved away recently. This plan was not satisfactory anyway, because he had to bathe the children and do everything else for them, except the cooking; and this all interfered with his business. He advertised for a housekeeper a few weeks ago, and Frances West came in answer to his ad. She is very good with the children, but he says he cannot pay her $9.00 a week. He realizes that this is a small salary but it is more than he can afford.

He thinks that if he places the children he will be able to live more cheaply and can pay some on his debts.

Paternal relatives.—Uncle, Mr. Joseph Tomchek. Lives at 5430 St. Francis Street. He has a small shoe store and repair shop. He is married and has five children.

Maternal relatives.—Aunts: Mrs. Hudec, 2513 Washington Avenue.

Mrs. Hudec has no children but would not be able to take her niece and nephew, as she is not strong.

Marian Krayes, a Sister, is in a convent at Chicago Heights.

Mrs. Droba, 2550 Hillside Avenue, has four children between the ages of fifteen and twenty-three. She does not think she could take the children, as both she and her husband suffer from asthma.

Grandfather.—Died in 1916 of heart trouble.

Grandmother.—Living in Jugoslavia with three sons. Mr. Tomchek said he wanted her to come to the United States to care for his children, but her sons would not let her come.

Case cleared. Found six medical agencies registered. They are:

Municipal Tuberculosis Sanitarium, No. 56348, April 3, 1925
County Hospital, No. 254, March 3, 1925
West Side Dispensary, No. 45262, January 21, 1925
Infant Welfare Station, No. 2372, January 6, 1922
Visiting Nurse Association, September 15, 1921
Warner Hospital, September 3, 1921

June 28, 1928.—Called at Mr. Tomchek's shop and talked with Miss West, housekeeper. She says she is willing to stay until the children can be admitted to the Home. She likes her work, but says Mr. Tomchek cannot afford to pay her. She seems interested in the children. She was dressed very neatly.

Called on Mr. Tomchek's brother, Mr. Joseph Tomchek. He is a very stooped man who coughs continually. He says he hopes his brother, the father, can place his children. The father owes this brother $1,600 and has three mortgages on his house and tailor shop. His wife's long sickness took all his savings. He has had bad luck ever since he built his home. It is very hard for him to care for the children, as they take so much of his time that he is not able to get all his own work done.

Mr. and Mrs. Joseph Tomchek have five children, the youngest of whom is three years old. Mrs. Tomchek assists her husband in the shop.

July 2, 1928.—Called at 2513 Washington Avenue. Mrs. Hudec was not at home, but talked with her sister-in-law. She says that Mrs. Hudec has no children, but that her husband is not willing for her to take the responsibility of the Tomchek children because she is not very strong.

July 3, 1928.—Case discussed by Application Committee. It was decided that the children might be admitted, rate to be $2.00 each a week, plus clothing.

July 5, 1928.—Called on Mrs. Hudec. She is a young woman, who seems interested in her nephew and niece. She says that she would like to have taken Veronica to keep as her own, but Mr. Tomchek refused to separate the children. She does not feel able to care for both of them. Mrs. Hudec has been married three years and she is very fond of children, but her husband does not think she is strong enough to have children of her own. He is afraid that she will die as her sister did, because she is delicate and has a similar heart condition. She has to have an operation next month.

Mrs. Hudec says that her sister Veronica came to the United States in 1913, just before the war broke out. She was never very healthy. She had a very difficult time throughout her married life, because both she and Mr. Tomchek were ill the greater part of the time. Mr. Tomchek had tuberculosis at the time he married Veronica, although he did not mention this to her. The doctor told Mrs. Tomchek that she should not have children, but she had several pregnancies and lost two children through miscarriages before Joe was born.

Mrs. Hudec says that Mr. Tomchek never treated his wife well. He is devoted to his children, however, and has tried his best to keep them with him. In spite of this she would rather see the children placed where they could receive good care. Mr. Tomchek's other arrangements were never satisfactory, because the children were left to themselves most of the time. She thinks having Miss West as a housekeeper is satisfactory, but she believes Mr. Tomchek cannot afford to keep her.

Called on Mr. Tomchek to tell him of the Committee's decision. He said he considered the rate very reasonable and realized that it must cost the Home a great deal more to care for the children.

July 6, 1928.—Called at the Municipal Tuberculosis Sanitarium. Mr. Tomchek and the children were last examined June 25, 1928. The children were both well, but Mr. Tomchek had active tuberculosis. The M.T.S. nurse believes the children will be much better off in an institution, away from Mr. Tomchek.

Reported situation at Mr. Tomchek's brother's home.

July 18, 1928.—Children admitted to Chicago Children's Home, rate $2.00 a week each, plus clothing.

AGREEMENT WITH THE CHICAGO CHILDREN'S HOME

I, Mr. Sava Tomchek, of 1853 West Lawrence Avenue, wish to place my children, Joe and Veronica, under the care of the Chicago Children's Home. I do hereby agree to pay the sum of Four dollars ($4.00) per week to aid in the care of the children.

I agree to provide my children with suitable clothing as needed and to pay for such clothing as I authorize the Home to purchase for them.

I agree to visit regularly and to try to be in all ways a responsible parent, looking forward to the time when I may be able to resume the full responsibility for my children.

[*Signed*] SAVA TOMCHEK

November 8, 1928.—Mr. Tomchek came for a conference about the children. He received a letter from his mother-in-law recently saying she might come to the United States, and if so she will keep house for Mr. Tomchek and the children. Mr. Tomchek suffers from asthma. About twenty-three years ago he had tuberculosis, but he believes this condition is cleared up now. He says he will never marry again because he is not well. Mr. Tomchek says people who don't understand blame him for putting the children in a home. He could earn much more by working for someone else rather than having his own business, but he would not be able to keep a position, as much of the time he is unable to work. Mr. Tomchek has recently had about five or six weeks of good business and has hired a helper during this time, but now business will be slack again until spring. He has recently rented his flat.

February 16, 1929.—Visited Mrs. Droba, who is Mrs. Tomchek's half-sister. Mrs. Droba lives in a very poor neighborhood. Her flat, however, was well furnished and was very clean. Mrs. Droba has four children between the ages of fifteen and twenty-three. Both she and her husband suffer from bronchial asthma such as Mr. Tomchek has. She says that nearly everyone who comes from Hungary seems subject to diseases of the lungs. Her sister was always well at home. Mrs. Droba does not believe that her home would be a healthful place for Veronica and Joe to live. Her children are grown now so that it does not make so much difference. Mrs. Droba says that all her people consider Mr. Tomchek a good responsible man. He is rather reserved and may be somewhat of a "mollycoddle" but he has no bad habits. Mr. Tomchek is not well and has very little money. Mrs. Droba says that the children were very much spoiled when they were with Mr. Tomchek. She thought they were much more polite and well behaved when she saw them last. Mrs. Droba's husband does not like Mr. Tomchek very well because he is too slow. She says that when they invite him to dinner, he always arrives at three-thirty and this annoys Mr. Droba very much. If anything should happen to Mr. Tomchek they would be willing to accept the responsibility for Joe and Veronica. Mrs. Droba has a sister in Gary, who is a Catholic and very bigoted. She was very angry when her half-sister married Mr. Tomchek, who was a Unitarian, and she will have nothing to do with his family. Mrs. Droba is Catholic also; but, if the difference in religion made no difference to her sister Veronica, she says she certainly has no right to object to Mr. Tomchek because he is not a Catholic. Mrs. Droba said Mrs. Hudec had sent a ticket to Mrs. Krayes, the children's grandmother, to bring her out to Chicago. She hopes that Mrs. Krayes will be willing to take care of Veronica and Joe. Mrs. Krayes is between sixty and sixty-five years old. She is Mrs. Droba's stepmother. Mrs. Hudec would be willing to keep the children but her husband objects very strongly.

June 24, 1929.—Called on Mrs. Hudec, maternal aunt. Mrs. Hudec is working at present. For that reason she does not feel that she will be able to take both of the children. Her husband is willing that she take Veronica as she can stay during the day with his brother's wife, who lives on the first floor of the same building. They would be glad to have Veronica for the entire summer and, if Mrs. Hudec could get a vacation, she would take Joe also. Mrs. Hudec will come into the office to discuss the situation with the social worker or superintendent.

June 30, 1929.—Mrs. Hudec took the children out for the day. She has talked the matter over with Mr. Tomchek and has decided that she will not take Veronica until August but during August she will take both Joe and Veronica as she will not work then and can give her attention to them. Mr. Tomchek prefers that the children be cared for by relatives rather than by strangers.

August 6, 1929.—Veronica was admitted to St. Martin's Hospital today with an infected jaw.

August 21, 1929.—Mrs. Hudec took Joe for a two weeks' vacation. She was disappointed because she couldn't take Veronica also.

September 6, 1929.—Veronica was discharged from St. Martin's Hospital and returned to the Chicago Children's Home.

November 3, 1929.—Letter written by Mr. Tomchek to the children:

DEAR JOE AND VERONICA:

I am sorry that I couldn't come yesterday because I had to work. I hope you are all right and I will come sure next Sunday. Please give this chek to the superintendent and be good!
and I will be ther early next Sunday afternoon.
Many kisses from

YOUR FATHER

February 18, 1930.—Visited at the Hudecs. Mr. Hudec was at home alone. Talked with him about the possibility of placing Joe and Ver-

onica in his home, under the supervision of the agency, with the Home
being responsible for their board. He seemed rather interested in the
plan but didn't want to commit himself to any decision. He said he
expected his wife's mother soon and does not want to add anyone to the
family group until after she comes; also he is hoping to move from his
present location and buy a home a little way out of the city and he
wouldn't like to make a change now. Mr. Hudec works in a brewery
making near-beer. His wife works occasionally two or three days a
week. He said she is not very strong and he is afraid it might be too
hard for her to take care of the children. He believes that his mother-
in-law is well and strong. He will talk things over with his wife and give
us their decision. (When this plan had been suggested to Mrs. Hudec
one Sunday when she came to visit the children, she seemed quite
enthusiastic.)

March 2, 1930.—When Mrs. Hudec came to see the children today,
she said they were still undecided as to what they should do. Her husband says they do not know in what condition her mother will be and
he thinks they should at least wait until she arrives. Mr. Hudec is very
much afraid his wife will overdo and because of her weak heart will die
as her sister did. For this reason they never plan to have any children
of their own. Mrs. Hudec doesn't seem to have any idea of the type of
heart trouble she has except that she has been told she has a weak heart.
The worker suggested that she go to St. Martin's Hospital for a complete examination. She seemed interested in this suggestion and took
the address. Mrs. Hudec said she would be willing to take Joe and
Veronica free during July and August for a vacation; then, if she gets
along all right, she will consider keeping them permanently.

Mr. Tomchek came in the other evening and asked about the Hudecs
taking the children. He said they would take Veronica at any time but
he doesn't want the children separated. Mr. Tomchek cannot understand their wanting his children when they don't want any of their own.
The worker talked with Mr. Tomchek about the fact that the main
building at the Children's Home is to be closed soon and other arrangements made for all the children, since life in an institution is not a normal or, in most cases, a desirable experience for children. Told him it
would be necessary to make a plan for his children sometime fairly
soon. He will be glad to have Mrs. Hudec take the children for the
summer.

May 30, 1930.—Mr. Tomchek came in today. He said he didn't
believe Mrs. Hudec could be depended on to take the children per-

manently. The last time he saw her she said she had been ill for a couple
of weeks and had to stay in bed part of the time. Mr. Tomchek said
she described her sickness, and it sounded like the spells his wife used to
have with her heart. He took his wife to many doctors, and they all
said the muscles of her heart were very weak and it was only a question
of time until they would give out. He thinks Mrs. Hudec may have
inherited the same thing from her father, as he died of heart trouble.
Mr. Tomchek would be glad to have the children go to her house for a
summer vacation but thinks it might be a mistake for them to stay on.
For one thing they would be disappointed if they had to leave if they
thought they were going to stay there; and also if Mrs. Hudec were ill
much of the time, they might not be able to go to school regularly.

Mr. Tomchek's business is very poor. He has had to reduce his prices
to comply with the union rules so now he makes practically nothing.
Since the department stores have gone into the business and do cleaning
at cut prices, it is still more difficult to make a living. He described the
racketeering in the dry-cleaning business and said he paid for the last two
years but this year refused to pay since he was made to cut his prices.
Mr. Tomchek talked at length about the present economic system. His
conversation showed that he has read and thought about conditions a
great deal. Mr. Tomchek has rented his house, but the income barely
pays for the upkeep. He will have two years' taxes to pay this year, and
his taxes two years ago amounted to $285, while a sixteen-flat building
across the street was taxed for only $150. He is disgusted with conditions
in Chicago.

Mr. Tomchek is feeling quite well now and would be able to do more
work if he could get it. He went to the M.T.S. dispensary last week and is
all right.

June 22, 1930.—Mr. Tomchek is not pleased about the children going
to Mrs. Hudec even for the summer. He thinks that relatives are always
liable to criticize. He feels that here he has had a purely business arrangement and that he could see the children at any time. When they are
at his sister-in-law's he is doubtful whether they will think that it is a
business arrangement. He will pay us the same as when we had them and
we can pay the Hudecs. He does not like to ask favors of relatives. His
brother-in-law would not take his own brother's children when they
needed a home. The Hudecs need the money and they will not want to
undertake the financial responsibility of two children. Mr. Tomchek was
definitely opposed to having the children there permanently. They talk
to him differently from the way they talk to the people at the Children's

Home. Mr. Hudec's brother wonders why they take the Tomchek children before his. Mr. Hudec is the "boss of the family and what he says goes."

June 28, 1930.—Veronica and Joe went to their aunt's home for the summer vacation. Mr. Tomchek will pay the Children's Home as usual, and the money will then be sent to Mrs. Hudec.

August 30, 1930.—Visited Mr. Tomchek today to ask if he would be willing for the children to remain with Mrs. Hudec if she felt that she could keep them. Mr. Tomchek said he was perfectly well satisfied to have them stay at the Children's Home, but if they have to be placed elsewhere he would rather have them remain with Mrs. Hudec than go to a stranger's home. He thinks they got along very well this summer.

August 31, 1930.—Talked with Mrs. Hudec. As far as she is concerned she would be glad to keep Veronica and Joe, but her husband will not consent. He would be willing to have her keep Veronica but he thinks Joe is too difficult to manage. He is very much like his father, is very stubborn, and has a bad temper.

September 1, 1930.—The children returned to the Children's Home today.

September 10, 1930.—Mrs. Hudec came in today to take Veronica and Joe to the chapel from which their aunt, Mrs. Droba, is to be buried. She died very suddenly on September 8. This is the fourth sister Mrs. Hudec has lost in three years. The one who was in the convent in Chicago Heights died this past winter. Mrs. Hudec said she supposed her husband would never consent to her having the children now. He is so afraid she will overwork and die as her sisters have. Mrs. Hudec said she loves Joe and Veronica so much she would enjoy having them permanently. This past summer has been the happiest she has ever had because of them.

April 16, 1931.—Mrs. Hudec said today that her mother has arrived in New York but is being held at Ellis Island. She has made the necessary arrangements and expects her in Chicago any time.

April 19, 1931.—Joe and Veronica spent the day with Mrs. Hudec and their grandmother. Each child carried a bouquet as Mrs. Hudec had requested.

May 16, 1931.—Visited Mrs. Hudec. She is planning to take Veronica and Joe for the summer. If she works part time her mother can take care of the children. Mrs. Krayes seems to be quite well. She is a very small old lady and speaks no English. Joe can talk with her quite well, and Veronica can remember enough Hungarian to talk a little.

Mr. Hudec has been fortunate in having steady work. Mrs. Hudec said she sent some money today to her brother in Jugoslavia to help him rebuild his farmhouse which recently burned.

June 24, 1931.—Talked with Mrs. Hudec. She will take the children on the twenty-sixth for the summer at least, and then in the fall will see what arrangements can be made to keep them. Her mother seems to be very well.

Called at Mr. Tomchek's store. He would like to have the same arrangement made as last year; that is, he will pay the board regularly to the Home and we will turn it over to Mrs. Hudec. He feels that this is much more business-like than giving it to her directly.

Mr. Tomchek's business is getting no better. He doesn't make much cleaning and pressing, and he almost never has any tailoring to do.

June 27, 1931.—Veronica and Joe dismissed to their aunt for a summer vacation.

July 21, 1931.—Called at Mr. Tomchek's store. He said he has had no complaint from Mrs. Hudec, so he presumes the children are getting along all right. She has been working some, and her mother has been looking after the children. Mrs. Krayes is quite "lively." The children have been having a good time. They have gone to the parks, and they spent a few days in Indiana. Mr. Tomchek said he takes them to the show once a week; otherwise they would have little opportunity to go. Mr. Hudec doesn't like to go out much. Mr. Tomchek went to a Hungarian outing recently and "although an old man danced every dance," while Mr. Hudec just sat and talked.

Mr. Tomchek is quite sure that Mr. Hudec feels better about having the children there now that Mrs. Krayes has arrived, for she can help his wife. If arrangements can be made for the children to remain with Mrs. Hudec, the father would like to have them stay there permanently if they continue to get along well.

July 22, 1931.—Called at Mrs. Hudec's home but found only the grandmother at home. The children were out playing somewhere, but Mr. Hudec's brother who lives on the first floor couldn't find them. Mrs. Hudec is working for two weeks at the hospital where she formerly worked.

August 12, 1931.—Mrs. Hudec and Veronica came today to bring a present to Mrs. Johnson, Veronica's matron at the Home.

Mrs. Hudec is having a rather hard time with Joe. He gets very stubborn and will not obey. He picks on Veronica and says hateful things to her, though she is very sweet to him. Joe has shown his bad temper many times. Mrs. Hudec spanked him once because she got out of patience with him after getting no response from being good to him. This did absolutely no good, and Joe told her the best thing to do was to leave him alone.

One night Mr. Hudec came in while she was having a session with Joe. He said to her, "Do you have to stand this?. Why should you wear yourself out with children like your sisters did?" He has told her that when they have a home of their own, she can try to keep the children if she wants to, but he won't let her have them permanently in this present flat. If Mrs. Hudec did not have to work this year, she might be able to persuade her husband to let her keep them, but she has to work as they have been under such heavy expenses. It was expensive to bring Mrs. Krayes to Chicago, and now Mr. Hudec and his brothers are going to send for their father and he has to pay his share of the expenses. They have also helped Mrs. Hudec's brother in Jugoslavia whose farm burned. The children are too difficult for Mrs. Krayes to manage by herself all day when Mrs. Hudec is away.

Mrs. Hudec has had very little trouble with Veronica on the whole, and she is able to manage her easily. One day, however, she went off with another little girl and was gone until supper time. She brought home a doll and a notebook she had taken from the near-by ten-cent store. Mrs. Hudec took Veronica back the following day and made her put the things back on the counter and tell the clerk. Veronica was very much embarrassed and was thoroughly ashamed. Mrs. Hudec said her husband thought her "crazy" to embarrass herself by taking Veronica back. Mrs. Hudec also spanked Veronica because she first denied leaving the little girl's yard. Mrs. Hudec had told her she should not go to the near-by business section without permission. Mrs. Hudec would like very much to keep Veronica permanently and then take Joe back when she moves. Joe had a godmother who might be willing to take him. She would have taken him gladly at the time of Mrs. Tomchek's death. Her name is Mrs. Michael Sauchek and she lives at 2324 Winchell Road. She has one boy, age seventeen, who has graduated from high school. Mrs. Hudec is quite sure Mr. Tomchek will never consent to have the children separated.

August 26, 1931.—Visited. Talked with Mr. Tomchek about letting Joe go to his godmother and letting Veronica remain with Mrs. Hudec. Mr. Tomchek would prefer to have both children return to the Home if they could stay there, but rather than have them placed in a foster-home, he would let them be separated. Mr. Tomchek said he didn't believe Mr. and Mrs. Sauchek would want to take Joe but he is willing to let Joe go to live with them if they want him.

Called at 2324 Winchell Road and talked with Mr. Sauchek at his barber shop. His wife was at Black Lake. Mr. Sauchek said he would talk to his wife about Joe. Personally he prefers Joe to Veronica. He said Joe was much better behaved during a visit to Black Lake this summer than Veronica was. Joe ate everything and obeyed immediately. Veronica, on the other hand, was very fussy about her food and complained when told to go to bed. Last summer it was the other way around, and Joe was the difficult one to manage. Mr. Sauchek said that Mrs. Tomchek on her death bed had asked his wife to take care of Joe. At that time, however, Mr. Tomchek would not let them take Joe. Mr. Sauchek said he did not know how his wife would feel about it now, but he would ask her and would call Mrs. Hudec.

August 27, 1931.—Visited Mrs. Hudec. She is very much pleased because Mr. Tomchek is willing that she keep Veronica. She would like to have Joe, also, if he were easier to manage. Mrs. Hudec hopes that Joe may appreciate being with Veronica if he is away for a time and that he may possibly return to her home and behave himself. Joe behaved very well at Black Lake this summer while visiting his godmother, so she thinks Mrs. Sauchek may like to have him.

August 28, 1931.—Telephoned. Mr. Sauchek told Mrs. Hudec that his wife didn't believe she could take Joe.

August 29, 1931.—Visited. Mr. Tomchek said he wasn't surprised to learn that Mr. Sauchek would not take Joe. He said Mr. Sauchek was Mrs. Tomchek's friend rather than his. Mr. Tomchek said Mr. Sauchek talks about doing more than he really will do. He is the kind of person who likes to make a good showing. He has two houses, but they are mortgaged for $20,000. He lives way beyond his means. While his wife is at Black Lake for the summer, Mr. Sauchek uses his car to drive back and forth daily. Mr. Tomchek said he thought he would try to manage with Joe at home as he prefers this to having him with strangers. The Roosevelt School is near by. He is going to see that Joe gets to bed early and is not out until eleven or twelve like many boys of his age in the neighborhood. He has a gas plate in the back of the shop, where he can cook.

Mr. Tomchek said he thinks he can get along if the Home will have Joe and Veronica in to see the doctor and dentist occasionally.

September 1, 1931.—Case discussed by the Case Committee, and they approved of Mr. Tomchek's plan for the children. They agreed that the social worker should continue to supervise the children and that the Children's Home might be responsible for the medical and dental work.

September 21, 1931.—Visited Mrs. Hudec. She is enjoying Veronica and is managing her very well. Mrs. Hudec said she is not going to ask Mr. Tomchek for any board for Veronica for the time being, because he has had such bad luck. His shop was held up a few days ago, and thirty-five pairs of pants stolen in addition to several other garments. The robbers posed as a couple who wanted to rent his apartment. After being shown around, they returned the following day with a third party, who, they said, wanted to see the apartment. When they got in, they bound Mr. Tomchek's wrists with wire and tied him to the bed while they ransacked the place. Mr. Tomchek was tied up for about three hours before Joe found him and released him.

September 26, 1931.—Joe brought Veronica in to see the doctor but left without seeing her himself. Joe arrived in a bad mood this morning because of a dispute with his aunt about whether to come on the elevated or streetcar.

October 3, 1931.—Joe came to the Home supposedly to see the doctor and dentist, reported at the main office, and then slipped out the back way without going to the hospital. Social worker went after him later in the morning and brought him back in time to see the dentist but he missed Dr. Robbins. Mr. Tomchek was quite angry and strapped Joe with his belt.

Mr. Tomchek seemed thoroughly discouraged because of his loss. He said he wished the robbers had killed him, for he had nothing to live for. His wrists were badly cut by the wire.

October 10, 1931.—Joe came in to see Dr. Robbins today.

October 30, 1931.—Visited. Mr. Tomchek seems to feel perfectly satisfied to have Joe at home, and he has very little trouble with him. Mr. Tomchek doesn't quite see how he is ever going to come out of his financial difficulties. He was unable to meet his payment to the building and loan association and had to increase the loan to cover his fire insurance because he had no way of paying it. He is having trouble with the cleaner because of the $60 bill he owes, but he had to get in arrears with this so he could reimburse his customers for the loss of their clothes. Mr. Tomchek learned through the Tribune Law Department that he was not liable for the losses because of the robbery, but he said it is either a question of making good or losing his customers.

November 20, 1931.—Visited Mrs. Hudec. She is getting along very well with Veronica. Veronica has a library card and goes after books by herself. Mrs. Hudec's mother is such a help with the housework that Mrs. Hudec feels she has plenty of time to go out to work now, but she has not been able to get a job. The hospital where she formerly worked has only about half as many patients as it could care for, so she gets a day's work there very seldom now. Mrs. Hudec thinks that Joe is getting along very well with his father.

December 23, 1931.—Called on Mr. Tomchek at his store to leave some work to be done for Children's Home. He is getting along well with Joe. They are going to spend Christmas with Mrs. Hudec.

The worker called at the store several times during October, November, and December with garments to be cleaned for various people at the Children's Home in order to help out Mr. Tomchek's business.

February 18, 1932.—Visited. Mr. Tomchek looked very ill and has had such a bad cold he could scarcely speak.

He said Joe is getting along all right. He keeps him busy and calls him in frequently to do something so he can keep his eye on him. Joe is doing well in school and passed this term. Asked Mr. Tomchek to have Joe come in to see the dentist Saturday.

February 19, 1932.—Called at the Hamilton School and talked to Veronica's teacher, Miss Ritter. Veronica is doing excellent work in grade 3A. She is a very sweet little girl and appears to be well cared for.

Visited Mrs. Hudec. She was getting ready for a birthday party to-morrow and was baking three elaborate cakes. Five brothers-in-law and their families are invited. Her mother and her father-in-law, who has recently come from Hungary, were chatting away in the parlor, while the old gentleman picked out nut meats and Mrs. Krayes beat the cake batter. Mrs. Hudec doesn't try to do any work away from home because it doesn't pay. She is so pleased with Veronica. At first she used to cry because she couldn't make grandma understand but now she can speak Hungarian quite well.

Mrs. Hudec is a little worried about Joe. She thinks he looks pale. She believes he gets proper food because Mr. Tomchek was always particular about the kind of food he had. Mr. Tomchek has to spank Joe about every day to make him mind.

April 6, 1932.—Visited to notify Joe and Veronica to come in Saturday to see the doctor and dentist.

April 8, 1932.—Worker stopped to leave some work for Mr. Tomchek. He showed worker the buttonholes which Joe had made in his own suit. They were very well done. He likes to sew. Mr. Tomchek has him work part of the time. He lets him go out to play several times a day but will call him in at intervals to work and in this way can keep track of him. Mr. Tomchek had to spank Joe to make him do his homework and since then he has had no trouble at school.

June 1, 1932.—Called at the store to leave some clothes to be cleaned.

June 4, 1932.—Visited Mrs. Hudec to find out why Veronica had not come in to see the dentist. Mrs. Hudec had telephoned and said Veronica's tooth was aching so badly that she had to come home from school. Soon after Veronica reached home she asked to go out to play and Mrs. Hudec wouldn't let her do it because she had been excused from school. After Veronica's grandmother looked at the tooth and discovered how loose it was, she pulled it.

Grandmother was at Mr. Tomchek's today. Every week end she goes to cook for him and Joe.

Mrs. Hudec said Mr. Tomchek has two men rooming with him now, and it is necessary for Joe to sleep with Mr. Tomchek on a day bed. Mrs. Hudec plans to have Joe spend a great deal of time with her during vacation, and they all will probably go for a week or two with Joe's godfather.

Visited Mr. Tomchek. He was very much pleased with the offer of a bed. He said he had been intending to buy one but hasn't been able to get the money together. Mr. Tomchek sold his best bed a long time ago and has never been able to replace it.

Mr. Tomchek said Joe's last report card was good.

June 6, 1932.—The bed was delivered to Joe.

June 9, 1932.—Worker called to ask Mr. Tomchek if he would like to have Joe go to camp. He said he would be very much pleased to have him go if he didn't have to pay but he couldn't afford to pay anything.

June 23, 1932.—Visited to weigh and measure Joe. Found he had gained. Joe is pleased to go to camp next week.

June 29, 1932.—Called to get Joe to take him to the station. He and Ralph Potter leave for two weeks at Indian Lodge, Fern Lake.

JOE'S RECORD IN INSTITUTION

Child.—Joe Tomchek.

Birth date.—October 7, 1921.

Birthplace.—Chicago, Illinois.

Date of Admission.—July 18, 1928.

Chronological history to time of admission.—Joe was born in Chicago, October 7, 1921. He lived with his father and mother and sister until his mother's death in March, 1927. After Mrs. Tomchek's death, Joe and Veronica were cared for by their father with the help of a neighbor, who prepared the meals. For the last few weeks Frances West, whom Mr. Tomchek hired as a housekeeper, has been taking care of them.

Health history.—Joe was born, full-term, normal birth, and weighed eight pounds. He was breast fed. The only diseases which he has had are measles in 1927 and whooping cough in 1928. Drinks coffee every day and eats a great deal of candy, as Mr. Tomchek's customers give him pennies.

November 8, 1928.—Reports given Mr. Tomchek at conference:

Caretaker's report.—Joe Tomchek is lazy, disobedient, and has pugilistic tendencies. Does not like to get up in morning. Always looking for trouble—"butts in." Talks about his father and mother and seems to remember his home very well. Won't eat desserts, puddings, etc. (rice pudding). Very slow about eating, but "gobbles" what he likes.

Medical report.—Examined July 18, 1928, by Dr. Howard. No findings. General condition good. Urine, Wassermann, Von Perquit, Schick Test—negative. September 1, 1928, dental examination—O.K. Habits good except he does not masticate food thoroughly—eats very fast which causes vomiting at times. October 11, 1928, examined by Dr. Robbins.

School report.—Quality of work—very good; attitude towards work—very satisfactory; general behavior in school—very good.

Mr. Tomchek seemed to understand the reports on the children. He seemed to feel that Joe's laziness was more a sluggishness due to retarded digestion. Unless he forced Joe to drink a great deal of water or gave him milk of magnesia occasionally, he would get very sluggish and dally about getting up in the morning.

May, 1929.—Reports for Parent's Conference:

Matron's report.—Gives a first impression of being very good-natured and being a very good little boy but really gets into a good deal of mischief and when corrected is sullen, stubborn, and pouts a good deal. Likes to talk and carries on quite an adult conversation.

Teacher's report.—In Grade 2A. Joe is an excellent scholar. Reading and spelling are exceptionally good. His handwork especially in clay shows real imagination. He is very much pleased with praise. Causes no trouble at school.

Medical report.—Ringworm has been cured. General condition good except that he needs tonsillectomy. Teeth are good.

November, 1929.—Reports for Parent's Conference:

Medical report.—Examined June 30, 1929. General condition good. Had a tonsillectomy July 3, 1929, at St. Martin's hospital. Good recovery. No other illness. Needs dental care. Average weight.

Matron's report.—Joe is a "big bully." Gets what he goes after. He is a bright boy. Good scholar. Loves drawing and music. Has a wonderful memory. Wants to be a leader, but his temper gets the best of him. If that can be corrected, he will be a great man some day. Tries to be honest and truthful in every way. Does not like work. Tries to get out of it.

School report.—Joe is in Grade 3A. Reading—good; arithmetic—fair; spelling—good; writing—good. Needs special help in arithmetic.

Former matron had stated Joe is very untruthful. She said that he likes to make a good impression and often told extremely cunning lies so that it was hard to detect them.

June 28, 1930.—Joe and Veronica went to their aunt's home for the summer vacation.

September 1, 1930.—Joe and Veronica returned to Children's Home today.

November, 1930.—Reports for Parent's Conference:

Medical report.—General condition—good; nutrition—good; weight—average. Gained 2 pounds during summer vacation, which he lost the first month he was back at the Home. Weight has remained the same since. There seem to be few foods he will eat in dining-room but he has no difficulty eating in the hospital. While patient is still up to weight, something should be done to encourage eating.

Acute infection in parotid gland was opened and drained—St. Martin's, January, 1930, no illness.

Teacher's report.—He is slow in arithmetic. Capable, but does not apply himself. Very inattentive. Needs silent reading to improve speed and composition in content subjects (history and geography). Good speller—100%. Will be given other words for homework. In English he needs sentence drills for recognition.

Matron's report.—Problems. At the table he refuses to eat anything that he doesn't like. He will give up any pleasure and go to the hospital rather than eat. Abilities: A born artist. Paints and draws very well. A good story teller. Wonderful student of the Bible. Perfect dramatic expression. Very much liked by boys. Loves his father, but is jealous of his sister. On returning from his vacation last summer, he ran to matron and said, "I'm so glad to be back." He seems to enjoy his school. Likes to be let alone to read, draw and paint. Should be given artistic training.

Note from teacher to Superintendent of Home:

In regard to Joe Tomchek. Inclined to be a nuisance. Attitude is rather silly and acts clownish at times. Thank you.

June 27, 1931.—Joe and Veronica were dismissed to their aunt, Mrs. Hudec, for the summer vacation.

January 5, 1932.—Joe stayed with his aunt until September 7 and then went to live with his father. Veronica remained with her aunt.

July 13, 1932.—Joe returned from camp today. He said he had a fine time. He can swim better than he could last year.

July 16, 1932.—Joe has visited since his return from camp.

VERONICA'S RECORD IN INSTITUTION

Child.—Veronica Tomchek.

Birth date.—April 16, 1923.

Birthplace.—Chicago, Illinois.

Date of admission.—July 18, 1928.

Chronological history to time of admission.—Same as for Joe.

Health history.—Veronica was born at full-term, normal birth and weighed about eight pounds. Breast fed. Mrs. Tomchek was confined to her bed with a serious heart attack for the last two months before Veronica was born. The only diseases which she has had are measles in 1927 and whooping cough in 1928. Drinks coffee every day and eats much candy, as Mr. Tomchek's customers give her pennies.

October 28, 1928.—When Mr. Tomchek came to visit Veronica, he brought a large sack of apples. Veronica at once began to cry because he did not bring her candy. At first he said he would not get candy for her but when she cried he decided to go out and get some. He agreed when told it was bad training for the child. Veronica began to scream and kick, so she was taken back to her department and not allowed to visit her father for the rest of the afternoon. This is a very typical situation of Veronica's attitude toward her father and his method of dealing with her.

November 8, 1928.—Reports given Mr. Tomchek at conference:

Caretaker's report.—Veronica is quiet and obedient. She seems to be happy and plays nicely with the other little girls. Others have complained of her impertinence, but I have never observed it. She has lied, but only a few times, and I believe due to some fear. She is very fond of her brother and has mothered him since she came. When she came back from the hospital, she was very naughty for a short time. At times I have felt that she was deceitful, but I cannot be really definite. She seems very fond of me. She always takes my part if the opportunity presents itself. We get along together excellently.

Kindergarten teacher's report.—Veronica is capable of being very stubborn when crossed in any way and sometimes pouts and cries when things don't go to please her. However, I have not found her unreasonable in her desires, and with a little encouragement she is often made to see she is in the wrong. She loves to help with practical work—such as washing cups and tables and sweeping, etc. She does splendid work in handwork.

Medical report.—September 18, 1928, examined by Dr. Howard—no finding. Abscess on leg opened by Dr. Howard, healing uneventful. October 11, 1928, examined by Dr. Robbins. Weight normal—48 pounds. General condition very good. No findings.

May, 1929.—Reports for the Parent's Conference:

Matron's report.—Veronica has temper tantrums sometimes but in general seems sweet and willing to do things. She is rather inconsistent in her behavior. Demands much attention. Seems to have a great interest in sex information at the time.

Teacher's report.—In Kindergarten. Will go into first grade next year. Finishes whatever she starts even though confronted with difficulties. Active, wide awake child. Very good in drawing and cutting. Is lovable, but very stubborn at times. When punished, screams and stamps her feet and cries for a long time.

Minnesota Intelligence Test for Pre-school Children: Chronological age six years. Mental age five years six months. I.Q. 92. Low average intelligence.

Medical report.—Veronica had a tonsillectomy. Talked through her nose for a while but has recovered her normal speech. Recovery good. She needs dental care. General condition good.

August 6–September 6, 1929.—Veronica in St. Martin's Hospital because of infected jaw.

November, 1929.—Reports for the Parent's Conference:

Medical report.—Examined September 10, 1929, by Dr. Robbins. General condition good. Average weight. Had a tonsillectomy in January, 1929. Infected tooth in August, 1929. Went to St. Martin's Hospital. Good recovery. Is in good condition.

Matron's report.—Veronica is quiet; makes no effort to attract attention. Is slower than "molasses in January." Likes to sew. Haven't as yet discovered any bad habits or traits. Loving disposition.

School report.—Veronica is in Grade 1B. She seems to be doing well in school. Adjustment normal.

June 28, 1930.—Veronica and Joe went to their aunt's home for the summer vacation.

September 1, 1930.—Veronica and Joe were returned to the Children's Home today.

November, 1930.—Reports for Parent's Conference:

Medical report.—Nutrition—good; posture—good; resistance—poor; no illness in past year. General condition—good.

School report.—Reading—fair; writing—good; arithmetic—fair; spelling—good.

Matron's report.—Problems: Dislikes to work, except "baby jobs" quickly done. Abilities: Neat and orderly, very lady-like; sings well. She gets on with the children; likes to play with them. Welcomes father and talks well of him. She likes the Home; enjoys school; and loves to figure and draw. She enjoys being out with father and going to the Field Museum.

May 25, 1931.—Veronica, with Nancy and Helen Schwartz, "ran away" to her aunt's (Mrs. Hudec) "because she wanted a good dinner." She had been punished at breakfast for rudeness to matron. The children left the playground at recess, about eleven; arrived at Mrs. Hudec's at one, having walked all the way. Mrs. Hudec had been asked by the Superintendent to tell the children that as they were "unexpected guests" she had no dinner for them. They were brought home and waited until 2:00 P.M. to see the Superintendent.

June 27, 1931.—Veronica and Joe were dismissed to their aunt, Mrs. Hudec, for the summer vacation.

January 5, 1932.—Veronica continued to stay with her aunt, but Joe went to his father in September.

July 16, 1932.—Telephoned Mrs. Hudec to tell her of Veronica's appointment for eye clinic at St. Martin's on July 19. Mrs. Hudec will take her.

SUMMARY OF CASE RECORD TO JANUARY I, 1935

Joe continued to live with his father. The Children's Agency sent him to camp for two weeks and saw that he had physical examinations and care. Veronica lived with the aunt until June, 1934, when she also returned to her father. Veronica and the grandmother visited the father and Joe on week ends, cleaned the house, and cooked for them. The grandmother continued these visits after Veronica moved back with the father.

Both children did good work in school and developed well physically. The worker continued visiting the home. The relationship between the children and the father seemed congenial. The father was quite strict; he insisted that the children assume certain responsibilities; he punished them if they did not mind; but the children seemed to accept his punishment, to understand him, and to be very fond of him.

3. The Harris Children

*(Three Children Are Supervised and Supported by the Children's
Agency in Their Grandparents' Home)*

March 26, 1931.—The Juvenile Court asked for placement by the Children's Agency for three Negro children, Chester, Mabel, and Edith Harris, the dependent children of Chester and Jennie Harris. The father died on October 21, 1929. The mother was granted a pension of $53 on November 21, 1930, with the provision that she give up drinking and remain in her mother-in-law's home, under the latter's supervision. When, in January, 1931, the mother moved to a furnished room, taking the two girls with her, she resumed her drinking and began to live with men. On March 31, 1931, the pension was stayed by the Juvenile Court because of the mother's moral unfitness.

FAMILY COMPOSITION

Father—Chester Harris......died October 21, 1929, at the age of 26

Age

Mother—Jennie Harris...... 25

Children:

Chester.................. 9

Mabel.................. 8

Edith.................. 6

Father.—Chester Harris was born February 5, 1903, in Williamsport, Maryland. He came with his parents to Chicago at the age of twelve years. He went to Sunnyside School and graduated from Toussaint L'Ouverture Grammar School at the age of sixteen. He enlisted in the Canadian Army in 1917, though under age. His father and stepmother sent his correct age, and he was released after a short period of service.

Father met the mother while attending Toussaint L'Ouverture School and after a long courtship he married her on May 3, 1921, to please his stepmother, who felt that he should not desert the girl as she was pregnant with his child. He did not love her, but, according to the grandfather, was very fond of the children born to them and worked hard to support the family. The father was a decorator. He learned the trade early by working with his father and refused to go to high school so that he might follow the trade. When business was good he frequently made $50 to $60 per week. He died October 21, 1929, of pneumonia.

Mother.—Jennie Harris was born May 21, 1905, in Auburn, Indiana. Her parents moved to Chicago when she was eighteen months old and were divorced shortly afterward. Her father remarried and moved to Kansas City. Her mother, Mrs. Rosena Bridges, then took up day work to support herself and child. Mother went to Jefferson Park High School for one year and then went to work as a waitress.

Mother began to drink after her marriage. She claims that her father-in-law taught her, although he stated in the Juvenile Court that her whole family drinks. Her marriage was unhappy, and she says that her husband's people were hostile to her. They, however, state that she had a terrible temper and would fight and scratch her husband without cause. After the father died she received insurance totaling $600. She paid part of the funeral expenses (grandfather paid the balance), the back rent at two previous addresses, bought clothing, and was confidenced out of $125 by a Mr. Spangler, who had worked with her husband at Branscum, Magill, and Edwards Real Estate Company and who promised to invest the money for her but later disappeared. The balance was spent on living expenses. When her money was gone, she applied to the Family Welfare Agency for assistance. They found her a job in a "chili parlor" on Cleveland Avenue, but when she sprained her ankle she lost the job.

On November 21, 1930, she was granted a pension of $53 by the Juvenile Court. There was some question at that time about her habit of drinking; her mother-in-law went to the Family Welfare Office and stated that she questioned the mother's morality. The mother admitted the truth of the statement, but cried and begged to be given another chance. She seemed to be genuinely sincere in her desire to remain with her children and to give up drinking and she joined the Villa Street Baptist Church. Under these circumstances the Court granted a pension, with a provision that she remain in the home of her mother-in-law under her supervision.

On January 30, 1931, her mother-in-law, Sally Harris, telephoned the Court that the mother had moved to a furnished room at 2615 Howe Street. On March 5, 1931, the Juvenile Court probation officer visited the mother and found a man, who gave his name as James Clark, in bed with her. At the same time, and in the same room, the two girls, Mabel and Edith, were lying awake on a cot. Mother had evidently been drinking rather heavily. On March 19, 1931, the Pension Committee of the Juvenile Court recommended that the pension be stayed because of the moral unfitness of the mother; and on March 20, 1931, before Judge Martin, mother admitted that she kept late hours and had been drinking heavily. The pension was stayed from March 31, 1931.

Mother was very unco-operative, and on several occasions refused to see the visitor at her home as she had been drinking heavily. She cried and insisted that she wanted to keep her children with her and stated that, while she wanted to give up the life she was living, it seemed impossible to do so. Before Judge Martin, she cried and blamed heredity for her habit of drinking. While receiving the pension, she spent the money mainly on herself and neglected to buy the necessary clothing for her children; however, she feels that she has not mistreated them.

Children.—Chester was born September 2, 1921, in Chicago, Illinois. He is in 3A in Dunbar School. His scholarship is fair, but his work is "sloppy" and careless. His teacher believes that he may become a problem. He is inattentive in class and daydreams. He is indifferent and refuses to do his best. He sometimes assumes a quarrelsome attitude toward the children without an apparent cause. He has been truant occasionally and whenever absent says that he has to go to the Juvenile Court. He was examined in October at Barnard Hospital and was reported to be in excellent health, but had carious teeth. After his mother moved to the furnished room at 2615 Howe Street, he remained in the home of his grandparents. He refuses to live with his mother.

Mabel was born February 8, 1923, in Chicago. She is in the 2B grade at Dunbar School. Her scholarship is fair. She is timid in class and is slow to grasp the work. Her conduct is described as perfect. Her attendance is irregular, as her mother is frequently too drunk to get her and Edith ready for school. She prefers to live with her grandparents because of her mother's drinking. Her health is normal.

Edith was born July 20, 1924, in Chicago. She is repeating 1B at Dunbar School. Her scholarship is fair but her attendance is irregular. She is a neat quiet child and gives her teacher no trouble. Her health is good. She has a slight speech defect. Both girls are well-mannered children.

Home and neighborhood.—Mother lives in a furnished room in the rear of a flat at 2615 Howe Street. There are several other roomers in the house, and someone sleeps in every room except the kitchen. The house is dirty, and poorly furnished. The landlord is reputed to drink and is of a questionable reputation. Mother's room contains a bed, an old dresser, a trunk, and a small cot, on which the two girls sleep. The room is always disorderly and dirty. The mother pays $6.00 a week rent. The flat is in a big building located in a fairly well-kept-up residential street, just south of De Koven Avenue, which is devoted mainly to business in that neighborhood.

Treatment by other agencies and interested persons.—Lester Morgan, a friend of the mother's, 516 Franklin Street, claims that he pays her rent. He has offered to marry the mother and would like to assume the care of the children.

Mrs. Louise Jackson, 5211 Center Street, maternal great-aunt, is unable to assist in the present situation. She lives with one of her three adult children.

Sam Bridges, maternal grandfather, when heard from last year promised to help the mother. He sent $10 and was not heard from again until two months ago, when he promised to help as soon as he got settled in Joliet. He is not living with his second wife. His present address is unknown.

Mrs. Rosena Bridges, maternal grandmother, 1724 Clark Street, is the housekeeper for a man who lives at that address. Her wages are low, and she is unable to help with the children. She frequently goes to mother's home to dress the children for school.

Albert and Sally Harris, 2032 Howe Street, paternal grandfather and paternal step-grandmother. Albert Harris was born March 22, 1879, in Williamsport, Maryland. In 1900 he married his first wife, Kitty, and a year later, their only child, Chester, was born. About that time he and his wife and child moved to Columbus, Ohio, where they stayed until 1907 and then came to Chicago. His wife died in County Hospital of pneumonia, January 8, 1915. Mr. Harris was the son of a colored woman and a wealthy white landowner. A half-brother, born to his mother after her marriage, died suddenly in 1919. Mr. Harris went to fourth grade, when he had to leave school and go to work to support his mother. He took care of her from that time until her death on October 9, 1928. After the death of Mr. Harris' wife, he placed his son and mother in the home of Mrs. Sally Davis. Shortly after, he married Mrs. Davis on December 4, 1916. Mr. Harris has been a decorator for about twenty-five years. During the war, he spent six months in Virginia working as a painter at Norfolk. At present he has irregular employment as a decorator, averaging about $10 per week. Mr. Harris drinks, but at such times he goes to bed and annoys no one. He owns no property and at present owes $55 on his rent. Mr. Harris has three policies with the Connecticut Mutual Life Insurance Company totaling $500, on which he pays 75 cents per week. Mr. and Mrs. Harris belong to the Lexington Methodist Church. Mr. Harris wants to take Chester, Jr., and rear him as his own, just as he did the child's father, Chester. He is willing to accept the two girls, if he can receive a little aid. He is very bitter toward the children's mother because of her conduct and her treatment of her children.

Statement written by Mr. Harris concerning the mother's conduct:

On July 1, 1930, Jennie Harris brought Chester Harris, Jr. here to live. She had broke up housekeeping. She storaged her furniture at 18th and Wallace. Edith and Mabel, the two girls, stayed with Mrs. Owens where the furniture was. She worked out in service about 3 weeks at which time she came back to Mrs. Owens. She got drunk and cursed Mrs. Owens out. Mrs. Owens beat her up and put her out doors. Jennie then brings the oldest girl over here to stay. In August, Jennie said that she would have to bring the other child over here. To this I, A. Harris, objected because I did not see a way to care for all of them, but Jennie said that she would find a place for all of them very soon. The 3 children and her stayed here all through August without a penny and after I raised cain she went back to the Welfare Agency for help. The Welfare Agency then started to giving her a $3.00 a week order for groceries, but this order only lasted about 2 days out of each week because they ate so much. My gas bill ranged from $2.50 to $5.00 every month and the electric bill doubled also. In September, the rent commenced to fall behind because instead of paying my rent I had to help feed the children. At this point my wife went to the Welfare Agency and told them that something would have to be done, because almost every night Jennie would come home drunk and start raising a rough house. The Welfare Agency consented to pay $20 of the rent every month and allowed $6 a week for groceries. In November they fell back to $4 a week. The Welfare Agency in the meantime was trying to get Jennie her pension, but they did not know of her drunkenness. After she saw that she was going to get the pension, she told us that we had been so good to her that the first check would be ours except for the kids some clothes. On the 2nd of January the check came and Jennie had it cashed. She bought the boy a pair of boots, 2 suits of underclothes, 2 pairs of stockings, and a pair of gloves. She got the girls 2 pairs of stockings, 2 suits of underclothes, a pair of gloves and a pair of overshoes apiece. The overshoes were left some other place until January 20. That same Saturday evening she went out and came back Sunday morning drunk and mad. She slept till noon, got up, and went out again. Sometime Monday nite she came back. Tuesday she stayed around practically all day, going out in the evening. When she returned Tuesday nite she tried to raise Cain and we had a big argument. Wednesday morning she left here about 9 or 10 o'clock, and the next we hear of her she was in the County Hospital. This brings us up until the present and now do you think that there has been any mistreating on my part. She has not cooked her kids as much as 3 meals since July 1 because she hasn't been sober long enough. The captain of my precinct can verify my words because he is a constant visitor at my house and he has seen her condition. This, however, is not the only witness, there are plenty more if you need them. I could have had the kids taken away sometime ago, but by them being my son's kids I thought that I would try to be as good to them as possible. When she leaves here, you will do well to keep an eye on her, because she is going to live with one of her men, and he will get the benefit of her pension instead of her kids.

Sally Harris, paternal step-grandmother, was born November 12, 1883, in Hopewell, Virginia. Her father died when she was a baby. At the time of his death he was buying some property in Hopewell, but as her mother did not know how to manage it, they soon lost it. They then moved to Covington, Kentucky, when Mrs. Harris was about six years old. There, she went to the third grade only, as she worked in wealthy families in order to obtain her food and clothing. The family consisted of three girls and one boy, all of whom are dead, except the brother, Jack Gaines, 618 Cleveland Avenue. The entire family moved to Chicago in 1895. On June 7, 1907, she married Donald Davis in Lexington, where her mother was then living. She divorced him three years later on the grounds of non-support and infidelity. She met Mr. Harris at the time he placed his mother and his son in her home at the rate of $10 per week. Chester was then eleven years old. She and the boy grew very attached to each other and she took his mother's place in his life. Mr. Harris and Mrs. Davis were married on December 4, 1916. At present, Mrs. Harris is unemployed. During her first marriage, she occasionally did work by the day. Since her second marriage, she has frequently cooked by the week and for three or four years she worked for the Midwest Utilities Company. Mrs. Harris is anxious to bring up Chester, Jr., as her own and is also willing to do all they they can to remove the children from the harmful influence of their mother. Mrs. Harris is an intelligent, sympathetic woman who has greatly impressed the Family Welfare Agency and the Juvenile Court. She is insured in the Connecticut Mutual Life Insurance Company for $600; weekly premiums total 50 cents.

The Harris home is a seven-room flat on the second floor of a rather poorly kept two-flat frame building. The home is poorly furnished but is clean and neat. The two girls will occupy one bedroom while Chester will have a room by himself. Mrs. Harris' niece and her husband, Wanda and David Washington, ages twenty and twenty-four, occupy one bedroom. Mr. Washington is a chauffeur and at present earns $15 to $20 per week. They pay $7.00 per week room rent.

The Municipal Tuberculosis Sanitarium Station registered December 30, 1930, when they examined mother and the three children. Negative sputums and no evidence of tuberculosis were found. The mother was placed under observation for a slight heart condition.

The County Board of Public Welfare was registered April 7, 1927. The County Agent gave monthly relief to mother and father at the request of the Family Welfare Agency. No case work was done.

The Family Welfare Agency registered October 7, 1930, and gave monthly relief after the death of father totaling $200. They placed her on the Mothers' Pension List of the Juvenile Court.

Plan.—Case Committee recommended placement in the home of the grandparents.

April 22, 1931.—Mabel and Edith Harris committed to the Children's Agency with an order on the county, $25 per month, each.

Chester Harris placed on probation by the Juvenile Court in the home of his grandparents, Albert and Sally Harris, 2032 Howe Street.

Later.—Mabel and Edith Harris placed in the home of their grandparents, Albert and Sally Harris, 2032 Howe Street; rate of board, $25 per month, each.

October 22, 1931.—The following letter was received by the Children's Agency from the Chief Probation Officer of the Juvenile Court:

The Harris children were before the Juvenile Court on April 22, 1931. Edith and Mabel were placed under the Children's Agency, and Chester was placed under the supervision of Mrs. Barnard, probation officer, to live with the grandparents.

Special arrangements were made by the Children's Agency with Judge Martin to leave the younger children with the grandmother, and we think it is useless for two agencies to visit in the home at the same time. I am therefore relieving Mrs. Barnard of the supervision of Chester and will ask you to give me a report on the case every three months.

October 31, 1931.—Case transferred to M. L. Burnett, visitor, Children's Agency.

November 4, 1931.—Mrs. Harris, grandmother, shows a genuine interest in the children and is intelligent in her method of handling them. She and Mr. Harris are both very bitter toward the children's mother. Mrs. Harris will not allow her in the house except for a short call when the children are home. But Mrs. Harris disapproves and tries to stop Mr. Harris from always trying to draw the children out to talk about the quarrels and discord that had existed between their father and mother. Mrs. Harris would like to have assistance in paying for the children's shoes and coats this winter, as Mr. Harris has had irregular work since August. Rent has been reduced to $35 per month.

November 11, 1931.—Mrs. Harris, in office, stated that she is in need of financial assistance and asked if she should go to the Family Welfare Agency or the Emergency Relief Station for temporary help.[1] She was advised to apply for assistance.

November 12, 1931.—Visitor went to deliver Mrs. Harris' check at home. She was out, but Mr. Harris was home with a young man who formerly worked for him. Mr. Harris had been drinking but was courteous and straightforward in his manner. He complained of being nervously upset because of the lack of work; his right eye twitches frequently. He says that he occasionally takes a drink and that he reported this to Judge Martin, but he does not get drunk. He was encouraged that he and Mrs. Harris were doing the right thing in applying for help because they must keep the children well and strong and he was reminded that he was

[1] [The Emergency Relief Station was a public agency set up in September, 1931, to furnish relief to needy families whose breadwinners were unemployed. See case of Paul and Molly Gray, p. 35 n.]

Chester, Jr.'s, ideal of a man and his conduct must be such that the boy could copy.

November 17, 1931.—Mrs. Harris in the office stated that she had been to the County Board of Public Welfare, where she was told it would be over a week before she could get help; then to Family Welfare Agency, where she was referred to the Emergency Relief Station at 2750 Lincoln Street. No relief was given at the last place, as Mr. Harris was recognized by Mrs. Draper, one of the workers. Mr. Harris had done some painting for Mrs. Draper, and the day he came to be paid, Mrs. Draper had noticed liquor on his breath and he had argued with her about his condition. (Mrs. Draper's address is 8234 Douglas Avenue.)

Mrs. Harris' budget was discussed:

BUDGET

Income—$50 from the boarding fund, $16 from Mr. Harris' work (October). So far during November, Mr. Harris has earned only $5.00. He has a promise of work after Thanksgiving.

Expenditure.—Food budget is about $42. Electricity bill averages $1.90. Gas bill is over $3.00 but will be less as a leak was found.

Mr. Harris' work will probably be sufficient to cover some payment on the rent each month, and the landlady will allow the balance to be paid in the spring.

Clothing was promised by the Children's Agency: leatherette jacket, shoes, flannel sleeping suits.

Coal is a big expense as the flat is heated entirely by stoves in the kitchen and in the living-room. Mrs. Harris was advised that the County Board of Public Welfare would be asked to furnish this.

November 24, 1931.—Letter written by Children's Agency to the County Board of Public Welfare, requesting temporary relief for the Harris family:

We should like to ask you to supply coal temporarily to Mr. and Mrs. Harris, 2032 Howe St., who are caring for their three grandchildren, Chester, Mabel, and Edith Harris. Mr. Harris has had only occasional odd jobs since August of this year. During October he earned $16. To date during November he has earned $5.00. The one regular source of income is $50 per month paid by the County boarding fund for the two girls. Chester is placed by Juvenile Court order; the grandparents have accepted responsibility for his care.

The family budget is:

	Per Month
Rent	$35
Food	41
Gas and electricity	4

This excludes clothing of which we are now supplying a part, incidental expenses, and coal.

However, we believe that if it can be arranged for the coal to be supplied to the family, they will be able to manage, by making part payments on the rent, until Mr. Harris' work picks up in the spring.

We realize that ordinarily the County would hesitate to help a family in these circumstances, but believe that this case is worthy of your consideration. If this relief cannot be put in the home, it will be necessary for the two girls to be removed, thus cutting off the only definite source of income, and leaving three people with only Mr. Harris' occasional earnings.

May we hear from you soon?

Mrs. Harris was notified to call at the County Board of Public Welfare, November 30, but after she had waited a whole day, she was sent home because the person who interviewed her could not find the letter referring her. Mrs. Harris returned December 1 with a copy of the letter and was sent back to the Children's Agency with a form face sheet to be filled out. December 3, 1931, after waiting all day, she was given an order for coal and groceries and told to return in a month.

December 2, 1931.—Mr. Harris asked if he could do any painting for the Children's Agency and get part of his rent paid as wages. The rent collector left a five-day eviction notice on December 1, 1931. He is nervous, hypersensitive, and somewhat irritable because of his lack of work and loss of self-esteem. But he assured visitor he had not had a drink for a month.

Mrs. Harris is quite protective and diplomatic in her attitude toward him. She goes with him to the County Board of Public Welfare as she is afraid he will lose his temper because of the long wait. She tries to keep him occupied and away from drink.

January 5, 1932.—Mrs. Harris stated that the mother of the children called Christmas Day for the first time in nearly three months. She brought a lumber-jacket for Junior and a doll for each of the girls. She could not stay, as she was very drunk. She is now living at 2513 Clifton Avenue, basement apartment. The children always look sad and cowed when she comes.

February 9, 1932.—Mrs. Harris stated she returned to the County Board of Public Welfare early in January and her coal and grocery orders were continued for that month. She returned again the first week in February but was advised that the County would give no further relief.

February 10, 1932.—Called worker at the County Board of Public Welfare to inquire about present conditions in the family.

Later.—Letter written by the Children's Agency to the County Board of Public Welfare:

This will confirm my telephone request of this morning, that your Bureau continue relief to Mr. and Mrs. Harris, 2032 Howe Street.

We first wrote you about this family November 24, 1931. During December and January we understand that your department supplied coal and rations. The family's financial circumstances are the same as at the time we first wrote you in November. We are enclosing a copy of that letter for your convenience.

In December Mr. Harris' landlord threatened eviction.

Whatever money Mr. Harris has earned since that time he has applied on the rent. During January he earned $13. He has had no work in February. We require that the children receive a nourishing diet. Mrs. Harris used the $50 board for food, gas and electricity, cleaning, and household supplies.

We trust that you will be able to continue your relief. We will notify you promptly of any change in the circumstances.

February 11, 1932.—Mr. Lindal, County Board of Public Welfare, telephoned that the County had given only temporary relief as requested but now would have to refer the case to the Joint Emergency Relief or Family Welfare Agency, where family was formerly registered.

February 17, 1932.—Cleared case of Albert and Sally Harris with Social Service Exchange. Found the following agencies registered:

Family Welfare Agency . . . . July 12, 1931
Emergency Relief . . . . October 14, 1931
County Board of Public Welfare . . . . December 24, 1931

RECORDS OF CO-OPERATING AGENCIES

FAMILY WELFARE AGENCY

January 5, 1931.—Albert Harris applied to the Family Welfare Agency for food as the Mothers' Pension was not enough to care for the children. The mother, Jennie Harris, had gone on a drinking spree and was in County Hospital. The Family Welfare Agency reported to Mothers' Pension Department of Juvenile Court that Mrs. Harris had been drinking.

EMERGENCY RELIEF

October 15, 1931.—Mr. Harris applied for work; said he was a decorator and that the Court had awarded him his grandchildren and paid him $12 a week. His work references had replied as follows:

Mr. Dawson, Tanner's Bookstore, 5816 South Seneca Street, stated that Mr. Harris had worked there as an interior and exterior decorator. Mr. Dawson found Mr. Harris perfectly honest and his work satisfactory.

Mr. Robert Thorpe, 1418 Pennsylvania Avenue, had known Mr. Harris for sixteen years. He has never given him any fine work to do but has found his work satisfactory.

October 20, 1931.—Referred Mr. Harris to Mrs. B. Draper, 8234 Douglas Avenue, for cleaning wall paper, etc.

October 28, 1931.—Mrs. Draper reported having given Mr. Harris work for one week. She paid him $22. Several mornings Mr. Harris came to work smelling of liquor. When he came for his money, he was quite liquored.

November 16, 1931.—Mr. Harris in office, asking for aid until the family gets caught up. Mr. and Mrs. Harris paid $200 back rent during the summer of 1931. Mr. Harris always brings his earnings home, and Mrs. Harris cannot complain of his spending his earnings on liquor. Mrs. Harris works every other week in Dr. Bryson's home, earning $2.75.

December 31, 1931.—Case closed.

February 18, 1932.—Miss Leonard and Miss Riner, Supervisors, Joint Emergency Relief, stated that Emergency Relief could not accept the case, as, according to the budget outlined, the family is living above the minimum standards they are considering. The rent is too high. Joint Emergency Relief cannot refer the case to the County for special relief unless they themselves are giving relief. They advise that the family let the rent go until Mr. Harris has work and live on the income from the children's board.[2]

BUDGET

Expense		Income	
Rent	$32.50	Board	$50.00
Food	41.00	Earnings (av.)	12.00
Gas and light	4.00		
Coal	7.50		
	$85.00		

It was explained that the family needing relief consists only of Mr. and Mrs. Harris and Chester, that the other two children are paid for by the County, and only about $15 of the $50 could be counted as income for the other three for whom aid is requested. In spite of this, Joint Emergency Relief refused to give relief.

February 24, 1932.—Mrs. Harris stated that a cousin of Mr. Harris' came from Gary last Friday and asked to stay because of a misunderstanding with his wife. He has the upstairs bedroom. He paid $3.00 when he arrived and will pay $2.50 this week for the room. The rent, which was

[2] [If the budget of the client is within 10 per cent of the budget allowed by the Relief Agency, the client cannot be accepted for relief.]

reduced to $32.50 late last fall, is two months in arrears. Mr. Harris needs clothes, and they need house furnishings.

Mr. Harris is more worried about his rent than anything else. He has not been able to realize that because of hard times he can let the rent get behind, although it has been pointed out to him that he has lived in the same place five years, and that he was further in arrears last winter and caught up, and that the landlord will trust him.

Mrs. Harris has not worked for Dr. and Mrs. Bryson since early in January, when they went south. Mrs. Bryson gave her clothes, which she had made over for the children.

Mr. Harris expects to have work sometime during the next week.

March 2, 1932.—Mr. Harris began work February 29, 1932. He will be paid $45 for the job but has already spent $5.00 of his own money for supplies, which will make his net earnings $40.

Rent has been paid as follows (rent receipts shown; paid to first of October, 1931):

10–6–31	$20.00	12–22–31	$20.00
10–22–31	12.50	1–7–32	12.50
11–12–31	20.00	2–10–32	17.00
12–4–31	12.50	2–25–32	6.00

He still owes the rent for January, February, and March (due 3-1-32). The landlord is Gilbert Lengel and Company, Real Estate. The collector is Mr. Hamilton, 516 East Thirty-seventh Street. Miss Reeves, 116 North Rock Island Avenue, owns the property and has been considerate, so they feel somewhat indebted to her.

Mrs. Harris asked that the visitor secure information about her insurance from the County Board of Public Welfare worker who called in December (and asked Mrs. Harris "hundreds of questions about her family affairs"—"why she had the children," etc.) This worker offered to exchange Mr. and Mrs. Harris' insurance policies so that they could have "rent money." Mr. Harris agreed as he was worried about the rent, but Mrs. Harris thinks they need the insurance. They have heard nothing further from the County Board of Public Welfare. When Mr. Harris went back in February, Mr. Lindal asked him if he was still interested in the insurance plan.

When discussing her food budget, Mrs. Harris stated that she has been spending about $7.00 or $8.00 per week. She gets cheap meats and mostly root vegetables, milk only every other day. The children have a glass of milk on their cereal every day. After discussing the diet, Mrs. Harris promised to allow more money for food, to buy at least one quart of milk per day, and not to use more than $10 of the boarding money on the payment of rent and back bills. Now that Mr. Harris knows that he will have $40 to apply on the rent, he will be less perturbed.

March 5, 1932.—County Board of Public Welfare, Mrs. Gallaher, case worker, explained the services of the Insurance Adjustment Bureau of New York.[3] The family is to receive cheaper policies and $40 in cash.

March 11, 1932.—Mrs. Harris took the insurance policies to be turned in. They should have $40 within ten days.

March 31, 1932.—Mr. Harris had been ill for two weeks with pneumonia but was out looking for work when the visitor called. He came in later; he had a very bad cough and asthma. He looks dreadful and was in low spirits. "If I had died everyone would say, 'He died of drink.' Well, I haven't had a drink in six weeks." He is worried about tuberculosis.

April 4, 1932.—Called on the County Board of Public Welfare; they cannot take the case as it is one of unemployment.[4]

Later.—Joint Emergency Relief consented to give relief.

April 5, 1932.—Letter to Joint Emergency Relief:

This will confirm our conversation of yesterday (April 4, 1932) in regard to Mr. and Mrs. Harris, who are in need of temporary relief due to Mr. Harris' unemployment.

The family consists of Mr. and Mrs. Harris and their three grandchildren: Chester, 10 yrs.; Mabel, 9 yrs.; and Edith, 7 yrs. Mr. Harris cares for Chester by Juvenile Court order. Mabel and Edith may be considered apart from the family, as far as the financial problem is concerned, for they are wards of the Children's Agency and are boarded with the Harris's at the rate of $25 per month for each. As our usual rate of board is $20 per month, the extra $5.00 for each may be considered as income for Mrs. Harris.

The $10 per month from the children's board has been the only regular income for the family during the winter. We understand that Mr. Harris earned $15 during December, $13 during January, nothing during February, and $10 during March.

---

[3] [The social worker many times must help make decisions regarding the expenditure for life insurance made by dependent families. In 1929 a Committee on Insurance was organized by the Family Section of the National Conference of Social Work. The John Hancock Mutual, Metropolitan, and Prudential life insurance companies agreed to organize a bureau to aid in adjusting, for dependent families, the life insurance in force in these companies. See *Life Insurance: A Handbook for Social Workers*, prepared in 1931 by John Hancock Mutual Life Insurance Company, Metropolitan Life Insurance Company, and the Prudential Insurance Company of America.]

[4] [At this time all families whose problem seemed primarily unemployment were carried by the Joint Emergency Relief.]

Coal and rations were supplied by the County Board of Public Welfare during December and January but were discontinued as the case was one of pure unemployment. Early in March, Mrs. Gallaher, the case worker at the County Board of Public Welfare, arranged for the Harris's to transfer their insurance policies for smaller ones, and to receive $40 cash from the Insurance Adjustment Bureau. There has been a delay in this transaction, and we do not know when the money will be available, but will notify you at once.

According to our computation with Mrs. Harris and following the Standard budget of March 1, 1931, the expenses for the family are as follows:

General Household Expenses		Personal Expenses	
Rent (as paid)	$32.50	Food	$42.42
Gas and electricity	3.00	Insurance	4.98
Coal	3.90	Miscellaneous (for children)	7.50
Household supplies	4.50		
	$43.90		$54.90

Total budget... $98.80

Deduction of all expenses of the two girls as follows:

Two-fifths of general household expenses	$17.56	
Food	15.85	
Clothes, school supplies, miscellaneous	6.50	$39.91
Amount over normal amount of board (as stated above)	10.00	$49.91
Total budget to be met by family's own resources		48.89
Average earnings of Mr. Harris for the past four months		17.00
Deficit		$31.89

This budget does not include clothing for Mr. and Mrs. Harris and Chester nor does it include carfare for Mr. Harris to be used in looking for work. We have supplied some clothing for the children during the winter, but will have to insist that this come from the board henceforth, as our funds are very low.

Mr. Harris has paid his rent through the middle of February, to the Gilbert Lengel & Co. Real Estate, 516 East 37th Street (rent receipts shown to us).

As the homes in which the Children's Agency may board children must be of a certain minimum standard laid down by the State Department of Public Welfare, this family, as well as our other families, must not be dependent upon the income from the children's board. For the two girls our organization is contributing to this family, $10 in cash (the difference between the normal rate of board, and the rate paid in this case), and $17.56 toward the household expenses (⅖ of the total household expenses), making a total benefit to the family of $27.50. Therefore, it would seem to be economically, as well as socially, advisable for these children to remain in this family.

We appreciate your interest in the case and will be glad to co-operate with you on the case work.

April 22, 1931.—Chester Harris, a light-colored Negro child, born September 2, 1921, was placed in the home of his paternal grandparents, Albert and Sally Harris, 2032 Howe Street, on probation to the Juvenile Court.

July 1, 1931.—Chester is very much attached to his grandparents, and they to him, and his adjustment in their home is highly satisfactory.

Appearance.—Chester is a slender, delicate boy who dresses neatly and is careful about his personal appearance.

Personality.—He is nervous and impatient; he jumps if only slightly frightened. When he wants something, he wants it immediately and, if unable to obtain it, becomes quite upset. He has quite a temper though he gets over it quickly. He was described by his 3A teacher as a delicate, high-strung boy. He cries easily when his will is thwarted. He seldom offers an apology for anything, and does not mean it if he does. He is a likable, appealing boy.

Behavior.—Chester is quite mischievous at times and teases his sisters and the girls in his room at school. He takes their pencils, whispers, and can make himself a general nuisance in school. However, he has no grave behavior problems. He never takes part in children's fights or arguments.

Control.—Chester's grandmother controls him easily by reasoning with him. He is used to her as he lived in his grandparents' home with his parents before his father's death.

Home Duties.—He is quite active in doing his share of household tasks. He mops the floors, empties the trash.

Recreation.—Chester plays with his sisters and the neighborhood children. He likes such games as baseball, football, and other boys' games. His grandmother takes him and the girls to Jefferson Park almost daily.

Health.—He hates to go to bed, but falls asleep immediately upon retiring. He arises as soon as he awakens. His appetite is rather poor and he is "choosy" about his food. He dislikes to eat.

September 22, 1931.—Chester was quite enthusiastic when informed that the visitor was going to take him and his sisters to Ringling Brothers' Circus on August 14, 1931, and jumped up and down in his excitement. The children greatly enjoyed the circus.

He is glad to be back in school. His nervousness is decreasing, and his general condition improving since he has been attending Harper Clinic.

January 6, 1932.—Chester and his sisters call Mr. and Mrs. Harris "granddaddy" and "Sally." All the children, as well as Mr. Harris, have respect for Mrs. Harris' quiet authority.

When Mrs. Harris is not in hearing distance, Mr. Harris often tries to get the children to talk about their mother and to describe brutal or disagreeable scenes between their parents. Mrs. Harris (grandmother) does not allow the children to talk about these things or against their mother. When Junior (Chester) asks Mrs. Harris why she doesn't talk about his mother and she says, "I haven't anything to say about her," Junior says, "Grandpa has got plenty to say about her."

Mrs. Harris does not try to prevent the children from talking freely about whatever is on their minds but does not encourage them to think about their earlier life and tries to give them full, happy lives so that their minds will be occupied.

Contact with own mother.—Jennie Harris has called only three times in the last three and a half months. One time she came with a young man with whom she was apparently living at the time. She brought a small automobile for the children. The second time she came in October. She was drunk at the time, and Mrs. Harris would not let her see the children. The children are not allowed to let anyone in the house, even their mother, when Mrs. Harris is not there. The mother came again at Christmas time and brought them gifts. When Jennie Harris is there, grandmother remains with them to see that the conversation does not harm the children.

All the children look a little cowed in the presence of their mother. Junior has no use for her. When she comes, he allows her to kiss him and then walks out of the room.

Personality.—Junior seems shy and quiet. He is less nervous and "jumpy," but still impatient. He does not cry so easily. He is popular with other children.

Behavior.—All the children are slow and forgetful about what they are told to do. Although Junior is willing to help, he has to be told many times before he carries out any instructions.

Control training.—Mrs. Harris shows great patience in training the children. She tells them over and over again how to do things and what to do. She explains their shortcomings and poor conduct to them. She does not believe in whipping children but is firm in her manner.

Daily regime.—The children arise a little before seven. After breakfast they wash dishes, put their rooms in order, and have a little extra time before going to school. They come home for dinner at noon.

In the afternoon they play until an early supper.

After supper Mrs. Harris often has a school for the children and helps them all read or spell. Bedtime is at nine. Mrs. Harris has followed advice and is gradually trying to get them to bed a little earlier each night until she can get an extra hour of sleep for them.

Recreation.—The children always have sufficient toys given to Mrs. Harris by people for whom she has worked. Junior has had a rocking horse, tricycle, sled, games, and an expensive electric train. Most of these things were lost when the mother's home was broken up. Junior now has a sled and victrola and some games. He likes to play cards and other games with the girls. They all enjoy the radio—the "Uncle Bob" stories particularly—and they enjoy reading the funny papers. They go to the show every week or two on Sundays. Junior plays mostly with the girls and as a family, as Mrs. Harris wants to supervise them.

Mrs. Harris gives Junior ten or fifteen cents spending money each week. She starts out with a nickel and then gives him extra pennies for helpfulness or good behavior. Junior runs errands for people in the neighborhood and earns nickels or dimes. The drug-store man has Junior dust for him sometimes. He always brings back this money to Mrs. Harris. He saved his money in a baking-powder can to buy Christmas presents.

Home duties.—He wipes up the floor and stairs, puts wood on the fires, empties ashes, and picks up papers in the yard.

School.—Junior is in the 3A grade at the Dunbar School. His scholarship is fair and good. His citizenship is good and effort very good. He is "very quiet, used to giving in to other children. He does not take any active part in schoolroom games."

May 17, 1932.—Mrs. Harris seems to be very intelligent and understanding in the handling of the children. She realizes that they were neglected and abused. She likes to think of them responding to affection and encouragement like plants to sunshine. She is especially fond of Junior, although she shows no difference in her attitude toward the children. She feels that she has his entire confidence. He comes to her with hundreds of questions, tells her all he does, and all his small doubts and worries. Mrs. Harris always takes time to answer Junior's questions, although sometimes she is a "little taken aback." She takes time to explain to Junior why she wants him to do a particular thing.

Mr. Harris is very fond of the children and, when he is in a good mood, plays and laughs heartily with them. On the few occasions when he has too much to drink, he goes directly to his room and stays until he has slept it off. Mr. Harris jokes with Junior sometimes and is likely to turn Junior's serious questions aside with a light answer (probably owing to his embarrassment at the searching questions the boy asks). When Junior comes to Mrs. Harris, worried about what he understood his grandfather to say, Mrs. Harris explains that Mr. Harris was joking. In some ways this has lessened Junior's respect for Mr. Harris. Junior tries to joke with Mr. Harris and does not take him seriously. When Mr. Harris tells him something, Junior is likely to answer, "Yes, that's what *you* say" or "I don't care nothing about that." He also laughs and makes remarks when Mr. Harris pronounces a word incorrectly.

Junior teases Mabel and Edith but not so much as he used to do. He is proud of them and takes their part when playing with other children. He takes Edith's part and brings her candy or nuts. He assumes responsibility for both girls. He is ashamed when Mabel wets her clothes.

During February and March Mrs. Harris was discouraged about financial difficulties and trying to make ends meet. She did not have so much energy for the children, and they probably felt some insecurity, but she has been much more encouraged and energetic for the last month.

Attitude toward own parents.—Junior's attitude toward his mother is the same as when last reported. Mr. and Mrs. Harris are proud of Junior and believe that he is brighter and shows more promise than his father. As advised, Mrs. Harris has been careful not to express this to Junior. He says of his father what Mrs. Harris tells him, that "the only mistake Daddy made was that he married a little too early."

Personality.—Junior is serious and conscientious. His quick temper is under better control. He seldom becomes angry at home. When he is playing with other children and they fight, he goes off, leans against the fence, and listens to them, but seldom joins in disputes. Sometimes he laughs so hard that he can't control himself. When Junior wants something he "wheedles and teases," or whines his request: "Sally, please I want to go to the park," looking very abject and as if he would cry if refused. Junior is well liked and popular among the boys in the neighborhood. He does not like to play with girls (except his sisters). During April his old nervous habits reappeared: tenseness, impatience, and flashing his eyes nervously. Mrs. Harris believes that he can overcome these again and that he will be better as soon as school is out. He resists going to bed as long as he can, makes up excuses, and wants to play or read, but the minute he hits the pillow he drops off to sleep. Mrs. Harris sends him to bed early.

Junior observes everything and asks hundreds of questions. This spring he has been interested in growing plants and wants to know how the different ones grow. He asks about the things he reads in the papers. He asks about the behavior of different people and why they do things or why they should do something else. He asks about his own development. He asks many questions about sex and marriage. From his experience at home with his mother he has become repulsed by the relations between men and women. "Sally, why do men and women be together like that? Do they always do that?" Junior's room is not very tidy. Mrs. Harris is not an immaculate housekeeper—her house is clean but frequently untidy.

Behavior.—Junior is obedient and does not misbehave. He sometimes gets into mischief—i.e., one day he shaved all the soap in order to blow soap bubbles. He is prompt and dependable in his habits.

Control.—Mrs. Harris is patient but firm in her control. When Junior teases for anything, she tells him that she will not listen to his requests. When he then asks for something, she explains the reasons for refusing his request. When his whining has been persistent, Mrs. Harris has threatened to whip his mouth. Mrs. Harris' usual punishments consist of depriving the children of something they want, keeping them from going out to play, or sending them to their rooms. The severest punishment is putting Junior in the closet. The thing that makes him most unhappy is being kept in from play.

Mr. Harris believes in being severe with the children and in whipping them. Mrs. Harris has tried to make him see that this is the punishment their mother gave them and that it was this which made them so cowed and nervous.

Recreation.—Beginning with spring weather Junior has been playing out of doors a great deal. He is an expert marble player; he describes with great earnestness the various ways to spin or roll marbles and has a large collection. He likes to roller-skate and play ball. His favorite sport is running his wagon, a fine "flyer," which he won early in May from saving grocery receipts.

Junior's room is decorated with pictures cut from magazines. He has movie stars, automobiles, landscapes, and many airplanes. His ambition is to be an aviator some day. He has his small victrola in his room, and his dresser is cluttered with trinkets. He has a tiny kitten of which he is extremely fond; he takes all the care of it and fondles it. He wants a puppy to grow up with the kitten.

During the spring Junior has been very much interested in growing plants. On two occasions he came home with flowers, a few tulips and a few lilies-of-the-valley, which he said he found on the street. (It is probable that he picked them from someone's garden.) With Mr. Harris' help he started several flower boxes on the back porch. In these he planted beans and a few other vegetables and has been interested in watering them and watching them grow.

During the spring Junior has been passing bills for a movie theater about once a week. He gets a pass to the show each time he distributes bills.

He with the girls was taken on an outing to the Aquarium during spring vacation. He was very much interested and enjoyed the whole trip.

Companions.—Mrs. Harris has restricted the amount of play her children have with other children in the neighborhood. She wants the children to play where she can observe them. Some of the children have told Mabel that her grandmother is too strict and thinks the Harris children are better than the others. Junior has a little more liberty than the girls. However, he is not allowed to go to Jefferson Park without either Mrs. Harris or a parent of another child in the group.

School.—Chester was promoted to the 4B grade. He is graded Fair in English and reading, Good in everything else.

Health.—Chester was seen in Pediatrics Clinic, March 30, 1932. He weighed seventy pounds. Nutrition and development good. Lungs and heart normal. Condition satisfactory. Was told to return in four months. He was not very clean about his person. Hands, ears, and feet very dirty.

Wassermann and Kahn tests done July 20, 1931, were negative.

Junior's eyes become tired when he reads. Moving-picture shows make his eyes so tired and red that he puts his hands on them to rest them.

MABEL

April 22, 1931.—Mabel Harris, a fair Negro child, born February 8, 1923, was committed to the Children's Agency with an order on the County for $25 per month.

Later.—Mabel was placed in the home of her paternal grandparents, Albert and Sally Harris, 2032 Howe Street. Rate of board $25 per month.

June 4, 1931.—Mabel is placed in the home of her paternal grandparents, who are very fond of her. The grandparents have little contact with the mother, as they do not approve of her conduct and drinking habit.

Appearance.—Mabel is nice-looking, plump and fair. She is careless in her personal appearance, but now that she is receiving training, she is improving in that respect.

Personality.—Mabel has a sweet disposition and obeys her grandmother readily. She talks but little and plays quietly with her sister and brother. She is an unresponsive child and has a serious, polite manner.

Behavior.—Mabel presents no behavior difficulties. She is quiet and obedient, and in school her conduct is described as "perfect."

Control and supervision.—Grandmother reasons with Mabel on the few occasions when she misbehaves.

Home duties.—She and her sister, Edith, make their own bed, clean their room and dust, and can wash dishes.

Recreation.—Mabel plays in the back yard with Edith and her brother, Chester. She stands apart from the children in their rougher games. She loves to roller-skate, though before the Children's Agency provided a pair of skates she and Edith owned only one skate.

Health.—A physical examination on October 30, 1930, at Barnard Clinics showed that Mabel is in normal health. An examination on December 2, 1930, at Municipal Tuberculosis Sanitarium Dispensary found her to be free from tuberculosis. She eats everything and sleeps fairly well. She has nocturnal and occasional diurnal enuresis, but this has improved slightly since the grandmother refuses to let her drink liquids after four o'clock in the afternoon.

School.—Mabel is in the 2B at Burke School. She attends regularly. Her scholarship is fair and her deportment excellent.

July 28, 1931.—Report from Harper Clinic on the initial examination of July 1, 1931, states that Mabel is in normal health. Wassermann and Kahn tests were negative for lues. Treatment for enuresis was given. Her nocturnal enuresis has cleared up considerably, and the diurnal enuresis has ceased.

Mabel is becoming fond of rough, tomboyish games and often plays with the neighborhood boys. She and the other children go to the park almost daily with the grandmother.

September 22, 1931.—Mabel is very glad to be back in school. She is becoming more careful of her personal appearance. She proudly showed the visitor dishes given her by one of her grandmother's friends. She divided them and gave half to Edith. She greatly enjoyed the Ringling Brothers' Circus on August 15, 1931.

October 16, 1931.—Mabel is slow and forgetful or careless. Grandmother has to ask her two or three times to do each little task. She does not like to go to bed, but she is not disobedient and rarely misbehaves.

Nocturnal enuresis has not been entirely checked. After ceasing for two or three weeks, enuresis will occur two nights in one week. Mrs. Harris has followed instructions of Harper Clinic and of visitor, taking care that Mabel observes regular hours, does not have any liquids after supper, and is awakened twice each night. Mrs. Harris praises Mabel for improvement and gives her a nickel as a reward for a week of dry nights. For the last month she has switched Mabel when enuresis occurred, as the doctor says there is no reason why it should persist.

Health.—Mabel sleeps well and has a very hearty appetite. She is still overweight. She has been taken regularly every month to Harper Clinic for treatment for enuresis.

School.—She is in the 2A grade at Dunbar School. Her scholarship is "good," and her effort "very good." She is "obedient, attentive, reliable —very quiet and kind."

Recreation.—The children play among themselves rather than with other children. Mabel and Edith like to play dolls. They all enjoy the radio. Mrs. Harris gives Mabel ten or fifteen cents a week, in small amounts, given as rewards for especially good behavior. She has been saving money for Christmas.

Personality.—Mabel is quiet, shy, and obedient. She is a little jealous of Edith. Neither wants to do any work unless she knows the other has to help, but they don't work well together.

May 17, 1932.—Mrs. Harris is fond of Mabel and tries to encourage the child; she gives her freedom to express herself and always takes time to explain why she wants her to do something or the kind of girl she wants her to be.

Mabel tells Mrs. Harris what the children she plays with do and say, although she does not confide her own thoughts as much as Chester and Edith do.

Chester always stands up for Edith when the children are playing together, and Mabel is not so close to them.

Personality.—Mabel is quiet and looks rather disinterested or unconcerned. Sometimes she has an expression that is almost unhappy or dissatisfied. The school report of March 3, 1932, states that she doesn't appear interested in anything. Mrs. Harris says that she used to smile more last summer. Early in the fall she began occasionally to look "droopy." Mrs. Harris thinks she may not feel well, but she always says she is all right. However, Mabel "giggles" and laughs a good deal—"she squeals and hollers." Mrs. Harris tells her not to act silly, and she is gradually overcoming this habit.

Mabel likes to play. She gets along well with other children. She is careless, forgetful, and slow. When Mrs. Harris asks her to get a glass of water or sewing material, Mabel will come back and say, "What did you ask me to get?" At school she is careless about personal habits and lessons (March 3, 1932). She is inclined to whine when she thinks she will be denied something. She used to "squinch" her eyes sometimes, and Mrs. Harris thought they were weak. She has "outgrown" the squint, but still frowns occasionally when someone is talking to her.

Behavior.—Mabel's slowness, carelessness, and forgetfulness are her worst faults. She leaves papers and toys all over the house. She is careless about her appearance—just washes the "high spots" when she is told how to wash her face carefully. She is supposed to wash her own stockings, but Mrs. Harris has to have her do them several times or do them over herself. Although Mrs. Harris goes over Mabel's lessons with her, Mabel is careless about them when she gets to school and seems to have forgotten them.

When the children and their mother were living with Mrs. Harris on a pension, Mabel was found engaged in mutual masturbation and exhibitionism with neighborhood children. Mrs. Harris did not observe any more of this conduct until this January and February. Then some twelve-year-old girls in the neighborhood gave out a lot of sex information, and the boys and girls hung around in the alley. At this time Mabel wrote some questionable notes to Jimmie, the boy next door. The children have told Mrs. Harris stories about what they have seen their mother do, and Mabel remembers distinctly her mother's conduct with men.

Control—Mrs. Harris talks to Mabel and explains why some things are forbidden and others expected. She is patient but firm about having Mabel take care of her possessions and room. She has not allowed Mabel to play with the neighborhood children whose influence was undesirable. She promises rewards and deprives Mabel of special treats or of going out to play. She whips Mabel whenever enuresis occurs.

Recreation.—Mabel has dolls, crayons, and games. She likes best to play out of doors with other children—strenuously and roughly—for example, a crowd of children pile on a sled or wagon while one pulls them. They fall off and wrestle or tumble. Mrs. Harris has had Mabel give up her rough play because of the advice about the enuresis. After supper Mabel is not allowed to go out. She plays games with Edith and Chester, draws, looks at funny papers, and listens to the radio. Mabel's drawings, made at the Clinic and one at the Office, are filed with the record.

Companions.—Some of the neighborhood children tell Mabel that her grandmother thinks the Harris children better than other children. Mrs. Harris has the children play by themselves because of the bad things Mabel was taught by other children.

Home duties.—Mabel washes the dishes after breakfast and helps Edith make the bed and put their room in order. After school in the afternoon she washes the dinner dishes. She washes her own stockings. She is slow about her work.

Enuresis.—For a while before Christmas, enuresis was much improved because Mrs. Harris told Mabel there would be no Christmas for her if she did not try harder. About two months after Christmas there was no enuresis. Late in February enuresis became more frequent, and there was again occasional diurnal enuresis.

School report, March 3, 1932, states, "She asks to be excused several times a day. When privilege is denied she has to be sent home for dry clothing."

Mrs. Harris visited school and was informed that the teacher had tried to help Mabel by reminding her to take care of herself during recess and not to drink any water, but she often forgets. Sometimes when she asks to be excused she only gets a drink of water.

Mabel was returned to the Pediatrics Clinic, March 16, 1932. The following advice was given for enuresis management:

    No playing after evening meal
    No movies
    No religious excitement
    No highly seasoned foods
    Cut down on celery and watery foods
    All the water she wants until the evening meal

Since there was a possibility that enuresis might be caused by some organic trouble, urinalysis was taken. Results were negative (March 30, 1932).

On March 30, 1932, Mabel was given a prescription for enuresis, and Dr. Moore stated that he would have to use a needle for treatment if she did not stop in the next two weeks. For the next two weeks there was no recurrence of the enuresis. Mabel reported again to Dr. Moore on April 13, 1932. In the period from April 13 to May 4, 1932, enuresis occurred twice. Dr. Moore stated on May 4, 1932, that he would give Mabel one more chance before starting the needle treatment. Enuresis has occurred once since then.

Mrs. Harris had cut down on her use of seasoning about a week before Mabel went to the Clinic on March 16, 1932. After the Clinic visit, she went to school and arranged for Mabel to stop gymnasium work and has stopped her playing so roughly in the neighborhood. Mabel is not allowed to go outdoors to play after supper. Every other time that the children would ordinarily go to a show, Mrs. Harris has taken them all on a special trip to the park so that Mabel will not feel that she is being punished.

It is noticed, however, that Mrs. Harris is constantly talking to Mabel about her enuresis. Mrs. Harris promises Mabel a special reward—something very nice—if she goes without wetting the bed for one month, and Mabel speaks about this almost every morning. Mrs. Harris gets up once or twice in the night with Mabel and of late has met her on her way to the bathroom by herself.

The difficulty at school has greatly improved. However, Mabel is constantly reminded about her weakness.

On the trip to the Aquarium with the visitor on April 28, 1932, Mabel kept asking for the toilet during the whole afternoon. Chester also asked visitor to watch Mabel because she couldn't be allowed to drink any water and should be taken to the toilet.

Health.—On her Clinic visit, March 16, 1932, Mabel weighed 69 pounds—nutrition and development good.

On March 30, 1932, Mabel weighed $70\frac{1}{4}$ pounds; on April 14, 1932, visit made only for enuresis; on May 4, 1932, Mabel weighed 74 pounds.

School.—School report received March 3, 1932, shows that Mabel's work has slumped noticeably. She was graded Poor in arithmetic, reading, spelling, and effort, and Fair in her other subjects. She was careless about personal habits and lessons and showed little interest in anything.

EDITH

April 22, 1931.—Edith Harris, a light-brown Negro child, born July 20, 1924, was committed to the Children's Agency with an order on the County for $25 a month.

Later.—Edith was placed in the home of her paternal grandparents, Albert and Sally Harris, 2032 Howe Street. Rate of board $25 per month.

June 4, 1931.—The paternal grandparents are very fond of Edith.

Adjustment.—Edith is adjusting well in the home as she has frequently lived with her parents in the grandparents' home before being placed there.

Appearance.—Edith is a rather pretty, fragile-looking, brown-skinned child with large, soft brown eyes.

Personality.—Edith has a sweet disposition and obeys her grandmother readily. She talks but little to outsiders and plays quietly with her sister and her brother. She is an unresponsive child and has a serious, pathetic manner.

Health.—A physical examination on October 30, 1930, at Barnard Clinics showed that Edith is in normal health. Toxin-antitoxin was given. Municipal Tuberculosis Sanitarium Dispensary found her to be free from tuberculosis. She eats everything and sleeps well. She has a slight speech defect.

School.—Edith is repeating 1B at Dunbar School. She attends regularly. Her deportment is excellent.

August 4, 1931.—Report from Harper Clinic of initial examination on July 1, 1931, states that Edith is in normal health. Wassermann and Kahn tests were negative for lues. Dr. Moore states that Edith's speech defect is due to the shedding of her teeth. She should talk normally when her new teeth grow in. Grandmother helps Edith to read every night and notes improvement in her pronounciation.

Church.—Edith, with Mabel and Chester, attends Lexington Sunday School regularly, and greatly enjoys going.

Recreation.—Paternal grandmother takes children to Jefferson Park almost daily.

September 22, 1931.—Edith is becoming more lively. She is trying to stop being a baby and cries less frequently.

October 16, 1931.—Edith is quiet and shy, and obedient. She is less sad-looking but almost never smiles. She is a little jealous of Mabel and does not want to do any work unless Mabel also has work.

Control.—Mrs. Harris shows great patience in training the children. She is especially patient in helping Edith to overcome her speech defect. She does not nag or make Edith feel discouraged, but has her repeat words and slows her speech when Edith gets careless.

School.—Edith is repeating 1B grade at Dunbar School, Miss Fairchild, teacher, because of her speech defect. She has improved slowly. December 3 her work was graded Good; citizenship, Good; effort, Very Good. Since school opened in the fall she has been given help by a special speech teacher, Miss Sullivan, in a small group which meets two mornings per week. Miss Fairchild reports that she is obedient, reliable, and independent.

May 17, 1932.—Edith, like Chester, talks freely to Mrs. Harris of all she does and what the other children do and say.

Personality.—She is cheerful at home. She skips, jumps, whistles, and sings. However, she never smiles except when she is playing very hard. She does not beg or tease for anything, but asks directly for what she wants. In spite of Mrs. Harris' punishment, Edith is determined to tell Mrs. Harris whenever Mabel has been disobedient or has not told the truth. Edith does not mix with other children as well as Mabel. Mabel is very friendly, but Edith is more reserved and holds herself aloof at first. Edith seems to have more delicate and refined tastes than Mabel. She is dependable and always does what she has been told to do. Edith's speech has improved, Mrs. Harris believes, but she still needs patient reminders.

Recreation.—Edith is happy playing with Mabel and Junior and does not seek outside companions. She likes to play dolls.

Home duties.—She makes the bed and keeps her room in order. She helps Mabel with the dishes and dusts.

Health.—Edith has attended Harper Clinic periodically. Her condition is satisfactory.

School.—Edith was promoted to 1A grade in February. Her work and effort are good. She is well behaved and obedient, trustworthy and diligent. Special help by a speech teacher has been continued.

SUMMARY OF RECORD TO JUNE 19, 1935

The children continued to live with the grandparents and developed nicely. An excellent relationship existed between the grandmother and the children. The grandfather was difficult at times; when he was out of work he became discouraged and drank, but the grandmother managed him rather well. The Children's Agency placed an eighteen-year-old Agency ward in the home as the grandmother's helper. The children did good work in school, and most of their problems were disappearing.

On June 19, 1935, while on a trip to the store with Mabel the grandmother dropped dead. The children's mother came in and took charge, proving herself to be capable. She asked that she be given the children, but agreed that it would be more advisable to place them in a foster-home until she could better care for them.

4. The Lane Children

(Three Orphan Children Are Placed in a Foster-Home. The Foster-Home Record of the Faville Home Used for the Lane Children Is Given Here)

FAMILY RECORD

Date of application to Children's Home.—February 9, 1931.

Applicant.—Miss Rosner, probation officer, Juvenile Court.

Child.—Mary Lane, born October 25, 1923, Chicago.

Parents.—Clayton Lane, deceased November, 1929; Ann Lane, deceased October, 1929.

Siblings.—Pearl Lane, September 23, 1921; Clayton Lane, February 11, 1925.

Reason for application.—Both parents are dead. There are no relatives able to care for the children. Mary has been examined at Child Guidance Clinic, and they recommended placement in an institution for a period of study.

Present situation.—Mary is in the Children's Refuge, where she has been since October 27, 1930.

Family history.—See reports from other agencies below and interview of February 10, 1931, with Mrs. Williams, maternal grandmother.

February 10, 1931.—Read record at Children's Refuge. Obtained a copy of letter to Child Guidance Clinic prepared by Juvenile Court officer and a report of Mary's adjustment in their institution.

SUMMARY OF CHICAGO CHILDREN'S REFUGE RECORD: LANE

Mary was admitted October 27, 1930, at the request of Miss Rosner of the Juvenile Court. Mary has been in the home of a maternal cousin, a Mrs. Walters, who lives on a farm near Centerville, Illinois. Mary is a full orphan. Mrs. Walters refused to keep Mary longer as she felt she was uncontrollable. Miss Rosner believed that Mrs. Walters did not understand the child and that she was giving her improper supervision, and asked that Mary be admitted for study prior to a mental examination.

Talked with the housemother on October 30, 1930. Mary seems lost in the department. She takes care of herself and pays little attention to the other children. She is a rather helpless little girl who is anxious to learn to do things like other children. She doesn't know how to play with the others but stands and watches them. She is an affectionate child who seems to have received little attention. Mary is unattractive in appearance; her hair is cut short, and she has a dull look in her eyes. She expresses no emotion. She has become angry with the children when they have taken dresses away from her, and it has been necessary for the housemother to interfere in her behalf. She has wet the bed once. Talked with the housemother on November 5, 1930. Mary is becoming accustomed to the group and tries to play a few simple games for short periods. She is a reserved child and seems inclined to be somewhat of an introvert; however, she seems happier in the department.

Mrs. Carter, the girl's housemother at Children's Refuge, reported on February 10, 1931, that Mary was making a fair adjustment. She gets along very well with the other children but is unable to compete with them. This seemingly does not bother her. Mrs. Rowland, Mary's teacher, reported that Mary was making no progress in school. Oftentimes she says, "I don't know," before she tries. She is inclined to be a source of disturbance in the room. Mrs. Rowland has seen her poke the other children, throw her number cards around, and, when approached regarding the matter, she states that she did not do it, although she is fully aware that Mrs. Rowland has seen her. At times her face is a complete blank. Mary is accomplishing nothing in 1B grade.

Later.—Called at 1452 Delaware Avenue and talked with Mrs. Williams, maternal grandmother. She keeps house for her sister, Miss Maggie Nevins, and her son, John Williams. Miss Nevins does day work. John has been out of work for several months but has a position now. Mrs. Williams seemed to take rather an impersonal interest in Mary. She first of all explained at length why it would be impossible for her to care for her. After Mrs. Lane's death, Mr. Lane placed Mary with Mrs. Walters, a relative of Mr. Lane's first wife. Mrs. Williams said that after a trip to Centerville she knew it was no place for a child, but she didn't know what else to do with her. The other two children were cared for by a friend of Mr. Lane's and he boarded there also until his death, which occurred shortly after his wife's death. After Mr. Lane's death, Mrs. Williams took Pearl and Clayton and kept them until last September, when she made arrangements for them to enter the Baptist Child Haven.

Miss Nevins came in before worker left. She is just mildly interested in Mary, but is very much interested in her brother and sister. She wishes it were possible to take them out of the institution and place them in a private home. She would be able to pay $5.00 a week for their care. The children are quite unhappy where they are, and it is very hard for Miss Nevins and the grandmother to go so far to see them. As soon as Miss Nevins mentioned moving the other children, Mrs. Williams spoke up and said she too was dissatisfied but had no way of caring for them. Mrs. Williams impressed worker as a person who would make no especial effort to change an unsatisfactory situation.

Mrs. Williams spoke freely of the family situation.

Mother.—Ann Williams was born in Aitkin, Illinois, February 13, 1898. She had two brothers—John, two years older than she, and Emmett, two years younger. Ann was a very small baby and was always delicate. She had convulsions until she was five years old. When she was grown up she had "peculiar spells" when she couldn't move or speak. Sometimes she was unconscious. Her mouth looked blue and her eyes looked queer. At the age of nine or ten she began to get very stout and pictures of Ann at the age of fifteen and sixteen showed that she weighed at least two hundred pounds.

Ann's father, Rollo Williams, died of apoplexy in 1904, when she was six years old. He drank heavily and was a drug fiend for a good many years. Mrs. Williams said a doctor who had examined Ann when she was a child said she showed very plainly that at least one of her parents was a drug addict. About two years after Mr. Williams' death, Mrs. Williams placed Ann and Emmett in the Odd Fellows Home at La Porte, Illinois; Mrs. Williams said she never had any complaints of her misbehavior while in the institution. After Mrs. Williams took her home, she had a great deal of trouble with Ann. She was a great worry to her. She couldn't keep a job and she would not come home directly after work. It was useless to send her to school because she could not learn. Ann met Mr. Lane when she was doing maid work in a hotel. He was janitor there.

Mr. Lane was between twenty and thirty years older than Ann. He was lame and had a silver plate in his leg. He weighed less than one hundred pounds. He did his best to make a home for the children. He had to take the entire responsibility because Ann was not capable of managing a home. He did all the buying.

Mrs. Williams knows very little about Mr. Lane. She thinks he was born in New York. He was married previous to his marriage to Ann Williams and had one adopted daughter.

Mr. and Mrs. Lane had rather a hard struggle financially. Mr. Lane had no trade and had to accept whatever work he could get. His last position was at the Universal Automobile Company, where he worked as watchman. Mrs. Williams said she worried about conditions in the home a great deal. Ann had the children close together and had several miscarriages.

Mrs. Lane died October 25, 1929, of apoplexy, and her husband died three weeks afterward of heart trouble.

February 13, 1931.—Read record at the Children's Bureau. Summary follows:

Mrs. Mathew Belknap, aunt, came to the office, asking for placement of Pearl and Clayton Lane. She said Mrs. Williams, grandmother who was caring for the children, was finding the burden too great. Mrs. Belknap is employed and her husband is chronically ill, so she could do nothing at all for her niece's children.

Mrs. Williams was in the office June 11, 1930. She said she had reported the case to the Juvenile Court seven months before and asked that the children be placed in an orphanage pending the decision as to their adoption. Mrs. Williams said she was dependent on her son for support. She was advised to return to the court.

A letter was written to the Juvenile Court, June 23, 1930, explaining Children's Bureau contact.

February 16, 1931.—Read record at Juvenile Court:

The case was reported November 19, 1929, by Sergeant Butler because Mrs. Milton, who had been boarding the children, said she could no longer keep them.

November 25, 1929.—Officer called at 450 W. 67th and talked with Mrs. Milton, a widow. She has several roomers. Pearl and Clayton were neatly dressed and seemed well cared for. Mrs. Milton said she had known Mr. and Mrs. Lane for a number of years. At Mrs. Lane's funeral, Mrs. Walters offered to take Clayton, thinking Mrs. Williams would take Pearl. However, she did not offer to do so. Mr. Lane, who was working as night watchman, slept at home during the day and took Pearl with him to the garage where he worked, and she slept there. After this arrangement had gone on for a week, Mrs. Milton agreed to take Pearl also and allow Mr. Lane to room there.

Mrs. Milton said there was bitter feeling between Mrs. Williams and Mr. Lane, who was many years older than his *third* wife.

Since Mrs. Milton asked the police to take the children, Mrs. Williams had been over and said she would take them and place them in an orphanage. However, Mrs. Milton, acting on police instructions, refused to give the children up to her.

December 4, 1929.—Officer had a conference with Mrs. Williams, her son Emmett, and his wife. Mrs. Williams said she had to support herself by housework—cooking, catering, etc. She planned to place the Lane children in the Odd Fellows Home. She thought perhaps the children would be accepted because their mother was raised in the institution.

Emmett Williams said he couldn't take any of the children because he had one of his own.

December 9, 1929.—A letter was received from probation officer, reporting his investigation of the Walters home where Mary was staying. The Walters owned a farm and were in very comfortable circumstances. They had had Mary since October 23 and would be glad to adopt her and her sister Pearl. Mr. and Mrs. Walters had had five children of their own, three of whom were married. They would take good care of a child and give her a good education. The probation officer reported that, were he placed in similar circumstances, he would be willing to have his children adopted by Mr. and Mrs. Walters.

March 3, 1930.—Visited. Mrs. Williams had not been able to place the children. Emmett said the care of the children was too much for his mother because she was used to having the house orderly and the children disturbed things. *Case closed.*

May 1, 1930.—Mrs. Williams was in court asking that the children be placed. She said she wasn't well, and her son had been out of work for six months.

May 13, 1930.—Another letter from probation officer said that the Walters were willing to keep Mary until she was eighteen, but were not willing to adopt her. However, he believed by persuasion they could be made to care for both girls for a few years.

July 23, 1930.—Mrs. Williams made arrangements to place the children in the Baptist Child Haven in Center in September. *Case closed.*

October 27, 1930.—New complaint. Mrs. Walters brought Mary to the office and refused to take her back. She despaired of there ever being any improvement. Mrs. Walters said her husband was a brother of Mr. Lane's first wife.

Mary was placed in the Children's Refuge.

February 17, 1931.—Case discussed by Application Committee of Children's Home. It was decided to accept Mary Lane for a trial period and later on to accept Pearl and Clayton for placement in a private home.

Mrs. Smith, secretary of the Application Committee, has known the Williams family for a good many years. Her mother knew them in Aitkin. Miss Maggie Nevins has worked as laundress in this family for years. She is a very conscientious, hard-working person. She has worried a great deal about Pearl and Clayton, and has talked with Mrs. Smith about them. She would like to have the children at home, but her sister, Mrs. Williams, will not co-operate in such a plan.

February 19, 1931.—Visited school at the Children's Refuge. Mrs. Rowland, Mary's teacher, said she had shown a big improvement. She is trying her in first grade. Mary does not grasp very much, yet she enters into all the activities. She sings with the other children but is not able to get all the words. She was cutting out pictures today and was doing quite well. She was keeping all the scraps in a neat pile.

Mary is a fair child with rather dull brown eyes. She is well built. Her appearance is not markedly that of a subnormal child.

February 26, 1931.—Attended Dependent Child Case Committee at Juvenile Court. Since there is no opposition to placing the children in the Children's Home, but a desire on the part of the relatives to place them there, the Committee felt that there is no need for court action. If at any time we feel court action is essential, they will accept the case at once.

March 3, 1931.—Application Committee at Children's Home agreed to accept the three children by private arrangement.

March 6, 1931.—Mrs. Williams and Miss Nevins came to the Home today. They are very anxious to have Pearl and Clayton brought here. Pearl has not been getting as much sleep as she should have because she has been having to sleep with a little girl who suffers with a rupture and screams out frequently during the night. Mrs. Williams has been getting bills which she cannot afford to pay. They are dissatisfied because it is so hard for them to visit.

Showed Mrs. Williams and Miss Nevins around the Home. They were very much interested in everything. It seemed to be very hard for Mrs.

Williams to go up and down stairs. She seemed much more interested in the children's future today and said she was getting along in years and wished she could be assured that they would be cared for if anything happened to her and Miss Nevins before the children were grown up.

March 17, 1931.—Miss Nevins came in today at worker's request. Worker had never had an opportunity to talk with her except in the presence of Mrs. Williams. Miss Nevins said she would like to pay $5.00 a week for Pearl and would like to have her have all the advantages possible. She would be very much pleased if Pearl could have music lessons because she is "crazy about music." If she pays for Pearl, she thinks Mrs. Williams and John should pay $5.00 a week for the other two children. When asked if John were interested in the children, she said he pays no attention at all to them and seems to care nothing about them. Miss Nevins said there was no reason why Mrs. Williams couldn't have kept the children if she had wanted to. She has always avoided work, and fussed if she had to work. When she used to go out to do catering, she always considered it a great hardship and made up excuses so she wouldn't have to go.

Miss Nevins said she always felt sorry for the children's mother. She had a miserable life with Mrs. Williams. She thinks she probably married Mr. Lane because she thought most anything would be better than being with her mother. Mrs. Williams has a terrible temper. "It would be awful for a person who can't fight to have to live with Mrs. Williams." She never took care of her own children. Miss Nevins said she raised John, and her other sister raised Emmett.

Miss Nevins works four days a week now.

March 19, 1931.—Visited Mrs. Williams to tell her that the Application Committee was willing to admit Pearl and Clayton to the Children's Home whenever she wanted to bring them. Mrs. Williams said she didn't know just how she could get the children. John has an automobile, but his work as an airplane mechanic keeps him busy every day unless there is a bad storm. She finally decided she might be able to go out in the streetcar. About the rate, Mrs. Williams said they could pay at least $5.00 a week. She mentioned voluntarily owning some stocks, but said they paid her only $5.00 or $6.00 a month now. Mrs. Williams has to pay $1.00 a week for insurance. She sat back in a big chair in an exhausted pose and talked very wearily.

April 10, 1931.—Called at the Baptist Child Haven in Center today. Talked with Rev. and Mrs. Silverthorne. They said Pearl was a very nice child. She did excellent work in school and adjusted very well in the institution. Her only fault was a tendency to be stubborn. They both agreed that she should be in a private home, preferably one where she could be adopted. Mrs. Silverthorne said Clayton was a "charge" particularly because he soiled himself. In other ways he wasn't especially troublesome, but did not make such a good adjustment as his sister.

Mrs. Williams paid only $5.00 all the time the children were there. When they were dismissed, they told her she could not have the children until the bill for incidentals was paid, so the children's aunt paid it. Mr. Silverthorne said they have a rule at the institution that people who place their children must either pay their board or give them up in three months. They allowed Mrs. Williams six months and then told her she would have to take the children.

April 10, 1931.—Pearl and Clayton admitted to the Children's Home.

Mrs. Williams brought the children. After she came back from the hospital, she sat down exhausted and began to cry. She said she was just worn out after having the children for a week. She said she wished she were young enough to take care of them. She complained of a nervous headache and said she would have to go home and get to bed. She is afraid to go out on the street alone because her legs give out.

She said to the worker before the children, "I don't see why someone won't adopt these two little children."

April 13, 1931.—Mary admitted to the Children's Home.

June 19, 1931.—Called at the Universal Automobile Company and talked with Mr. Boyles. He said he is perfectly willing to pay the ten days' salary due Mr. Lane to whoever is caring for his children, but the company's lawyer advised him not to pay out this money until the Court appoints a legal guardian because the children could sue the company twenty years from now and collect the salary plus interest. Although this sounds quite improbable, such suits have been brought up by shyster lawyers who are looking for just such chances, so Mr. Boyles prefers not to take the risk.

July 25, 1931.—Visitor talked with Miss Nevins and Mrs. Williams in their home. Both would be pleased to have the children placed together in a boarding-home.

July 27, 1931.—Placed Pearl and Mary Lane in the boarding-home of Mrs. George Faville, 721 South Alden Avenue. Boarding rate $25 a month for each child.

August 12, 1931.—Visitor talked with Miss Nevins, who said that she was not surprised at Pearl's display of temper and jealousy. Miss Nevins likes the foster home and will co-operate with Mrs. Faville in every way.

Placed Clayton Lane in the boarding-home of Mrs. George Faville. Boarding rate $25 per month.

August 14, 1931.—See letter from Juvenile Court regarding collection of money from the Universal Automobile Company.

August 27, 1931.—Visited Juvenile Court and spoke with Miss Johnson. She would not like to bring the children into Juvenile Court for a guardianship order for the purpose of collecting the money. The Public Guardian in Probate Court can take care of the matter for a small charge. Miss Johnson cannot see why it could not be advisable for the Children's Home to have guardianship of the children through Juvenile Court as long as relatives are co-operating.

October 16, 1931.—Spoke with Mr. Theodore James, by telephone briefly, after many unsuccessful attempts to make an appointment for an interview. Mr. James is attorney for Universal Automobile Company. He can see no way of collecting the money due the children except through appointment of a guardian of the estate of the children.

October 17, 1931.—Miss Nevins called to explain that she has lost one day of employment and she cannot contribute to the Children's Home for Pearl's board on this account. She worked for this one family many years, and a death in the family brought about the change in the arrangement with Miss Nevins.

Mrs. Williams could sign an affidavit regarding Mr. Lane's funeral expenses and other indebtedness.

Miss Nevins sees the children frequently. She gives Pearl as much attention as possible as she realizes she was spoiled by her father and demands more than the other children.

December 18, 1931.—Visitor saw Miss Nevins at Children's Home. She would be willing to have Children's Home get guardianship of the children through Juvenile Court if this seems advisable.

January 16, 1932.—Visited Mr. James. There has been recent legislation which will enable Children's Home to collect the money from Universal Automobile Company if Mrs. Williams and Miss Nevins will sign an affidavit before a notary. Mr. James dictated the form for signature.

January 21, 1932.—See letter to Mrs. Williams.

Talked with Mrs. Smith of the Children's Home Board regarding Miss Nevins. She does not believe Miss Nevins should be pressed for payments on the board of the Lane children. When she did pay, Mrs. Smith thought it a very generous thing. Miss Nevins has worked very hard all her life, assumed the major responsibility regarding care of her aged mother, and has had little opportunity to save for her old age. Mrs. Smith believes she is trying to save enough to buy her a place in a home for aged people when she can no longer work. She is employed by Mrs. Smith two days a week and receives $8.00.

February 5, 1932.—Took Miss Nevins and Mrs. Williams to Universal Automobile Company, where check was accepted by Mrs. Williams for $66 and signed over to Children's Home to apply on board of the Lane children.

Talked with Miss Nevins about board payments to Children's Home. She will resume payments as soon as she has more work. Mrs. Williams pointed out that at present she is barely able to make ends meet. She is buying a much-needed winter coat on the instalment plan. Mrs. Williams' son supports her entirely, and he has been cut to $150 from an income of around $300 a month. Mrs. Williams and Miss Nevins pay $50 a month rent in addition to the janitor work they do, which reduces the rent. Mrs. Williams' son has to keep up an auto as he is often called to the aviation field on short notice outside of the regular working hours.

Both Miss Nevins and Mrs. Williams spoke enthusiastically about the foster-home. They appreciate the simplicity as well as the wholesome good care the children receive.

September 21, 1932.—Visited and saw Mrs. Williams and her sister. For several months Mrs. Williams' son has been unemployed. He has some prospect of going back to work soon, but both she and her sister have had to be very saving, even on carfare. They have not seen the children much on this account. Miss Nevins continues on about the same schedule of day work.

Visitor urged Mrs. Williams and Miss Nevins to show Mary and Clayton just as much attention as Pearl. They will have all three children over to spend a week end soon.

November 29, 1932.—Visited Mrs. Faville, who stated that Mrs. Williams' son has been ill. He has ulcers of the stomach, and there have been hemorrhages. His heart was affected.

March 1, 1933.—Visited Mrs. Williams and Miss Nevins. Mrs. Williams' son has recovered from his illness but is still unemployed. They are back on house rent. Maggie's wages are all they have to live on. She earns $9.00 a week now. She has only three days' work.

Mrs. Belknap came in while visitor was calling. She was nicely dressed and seemed to be interested in the Lane children. She said she had given Pearl a new coat and that she tried to give the children clothing from time to time as she had it.

August 4, 1933.—Visited Mrs. Williams and Miss Nevins. Mrs.

Williams' son has prospect of work but has been out of employment for a year. It has been so difficult for them to manage financially that at times Miss Nevins has not been able to visit the children because of the carfare expense. She works three days a week and has been reduced to $3.50 a day by Mrs. Smith. She is given nothing extra for carfare and often has to work overtime.

Miss Nevins stated that she would be glad to have visitor call on her sister-in-law. Her sister-in-law is a widow and receives a pension as her husband was a veteran of the Spanish-American War. She has married children and lives comfortably. Miss Nevins is very fond of her and knows that she has a kindly interest in the Lane children. Pearl did not behave very nicely when she visited her aunt's home a year ago, and the aunt has not mentioned having her again; but Miss Nevins thinks she might be persuaded to take a more active interest if visitor called on her.

They enjoyed the visit of Pearl and the two other children. The little ones made Mrs. Williams nervous after a short stay, but they were glad to have Pearl stay on for a longer period.

November 29, 1933.—Visited Mrs. Williams. She would like to take Pearl but is in no position to do so at the present time. Mrs. Belknap and Miss Nevins are also living with her, as well as John. Just two weeks ago John went back to work, and so they will begin paying on their back rent.

Mrs. Williams impressed worker as being a very conscientious person and one who would try to understand Pearl but would need suggestions in dealing with her. She is an active woman, quick in her decisions, which no doubt causes Pearl to judge her as "bossy."

Mrs. Williams would like to have Pearl visit her during the Christmas holidays but does not wish to seem partial so will work out a plan whereby each of the children will have a few days with her.

January 17, 1934.—The worker visited Mrs. Nevins, 45 Westover Avenue. Mrs. Nevins lives with her daughter, Mrs. Davis, and her husband, in a comfortable five-room apartment. Both the daughter and the son-in-law work. Mrs. Nevins keeps the little girl, aged six, and keeps the house. She is a woman perhaps fifty years old, neat and energetic. She was eager to hear of the Lane children and related different stories of her own childhood and the experiences of the Nevins family. Mary, she thought, must be much like her mother, who was lovable, pretty, and oversexed. She became very fat at nine years and was always too fat.

She asked particularly about Pearl's disposition and related two incidents five years ago that made her think Pearl would be a problem. One was that she told Pearl to remain at home while she attended a funeral. Pearl pouted five days from the disappointment and said her father let her go to funerals. Later, Mrs. Nevins heard Pearl tell some children that Mrs. Nevins was mean to her. Mrs. Nevins called her in the house, after hearing the conversation, Pearl was restless for several weeks following this, so Mrs. Nevins decided to let her alone.

She said that the children were welcome for visits but she could not take anyone into the home. When Mr. Nevins was living and had an income, they did a great deal for the children, but she is not in a position to do so now. She and Mrs. Williams never got along harmoniously; but she never had a cross word with "Aunt Maggie" and she lived under the same roof with her for sixteen years. "Aunt Maggie" always took heavy responsibilities. She and Mrs. Williams talk to each other over the telephone, though they do not see each other often. This is because both are busy and do not live near each other.

Mr. Nevins has been dead eight years. Mrs. Nevins did cleaning jobs until her daughter took a switchboard job several years ago. She has two children. The son is working for the Grace Line and is now in South America. He is ambitious to be a captain and had a promotion Christmas. She showed considerable pride when she asked the worker to tell Pearl of his promotion.

CHILDREN'S RECORD

Children.—Pearl Lane—September 23, 1921; Mary Lane—October 25, 1923; Clayton Lane—February 11, 1925.

Birthplace.—Chicago, Illinois.

Date of admission.—April 10, 1931.

Chronological history to time of admission.—Pearl was born in Chicago and lived here all her life with her parents until her mother's death in October, 1929. After her death, Pearl stayed with her father and brother in a rooming-house. In three weeks Mr. Lane died, and Pearl and her brother continued to stay with the proprietor of the rooming-house for about two weeks longer. Then they went to their maternal grandmother's house and stayed until they were admitted to the Baptist Child Haven in Center, Illinois, in the fall of 1930.

Mary lived with her father and mother until her mother's death, which occurred on her sixth birthday. She was taken to the home of friends of her father, Mr. and Mrs. Walters, in Centerville, Illinois, where she remained for a year. At the end of this time, she was placed in the Chicago Children's Refuge and remained there until her admission to the Children's Home.

Clayton was born in Chicago and lived with his parents until his mother's death in October, 1929. After her death, he lived with his father and sister in a rooming-house and three weeks later when his father died, he continued to stay with the proprietor of the rooming-house for about two weeks. He then went to stay with his maternal grandmother and remained with her until his admission to the Baptist Child Haven in Center in the fall of 1930.

July 27, 1931.—Placed Pearl and Mary Lane in the home of Mrs. George Faville, 721 South Alden, at a boarding rate of $25 a month for each child.

August 3, 1931.—Visited Mrs. Faville and saw Pearl and Mary.

Pearl was contentedly sewing for dolls on the back porch. Mrs. Faville has had some difficulty with her on account of little temper displays caused by what seems to be jealousy and desire to have her own way. Mrs. Faville just lets Pearl "cool off," and then she is as co-operative and friendly as can be.

Mary is getting along splendidly and gives Mrs. Faville no cause for worry. Mary asked visitor to tell her grandma that she liked this home and wished to stay here.

August 12, 1931.—Placed Clayton Lane in the home of Mrs. George Faville with Pearl and Mary. Clayton went with his face beaming. He made himself at home quickly.

Mary seemed happy and well.

Pearl left with her relative for a two weeks' visit. They assured her they had an understanding with the office, and Miss Nevins said on Sunday that it was all right. She will be at 4702 Ransom Street. Pearl has been better since Miss Nevins' visit. She had one pouting spell and said she was going back to Children's Home but got over it all right.

Mrs. Faville takes the girls to Jasper Park once a week. They take their lunch and spend the day. Both girls are good workers and help her with the housework. There is some friction between them, but on the whole they play well together.

August 26, 1931.—Mrs. Faville brought Clayton to the Children's Home to go to the circus. He has been getting along well.

Mrs. Faville reported that Pearl came back after two weeks. She seemed to have a very good time but has been happy and contented since her return.

August 31, 1931.—Mrs. Faville telephoned and reported that Clayton was making a good adjustment. There have been only a few minor behavior problems.

September 23, 1931.—Mrs. Faville telephoned. Pearl was very rude today. She called her names and told her she did not have to mind. Lately Pearl has been difficult; she was rude to her aunt and also said "The Home" did not have anything to say about her affairs. She seems jealous of Mary and Clayton and teases him especially. Mrs. Faville put Pearl in her own room for punishment and shook her. Miss Nevins had told Mrs. Faville to spank Pearl, but Mrs. Faville "does not like to do that." She just wanted the Home to know she shook her. She will try to praise Pearl's good points so she will feel less jealous of Mary and Clayton. She feels sure she can manage things in the long run.

October 5, 1931.—Visited Mrs. Faville and saw the children. Pearl continues to have moody spells when she behaves in a disagreeable manner. Sometimes she gets up in the morning out of humor with everyone. Mrs. Faville pays as little attention to her as possible. Shaking her the one time seemed to have a good effect. She usually punishes her by depriving her of pleasures. When she asks for something she cannot have she does not act so naughty as she used to. She is quite selfish in her relations with Mary and Clayton.

Pearl is very good help sometimes. She likes to cook, and Mrs. Faville encourages her by giving her praise and special recognition.

Mary has wet the bed twice. She sleeps very soundly, and Mrs. Faville does not believe she will have difficulty with this if she checks on liquids. Mary is of a very different temperament but sometimes copies Pearl's behavior. She tore a pillow to pieces and picked the fringe from the bedspread when she was being punished by sitting on a chair in her room.

Mary has considerable difficulty with her reading. Mrs. Faville helps her every night because she knows Mary would be so sensitive if she did not keep up with Clayton.

She is disrespectful sometimes and says she does not have to mind. Mrs. Faville said she would like to have the privilege of switching Mary's legs when she is naughty and disrespectful. She does not believe she would have to do it more than once.

Clayton is more like Pearl in that he has a tendency to be moody. He is disrespectful like Mary sometimes, but Mrs. Faville thinks he is doing quite well.

Clayton is quick in his studies and does not need help at home.

November 10, 1931.—Visited at 8:00 P.M. The children were all in bed. Mrs. Faville spanked Pearl because of her disrespectful attitude one day. Mrs. Faville realizes that such punishment is probably unwise for

Pearl but she felt that she could not do otherwise because of the example Pearl was setting for the other children. Mrs. Faville does not think this will be necessary again as she is responding better. She will try ignoring her when in disagreeable moods.

Mary is making little progress in her reading. Both Clayton and Mary have a tendency to take things at school such as pencils and other little articles belonging to children. Mrs. Faville is checking carefully on this and makes them return the things. She does not believe it is stealing in the ordinary sense but lack of appreciation of individual ownership. Mary has had no trouble with enuresis.

November 20, 1931.—Pearl at the Children's Home. She appeared happy, friendly, and contented with her home.

December 9, 1931.—Pearl and Mary have been well.

Mrs. Faville has had some difficulty with Pearl because her little girl friend who lives in the same block buys a lunch at school and she wants to do the same thing. Mrs. Faville explained to Pearl that the Children's Agency wished her to have a warm lunch at home instead of taking her lunch to school as she wanted Mrs. Faville to permit her to do. Today Pearl did not come home for lunch. Mrs. Faville feels sure that she was the guest of her little friend for lunch. Pearl is sweet and obedient most of the time now, and Mrs. Faville believes she can reason with her about this.

Mary is grasping her school work some better.

Clayton has chicken pox. He has a very light case.

December 18, 1931.—Talked with Miss Nevins at Children's Home. She believes Pearl is happier and better adjusted in the foster-home than at first. She did want to go back to the Home. She told her aunt she liked to be with the girls at the institution and found it more pleasant there. She had no specific complaints about the foster-home. Pearl has always been selfish and is inclined to be jealous. When the children were home on the occasion of Mary's birthday, Pearl was in a disagreeable mood because Mary was getting so much attention. Miss Nevins believes Pearl is jealous of Mary and Clayton in the foster-home and is inclined to want to be first in everything. Miss Nevins believes she likes Mr. and Mrs. Faville and that there will be less trouble in the future.

December 29, 1931.—Visited the school and saw Pearl's teacher. The conduct of Pearl in school is perfect. She gets along well with other children. Her scholarship is a little better than the average. She has special ability in art work.

Pearl is sensitive about any mention of her mother. She does not seem to want anyone to know her mother is not living. She made a glove box to give to her mother for Christmas just as the other children did. Her teacher discovered through the other children that she does not live with her parents. Some time ago Pearl's little girl friend was telling the teacher about her. She said, "Pearl lives with her stepmother, and her stepmother does not even buy her gloves to wear."

Pearl's attendance has been good, and she has come clean and comfortably dressed.

Mary is a carefree child and does not conform to classroom routine. She often asks the teacher if she is good but does not remember what she is told to do and does not concentrate on her work. She is improving in her school work, and her teacher is appreciative of the help Mary is getting at home. She will not pass, but the principal will arrange to place her in another 1B room so that she will be less sensitive about it.

Clayton was restless and not very good at the beginning of school but he responds to reasoning and instruction better than Mary. He has a good mind but is a little behind the class now on account of his absence when he had chicken pox. He is a more sensitive child than Mary.

January 4, 1932.—Visited and talked with Mrs. Faville about school reports. The children were at home.

Pearl tries to control her temper. She is anxious to be very good after she has been disagreeable. One day she said, "You don't like us so well when we get mad, do you?" She is an affectionate child. Pearl gave Mrs. Faville the glove box for Christmas. She takes real interest in housework and especially in the preparation of meals. As visitor called, Mrs. Faville asked Pearl to set the table for lunch, and she went about this cheerfully. Pearl shows some talent in reading and oral expression. Mrs. Faville believes she should have elocution lessons instead of music as her aunt had planned.

Mrs. Faville will get acquainted with the family of Pearl's girl friend. They have not lived in the neighborhood a great while. They appear to be well-to-do. They have given Mary several suits of wool and silk underwear and other garments that were almost new.

All the children are becoming more reliant. Mrs. Faville does not think there is anything wrong with Mary's mind. She believes that she has not had time to get adjusted to school. Clayton attended school much younger and should make more rapid progress. Mrs. Walters and her daughter called to see Mary.

Mrs. Faville will give Clayton special help in reading at home. He is always trading things and often gets the worst of the bargain. Older boys take advantage of him. He had traded off his Indian suit and gloves. Mrs. Faville made the boy give the things back to him. He makes friends easily. He is fond of Mr. Faville. The Favilles have a little dog which is the special playmate of Mary and Clayton.

January 28, 1932.—Visited and saw the children. Mrs. Faville showed visitor an examination paper marked 100, on which Pearl's teacher had written, "Best wishes for the future to one of the sweetest little girls in the world."

Talked with Mrs. Faville about Clayton's underweight condition and left cod-liver oil. He had refused to eat cooked cereal in the morning until recently. Pearl has had the same attitude. They got sick of the cereal which they had to eat at the Baptist Home because they were not given sugar with it. Both Pearl and Clayton are eating oatmeal and Cream of Wheat now.

February 6, 1932.—Saw Mrs. Faville, Mary, and Clayton at the Children's Home, as Clayton came in to have a physical examination. Mary did not pass, but the teacher put her in another room.

February 20, 1932.—Report from Child Guidance Clinic regarding the results of the examination of Mary:

We should like to report the results of our re-examination of Mary Lane on February 16, 1932. Re-examination was requested because there was found to be a degree of mental retardation, at the time of our former examination, which could not be determined accurately. Mary is having trouble doing her schoolwork at present, but is not presenting any behavior problem otherwise.

At the time of Mary's first examination at the Child Guidance Clinic on January 9, 1931, her chronological age was 7 years 2 months; her rating on the Stanford-Binet test was 3 years 8 months, with a resultant intelligence quotient of .51. We questioned this rating not only because of the unreliability of the test at this low level, but also because Mary had had an unusually bad home and training background. Therefore we felt it unfair to accept that rating as final and asked for a re-examination after a year in an improved environment.

When Mary was re-examined on February 16, 1932, her chronological age was 8 years 4 months; her rating on the Stanford-Binet test was 5 years 2 months, with a resultant intelligence quotient of .62. During this examination the child was co-operative and responsive and showed spontaneous interest. The result of the test indicates a higher rating, but still places Mary in the group of high-grade mental defectives. She seemed a rather imaginative child, and gave the impression of being a younger and brighter child than she really is.

Physical examination showed no positive findings for which any recommendations are needed.

Our psychiatrist interviewed Mary briefly, and observed her at play. Her general behavior appears like that of a fairly "normal" girl of about six years. She does not give the impression of being as mentally retarded as tests show. Her actions are orderly; she is persistent, her co-ordination is good, her manner is pleasant and co-operative.

Mrs. Faville, the present foster-mother, was interviewed by the psychiatrist, She describes Mary's behavior as greatly improved, and she says that she would like to keep her. Mary is "somewhat slow" but does not impress the foster-mother as being "feeble-minded." The child is helpful, busy, and has an unusually "sunny disposition."

It is impossible for us to give any prognosis about the possible future mental development. We believe that the examination at this time gives a fair representation of the child's ability, so far as test-performance goes. However, we cannot say that there may not be a further improvement in her ability on tests. We recommend that she remain in her present foster-home, and that she be re-examined again in another year's time.

March 7, 1932.—Visited Mrs. Faville and saw children. Pearl was much pleased to be able to take a little girl chum to "The Three Musketeers." Clayton took a boy chum. Pearl no longer plays with the little girl whose family seems so well-to-do. She has found another little friend about nine, and Mary joins them more often than formerly.

Pearl did not like her teacher so well at first as the one last term, but she is enthusiastic now. She is having some difficulty with long division and sometimes gets impatient and cries.

Mary has always played more with boys than with girls. Recently she complained that Clayton and another boy urinated out of doors, and then Clayton said Mary did it too. Mrs. Faville has discovered Mary wetting outside before. She is trying to encourage her to make girl friends at school and play with girls in the neighborhood. There is one little boy in the neighborhood who has bad habits.

Mary has been receiving good marks at school. She showed visitor several hundred marks. Her handwriting has improved.

March 25, 1932.—Visited and weighed the children. Mary looks plump and rosy. She has gained six pounds since October. Both Pearl and Clayton continue to gain.

The grandmother and aunt have not visited for two months.

Visitor noted the affectionate and confidential relationship between all the children and Mrs. Faville. "Aunt Margaret" seems to be the center of their universe. They consult her about everything and want her approval and praise for all their little triumphs.

April 28, 1932.—Visited and saw the children. Spoke with Mrs.

Faville about taking Andrew Thomas. She believes Clayton would enjoy having a little boy in the home.

All the children are doing well in school.

May 2, 1932.—Visited and placed Andrew Thomas. He will share the room with Clayton.

May 12, 1932.—Visited. Pearl has taken a special liking for Andrew. She praises him and babies him more than her own brother. All the children get along well with Andrew.

Mary continues to do well in school. Mrs. Faville praises her generously for every 100 she brings home. She still does not like to play with girls.

Clayton and Andrew quarrel very little.

June 20, 1932.—Visited and saw the children. All the children passed.

Mrs. Faville believes Clayton's failure to gain in proportion to the others is due to the fact that he gets so excited and tense. He just swallows his food without chewing unless checked.

He soiled his trousers once last year, but otherwise toilet habits have been good.

Clayton passed in school to 2B.

Mrs. Faville believes she can see improvement in Mary's hearing. Mary passed to 1A.

Pearl pays less attention to Andrew. She passed to 5B grade.

June 29, 1932.—Visited and saw the children. Mrs. Williams has visited. She purchased a pongee dress for Mary and pajamas and socks for Pearl.

Mrs. Faville asked permission to let Clayton visit her sister a week. She has a little boy his age and is very fond of Clayton. (The sister's address is 452 South Kahler.)

Pearl shows a definite dislike for meat and fish. She will eat steak. Mrs. Faville does not force a great deal of meat on her as she seems well nourished.

July 15, 1932.—Visited. The children were just up from their nap at 3:00 P.M. They were wearing sun suits and have acquired a good tan. Mrs. Faville has taken the children to George Park for swimming.

August 1, 1932.—Visited.

Clayton is looking well. He finishes his dish of oatmeal without complaint this summer. Last week he had a cold and complained of earache. Mrs. Faville took Clayton and Andrew to Field Museum on Saturday.

Mary is a little mischievous and likes to tease Andrew. She will tell stories sometimes. She is a little nervous and fears scoldings. She will just sit after being scolded. She "buries her feelings."

Mrs. Faville dreaded the summer with Pearl, remembering her problems last year. She has had a pleasant surprise. Pearl is such a good helper. She does her work thoroughly. She is truthful. She cries and shows that she is hurt when punished but wants to come up and be friends again soon. Pearl is very serious about Sunday School. After she has been home to her aunt and grandmother, she always acts up for a few days. She seems to have been spoiled by her relatives.

September 14, 1932.—Visited. All the children entered school enthusiastically except Clayton, who prefers vacation all the time.

Mrs. Faville asked that Clayton and Mary be included on future visits to the grandmother's home. Pearl has had one visit and is asking to go again.

A maternal great-aunt gave her a dress and coat. Pearl takes excellent care of her clothing, and things look well and last a long time.

September 23, 1932.—Visited and weighed the children. All have gained over the summer.

September 24, 1932.—Pearl Lane in for annual examination by Dr. Meek; general condition very good, no findings. Dental O.K.

October 31, 1932.—Visited. Pearl was pouty and a little disagreeable after her last visit to the grandmother and aunt. She accused Mrs. Faville of telling everything she did to visitor and said visitor tells her Aunt Maggie (see entry on white sheet of September 21, 1932). Pearl was naughty last Sunday. Mrs. Faville believes it was because she bought caps for both Mary and Pearl. They were of different color, and Pearl probably thought Mary received the better one. Mrs. Faville ignores her at such times, and Pearl feels ashamed of herself and comes to apologize of her own accord later.

Mary and Clayton have been placed in the same room at school. So far this has not worried Mary, but the children like to tattle on one another, and Mrs. Faville would prefer to have them separated.

November 12, 1932.—Mary in for annual examination by Dr. Meek; she has gained twenty pounds in the last year. Dr. Meek advises cutting down on starches. Her permanent front teeth are missing; is to have X-ray.

November 23, 1932.—Visited the school. Miss Palmer, Pearl's teacher, stated that attendance has been good. Pearl is always neat and well dressed. Her work is above average. Miss Palmer said that she had never known Pearl was not in the home of her own parents. There are no behavior problems. She gets along nicely with other children.

Clayton and Mary are in the same room. It is evident that Clayton is brighter and more capable. The principal stated that she would have placed Clayton in a 1A-2B room on second floor but that teacher is not good for nervous children. She will have Mary transferred into another 1A grade on first floor. The teacher will come to the room and ask for a big girl who can be of some help to her. Mary does not concentrate. She bobs up and down a great deal. It seems hard for her to keep up with her class. She will probably not be promoted. The teacher spoke appreciatively of the good co-operation she has had from Mrs. Faville.

Miss Bailey spoke of Mary's facial disturbance, squinting, etc., and thought it might be indicative of eye strain. She has noted a facial disturbance with Clayton, which has taken a little different form.

Aside from the fact that Clayton is a nervous child, he makes a good adjustment in school.

November 29, 1932.—Visited. Enuresis occurred with Mary last night. This has not happened since last summer. There were only a few incidents then. Mrs. Faville restricts liquids. She has noted that it is hard for Mary to control her kidneys even during the day. She wet herself in the schoolroom once. She said she held up her hand, but the teacher did not notice. Clayton spoke of Mary's accident to the other boys, and Mrs. Faville punished him for this when he arrived home.

Mary has been transferred to Miss Collman's room. She helps Miss Collman take care of library books and is very happy in having the responsibility.

Mary plays with Pearl almost all the time when at home. The neighbors think Mary is a wonderful little girl. She has a cheerful disposition, is lively, and affectionate.

December 16, 1932.—Visited. Mary and Clayton were getting ready for bed at 7:15. Clayton has gained five pounds since October 1.

Mrs. Faville mentioned Clayton's and Andrew's runaway escapade recently. They left school at 3:00 o'clock and came home round 4:00 or 4:30. They had planned to run away, Clayton taking the lead because "Aunt Margaret had scolded him." It was raining, and they were quite chilled when they arrived home. Mrs. Faville sent each to his room for a time and later told them she would put up a lunch for them if they decided to go away again. Clayton gets little spells of wanting to run away if scolded for something but he makes up with the family and is as friendly as ever in a short while.

Mary has had a cold and has been coughing. She has about recovered. Mrs. Faville mentioned Mary's good handwriting, and visitor noted that Pearl was anxious to impress visitor with her little sister's accomplishments as she brought a sample of writing Mary had done at school. Mrs. Faville finds that Mary does fairly well in her reading unless she becomes excited. It is useless to try to work with her if she is excited.

Mrs. Faville believes Mary is about broken of her habit of biting her fingernails. Mary has had no recurrence of enuresis.

December 20, 1932.—Mary was in for a check by Dr. Meek on possible need for glasses.

Mrs. Faville reported that Mary's behavior is good but she continues to have difficulty in school. At times Mrs. Faville has to remind her about once a day about biting her fingernails. Sometimes she has let her fingernails grow for a week or so. Mrs. Faville thought that it might help if she secured a simple manicure set for Mary. Mary sleeps well; she usually snores.

The children had a nice time at the aunt's and grandmother's during the holidays. Pearl was cross with Clayton when she came back, and Mrs. Faville had to remind her that if she did not straighten out she would have to call and report the matter to the worker. At times Pearl still shows quite a temper which she gets over in a hurry.

Clayton has a wonderful appetite now. He wanted Mrs. Faville to tell visitor that he could eat cereal even without sugar. However, he does not have to eat it without sugar. He continues to show some of the same characteristics as Pearl—jealousy, quick temper—although he seems better than Pearl on the whole.

Mrs. Faville is trying to plan Clayton's food so that he has more nutritious things and in somewhat concentrated form. She is now working some for the Famous Cookie Factory. She is able to secure graham crackers and wholesome cookies in some quantities and inexpensively. She gives the children frosted cookies at the close of meals instead of candy. Mrs. Faville is giving Clayton orange juice both in the morning and for lunch. She gives him milk before he goes to bed and some milk with his meals.

March 4, 1933.—Pearl Lane—Dental O.K.

Clayton Lane—Dr. Meek—annual examination—general condition good—good weight gain. Dental O.K.

March 8, 1933.—A previous visit was made on February 22. The children were all well and Mrs. Faville remarked that she had not put Mary on such a strict diet because she had noticed that she had better resistance this winter from colds and had had earache only twice when last winter she had had it frequently. She believes that her health is better when she is a little stout. Mary's hearing seems fairly good now.

Mrs. Faville accompanied visitor to the school where the teachers of Mary and Clayton were interviewed. Mary is now in 2B grade. She has the same teacher as she had last term. Mrs. Collman stated that she has had considerable difficulty with Mary on account of her tendency to take things belonging both to her and other pupils. One day she was found with a dime and once she took some pieces of seat work from the teacher's desk. The unfortunate part of it is that when anything disappears in the room Mary is thought of by the other pupils. Mrs. Collman believes that Mary is gradually learning and she has tried to talk with her alone and point out the effects of her dishonesty. At times Mary has destroyed seat work. When this work is destroyed, it means that the children have less to do. Some of the other children have done this as well. Mary is very willing and craves affection. She will come up and put her arms around Mrs. Collman. She likes being given responsibility, and Mrs. Collman makes her feel that she is important to her. She calls her her housekeeper. She made her a captain in the line but she did not get along so well. She was so bent on having a perfect line that she would slap or hit a child who did not come up to the standard. She is older than the others and thinks she should tell them what they can do. She is inclined to be very dictatorial. She used to take care of Andrew like a grandmother when he was in the same room. The teacher has noted that she has a motherly instinct.

Mary is doing better school work. She is conforming better. Mrs. Faville stated that she is impressed with the fact that Mary is waking up. She continues to help her with reading at home. Her writing is lovely.

Mrs. Faville has noted that Mary has a girl friend by the name of Shirley Jones. Mrs. Collman said that Shirley is in the same room and is a fairly new girl. She is older than the other children just as Mary is. As far as Mrs. Collman has observed, Shirley is a sweet, wholesome little girl, but rather dull.

Mrs. Faville pointed out that Pearl is not such a companion to Mary now. She has a rather superior air.

Mrs. Collman stated that Mary will do any old dirty work there is just so she feels that she is helping and pleasing.

Clayton was promoted to 2A. He seemed to go down about the time the cards were made out last term. If he knows he can get out of doing things he will. Mrs. Faville stated that he brings no work home although the teacher pointed out that he should have home work. She will notify Mrs. Faville in the future if he does not do his home work. She will give him a second reader so that Mrs. Faville can help him at home. Clayton gets along with the other children fairly well. His behavior is all right. He is a little slow about taking up new things and sometimes has to be told two or three times.

Mrs. Faville was inclined to think it is play on Clayton's mind instead of daydreaming. The teacher was uncertain what interpretation should be placed on it. Mrs. Faville pointed out that Clayton never has liked school and this term has had more to say about it than usual. His averages for the last terms have been as follows:

	1B	1A	2B
Mentality..................	E*	E	G
Interest....................	A	A	A
Industry...................	A	G	A
Scholarship...............	A	G	A—
Conduct..................	A	G	G—

* (E—Excellent; G—Good; A—Average.)

Mrs. Faville stated that Pearl was promoted and is doing her usual good work in school, according to grade cards and papers she brings home. Pearl's aunt recently gave her a new coat. Mrs. Faville had some trouble persuading her not to wear the new one to school. Mrs. Faville has found that she gets the best response from Pearl when she talks things over quietly with her Aunt Maggie and then Aunt Maggie has a chance to talk with Pearl alone. Pearl thinks more of Aunt Maggie than anyone else. She wonders sometimes if Aunt Maggie tells Pearl she may not live very long because some times when she has taken her to the corner she comes home in a saddened mood. Pearl's grandmother seems to upset her and does not seem to have any understanding of the child.

April 3, 1933.—Miss Davis, household manager of Children's Agency, reported that Mrs. Faville had come in for advice on diet as suggested by visitor. Miss Davis advised reducing Pearl to one slice of bread per meal. She advised further reduction of starchy foods and more vegetables for Mary.

April 7, 1933.—Pearl Lane—St. Martin's Eye Clinic—Dr. Green—new glasses.

See letter from Child Guidance Clinic arranging for basal metabolism test as requested for Mary.

April 8, 1933.—Mary Lane—Dr. Denton—dental care—has lost one pound in the last three months—to return to see Dr. Meek when we have the report from the Child Guidance on her basal metabolism.

April 10, 1933.—Visited. Mary, Clayton, and Andrew were playing with the dog, and Pearl was reading the evening paper. Explained to Mrs. Faville the requirements for Mary's basal metabolism test Friday, April 15. Told Mary about her coming Child Guidance Clinic examination. The children met the new worker easily. Mary showed a 100 paper in arithmetic and spelling and a picture book colored with crayons.

April 12, 1933.—Delivered clothing and visited with the children. Mr. Faville was alone with the children.

April 14, 1933.—Visitor took Mrs. Faville and Mary to the Clinic for a basal metabolism test. Mrs. Faville stated that Pearl co-operated nicely in the reduction of bread in her diet.

April 20, 1933.—Mrs. Faville accompanied Mary to the Child Guidance Clinic for re-examination.

April 24, 1933.—Visited and saw Clayton. Mrs. Faville understands Child Guidance Clinic recommendations and is prepared for the fact that Mary may never reach normal intelligence, although she may gain slightly. However, she is hopeful that Mary can be helped to make those gradual adjustments to her social environment so that in the future she may be self-supporting and have an emotional and economic adjustment which will allow her, with her limited intelligence, to be happy and at the same time be safe and responsible outside a feeble-minded institution.

Mrs. Faville will increase her stress on housekeeping and try to build up Mary's sense of achievement in cooking, sewing, and cleaning. She will lessen her stress on school achievement. The children helped clean the attic during vacation. Mary is patient, efficient, and thorough when she understands her job.

Clayton is gradually getting over his tenseness and excitement. He still is a little lazy in his school work but can do well when he tries. Clayton willingly does the shopping for Mrs. Faville any time she asks. He is very efficient and always brings back the correct change.

Pearl is well, but still has not completely overcome her jealousy. She is occasionally jealous of Andrew, has a temper, and sometimes hits the children if they have something she wants. Mrs. Faville says she was spoiled by her father. These moods are only occasional, however, and she is much more reserved in receiving the visitor than the younger children.

The younger children put their arms around the visitor and want to be kissed when the visitor leaves, although the visitor made no unusual affectionate advance to encourage them.

Mrs. Faville had taken the children to the church minstrel show, and they enjoyed it very much. Mr. and Mrs. Faville go out with the children every other Sunday.

April 27, 1933.—Report from Child Guidance Clinic of re-examination of Mary:

The following is a report of our re-examination of Mary Lane on April 20, 1933. She was referred at this time in order to determine what progress has been made in mental development. A basal metabolism test was also requested because of a rapid gain in weight during the past year. We understand that no personality problems have appeared during the past year.

On the physical examination Mary was found to appear to be more overweight than was actually the case. She was found to be six pounds overweight. However, there was nothing to indicate that this increase in weight is due to any particular endocrine disorder. Her physical development in every other respect is normal. The basal metabolic rate was found to be plus 4 per cent. This is a normal metabolism rate and rules out the possibility of a hypothyroidism. We believe that a restriction of fats and carbohydrates in the diet should be continued in order to prevent further increase in weight. Mary was found also to have developed a slight heart murmur, which has the characteristics of an organic valvular defect, and it may be a result of an early attack of diphtheria. However, there is no cardiac enlargement or other evidence that this is causing any particular difficulty, and we see no reason for a restriction of activity. We feel, however, that this should be checked by periodic examinations of the heart.

In the psychometric examination at this time, Mary was found to have a mental age of six years four months and an intelligence quotient of 67 on the Stanford-Binet scale. Although this is five points higher than that obtained in our examination of a year ago, it does not change the classification of high-grade mental defective. During the test Mary was quite spontaneous and eager but showed no insight into successes or failures. The results of the test are considered reliable. We understand that she is now in grade 2B which is beyond her ability. However, we understand also that her placement in this grade was made in order to give her a sense of promotion and that she is not expected to do grade 2B work. It will probably be necessary some time to place her in a special room or to work out a special program for her in school.

In additional observations we were impressed that there has been no particular change since our examination in 1932. Mary was found to be very much attached to Mrs. Faville and her brother and sister and to be quite happy in this home. She apparently does not realize as yet her limited mental ability and in order to prevent her from becoming suddenly aware of this, our psychiatrist suggested to Mrs. Faville that she avoid comparing Mary's scholastic achievements with that of the other children. She was also warned to avoid pushing the child beyond her ability and to emphasize rather the value of her good work about the house.

From the results of this and preceding examinations, it appears to us that Mary will always be considerably below the average in mental ability.

However, we feel that her chance for social adjustment is fairly good and probably will remain so if your agency remains active on the case. There is reason to believe that she may eventually become self-supporting in doing housework or some similar type of occupation.

May 6, 1933.—Mary Lane—seen by Dr. Meek—slight basal systolic murmur—does not seem important—return in one month.

May 15, 1933.—Visited Mrs. Faville. She was very much upset about Pearl's stubbornness and failure to co-operate. All Pearl's friends are able to stay out until nine or eleven o'clock at night, and Pearl must get ready for bed at eight. Pearl objected to taking Mary to the Children's Home so much and to going to the store. Mrs. Faville thinks Pearl places too much importance on favorable notice from Mr. Faville, and Mr. Faville "is afraid to pay much attention to her." Mrs. Faville, although reduced to tears, seemed somewhat heartened by the assurance of the confidence the agency placed in her and the reminder that she might expect to see Pearl's stubbornness and temper tantrums aggravated in adolescence and that with careful and tactful handling she could outgrow them.

Talked the matter over with Pearl on the way to the streetcar and she promised her co-operation. She notices and is hurt by the restrained attitude of "Uncle George" (Mr. Faville).

May 29, 1933.—Visited Mrs. Faville and brought a new slip for Pearl. The dining-room and living-room had just been repapered, the Favilles doing the work themselves. Mrs. Faville promised the children new paper in their rooms if they would promise to keep it clean and help tear the old paper off.

Mrs. Faville did not think a visit to Pearl's girl friend's mother would be advisable as Pearl's behavior had improved since the worker's last visit, and Pearl had been seeing much less of this little girl. It was thought that a visit might overemphasize the situation.

Pearl and one other girl had been chosen as the best writers in their room and were to write before the principal the next day.

Pearl may stay out to 8:30 on school nights and be in bed by 9:00 but she may stay out until 9:00 Friday and Saturday evenings.

June 14, 1933.—Mrs. Faville called. The Lanes' aunt came over this morning and took them to visit until Sunday night.

June 18, 1933.—Mrs. Faville called and stated that Pearl's grandmother wants to keep her the rest of the week. She felt it would be good for Pearl and that it would not seem discriminating against Clayton and Mary.

July 6, 1933.—Visited. Pearl has been a good girl. Before her visit to the grandmother's house Mrs. Faville told her she would be deprived of a visit there in the near future if she came home disrespectful and ill-tempered this time. This may have helped as she has been in a good frame of mind. She visited a week longer than the other children.

Pearl began menstruating last Saturday. She seemed prepared, and told Mrs. Faville her mother talked to her. Mrs. Faville also talked with her about personal care.

Visitor arranged for an allowance for Pearl of ten cents a week. Mrs. Faville has been giving all the children a nickel.

Pearl is assisting some with cooking. She makes excellent apple sauce. The boys take turns washing dishes. Mary likes to make the beds.

Mrs. Faville plans to take the children to the park once a week for swimming this summer. She is taking them to the Fair next week.

August 4, 1933.—Mary Lane—Dr. Denton—dental care.

Clayton Lane—Dr. Denton—dental care. Fell while playing and broke one of his front teeth.

August 7, 1933.—Dr. Meek found a slight systolic murmur and asked that Mary be put to bed immediately if she has a cold or pain. She has lost considerable weight and is to be put back on regular diet and allowed to have two slices of bread at a meal.

August 16, 1933.—Visitor met Pearl at the Northwestern Station after two weeks' vacation at Glenn Camp. Pearl had had a happy time and hoped that she might repeat the camp experience another summer.

Visitor saw Mary and Clayton. Both were beginning their nap period at 1 P.M. Mrs. Faville stated that she has given Mary an additional portion of bread since receiving instructions from the doctor. Mary has been well, but Mrs. Faville had noticed that she was getting thin-looking. She is not giving her all the potatoes and bread that she would normally eat if left unsupervised, but she believes that she will pick up when the proportion of starch is greater.

Mrs. Faville has to supervise Mary closely when she is with boys. Recently she was away, and Mr. Faville was in charge of the children. Mary and Andrew went across the street to play. An older boy who has bad habits himself persuaded them to expose themselves to one another. Mary did not speak of this, but that night Clayton came and told Mrs. Faville what had happened. He said that the boy told him to do the same but he did not want to. After talking with Mary and Andrew, Mrs. Faville gave each of them a spanking. Mary is all right when playing with Clayton and Andrew in the home or the immediate yard. There are two little girls in the neighborhood with whom Mary plays, but her preference would be boys.

Mrs. Faville finds that it is very hard to build up Clayton. He is inclined to eat his food very fast and does not chew it properly. In spite of the fact that she arranges for him to rest before and after meals, he seems to be in a somewhat tense, excited state during his meal.

September 27, 1933.—Visited Mrs. Faville and saw the children. She cannot account for the loss of weight of each of the children except through the fact that she had definitely restricted diet for a time and during the summer they were all very active in their play. She has made an adjustment in the diet so that she feels they will regain the weight which they have lost. She is careful that Mary gets her rest. Both Mary and Clayton continue to bite their fingernails. Mary does it less since she is resting more.

Pearl has been happy and enthusiastic about her vacation at camp and is looking forward to another camp vacation next summer.

Visitor talked with Mrs. Faville about the report from a friend of Andrew Thomas' grandmother to the effect that they were receiving relief from the county. She stated that she had never received relief even when Mr. Faville was out of employment and would not think of getting it now when he has regular work. Visitor could not sense any strain in the family situation which would account for the physical findings of the children.

Mrs. Faville stated that Mary and Andrew Thomas had been put in the same room at school but that she had a conference with the principal and the rooms were changed. Mary has a teacher who does not impress Mrs. Faville as very understanding or co-operative, but she feels that it will be better for Mary than to be with Andrew. When they are together they are constantly tattling on one another, and there is more chance that Mary will feel more self-conscious and sensitive because of her retardation.

October 7, 1933.—Mary—gain of two pounds—has definite heart murmur—to continue moderate exercise. Return here in one month.

October 27, 1933.—Mrs. Faville telephoned about a Halloween costume for Pearl. Pearl has $2.00 which was a Christmas gift and she wants to buy a devil costume for $1.90. Later visitor talked with Pearl and suggested that she come in as there are costumes at the Home. Visitor sensed a tightening in Pearl's voice and she said, "But I want the devil's costume." She agreed to come in.

October 28, 1933.—Visitor saw Pearl. She was not satisfied to use the costume available here. She seemed to feel that she should be allowed to spend her own money in any way she liked, even after visitor talked with her about agency expenses and present financial problems. She agreed to go without her allowance for two months. "I have thirty cents saved already, and my aunt will give me a dime now and then when she visits." Visitor pointed out that the aunt would not be able to give her this extra spending money as whatever she can afford must be applied on clothing expenses for the children.

November 1, 1933.—Visited. Mrs. Faville let Pearl go to the aunt's house. She was given the $2.00 and spent $1.00 for a costume. She was unable to get the devil's costume, but the one she selected was of black sateen with interesting printed figures. Mrs. Faville finds Pearl very stubborn in her opinions about clothing. The aunt gave her a brown dress suitable for Sunday wear, and she insisted on wearing it to school when she had plenty of other school dresses. Soon she was asking Mrs. Faville to fix up her black skirt and a blouse to wear to assembly for a special program as the brown dress was soiled. Mrs. Faville said she was sorry Pearl had spoiled her good dress and she would have to make the best of the situation. One day Mrs. Faville saw Pearl had put on her silk stockings for school. Mrs. Faville learned at school that Pearl might be given a double promotion. She is doing excellent work.

Clayton did such poor work in 3B the principal thought he might have to be demoted. Mrs. Faville has visited his teacher, and he is showing improvement. The teacher thinks he is lazy. He would do one problem in the time he should have done ten. His behavior is fair. He had such a poor teacher last year Mrs. Faville thinks it may have affected his attitude toward school. Clayton has had one cold. Mrs. Faville asked that the nurse look at the wax in his ear. He has a great deal.

Mary has the same teacher as Clayton had last year in 2A. She is doing fairly well. Mary shows less nervousness since she has more rest. However, recently Mrs. Faville noted that she is picking her toenails as well as fingernails.

Mrs. Faville believes both Pearl and Clayton have had a somewhat antagonistic attitude toward the Agency and it may have been a carry-over from their experience at the Baptist Home. Clayton seems to have gotten over his largely. It helped Pearl when the worker gave her a little special attention and had a confidential talk with her.

November 6, 1933.—Miss Baker, the Agency nurse, stated that Pearl has told her several times that she is dieting and intends to get thinner yet.

November 7, 1933.—Visited boarding-home.

Mary was kept home from school today on account of a severe cold. She was in bed but she made no fuss about it, although she cried a little at first because she couldn't go to school.

Clayton has been doing a little better at school recently. Last time he did all his arithmetic problems in the allotted time.

Pearl plays with a little girl Mary's age who lives in the next block. She often brings her home from school with her. Pearl does not seem to be interested in girls her own age.

Later.—All the children came home from school and speedily changed to their play clothes. Pearl had her little friend with her, and the two went out to play. Mrs. Faville remarked that Pearl is the odd one in the the family and never seems to know quite what to do with herself.

November 11, 1933.—Pearl Lane—has recently gained four pounds—looks better.

Clayton Lane—wax removed from ears.

November 29, 1933.—Visited boarding-home. Mrs. Faville was upset because she has recently had two arguments with Pearl. Last Saturday afternoon she allowed her to go to the movies with her little girl friend, but she wasn't satisfied with this and begged to go over to her house for the rest of the evening. Mrs. Faville thought she had been out enough so she told her "no," and Pearl has acted ugly since. Mrs. Faville reported that Pearl had been acting foolish with the boys and for proof she brought a crumpled piece of note paper on which Pearl had drawn a heart and put her initials coupled with a boy's initials on it. Worker advised Mrs. Faville not to take this seriously as it was customary behavior for boys and girls. Pearl kept her eyes downcast while she explained that her aunt had told her never to make a fool of herself with the boys and she said she didn't want to either. The matter was dropped.

Pearl talked about her grandmother. It was apparent that she holds a grudge against her grandmother for having placed Mrs. Lane and Emmett in an orphanage while she kept John. She thinks her grandmother is very crabby and disagreeable on the whole. Worker talked to her about her attitude toward her grandmother. Pearl asked if she could go to her grandmother's for Thanksgiving Day to stay over the holidays. As worker was planning to visit Mrs. Williams, she agreed to learn whether Mrs. Williams had room for Pearl or whether she had other plans. Pearl sent a note to her grandmother.

Pearl showed her school notebook to worker. The penmanship is beautiful, and the work well organized. Pearl's grades were practically all E's. Her ambition is to be a movie star, secretary, or teacher.

Mrs. Faville believes that Mary is doing much better at school since she is separated from Andrew. She seems to remember things better.

The three younger children play nicely together, but Pearl seems out of place in the family group.

Clayton seems less nervous. He has difficulty in studying, so Mrs. Faville takes him out in the kitchen alone and helps him study. He does more of his number work at school; he used to do only two problems when the others were doing ten.

December 2, 1933.—Mary Lane—St. Martin's—Dr. Gilson—has slight systolic murmur—to return in three months for check-up.

December 3, 1933.—Mary—seen by Dr. Meek—general condition good—to return here in one month.

Clayton Lane—seen by Dr. Meek—does not gain very well—to return in one month when Mary does.

December 8, 1933.—Mrs. Faville phoned that she has an appointment at the school next Wednesday to see all the children's teachers. She would like worker to accompany her to hear the reports. All those children who are not doing well at school were given notes. Pearl did not bring a note.

December 13, 1933.—Visited Franklin School. Miss Evans, principal, talked with worker about Mary before sending for her teacher. She would like to refer Mary to the Child Study Department for a recommendation to a special room where she will make a better adjustment. Mrs. Evans stressed the point that she was looking toward Mary's future and that in another year she would not belong socially in a regular classroom. She can attend the Sayman School, where there is a room for subnormal children.

Later Miss Grimes, grade-2A teacher, talked with worker. Mary has a reading disability and will never be able to do third-grade work. "She is a slow child—pushes and strikes at other children."

Miss Rosen stated Clayton is very poor in reading. He is making a real attempt to do his arithmetic problems and will put down some kind of an answer for each one although he does not as a rule get them all correctly. His attention is spasmodic, and this probably accounts for his poor work in general.

December 18, 1933.—Mrs. Faville phoned that she had received a note from the teacher regarding Pearl's laziness at school. Worker promised to visit the schoolroom with special reference to Mary and she would see Pearl's teacher.

December 28, 1933.—Visited boarding-home. All the children were excited about the gifts they received and clamored to show them to worker. They are well and happy.

December 30, 1933.—Pearl, accompanied by worker, visited the Aquarium and Field Museum.

During the course of the conversation Pearl said, "I like to play with younger children because they are not so bossy as older ones." Pearl did not seem to realize that she in turn becomes the boss to the other children. She enjoyed visiting her aunt's sister-in-law on the North Side a year ago because she played with the little girl whom she referred to as "cousin." However, she does not believe that she would like to live there because she would be too far away from her own family. She prefers also to continue at the same school.

Pearl remembered this time to mention that she had enjoyed the outing.

January 6, 1934.—Mary Lane—Special examination—Dr. Meek—general condition good—good weight gains—to return in two months.

Clayton Lane—no gain in weight in the last month—to return in one month for check-up.

January 13, 1934.—Pearl Lane—about 12 per cent underweight—general condition good—has recently gained two pounds.

January 26, 1934.—Visited Franklin School. Miss Evans will arrange for Mary's transfer to the Sayman School, where there is a room for sub-normal children. Worker left summary of Child Guidance Clinic report of 1932 on Mary. It will be necessary for Mary to cross the boulevard, but she can go an extra short block and cross where there are traffic signals. The only other alternative would be to have Pearl transfer, but it is not likely that she will care to do this.

Later.—Visited boarding-home and discussed the possibility of Pearl's wishing to change schools in order to be of help to Mary. Pearl said she did not want to leave Franklin School. She has made excellent grades there and feels at home with her classmates.

February 3, 1934.—Clayton Lane—annual examination—Dr. Meek—general condition fairly good—has gained three pounds in the last month—to return in two months—Dr. Denton—dental care.

March 3, 1934.—Clayton Lane—lost one pound in the last month—came prepared to repay two cents for the pound that he had lost—to return in one month.

Mary Lane—has gained four pounds in the last month—to return in one month.

March 10, 1934.—Pearl Lane—has gained one pound in the last two months—dental care. Posture very poor—does she have a good corselet?

March 12, 1934.—Visited boarding-home. Mary, Clayton, and Andrew Thomas were playing school. They all looked well. Pearl was pouting because she could not go out again because of the cold. She was even rude to worker, although the latter had nothing to do with the refusal.

March 16, 1934.—Clayton Lane—Dr. Denton—dental care.

March 24, 1934.—Mrs. Faville called saying the Child Guidance Clinic wanted to see Mary Thursday afternoon, and she will go with her unless worker wishes to do so.

SUMMARY APRIL 1–JULY 1, 1934

Visits were made April 12, April 24, and June 8. The children were all seen in the office on June 16.

Health.—Pearl had been having nosebleed so was seen by Dr. Meek. She advised the use of vaseline in the nose.

Clayton has gained three pounds in the last month and is looking unusually well.

Mary's general condition is good and there were no cardiac findings when she was examined by Dr. Meek on April 14.

School.—Pearl is doing good work at school and all her papers are especially neat. She was passed to 7A in June. Her grades were as follows:

English—A	Geography—A
Reading—E	Music—E
Writing—E	Nature Study—G
Arithmetic—G	Effort—G
Spelling—E	

Clayton has improved in his school work and frequently brings home 100 in arithmetic. However, he is still weak in reading. He passed to grade 3A.

Mary was transferred to another school in May after a study had been made by the Child Study Department of the Board of Education. Miss Evans recommended this in view of a long-time plan for Mary. She is very happy in the special room and industrious about the handwork.

Adjustment in foster-home.—Pearl is getting along better now than at any other time, although she is still inclined to pout when her will is crossed. At these times she is even "sassy." The main disagreement is usually over clothes as Pearl likes to wear the best she has on all occasions. Pearl is a little jealous of Andrew Thomas and seems to feel that any attention he receives should have been given to Clayton.

Clayton is a happy, rather shy boy. He seldom has to be punished but when he does it is all over in a hurry and he never holds a grudge. He is inclined to be a bit selfish but not so much as Pearl. Clayton spends much of his time in drawing.

Mary occupies a good deal of her spare time in playing school. She is easily pleased, readily following suggestions, so that she is seldom wilfully disobedient.

Since she has transferred to the special room at the new school she is even happier. She seems to feel that she is really accomplishing something when she is able to bring home samples of her handwork.

SUMMARY JULY 1–OCTOBER 1, 1934

Visited July 6 and September 27.

July 28.—Pearl was given her annual physical examination by Dr. Meek. Her general physical condition was only fairly good. She had insufficient weight gain and her posture was very bad.

August 1.—Mary was examined by Dr. Gilson at St. Martin's Cardiac Clinic. No organic cardiac condition was ascertained. She is to return in six months. On August 25, it was noticed that Mary had lost one pound, but her general condition was considered good when Dr. Meek gave her her annual physical examination. Dr. Denton asked for an X-ray of her teeth. Mary had the mumps the first week in July.

July 28.—It was noted that Clayton recently lost two pounds. He gained two pounds by September 29.

Summer vacation period.—When worker visited on July 6, Mary was in bed on account of the mumps. She was being a very good patient and made Mrs. Faville no extra trouble at all.

Pearl still pouts when she wants her own way and cannot have it. Not only does she pout but she continues begging to do things until she wears down Mrs. Faville's resistance. This is particularly true about going out of doors after hours. Pearl seems to need a wider group of friends. She still continues to cling to the companionship of the little neighbor girl who is so much younger than she.

Pearl said that her Aunt Maggie is not with her grandmother any more but is working full time for Mrs. Smith.

Clayton is a happy little boy. So far he is satisfied to stay home and play with Mary and Andrew Thomas. He is growing quite tall now and seems more alert and less shy.

SUMMARY OCTOBER 1, 1934—JANUARY 1, 1935

Visited October 31, November 22, and December 15. Mary and Clayton were seen at the Home on October 24. Visited Mary's school teacher on October 31.

Health.—Mary had an X-ray taken of her front teeth October 21 at the University of Illinois Dental Clinic. Mary's school nurse advised surgery for nasal obstruction. She was seen at St. Martin's Clinic on November 12, and no nasal obstruction was found except a moderate amount of adenoid tissue, which does not need to be removed unless there are frequent colds and mouth breathing.

November 24, Mary was examined by Dr. Meek. Her general condition was good. November 30, Dr. Gilson, St. Martin's Pediatric Clinic, examined Mary and found her general condition good. The heart murmur was less distinct than at any time previous.

When Clayton was weighed on November 24, he showed a loss of two pounds but by December 22 he had gained three pounds.

School.—Pearl's grades are always good, as she applies herself well to any work and strives to do it neatly.

English—E		Geography—G
Reading—G		Physical Education—A
Spelling—S		Music—G
Arithmetic—G		Drawing—G
Nature Study—G		Deportment—E

Clayton does not like school but he is doing average work and there is no complaint about his behavior at school.

Mary is doing good work in the special room. She is a happy child and responds well. She writes well but often confuses words.

Foster-home.—According to Mrs. Faville, Pearl does not pout so much as formerly. She seems to be more broad-minded, and Mrs. Faville attributes this to mixing with other girls and boys at the Confirmation Class. She has also joined the Girl Scout group and likes it very much. Pearl helps with the dishes and takes care of her own room. Pearl is still very sensitive about her clothes, and one day she refused to go to school because she did not have a suitable dress to wear. Pearl agreed to wear the best that she had on hand, and worker promised to look over her clothes. Pearl had a number of old-fashioned but good dresses. She said she felt queer in these dresses and she would not wear them. A new school dress was given to her. Pearl has $3.00 saved. Some of this money was given to her at Christmas.

Clayton is inclined to be a little selfish but he is well liked by the children in the neighborhood. He is good-natured in playing with them, so has many more friends than Andrew Thomas.

Mary likes to practice writing at home. She will sit for hours at a time doing school work. Mrs. Faville has no trouble with her at all, and she is a good little worker about the house. She likes to save her money and now has $5.00 saved at the church.

Family relationships.—Aunt Maggie is in better humor since living at Mrs. Smith's home. This arrangement seems to have relieved the strain between the various relatives so everything is going along so much more smoothly. Aunt Maggie gave Pearl a pair of shoes for her birthday.

SUMMARY JANUARY 1–APRIL 1, 1935

Visited February 1, February 21, and March 15. Pearl was seen in the office January 5, and Clayton February 8.

Health.—Clayton was given his annual examination by Dr. Manly on February 9. His general condition has improved, and he has gained five pounds in the last year. Dr. Denton gave dental care.

Pearl has made no weight gain in the past year. She was seen at St. Martin's Clinic March 26 and advised to wear the same glasses for another year, as she needs them for close work.

School.—Clayton had trouble at school. He had not passed so tore up his slip. He did not like the idea of going into Mrs. Campbell's room and was not doing his work at all. He would spell perhaps two words out of the entire list, when he used to receive hundreds in spelling. It was noticed that he would sit and dream and he would not visit with the other children. After foster-mother's conference with the principal, it was decided to put him in 4B. Mrs. Faville said Clayton had an average card and it was not clear why he had failed to be promoted in the first place. Clayton is bashful and did not do well in the previous room partly because there were so many substitute teachers.

Personality and interests.—Worker visited February 1, to check clothing. Mary chats freely, as usual, and is a very out-going little person. Mary walks to school with a subnormal boy who lives in the next block. Mrs. Faville is trying to persuade her to associate with little girls instead. She still likes to play school but best of all she likes to take care of children and continually teases Mrs. Faville to get a baby. She has a great deal of patience with children. Mary is an active child and likes to help with little chores, especially around the house. She always sets the table in the morning.

Pearl does not get along well with Mary and regards her as a nuisance. She likes the girls at the Scout troop, but none of them lives in her neighborhood. Pearl takes care of her own room, helps with the supper, and dries the dishes in the evening.

Pearl is being confirmed in the Lutheran church this Easter.

Clayton remarked at the dinner table one evening that he wished his parents were living. Pearl retorted, "Maybe we would be poor then."

Pearl is less irritable since she has new interests. Mrs. Faville considers the Scout leader excellent and feels that her influence will help Pearl a great deal.

Clayton thinks that he can do things at his grandmother's house that he is not allowed to do at the foster-home. He likes the freedom to run the streets, and, of course, Mrs. Faville does not allow him to do this. He is growing quite tall recently.

SUMMARY APRIL 1–JULY 1, 1935

Visited May 6 and June 20. All three children were seen in the office April 27.

Health.—Pearl was given dental care during May. She has gained a little weight and looks better. May 27, Pearl and Mary had German measles.

Mary had gained four pounds when she was weighed June 8. This was gained in the last two months. She was seen by Dr. Meek. Her general condition was good.

School.—Pearl was promoted to 8A. She received all G's and E's. Her strongest subjects are reading, writing, spelling, and drawing.

Worker visited school at the principal's request. Clayton's attitude seems all right in general, although the principal thought Andrew leads him into mischief, as hopping on trucks. However, Clayton is accomplishing very little in school. His reading and arithmetic are poor and spelling spasmodic—sometimes fair. Clayton is extremely listless as though sleepy or fatigued. Worker told her Children's Agency would give a special physical examination, and he might be referred to the Child Guidance Clinic.

Clayton was promoted to 4A on trial.

Foster-home.—Mrs. Faville is greatly discouraged with Pearl as she is sensitive to even the slightest correction. One evening she stayed out until ten-thirty without permission. She went to church with a girl friend. Pearl has frequently told Mr. and Mrs. Faville that they hated her and she feels that she is blamed for everything that goes wrong in the home. Mrs. Faville suggested to her that she go to worker and ask for another placement but Pearl said she would run away if placed in another home.

Mrs. Faville cited another instance of Pearl's carelessness. Mrs. Faville had to leave one afternoon at two o'clock so gave Pearl the key. Pearl left the house open, and no one was around when Mr. Faville came home at four o'clock. Mrs. Faville says Pearl doesn't take responsibility as well as Clayton.

Pearl acted disgruntled with her aunt and grandmother at her confirmation because they didn't give her the clothing she wanted. Her grandmother brought two dresses and Pearl didn't like either one.

SUMMARY JULY 1–OCTOBER 1, 1935

Visited July 12 and September 30, 1935.

Health.—September 12, Pearl was given her annual examination by Dr. Meek. Her general condition was good, and she had gained nine pounds in the last two months. She was given dental care September 20.

July 1, Dr. Gilson at St. Martin's Pediatric Clinic saw Mary. There is no organic cardiac condition.

August 1, Mary's general condition was good. September 12 she was given her annual examination by Dr. Meek. Her general condition was good and her eyes were all right. She was given dental care September 20.

August 1, Clayton was seen by Dr. Meek. His general condition was good, but he had made insufficient weight gains. September 12, he was again weighed. He had gained two pounds. September 24, nurse visited him at home. He had an upper respiratory infection with swollen glands. He was improving.

Summer vacation.—Pearl went to Scout Camp one week this summer. She was disappointed because the captain of their troop was unable to go. All the girls are fond of this captain. She sent her daughter and another woman along, but they were unable to manage the girls very well. There was quarreling among the girls, and one girl who is known to be excitable left camp a day or two early. Pearl and another girl left in sympathy with this girl.

August 24, Mrs. Faville took the three Lane children to visit with her sister for a week. Pearl liked it so well she stayed a week longer than the others. She was in very good humor when she returned.

Mrs. Faville said that most of Pearl's irritability is over clothes, for she has strong likes and dislikes in the matter. If she likes a dress real well she wears it over and over again, but if she has dislike for it she won't even put it on.

Pearl doesn't get along well with her friends for she quarrels with them. At home she likes to read and listen to the radio. Mrs. Faville subscribes to three magazines especially for Pearl. They are the *Delineator*, *Radio*, and a movie magazine.

Mary took care of the neighbors children frequently this summer. She earned twenty cents each time and at first had difficulty in saving any of her money for she was inclined to spend it all on ice cream. Mary likes to iron and take care of children better than anything else. She is doing better at school this term and is fond of her teacher.

Clayton was offered the opportunity to go to Camp with Andrew but he refused it even though the date did not conflict with going to the country with Mrs. Faville.

At the beginning of the term Clayton had trouble at school. He was promoted to 4A on trial and now has the teacher he wanted. However, he is so easily excited he is often misunderstood. Clayton turned around in his seat because the boy back of him poked him. When the teacher corrected him he smiled at her but she was angry. He was so upset he couldn't read his lesson. This brought him further disapproval. Clayton has been smoking in the washroom at school. Clayton's main difficulty in school is his inability to pay attention for any length of time. In long division he forgets to finish the problem.

Clayton is helpful in the home. He always makes the bed and is willing when it is his turn to dry dishes.

SUMMARY OCTOBER 1, 1935—JANUARY 1, 1936

Visited November 6 and December 4.

Mary in office October 26.

Pearl shopping October 5 and December 23.

Health.—October 6, Mary had temperature of 103.4, pain in right hip and back but more in the joint than in the muscle, slight systolic heart murmur. She was seen by Dr. Seeley in the boarding-home. Urinalysis negative for pus and albumin.

October 7, Mary seen by nurse; temperature 100, pulse 98, respiration 24; general condition seemed better.

October 8, nurse visited Mary; temperature 103.6.

October 19, Mary seen by Dr. Meek; general condition good but she still has a few rales.

October 26, Mary again seen by Dr. Meek; general condition good.

School.—Pearl graduates in February from the Franklin School. She has continued to do excellent work.

Mary is slow in school and is becoming more and more aware of the significance of a "special room." She does not like Andrew to brag that he is ahead of her. She talks babyish and still confuses breakfast, dinner, and supper. Mrs. Faville, foster-mother, has been called to school on Clayton several times. He does not grasp long division. He seems to forget to finish the process. Some of his poor work is due to inattention.

Recently Clayton has been smoking at school. His teacher has talked with him about this. She does not feel that his behavior is serious and is confident that she can handle the situation because there are only eleven in his class and they are all slow.

Worker visited Franklin School on December 4. Clayton's teacher and Miss Evans, principal, agreed that it might be well at this point to refer Clayton to the Child Guidance Clinic so that a suitable school program may be planned for him.

Foster-home.—Mrs. Faville still feels that Pearl is somewhat of an irritant in the home. She does not find anything in common with the younger children and is inclined to stir up trouble.

Pearl does not want to accept a change in homes and has told Mrs. Faville that she will not stay if she is placed anywhere else. This may be due to Pearl's rejection of a wage home. She met several of the girls at a tea at Children's Home who were earning their room and board. She said she would never do that.

Relatives.—Pearl likes her aunt, Mrs. Nevins, and would like to live with her. However, she is perturbed over the situation because Mrs. Williams does not get along with her at all and Pearl knows it would create more trouble. Mrs. Nevins is now living with a married daughter, Mrs. Ella Davis, 45 Westover Avenue. Pearl said she likes Ella too. She planned to visit them during the holidays.

Mrs. Nevins visited Pearl when she was confirmed, but Pearl was in a disagreeable mood and did not treat her aunt nicely. Mrs. Faville wonders if the aunt will feel kindly toward Pearl after this incident. Pearl treated her Aunt Maggie and grandmother in much the same manner on that occasion.

Shopping.—December 23, worker accompanied Pearl to select a winter coat. She had saved four dollars to apply on the cost of the coat. Pearl knew exactly what she wanted and although the selection was small she found a coat that suited her.

Pearl's inclination to avoid new situations was noticed when worker suggested another way for her to return home and thus save a walk of several blocks. Pearl said she would rather go home the way she came because she was used to it.

Mary continues to be well adjusted in the foster-home. She occasionally earns a little extra money by helping the next-door neighbor. The woman is fond of Mary and "makes work" for her because she is so happy in doing little odd jobs.

Clayton has grown quite tall recently and is now asking for long pants because "he feels better in them."

SUMMARY JANUARY 1–MARCH 15, 1936

Visited in the home of Mrs. Faville, January 8, 9, 13, 15, February 5 and 17. Visited Franklin School, January 8, 15, 30. Shopped with Pearl Lane, Saturday afternoon, January 25, and Saturday afternoon, February 15. Mrs. Faville, Pearl, and Mary visited the worker at her home February 8. Visited Mrs. Nevins, aunt of Pearl Lane, January 17.

Mary has been a happy, responsive child at all visits, showing her Christmas presents, her lessons, drawings, and telling of different experiences. She is very fond of "Uncle George," who helps her with her lessons. She enjoys his jokes and does little personal things for him such as "tucking him in bed," and saving parts of special foods for him. She is usually so delighted with small children that she has little interest in girls her own age. She greatly enjoys helping take care of the neighbor's baby.

January 18, Mary has gained seven pounds in three months—restrict starches. March 13, Mary given dental care O.K. March 13, Mary at St. Martin's Pediatric Clinic, Dr. Gilson. Heart normal in size and position; does not need to return.

During the severely cold days, Mrs. Faville kept Mary at home, and she was allowed to stay away from school to attend Pearl's graduation on January 30. She was very proud of Pearl and called the worker's attention to Pearl each time she appeared on the stage.

One very cold day, Pearl and Mary started to school and Pearl thought it might be too cold for Mary. She asked her principal about it and later called Mrs. Faville who advised that she send Mary home.

Recently, Mary took twenty cents from off the refrigerator of Mrs. Shelly, where she sometimes takes care of the baby. Later, Mary told Pearl about it. Pearl told her to talk to Mrs. Faville and tell her all about it. Mrs. Faville and Mary returned the money to Mrs. Shelly.

During the visit to Franklin School, January 8, the principal said that it might be advisable to have an examination of Clayton at the Child Guidance Clinic, though she would give his situation more thought. Mrs. Faville said that Clayton was having difficulty with his arithmetic. When he does not understand it, he does not like to go to school. In preparation for a possible examination at the Clinic, a social history was written of Clayton.

On January 30, the worker again talked with the principal and Clayton's teachers last year and this year. He was promoted January 30 to 5B. He is showing some improvement in arithmetic. The day before he was one of four to get a "thought problem." He is in a class of eleven who are retarded, so the competition is not so severe.

The principal said that she would like to work with Clayton. Her plan would be: (1) to give an individual intelligence test; (2) through a general achievement test find where he is weakest; (3) then, do some individual work on one of the weaknesses.

His last teacher showed the worker a letter Clayton had written her telling her that he was sorry to leave her room, that some day he hoped to be in 8A as his sister, Pearl, who was going to high school. The teacher of last year thinks he is mentally handicapped. She pointed out that he is dreamy and faraway; that he is temperamental and artistic; that he is responsive to personal interest but he is a listener and not a talker.

FRANKLIN SCHOOL, CHICAGO, ILL.
January 30, 1936

DEAR MRS. MUS,

I wold like to stay in the room. You a verry good to me and I am going to be verry good to the teacher I get. I hope you will rember me when I am in 8A. I heard that Miss-Hellgren is a verry good teacher but you are verry verry good and I dont want to go a outher tacher. When I an in 8A I will be thanking off you. I hat to be goinning to a outher tacher. When I am in 8A I will come to see you and I hope you will rember me. I now I will rember you. My sister will be working than and I will be working in school. You may not be here but I will thing of you. and I hope you will do it to. Miss right is a verry nice tacher and I like her and you to. Will I must say goodby.

Your Pal
CLAYTON LANE

The principal told of an incident that happened before the Christmas holidays. The pupils in Clayton's room were given a pledge card asking that they promise not to play with guns. All the children in the room except Clayton signed the cards. This focused attention upon him for not doing it. The principal talked to the room and told them that Clayton probably did not know the danger there was in playing with guns and he had been altogether honest in not signing the pledge; that he should not have signed it unless he understood what it meant and unless he knew he could keep his promise. Clayton told Mrs. Faville that the teacher did not scold him and thought he did right.

After the conference with these teachers, the principal suggested that the Child Guidance Clinic examination be withheld for a while until he was observed a little more closely.

Clayton plays with his friends in the neighborhood. He has more friends than Andrew, according to Mrs. Faville. He enjoys playing with the boys and enters into most games. He likes his bicycle. He gets along fairly well with Andrew Thomas.

Relatives.—Mary and Clayton told the new worker on her first visit of incidents about their parents and other relatives. Mary took the initiative in this and brought their pictures of the different members of the family. Often, Pearl would correct them in some detail of their statements. Clayton was pensive and quiet most of the time. He told of the death of both parents.

Health.—January 18, Clayton gained three pounds in three months.

January 25, Clayton's eyes checked—referred to eye clinic.

February 7, Clayton given dental care.

February 14, Clayton at St. Martin's Eye Clinic, to return for refraction.

February 15, Dr. Meek gave Clayton annual examination; general condition fairly good, has small swelling around right nipple which should be watched, to return in one week to see Dr. Meek and if not better should be referred to the Children's Hospital Clinic for diagnosis.

Dr. Denton gave dental care to Clayton, to return if front tooth is too sore.

February 22, Clayton seen by Dr. Meek; has a slight cold and temperature of 99, nothing serious; also had a bruised place in right groin, mostly skin abrasion, small swelling of right breast around the nipple. Referred to Dr. Grant at Children's Hospital.

February 24, Clayton at Children's Hospital Surgical Clinic, seen by Dr. Hamaker; need not return.

February 25, Clayton at St. Martin's Eye Clinic, seen by Dr. Green; does not need glasses.

Mrs. Faville says that Clayton is very nice about his eating, even eating things he does not like. He does not care for peas and custards but tries to learn to like them. She says his digestion is much better than last fall, when he often became nauseated and lost his breakfast. Mrs. Faville thought this was partly due to his nervous hasty eating. She tried to help him overcome this by telling him to eat slowly.

Special problems.—The teachers think that Clayton is not smoking now. He still bites his fingernails to some extent. He is quick tempered and reacts hastily but gets over it. Mrs. Faville told of an incident last spring when Clayton quarreled with her nephew. He hit his jaw and knocked out a tooth. Later, they made up and Clayton visited him during the Christmas holidays. No special problems have occurred for sometime. The worker's impression is that Clayton is shy and quiet, particularly when he is with older people; that he is conscious of his limitations in school and that this influences his attitude about school; that he is aware of the fact that Andrew makes contacts more quickly than he though he is not able to understand that he may have more friends than Andrew in the community.

When a visit was made on the evening of January 9, Mary ran to the door to greet the worker and began telling her all about her Christmas toys, the dog, her books, and other interesting things. Andrew soon joined in with the same spontaneous manner, showing his things. Clayton stood by the table quiet and smiling but saying little except in answer to questions. On a later visit, February 17, the worker planned to focus attention upon Clayton. He and Andrew were shoveling snow as she reached the house. Clayton called from a distance. Later, in answer to questions, he told of his school and what he had been doing. He said that he did not like his new teachers so much as he did the teacher last term. Again, he took little initiative in the conversation, though he always answered the questions with a smile. Andrew asked if he and Clayton could go to International House and see it and the Chapel chimes as Pearl and Mary had done. When the two boys went into the kitchen, where Mr. Faville was helping Mary with her lessons, Clayton said, "Uncle George, I saw Mrs. Sayles (worker) first, before Andrew did."

March 9, talked to Clayton over the telephone, asking how he and Andrew would like meeting the worker on Saturday, March 21, with two other boys at the Field Museum and seeing a picture show of the Cliff Dwellers. He said that he would go talk it over with Andrew.

He said that school was "not so hot."

Pearl was graduated from Franklin School January 30 and entered Hillman School the following Monday. She will remain in Hillman one year and then go to Lincoln High School. The principal of Franklin School said that Pearl was being sent to Hillman instead of the Technical High School because she was "academically minded." Pearl said she did not want to go to the Technical High School because it was a "sissified" school where they taught home economics.

Pearl is very artistic. Her work in everything except arithmetic has been excellent. Her plaque, completed before the holidays, was well done and artistic. When an occasion came for the selection of a few of the best for a display, the children in the room all voted for Pearl's plaque. She was in a play at the graduation program, taking the part of Judith in *Rip Van Winkle*. She gave the part with some reticence and reserve. At no time was she demonstrative. She looked very attractive in her new dress, which she told the teachers she liked. Mrs. Faville had taught her to make paper tulips, and she in turn had taught a group of girls. They had made a large box which made the decoration for the stage. She participated in all the numbers given by the girls. The program was attractive and carried out well. Later, when the worker asked Pearl if she enjoyed the graduation, she said that it was not so good as the graduation programs had been in the past.

She apparently made an easy adjustment at Hillman. She and her friend, Martha Haines, had planned how they would meet and walk to school each day. Pearl told the worker that she and Martha would try out for the Glee Club, that she would rather be in that than in any other organization of the school. Later, when the worker told her she was glad to know she had made the Glee Club, she answered, "It is not much. We are learning scales now. It is not much. No songs."

Pearl is inclined to make negative statements a great deal. She said the Hillman School looked very well outside but "not much inside." "The rooms," she said, "are filthy, walls are smudgy. It's lousy. It's not like Franklin. I hate the principal. She is a Jew." On a shopping trip with the worker, as they stopped to look at displays, Pearl would often say, "There is not much to that."

Foster-home.—Pearl has been something of an irritant to Mr. and Mrs. Faville. Mrs. Faville had been thinking of a possible change but reconsidered because of Pearl's plan to go to Hillman School with girls in the neighborhood, because Pearl had said she would run away should she leave, because of her influence with Clayton and Mary, and because of the stay at Hillman School being but one year. (See foster-home record.)

Mr. Faville gets out of patience with Pearl, so Mrs. Faville has asked that he leave Pearl's control to her. When Pearl, Mary, and Mrs. Faville visited International House, Mary left with a bag of popcorn to take to Mr. Faville. On the car, when Mary refused to let Pearl eat it, Pearl said that Mr. Faville "was a pig." Mary told Mrs. Faville of the incident the following morning. Mrs. Faville sent Pearl to her room to be alone. As she left the group she said, "You hate me, anyway."

Special problems.—Mrs. Faville says that most of Pearl's problems relate to clothes. Recently, Pearl said that people on relief had better clothes than she. She is a bit jealous of Anna Gibbs, who is fourteen and in the same school. Anna's parents are on relief, but her aunt gives her clothes. Mrs. Faville says that Pearl is always finicky, she can never foretell her taste or standards in clothes; that unless she likes a dress, she refuses to wear it. She mentioned particularly her not wearing her confirmation dress—now dyed powder blue—and not wearing a blue plaid blouse Pearl and the worker had selected.

Pearl's teachers had suggested that she was quite self-conscious of her rapid physical development at this time. Mrs. Faville reported that Pearl refused to wear a blouse because a girl had told her it was too tight. During one visit, Pearl put on her blue dress and showed why she did not like the tightness in the hips. Mrs. Faville then took out the pleats instead of remaking the dress for Mary as she had contemplated.

On January 8, Pearl's teachers at the Franklin School said that they had recently noticed a change in Pearl's attitude in regard to Mrs. Faville. One particular instance related to a form letter sent out by the principal to the parents and guardians of the graduates. The following is a copy of the message:

Are you in favor of your child having a pin and all or any of the listed items below? None is necessary to graduation. If just one is chosen, we suggest that it be the class ribbon. Please write "yes" after any article you wish to buy, and sign your name below. Be free to make any comments.

Pin.................. $0.90   Ribbon.............. $0.20
Guard................ .50   Picture............. .60

The paper had a marked space for the signature of the parent or guardian. Pearl marked the paper "All" and signed her own name saying to the teacher, "Mrs. Faville says that I may have none of them." They had never heard her refer to Mrs. Faville other than as "Aunt Margaret." The teacher asked if Pearl was worried about her dress.

On Saturday, January 25, Mrs. Faville and worker went with Pearl to buy her graduation dress and shoes. Pearl was articulate in her dislikes but not clear in her preferences. She did not find shoes to her taste so decided to have a good shine for her old ones and wear them. She asked for shoes that were "growner" and seemed to dislike low and Cuban heels.

She selected a dress that she evidently liked although she was not demonstrative. Later, she told her teachers she had a new dress for graduation and liked it. The teacher told the worker that the disturbed feeling about Mrs. Faville had passed, she thought.

On Saturday, February 15, worker shopped with Pearl for shoes. It was very difficult to discover just what Pearl really wanted though it was very clear what she did not like. Worker thought that she must have a definite idea but for some reason was a little restrained about actually saying. She finally decided on a pair. Later, as she and the worker walked down the street, she pointed to shoes in a window that she had had in mind. On Monday afterward, worker asked if she would not like to return her shoes and try to find some like those in the window. She said that she had decided she liked her shoes and it did not matter.

During the shopping trip, she said that she wanted a leather brief case. She found one she liked particularly. A few days later when the worker showed her pictures of brief cases less expensive, she said that she preferred having the one she selected and paying for part of it with her allowance. Even when it was learned that the particular brief case had been sold and it might be several weeks before another would be in, she preferred waiting. Several weeks later, the brief case bearing her full name was delivered. Andrew Thomas told a worker at Children's Agency that Pearl was "just crazy" about her new brief case.

Pearl wants to be a stenographer. She has apparently sensed a little insecurity about her foster-home. One time, she told Mrs. Faville that she hoped the Home would never place her where she would have "to care for brats." On the other hand, upon her own initiative, she has cared for Mrs. Shelly's baby and has earned a little money in this way.

She is reserved and lacks graciousness. It is not clear that she is having spontaneous social life. She no longer takes part in the Scouts. The girls belong to a different neighborhood, and she has little common interests with them. Then, she does not like the new leader. Her interest in the church is passive more than active. The Rev. Mr. Coble, pastor of the Lutheran church which she attends, says that he sees her daily as she passes to school and that she is in his Bible Class. Her rating in Sunday School is between 80 to 95 per cent. He said that her background was not so religious as some but her interest was there. However, he added that she is a little reticent and reluctant, as though she felt inferior or a little strange. He said that he had noticed this but has assumed it to be an adolescent quality and, because Pearl did not give encouragement to spontaneous co-operation, he had not made any particular effort to learn if he could help her. He said that he would be glad to seek out an opportunity to give her some natural expression. On one shopping trip, she and the worker browsed about from one counter to another, noting things. Pearl would perhaps say, "That is not much," "They are wearing that now," "That costs so much, I guess no one ever buys it," or remain silent. Once before a table of fancywork, she said, "Oh, I begin things, but I never finished one." Twice, however, she spontaneously explained, "This is pretty." She showed more than the usual enthusiasm about a display of a great variety of paper flowers. On Monday when the worker asked if she had told Mrs. Faville about these, she told her for the first time, adding a number of observations which the worker had failed to note.

Worker explained to Pearl when she entered Hillman that her allowance would be increased; that it might be well during the first weeks for her to keep a record of her needs and expenditures in order to know what would be an adequate allowance. After the initial expenses were met, it was decided to see, for a while, how twenty-five cents a week met her needs.

Pearl showed some humor and co-operation during a visit February 17. The boys told of their interest in airplanes, and Pearl answered, "Well, we are all air-minded. I want to be an aviatrix." Later, when Mrs. Faville was giving information for a questionnaire, in answer to a question about keeping animals, Pearl said, "You know, Aunt Margaret, you keep us and we are four domestic animals.

When Mrs. Faville was hesitant about the question of her preparation for a foster-mother, Pearl intervened by saying that Mrs. Faville was a practical nurse in a state institution three years before she was married.

February 1, 1936, Pearl was at St. Martin's Eye Clinic, Dr. Green; to discontinue glasses, need not return.

February 21, 1936.—Letter to Pearl from the social worker:

You know we were uncertain about what extra things you would need when you entered Hillman School. It was for that reason that I suggested your keeping a list of the items you bought. I appreciated the neat way in which you listed your purchases. Since you think you have all the extra things for a time, you need not furnish me a list of your other purchases.

What do you think of this plan? The Children's Agency will allow you two dollars for the month of February. The additional is to take care of these extra needs. It will cover all you have bought except eighteen cents. Beginning March first, you will receive a weekly allowance of twenty-five cents. With your good management, I am sure that you will be able to buy your school supplies and personal things with this. When you were talking about the show, I did not ask you about the price of admission; but since twenty-five cents is an increase, I am confident that it will do a lot for you.

I know that you greatly prefer the rough leather brief case at the Davis Store. You know, of course, that there have been several purchases recently, so it seems that one dollar and fifty cents for the brief case is as much as we should spend at this time. If you wish to save from your allowance or to use some of your present money to add to this for the brief case you like, it is entirely all right and we shall appreciate your co-operation.

I shall not be seeing you for a while, so I wanted to be quite sure you understood about your allowance.

Visited in the home of Mrs. Faville on Wednesday, March 23; Saturday, April 18; and Thursday, April 30. On Saturday, March 25, Clayton Lane, Andrew Thomas, and four other boys went with the worker to the Field Museum for a visit.

Clayton and Andrew with two guests met the worker early Saturday morning at the Children's Home for the trip to Field Museum. Clayton politely introduced the two boys. Clayton joined with Andrew in telling what they had for lunch.

As the group approached the Museum, Andrew suggested that the boys race. Later, Andrew called back, "I beat Clayton." Clayton answered, "I was not trying to beat." After the boys reached the Museum, they were joined by Jimmy Parker and another lad older than the others. They all enjoyed the Museum. Suddenly, Clayton saw a woman with an easel and paintbrushes. He said that he wanted to watch her. He stood for sometime and later said he wanted to learn to paint some day. Recently, during a visit in the home, Clayton said that he was going to study at the Art Institute sometime; that he used to be able to draw but he had not kept it up and he wanted to.

At the Museum, Clayton told a great deal about the birds showing a surprising fund of information. In contrast with Andrew, Clayton was not competitive. He did not strive to excel in giving directions, racing, or explaining though he met each situation adequately. He got along well with the boys and was agreeable to plans.

In the afternoon, the boys played on the rocks, and Clayton like the others said that he liked that best of all. There was some risk about jumping on the rocks, so it was agreed that they could jump provided they did not jump on the rocks touching the lake. Andrew several times ventured quite to the water's edge; Clayton was conforming. When Andrew persisted in venturing too far, the game was called off and another interest followed. Clayton was agreeable though he said that he surely liked to jump the rocks.

Mrs. Faville says that Clayton holds his own with the boys; that he does not take anything from them. He has a quick temper and the boys know it and respect it. Mr. Faville stated that when the boys first came to their home, he told them never to strike first but not to be imposed on. Andrew sometimes runs to Clayton crying and asking him to take his part.

Recently, the worker had supper with Mrs. Faville. Clayton was not in the room when she arrived. Later, he came in clean and well dressed.

He came directly to the worker and shook hands with her. This is the second time the worker has observed that he meets "greeting situations" with noticeable ease for a boy of his age.

Mrs. Faville says that Clayton is an excellent person to send to the stores, that at first he was timid and held back but now he has overcome that. She thinks that in recent months, in particular, he has gained control of himself; she thinks his health is better.

School.—In March, Mrs. Faville phoned that she had had a note from Clayton's teacher asking to talk with her about his work. Since the worker was at Franklin School the following day, she explained to Clayton's teacher that Mrs. Faville would see her the following day but she would like to know the difficulty. His trouble was with subtraction. She said that Clayton seemed to be trying but that he lacked concentration. The principal said that she would give him the Otis Test the following week. Both reported that Clayton was showing no behavior problems. Mrs. Faville thinks that Clayton is now doing his school work. He is doing home work.

Special problems.—On Good Friday evening, the Favilles and the children attended services. Mr. and Mrs. Faville and Pearl went to the front for communion and left the three children in the rear. Clayton and Andrew misbehaved. An elder in the church led Andrew to his seat and had him stay by him. When Clayton returned home, he told Mrs. Faville that they had been naughty in church.

On Monday after this, Mrs. Raney, Andrew's mother, talked with Mrs. Faville over the phone. She told her that Clayton and Andrew had been talking of running away. Mrs. Faville talked to Pearl and asked her if she could learn anything from Clayton. Clayton told her that they had talked of running away but had no place to go, so had given it up. Later, Clayton talked with Mrs. Faville about it.

Adjustment with relatives.—Recently, Clayton went for a visit to his grandmother's. He planned to spend the night but returned and seemed very moody. Mrs. Faville knew that something had hurt him. Later, Pearl told her that Clayton's grandmother came into the room and spoke as though she did not want him and said, "Are you here again?"

Adjustment in foster-home.—Mrs. Faville says that Clayton has made noticeable improvement in several ways in recent months. Worker observed him with Mr. Faville. Clayton told him of catching crabs and mentioned that he wanted to hike to a certain place. Mr. Faville suggested that they could go some Sunday afternoon. Clayton referred several questions to him, suggesting a wholesome natural relationship.

Worker's impression.—Clayton finds it hard to carry his school work well but he is gaining confidence. Mrs. Faville suggests that he has more confidence for untried situations than Pearl has. He is pleasing in his relationships with people. He is not competitive as Andrew is, but he holds his own and usually has a rather winsome manner. It might be well to follow his interest in drawing.

Mary remains practically the same with the different visits. She is invariably affectionate and thoughtful. At a recent visit, she drew several pictures, and carefully wrapped an Easter egg for the worker. She helped to care for the neighbor's baby. When she returned from taking him home, she had a quarter which the neighbor had given her. She went immediately and pushed it into her savings bank. She saves her earnings and has more than $10.

March 28, Mary given vaccination.

Pearl likes Hillman better now than she did at first. Her grades did not come up to her usual standard, but Mrs. Faville credited this to her not being known yet and her timidity about asserting herself. Pearl has not, from the beginning, liked the principal at Hillman. Recently, when her teacher checked the home work, Pearl did not have hers done. This was exceptional with Pearl, and it happened at the time that the principal was in the room. She asked all those who were not prepared with home work to report to her office. The principal made Martha Haines, Pearl's friend, cry.

A day or two later, Mrs. Faville was at Franklin School and told Miss Evans, the principal there, of the incident. Miss Evans talked with the Hillman principal, who later called Pearl to her office, told her that she heard that she had made a very good plaque at Franklin and she would like to see it, and if possible arrange for her to be in an art class at Lincoln. This was very heartening to Pearl. Soon afterward, when she saw the worker, she said, "I have something to tell you." She then told of the latter part of this incident. Pearl said that she could not say that she liked the principal yet but she did like her assistant. She sang in a minstrel show given at Hillman and said that it was very good. Not long ago, someone asked Pearl how long it would take her to get through high school. She answered that she could quit after two years if she did not like it.

Vocational guidance.—Pearl has been saying that she wanted to be a stenographer. It seemed that she decided on this because it was the most familiar. It was suggested to Mrs. Faville that vocational advice at Child Guidance Clinic could be given Pearl if she wanted it; that Mrs. Faville might from time to time make suggestions about different vocations for girls and lead up to her really wanting such help. Pearl is good with hair arrangement; then, when she wants to sew, she always does neat work.

Mrs. Faville has had several satisfactory conversations with her though the time is not yet opportune for suggesting the vocational help.

Health.—March 28, Pearl was vaccinated.

Social adjustment outside the home.—Pearl shrinks from new experiences. The girls in the new confirmation class are together a great deal because of the preparation for confirmation. Because of this, Pearl has withdrawn and come to Mrs. Faville's class. Mrs. Faville says that she knows she should not be there but, for the time, it looks as though nothing can be done about it.

Mrs. Shelly, a neighbor, asked Pearl to go for a package. Mrs. Faville thinks that Pearl declined simply because it was a new and strange place and she was not sure just what to do. She was to go to a laundry for the package.

Pearl has had several satisfactory experiences recently, however, and they seem to influence her attitudes considerably. She is going on hikes regularly. When she walks one hundred miles she will receive a bar. These hikes take place two and three times weekly. Mrs. Faville has told Pearl that she may have a party before very long. Pearl had withdrawn from the Scouts because she did not understand and like the substitute captain. When the old captain returned, she called Pearl and invited her to come back. She asked her especially to sing in the quartet which would be known as the Scout Quartet. Pearl is enjoying this and practices in the quartet regularly. Mrs. Faville thinks that Pearl's widened activities are helping her.

Pearl was quite a different person the evening the worker was a guest in Mrs. Faville's home. She took the lead as hostess and did it with graciousness, though with some reserve. She suggested that she and Mary would walk to the car with the worker and she waved goodbye in a very girlish manner.

Mrs. Faville says that she has difficulty in getting Pearl to go to the Children's Agency for the different appointments. Recently after the dentist was at the Home and Pearl was to come for service, Mrs. Faville called that she could not get Pearl to come. It was learned, though, that Pearl had additional home work assigned for the following day.

Special problems.—Pearl still brings problems about her clothes. She now dislikes a coat which she and worker bought during the winter, and it was thought at the time that she liked it.

Pearl's attitude toward Andrew was clearly indicated one evening when Mrs. Faville was telling an incident when Andrew misbehaved. Pearl injected such remarks as, "Gee, I wish that he would live somewhere else. I could tell him goodbye at any time. He is such a cry baby."

Mrs. Faville has asked if it might be possible to find some kind of work for Pearl during the summer vacation, that she rather dreads the summer since Pearl is so easily irritated by the other children. Then, she thinks that it will do Pearl a great deal of good to come under the influence of someone else and learn how other people do things. Recently, she and Pearl had an argument. Pearl was going on a hike and put on her best blouse when there were two slightly soiled that could have done as well. When Pearl was dressed, she had some extra time, so went to the basement to do some cleaning. Mrs. Faville told her that she must not do dirty work in that clean blouse.

Mrs. Faville has reported, however, several favorable experiences with Pearl in recent weeks, and she is quite eager to help her.

On April 13 the problems of Pearl were discussed in staff conference. The following points were stressed. The adjustment of the other two children is always emphasized. Mary, quite in contrast with the report given by Mrs. Walters, had made a happy adjustment. Early, she showed that she was desirous of affection and had made her adjustment with reference to this desire. She had made a place for herself with the family and the neighborhood. She would do anything for approval and continuously intrenches herself.

Pearl, on the other hand, made a different kind of adjustment. She was always on the defensive; inclined to come in conflict with foster-mother; has much pride and wants the best clothes, best of everything; closes up and sulks; she has different standards and ideas and is inclined to transfer her affectional needs into material demands. Pearl does not face the fact that she needs affection, will not admit it, but she does need affection. On the whole the children have made a pretty good adjustment. It is a rather usual family life, pretty normal; but Pearl does not make her adjustment as the other two. The suggestion of her going to another place has been a traumatic one for Pearl. *She is deprived and suffering.* She transfers these affectional needs to various demands. She needs relationship with someone who means something to her. She is entering adolescence with a good bit of difficulty. She has difficulty in relating herself to people. Note that she is immediately defensive—she has the attitude of a youngster deeply hurt, who cannot substitute any other relationship where her demands can be met. It was thought that it would be a mistake to remove Pearl from the home of Mrs. Faville. There must be a strong achievement satisfaction for Pearl.

Interpreting.—Worker told Mrs. Faville that several of the workers familiar with Pearl's history had talked over her problems and were so eager to find the underlying cause of her difficulties. It was emphasized that Mrs. Faville's work was appreciated and her own eagerness to get suggestions had helped so much in studying the case. Worker then suggested to her Pearl's need for affection and her urge for achievement, emphasizing the point that Pearl had a deeper sense of affection and security with Mrs. Faville and her home than her behavior overtly suggested.

Mrs. Faville recognizes that Pearl is happier when she has some recognition and she named many experiences that had seemed happy.

During the evening that the worker was in the home of Mrs. Faville she observed several indications that showed Pearl was intrenched in the family. She took the role of the oldest daughter and met the requirements as far as the evening went, in a way to make parents proud. She was the hostess to some extent, meeting the worker at the door, taking care of her coat and hat, seeing that she was given a napkin, addressed conversation to her, and later when Mrs. Faville was telling of incidents relating to the other children, she entered into the conversation.

Relatives.—Not long ago the worker visited Mrs. Williams and Miss Maggie Nevins. Mrs. Williams said that Pearl had been her father's idol; that he gave very little attention to the other children. Pearl refused to obey her mother and took everything to her father. He was a janitor, and Pearl followed him to all his places of work, even going, up until midnight, on firing trips, returning home dirty and worn out, going to bed in her clothes. Mrs. Williams often had disputes with Mr. Lane about this. When Mr. Lane died, Pearl could hardly be reconciled, though she showed little emotion when her mother died.

Mrs. Williams said that Pearl had a peculiar stubborn disposition and she thought that nothing could be done about it; that she was not appreciative and not at all gracious. She thinks she inherited her stubbornness. Mrs. Williams once gave Pearl a dress; Pearl liked it at the time but soon she disliked it and tried to sell it. Mrs. Williams said that she would never again give her clothes. Not long ago, Pearl was in her home when the insurance collector came for the weekly insurance which Mrs. Williams carries for the children. Pearl withdrew to the bathroom and did not want to come out to see him though Mrs. Williams made her come out. The man gave her a dime. Mrs. Williams was critical because Pearl did not thank him and scolded her severely after the man left. She thinks that she does not appreciate what Mrs. Faville does for her.

Miss Maggie Nevins said that Pearl turned up her nose at a girl with whom she once played because the girl was going with a boy; that she, Miss Nevins, thought it was because Pearl could not do that herself. Miss Nevins mentioned that it had been suggested that Pearl live with them because the other children irritated her so. She thought that this was foolish because there are usually younger children and an older one has to accept it.

Mrs. Faville thinks that Pearl had her feelings hurt at her last visit to her grandmother's and will not want to return.

Worker's impression.—Pearl is making some progress and really needs help. It is clear that she shrinks from new experiences and the repetition of unpleasant ones. Some help could be given in making new experiences more pleasant. If adjustments can be made, it does seem wise for Pearl to remain in the Faville home.

Mrs. Faville needs more help in understanding the basic reasons for this behavior, and Pearl needs more praise for what she does accomplish. It was surprising how adequately she met the situations as hostess in Mrs. Faville's home. At a later visit, her manner was more gracious and she called out goodbye with a spontaneity which had been absent in earlier contacts. Care should be taken to help Mrs. Faville to adjust to the rather extravagant needs of adolescence. Does Pearl really have a large-enough allowance, even though Mrs. Faville is sure she does?

Miss Evans, principal of Franklin School, is thinking of organizing an Alumni Association of Franklin School. The primary purpose of the organization will be to have a group of students at the high schools that will help the incoming Franklin students to make adjustments. If Pearl could be a part of this and feel a sense of purpose and responsibility next fall at Hillman, it might help her to feel less concerned about her own security.

FOSTER HOME RECORD

A. FACTS FOR IDENTIFICATION AND REFERENCE

Surname __Faville__   Address in full at Application __721 S. Alden__   Date of Application __5–29–31__

Parents (Present marriage)   *Birth Date Birth Place* (Mo.Da.Yr.)   *Present Marriage*

Boarding Father: __George__   __'45__   Date __9–11–1920__

Boarding Mother: <u>Margaret 5-30-1887</u> <u>Barney, Ill.</u> Place <u>Kenyon, Ill.</u>

Indicate which Parent	Time in City– County– State–U.S.	Citizen	Race	Nation- ality	Religion	Usual Occupa- tion and Weekly Earn- ings
Boarding Father		Yes	Amer.	Ger.	Luth.	
Boarding Mother		Yes	Amer.	Ger.	Luth.	

Relatives (Including Married Children. State whether relatives
are paternal or maternal)

Relationship	Full Name	Address (or, if dead, age and cause)
Sister—Man	Mrs. Jacob Miller	452 S. Kahler
Sister—Man	Mrs. Nellie Dorbeck	728 N. Oakdale
Brother—Man	Frank Faville	Clayborn, Ill.

References and Others Who Know Family		Agencies Registering with Social Service Exchange	
Connection (as employer, physician, etc.)	Name and Address	Registered (Date) 7/1931	Known Not Known
Friend	Bertie Goeber, 645 Sampson Avenue	No record	
Friend	Ben Wiley, 630 Finlay Street		
Friend	Mrs. Grace Ziegman, 503 Hanover Avenue		
M.D.	Dr. O. Zorber, 521 W. 14th Street		

AGENCY___Chicago Children's Agency___ DATE_____

What persons live in your home (including hired help)?
(Give full name and age and sex of each)

George Faville
Margaret Faville

Location of your home: On what line of railroad?
Railroad Station? I.C. Railroad. *How far from house?* 6th and Davis.

Give full directions for reaching your home by railroad, trolley, or otherwise. If necessary to drive, where is nearest garage or livery?

Can reach us by trolley. We live one block and half from Kedvale and 6th Street.

How can you be reached by phone? Harris 421.

What is your religious preference? Lutheran. *Race?* White. *Nationality?* German.

Name and address of your pastor?

Rev. Harry Coble, 764 S. Sennett Street.

What is the state of health of the members of your household? Good.

Name and address of your physician?

Dr. O. Zorber, 521 W. 14th Street.

Why do you want to take a child?

I have spare time and am interested in children.

What kind of a child would you consider taking?

Between what ages? Any age from 3 yrs. up. *Boy or girl?* Either one.

Would you take more than one? Yes.

What kind of child would interest you? Any of them.

What would be your plans for a child's future (his position in the family, education, etc.)?

Would see that they were sent to school and Sunday School if desired.

What are your present circumstances and your probable ability to carry out your plans? (Give occupation and employer of husband)

Very good.

Excel Roofing Company   1340 West 12th Street.

What facilities are there in your family and neighborhood for giving a child:

Schooling? (Distance of school from house, kind of school, length of term)

5 blocks from Franklin School. Public school.

Religious life? (Accessible churches and distance from house)

1½ blocks from house.

Recreation?

Manley Park, Sixth and Kedvale Avenue.

Have a nice yard and radio.

Please give as references:

At least three persons (not all relatives) who are well acquainted with your family life.

Name	Address	If related how?
Bertie Goeber	645 Sampson Avenue	None
Ben Wiley	630 Finlay Street	None
Mrs. Grace Ziegman	503 Hanover Avenue	None

[*Signed*] MRS. MARGARET FAVILLE

P.O. Address: 721 S. Alden, Chicago, Illinois

*Date:*5–29–31

Applicant.—Mrs. George Faville.

Address.—721 South Alden Avenue.

Date of application.—May 29, 1931.

Source.—Mrs. Faville learned of Children's Agency through Mrs. Ziegman, who had formerly applied to board children for the Agency but who now boards children through newspaper advertising.

Date of investigation.—July, 1931.

Location of home.—Take Fifth Street car to Kedvale and south to Sixth. Walk one block west.

Community.—The Favilles live in a quiet residential section where the homes are fairly simple brick bungalows but well kept. The residents are of no predominating nationality but for the most part are northern European stock. A German Lutheran church which the family attends is one and a half blocks from the home. Manley Park is located at Sixth and Kedvale. This is not one of the better-equipped parks. The Franklin School is five blocks distant.

Home.—The home is a five-room bungalow valued at $8,000. There is a small back yard with flowers. The porch in the rear is inclosed.

There are two bedrooms and in the living-room a folding davenport. The Favilles sleep on the davenport much of the time in the warm weather. The rear bedroom, which would be used for boarding children, is 10 × 8½ × 9 feet high. There is one window 3 × 5 feet and cross ventilation. The basement is cement, and there is a hot-air furnace. The house was neat and orderly when visited.

The furnishings are plain and simple but adequate. The Favilles have a radio.

Household.—The household is made up of Mr. and Mrs. Faville.

Mrs. Margaret (Newman) Faville was born May 30, 1887, in Barney, Illinois. There were six children by her mother's first marriage and four more by her second marriage. Mrs. Faville's father died of pneumonia at the age of sixty-nine, and the mother of cancer at eighty. Both of Mrs. Faville's parents were born in Germany. Mrs. Faville stayed at home as long as her mother lived, even after her marriage on September 11, 1920.

She was married in Kenyon. She completed the eighth grade, clerked in a bakery, and for four years was a practical nurse in the State Hospital for the Insane. She quit this work in 1912. Her experience was in the receiving ward and in the ward for violent patients.

Mrs. Faville belongs to no clubs or lodges. She has been active in the church and at present has a Sunday School class of girls between ten and twelve. She has enjoyed this class a great deal. She takes the *Ladies' Home Journal*. While Mrs. Faville has not danced since her marriage, she learned to dance while working at the State Hospital and liked it. She does all her own work and has often gone out to do cleaning or take charge of a home during temporary absences of members of a family. Mrs. Faville stated that Mr. Faville took no part in outdoor activities but she would enjoy such activities if she had an incentive through caring for children.

Mrs. Faville is a tall well-built woman, neat, with fresh complexion and wholesome appearance. She uses fairly good English, is quiet, and well composed. One feels in talking with her that she has a broader knowledge and understanding of life through her earlier nursing experience than her present simple home and community life would imply.

Mr. George Faville, forty-five, was born in Chicago. He is of German descent and his own family consisted of four brothers and two sisters. The sisters and a brother live in Chicago. His parents are dead. Mrs. Faville does not see much of these relatives because all of them live at some distance.

Mr. Faville completed the seventh grade and started the piano-tuning business as an apprentice. He has worked in a number of piano factories.

Mr. Faville's first wife and little girl of five died about the same time of influenza. They lived in Kenyon, Illinois, at the time.

Mr. Faville has always had good health and has not needed a doctor since their marriage. He is a man who appreciates his home and seldom goes out except to the church meetings. He likes his radio. He belongs to no lodges or clubs. Mrs. Faville described him as a man of good habits who smokes but does not drink or use bad language. He takes the *Master Mechanic* magazine.

Financial condition.—The Favilles own their home, which has a $3,500 mortgage with taxes of $100 a year. Some of their savings are tied up at present in a closed bank (Bently) at Eighth and Kedvale. Mr. Faville works at the Excel Roofing Company and earns altogether between $75 and $100 a month. He is working only part time, but gets some piano-tuning on the side.

Relatives.—Mrs. Jacob Miller has one daughter, and her husband does piano repair work. Mrs. Dorbeck is a widow. She has five children who work and help support her. Frank Faville has a daughter, nineteen, and a son of six. He works at the King Washing Machine Company.

REFERENCES

Mr. and Mrs. Ben Wiley, 630 Finlay Avenue.—Mrs. Wiley stated that she had known Mr. and Mrs. Faville four years and would recommend them highly for the care of children. Mrs. Faville is an energetic woman, practical, and with sound ideas about child care. She has helped Mrs. Wiley from time to time in her home. Mrs. Faville is not a person "to put everything on her back." She dresses simply but believes in setting a good table. She has discussed with Mrs. Wiley the necessity of plenty of milk for children and was more successful in getting Mrs. Wiley's little girl to drink it than Mrs. Wiley herself. She is quite saving. She likes to read and often asks to borrow a magazine from Mrs. Wiley.

Mrs. Wiley spoke of how fond the children were of Mr. Faville when he was janitor at the church. When there was a change in janitors, they made a great fuss and said Mr. Faville was not cross and he let them have more privileges. Mr. Wiley stated that Mr. Faville works on the finance committee at the church and is considered a conscientious, good man.

Mr. and Mrs. Wiley have an elaborately furnished and well-kept home. They appear to be people without much education and few cultural advantages but straightforward and honest.

Dr. O. Zorber, 521 West Fourteenth Street.—Dr. Zorber has known Mrs. Faville for several years and took care of her when she had a tumerous growth. She has been in good health except for this. The growth was not malignant. When Mrs. Faville first consulted Dr. Zorber, she told him she had no children but would welcome them if they came. There is no indication of ill health on the part of Mr. Faville and Dr. Zorber has known Mrs. Faville well enough to have information of this nature. Dr. Zorber got in touch with Mrs. Faville, through the Wileys, who are good reliable people.

Mrs. Grace Ziegman, 503 Hanover Avenue.—Mrs. Ziegman has known Mrs. Faville for the past year, and two of her children have had her as a Sunday School teacher. Mrs. Ziegman stated that one never felt that one knew Mrs. Faville well as she is so quiet and reserved. She was president of the Ladies' Aid but resigned because she did not like the way the ladies quarreled among themselves. You never hear Mrs. Faville say anything "out of the way." She feels sure that Mrs. Faville will give children good care. Mrs. Ziegman has a license from the Department of Public Welfare and boards children privately. She impressed visitor as being quite ordinary, though respectable.

Rev. Harry Coble, 764 South Sennett Street.—Rev. Coble has known the Favilles for four years. Mrs. Faville has had to help toward the family income in the last two years because Mr. Faville's work has been so irregular. She has done cleaning for various members of the church and is well thought of. She has been active in the church, especially in Sunday School. She has a way of commanding respect and disciplining children but at the same time keeps their affection and interest.

The Favilles get along well together. Mr. Faville is a quiet fellow, overserious at times. He works hard and conscientiously at anything he undertakes. He is not well read. Rev. Coble thought Mrs. Faville more resourceful and intelligent. However, Rev. Coble assured visitor that the Favilles would make good foster-parents. They would give good physical care and set them a good example.

. Visitor was impressed with Rev. Coble's frankness, his intelligence, and understanding of the problem of foster-home placements.

Visitor's impression.—This is a simple home where children would be welcome for themselves as well as for the income. It should prove suitable for children requiring permanent care. It should probably not be used for children requiring considerable resourcefulness on the part of the foster-parent, although Mrs. Faville impresses one as patient and persistent.

July 27, 1931.—Placed Mary and Pearl Lane at a boarding rate of $25 a month each.

August 12, 1931.—Placed Clayton Lane at a boarding rate of $25 a month.

May 2, 1932.—Andrew Thomas was placed with Mrs. Faville at a boarding rate of $20 a month.

April 13, 1933.—See letter to Mrs. Faville arranging for boarding rate of $22 a month for each of the four children, to begin June 1.

July 21, 1934.—Mrs. Faville is a calm, patient foster-mother with a good measure of common sense. Mr. Faville has readily entered into the the plan of boarding children, and his good, jovial nature is felt by all the members of the household. It is evident that there was a need for children in the home. Although the Favilles are not financially well off, they do not hold on to the children for money. This fact was evidenced by Mrs. Faville's willingness to give up Andrew if the Children's Agency thought it best for him to be in a home by himself. She is fond of Andrew but is sincerely interested in his welfare.

Revaluation of the home, October 1, 1935.—Worker's first impression of the home has not changed. It is excellent for an average child. Probably Mrs. Faville will not do well with an adolescent child because of her rather rigid standards.

SUMMARY JANUARY 1–MARCH 15, 1936

Mrs. Faville is a calm, systematic, practical woman. Her home is well run, and her manner is that of one punctilious and sensible. She is not imaginative or particularly creative where diversified situations arise. Since she is remarkably co-operative, it may be possible for the worker to stimulate her creative imagination.

She says that Pearl is a problem and she invites every suggestion for understanding her better. She seriously considered asking that Pearl be placed elsewhere when she was graduated from the Franklin School but she decided against this for several reasons which she carefully gave. These were: (1) Pearl and some of the girls in the neighborhood had planned to go to Hillman School together. (2) Pearl takes a certain responsibility for Clayton and Mary. This was shown in the instance when she sent Mary back when the weather was so severely cold. Again it was shown when she told Mary to talk with Mrs. Faville about her taking twenty cents belonging to Mrs. Shelly. (See Mary's record.) (3) Then, Pearl had told Mrs. Faville that she would run away if she were placed elsewhere. (4) Since Pearl is to be at Hillman but one year, Mrs. Faville felt that it would not be wise to have a change before that time.

Two weeks after this decision was made, when Mary refused to give Pearl some popcorn because she wanted to take it to Mr. Faville, Pearl called Mr. Faville a pig. For the moment, Mrs. Faville thought perhaps the question of Pearl's removal should be opened again. The matter passed out of significance in a few days, however. Mrs. Faville nearly always judges an article or a dress by whether or not it is practical or sensible. Her judgment on an activity is whether or not it is educational. As the worker has talked with her about possible ways that girls and boys entered into activities, she usually says, "That would be so educational." Her comment about Pearl's dress, which was colorful and artistic, was, "I think it will be real practical."

Apparently, she is creative in handwork. She showed Pearl how to make a puppet for a school play and she taught her to make some paper tulips.

The younger children are obedient to her quiet statements of what to do. One evening at bedtime, she said, "I think it is time for you little folks to go to bed." There was no question. They all called good night and went to their rooms.

Mr. Faville was present during three visits. One evening, he sat by the radio, taking little part in the group conversation except now and then to insert a little teasing with Mary. One evening, he washed the dishes as the children and Mrs. Faville sat in the living-room talking to the worker. At another time, he remained in the kitchen helping Mary with her lessons. When the worker stepped to the door to talk with him, he asked if she knew how smart the two boys were, that they had shoveled off the snow on the front walk.

SUMMARY MARCH 15–MAY 1, 1936

On Saturday, April 18, the worker had supper with Mrs. Faville. Pearl was really the leading hostess. She was at the door when the worker came up the stairs and she took care of her hat and coat. Andrew and Mr. Faville were in fresh clothes sitting in the living-room. Mr. Faville was talkative and took a definite role in the family circle. Later in the evening several times Mr. Faville referred questions to Mrs. Faville since "she has more information on that subject than I."

Clayton and Mr. Faville talked of catching crabs and going on a proposed walk. Mr. Faville said that always when they were out with the boys Andrew would venture farther than Clayton but that he really did not meet hard situations so well. Mr. Faville told the boys when they first came to live in the home that they must never strike first but were not to be imposed on. He says that Clayton has learned this pretty well and holds his own, but Andrew has not. At the table, at the beginning of the meal, Andrew gave a short prayer. At the close of the meal, Clayton gave a short prayer. Both were prayers for the purpose planned for children.

The evening was one that offered participation to every member of the household. Pearl took the leading part and seemed to get satisfaction from it. A neighbor's child, two years old, ate supper and stayed until eight. Considerable attention was given to him. The dog entered into the picture. The whole setting seemed to be a home with considerable naturalness.

Mrs. Faville is always dignified. She is a woman who places very high values on basic principles. In talking with Andrew about his attitude toward his mother, she showed him the Fourth Commandment in his Sunday School book.

Background for understanding Agency work.—Mrs. Faville has a background that may be utilized for interpreting Agency work. She was for four years a practical nurse in the State Institution at Kenyon. In talking with the worker, she told of her interest in reading the records to understand the cases better; that she often thought that foresight and training could have prevented such serious situations.

Mrs. Faville is responsive to suggestions, particularly about Pearl. Worker at one time suggested that if Pearl would like it, during the coming year perhaps before she left Hillman, she could have the services of a Vocational Guidance Test at the Child Guidance Clinic; that this could come advantageously only if Pearl wanted it. In the conversation, it was suggested that as the opportunity came naturally, she might talk to Pearl about various kinds of vocations since Pearl might be thinking of the most familiar only. Mrs. Faville responded to this and has reported several conservations with Pearl.

Mrs. Faville plans to let Pearl have a party during her early vacation. She thinks her increased interest in girls and activities has helped her disposition.

At a recent visit, worker expressed appreciation of Mrs. Faville's work and told her that several of the workers familiar with Pearl's history had talked over the problem and had talked along the following lines.

1. Pearl has a deep need for Mrs. Faville's home; regardless of her record at school she has not felt the affectional security in the home and with her associates that the other two children have gained. Her behavior may be the symptom of her real need for that. Any suggestions of her going from Mrs. Faville's home at this time are a real shock to her; for she has found with Mrs. Faville and in her home more affection and security than at first seemed true.

2. Because of her reticence, Pearl needs a good many successful experiences. Worker and Mrs. Faville talked along this line, illustrating from different things the satisfactory experiences she had had and those from which she withdrew. Mrs. Faville stated that Pearl seemed to dread new experiences but in other things was quite determined.

Worker's impression.—The worker thinks that Mrs. Faville is usually co-operative. She is not creatively imaginative but quickly follows interpretations. She may be a little too thrifty to understand the extravagancies of adolescence very easily. It seems wise to spend considerable time talking with Mrs. Faville. There is a question with regard to Andrew's remaining in the home. The three Lane children do make a family unit, and Pearl holds considerable feeling about Andrew. On the other hand, the situation has not been studied sufficiently to make recommendations.

5. David Levy

(The Permanent Placement in Adoption of an Illegitimate Baby)

May 20, 1927.—A letter was received by the Children's Agency from the Welfare Council[1] asking for boarding-home care for the illegitimate baby boy (born April 13, 1927) of Miriam Levy. The following letter from the Girls' Department of the Family Agency was inclosed:

May we ask for a home for Baby Levy, who will be ready for discharge from the Salvation Army Maternity Home and Hospital within the next week?

Several weeks ago the hospital telephoned us that Miriam Levy had entered as a waiting mother on January 17. At the time the girl entered, both she and her mother refused to be referred to the Family Agency, claiming that they could make their own arrangements. This family had not been known to social agencies previously. Mrs. Levy expected to take Miriam home after her discharge from the hospital and leave the baby there. However, when she learned that this was impossible, she was willing that the Family Agency be asked to help.

Miriam was born in Chicago on February 9, 1904. Several months after her birth her father died, and she was placed in a private home where she remained until Mrs. Levy later remarried. Miriam entered the first grade at the Lincoln School at the age of six. She disliked school and in her first year was a problem as she was a continual truant. She left school at the age of fifteen when she was in the sixth grade. After leaving school she worked at Wellington's Store for two and a half years, making $12 a week. At the age of seventeen she ran away and married an Italian man named Juliano. She lived with him for about three months. According to her mother, he beat her and they could not get along. Consequently she secured a divorce from him. The girl has worked irregularly, clerking in department stores and working in factories. Her last job was with the Alpha Chocolate Company, where she worked as a packer, earning $15 a week.

In December, Mrs. Levy began to suspect that Miriam was pregnant. The girl firmly denied this until Mrs. Levy took her to a neighborhood doctor. After pregnancy was definitely established, Mrs. Levy knew that they could not keep the girl at home, so made her own arrangements at the Salvation Army Maternity Home and Hospital. Miriam refuses to give any information regarding the father of her baby, although her mother has questioned her time and again. She also refuses to tell our worker, who believes that she does not know the name of the father of the baby.

Miriam is physically very unattractive. She is very slovenly in appearance and is very dull in her conversation. She is a girl who is easily led by other peo-

[1] [The Welfare Council is a clearing agency for the Jewish child-caring agencies of Chicago. See the Stern case, p. 182.]

ple. Although while at the Salvation Army Home she has made a fair adjust-ment, they feel that she is extremely childish and is unable to make any decisions herself.

Mrs. Levy, aged fifty-seven, came to America when she was thirteen years old with her two brothers, her parents having died in Russia. The family came directly to Chicago. Mrs. Levy worked in a fish store on Franklin and St. Patrick streets. Her first husband was also employed in this store. She married him at the age of eighteen. There are four children by this union. Mr. Wein-burg, the first husband, died of pneumonia in 1904. After the death of her husband, Mrs. Levy returned to work in the fish store. Several years later she married her present husband. There is one child by this union. Since her second marriage Mrs. Levy has always assisted her husband in his business. For fifteen years the family had a grocery store on Eighth Street and Superior Avenue. Five years ago they moved to their present location.

According to Mrs. Levy her husband is unaware of the birth of Miriam's baby. Mr. Levy has not been on very friendly terms with Miriam since she married the Italian boy. Although the girl has lived in his home, he has not talked to her.

Richard, the oldest son, is practicing law near Denver. He comes home to visit once a year.

Ben is single and works in an overall factory. He has held the same position for the past fifteen years. During the War he was overseas and was reinstated in his job upon returning home.

Fred has been married for the past four years. His wife is pregnant and ex-pects to be delivered within the next two months. He is employed in a laundry.

Cynthia, aged eighteen, is employed as a stenographer and is earning $17.50 a week.

Since the Levys have a store with only one room in the rear for living quar-ters, the two youngest children live in an apartment over the store, with Fred and his wife. Mrs. Levy allows her son $30 a month towards his rent. The chil-dren eat their meals downstairs with the parents. The Levys pay $125 a month for their store. At the present time, Mrs. Levy complains that they are unable to make a living from their business.

Mrs. Levy has a brother, Frank Curman, who is a widower, living in the Piccadilly District. He is a harness-maker by trade and has been unemployed for the past two years. Mr. Curman has five children, who have been supporting him.

Mrs. Levy's other brother died a year and a half ago, leaving a wife and six children. None of the relatives is able to take the baby.

Mrs. Levy says that she is willing to pay $25 a month for the support of the baby.

As soon as we have obtained information regarding the baby's birth, delivery, et cetera, we will send you the additional information.

Later.—The following report was received from the Salvation Army Maternity Home and Hospital:

Re: Baby Levy
Mother: Miriam

Baby Boy: Born April 13, 1927.
Type of Delivery—Doctor delivered by midforceps, male child.

> No progress had been made in last three hours of labor; therefore forceps were applied but not a difficult delivery.

Laboratory tests—Negative.
Child is being breast fed.
Hours of Labor—12 hrs. 57 minutes.
Baby being circumcised at Salvation Army Hospital.

July 3, 1927.—Letter from Welfare Council stating that they have referred Baby Levy to the Juvenile Court, asking that the Children's Agency be given guardianship with the right to place and that the baby be put on the County Boarding Fund.

July 17, 1927.—Baby David Levy placed.

July 26, 1927.—Miriam was in the office to get the address of her baby. A letter of introduction to the foster-mother was given to her.

The following letter was received by the Family Agency from the Juvenile Court:

> We have a letter from you referring Baby David Levy to us for placement on the Boarding Fund. We wonder if it would be possible to give this child in adoption, as the mother apparently is not interested in keeping the baby. If adoption is to be arranged, perhaps this could be done directly through the County Court.
>
> If it is not yet determined whether the child is adoptable, would it be possible for the family or the girl to contribute to the support of the child until this has been determined. We believe that, when a girl is not willing to assume the responsibility for her illegitimate child, it should be given in adoption. This, of course, does not necessarily have to come through the Juvenile Court.
>
> We shall await your reply before taking action in this case.

August 4, 1927.—Letter to the Juvenile Court written by the Children's Agency:

> In reference to the Levy case, I wish to say that we are not ready to go ahead with the adoption and that the reason the petition was filed in the Juvenile Court to put this child on the Boarding Fund is because there is no one to support him. We asked that the baby be placed on the Boarding Fund until we know that he is adoptable.
>
> As far as the adoption proceedings are concerned, we, of course, know that we can take the matter up at the County Court, but it has been our practice

for a great many years to bring all our cases for guardianship with right to consent to the Juvenile Court, and we intend to follow this procedure unless the Juvenile Court refuses to act upon our petition.

August 21, 1927.—The foster-mother reported that Miriam visits the baby on an average of once a week and has not interfered with his routine in any way. She advised the foster-mother that she has not been able to secure a job as yet.

August 29, 1927.—Letter received by the Children's Agency from the Girls' Department, Family Agency:

Enclosed you will find a copy of the psychometric and vocational examination on Miriam Levy, who was examined on August 25, 1927.

Since our conference the worker has interviewed Mrs. Levy and Miriam. Mrs. Levy says that she has questioned the girl numerous times regarding the father of the baby and that Miriam has refused to answer. Since the girl returned from the Salvation Army Maternity Home and Hospital she has been unable to find work, and has remained at home all the time. Mrs. Levy has no plans to offer for the baby other than that he be given in adoption.

When Miriam was interviewed she insisted that she had no idea of the last name of the father of the baby; that she never asks men their last names nor does she tell them hers. We feel sure that the girl has no idea who the man is. Miriam has no plans for the future. She visits the baby occasionally but does not seem to be very much interested in him.

If there is any additional information that you wish, we shall be glad to obtain it.

PSYCHOMETRIC AND VOCATIONAL EXAMINATION

Miriam Levy—Age: 23   Examined: August 25, 1927

   I. *Test Results:*
      General Intelligence
         Mental age: 10 yrs. 3 mos.
         (Stanford-Binet) I.Q.: 64
         Mental rating: Mentally defective
         Performance Test I.Q.: 64
      Mechanical Ability: Average

  II. *Interests and Personality.*—Her interests are entirely in work of an unskilled type. She is not interested in learning a trade. Work as a cashier would appeal to her most.

      She gave the impression of being dull. Her comprehension during the interview and during the tests was very low.

 III. *Recommendations.*—Her abilities would be best adapted to work requiring very little intelligence. Work of an unskilled type is in keeping with her interests.

September 4, 1927.—In accordance with the arrangement made through correspondence with the Court, a representative of the Children's Agency was present at the committee meeting where the advisability of putting the baby on the County Boarding Fund was discussed. At the previous meeting the committee decided that this child should either be returned to the mother or that she should be compelled to give the child in adoption at once unless she is willing to support the baby herself. However, it was pointed out to the committee that, according to the Family Agency's investigation, the mother is apparently subnormal and a serious delinquent, and, since her stepfather does not know of the existence of the child, it is probably impossible for her to take the child home. With regard to the adoption of this child, it was explained to the committee that the child is entirely too young for the Children's Agency to consider giving him in adoption at the present time, since practically nothing is known of his paternity and the maternal history is poor. The committee therefore decided to put the baby on the County Boarding Fund until he is a year old, when the case will be again reconsidered with a view of either returning the baby to his mother or compelling her to give him in adoption, providing the child is adoptable.

Later.—Sent report to the Juvenile Court on the psychometric and vocational examinations of the mother.

September 26, 1927.—Letter received from the Welfare Council approving David's placement by the Children's Agency.

November 3, 1927.—Miss Levy, David's mother, was brought to the office of the Children's Agency by the worker from the Family Agency, Girls' Department; she says she is now willing to give her child in adoption. However, since it has been reported several times that she is interested in the baby and visits him regularly, she was questioned thoroughly as to whether she realizes that by consenting to the child's adoption she is forfeiting the privilege of ever seeing him again. The girl, with tears in her eyes, said that she understood this but that since she has no means of providing a home for the child herself, since her mother is absolutely opposed to her keeping in touch with the child, and since her stepfather does not even know of the existence of the baby, she is sure that she will never be able to care for him herself. In the girl's presence, the worker telephoned the Juvenile Court, where the case is pending, and requested that the investigation be completed and the baby be put on the County Boarding Fund until he is a year old, at which time we will agree to take him with consent to adoption providing we find him adoptable at that time. Meanwhile, the mother is to sign the Appearance and Consent, and when we are ready to place the child in an adoptive home we can then request the Court to change the order from "guardianship with right to place" to "guardianship with right to consent."

November 10, 1927.—A case conference was held with Miss Stone and Miss Stern of the Girls' Department, and the Superintendent of the Children's Agency was present. The purpose of the conference was to establish the present family situation and to ascertain what future plans should be made for the baby. Miss Stern reported that the Girls' Department is active on this case and will continue until the baby is given to us with consent to adoption. Our plan is, first, to have the mother release the child to the Court and, second, to ask the Court for County Boarding Fund until it is definitely established that the child is adoptable.

December 3, 1927.—The case was heard in the Juvenile Court. The mother was present. The Children's Agency Committee decided to consider the Levy child for adoption at this time, so informed the Court that they were willing to receive guardianship with right to consent on this child at the present time. The Court therefore gave guardianship with right to consent.

While waiting for the case to appear before the judge, the mother held the baby in her arms and played with him very affectionately. She, however, admitted that it is best for the welfare of the baby to be placed in adoption. When she said goodbye to the child she shed a few tears but became cheerful after she was assured that every possible care would be exercised to place her child in a home where the people would take him because they were sincerely fond of him and where he would be provided for adequately.

December 5, 1927.—Received Decree from Juvenile Court.

In re: 103056 David Levy	Warner—Probation Officer
DEPENDENT	December 3, 1927
Before JUDGE MARTIN	MOTHER

MISS WARNER: Miss Apel of the Children's Agency is present. David is an illegitimate child who has been boarded by the Children's Agency since July of this year. Nothing is known of his father. Very few relatives know of this child. Mother is willing to consider giving him in adoption.

Q.: What do you wish to say?

MISS APEL: Just as Miss Warner says. David was born out of wedlock, and we have had him since July. Mother was undecided whether she would give him in adoption but realizes she is not in a position to care for him, and stepfather in whose home she is living does not even know of his existence. I think for the protection of the baby that the child should be given.

Q: Your name?

MOTHER: Miriam Levy.

Q: Who is the father of the baby? A: I don't know.

THE COURT: You are ready to give your child in adoption?

MOTHER: Yes.

The court reads the adoption paper.

THE COURT: (indicated adoption paper) Is that your signature?

MOTHER: Yes.

Q: You are willing to give your child in adoption at this time?

A: Yes.

ORDER: Children's Agency appointed guardian with right to consent to adoption.

CHILD'S HISTORY

First Health Sheet

Name: LEVY, DAVID. Born April 13, 1927

FAMILY HEALTH HISTORY

Father: No medical history

Mother: Wassermann   neg. } Salvation Army Maternity Home and Hospital,
Test for G.C. neg. } 1927

CHILD'S PAST HEALTH HISTORY

Full term, midforceps delivery

Birth weight, 8 lbs. 4¾ oz.

Breast fed for several weeks

CHILD'S PHYSICAL CONDITION

7–18–27   Examined at Warner Hospital, Dr. F. R. Harris
    (*Placed* 7–17–27)
    Weight 10 lbs.   Bow-legged
    Simple dystrophy   Insufficient food

7–31–27   Examined in Pediatrics Dept., Warner Hospital, Dr. F. R. Harris
    Temperature 99.2° (R)   Formulae—milk ⅔ now. Increased
    Weight 9 lbs. 12 oz. (?)   Cereal added to diet
    General condition good   R$_x$: Viosterol 10 drops

8–21–27   Examined in Pediatrics Dept., Warner Hospital, Dr. H. Williams
    Temperature 98.8°   Not gaining much
    Weight 10 lbs.   Practically no vomiting
    Bowels O.K.; Takes feeding well; Exam.: Moderate undernourish-
        ment

9–17–27   Attended Pediatrics Clinic, Dr. Harris
    Weight 12 lbs. 5 oz.   Exam. negative

10–16–27   Examined in Pediatrics, Dr. Harris
            Weight 14 lbs.   Recom.: Vegetable soup added
            Exam.: No teeth   to diet
            No cranio tabes
            No rickets
10–30–27   Attended Infant Welfare Station
            Weight 15 lbs. 10 oz.
10–31–27   Slight cold and cough
            Dr. Cohen called   Regulated diet pro tem
            Prescribed Argyrol for nose
11– 6–27   Sitting up (6 mos. 3 wks.)
11–12–27   Attended Infant Welfare Station
            Weight 16 lbs. 2 oz.   Put on whole milk
11–13–27   First tooth erupted (age 7 mos.)
11–28–27   Attended Infant Welfare Station
            Weight 18 lbs. 8 oz.
12–22–27   Attended Infant Welfare Station
            Weight 20 lbs.
  1–2–28   Dr. Rosenbloom called
            Child had red throat   Prescribed
  1–12–28   Attended Infant Welfare Clinic
            Weight 21 lbs. 14 oz.

July 17, 1927.—David was placed in the home of Mrs. Michelson, 5246 North Yesler Avenue. Rate, $25.

Opening summary.—David Levy, born April 13, 1927, was accepted for placement through recommendation of the Welfare Council, to whom case was referred by the Girls' Department of the Family Agency because the child is illegitimate and the mother is unable to make her own arrangements for the placement of her baby.

The child.—David, three months, has been diagnosed as a case of simple dystrophy. Up to the present time he has not been able to retain his feedings and cries considerably.

Foster-home.—The Michelson home is new to the organization. The family occupies a five-room apartment on the northwest side. The family consists of Mr. and Mrs. Michelson, a grown daughter, and son. The latter lives upstairs with Mrs. Michelson's sister, but the family relationship seems to be a very congenial one. At the time the worker discussed the placement with Mrs. Michelson, she was unaware of the baby's physical condition. However, he was received very warmly, and the entire Michelson family has a sympathetic attitude toward him.

July 10–30, 1927.—During this period the baby has been examined twice. He has not made any gain in weight, but he is more satisfied with his feedings, does not vomit so much, or cry as before. His nights also are better.

August 8, 1927.—Visited. Baby seems more contented, is interested in his surroundings, and enjoys attention. When examined last, he was put on cereals, which he takes reluctantly and vomits occasionally.

August 21, 1927.—Worker brought David to the Clinic, accompanied by the foster-mother. His weight remains stationary, although he seems much stronger and there is practically no vomiting at present.

Foster-family moved a few days ago to 5215 North Columbia Avenue, second floor, to a four-room apartment, which is stove-heated. The baby's crib will be put in the daughter's bedroom as before.

September 4, 1927.—Visited and saw Mrs. Michelson and the baby. Mrs. Michelson said that David raises himself up when in his carriage and is able to roll over. He likes to have some one near him and, when he finds himself alone, cries and screams, and gets himself all worked up into a temper. He woke up last night and would not quiet down, and Mrs. Michelson was forced to give in to him so as not to disturb the household.

September 17, 1927.—Called and took David to the Clinic. He has made a satisfactory gain in weight during the past month. Mrs. Michelson said that when she moved to her present apartment she fell and injured her back and finds that she is physically unable to continue caring for him. She therefore requests that another home be found for him.

September 26, 1927.—David transferred from the home of Mrs. Michelson, 5215 North Columbia Avenue, to that of Mrs. H. Wallenstein, 1356 Lake View.

The Wallenstein home is new to the organization. Mr. Wallenstein is forty-five years old, Mrs. Wallenstein forty. The bungalow which they occupy and own is attractive and comfortable and offers every advantage conducive to the bringing-up of a healthy child. It is located in the far northwest section of the city.

The Wallensteins have no children of their own, although Mrs. Wallenstein has often assisted her sister in caring for her baby. Mrs. Wallenstein was all prepared for the baby's arrival and received him very warmly. Instructions were given her regarding routine and food formula.

Later.—Telephoned. Foster-mother reported that David cried almost the entire afternoon. It was explained to her that his behavior may be due to the fact that he is in a different environment and that he will probably get accustomed to the change in due time.

The worker has communicated with Mrs. Wallenstein several times by telephone. She is discouraged because the baby seldom is quiet before midnight; and because of lack of sleep, she does not feel physically fit to care for him during the daytime. He does not present any feeding difficulty at this time but seems to be spoiled.

October 3, 1927.—Visited. Observed that the baby sucks his finger and sometimes puts the entire hand into his mouth. Advised foster-mother regarding treatment.

He slept well last night. He is contented when awake as long as he hears and sees people around.

The worker accompanied the foster-mother and the baby to the Clinic. David is making satisfactory progress, physically. The foster-mother reports that he sleeps well at night and does not demand attention during his waking hours as previously.

October 30, 1927.—Foster-mother telephoned that she registered David at the Infant Welfare Station, since his condition no longer necessitates Clinic attendance.

October 31, 1927.—Foster-mother telephoned that she called the doctor as David became ill during the night and she was unable to reach worker at her home (see medical write-up).

November 20, 1927.—Visited. Found David outdoors in his carriage. He has improved considerably. Foster-mother reports that he is cured of sucking his finger. He drinks water from the cup. He is awakened for his night bottle.

Instructions were given in order to establish toilet habits.

December 3, 1927.—Case in Juvenile Court. Children's Agency given guardianship with right of consent (see family record). Worker called for David and brought him home from the Court, accompanied by the foster-mother. Mrs. Wallenstein states that the baby presents no problems. He is good-natured and happy. Mrs. Wallenstein has had no difficulty in training him in routine toilet habits.

January 30, 1928.—Visited. Brought the baby a toy (stuffed animal) in which he seemed quite interested. The foster-mother's reports continue to be favorable.

When Mrs. Wallenstein had him examined at the Welfare Station, he was put on cereals twice a day—10:00 A.M. and 6:00 P.M. Since this addition to this evening meal he does not wake up for the 10:00 P.M. feeding. Foster-mother has to awaken him. He usually takes part of the feeding but seldom the entire amount, and the foster-mother feels that he would sleep through without it. He is not underweight and has reached the age when he does not require a night feeding. However, since he attends the Infant Welfare Clinic, the worker did not wish to make the change and advised the foster-mother to ask the doctor if this feeding could be discontinued.

Off and on, Mrs. Wallenstein has attempted to give the baby cod-liver oil, resulting always in emesia. The former foster-mother reported likewise. He has been getting viosterol instead. Mrs. Wallenstein has finally succeeded in getting him to take the cod-liver oil (Squibbs), starting with a few drops until now he takes the required amount, one teaspoonful three times daily.

He pronounces such words as "mama," "papa," "bye bye," and "up." He gives positive evidence of understanding when spoken to.

February 10, 1928.—Worker telephoned Mrs. Wallenstein advising her not to take the baby to the Infant Welfare Clinic on account of the present "flu" epidemic.

Worker accompanied Mrs. and Mrs. Henry Steiner, prospective foster-parents who intend to give the child a permanent home, to the home of Mrs. Wallenstein, where they saw the child and were favorably impressed with him.

February 20, 1928.—David transferred from the home of Mrs. H. Wallenstein, 1356 Lake View, to the home of Mrs. Henry Steiner, 8641 Kendall Avenue.

February 20, 1928.—Accompanied Mr. and Mrs. Steiner to the baby's foster-home, from where they took him to their own home. The application of Mr. and Mrs. Steiner was recently accepted by the Board, and the following plan was made for the placement of the child in their home. They are to give the child a free home for an indefinite length of time until it is definitely determined through psychiatric examinations that the child's mental development is normal and that it would be possible for them to adopt him.

The foster-mother gave the Steiners a list of instructions regarding the child's routine and informed them that the child is trained to use the nursery chair.

February 21, 1928.—Telephoned Mrs. Steiner and learned that the child had a restless night, but she understands that that may be due to the newness of his surroundings and his lonesomeness for his foster-mother. He was put on the nursery chair this morning in accordance with instructions from the previous foster-mother, but he did not have a bowel movement. Later he soiled himself. Warned Mrs. Steiner to continue putting the child on the nursery chair until his habits are re-established. Mrs. Steiner stated that she had not had the child examined yet because Dr. Winslow, whom they want regularly, is now out of town. If he does not return by Monday morning they will take a pediatrician in the neighborhood. Instructed them that if they have further trouble with the baby to call worker.

February 22, 1928.—Worker was in the neighborhood of the Steiner home, and upon their request called at the house. Last night they again had considerable trouble getting the baby to sleep and he woke up twice during the night. The worker visited at six o'clock, and after the baby was fed, he was put in his crib and the bedroom door was closed, which procedure was also followed in his previous foster-home. However, he at once began to cry and continued to cry until seven-fifteen, when he finally fell asleep. The child eats well and is otherwise a cheerful, pleasant baby. Mr. and Mrs. Steiner requested that we suggest some books for them to read on the problem of child training. This was promised to them.

February 23, 1928.—Letter sent giving list of books on child care in accordance with the Steiners' request.

February 25, 1928.—Telephoned and learned that since Dr. Winslow will be out of town for several days, Mrs. Steiner took the baby to another pediatrician in the neighborhood and that he changed the child's entire schedule with the result that he seems to be more contented and last night was not at all restless. On the whole, Mr. and Mrs. Steiner are extremely happy with the child.

February 27, 1928.—Telephoned Mrs. Steiner and learned that the baby is doing very nicely on his new schedule. Informed Mrs. Steiner that Miss Rothman, our worker in her district, will visit her home from time to time to consult with her regarding the care of the baby.

Supervision turned over from Miss Apel to Miss Rothman.

March 19, 1928.—Visited. Mrs. Steiner stated that David now has six teeth, two of which erupted in the last two weeks. She thinks that he is now learning to understand; for example, he shakes his head when he does not want his food or when he does not want a certain toy. He now stands up in his play yard; this has developed in the last two weeks. When he gets angry, he stiffens but he does not become red or change color at all. Also he now has acquired the ability to lift himself up from his buggy. Mrs. Steiner remarked that for the last week he has been mumbling to himself, making such sounds as "mum, mum." She finds him a friendly child, one who laughs frequently.

Worker suggested to Mrs. Steiner that she keep as complete a record of her observations of the child as possible, in order that we may have a careful record of his development. The importance of not becoming too emotionally attached to him was also emphasized in an effort to make her understand that if she has a more objective attitude toward the baby she will be much better able to train him correctly.

Mrs. Steiner is very much delighted with the child and believes that he is making a splendid adjustment in her home.

April 7, 1928.—Visited. Mrs. Steiner reported that the child now stands in his play yard and is able to walk around in it when he holds his hands on the rods. He has acquired the habit of imitating Mr. and Mrs. Steiner; for example, when they make any loud or unusual noises, he copies this sound to the best of his ability. Whenever Mrs. Steiner says "ma-ma," he repeats it after her by saying "mamamamama." He is very fond of Mr. Steiner and refuses to go to anyone else when his foster-father is home. He has learned to crawl on his stomach backward and can stand up in his high chair. He appears to be fond of his toys, but he destroys them very readily. Mrs. Steiner believes that he is a very "strong" child, since she has, on several occasions, observed him lifting up a small chair.

He is a friendly baby; whenever he sees any children in the street, he laughs and appears to wish to play with them.

Mrs. Steiner gave worker his daily schedule, which is as follows:

Breakfast................	8:00	Toilet.....................	
Toilet....................	8:30	Afternoon nap until..........	3:30
Playing in yard from then until	10:00	Outdoors until..............	6:00
Outdoors to..............	11:45	Dinner until................	6:30
Lunch to.................	12:00	Bed......................	

He eats everything that is served to him. Mrs. Steiner believes that he would eat even more if larger portions were given to him. However, he dislikes drinking water at all times.

Mrs. Steiner commented upon the fact that the child had started to suck his fingers. However, when she had shaken her head at him and said, "No, no," he appeared to understand her because he took his fingers out of his mouth and has not engaged in this habit since.

Worker complimented Mrs. Steiner on the excellent progress which the child is making in her home. The necessity of being objective in dealing with a child and not becoming too emotionally wrapped up in him was again discussed with her, in an effort to make her understand that if she is not objective she will never be able to perfect her training of the child.

May 18, 1928.—Visited. The physician who examined the baby is Dr. Edwin Gebhardt, 7436 Villa Street.

Mrs. Steiner said that all her friends are very fond of the baby and feel that she was sensible in taking him into her home. David now stands up and gazes about in a most knowing manner. He repeats any word that the Steiners say. He is a friendly, cheerful child; he laughs out loud frequently. He is fond of other children and desires to have their attention whenever he sees them. Mrs. Steiner is attempting to teach him to share his toys with other children, and whenever he is asked to do so, he will hand over a toy to a child very willingly.

Mrs. Steiner is attempting to teach him by saying very firmly to him, "No," whenever he does anything undesirable. On one occasion she spanked him immediately after some misbehavior, and he evidently understood as he has not repeated this behavior.

The worker again cautioned Mrs. Steiner about paying the child too much attention. However, the foster-mother assured the worker that she is very firm with him and there is no possibility of his becoming unruly in her home.

May 25, 1928.—A letter was written to Dr. Edwin Gebhardt, asking that he send us a report of his examination of David.

June 20, 1928.—The worker telephoned Mrs. Steiner several times during the month to ask if she might call, but was never able to speak with anyone in the home. Finally on this date the worker wrote a note to Mrs. Steiner, asking if it would be convenient for her to allow worker to call the following week.

June 26, 1928.—A letter from Mr. Steiner stated that in answer to the worker's letter he wished to advise that Mrs. Steiner and the baby were in the country and would probably remain there until after Labor Day. He added that, in order to lessen any worry that this plan might cause the worker, he wished to say that they own a cottage in a lakeside resort in Wisconsin and that they had a maid with them to assist Mrs. Steiner with the work, so that he thought the child would get every possible attention.

August 25, 1928.—Visited. Mrs. Steiner said David had done very well during the summer months. He enjoyed the beach and was kept outdoors most of the time. The Steiners own their cottage on Little Lake, Elkhart, near Plymouth, Wisconsin, and go there every summer. David now walks; he began to walk at the age of fourteen and one-half months. He now has nine teeth.

He is also learning to talk. According to Mrs. Steiner, at the present time he says, "Mama," "Daddy," "bottle," "baby."

Mrs. Steiner believes that the child has a very good memory. He is fond of people and cries when anyone leaves the home. He especially likes the outdoors and plays in a very socialized manner with the other children in the park.

Mrs. Steiner is continuing to carry out a regular routine in dealing with David.

September 14, 1928.—The worker visited in the evening and spoke with Mr. and Mrs. Steiner. Mr. Steiner is a very pleasant, agreeable, intelligent person. He is very fond of David and spoke at great length of his interest in the boy and of his pride in the fact that David is developing so well. He is a very observant child, eager to watch the other children at play, but uses a great deal of originality in deciding which games he will follow. He has numerous toys that interest him. According to the Steiners he is very sociable and friendly, and causes them no difficulty.

October 20, 1928.—Visited. Mrs. Steiner believes David is showing growing signs of intelligence. For example, the previous day when he had been playing underneath the baby grand piano, Mrs. Steiner said to him in a low tone, "Be careful not to lift yourself up because you will bump your head." The child then crawled out from underneath the piano, keeping himself at a very low level, and showed definitely that he had understood Mrs. Steiner's comment to him. Mrs. Steiner stated that for the past month David has been asking to go to the toilet. He can now put two words together and is able to say such phrases as "All gone," "All there," etc.

David has a temper which is easily aroused; however, Mrs. Steiner always speaks to him in a very low tone of voice and attempts to quiet him and make him feel composed before she asks him to carry out any request.

October 29, 1928.—A letter was written to the Child Guidance Clinic, inclosing a report on David and asking that he be examined at their earliest possible convenience.

November 11, 1928.—Visited. Mrs. Steiner said that Davy, as the Steiners call him, no longer has as many temper outbursts as he had previously. He now stands up in his high chair.

Mrs. Steiner related an instance to prove that the child does not bear a grudge against anyone. During the previous week she took him to Dr. Gebhardt because of some skin condition on his hand. The doctor gave him some treatment that must have been very painful because Davy cried; but when he got ready to leave the office and Mrs. Steiner asked him to say goodbye to the physician, he approached the doctor and kissed him. Mrs. Steiner also talked at great length about the fact that the child understands everything that is said to him.

Recently Mrs. Steiner was gone from her home for an entire day, and the child appeared to miss her very much; he greeted her in a most cordial manner when she returned, and showed every evidence of being pleased that she was back.

Davy continues to be exceptionally fond of sweet foods. Mrs. Steiner and worker had a discussion about such foods, and the point was made that it is harmful for any child to have an overabundance of carbohydrates.

Mrs. Steiner has recently subscribed for the *Parents Magazine*, as she is eager to become acquainted with newer ways of dealing with children.

December 18, 1928.—Visited. Mrs. Steiner reported that David is now able to use two-word phrases; he says, "Oh, boy," "Thank you," "Please," but he speaks in baby talk. She also remarked that he is very eager to be outdoors. As soon as he awakens in the morning he asks Mrs. Steiner to take him "bye," and will stay close to her until this suggestion is carried out.

The worker observed that David is a very cheerful child; he runs about the home and is content to play by himself. He is active and does not appear to need a great deal of attention. Mrs. Steiner attempts to instil habits of tidiness in him. For example, on that afternoon, she insisted that he straighten out the rugs which he disturbed while he was running about the house, and he carried out her suggestions.

During this interview, the worker spoke with Mrs. Steiner about the impending examination at the Child Guidance Clinic; Mrs. Steiner was sure that the Clinic would definitely find that the boy is very bright, and she is looking forward to this test.

December 22, 1928.—David at the Child Guidance Clinic for an examination. The worker attended the conference which was held at that Clinic in the afternoon. The psychiatrist reported that David has average intelligence (I.Q. of 100) and is making a very satisfactory social adjustment. He had spoken with Mrs. Steiner for a short time and believes that she has good insight into the child's personality and that she is giving the child good care.

Upon worker's suggestion, it was decided that the psychiatrist should have a further interview with Mr. and Mrs. Steiner in an attempt to help ascertain whether or not they are emotionally fit to adopt a child. The worker told the psychiatrist that there was some thought that Mr. and Mrs. Steiner were not entirely compatible (see foster-home record), and it is advisable that this matter be cleared up before the child is definitely given in adoption to them.

January 8, 1929.—Letter received from the Child Guidance Clinic confirming the findings at the recent examination:

This letter will report our examination on David Levy, December 22, 1928.

David was found to be in excellent physical condition. The Merrill-Palmer psychometric examination indicated that his mental and chronological ages are the same.

The boy impressed all those who had anything to do with him, with his good social adjustment and pleasant cheerful attitude.

At the present time there is nothing which we could discover to indicate that the boy is abnormal or inadequate. We do not feel that we are able to venture a prognosis based on his heredity and are inclined to doubt that the science of genetics is sufficiently advanced to be of much value in the individual case.

We should like to have the boy return in a year for a re-examination. In the meantime, the psychiatrist would like to interview the foster parents and is saving January 19, at 9:30 A.M., for this.

We would appreciate it if you would send us a record of David's former Wassermann to complete our files.

January 12, 1929.—Visited. Mrs. Steiner stated that David now plays such games as peek-a-boo, hide-and-go-seek, etc. Mrs. Steiner believes that he has very good judgment and that he is inclined to be serious-minded. He laughs most heartily.

During the Christmas vacations, Mrs. Steiner took David to Omaha, where they visited some relatives. He made a very good adjustment there, and all the people whom they visited became very much attached to him.

Mr. Steiner remarked that the child is now beginning to have some fear of the dark; he refuses to go into his bedroom alone at night, although he does not cry or give the reason for this hesitation. The worker suggested that Mrs. Steiner turn on the light whenever he is afraid; then quickly darken the room so that he will realize that the room is much the same whether darkened or light.

The worker discussed the Child Guidance Clinic findings with Mrs. Steiner. She was very pleased to learn that the boy is developing normally and stated that she thought she would have no difficulties with him. Mr. Steiner and she will be very glad to have another interview with the psychiatrist, since he suggested that he would like to see them again.

During this interview, the worker also discussed with Mrs. Steiner the importance of being truthful with the child about everything. Mrs. Steiner does not want the child to know that he is adopted, but the worker pointed out to her that he would undoubtedly become aware of this fact at some future date, and in order to avoid any possible conflict on his part, she should begin by telling him the truth as soon as he questions her. She was assured that if she gives the boy good care and a great deal of love, he will respond to her attentions and she will not lose in any way through the fact that she is being truthful with him. The worker suggested that Mr. and Mrs. Steiner discuss this matter with the psychiatrist, in order that they might get his opinion also.

February 2, 1929.—Letter received from the psychiatrist at the Child Guidance Clinic, reporting his interview with Mr. and Mrs. Steiner:

In compliance with your request, Mr. and Mrs. Henry Steiner, who wish to adopt David Levy, visited the Clinic and interviewed the psychiatrist.

Our psychiatrist finds both Mr. and Mrs. Steiner extremely devoted to David. They recognize that the mother was subnormal but, as Mr. Steiner said, "you take a chance no matter how you get a baby," and they are both very anxious to take this chance. They appear to have handled the boy quite wisely during the months they have had him.

Miss Rothman indicated that there was some marital disharmony. However neither Mr. nor Mrs. Steiner raised this question, and the psychiatrist felt, under the circumstances, that it would be decidedly unwise for him to broach the subject himself by direct questioning. However, he gains the impression that they are at least as well adjusted as many parents who make a fair success of raising children. Moreover, he feels that as far as emotional facts go David is already the son of Mr. and Mrs. Steiner and that any interference with this will result in an unwarranted wrench to all three personalities.

Therefore, it is our belief that the wisest thing to do is to arrange for the formal adoption as soon as possible. Our psychiatrist is particularly inclined to this view, since both Mr. and Mrs. Steiner have a very friendly and appreciative attitude toward the Clinic and intend to keep in touch with us for advice in the care of David. With this attitude it seems probable that, if the marital maladjustment should cause difficulty for David, we will be in a position to help.

February 15, 1929.—Visited. Mrs. Steiner reported that David is good-natured, kind, friendly, cheerful. He sings frequently when he is playing by himself. Mrs. Steiner has observed that he is eager to be friendly toward other children and never hits them, although he sometimes receives this type of treatment from his little playmates.

Mr. and Mrs. Steiner had an interview with Dr. Leighton of the Child Guidance Clinic two weeks ago, and they enjoyed the talk with him very much. Mrs. Steiner discussed David with Dr. Leighton in some detail, and asked his advice as to whether or not to tell David that he is adopted. The psychiatrist told her he thought definitely that she should give the child this information at an early age, but that she should not stress the point continuously as David grew older. The worker spoke with Mrs. Steiner about the work that is now being done by the nursery schools, and suggested that at a very early age she enrol David in one of them, in order that he might receive the socializing training that they offer.

Worker also suggested to Mrs. Steiner that she make every effort to have as many outside interests as possible, in order that she might not devote herself excessively to the baby, to both his detriment and hers.

February 25, 1929.—David discharged to Mr. and Mrs. Steiner. Permanent home.

February 13, 1930.—Letter received from M. L. Rosen, lawyer for the Steiners:

I acknowledge receipt of the signed consent with regard to the adoption of David Levy and as soon as Decree is obtained a copy will be sent you.

FOSTER-HOME RECORD
CHILDREN'S AGENCY OF CHICAGO
24 South Justin Street

APPLICATION FOR ADOPTION OF A CHILD[2]

[*Name*]
[*Address*]
MY DEAR MRS.

In reply to your inquiry regarding the adoption of a child, we assume that you are fully cognizant of the responsibilities you seek to assume. Before we can give you a reply, we will need to have the following information. It is hardly necessary to say that all facts presented by you or our office, are sacredly confidential.

The organization carries a heavy responsibility for the proper placing of children committed to it. It, therefore, reserves the right to make as complete and full an investigation as it deems necessary, and to reject any unsatisfactory applications. A visit to the home at the expense of the applicant is necessary before any child is placed. The child is placed on six months' probation to protect both parents and the child. If the probation period ends satisfactorily, the adoption is then consummated.

SUPERINTENDENT

We hereby make application to the Children's Agency to have a child placed with us on the above terms, realizing in full the responsibility we assume in so doing.

What is the husband's full name, place and date of birth?................................

Address: Business................................   How   Bus
        Residence...... ....   Reached   Car

[2] [Application blank shown here for illustrative purposes.]

What is the husband's occupation?

If foreign born, when and where did he land, and when reached present residence?

In what city and court was he naturalized and on what date?

Please state his education.

What is the wife's maiden name, place and date of birth?

Has she any gainful occupation in or out of the home?

Has she any income other than her husband's?

What occupation did she follow previous to her marriage?

If foreign born, when and where did she land, and when reached present residence?

With whom did she live previous to her marriage?

When, where and by whom was your marriage solemnized?

Has either been married before, and if so, please give place and date of deaths or divorce.

Have you any children at home—away—not living?

Who are the other members of your household including servants?

What is their age and relationship?

What is your house—Apartment?   House?   Owned?

How large?   Rent how much?

Have you ever made application for a child to any other agency, and have you received a child from them or elsewhere?

Of what church are you a member?

What is the minister's name?

In what lodges, organizations, or clubs do you hold membership?

What schools are in your neighborhood and how far are they?

What investments have you outside of your business? What property do you own?

What is your approximate annual income?

Investments?   Property?   Business?

How much insurance do you carry and with what company?

Husband?   Wife?

Why do you want a child?

In case of your death what provision would be made for a child?

What are your plans for the child's future and how do you contemplate carrying them out?

What is the name and address of your family physician?

Please give us the names and addresses of at least three citizens, not related to you, to whom we may refer before we take action.

Please state your preference as to the child—Sex?   Age?   Complexion?

Remarks:

[*Signed*] HUSBAND
[*Signed*] WIFE

Date submitted:

December 22, 1927.—Mrs. Steiner in the office. She was accompanied by Miss Becker of the Family Agency office, who introduced her as a friend of one of her relatives. Mrs. Steiner stated that she is interested in adopting a baby and was referred to us by Mr. J. S. Seligman, who has a child from us in adoption.

Mrs. Steiner is a very attractive-looking, well-dressed woman. She stated that she has been married eight years; and, as she is fairly certain that she can have no children of her own, both she and her husband are extremely anxious to adopt a little boy not over one year of age. Told Mrs. Steiner about the scarcity of adoptable children, also that occasionally we have a young baby who can be given in adoption but we often hesitate to do so when the baby is under one year of age because of the many unknown factors that enter into the heredity of these children. Told her in those instances we prefer to place the child in a home without a definite obligation on the part of either the organization or the family until after it is certain that such a plan is advisable from the point of view of both the organization and the family.

The worker related to her in detail the background history of David Levy, a nine-month-old baby, who is illegitimate and whose mother is a mental defective with a poor school, work, and behavior history. Told her that, while the child at his present age shows no indication of being either a medical or a mental problem, it is entirely too early to ascertain definitely his prognosis in the future, especially his mental development. No definite information can be secured about the mental status of the baby until the baby is at least from one and one-half to two years of age. Mrs. Steiner at first asserted that she is confident that any child who is given a good environment from such an early age is bound to respond. However, she could see the inadvisability of taking a child who might become a mental problem as he grows older. She was therefore willing to consider taking the Levy baby, or any baby that we might place in her home, for an indefinite period, giving him a fine home but not urging adoption until such step would be advised by a competent psychiatrist.

Mrs. Steiner made an excellent impression, being a refined, sensible woman who, although not having much education, has some good insight into various problems which arise in rearing children.

January 2, 1928.—Following letter of inquiry was sent by the Children's Agency to the three references furnished by Mr. and Mrs. Steiner:

We are interested in the family of Mr. and Mrs. Henry Steiner, 8641 Kendall Avenue. Mrs. Steiner tells me you are a friend of theirs. As you undoubtedly know, placing a child is a very serious responsibility, and the organization charged with it must assure itself of the abilities of those desiring to undertake the responsibility of foster-parenthood. Will you be kind enough to let me have at your earliest convenience your estimate of the family life of this couple and their possibilities for directing the life of a child?

What is their attitude toward childhood in general? What type of social life do they lead? What do you believe are their mental and moral standards? What seems to be their chief interest in life? Are their domestic relations above question? What is your opinion of their economic future?

Everything you can tell me will be of great value to us, and I need not assure you that it will be held in the strictest confidence.

I should appreciate your early reply,

Very truly yours,

SUPERINTENDENT

The following letter was sent to the doctor:

We are interested in the family of Mr. and Mrs. Henry Steiner, 8641 Kendall Avenue. Mrs. Steiner tells me you are their physician. As you undoubtedly know, placing a child is a very serious responsibility, and the organization charged with it must assure itself of the physical condition of those desiring to undertake the responsibility of foster-parenthood, as it may relate itself to the future of the child placed with them.

I should appreciate from you a very frank statement regarding the physical condition of Mr. and Mrs. Steiner with particular reference to specific and infectious diseases that may affect their future or jeopardize the future of a child.

I assure you that any and all such information submitted is sacredly confidential and will be held as such.

Thanking you for the courtesy of an early response,

January 6, 1928.—Letter received from Dr. Solomon:

I hasten to respond to your inquiry of the second instant regarding Mr. and Mrs. Henry Steiner. I know of no specific or infectious disease in either of them nor of any ailment that could in any way be transmitted to a child or otherwise affect its health and development.

Such ailments as I have observed in them have been of a superficial and transitory nature.

Physically as well as temperamentally I can recommend them highly as desirable foster parents.

Yours sincerely,

January 10, 1928.—Letter received from Mr. J. L. Seligman, reference:

Owing to the absence of the writer, your letter of the second instant was not answered sooner and I regret this delay exceedingly, as I can imagine how anxious both Mr. and Mrs. Henry Steiner must be.

I have known Mr. Steiner for the last seventeen years and I have become very intimate with him within the last ten years.

I can only say that both Mr. and Mrs. Steiner would worship a child in their family and that they are worthy of receiving a child from your home.

It is my privilege and pleasure to recommend their application.

Yours very truly,

J. L. SELIGMAN

(The agency received similar responses from the other references.)

Discussed the application at a meeting of the Adoption Committee at which Mr. Leopold, chairman of the Adoption Committee, and Miss Appelman of the Board were present. The Committee recommended further investigation of the Steiner application, especially in order to ascertain details regarding Mr. Steiner's first marriage, as the application indicates that he was married twice.

January 22, 1928.—Telephoned Mrs. Seligman inquiring as to her knowledge of the Steiner family. She stated that she has met Mrs. Steiner only twice on social occasions and was very well impressed with her. Mr. Seligman, however, has known Mr. Steiner intimately for a number of years and every time he talks about him he refers to him as a man of unusual integrity and fine character.

January 23, 1928.—Telephoned Mrs. Sampson, who also has two children from us in adoption, to inquire about Mrs. Steiner, since the Sampsons live in the same neighborhood with the Steiners. Mrs. Sampson stated that she has a number of friends who know the Steiners although she herself does not know them very well. She knows, however, that Mr. Steiner is the city champion of volley-ball players and that he is a member of the Men's Athletic Club. Their friends in common talk very highly about the present Mrs. Steiner. They also knew the first Mrs. Steiner. She thinks the reason for Mr. Steiner's divorcing his first wife was because he married when very young and found that he and his wife were incompatible. He was married to his first wife only for four years. He has been married to the present Mrs. Steiner about eight years, and according to their friends their married life is an extremely happy one. Mrs. Sampson promised to talk to her friends who know the Steiners very well and to inform the worker if she gets any other information regarding them.

January 24, 1928.—Interviewed Mrs. Sampson who stated that she spoke to three men who live at the Hyperian Club, and they all spoke very highly of Mr. Steiner and also think very well of Mrs. Steiner, whom they met on numerous occasions. She told these people that the Steiner family is contemplating adopting a child and as they all have children of their own she felt that their opinion favoring giving a child to this family is well worth considering.

January 26, 1928.—The worker called by appointment at the Steiner home and secured additional information regarding the family. Found the Steiners occupying a modern four-room apartment on the exclusive East Side. The home is luxuriously furnished including a baby grand piano, some expensive oil paintings, and fine furniture, arranged in good taste. The condition of the kitchen indicated excellent housekeeping, although Mrs. Steiner stated that she does all her cooking and most of her housework as she gets a woman in only twice a week for her laundry and heavier work. Mrs. Steiner on this visit made even a better impression than in the office, as she had no make-up on and was dressed in a simple housedress. She gave information freely, and her facts were consistent. She gave the following information regarding her own and her husband's families.

Mrs. Steiner is twenty-nine years of age. She was born in Chicago; her family name was Stern. Her parents owned a small sausage factory called the United Sausage Company. It was located on Emerson near Fourth Street. They were all born in that part of the city. In 1914 her father died of pneumonia. He was then forty-two years of age. There were eight children. The mother was then only thirty-seven years of age. Mrs. Steiner was the oldest of the eight children and was then only sixteen years of age. The mother at once sold the business and with the money bought a six-flat apartment building at 416 Greely Street. She moved there with the children and maintained herself and her family on the income she received from the building. The mother never remarried. At the present time, besides Mrs. Steiner, there are two other married children, and five children, all boys, are still at home. All except one are still attending school. Mrs. Steiner was graduated from the Cox Grammar School on the East Side at the age of fourteen. She started high school but after the death of the father she discontinued high school and entered business college. After she took a complete secretarial course, at the age of seventeen she took a secretarial position at the General Electric Company. She worked there for two years. After that she stayed home for about a year, as the mother needed her, and then again took a position as a millinery saleslady, working three days a week. She earned enough as a millinery saleslady to maintain herself and since this work enabled her also to assist her mother, she preferred it to full-time work. At the age of nineteen she met her husband and after keeping company with him for one and one-half years, married him. They were married in December,

1920. When she first met him he was just separated from his first wife and she had occasion to meet her. She is convinced that their separation was due to the fact that they were not compatible and that their continued married life would have been an unhappy one for both of them. Mrs. Steiner studied piano for a number of years and attended both the City Musical College and the Central College of Music. She plays well but did not take every advantage of her opportunity and therefore has not made the best of her talent. She resumed lessons since she has been married but lost interest in it about a year ago when she became anxious to adopt a baby. Mrs. Steiner describes her early home life as a very happy one, although she says they did not always have all the essentials in life; since the mother had to rear all the children practically alone she was often compelled to deny them even necessities. She was sent to Chader and received some Hebrew education. Because of the presence of the maternal grandmother in their home, until her death several years ago, they were all taught to speak Jewish although her own parents came to the United States when they were only ten and eleven years of age and therefore spoke English freely. Mrs. Steiner has a number of relatives, both on the paternal and maternal side, in Chicago, most of whom are in the wholesale meat business.

Mrs. Steiner stated that she spends her leisure time either visiting her husband's or her own relatives. They also attend the theater and frequent the movies. Every summer she goes with her sisters-in-law to California, where they spend the months of July and August. They own some land in Wisconsin and plan to build a summer home there, especially if they take a baby into their home, as she feels it would not be advisable for her to travel with a baby long distances. Mrs. Steiner stated that she has always been in good health except that she has occasional sinus trouble, which has not been troubling her very much of late.

Mr. Steiner is thirty-five years of age. He was born in Chicago. He has five brothers and one sister. He was also reared on the East Side as his parents were orthodox middle-class Jews. His father died when he was a baby. He was the sixth of the seven children in his family. His mother never remarried but supported herself with the assistance of the two older children who were self-supporting at the time of husband's death. Mr. Steiner was graduated from grammar school, and he immediately entered the insurance business in which his four older brothers were already engaged. He has been in this business since, although several years ago he also owned a garage as a side line. At the present time, however, he devotes his entire time to the insurance business. All his five brothers are

insurance brokers. Three of them are in partnership. Mr. Steiner's brothers are as follows: Mr. George Steiner, age fifty-three, married but has no
children. Gordon, age forty-nine, is married and has one son, who was
recently graduated from St. Andrews Academy. Mrs. Mable Gold, forty-
three, is his only sister. She used to own the Gobels Furniture Store.
Several years ago she turned over the store to several old employees and
is now engaged in the manufacture of furniture at Grand Rapids, Michigan. Mrs. Gold also lives in the same apartment building with Mrs.
Steiner, and is exceedingly friendly with her. Mrs. Steiner states that
their relationship is more like that of mother and daughter than two
sisters-in-law. Mrs. Gold has four sons, one of whom is graduating from
the University of Wisconsin, another from St. Andrews Academy, the
third is at the University of Illinois doing social research, and the fourth
is still at high school. Mrs. Steiner stated that this sister-in-law is extremely anxious for her to adopt a child and in fact urges her to take two
or three children eventually. The third brother is Joe, age thirty-eight,
who is married and has no children. He lives in the same apartment
building with the Steiners. Harry, age thirty-seven, is the fourth brother.
He is married, and has two daughters. One is attending the University of
Illinois and the other is at the Parker private school. This brother is
married to a non-Jewish girl who, however, accepted Judaism shortly
after they were married and is observing all the Jewish rituals even more
than her husband. She is sending the children to Solomon Temple. After
Harry is Mr. Steiner. The youngest brother is Roy, age thirty. He is
married and has two children. Mrs. Steiner describes the relationship
between all the brothers and the sister and their families as most congenial.
During the interview Mrs. Steiner received several telephone calls from
her sisters-in-law and she stated that this is a daily occurrence, that they
all call her daily. Mr. Steiner is exceedingly interested in volley-ball
playing and has been city champion for several years. He spends a great
deal of his leisure time during the winter months at this form of athletics.
He is a member of the Men's Athletic Club, where he does his practicing.
She, however, spoke of her husband's athletic achievements very modestly
and did not give the impression of being boastful. In the summer Mr.
Steiner plays golf, and they are members of the Highland Golf Club, which
they joined a short time ago. Among Mr. Steiner's other hobbies are
reading and collecting pictures and oil paintings. There are about a dozen
expensive oil paintings and other pictures. Mrs. Steiner describes her
husband as a home body with the exception of his ball playing. He does
not enjoy social gatherings nor does he play cards.

Mrs. Steiner knows Mr. Steiner's first wife as they have occasionally met at friends' homes. The first Mrs. Steiner is now married to a Mr. Andy Krevitsky, owner of a fur store. Mrs. Steiner had no objection to our interviewing the first Mrs. Steiner. Mrs. Krevitsky's present address is 6400 Greenleaf Avenue.

Mr. Steiner banks at Younker's Bank and according to Mrs. Steiner he is known socially to one of the Younkers; she was not certain which one. Mrs. Steiner stated that she talked over with her husband the conditions under which we are willing to place the Levy baby in her home and he agreed to this plan, providing the baby appeals to them after we permit them to see him. Told Mrs. Steiner that we shall arrange for her and her husband to see the baby upon the completion of our investigation. She was extremely anxious that the matter be attended to at once.

January 27, 1928.—The worker met Mr. and Mrs. Steiner by appointment downtown and took them to see the Levy baby. Both were much impressed with the baby and agreed to take him into their home for an indefinite period before they ask for his adoption, in accordance with our suggestion. Again told Mr. Steiner in detail of the facts concerning the child's heredity and social background, and he was much impressed with the precautions this organization is taking in placing a child of doubtful heredity in adoption. He felt that such a procedure is just both to the child and to the family that takes him.

Mr. Steiner is a tall, attractive-looking young man, who appears to be younger than his age. During the interview he was very direct and frank in his statements. The worker observed him when he was visiting with the baby and felt certain that he was very much attracted to the child and would doubtless contribute considerably to the rearing of the child.

Later.—The worker presented the facts she secured in her interviews with Mrs. Steiner the previous day, and with Mr. Steiner on this day, to the Adoption Committee. Mr. Leopold, chairman of the Adoption Committee, also reported that he had spoken to two independent references, and both men told him that Mr. Steiner is a man of unusual character and integrity, and that they have full knowledge of the fact that he is very happily married. One man reported that to his knowledge the reason for Mr. Steiner's first divorce was that he wanted a child and his wife could not have children. Mr. Leopold thought from the information he had secured and that secured by the office that we would be justified in appointing a committee to visit the home and also arrange for an interview between Mr. and Mrs. Steiner and the president or vice-president of the organization. If the reports from both of these sources are favorable we may proceed.

January 31, 1928.—The worker visited Mrs. Krevitsky, Mr. Steiner's first wife. Mrs. Krevitsky was telephoned a few days ago and was asked for an appointment. When told about the nature of the interview sought with her she was greatly astonished to hear that Mrs. Steiner gave us her name and agreed that she be interviewed. Mrs. Krevitsky is a young woman but is considerably plainer-looking than Mrs. Steiner. She admitted being bitter against Mrs. Steiner as she blames her as being instrumental in her divorce. She stated, however, that the reasons for the incompatibility were manifold; when they were married both of them were very young and unstable. Mr. Steiner was not making enough money for them to establish a home and they went to live with his mother. The latter was very orthodox, while Mrs. Krevitsky was reared in a reformed home, and she found it difficult to adjust to the routine of the Steiner home. Mr. Steiner and his brothers all were very much devoted to their mother and resented her inability to fall in with the routine of their mother's home. She also claimed that Mr. Steiner was then very flighty and had many friendships with women.

When the war broke out they were separated, and she went to live in the home of her mother. Mr. Steiner remained in the war for over a year and during this entire period was sending her money. Upon his return from the war they lived together for a while but at that time she found that he was courting Mrs. Steiner. She went to Mrs. Steiner in an effort to have her give up her husband but she realized that it was as much Mr. Steiner's fault as Mrs. Steiner's and finally agreed to divorce him. He continued supporting her until she remarried. Mrs. Krevitsky now has two children, a little girl of six and another child of two and one-half years of age. She has married successfully. Although she apparently is still fond of Mr. Steiner and feels bitter about the divorce she says that he is an unusually fine person and that a child intrusted to his care would be amply provided for and would receive excellent care. She also feels that Mrs. Steiner would doubtless make a good mother, as she comes from a large family and has always had the responsibility of her younger brothers and sisters. At the end of the interview she urged the worker to see that Mr. and Mrs. Steiner are given a child, as she felt that her contacts with them were eight years ago and that both people by now have doubtless matured and settled.

February 17, 1928.—The worker brought to Mr. Schaar's office the adoption application of Mr. and Mrs. Steiner and our investigation of the case. After carefully reviewing the entire record, he agreed that we place the Levy baby in the home of Mr. and Mrs. Steiner with the agreed provision that this child should not be given in adoption until he reaches an age when it would be possible to ascertain his mental condition. He also suggested that a letter be written to Mr. and Mrs. Steiner before the child is placed in their home so that we may go on record that at the present time we will not consider this child for adoption and we will consider their home only as a free home.

February 19, 1928.—Letter to Mr. and Mrs. Steiner from the worker:

We are glad to inform you that your application for the adoption of the Levy baby has been passed upon favorably by our Adoption Committee with the reservation that we confirm in writing to you, the agreement we made, namely, that the adoption of this child be postponed until such time when it will be possible to secure a competent examination of his mental condition. We find that usually it is impossible to ascertain the mental status of a child through tests until he is at least two or three years of age. You understand, of course, that this step is taken as an extra protection to yourself.

We hope, however, that the child will fulfill all your hopes and ambitions for him.

Very sincerely yours,

February 19, 1928.—Letter received from Mr. Schaar, confirming the results of our interview in his office on February 17, 1928.

Later.—The worker telephoned Mrs. Steiner informing her of the Board's decision in regard to the Levy baby. Also reminded her that we have not as yet received hers and her husband's medical report, that the report they sent us was not of a recent examination. Mrs. Steiner was extremely happy with the Board's decision and promised at once to secure the necessary medical data. She also stated that they are anxious to receive the baby into their home the following day, providing the reports reach our office before them. Made a tentative appointment with them to call for the baby on February 20.

Later.—Medical reports received. (See letters on file.)

February 20, 1928.—The worker accompanied by Mr. and Mrs. Steiner called for the Levy baby and they took him home with them. They have purchased a complete outfit of clothes and furniture for him. They will at once refer the baby to Dr. Winslow, who is going to see him periodically from now on.

February 20, 1928.—David Levy transferred to the home of Mrs. Henry Steiner. Free home.

SEPTEMBER 17, 1928

I. FOSTER-FAMILY

A. *Change in location.*—On September 1, 1928, the Steiners moved to 32 Madison Park, Apartment 2-C (this building is an annex to the building in which they formerly lived). They now have a large six-room apartment, furnished in excellent and lavish style. The child has a bedroom for himself.

B. *Changes in personnel.*—Throughout the period of time the child has been in the home the Steiner group has consisted of Mr. and Mrs. Steiner and a maid.

C. *Additional information on family background.*—Mrs. Steiner has spoken with the worker on numerous occasions about her early life. She speaks of her mother with a great deal of affection and often remarks about her mother's many excellent qualities. Mrs. Steiner was raised in a typical orthodox family. Her family was always in very moderate circumstances but Mrs. Steiner feels that she was never deprived of many things which she desired.

D. *Additional information on interrelationships.*—According to Mrs. Steiner, Mr. Steiner and she are most congenial. She looks to him as a person with a great deal of intelligence. During this period worker met Mr. Steiner and found him to be a very intelligent person, who is much interested in his business. He is friendly, congenial, but has dignity and reserve. The worker felt that he is a very serious-minded person and not a particularly good conversationalist. He is very much interested in the child and eager that he be allowed to remain with them permanently.

E. *Additional information on family attitudes.*—Mr. and Mrs. Steiner frequently have bridge parties and other gatherings at their home, entertain people for dinner, and are in turn invited out frequently. They are not interested in any educational projects, do not read extensively, and are not particularly desirous of improving themselves along intellectual lines. They attend the Solomon Temple on the high holidays, but this is the only evidence of a religious spirit in the home. Both Mr. and Mrs. Steiner believe that worldly possessions are an indication of success and are proud of the fact that they have been able to acquire so much. It is the worker's impression that Mrs. Steiner also believes that material possessions are an indication of culture, since she has several times indicated that she feels that living in the more crowded sections of the city is an indication of being uncouth.

F. *Present economic status.*—Mrs. Steiner has never discussed with worker the economic situation of her family. However, from all outward indications, they have managed to keep a high standard of living.

II. FOSTER-FAMILY IN RELATION TO CHILD

A. *Changes in attitude toward the child.*—Mr. and Mrs. Steiner are very much interested in the child and eager to have him remain with them permanently. They look upon him as their own, are very proud of him, and always wish to speak of his many accomplishments. All the Steiner relatives have taken over this attitude and the child receives numerous gifts from them, etc., and is in general treated as a member of the family group.

B. *Growth in understanding of the child's personality.*—Mrs. Steiner understands David very well. She has given the worker fairly complete observations about the child and is conscious of the various changes that are occurring in his personality as he grows. Mrs. Steiner has been inclined to emphasize his physical health, has been very careful about taking him to her family physician once each month, but the worker does not think that she has a good understanding of the mental development of the child. She has not read literature on child care, throughout this period, although the worker has suggested from time to time that she do so. Mrs. Steiner has carried through a regular routine in dealing with David, has carried out the doctor's suggestions about food, sleep, habit formation, etc. The child has made very good progress while with the Steiners and from all indications, appears to be very contented. The worker always found him being cared for physically in a most excellent manner; he is always very neat, dressed in very good taste, and has been outdoors a part of every day. Mrs. Steiner has had a maid to assist her with the care of the baby, but she has assumed supervision since she does not believe that she should trust a maid entirely with the child.

C. *Attitude toward the child's parents.*—Both Mr. and Mrs. Steiner have an excellent attitude toward an illegitimate child. They believe that such children should be given as much opportunity to develop as children born into a normal family group. However, because they realize that many of their friends and acquaintances do not share this attitude, they have refrained from telling the child's background history.

III. FOSTER-FAMILY IN RELATION TO THE CHILDREN'S AGENCY

Mr. and Mrs. Steiner have had a very good attitude toward the organization. They have accepted supervision willingly and have always made the worker feel very welcome. At the present time they are eager to pursue the plans for the child's adoption, so they may be completed as soon as possible.

November 3, 1928.—An anonymous telephone message was received in the office from a woman who refused to give her name or address but stated that there is domestic difficulty in the home of Mr. Henry Steiner. However Mr. Steiner claimed that he and his wife have no trouble and, although he is fond of the baby, if he had to choose between the two, he would choose his wife because he is exceedingly happy in his relationship with her and he cannot account in the least for such a report. He appreciated our position and did not feel badly that we questioned him. He thought that this report might have been initiated by one of his sisters-in-law, Mrs. Roy Steiner, who is not on speaking terms with her husband and blames the paternal relatives for her family discord.

November 5, 1928.—Telephoned Mrs. Roy Steiner, explaining to her that our organization has placed a baby in the home of her brother-in-law, and we wanted to know her opinion about the marital relationship of the family and whether in her opinion the child is rightly placed. She spoke very highly of both Mr. and Mrs. Steiner and of the care the child is receiving in their home. It is therefore not likely that she is the person who telephoned the office.

FEBRUARY 5, 1929

I. FOSTER-FAMILY

A. *Change in location.*—The Steiners continued to live at 32 Madison Park.

B. *Changes in personnel.*—The group continues to consist of Mr. and Mrs. Steiner and a maid.

C. *Additional information on family background.*—Mrs. Steiner has spoken frequently to worker about her family. She is evidently very much attached to her brothers and sisters and always speaks with a great deal of pride about them. During this period, she took Davy to visit her sister in Oklahoma and upon her return to Chicago, reported very proudly that her sister had considered him a "very fine boy."

D. *Additional information on interrelationship.*—In spite of the doubt that had been raised about the relationship between Mr. and Mrs. Steiner because of the telephone message which was received in this office, the worker believes that a good relationship exists between these two people.

Mrs. Steiner has often told the worker how fond she is of her husband and how very congenial their married life is and how happy she has been.

She is very eager for her husband to succeed in business, but feels that no matter what would happen in a business way, he would always find happiness through his congenial home life.

E. *Additional information on family attitudes.*—Mr. Steiner is very much interested in his business career and spends a great deal of his leisure time planning for his business activity. In spite of this fact, he is interested in his home and is always happy to have guests.

F. *Present economic status.*—As stated in the write-up of September 17, 1928, Mrs. Steiner and worker never discuss the economic situation in the family; however, from all indications, they do appear to have consistently had plenty.

II. FOSTER-FAMILY IN RELATION TO CHILD

A. *Changes in attitude to child.*—Mr. and Mrs. Steiner continue to be interested in the child and continue to be eager to have him remain with them permanently. They have become somewhat annoyed recently because adoption proceedings have not gone through as quickly as they thought they would.

B. *Growth in understanding of child's personality.*—Mrs. Steiner has a very good understanding of the boy's personality. She gave the worker very detailed observations about the child for a Child Guidance Clinic report which was written during this period. She also co-operated in taking the child for an examination to the Clinic and appeared to be very pleased to get the advice of the psychiatrist in regard to the boy.

During the past summer, Mrs. Steiner took the baby to her summer home for a period of two months, since she felt that he would benefit by this change in environment.

Both Mr. and Mrs. Steiner are very proud of David and are happy in the realization that he is making good progress in the home. During this period, Mrs. Steiner subscribed for the magazine, *The Parent*, a magazine devoted to the newer methods of dealing with children. She shows a great deal of insight in training David; for example, the boy has shown evidence of having a temper, and she has dealt calmly with him.

C. *Attitude toward child's relatives.*—No member of the Levy family has been to visit in the Steiner home. Mrs. Steiner feels definitely that she ought never to tell the child of his heredity; she is eager to have him grow up feeling that he is their own child. The worker has attempted to dissuade her from carrying out such a plan, by pointing out to her that adopted children always find out about their parentage and then show resentment to their adopted family for not having been truthful with them. The worker has suggested to Mrs. Steiner that she attempt to be truthful with David from his earliest childhood, in order that he might have a good attitude toward Mr. Steiner and herself. Mrs. Steiner has not been willing to carry through such a suggestion thus far, but has stated that she will talk this matter over with the psychiatrist at the Clinic before making a definite decision as to which plan to pursue.

III. FOSTER-FAMILY IN RELATION TO THE CHILDREN'S AGENCY

Mr. and Mrs. Steiner have continued to have a very good attitude toward this organization throughout this period. They have accepted supervision very willingly and have carried out all suggestions which have been made to them. During this period it was suggested to them that they visit the Child Guidance Clinic to have an interview with the psychiatrist, before adoption proceedings are completed, and they carried out this suggestion very willingly.

In the letter which was received from the Clinic following this interview, the psychiatrist stated that he found both Mr. and Mrs. Steiner to be extremely devoted to David. They recognized the fact that the mother was subnormal, but are very eager to adopt the child in spite of this. The psychiatrist thought that they had handled David wisely during the time they have had him in their care. The psychiatrist got the impression that both Mr. and Mrs. Steiner were at least as well adjusted as many parents, and would make fair success of raising children. Moreover, the psychiatrist felt David is already their son emotionally and any interference with this would result in an unwarranted wrench to all three personalities. The psychiatrist therefore thought that the only thing to do was to arrange for final adoption as soon as possible. He was particularly inclined to this view since both Mr. and Mrs. Steiner have a very fine and appreciative attitude toward the Clinic and intend to keep in touch with them for advice in the care of David. (See letter on file.)

February 22, 1929.—Case reported to the Adoption Committee, informing them that the family now is very anxious to consummate the adoption. After reviewing the reports from the Clinic on the child and the family the Committee decided to permit the family to adopt the child at the present time, subject to the approval of the Board of Directors at their next meeting to be held February 24.

February 24, 1929.—Miss Appelman of the Adoption Committee presented the case to the Board of Directors at their monthly meeting, and it was unanimously approved that the child be given in adoption to Mr. and Mrs. Steiner subject to their interview with the president or vice-president.

Later.—Telephoned Mr. Steiner giving him this information. He received it with considerable joy and at once asked whether by next year he could reapply to the organization for the adoption of a little girl.

February 29, 1929.—Letter from Mr. Foresman, president, stating that he and Mr. Schaar approve of the Steiners adopting the child.

March 21, 1929.—Letter from Mr. Maurice Kepler, attorney-at-law, advising that he is the attorney for the Steiners, and asking that we send him certain information regarding the child.

March 22, 1929.—Letter to Mr. Kepler:

In reply to your request for information regarding the child who is being adopted by Mr. and Mrs. Steiner, we wish to furnish you with the following information.

The child's given name is David Levy, born April 13, 1927. This child was born out of wedlock; and shortly after his birth the mother refused to care for him, and he was placed with our organization. On December 3, 1927, the Juvenile Court gave us guardianship with right to consent to the adoption of this child, as per docket 103056. A copy of this decree will be sent to you upon request through the County Clerk's office of the Juvenile Court. The mother has never shown any interest in the child. On February 20, 1928, he was placed in the home of Mr. and Mrs Henry Steiner with the view of their taking him in adoption. The child has been in their home since that date; and they have given him excellent care, and we heartily approve of their taking him in adoption.

We do not know the mother's present address; her name is Miriam Levy. She was born on February 9, 1904.

If there is any other information you may need in petitioning the County Court, we shall be glad to submit same upon request.

November 17, 1929.—The worker visited the home and interviewed Mrs. Steiner and saw the child. The Steiners now occupy a spacious six-room apartment, which, like the previous home, is beautifully furnished, They keep a maid. The child, although not three years of age, speaks quite plainly and appears to be a very happy, contented youngster. He shows evidence of good training and according to Mrs. Steiner he has completely overcome his temper tantrums. He is amenable to suggestion, and she controls him primarily by talking to him in a low voice. Mrs. Steiner stated that both she and her husband are exceedingly fond of the child and cannot picture themselves without him.

Mr. and Mrs. Steiner are very anxious for another child but realize that at the present time their financial status would not permit them to take on this extra responsibility. Mrs. Steiner is very grateful to the organization for placing a child with them and is anxious to be of assistance to us if we can use her services. Told her that we may call upon her soon to do some volunteer service.

December 30, 1929.—Mrs. Steiner in the office, stating that although they requested Mr. Kepler, attorney, to proceed with the adoption last March, they recently discovered that he has never filed a petition for the child's adoption. They have therefore decided to take the case out of his hands and are now asking Mr. M. L. Rosen, attorney, to proceed with the adoption. Advised Mrs. Steiner to have the attorney write us a letter and we will send him the desired information.

January 4, 1930.—Letter from M. L. Rosen, asking for information to proceed with the adoption of the child.

Later.—Necessary information sent. (See letter on file.)

March 15, 1930.—The worker visited the home and interviewed Mr. and Mrs. Steiner, also saw Davy. It seemed to the worker that the child on the whole appears undersized for a three-year-old. However, Mr. and Mrs. Steiner both feel that he has grown considerably since he has been in their home and, while they realize that he is not robust or tall, they consider him average for his age. According to their family physician, the child is in good physical condition. He still talks indistinctly and in a decided babyish manner. Otherwise, he shows evidence of excellent training and good physical routine. Mr. Steiner stated that for the past two years he has had considerable business reverses and is now hardly able to make his current expenses. He therefore intends to move into a smaller and cheaper apartment. Since he bought a summer home two years ago, he will probably send Mrs. Steiner and the child to the country in June, store the furniture, and not take another apartment until the fall. In this way he intends to economize on his expenses during the summer. Mr. Steiner lost over $25,000 in investments and admits that he now has no savings except his insurance. Suggested to Mr. and Mrs. Steiner that they have Davy re-examined at the Clinic to establish the cause of his speech retardation, and they were very much interested. Both Mr. and Mrs. Steiner were seen by Dr. Leighton when the child was at the Clinic formerly, and asked that if possible the child be seen by the same psychiatrist.

March 17, 1930.—Letter to the Child Guidance Clinic requesting re-examination.

Later.—Mrs. Steiner telephoned that she is leaving for the country at the beginning of May and if re-examination cannot be made by then, she will be obliged to postpone it until the end of the summer. The worker

learned that the earliest date for re-examination will be in June. Therefore postponed the re-examination until the fall.

September 20, 1930.—Mrs. Steiner telephoned stating that both she
and Davy had a marvelous summer. According to her the child grew considerably during the summer and is now speaking plainly. She is anxious
to enter him in a nursery school and wants the Clinic's advice.

October 25, 1930.—Letter from the Clinic stating that they re-examined
the child and find that he has average intelligence. His general behavior
and attitude are that equivalent to the average three-year-old child.
They suggested that he be entered in a nursery school because of a speech
defect and because he shows a tendency to be overly stimulated. They
also thought that the school could assist him in establishing proper eating
habits.

October 26, 1930.—The worker visited Mrs. Steiner and discussed the
report from the Clinic. She was very anxious that the child be entered in
a nursery school and through the Clinic the worker later made several
inquiries and sent the report to her regarding possible schools.

January 15, 1931.—Mrs. Steiner telephoned that in accordance with
our suggestions, she entered Davy in the Layton Nursery School which
he attends every morning from nine to twelve. He enjoys it very much
and attends willingly. Mrs. Steiner feels that it helps to "socialize him,"
and since he has been attending his speech is also improved. She intends
to have him continue attending nursery school until they go to the country
in early summer.

September 18, 1931.—Mrs. Steiner in office with Davy. She stated that
all last year he attended the nursery school, which he enjoyed immensely.
The worker observed a change in the boy as he has become more independent and self-reliant. He played by himself during the entire interview
with his mother and took a great deal of pleasure in playing with the
blocks that were given to him. He is able to tell all colors and used a great
deal of initiative in building various things with the blocks. During the
summer, Mrs. Steiner spent four months with the child in their country
home in Wisconsin. According to Mrs. Steiner her husband is still able
to make a fair living, although his earnings are not so great as they were
at the time they adopted the child. Both she and her husband are exceedingly happy with the child and find that their whole family life has meant
a great deal more than formerly. To insure his education, Mr. Steiner
recently took out an additional policy for the child. Mrs. Steiner stated
that both she and her husband are still planning to adopt another child
but are waiting until the times become a bit more certain. They are grate-

ful to our organization as they think that Davy is a very fine bright youngester.

November 5, 1931.—The worker visited the home. She went without an appointment and did not find Mrs. Steiner at home. Visited, therefore, for some time with the child and had an opportunity to observe him not in the presence of his mother. Although the child had a cold that day, he was very cheerful, friendly, and, as usual, talkative. He related in considerable detail his activities in the nursery school, also his daily routine at home. The maid spoke of the child as being unusually easy to handle and exceedingly well trained. She cited the fact that, unlike other children of his age, he never objects to the parents leaving home and when saying goodbye, usually accompanies this with a remark, "Go and have a good time." After he got through playing with his toys, he put them away in his box of his own accord.

Later Mrs. Steiner came home. Although she had been away the greater part of the day, the child made no fuss over her return although he was very affectionate with her. Mrs. Steiner stated that the child is exceedingly anxious to have a playmate in the home and often talks to them about his coming brother or sister. Recently when they wanted to remove his crib when they purchased him a larger bed, he asked that it remain in the room in the hope that his sister will come soon.

Both Mr. and Mrs. Steiner are very anxious to adopt another child at this time as they realize that Davy is now quite self-sufficient and yet young enough to accept another child as a playmate. For the past year, Mr. Steiner's business has improved and they now feel financially able to assume this extra responsibility.

Discussed with Mrs. Steiner briefly the case of Sarah Manitz, a child two and one-half years old, and she was very much interested. However, since the child is this old, she would like to see her before she applies to the organization formally.

November 9, 1931.—Mrs. Steiner in the office. She came in order to discuss Sarah's record in greater detail and to secure complete background history. She was given this information but was told that we would not consider her application until Mr. Steiner calls at our office with her or alone and is given the child's background history, directly through the office. The object of the interview with him would also be to ascertain his interest in adopting another child at the present time, and should we suspect in the least that she is inducing him to do so against his desire, we will not take any action in this matter. The worker pointed out to her how important it is not only for the child's future well-being, but also for her own good to be certain that her husband is as much desirous of adopting another child as she is. The importance of this point of view was evident to Mrs. Steiner, and she assured the worker that she had talked the matter over with Mr. Steiner and he is interested in adopting another child at this time. He realizes that it is unwise to rear an only child and, if he does not take another now, he will probably never take such a step, as he is getting older and will not care to assume the responsibility of rearing a young child. They discussed the matter pro and con and are very anxious to consider Sarah, providing she appeals to them after they see her. The worker made an appointment to bring the child to their home on Wednesday, November 14. The object of this visit would be to observe the child's reaction to the home and especially to observe how their child would take to her and to what extent he himself is emotionally ready to accept another child.

November 14, 1931.—The worker accompanied by Sarah and Miss Graber, the child's worker, visited the home; Sarah went from her foster-mother without any emotional disturbance, was playful on the way, and was exceedingly at ease and joyful during this visit. Mrs. Steiner and Davy met her at the door, and she greeted them affectionately. After her hat and coat were removed she was taken into Davy's playroom, and at once both children began to busy themselves with the toys. When it was announced that the older people would leave the room, Sarah said, "O.K., I will play here with Davy." He took to her very readily and was very affectionate with her throughout the visit. He pleaded that she be left in the home. Sarah at first refused to accompany Miss Graber, but was told that she might come again.

Later Mr. Steiner came in and the child greeted him at the door, giving him her name. He was apparently quite impressed with her friendliness and intelligent way of responding to his questions. He was told that although the child apparently appeals to them, they are still at liberty to think the matter over and if there is the slightest doubt about their interest in the child, or their ability to take this step at the present time, they should not do so for their own as well as for the child's sake. Mr. Steiner, who is an intelligent man and who is serious-minded, appreciated the importance of this step and asked for a few days in which to think the matter over. Mrs. Steiner, however, was so emotionally taken with the child that she appeared to be somewhat impatient.

November 16, 1931.—Mr. Steiner in office. He said that since the child's visit to their home, he has been thinking about her and he is now determined to apply for her adoption. He feels that economically his situation is much better than it was at the time they adopted the first child. Both he and his wife feel that they are able to give affection and good care to another child and since the child made such an excellent appeal not only to him and Mrs. Steiner but also to Davy, he is anxious to proceed with the adoption. He was given a detailed background history of Sarah and was asked to write a letter to the organization making formal application. It was suggested that he mention in the letter his present economic status, his reason for desiring another child, and what the status of his and Mrs. Steiner's health is at the present time. Mr. Steiner stated that he recently took out a $10,000 insurance policy making Davy the beneficiary and also is carrying a $2,000 educational policy on the child, which will become due when he is twenty-one years old. He intends to increase insurance when Sarah comes to their home and also take an educational policy out for her. Mr. Steiner is so essentially a stable and innately refined person, that the worker feels certain that he will meet his responsibilities toward this child as well as he has met them for the first child. Mrs. Steiner is essentially a homemaker who is very fond of children, yet being somewhat unemotional, she is able to give a child excellent training without tying him up too much to herself. This is very evident when one observes Davy.

November 21, 1931.—Case presented before the Adoption Committee which consisted of Mr. Leopold, chairman, Miss Appelman, and Mrs. Seder. The Committee favorably considered giving Sarah Manitz to the family, subject to a visit to the home by a committee consisting of Miss Appleman and Mrs. Seder, also subject to Mr. Foresman's approval. Unless objectionable to Mr. Foresman, after he sees the family, the Committee would have no objections if the child is placed in the Steiner home before the next regular Board meeting.

November 22, 1931.—Letter to Mr. and Mrs. Steiner, informing them of the Adoption Committee's decision and of the pending visit by that Committee to their home.

November 27, 1931.—Report received from the visiting Adoption Committee approving the giving of the child in adoption to the family, subject to the president's interview of the couple.

Later telephoned Mr. Foresman for an appointment between himself and Mr. and Mrs. Steiner and was informed by his secretary that he will be out of the city for the rest of the week and he therefore authorized Mr. Leopold, vice-president, to interview this family.

November 30, 1931.—Telephone message received from Mr. Leopold that he had just interviewed Mr. and Mrs. Steiner and confirmed the opinion of the visiting committee of giving the child in adoption. He will forward the report.

Later.—Case presented at the Board of Directors' meeting, and they unanimously approved the giving of Sarah Manitz to this family.

December 1, 1931.—Telephoned Mrs. Steiner informing her of the Board's decision, and she was overjoyed. She asked that we delay bringing the child into the home until Thursday, December 6, because both she and Davy are ill with the grippe. She was sick yesterday, but went to see Mr. Leopold, fearing that if she did not do so there might be a delay for a whole month. Arrangements were made with the worker to bring the child to the home next Thursday, December 6.

December 6, 1931.—Sarah was transferred to the home of Mr. and Mrs. Henry Steiner.

All information on Sarah Manitz, to be known from now on as Anna Irene, will be found on sheets beginning with No. 1 under her name.

[The remainder of the record covers the next two years and shows a continuation of this most satisfactory situation with both children.]

6. The Robinson Family

(The Placement of a Large Family of Children Who Have Very Inadequate Parents)

FAMILY RECORD

July 17, 1929.—Case referred to the local supervisor of the Children's Agency (Central Office in Chicago) by Rev. Emery of the First Baptist Church, Dalton, Illinois. The family had been helped by the congregation since 1926. The eldest child, Helen, born August 13, 1913, was very ill in St. Xavier's Hospital with venereal infection. She will probably lose her sight. There are eight children, and the mother is to be confined soon. The father earns $24 per week, on which the family barely exists. Rev. Emery thinks that the children are neglected and wishes the assistance of the Children's Agency in working out a plan for them.

Following material copied from family agency record in Dalton:

July 17, 1929 to July 20, 1929. Father.—Henry Robinson was born at Dalton, Illinois, December 24, 1876, of Protestant parentage. He attended school to the fourth or fifth grade. He has been a steady worker; of late years has been employed at the Dalton Foundry. He has nine brothers and sisters; his mother is living, but his father is dead. He was married to Jessie DeFrere Krause (his second wife) January 1, 1913, Saybrook, Illinois. She came from Murray or Saybrook.

Family.—The family has always been poor. In the past ten years they have been known to every social agency and practically to every church, society, or club in Dalton for assistance with Christmas boxes, clothing, etc., and the township supervisor has sent coal almost every winter and grocery orders at least once a month during the winter months. The father was previously married and had six children while living in Jefferson County. During his first wife's last illness, he employed his present wife as housekeeper and was married to her two weeks after his wife's death. She mistreated the six children, so that the family came to the attention of the Jefferson County authorities, and the children were removed and placed for adoption.

Since the birth of the second child of the second group the family has had to be assisted. At that time the father was earning $35 per week. The mother is regarded by all who know her as incapable and as inadequate mentally, but she is probably not committable. Although the father works steadily enough and tries to support his family, the mother has never managed well. A quantity of clothing has been supplied by organizations and private individuals, but it is never washed when dirty and is generally worn until it is in rags. The mother often takes much of the clothing for herself and has been known to take shoes off the children's feet to wear. The mother has not learned how to co-operate with the organizations helping her, and a contact usually ends with her becoming angry when questioned or supervised. Helen, the oldest daughter, became seriously ill over a week ago, with an infection which settled in her eyes; this became so severe that the child had to be sent to St. Xavier's Hospital, where the infection was diagnosed as gonorrheal infection and her eyesight was despaired of. A specialist and two private nurses were engaged, and the girl placed in the quarantine ward. Although she had been ill in the home for several days before being removed to the hospital and a public health doctor came from Springfield to see her, no Wassermann was taken or examinations made of any of the rest of the family. The family live in a two-story frame house in quite a good section of Dalton. The house is somewhat dilapidated-looking from the outside and has every appearance of neglect and disorder inside. The children have only one or two garments and are often barefooted, even the thirteen-year-old girl.

Mother.—Jessie Robinson was born at Saybrook or Murray, Illinois (date unknown). Since the visitor of Children's Agency was not introduced in the home in her own role but accompanied the probation officer, Mrs. Avery, as a friend, she was able to question Mrs. Robinson very little regarding her parentage, early education, environment, etc. The father's sister, Mrs. Silverthorne, did not know her maternal name but thought she came of a good family near Saybrook and that she has a very nice sister living in Saybrook. There has never been any friendly contact between Mrs. Robinson and the father's relatives. She is a slight, very thin woman; looks badly nourished and has scars on her face, neck, and hands. She is regarded as a very bad-tempered woman by people who have helped her, also by neighbors and relatives. She has no idea of home management or of caring for her children; she spends much time in bed or on the streets. Last year a carnival was in Dalton, and the mother wished her eldest daughter, Helen, to elope with her and one of the carnival men. She stayed away from home two nights and would have gone with the man except that he did not give her a ticket and went on without her. In the past ten years she has written letters to Mrs. Cole of the Associated Charities, Mrs. Avery, probation officer, and Mr. Holmes, township supervisor, requesting coal, food, and clothing for children. She has also enlisted the support of the Catholic Circle and the Baptist Church for the past couple of years. When she gained the disfavor of one organization she misrepresented it grossly to the next one which helped her.

Children.—1. *Helen*, born August 13, 1913, is a very bright, quite pretty girl. She shouldered much of the family responsibility, caring for children, etc. She joined the Baptist Church in 1926 and has been quite in earnest in her church obligations; enjoyed Sunday School and wanted the little ones to attend. She finished the elementary school and wished to go to high school. In the last year she has been very "flighty and people thought her too familiar with boys."

2. *Mary*, born April 19, 1915, is very small for her age; she does not look healthy. She is rather plain in appearance. She had very badly diseased tonsils over a year ago. Mrs. Cole of Associated Charities made plans for an operation; but the mother refused, and the child was not benefited by the treatment of a chiropractor.

3. *Rachel*, born September 28, 1917, is also a rather plain-looking child, light brown hair, gray eyes. She looks very healthy.

4. *Henry*, born September 12, 1919, has brown eyes, light brown hair. His teeth are prominent. He is plain in appearance and does not look well nourished.

5. *John*, born March 4, 1921, has black eyes, brown hair, and a nice appearance.

6. *Harold*, born September 17, 1922, has black eyes, brown hair, and a quite nice appearance.

7. *Jean*, born February 3, 1925, has light brown hair, blue eyes, is fairly nice-appearing, and looks fairly well nourished.

8. *Clarence* was born September 8, 1926.

Maternal relatives.—The visitor has not investigated the mother's side of the family.

Paternal relatives.—*Grandfather, James Robinson*, died one year ago, age eighty-one, following a stroke of apoplexy. He spent most of his life near Dalton.

Grandmother, Mrs. Fannie Robinson, seventy-two years old, has had no home of her own but has lived most of the time with her daughter Pearl. She has had ten children. She is bothered with rheumatism and has grieved over the shiftless ways of Henry's wife and the situation of his family.

Aunts.—*Mrs. Blanche Goode*, Dalton. Her husband is dead. She has four children and works for the Dalton Watch Factory, or helps her sister, Ida Silverthorne, in her beauty shop.

Mrs. Ida Silverthorne, Dalton, was divorced from Paul Silverthorne seven years ago. She has two children, Joanne and Tommie. She supports herself and the children by running a beauty shop in her home. Her home is a two-story house, comfortably furnished. Mrs. Silverthorne is a nice-appearing, pleasing woman with blue eyes and brown hair. She has tried to help her brother's family many times; has given them furniture and clothing but has to fight her sister-in-law's disinterest and dislike continually.

Mrs. Frances Gamble, age forty-four, lives at 903 K Street, Park, Michigan. Her husband works for the Michigan Central R.R. in the office at Park. The family is in very comfortable circumstances and has one adopted child.

Uncles.—William Robinson, age fifty-six, of Grant, Michigan. He is married but has no children. His wife has four children by a former marriage in the home. He works at the Wilson Factory in Grant. They are buying their home.

Charley, age fifty, who has not been heard of for fourteen or fifen years. He deserted his wife and two children who live in Chicago. His wife remarried and runs a beauty shop in Chicago. Her name is Mrs. Janie Gowans.

Oren, age forty-six, lives at 405 Austin Avenue, Milton, Illinois. He is married and has three children. He works at the stocking mills and owns his own home.

Joseph, age thirty-six, Dalton. Works at the Dalton Watch Factory, in the Assembling Room. He is married and has two children. He is buying his home.

Stevie, age twenty-nine, is married and has one child. He lives in Dalton, and works in the Illinois Watch Factory.

Bernard is twenty-three or twenty-four years old and works at the Dalton Watch Factory. He is married but has no children.

Environment.—The Robinson family lives at 735 Grove Street, Dalton. The house shows poor care and very little housekeeping. There is an odor of unwashed clothing everywhere. During the friendly call of visitor with probation officer, the children scampered up and down the stairs but would not come near to talk or answer questions. The mother talked in a strained high voice about her confinement and the condition of Helen. The children's clothing was dirty and inadequate. Their faces were not clean, hair needed combing, and all were barefooted.

Treatment by other agencies.—Rev. Emery of the Baptist Church has been urged by the Board of Deacons in his church to present the case to the Children's Agency, thinking they might place the children in foster homes or could advise Dalton people as to treatment. The visitor said that the Children's Agency could not assume the responsibility of such a family without the co-operation of the agencies and resources of the town and advised a conference with Mrs. Avery, probation officer, and Mrs. Cole, the Associated Charities worker, who visitor thought should be working on the case. Mr. Holmes, the township supervisor for several years, has helped the family every year since being in office. They sent coal by half-tons, sent grocery orders and supplies of clothing. Mrs. Cole of Associated Charities has supplied much clothing, has sent baskets of food at holidays, and has also offered medical aid, which was refused. Mrs. Avery, the probation officer, has been asked several times by Mrs. Cole to bring the family into Court because so many complaints from private citizens and other organizations were coming in. The Baptist Church has for the past two years given food and clothing, Christmas gifts, etc., generally. The family joined the church, and an effort was made to keep the children in Sunday School and to advise the older girls. The Catholic Circle has contributed aid also. Mayor Stevens ran a public appeal in the Dalton paper for assistance for this family, not knowing they had been assisted by most organizations in town. The American Legion has sent food and clothing.

Judge Baker at Baylor was interviewed regarding the family. He was in favor of the Dalton authorities taking the responsibility if at all possible. He thinks the County may object to financial support of all eight children but that it would be possible to allow $70 per month for a short length of time. He advised Mrs. Avery to have Wassermanns and complete physical examinations made of the entire family at once. He would be willing to go into the home with Mrs. Avery and talk with the mother and father concerning a plan for the children either in their home or outside.

Plan.—The visitor attempted to make clear to the Dalton authorities that this family is primarily their responsibility and should be dealt with as a whole for some time before being referred to the Children's Agency.

If the children prove adoptable and foster-home placement seems the better plan and the County will finance the children until permanently placed, the Children's Agency might be willing to plan for and supervise them.

July 27, 1929.—Mrs. Avery in the office to report that the Wassermanns taken on the children last week were all negative.

August 1, 1929.—A baby boy, James, was born to the mother at St. Xavier's Hospital, Dalton.

August 8, 1929.—The following letter was written by Children's Agency worker to Mrs. Cole, reporting the case closed at this point:

Regarding the Robinson case which Rev. Emery referred to our notice some time ago.

In my efforts to learn of the situation in the Robinson family and of the previous contact which Dalton authorities had had with the case, I inadvertently took over more responsibility than I should have. As a matter of fact, I should merely have reported to you and to Mrs. Avery that Rev. Emery had asked our assistance, but after learning that both parents were living and that it seemed to be a family problem to be worked out by closer supervision than has been given in the past, we had withdrawn.

It is our opinion that you might give very close supervision for several months, in spite of the fact that your contact with Mrs. Robinson has been far from agreeable. By "you" I mean the Dalton agencies. We consider it quite impossible to take over a family of eight children when both parents are living, without a history of more intensive work having been done on the case in its own community.

We were glad to hear from Mrs. Avery that Wassermanns on the family were negative.

We are closing our case at this time.

January 10, 1930.—Called upon Rev. Emery at his home in response to a request from him that we reopen the Robinson case, since it was still very active in Dalton. He believes it inadvisable to leave the children with their parents. An effort was made to get a few other interested people to have a conference in the afternoon, but, owing to a good deal of illness, this was not possible. The worker promised to make arrangement for a later conference to determine what steps to take.

Case reopened upon receipt of a letter from Mrs. Cole, of the Associated Charities of Dalton.

January 23, 1930.—Conference in Mrs. Cole's office with the following people present: Mrs. Evans, of the Charity Board; Miss Kane and Miss Coleman, community nurses; Mr. Holmes, county supervisor; Mr. Engle, assistant State's attorney; Mrs. Scott and Mrs. Brady, members of the Baptist Church; Rev. Emery, minister of the Baptist Church; Mrs Meredith, the school attendance officer; Mrs. Avery, probation officer; Mrs. Chase, visitor of the Children's Agency; and Mrs. Cole, secretary, Family Agency.

It seemed to be the desire of the group that the Robinson children should be taken from the mother and father and placed in adoptive homes. Rev. Emery was asked what charge might be made, which would be just and legal, in order that the children might be removed. He replied, "Poverty." He said he would expect the children to be taken away from the family if they could not provide for them. State's Attorney Engle felt certain that the mother is a mental case, although there has never been any study made of her, or of the children. When asked if any constructive work had ever been done, County Supervisor Holmes presented a statement showing that the County had contributed to the extent of $1,044.05 to the maintenance of this family since January 30, 1918, but out of this amount $872.25 was for hospital and medical care for Helen, making a total contribution of about $150 in actual supplies to the family in twelve years. Mrs. Cole said the mother had "deliberately lied" to her on one occasion about two years ago, and she had forbidden her to return to the office again, although she has sent baskets of food and clothing from time to time. Each member had some complaint to make as they had all contributed more or less, and they could not seem to understand why this mother has not been able to manage on her husband's income of $35 a week, although he has not been receiving that amount for several months.

After much discussion it was finally agreed that a housekeeper should be placed in the home, or the children placed for a period of two or three weeks; that the mother be placed in the hospital for a thorough physical examination and treatment, if necessary, as well as mental study. If at the end of this period she is declared unfit mentally, the case will then be reconsidered.

Note to the School Principal from Mrs. Robinson:

DEAR SIR:

About that woman that you have at your office looking after children's that dont go to school.

Now my children's are all shut in by Health Dept with Whooping Cough. First they had measles. Its the four small ones got the Whooping Cough. So the big ones can't go to school because there's no record to show that they had its years back.

Now that's not all either. I want that woman to stay away from my house from now.

She talks to overbearing to me. I run my children's home and not her.

People that haven't children now a day are always around trying to run others that have family's.

When the Health Dept says they can go to school then they will go not before.

Now see that she don't never come here agin. if she does I have it stop.

Thanks

TOTAL HELP GIVEN THE ROBINSON FAMILY FAIRFIELD COUNTY FROM JANUARY 30, 1918 TO JANUARY 23, 1930

January 30, 1918............................ $	3.00
For 1925. Groceries $10.00....................	10.00
For 1926. Groceries $5.00. Hospital $37.00.....	42.00
For 1927. Groceries $3.00. Coal $13.25. Rent $35	51.25
For 1928. Groceries $10.50. Coal $24.50........	35.00
For 1929. Groceries $2.44. Coal $20.68........	23.12
Doctor $151.00. Hospital $319.75...........	470.75
Nurses $383.00. Prescriptions $18.50........	401.50
For 1930. Groceries $3.43. Coal $4.00........	7.43
	$1,044.05
	872.25
	$ 171.80

Total amount given in relief over period of twelve years. Balance medical service for Helen when contracted gonorrhea.

Later.—Worker visited the family and learned that they had just moved into an attractive house, all outside windows, allowing for plenty of air and sunshine, with furnace heat. There were three chairs in the living-room, but no other furniture. There was a dining-table in the dining-room, and a stove but no chairs, there were two beds in the two bedrooms downstairs on which the family of eight children and father and mother are expected to sleep. There was no furniture for the upstairs rooms. The children were all dirty but fairly healthy-looking, with the exception of Rachel, who looked pale and "hollow-eyed." Mary looked healthy, but said her throat was sore most of the time and there was a swelling on the side of her neck. John, eight years of age, is a pathetic little fellow; he seemed entirely different from the rest. He is in 3A grade and, when a remark was made that he would have to drink more milk to get fat, he said, "Oh, I guess I am the skinny one of the bunch." He said it with an air of resignation which was truly pathetic. He also had an abscessed tooth which was in need of attention.

The mother, a very slight woman weighing about 90 pounds, has double goiter, her teeth are very much neglected, and she was in an extremely nervous state. It was plain to be seen that the children irritated her, which was not surprising, as they were tumbling all about in every direction, falling over her, knocking the chairs over, running in and out with complete abandon with no evidence of ever having been disciplined.

The total income now is about $10 a week. Mrs. Brady, who drove us to the home and who seems to be the one person on whom Mrs. Cole depends for advice and financial support, has no patience with the family now and sees no other alternative to removing the children.

January 28, 1930.—Letter written to Mrs. Cole by the Supervisor of the Eastern Illinois Division of the Children's Agency:

I have been thinking very seriously about the Robinson case since my return from Dalton and am going to ask that you give us a little time. We shall go into the mother's family history, also try to learn from Jefferson County just why the father's first children were taken from him.

May we ask that you check up on the earnings of Mr. Robinson. It would appear that, if he is working only three days a week, earning possibly not more than $4.00 a day, they cannot possibly live on that amount and their income will have to be supplemented. Do you think it should be explained to Mrs. Robinson that the children might have to be taken from her if she does not improve conditions in her home? Do you not think it would be well to try to work out a budget with her, checking up pretty closely as to the expenditures and the amount which she receives per week?

I do not know what Mr. Robinson's income has been throughout the past twelve years; but according to Mr. Holmes' report there has been only about $150 in supplies, coal, and rent given the family throughout the twelve years. The balance was for medical service given Helen and could not be counted as relief to the family.

I would appreciate, too, if possible, a pretty thorough medical check-up on the mother and children. She stated very frankly that she was sorry she had had the misunderstanding with you regarding Mary's tonsillectomy, as she is having a great deal of trouble now. Rachel does not look well, and John complained of an abscessed tooth. If this can be done, explaining to the mother that she is on trial; that this comes as a result of her making so many appeals to the citizens of Dalton; and that the county will supplement enough to give her an adequate income for her family providing she cleans up her house and keeps the children in better condition, then we would feel that the last attempt had been made to bring about the proper solution of their difficulties, whether it be taking the children away, or whatever plan might be worked out.

It would be a very expensive proposition to take eight children out of the home and place them in boarding-homes, and I am sure the county would be willing to contribute enough to give this trial, if you are willing. May I hear from you as to just how you feel about such a program. Let us be frank with each other, and I am sure we can work this out to the satisfaction of all concerned. Mrs. Chase (Children's Agency Worker) will call upon you often, and you will find her very co-operative and willing to work with you. I was so glad to have met you and the other members of your organizations. You certainly have a splendid group and you are fortunate to have them working with you.

May I suggest a mental examination on the mother too; I believe this would help us to determine whether she is capable or not.

February 4, 1930.—A memorandum was sent to Miss Carroll requesting a worker in Jefferson County to look over the records for some account of Mr. Robinson's six children by a former marriage who were declared dependent in Jefferson County and supposedly placed for adoption.

February 13, 1930.—The visitor held a conference with Mrs. Cole and Mr. Robinson. Mr. Robinson feels that he must give up the children for placement. His wife has never cared for them properly and has never kept house as she should. He was practically forced into this marriage, and he feels that Mrs. Robinson's mentality is not normal. He has tried to teach her how to cook, but it has been hopeless. If he earned $100 a day she would waste this amount.

March 1, 1930.—A memorandum from the Supervisor of the Eastern Illinois Division was sent to Mrs. Cole with regard to the Robinson case:

I judge you have received the information which is enclosed concerning the Robinsons but in case you have not, I thought it would be well for you to read it over very carefully, and my only suggestion can be that if the county is willing to pay the board for the children for a period until we can determine whether they are placeable, we will be glad to accept them. This, however, only with the understanding that if for physical or mental reasons they will not be fit for free home placement, the county will continue to be responsible.

There is no vacancy in the Receiving Home right now; but, if the Robinson children are definitely adoption cases, we can begin to place some of them very soon. The decrees have not come in yet, and we would like to be absolutely sure that there will be no difficulties before they are placed.

If we are to place any of the children we would feel that we should place them all. I am not in favor of Mrs. Avery placing one out in the community and having us responsible for the rest.

March 3, 1930.—A conference was held with Mrs. Avery, the probation officer, and Mrs. Cole of the Family Service. A decision was made that the children should be placed for adoption. Mr. Robinson was present at this conference and consented to this plan.

March 12, 1930.—Hearing was held at Ranson, Illinois. Mary, Rachel, Clarence, Jean and James were committed to the Children's Agency. Henry was sent to the State School for the Feeble-minded, and John and Harold sent to Rosedale Sanitarium at Baylor, Illinois. History sheets on all these children were sent to the Children's Division of the State Department of Public Welfare.

April 25, 1930.—The visitor called at the State Hospital to secure a diagnosis of Mrs. Robinson. She was found to be subnormal, but with no psychosis. Institutional care was recommended.

May 26, 1930.—Letter from Mrs. Avery regarding birth dates for the Robinson children.

June 9, 1930.—Conference with Mrs. Cole, Family Service, Mrs. Avery, probation officer of Dalton, Illinois, and Mr. Robinson. Mr. Robinson has gained twenty pounds. He looks cleaner and much happier. He is living with his mother in Dalton and is working on an average of four days a week. He has not yet caught up with the payments on his accounts. He does not go to see Mrs. Robinson and will never live with with her again. He sees no way of ever establishing a home for the children and wants them placed for adoption.

Visitor called at the State Hospital. Mrs. Robinson has gained 31 pounds; her hair and clothes were so clean that visitor hardly recognized her. She asked only about James, the baby. Mrs. Adams, the social-service worker at the Hospital, stated that Mrs. Robinson was the filthiest person who had ever entered the Hospital. Hospital staff diagnosis:

"Subnormal, no psychosis and needs institutional care." Mrs. Avery will prepare new petitions so that children may be committed for adoption.

June 13, 1930.—A letter came from Mrs. Avery, stating that Judge Baker is going out of town for a few days and the hearing will be on the twenty-fourth of June.

June 20, 1930.—A letter came from the Managing Officer, State Hospital, stating that Jessie Robinson has been diagnosed "mental deficiency." Prognosis is poor. He does not believe she will ever be able to establish herself and her children.

Letter from Mrs. Avery inclosing an appearance to be signed and returned.

July 3, 1930.—Decree mailed to office of John Miller, County Clerk, Fairfield County, Ranson, Illinois.

July 31, 1930.—Letter written to Mr. Granger, lawyer, inclosing decrees for his review:

We are enclosing herewith a decree for the Robinson children. We desire decree good for adoption.

State of Illinois ⎫ ss.
County of Fairfield ⎭

In the County Court of Fairfield County
June Term A.D. 1930

In the matter of:
James Robinson
Rachel Robinson
Mary Robinson
Jean Robinson   Juvenile General No. 8075
Clarence Robinson
Harold Robinson
John Robinson
Dependent Children

This cause having again come on to be heard upon the petition of Margaret T. Avery, for leave to enter an order appointing P. A. Whitaker, Superintendent of the Children's Agency, Chicago, Illinois, guardian over the persons of John Robinson and Harold Robinson, and for leave to give said P. A. Whitaker as guardian the power to consent to the adoption of James Robinson, Mary Robinson, Jean Robinson, Clarence Robinson, Rachel Robinson, Harold Robinson, and John Robinson, all heretofore having been declared dependent children; and all of the persons interested in the said above entitled matter having either filed their written consent, consenting to an immediate hearing of the above entitled petition, or having been served with notice of the hearing on said petition; the Court having read said petition, having heard the testimony in support thereof, and being fully advised in the premises, *doth find:*

That heretofore on, to-wit, March 12, 1930, the said James Robinson, Mary Robinson, Rachel Robinson, Jean Robinson, and Clarence Robinson were declared to be dependent children, in accordance with the Statutes of the State of Illinois, and that they were, at said time, committed to the Children's Agency of Chicago, Illinois, and that P. A. Whitaker, Superintendent of said institution, was then and there appointed guardian over the persons of the said last above named children.

The Court further finds, that heretofore, on to-wit, March 12, 1930, the said Harold Robinson and John Robinson were declared to be dependent children in accordance with the Statutes of the State of Illinois, and that they were then and there committed to Rosedale Sanitarium at Baylor, Illinois, and that Hubert Adel, Superintendent of said institution was then and there appointed guardian over the persons of the said two last named children.

The Court further finds, that it is now for the best interest of the said Harold Robinson and John Robinson that they be committed to the Children's Agency of Chicago, Illinois, and that P. A. Whitaker, Superintendent of said institution be appointed guardian over the persons of the said Harold Robinson and John Robinson.

The Court further finds, that it is now for the best interest of the above named dependent children that the guardian of said dependent children be given authority to consent to the legal adoption of said dependent children.

It is therefore ordered, adjudged and decreed by the Court, that Harold Robinson and John Robinson be and they are hereby committed to the Children's Agency of Chicago, Illinois, and that P. A. Whitaker, Superintendent of said institution be and he is hereby appointed guardian over the persons of the said Harold and John Robinson.

It is further ordered by the Court that the said P. A. Whitaker as guardian over the persons of the said James Robinson, Mary Robinson, Jean Robinson, Rachel Robinson, Clarence Robinson, Harold Robinson, and John Robinson, dependent children, be and he is hereby authorized to consent to the legal adoption of any one or all of said dependent children.

JUDGE

Dated at Ranson, Illinois, this 1st day of July, A.D. 1930.

Clerk's Certificate of Copy—General

State of Illinois ⎫
Fairfield County ⎰ ss.

I, JOHN MILLER, Clerk of the County Court, in and for said County, in the State aforesaid, and keeper of the records and files thereof, the same being a Court of Record, do hereby certify the foregoing to be a true, perfect and complete copy of Order of Court entered July 1st, 1930, *in re* James Robinson, *Et Al,* Dependent Children.

In testimony whereof, I have hereunto set my hand and affixed the seal of the said Court at my office in Ranson, in said County, this 2nd day of July A.D. 1930.

[*Signed*] JOHN MILLER, *Clerk*

Seal
County Court
County of Fairfield
Ranson, Illinois

August 11, 1930.—The following letter was received by the Superintendent of the Children's Agency, written by Mrs. Robinson regarding her children:

DEAR SIR:

I am sending you a line abart my children's that are under your care Why I am in the State Hospital—for my health. Don't think I am insane or feeble minded I feel fine eve since I been here. I came here as Voleenteer. I have been five months in here. I am Mother of nine babys. Which I am entitled to after I am release from here. There are six children's in your care. Now will you please let me know some how if my babys are all right and in good health. I haven't heard a word from any of them. I hope they all will be return to me soon. I can't stand it much longer without them—In place like this.

No one knows what it is to be a mother without her children's.

So kindly answer this.

August 12, 1930.—The following letter was written by the visitor to Mrs. Jessie Robinson, Dalton, Illinois, inclosing a picture of Rachel, Clarence, Jean, and Mary:

Your letter asking about your children was received.

Enclosed you will find a picture of Rachel, Clarence, and Jean, and Mary. They are all well and so happy. Mary and Rachel show some artistic talent and have made posters which have received quite a bit of notice.

James weighs about twenty-eight pounds, and can walk. He is a very lovable baby, and everyone who sees him loves him.

We are so glad to know you feel better, and that you are gaining in weight. Next time I go to Dalton, I will try to see you.

August 16, 1930.—Letter received from Mr. Granger returning the decree, which he considers only sufficient to give custody of the children to the Agency. He asks that the original decree be sent to him and he will review them together.

September 2, 1930.—The following letter was received from the mother:

DEAR SIR:

I received your welcome letter—and all so of my children's pictures.

Would you please send me James, baby and Harold and John picture to me.

I hope you will take good care of them all till we all get together some day.

If you see Mary, could she write to me.

Would you please report to me—two times a months, so I know they are O.K. there. I hope they will all have good health and be treated kind there. So when the visitor calls to see me call at State School for Feeble minded.

I am here with one of my boys. I was transfere here Aug. 15.

I hope I don't have to stay long here.

No one knows. What a life it is to be a way from her babys.

God bless them all.

                                        I remain.

Please answer.

P.S. I wish I could see all my children's. It is six months I haven't seen my home or little ones. Call or write

                                        MOTHER OF NINE BABYS

September 4, 1930.—The following letter was received from Mr. Granger, lawyer:

I received the original decree and also the subsequent orders entered in the case of the Robinson children. It appears at the bottom of page two and on page three that the mother, Jessie Robinson, is suffering from "mental and physical ailments," and there is a finding that it will be necessary for the mother to enter a hospital to receive treatment for her "mental and physical ailments."

I judge, therefore, that the mother is either feeble-minded or mentally abnormal in some way. In view of the finding of the Court, regarding her bad mental condition, I think it doubtful whether the children could safely be committed for adoption.

Assuming that the mother's mental condition is sound, before the decree would be good for use as the basis of an adoption proceeding, there should be a finding either that the parents consent to the appointment of a guardian authorized to consent to the legal adoption of the children; or there should be a finding that the parents are unfit to have the custody of the children on one or more of the six grounds of unfitness set forth in section 15 of the Juvenile Court Act.

Mr. P. A. Whitaker should then be appointed as guardian with authority to consent to the legal adoption of the children without notice to or consent by any person other than such guardian.

I think that the enclosed decrees are sufficient for custody only. Unless it can be ascertained that the mother is not insane or feeble-minded, it would be useless to ask the Court to make any further amendments. It may be that your worker can ascertain the real facts.

October 8, 1930.—The following letter was written to Mrs. Robinson by the Supervisor, Eastern Illinois Division, Children's Agency:

I know how worried you have been about your children and am sorry I cannot write more frequently to you, but you must realize that with 1,800 or 1,900 children under the care of this society, it is quite impossible to write to each mother once a month as you requested. Could we have an understanding that if at any time anything unusual happens, we would then let you know, but if conditions remain the same, you will not hear from us so frequently.

Mary and Rachel were at the office a couple of weeks ago. They were looking well. Mary has shown decided talent in art and is going to be allowed to continue in that study. She is in the 8th grade. I hope she may be able to graduate in February. Rachel is in the 6th grade and is looking very much better physically than when you last saw her. Harold and John are now in a boarding-home, having been removed from Rosedale. Harold is as fat as a little butter ball. John looks quite well, but we are feeding him plenty of milk and eggs, hoping he will gain weight.

Jean and Clarence are in the same home. They have a big dog, a kitten, and are indeed very happy. James is in another home and he is loved as an own child. The foster mother said she did not believe that she could do without him now. He is always smiling. You have lovely children, Mrs. Robinson, and I know you are going to be quite content knowing they are receiving the very best of care and will be given an education which will help them to become self-supporting in a few years.

October 18, 1930.—Letter received from Mrs. Robinson acknowledging our letter of October 8:

In regards to my letter abart my babys. I am glad to know that they are O.K. there.

I am well here and all so my boy Henry Jr. is well but he don't look good. I hope I don't have to stay here long.

Miss Thomas wrote that my baby had a *foster mother* It made me feel so bad, every time, I think of it—Will you let me know. When you write again (later) was my babys taking from me—not for good I hope. I want my babys to have good health and education but no step parents for them. So let me know from my babys once in a while. I wish I could come and see them. It's seven months I have been away from home. Won't you please send me a picture of my John— Harold—James—God bless them all— I remain—

THEIR MOTHER

Later.—Memorandum regarding Henry Robinson at State School for the Feeble-minded: His I.Q. is 79. Miss Rudovicz at the State School feels quite definitely that he should not be there. He has done well in school at the institution. They intend to give him another test soon and will report to our office.

April 16, 1931.—A letter came from the State School for the Feeble-minded regarding Henry. See letter regarding findings of physical examination, laboratory tests, and a new psychometric examination. They recommend a country home for him.

April 23, 1931.—The visitor talked with Mr. Robinson at the Lane Foundry, Dalton, in regard to assisting in the care of Rachel and Mary.

The visitor explained to him that both girls would graduate in June, which seemed to please him. He was told that we wanted the girls to have an education and at the present time were planning to have them remain at the Parkins School for Girls and attend the high school at Springville. He said that he is earning only $17 every ten days and he can do no more than pay house rent and groceries for himself and his mother. He is paying $25 a month rent. He says that his mother is dependent upon him and until his earning capacity increases he will be unable to do anything for either Mary or Rachel. Should he be able to put in full time, he will give something toward the children's support. The visitor thought that Mr. Robinson had lost weight, and his teeth are in very bad condition.

April 30, 1931.—Letter from Judge Baker asking that Dr. Munger write him regarding the change of order for Henry Robinson.

May 12, 1931.—Letter from mother inquiring about her children. She expresses a wish that Henry be removed from the State School for the Feeble-minded.

May 14, 1931.—Letter from Judge Baker stating he will have an order entered in court Thursday committing Henry to the Children's Agency, according to recommendation made by Dr. Munger, Managing Officer of the State Hospital for the Feeble-minded.

July 22, 1931.—Called on Mrs. Jessie Robinson in the State Hospital for Feeble-minded. Mrs. Robinson is glad that Henry is having a chance outside, but feels bitter that she must be kept there. She wonders why she does not hear from her husband. She insists that she was a voluntary patient at the State Hospital for the Insane and that they had no right to send her here. Her work at present is in the paring-room of the kitchen. She was given this work because she cannot be on her feet very long.

November 10, 1931.—The visitor interviewed Mrs. James Robinson, paternal grandmother, at Dalton. She was able to secure very little information concerning Henry's first wife and children. She claims that Henry was "roped into" the second marriage and tells about the same story as his concerning the matter. She states that the children were always neglected; no matter how much food or clothing was brought into the house, the mother did not know how to manage. She said that several years ago when Mr. Robinson was very ill with pneumonia his wife refused to care for him at all or to give him anything to eat. His mother learned that he was ill through one of the children and went to the home and cared for him. Many times she has gone into the home and cleaned and mended clothes, only to find that a few days later everything was in disorder and dirty.

Grandmother says that she was born in Canada and when she was seven years old had lost both her father and mother. After her mother's death she was taken by a friend of her mother's and had to work for her room and board wherever she went. She met Mr. Robinson, who was a painter and paper-hanger by trade, in Michigan, and they were married there. She is the mother of ten children, nine of whom are living. She states that Henry was born 54 years ago at Sewall, Illinois, and finished the eighth grade. He always has been very ambitious and has worked whenever he could secure work. As a boy he was no problem. Mrs. Robinson states that her husband was always able to provide for their family. Stevie and Bernard had two years of high school. The rest of the family finished the eighth grade.

The home in which Mrs. Robinson and her son James live is in a nice neighborhood where the houses are small but well kept. They have a six-room story-and-a-half house. It is very well furnished and excellently cared for. Mrs. Robinson states that all the furniture is her own. During the last year that she and Henry have kept house together she has contributed $250 toward the budget, Henry furnishing the remainder. Mrs. Robinson, although seventy years of age, is very well preserved and shows some refinement. She is quick mentally and evidently a good manager. There are many things about her home that show good taste.

Later.—The visitor interviewed Mr. Robinson at Lanes. During the summer months he has averaged about four days a week work; however, the last three weeks he averaged only two days. Although Mr. Robinson does not help his children, his mother insists that he thinks of them and often she has found him in tears.

When the visitor questioned him about his first wife, he did not want to give any information. After the visitor explained to him that we had never completed our history of the case and tried to show him it was essential, he gave the following information.

His first wife was Susie Jones Shafer. She was adopted by a Miss Shafer, a maiden lady at Murray, Illinois. Her father's name was Jones. She died December 8, 1912, a diagnosis of illness given as "cancer of the heart, caused by a goiter." During the time she was ill, his second wife, Jessie Krause, and her mother came to the home and helped him to take care of his house. Less than a month after the death of his first wife he married Jessie Krause. She neglected his children, and the case was heard in the County Court at Saybrook, Illinois.

Mr. Robinson reports that Alfred Krause married his wife's mother just a few months before Jessie's birth. He told Mr. Robinson that he was not her father. Alfred Krause had told him on many occasions that Jessie's mother had attempted to bring about an abortion and he felt that this was the cause of the mental condition of Jessie. Mr. Robinson gives the names of the following brothers and sisters of his second wife:

Ben Krause, San Francisco, California
Anna (married), last name unknown, living at Franklin, Illinois
Jay, living in Wisconsin
Cecil, who is reported to have committed suicide some place in Texas

Mr. Robinson stated that Alfred Krause lived in Milton, Illinois, about four or five years ago and worked in a hinge factory.

November 14, 1931.—Mr. Alfred Krause, alleged maternal grandfather, is now in the County Poor Farm at Saybrook. Until recently he had been living with his daughter (maternal half-aunt), Mrs. Anna Merrick, whose husband has been the manager of the Atlantic and Pacific store in Saybrook and is now selling Prudential life insurance. Rev. Pardee of the Methodist Episcopal church knows this family well and speaks highly of them. Mr. Krause went to the Poor Farm when a child was born at the Merrick home. His daughter states he is happier there.

Later.—Mr. Krause when interviewed gives the following information regarding his daughter, Mrs. Jessie Robinson, mother. Mrs. Robinson was born after his marriage to her mother, Ruth DeFrere, but Mr. Krause feels very certain that he is not her real father. The maternal grandmother, Ruth DeFrere, was a member of a family of fourteen, many of whom still live round Collins, Illinois, and are well known. He states that one of her older brothers was rather queer. He did not say anything definite as to his wife's reputation, but from his reaction to questions visitor would judge that she did not bear any too good a reputation. He excused her by saying she had little chance at education because she was a member of this large family.

Cecil Krause, the oldest son of Alfred Krause and Ruth DeFrere, committed suicide in Austin, Texas, in 1921. He was the building superintendent for a large contractor. He was married and had one child, George, and had had trouble with his wife. The wife is probably living in San Antonio, Texas. Mr. Krause attributes his son's suicide to despondency over family troubles and to injuries. He had lost a leg and an eye in two severe accidents.

Jay Krause (married, no children) lives in Wapello, Wisconsin, and works either in a cement factory or a tobacco warehouse.

Another son, Ben Krause, lives in San Francisco. Street address unknown.

The Krause family lived next door to the Robinsons for a year or two before their daughter married Henry Robinson. Mr. Krause's opinion of Henry Robinson is that he has always been improvident and irresponsible. He bought this house in which they lived at Saybrook and had great plans about fixing it up. He put wall board on half the dining-room and left the rest undone. He painted one side of the house and left the rest unpainted, etc.

His first wife was very untidy and had no control over her children. She dropped dead on the street. (Verified. Visitor saw coroner's report.) Mrs. Jessie Robinson kept house for about two weeks before she married Henry Robinson, but Mr. Krause states that nothing was wrong at that time because his wife kept very close watch over her.

Mrs. Jessie Robinson is said to have been of a quarrelsome nature and hard to control while at home. She quarreled constantly, especially with the brother next younger than herself. Mr. Krause did not oppose her marriage because she was a disturbing factor in his own home and practically uncontrollable.

SUMMARY OF FAMILY RECORD TO DECEMBER, 1935

The father continued to live with the paternal grandmother and was employed as a day laborer earning $25–$30 per month, in the spring of 1932. In April, 1933, he told the worker that he had rented an 80-acre farm, where he was working "on shares." His mother was living with him and keeping house for him. He seemed more interested in Helen than in any of the other children. On April 17, 1933, the father told the worker that he was convinced that Helen, Mary, Rachel, Henry, and John were his children, but he doubted the paternity of the others. On the same date the father showed a picture of a woman in whom he was interested and whom he wished to marry if he could obtain a divorce from his wife.

When Rachel was seen October 11, 1935, she reported that her grandmother had died of pneumonia. She said that her father had attended the funeral with his "girl friend." She said he was still working on the farm.

The mother was transferred from the State Hospital to the State School for Feeble-minded. When the worker visited the institution August 15, 1935, the physician reported that the mother was restless, had a very bad temper, and that she had difficulty in getting along with others. In an interview with the mother, she asked about first one child and then another, and appeared emotionally upset. She was concerned because Mary no longer wrote to her. She was most interested in hearing about Mary and Clarence, who she said were her favorites.

HELEN ROBINSON

There was no record of Helen Robinson except that she was placed in the State Industrial School for Girls. She was paroled to her father and grandmother on April 1, 1932; however, she was returned to the institution eight months later for breaking her parole by staying out late and refusing to conform to any discipline. After her return, she became very ill, and lost control of her arms and legs. This was attributed to active syphilis again, which affected her spine. She was transferred to a hospital. She was found to be pregnant and gave birth to her baby in the middle of the night without an attendant, as she was unaware of the birth owing to her paralyzed condition. She died April 18, 1933.

MARY ROBINSON

March 13, 1930.—Mary was committed to the Children's Agency on a temporary custody order. Fairfield County is to pay board at the rate of $5.00 per week.

Mary was removed from her home at Dalton, Illinois, and temporarily placed to board with Mrs. Rebecca Wood, 330 North Capitol Street, Compey, Illinois, until she could be placed in the Receiving Home.

REPORT OF CHILD LEAVING RECEIVING HOME

Name: Mary Robinson   Entered March 21, 1930
  I. Behavior
      A. Stealing..............Not to our knowledge.
      B. Lying................No. We have found her truthful, although she has pretended illnesses.
      C. Truancy..............Always on time.
 II. Personality Traits
      A. Cheerful—Sulky........Cheerful as a rule—when corrected she will pout for a time.
      B. Aggressive—Shy.......Very aggressive. Free to ask for anything she fancies as though there was no limit to supplies.
      C. Affectionate..........Yes, but one does not discover it until after longer acquaintance.
      D. Impertinent..........Very sharp with the girls.
      E. Good sense of humor....Fair sense of humor.
      F. Worrisome...........No.
      G. Temper tantrums.......Has a quick temper—does a great deal of sputtering—remains somewhat depressed for a short time—decided opinions.

H. Destructive...........No.

I. Imaginative...........Yes, and she is clever in making use of her imagination. Loves to plan programs and can do very well.

J. Tendency to cry.......Cries easily and so loud.

K. Energy well directed....Yes.

III. Interest

A. Flitting—Persistent.....Persistent when she once gets at a thing.

B. Responds quickly— slowly..............Responds quickly.

C. Lack of interest.......Keenly interested in everything.

D. Daydreaming..........No.

IV. School

A. Scholarship...........Promoted to 7A. By going the six weeks of summer school she hopes to skip a grade and be in 8B in the fall.

B. Special ability.........She does freehand drawing very well.

C. Conscientious

D. Backward

V. Relationship with Other Children

A. Plays in a group— By self..............Inclined to be bossy when playing with the group.

B. Leader—Follower.......A leader.

C. Bully.................Not a bully, but likes to tease.

D. Tease

E. Cruel—Kind..........Kind-hearted, but not so tender as her sister.

F. Quarrelsome..........Very touchy.

G. Selfish—Shares with others..............Not as unselfish as we would like.

H. Associates............Is well liked.

VI. Habits

A. Pride in personal appearance............Extremely proud, wears her clothes well, and keeps neat.

B. Ability to assume responsibility.........Yes indeed. She is very capable, rather quick in performing her little duties.

C. Care of personal possessions.............Not in the sense of being orderly.

D. Attitude toward work...Much better now. At first, she cried whenever we asked her to do any work. Would say she was not here to work.

E. Food..................Very good appetite. Table manners very good.

F. Sleep.................Sound sleeper.

G. Enuresis..............No.

H. Sex...................Not to our knowledge.

VII. Control and Supervision.
Type Productive of Best
Results

Response to discipline......Firmness. One must always be emphatic with her, and then she is amenable to reason.

A. Defiant................Yes.

B. Indifferent.............No.

C. Co-operative...........Not always.

VIII. Health...................Very good. She is still a few pounds underweight, but has gained since here. She frequently had headaches and backache, would go to bed, and cry loud and long, but as she adjusted they have practically disappeared. After frequent backaches, I forbade her using the roller skates thinking they were the source of her trouble. She seemed to feel better after a few weeks, and I then gave her permission to skate, and since that time she has not complained of her back.

IX. Remarks.................She is exceptionally bright and is so capable. She is abrupt in her talk, often it seems rude, but she does not mean to be. She is emotional. The day we outfitted Jean to go to a home, Mary was so upset, and cried bitterly. I explained to her that she was going to a boarding-home and that no doubt she herself would go when summer school was over. She calmed down then and was reasonable. A few hours later, when she was asked to dress her little sister, she was so indignant and made quite a fuss over doing it for her.

April 18, 1930.—Report from Mrs. Haines, Receiving Home:

Mary in Grade 7B, she is a good student. If she would do her best in her written work, her papers would be satisfactory. She has a good spirit. She has done most of the work assigned.—Myrtle Winter, teacher.

July 15, 1930.—Worker went to the Receiving Home to visit Mary and Rachel Robinson, also to see Clarence and Jean before having the children brought in for the Child Guidance Clinic examination. Mary is tall and quite mature. It is hard to realize that five months ago these girls came from such a wretched home. Both of them were neat and very spontaneous, particularly Mary, who did most of the talking. She was friendly and showed a great deal of poise and self-control. They stated that they did not hear from their parents and they often became lonesome because of this; both of them desire to be artists. They have been promised that placements would be—Clarence with Mary, and Jean with Rachel. They do not seem to doubt but that it will be possible for such a placement to be made. Both girls like arithmetic best in school. Mary said she was behind in school because of moving and also because of ill health, said she had trouble with her throat for ten years—now that her tonsils are out she is getting along better.

August 26, 1930.—Attended the Staff Conference on Mary at the Child Guidance Clinic. Dr. Pevonka, psychiatrist, thought that Mary shows potentialities of adjustment and that she is worth the expenditure of money. He advised placement in a suitable boarding-home where she would have the opportunity to go to school and to learn to be self-supporting. On the intelligence test she rated as average or above average. She is anxious to return home and is somewhat rebellious because she has not been allowed to do so. She feels that she was brought here under the false impression that she was to be able to see her father soon and that she would not have to remain at the Receiving Home long. She is a very mature child for her years and quite a leader. Among her sisters and brothers she is evidently the spokesman. Dr. Pevonka would advise separating all the children and placing Mary in a foster-home where foster-parents are capable of understanding her problem; for he feels, she will, to some extent, be a problem child, with the background attitude she has. In spite of all this, he feels that she, more than the others, is worth "salvaging," and every effort is to be made to do so. She has more ability than she has shown. The situation at home was discussed with her, and it was explained why she could not return home and also the fact that her mother is no longer there.

September 4, 1930.—The following letter was received from the Child Guidance Clinic, giving the report of their examination of Mary:

We have examined Mary Robinson on the 26th of August, 1930.

Psychological tests show her to be of high average intelligence. This would indicate that she is beyond her present grade in school and might safely be advanced. We would like her to return for vocational and art tests and have reserved Wednesday, September 17th, at 10:00 A.M.

Physically she is fit but gave us a history of abdominal attacks which suggest appendicitis. In the next attack she should be brought to a physician's notice.

In her interviews she was quite co-operative. As the other members of the family, she shows evidence of her hard upbringing, she has a sullen expression and perhaps defiant attitude. She seemed to have a very fair insight into her whole situation, but in spite of this she had only one desire and that was to go home. It was felt that this was a reaction to the past five months in the Home when she did not know what the future held for her. She does not know her mother is in the hospital. We think that this girl will do quite well if her interests can be followed, and she should be encouraged to train herself for some job, this in spite of her background. We would suggest a foster home placement where there are children of her own age. We do not think she should be placed with any member of the family.

September 18, 1930.—Mary was removed from the Receiving Home and placed in the Parkins School for Girls, Springville, Illinois.

September 28, 1930,—Miss Thomas, Supervisor, Eastern Illinois District, received the following letter from Mary:

How are you I am fine Will you please tell me where Clarence and Jean are. can I write to my mother and father if I can will you please tell me. You're write I do like it here, and I love Miss Paul and Miss Withrow and all the other ladies. thier all so nice to me. can I see Clarence and Jean soon. I'm so lonely without Clarence. I love to ride Black Beauty Cathrine said for him Gid ap and he did. He come near to throwing me into the tree.

P.S. Don't forget to write me soon and tell me about Clarence. Sending love. Come and see me soon.

Love yours

October 7, 1930.—Letter written to Mary by Miss Thomas:

Your letter made me very happy for you said you liked Parkins. I know how hard it was to go away and leave little Jean and Clarence, but you remember the talk we had and I am sure if you will try real hard it will not be long until everything will come out right

You asked for the address of Jean and Clarence. Won't you take my word for it right now when I tell you they are very happy? When Mrs. Chase took them out on the train Clarence cried; but when he got to the home and saw the big dog and the very kindly, motherly woman who has so generously offered to care for them, he said no more, and Mrs. Chase has later heard that they are just as happy as can be and not at all lonesome. I am of the opinion right now that it would be better if you did not write to them. Wait until they are a little more firmly established.

Mrs. Chase said she would not be at all surprised that, if you finished the

8th grade and if you do well at Parkins, there might be a possibility for you to go into the same home. If not in the same home, we will try very hard to place you somewhere near them in order that you may see them frequently.

Remember me very kindly to Rachel. We are expecting a great deal from both of you girls, for you can accomplish more than some girls can—you have the ability.

With best wishes, I am,

October 12, 1930.—Letter received from Mary in reply.

October 19, 1930.—Another letter received from Mary:

I received your letter and enjoyed it very much. But I would like to know for sure if I could go with Clarence and Jean. I'd love to. You don't know How I miss them. I most certainly wish I could see them.

It was a nice crisp morning and we walked to Sunday School. My finger tips and my nose got rather cold. Rev. Merrill preached a very good sermon about drifting in life.

I'm trying my best to make good and I think I will come out all right.

About where Clarence & Jean are. I would like to know where they are but I promise if you tell me I won't write to them.

We are having a nice time. sending my Love to you

P.S. I think Rachel is writing to. Can I write to mother & father You didn't tell me about that in your letter.

Love

XXXXXOOOOO

Don't forget to write.

November 10, 1930.—Letter written by Miss Thomas to Mary and Rachel:

MY DEAR GIRLS:

I was so glad to get your little letters and to know you are doing so nicely at Parkins, and, Mary, I expect you to be able to cook most anything when I come to Parkins to visit you in the near future. If you like it, you will succeed I know. Rachel, I called Mrs. Haines yesterday concerning your butterfly skirt and Mary's red silk dress. She seems to know nothing about them. Could you tell me where you left them? I will send them on to you if I can locate them.

Mrs. Chase went out to see Clarence and Jean the other day, and they are very, very happy. Clarence particularly chatters all day long. There is an Uncle in the home who is extremely fond of them and said he hardly knows how he could get along without them now. I know this will make you happy.

Give my love to all the girls.

Most sincerely,

November 11, 1930.—Report from Miss Paul of the Parkins School:

Mary is an intelligent, subtly domineering girl who smiles her way into people's good graces for purposes of her own. She is thoroughly unscrupulous in her treatment of her younger sister. She will tell her anything to gain and retain her domination over her. She made Rachel afraid to speak in school, for fear Rachel would be promoted to her own grade. The tests showed the little sister's ability to be so high that the promotion was made anyhow. Mary was the first one to come and rejoice and wish her sister well—she knew when she was licked. Just how much Mary has to do with Rachel's bad habits I have not yet discovered. When she has been here longer we can give a better report.

November 11, 1930.—Report from Parkins School:

MARY IN GRADE 8

Geography	92	Reading	92
Writing	90	History	90
Drawing	95	Language	90
Health	90	Spelling	94
Arithmetic	98	Average	93

November 23, 1930.—Letter from Mary to Miss Thomas asking if she may write to her father.

November 26, 1930.—Mary received a prize for the best Thanksgiving essay in grade 8.

December 7, 1930.—Letter written to Miss Thomas by Mary:

I got a letter from my Mother and it made me so happy. I missed your letter very much. I hope you will write me next week. I am writing to mother today.

How is Clarence & Jean. I do so wish I could see them.

Do you know what I want for Christmas. I want to see them and my folks and then I will be satisfied for a little while.

Don't forget to write

December 13, 1930.—Mary received the following letter from her mother:

My dear Daughter Mary,

I got your letter today. I was so glad to have you and little Rachel write me. I am glad you like school. all so well please to hear that they treat you fine. Yes I please to received your picture and the other childrens. Gee I wish I could get one of Harold, John and James Your Brother Henry is doing fine here now— Since Dr. Hardy been on his Ward. 2 I have a fine Dr. on my Ward. Your sister Helen is getting along fine. She is so please to be where she is on a count of her health is O.K. now.

Your father address is Lane Foundry & Co. South Dalton, Ill. He will be surprise to heard from his childrens. God will take care of you. I always think of you and Rest on Holiday away from home. It will be the first year all of us was away from each other. I am glad you won prize in eight grade and having highest honor in average in school.

I hope your girl friends will treat you fine. I always cry when I think. I dont expect any of my children's to send me a Xmas present. All I care for is their Love in life for me and theirs.

Your father goes to see Sis Helen once a month.

I received a letter from My Judge. stating that he wrote to the doctor here—about my release. And the Judge is going to write to me as soon he heards from the Doctor. I be so thankful if I get to go home for two weeks.

I surely will repay the Doctor and Judge Baker if they release me

Don't weary Mary. after your mother gets out I and Daddy will take of you and my baby's

Helen does write's to me, abait your father. I send a note to Rachel. Be a good girl for your mother's sake. God bless you. I always hope you will have good health till we all get home together. I wish you a Merry Xmas and a happy new. I will always write to you and Rachel Long as you have wrote. Weather is fine here. Love to you. Kisses.

YOUR MOTHER

(Many such letters were written to Mary by her mother.)

January 18, 1931.—Letter written by Mary to Miss Thomas:

I have missed your letters very much. I am awfully sorry I didn't write but I lost faith and when you didn't answer I thought you had put me way out here then forgotten me

I do hope you haven't forgotten so you will answer this letter. I wish I could see you. I have so many things to ask you   Where am I going if I graduate in May? Is one thing.

That worries me a lot lately. But then I have your word and I trust it. Closing with hopes you will write soon.

P.S. Don't forget to write.

January 24, 1931.—Letter written by Miss Thomas in reply:

Please do not think for one moment that I put you way out there and forgot you, as you stated in your letter. I am sure you realize, Mary, that it is not possible for me to carry on very active correspondence with all my girls in their various homes. I know you are being well cared for and I know too that you like to receive letters, but just be assured that I am always interested in you.

Clarence and Jean are very happy indeed, and the foster parents are extremely fond of them   Of course you miss them much more than they miss you —in fact they are so little they have forgotten that they had any brothers or sisters, but you know I promised you I would always keep you informed as to how they are getting along and I will keep my promise.

Give my love to all my girls, and much to yourself.

June 8, 1931.—Mary was removed from the Parkins School, Springville, Illinois, and placed with Mrs. Chester Phillips, 460 Pine Street, Perry, Illinois. Free home. She is to be given allowance of $1.00 per week. Clothing furnished by Mrs. Phillips.

June 10, 1931.—Letter to Mrs. Chase from Mary:

I don't suppose you expect a letter so soon from me. But I just had to tell you that I'm getting along fine. I just love Mrs. Phillips she's so sweet and nice.

Rosemary and I are great friends already. She took me to a show yesterday. It's just 10 min. to 11. I've finished my work and so I decided to write you. I hope you come down next week.

May I have Daddy's address. You said he acted as though he didn't care. Alright when I get through with him. *He'll care* more than he ever did. He needs a waking up and seeing you can't quite succeeded in doing it, I'm going to. Please don't try to stop me. I had enough disappointments with out more. I didn't say anything about Monday. But not going to Clarence and Jean was a big disappointment. But coming here made up for it. I'm so glad Rachel is happy there. Does she get to see my Mother. *I hope so.* As we were coming down here you said it was not Helen's fault. But oh if you only knew. Its just because you don't like my mother that you say its her fault. But it isn't. It never was and never will be.

Mother and Dad both begged and cried, pleaded with Helen to stay home nights and not go out every night. They knew what would come of it. But Helen was stubborn and she absolutely refused to stay. Called both of them old fashioned for not wanting her to go out nights. She said she was out for a good time. So she brought it on her self you see. But then I know how you feel toward my Mother.

Miss Paul told me so many horrid lies. Layed all the blame on mother. Broke her promise and so I *hate* her, I *despise* her.

Please don't let any one see this letter. I don't want any one but you to know how I feel about this. Until I've succeeded. That's why I want to get through High School as quickly as possible. So I can go back and start over. But don't you tell. Because thats my plan after School has been finished and I get a steady job.

I am sending a letter to Daddy as I send you this one. I don't know his address but I'm going to send it to Mr. Henry Robinson, Dalton, Ill. But I'm not going to send it through the City Office, because it wouldn't go through. I tried it before many a time But it never worked. I have tried to get a letter to him ever since I left and I'm going to now. So please don't try to stop me. It's almost lunch time so I'll close.

Love to all

P.S. Dont forget the addresses (Rachel's & Daddy's) Also the picture of Clarence and Jean. Harold's to.

June 25, 1931.—Miss Thomas wrote to Mary:

Enclosed please find the letter from Rachel. I hardly know what to say to you, Mary, for I am afraid you have gotten the wrong impression entirely of this Society and what we have tried to do for you.

I am going to take this opportunity to explain to you that at the time, or rather, previous to the time that your family was broken up, I personally, with Mrs. Chase, attended a meeting where a good many people were present who were interested in your family. We absolutely refused to consider removing you children from your home until further effort had been made to keep your family together. We worked on this basis for a long time. We were finally notified that if we did not accept you, you would be sent some place else.

Mary, you are old enough I am sure to understand and realize some things. You made a statement in your letter that we were keeping your mother from you. May I correct you? We have no responsibility for your mother. We at no time have recommended that she be kept at the State Hospital for Feeble-minded, nor did we ever recommend that she be admitted. You also stated that you had written your father several letters, sent them to the office, but they had never gotten to him. This again is incorrect, for every letter you wrote was forwarded to him. You also made some very unkind statements about Miss Paul and the people at Parkins. I believe you have received the kindliest treatment from everyone—at the Receiving Home, at Parkins, and here at the office, and it is not quite fair for you to say the unkind things you say about each and every one of them. We have many more boys and girls right now than we can afford to take care of, yet we are not turning down one of them. It is our aim and desire to give each one of them an education, after which they may earn their own livelihood and return to their families whenever it is possible.

You will admit too, Mary, that we got in touch with the foster mother of Jean and Clarence and she has written you a very nice letter, and Rachel is now with her baby brother and you are in touch with her. What more could we do? When I sent word to Parkins that I wished to have one of you girls for the home in which James is, I felt that you were the older of the two and could more rapidly adjust in a home in which we could place you. Miss Paul *did not* know that Rachel was going to that home and could not tell her when she left.

Now, Mary dear, I have written very plainly because it is not well for any little girl to go on under false impressions, and I did wish to clear up with you some of the impressions that you have had.

Won't you please get a more cheerful outlook on life; take all the education you can possibly get, fit yourself to be self-supporting, and you can depend upon every one of us being your friend. Work with Mrs. Chase, as she will be your visitor.

You probably felt that we were being very slow in getting certain information to you but you can realize, I am sure, that we have been in this work a long time and may have a little different way of working out some problems, and knowing that it will all come out right in the end.

Won't you sit down Mary and write me a little note telling me you do trust us, for without that I do not see how we can work together.

Sincerely,

Letter written by Mary to Miss Thomas in reply:

I didn't write before because I just couldn't bring myself to. If this letter is cold and hopeless forgive me. But I've got to tell some one my trouble's and thiers no one here. I have just got to see my dad Why Oh Why do you keep stalling me off. Helen wrote to me yesterday and she expects me to come and visit her. Oh but I've got to go. I wish I were dead. Thier's no use living. Because everything's gone. But I'm telling you this. I will fight till death to get our family back together and I will someday. Oh you don't know what torture it is for me to be so near yet so far from happiness. Please give me permission to go both to Helen and to Dad. I haven't ask Mrs. Phillips she's on her vacation now. But what I said in my last letter goes if I don't get to see them by your permission I'll have to go without. I don't want to do this but you force me to.

You told me to tell you that I trusted you. I do as much as I can, after everything that has happened forgive me if I have hurt you

June 28, 1931.—Visitor called at the Phillips home and while Mrs. Phillips was in the garden had a talk with Mary. Mary greeted her with a happy smile and insisted that she was very happy in her new home. She felt that Mrs. Phillips had been exceedingly kind to her and was making every effort to make her happy. Almost every afternoon she and Rosemary Gamble go swimming. If they do not go swimming they go to a movie. The visitor later talked to Mrs. Phillips, who believes that Mary is going to fit into her home. She said she felt sorry for Mary because she felt homesick for her friends at the school. She believes that she will be able to do her duties in the home well enough to satisfy her. She has entered a class in the Congregational Sunday School.

July 8, 1931.—Report from Parkins School. Received a County Diploma. Eighth grade.

Spelling	97	Geography	87
Writing	85	Physiology	93
Arithmetic	100	U.S. History	92
Grammar	94	Reading	87
	Average	92	

July 23, 1931.—Letter written by Mary to Rachel:

I'm sorry I didn't write earlier than this but I thought you were coming up so I didn't write. No I did not go with Clarence and Jean. I was supposed to But you know how they tell stories. Thanks for the picture. I got to from the Lady they are staying with. Did you write to her and to Mother. Please write to Mum every week to keep her cheered up.

Are you sure you are all right from the car accident. Are you sure Jamie was alright. I don't want you to call him Richard in my letters. Please call him Jamie or Baby Jamie.

And *don't you dare* write calling her mother. Call her anything but that. I'll tear the letter up if you do Have you been to Dalton yet. I went through South Dalton and Dalton the other day but we didnt stop. We went to Green Lake and had lunch and then we went swimming. I can swim, float, or dive. No high diving but low.

What color is Jamie's Hair. Is it still black. Please send me a picture of him and you.

Have you been to see mother yet you should go up and see her. She needs some stationery and stamps can you send her some. Do you get any money. I get a dollar a week And I save half. I can't get any stationery till next week or the week after. So maybe you could take her some when you go up.

Helen has not written to me yet. I m sure now that she has left the school now Mrs. Chase told me she was going.

Mrs. Gardner, I recall the name But I can't remember her.

I can't tell you much about Jean and Clarence because I don't know. They are getting awfully big now.

I broke my pen so I had to finish in pencil.

Do you like it there. I like it here. I'm going to Dalton and find Daddy Next week.

I must close now Will write later. Here's a picture of Clarence and Jean and the Lady that has them. Write soon if possible. Rosemary Gamble is my neighbor. Have you got any letter's from School. I haven't got a one and I wrote 2 times and I won't write any more.

Don't forget the picture and stationery. Also love to Jamie.

Love,

Send my love to Mum.

August 22, 1931.—The visitor called to talk with Mr. Henry Robinson at the Lane Company, Dalton. She asked Mr. Robinson if he could accept Mary for care as she seemed to be causing a great deal of difficulty and disturbing the rest of the children. Mr. Robinson said that he could not care for Mary. While she was at home she never did anything to assist him. He is in no position to give her an education. A few days ago he received a letter from Mary which had angered him a great deal. She was upholding her mother and criticizing him most scornfully. He advises that Mary not be permitted to hear from any of the members of the family especially her mother. When questioned by the visitor if he were willing to face Mary with these facts, he answered by saying, "Yes, I will be glad to tell Mary to her face how I feel."

Later that day the visitor talked with Mary and again told her of the attitude of her father. Visitor also explained to her that we could not allow her to write to her sisters and brothers if she continued to write the same kind of letters she had in the past. She was told that Rachel was about to lose her home owing to the fact that Mary had written discouraging letters to her and dictating what she should do for her mother. The visitor also explained in detail about her mother's condition, showing her that it was necessary for the state to care for her since no relatives could give her a home. Visitor also tried to show Mary that she was in no position to do anything for her mother at the present time but gave her a ray of hope that perhaps in the future when she had finished her education and was capable of supporting herself she might help her mother. She promised visitor she would do nothing in the future which would have any bad effect on Rachel and said that she was very happy in her home and was treated as a real member of the family.

The visitor explained to Mrs. Phillips, foster-mother, the type of letters Mary had written to Rachel and also explained to her the interview visitor had that day with Mr. Robinson. This was the first week that Mary had been left to do the work about the house alone, and it was done quite well. The family like Mary but as yet do not feel that they know her at all. She talks very little about how she feels. They had assumed that she was lonesome and that was the reason for her quiet manner. The visitor arrived just at the time when the family and Mary were going to Baylor State Fair. Mary was very well dressed and looked attractive.

September 22, 1931.—Visitor called to talk with Mary at the Community High School. Mary approached visitor with a very happy smile and an attitude of great pleasure at seeing her. She was dressed attractively in a white mesh dress. She had on slight coloring, but it was very cleverly done. She has a lovely coat of tan. Mary expressed great joy in her school work and with a great deal of enthusiasm told visitor how she was enjoying every subject and receiving good grades in her tests. She is taking English, community life, cooking, and science. She was able to purchase all her books second hand. She says she is making many friends in the school and again told visitor she was very happy in her home.

She gets $1.00 a week. She is furnished with very good clothes. Her schedule for the day is as follows: Arises at seven-thirty, gets her own breakfast as the family has already eaten, washes and wipes the breakfast dishes, straightens up the house before she goes to school. She does her own laundry work but has nothing to do with the family's laundry. At dinner time she helps set the table and prepares the vegetables, after dinner she does the dishes, and on Saturday she does the cleaning.

Mary is attending Congregational Sunday School, Rev. Jonathan

Evans, minister. She said she did not have a regular Sunday School teacher at the present time. Her Sunday School class has organized as a social group, and she is planning to attend all their social meetings this winter. (Carbon copy to State Department.)

November 10, 1931.—Visitor called at the Community High School to talk with Mary. Mary again showed pleasure to have visitor call. She is extremely interested in her school and says she is very happy in her home. She feels that Mrs. Phillips is strict but is fair with her. She attends a movie every Saturday with Mr. and Mrs. Phillips. She dislikes spending any of her savings. She is supplied with plenty of clothes and can save something every week. She expressed a desire to call to see her father as they frequently go to Dalton. Visitor noticed that many of the girls passing the hall spoke to Mary. Some of them were very fine-looking girls. They spoke to her in a friendly sort of a way.

She expressed a liking for her Sunday School teacher. She is planning to take a business course the last two years of high school and is hoping to stay with the Phillips family until she finishes school. She said that Mr. Phillips had promised to get her a position with Crane and Company and she is looking forward to this.

November 14, 1931.—Visitor called to tell Mary that she would permit her to see her father if she promised she would be friendly with him. Visitor asked her not to criticize her father in any way. Mary expressed happiness in being permitted to carry out this wish.

Visitor interviewed the foster-mother. Mrs. Phillips likes Mary very much and is extremely interested in her success at school. Mr. Phillips has promised Mary $1.00 for every A she receives. She received three A's and put the three dollars in her savings account.

Mrs. Phillips says that Mary at times is quite careless about her work, but she also realizes this is Mary's first home and tries to have a great deal of patience with her. She does persist, however, in having her do her work well. Every morning she puts the house in order and does the light dusting before going to school. If she does not finish it then, she does it after school.

At first Mary selected girls for her friends who were not the type that Mrs. Phillips would have chosen for her. Mrs. Phillips, not knowing definitely the group of girls that Mary might associate with, took the matter up with the eighth-grade teacher, who is a personal friend of hers. Through her help, Mary has met some of the nicer girls, who seem interested in her.

Every Saturday night Mr. and Mrs. Phillips take Mary to a movie. A week ago Saturday they noticed she spoke to two taxi drivers. She spoke to them both coming and going to the theater. So far Mrs. Phillips has said nothing to her about it, but plans to talk to her, trying to show her why it would be better to make the acquaintance of other boys in the community rather than older men. She is encouraging Mary to attend all the school parties and the church parties. The visitor believes that Mrs. Phillips is sincerely interested in Mary. She expects a certain service from her in return for her kindnesses to her.

January 7, 1932.—Visitor talked with the foster-mother, who states that Mary is making every effort to get along in the home. Foster-mother realizes that it is difficult for her because of her early training. The foster-mother is a very determined type of person, who has a great deal of patience and insists on Mary performing her duties well. She never permits her to form a slipshod habit.

Mary still keeps in touch with her mother, but the letters are less frequent.

Mary is very thrifty and unselfish. At Christmas time she wished to withdraw her bank account to provide gifts for her family. She remembered every one of the family. Mrs. Phillips provided her with materials and showed her how to make gifts. She also fixed up a box of food and gifts for Helen, her sister at the State Training School. Mrs. Phillips took her there and she said that Helen did not know Mary. They had a very happy time together. Visitor talked with Mary at school, and she is gaining in weight. She has excellent color and is very happy. She seems to be making splendid contacts in school and is taking an active part. She is afraid this month she will have two B's instead of two A's.

January 20, 1932.—Letter written by Miss Thomas to Mary:

Thank you for the pretty Christmas card which you sent and I did not reply to your little note in which you asked if I approved of your school grades. Indeed I do, Mary, and I am watching with real interest your progress.

I believe our little difficulty of a few months ago has entirely blown over, or am I wrong? You know you never did reply to my letter and I often wonder just how you felt, or if you thought I was unfair. Could you take time to drop me a little note and tell me what your attitude is now and whether or not you think we have been your friends.

I saw John and Harold the other day. They look fine and were so happy to have gotten a remembrance from you at Christmas time. Henry, too, is doing very well indeed, and we were so glad that it was possible to remove him from the State School and give him a chance.

Keep up your good work Mary and you will never be sorry.

With best wishes to you I am,

February 1, 1932.—The visitor called to see Mary at the high school, during the noon recess. Mary and Rosemary were watching the basketball practice. Visitor called to secure grades. Following are Mary's grades for the semester, with the examination grade and average in all subjects:

English	A A B A.	Exam.: A. Aver.: A minus
Civic Life	B A B B.	Exam.: B. Aver.: B plus
Foods	A A A B.	Exam.: A. Aver.: A minus
General Science	A A A B.	Exam.: A. Aver.: A minus

February 15, 1932.—Letter written by visitor to Mary:

When I saw you the last time I told you I wanted to have you and Rosemary come over to spend a Sunday with us. I also discussed it with Mrs. Phillips, who said she was willing to have you come.

I have decided to ask you to come this next Sunday, Feb. 21. I am also planning to invite another girl, Roberta.

I do not know the schedule on the Electric Railroad, but be sure and take a local car so that it will stop at Poplar Ave. This station is only about three blocks from our house. If you will let me know what time you will arrive, I will plan to have someone meet you and Rosemary at the station. I will reimburse you for the fare, so that it need not come out of your allowance.

Please let me know at once if this date is convenient for both you and Mrs. Phillips.

February 21, 1932.—Mary spent Sunday at the visitor's house. She picked up the book *The Mind with the Iron Door* and spent most of the day reading. She became too deeply interested in reading to be at all interested in any type of conversation. Mary was very well dressed. She makes a very attractive appearance. At present she is afraid of getting too heavy and talks of dieting.

Mary thinks that there may be a possibility of her not being able to keep her home. She feels that Mrs. Phillips is too particular and exacting about her work, especially the cleaning. Mary expressed a great dislike for cleaning, said she never did like it and never would. She does express an appreciation of the fact that she is securing an education and realizes that she must do something in return for this chance. The visitor thinks that Mary is getting a very practical viewpoint of her own situation and her future. Mary expressed a great desire to see her mother. Visitor explained to her that an effort would be made during the summer to plan this visit. Mary said she would be glad to pay the expense of this trip. At present she has a savings account of about $26. This includes the money she has saved out of her allowance plus the dollars she received for every A.

Mary also inquired especially about Jean and Clarence. She was very happy to have the visitor's report of them.

SUMMARY OF CASE OF MARY ROBINSON, FEBRUARY 21, 1932—
NOVEMBER 2, 1935

Mary remained in the home of Mrs. Phillips until January, 1934, when she said she would like to be free to make her own plans. She found a work home where she earned five dollars a week and later seven dollars a week. She reported this to the Agency.

Mary apparently always disliked authority. She was open in the expression of her hate for her father, because of his inadequacy in providing for his family. She did not have a kindly feeling for the Agency and those persons responsible for breaking up the home.

She finished two years in high school with exceptionally good grades and had one semester in her junior year, but left school two weeks before the final examinations. She did not get along well with children her own age. She was very dictatorial with them.

Mary made contact with an aunt and visited her occasionally.

On October 11, 1935, a card was received from Mary saying she was married. She gave the name of her husband and her address. Later she was visited, and it was learned that her husband was employed as a laborer earning about twenty dollars a week. They were living with his mother. On the day she was married she drove with her husband to see Rachel and James.

RACHEL ROBINSON

March 12, 1930.—Rachel was committed to the Children's Agency on a temporary custody order, Fairfield County to pay board at the rate of $5.00 per week.

Rachel was removed from Dalton, Illinois, and placed in the Receiving Home.

March 24, 1930.—Letter to State Department inclosing history sheet.
April 18, 1930.—Report from Receiving Home:

Rachel is in Grade 5A. She is a good student and has a sweet disposition. Her written work can be improved.—Mary Belknap, teacher.

June 13, 1930.—Report from Receiving Home. Rachel is in grade 6C. She will be promoted to 6B.

July 17, 1930.—Letter to Child Guidance Clinic, inclosing psychiatric history and requesting early appointment.

July 18, 1930.—Worker went to the Receiving Home to visit Mary and Rachel Robinson, also to see Clarence and Jean before having the children brought in for a Child Guidance Clinic examination. Both girls like arithmetic best in school. Rachel is very quick in her movements and in making decisions. The worker watched her as she was playing jacks; and out of a group of about ten who were playing, most of them boys and some of them older, Rachel was by far the most skilful, being able to figure out at a glance the best method of gathering up the jacks. Clarence and Jean are much slower and quite shy. Clarence seems somewhat duller than the other three children.

August 28, 1930.—Visitor attended the Staff Conference on Rachel Robinson. Dr. Pevonka reports that Rachel is in the low, borderline group, which will mean that she will probably not be capable of progressing very far in school. This, coupled with her very seclusive, antagonistic nature because she wishes to return to her family, and the background from which she has come, means that she will probably always be a problem. He does not feel that it is worth while spending a great deal of money and placing this child in a boarding-home. He would suggest if possible putting her in the Parkins School for Girls or some other institution of a like nature or into a free home where she could get some training in housework. She is to return for future tests, particularly to determine her artistic ability.

September 3, 1930.—Letter received from Mr. Granger, lawyer, inclosing decrees for the Robinson children. It is his opinion that the decrees are sufficient for custody only.

September 4, 1930.—The following excerpts are from a letter received from the Child Guidance Clinic, giving a report of their examination of Rachel:

Psychological tests show her to be a dull child, she being twelve years and eleven months of age with a mental age of ten years and three months. We should like her to return for further psychological and vocational tests and have reserved Wednesday, September 17, at 10:00 A.M.

This girl was more sullen and had less vitality than her sister. Her insight is considerably less. Much of her discontent seemed to be copied from her sister, particularly in regard to her going home. She could give no reasons for desiring this nor did she seem to realize the type of home she had lived in. Her ambition is to be an artist, but she has no idea of how to proceed. She gives marked preference to the country as against the city. We would recommend that she be placed in a foster home and, if possible, in the country. This girl's future lies in simplified surroundings. It is felt that her background seriously handicaps her, together with her mental retardation, and that only in being away from her parents can she hope to make any adjustment. It might be kept in mind that the children might be returned to the father should he ever be able to afford to keep them at home.

Both for this girl and her sister, we would suggest proper sex instruction as their information has only been gained from a psychotic mother.

September 18, 1930.—Rachel was removed from the Receiving Home and placed in the Parkins School for Girls, Springville, Illinois.

October 2, 1930.—A letter came from the Child Guidance Clinic, stating that both in arithmetic and in reading Rachel has eighth-grade ability.

October 17, 1930.—Copy of Child Guidance Clinic report mailed to Miss Paul, Parkins School for Girls.

November 9, 1930.—Letter received by Miss Thomas, Supervisor of Eastern Illinois Division of the Children's Agency, from Rachel:

I haven't been writing for quite awhile so I thought I would write. I haven't been in seventh grade very long so I didn't get very good grades on examinations. In Arithmetic I got 58, in Reading 80, Geography 49, English 75, History 72, Orth. and Spelling 71. My average is 69. I am writing mostly to ask about my butter-fly skirt. You said you would get it for me in the train and Mary's red silk dress. Miss Thomas, I made a mistake because it was Miss Carroll but will you see If you can get it. I want it so bad. I haven't much to say so I will close.

November 11, 1930.—Report from Miss Paul, Parkins School for Girls:

Rachel is a disappointment in some ways. She is "sneaky and dishonest," underhanded, and has atrocious sex habits and a filthy mind backed up by plenty of boy and girl experience. These things, of course, do not brand the child; they simply set our task for us. She is likable in many ways but thoroughly unreliable. I am sorry that she is so far advanced in school because she is going to need time here to straighten out these other things. However, she will not be through the eighth grade until June, 1932, so there is time to work on her. None of us has her confidence as yet, though both Miss Withrow and I have been courting it. She has the ability to anything she wants to do and if she is in the right mood can work all around many older girls.

December 1, 1930.—Report from Miss Paul, Parkins School:

This may be undue concern on my part, but I am going to have Dr. Barnard see Rachel Robinson for possible tuberculosis. She has lost five pounds in the last four weeks and runs a slight temperature in the afternoon. She is always tired. She eats between meals because I insist on it but has a poor appetite. The loss in weight is unusual; all the others have gained.

Report from Parkins School:

Arithmetic	58	Geography	49
Reading	80	Writing	80
History	72	Drawing	90
Language	75	Health	90
Spelling	71	Average	74

Child entered the 7th grade a week ago and can do the work. She took examinations without study.

December 13, 1930.—Letter written to Rachel by her mother:

Gee I was glad to get a letter from you and Mary all so. I got a letter from Helen and your Uncle Jay and Judge Baker last week. You don't know your Aunt Bell any your back relative. Never mind, Rachel, your father and mother will take care of you and the Rest. Soon as I get home. I hope we will all be home together some day. I don't want any Xmas present from any of my babys. Only their (love) is worth more to me. I hope you keep in good health. Everytime you write. Tell me some thing about yourself. Wishing you a merry Xmas. Be a good girl. I always see your Bro Henry. But it isn't like being all home together. I write later. Don't fail to write.

March 31, 1931.—Letter to Rachel from her mother:

I will write a line to you. Why is it you don't write the last time Mary wrote to me.

Are you well now. I am well at present. All so your Brother Henry.

Everyone got two more shots again last week. Myself and Brother passed O.K. I had five shots now. passed O.K. On everyone so farth.

I received a letter about John and Harold. They both are in Chicago. Doing well and happy. Go to school every day there. They are not in Rosedale Sanitarium now.

Rachel try and get your County Diploma. It means a whole lot to you and Mary. I hope you don't have to work hard.

I don't care of babys anymore. Henry don't do much work either. He goes to school in the afternoon. His work isn't either.

Brother goes to church every Sunday. And shows. I write more after I got word from Sister Helen. Weather is very cool here. And has been raining to. Pray every day and night for God to help you through are sorrow.

Be good girl.

Love—Kisses

April 24, 1931.—Note written to Miss Carroll regarding the possibility of keeping Rachel at Parkins another year and allowing her to attend high school at Springville.

May 7, 1931.—Miss Carroll says it has been decided that it will be unwise to keep the graduates from Parkins; the girls are away from the school many hours each day when the workers have no supervision over them.

June 4, 1931.—Rachel was placed with Mr. and Mrs. S. J. Gardner, Stanhope, Illinois.

The foster-parents and visitor met Rachel at the train. She had not been told that she was to be placed with her baby brother and was overjoyed when she found that James was in the same home.

June 16, 1931.—Letter received by Rachel from her mother:

MY DEAR DAUGHTER RACHEL

I am writing you a line I am well. I hope you are the same there. Why is it Honey I don't get any letters from you and Mary? over two weeks now.

I am not on the Hospital any more. on W^2 and B^4 where it is better Ward.

Did you know that Bro Henry is gone from here. I am glad of it. but I miss him so. I have got any letter from Sis Helen last month.

What kind of work are you doing now.

I work at the North Dining Room as extra helper. I work from 6 in the morning till 7:30 at nite. I worry when I don't get any mail from you.

When I don't heard from Sis Helen, then I don't know abait your father.

Be good girl. Cheer up.

Always write

Love and Kisses

YOUR LONELY MOTHER

July 8, 1931.—The Gardners are delighted with Rachel. They are making many plans for the summer and the school year. They think Manning schools are better than those at Stanhope and hope to move back before September.

Recently on a visit to Dalton to the foster-grandmother, Mrs. Gardner wrecked her car; Rachel received a severe sand burn, the skin was scraped from most of her thigh. At the time the visitor called, however, it was healing nicely. The chief injury was the shock to Mrs. Gardner, who became hysterical at the idea of the danger, particularly to the children.

The foster-father used to be a life-saver and plans to teach Rachel to swim this summer. She has joined a little sewing club of girls in Stanhope. She visits with the relatives of her foster-parents in Manning and Dalton frequently and so far seems to be accepted as one of the family. It is the wish of the foster-parents that their relatives do not know too much of the children's history. Recently on a visit to Dalton, however, Rachel was recognized by a foster-aunt who knew her in school, and the foster-mother was quite indignant when she insisted on telling some of the Robinson family history.

August 5, 1931.—Mrs. Gardner called on visitor to discuss the letters which Rachel has received from Mary. Mary particularly tells her sister not to dare call Mrs. Gardner "Mother" and urges her to get in contact with their mother at the State Hospital. Mrs. Gardner allowed Rachel to write to her mother and to send her some stationery. The foster-mother herself wrote the mother telling her that she had the two children and planned to give them a chance in school and treat them as her own.[1] All this has been very disturbing to Rachel, who doesn't seem like the same girl after receiving one of these letters. The foster-mother feels that this must stop, or it will upset all their plans for Rachel.

September 8, 1931.—Report from Parkins School. Eighth Grade. Rachel received a county diploma.

Spelling	88	Geography	75
Writing	80	Physiology	81
Arithmetic	85	U.S. History	91
Grammar	88	Reading	82

Average............... 84

October 13, 1931.—Rachel is taking algebra, history, English, Latin, and Glee Club work. She also has gym once a week. She is doing satisfactory work in her studies, according to her teachers, but no reports have been sent home as yet. She had a little difficulty with algebra in the beginning. The foster-mother talked with the teacher over the telephone, and with a little extra help she has now caught up with the class and seems to be understanding the work better.

Rachel has changed in appearance enormously since she was placed in this home. She now weighs ninety-six pounds. She takes more pride in her personal appearance. She has a permanent and manicures her finger-nails, and her foster-mother dresses her nicely. Her birthday was celebrated with a surprise party, to which a number of relatives were invited. Rachel knows few girls, as the family lived in Stanhope during the summer

---

[1] Mother's reply to this letter:

DEAR FRIEND:

I will answer your welcome letter I got with my Daughter Rachel.

I was glad to get good news. Hopeing your letter means just what it says.

I worried over that baby ever since they left me.

My children's are mine, and I want them all to know that their mother lives for them.

I am glad Rachel gets a High School Education. I have (nine) children's—oldest 18 years., Baby 17 months old. And I have none to spare either. I hope you will give them good care. Please don't take them a way—without me know-ing it.

I like to have them visit me. Only it make me feel bad. Please let Rachel write often. I was well please with the stationery and stamp I received from Rachel.

I suppose when you got my baby they told you that he didn't have any mother.

Say—Friend—Would you let my Daughter send me toilet soap and Powder and Rouge. I have no things here at all. I thank you for the Picture of baby. I cry over it so long and never sleep at all that nite.

God bless you. Always write.

YOUR FRIEND

and they only recently moved to Manning. The foster-parents are quite intimate with the Fosters, who run a lunch counter and ice-cream parlor across from the high school. This family has taken an interest in Rachel and is giving her her noonday lunch free. She also occasionally stays there when the foster-parents work overtime ·at the office. She occasionally waits on tables or washes dishes in return.

November 16, 1931.—The following letter came to Miss Thomas, Division Supervisor of Children's Agency, from Rachel:

I received your letter. I told you my grades last Sunday and my average was 69. Monday I got my grades for writing, drawing, and health. I got 80 in writing, 90 in drawing, and 90 in health, and that brought my average up to 74. You asked me where I put my butterfly skirt. It was in my package when I went to the Receiving Home. I haven't seen it since and say when are you going to give me the address of the people who are taking care of Jean and Clarence. I haven't much to say now so I will close with love

Yours truly

January 22, 1932.—Foster-grandfather, Mr. Gardner, who lives next door to the S. J. Gardners, recently dropped dead on the street. The shock to the relatives was very great, and Mrs. S. J. Gardner especially grieved a great deal. She said Rachel won everyone's heart by her helpfulness and sympathy, and they all feel that she is more one of them than ever since that experience.

She is quite capable of going ahead with the work and the cooking when the foster-mother is busy or away from home.

The foster-mother has been worried somewhat because Rachel seems to object to certain foods and occasionally leaves a meal without eating enough for a girl her age. She is of the opinion that Rachel is afraid she will gain weight and has the idea of dieting from some of the other girls. Finally she had a long talk with her and told her, if she wanted to be well, she must eat what was put before her and not be so "choosy." She has had little trouble since that time. Foster-mother is willing to recognize her likes and dislikes, especially her dislike of the things which she had so frequently in the institution, but does not want her to neglect really necessary foods as vegetables and some meat. Rachel, however, has always been willing to drink milk and from her appearance would not seem to be in any danger of being undernourished.

SUMMARY OF CASE OF RACHEL ROBINSON, JANUARY
1932—OCTOBER, 1935

Rachel continued to live in the Gardner home until February, 1932. There was some difficulty between Rachel and the Grandmother Gardner, who had moved into the home. The grandmother was very attached to James and Rachel resented this somewhat. She was in two different homes, but was not happy, and finally in May, 1935, she moved back with the Gardners. The grandmother had died soon after Rachel left.

In May, 1935, Rachel graduated from high school. She expected to enter nurses' training in the fall; however, as she did not get the necessary papers, this had to be postponed until the first of the year.

On October 1, 1935, Rachel wrote a letter to the Agency as follows:

I appreciate everything you have done for me. I think the society is a wonderful place for homeless children. I am eighteen, however, and I would like to break all relationship between me and the society. My birthday was September 28. Please give me my walking papers.

HENRY ROBINSON

[The early part of the record concerning Henry while he was still in the School for the Feeble-minded is in the correspondence in the family record.]

July 18, 1930.—Letter to the Children's Agency from the School for Feeble-minded:

Replying to your letter of the 15th inst. concerning Henry Robinson we wish to advise that he was committed to this institution as a feeble-minded patient by the County Court of Fairfield County. He was admitted here on March 12, 1930.

A mental examination was made on March 18, 1930, when his chronological age was 10-6, which showed him to have a mental age of 8-4, I.Q. 79, classifying him in the borderline group. He has attended school regularly and has made good progress.

At the time of admission his physical condition was rather poor. He was undernourished and had râles in the apex of his left lung. There were no abnormal neurological findings. Since being here he has gained in weight and improved physically.

We have no definite plans for the future of this boy. He will be given every opportunity for development that the institution can offer. In regard to his placement on the outside, we think he would be able to get along if placed in a home where proper supervision and care could be given him. He is a well-behaved boy.

April 14, 1931.—Report of the visitor of the Children's Agency:

While in the State School recently on my usual visit, I made further inquiries regarding Henry Robinson of Dr. Munger, who immediately sent for his record and went over it quite thoroughly. He said that since the boy had been in there a year, it seemed to be a good time to discuss his adjustment and possible placement outside. He promised that the boy would be made the subject of a staff meeting before very long. His I.Q. is 79. He weighs 59 lbs. When admitted he weighed about 50 lbs. and gained the first 9 lbs. in about a month but hasn't gained since. His teacher describes him as rather listless. He is still doing first-grade work. Dr. Munger remarked that perhaps there was nothing in the School that really interested him. If you do take the matter up with the judge of Fairfield County it might be just as well to wait until they have some recommendations. I will try to keep Miss Rudovicz and Dr. Munger reminded of the child and perhaps you can get some recommendations to present to the judge.

April 16, 1931.—Letter to the Children's Agency from the State School:

I am writing to inform you that we have made a physical examination, laboratory tests and a new psychometric examination on Henry Robinson. The following are the findings:

April 10, 1931: Temperature, 98 6/10; pulse, 86; respiration, 20. Physical condition fairly good; nutrition, fair; weight, 59 pounds; skin dry and normal. Sight normal in both eyes; hearing normal. Teeth fairly clean; dental arch of upper jaw projects about one-half inch beyond the lower jaw. Mouth normal; throat normal; tonsils normal. Thyroid not palpable. Lungs and heart normal. Abdomen normal in shape. Speech normal, except slow. Walks normally. Thought processes are very slow; and, while he is orientated as to time and place, he requires considerable time to determine and formulate his answers. Is rather nervous in temperament. He behaves fairly well and goes to school each day. (Detailed laboratory findings.)

You will notice that his red blood corpuscles and haemoglobin are quite low and show evidence of some anemia. This might be corrected by good food, proper diet and fresh air in a country home.

Mrs. Carter, the school principal, reports as follows:

He is the slowest in the group at school. Appears listless and apathetic. Educational age is 2.5 but he can only do first-grade work—does not seem to have ambition or energy to do more. Behavior O.K.

Taking everything into consideration, I feel that if the person who takes Henry is informed as to the nature of his trouble, that he might be given a trial on the outside. I would recommend, of course, a country home for him with people who would realize his handicaps and if you wish to make arrangements to place him after changing the Court order, we feel that we would be doing him a justice and giving him an opportunity that we believe he should have.

April 29, 1931.—Letter to the Children's Agency from the Fairfield County judge:

I understand you were at the office recently in regard to a boy named Henry Robinson, now confined at the State School for Feeble-minded, and that you are of the opinion that it will be better for him to be released and placed in some boarding-home.

I am willing to rely upon your judgment in this matter, and, if the Superintendent of the School will consent to an order being entered, I will sign such an order, directing that the boy be under the guardianship of the Superintendent of the Children's Agency. This will enable you to put him in a boarding-home. I would suggest that you have Dr. Munger write and advise me that he does not object to an order of this nature being entered. This will give the court jurisdiction to proceed without the formality of serving a ten-day notice upon the Superintendent of the School

May 12, 1931.—A second letter to Children's Agency from the Fairfield County judge:

I am in receipt of a letter from the Managing Officer of the State School for the Feeble-minded, in which he states that he believes the desire of the Children's Agency that Henry Robinson, now at the School, be placed in the country, so that he may receive plenty of fresh air and good food, is very commendable, and he recommends that a variation order be entered.

Accordingly, I will have such an order entered when I am at court next Thursday, and will request the clerk to send you a certified copy.

May 28, 1931.—Decree for custody of Henry sent to Superintendent of Children's Agency.

SUMMARY OF CASE OF HENRY ROBINSON, MARCH 4
1932—DECEMBER 3, 1935

Henry was placed from the Receiving Home on September 1, 1932, in the home of Mrs. Robert Corey, Parkview, Illinois, where he has been until the present time, with the exception of two days spent at the Receiving Home, April 11–13, 1933, for the purpose of receiving medical attention for his eyes.

On June 22, 1932, Henry was examined at the Children's Clinic, where it was found that he had an I.Q. of 82. It was noted at that time that he had marked astigmatism, which was partially corrected by glasses. The foster-parents have been quite interested in the boy and have made an effort to have him develop properly. He is rather slow in making new friends, fears criticism of any kind, and does not always feel free to talk. He often stays in the kitchen and wants to help the foster-mother with her work.

In the fourth grade he did very poor work and as a result of another examination of his eyes he was placed in the Sight-saving Class at school in January, 1933, where he has continued until the present. His last report, December 3, 1935, indicated that he was in the seventh grade, where his work seemed to be only fair.

For a time there were apparent such problems as stealing, lying, temper tantrums, etc. At one time he took $45 from the foster-mother and gave some of it away to older boys and spent the rest lavishly. Recently there have been no problems of any kind.

JOHN AND HAROLD ROBINSON

[The records were kept separately for the two boys by the Agency, but as the boys were placed in the same home the two records have been written up together.]

July 1, 1930.—John and Harold were committed from Fairfield County to the Children's Agency for adoption. Both boys were placed in Rosedale Tuberculosis Sanitarium, Baylor, Illinois; Fairfield County to pay $5.00 a week for each child when they were placed.

July 24, 1930.—Letter received from Rosedale Sanitarium, stating that both boys were in good physical condition. They have not caused any trouble and get along nicely with the other children. Harold is especially affectionate and likes to have attention.

September 30, 1930.—John and Harold were removed from the Sanitarium and placed with Mrs. Mabel Hutchins, 3347 California Avenue, Chicago. Mrs. Hutchins is a widow with two grown boys.

December 12, 1930.—Visited the Ross School. The principal reports that both boys are doing well in school.

The worker commended foster-mother for the control she has of the children; they love her and mind her instantly. The children are always very clean and extremely neat.

December 24, 1930.—Called at Hutchins home late tonight with toys. Children all happy and excited over prospects of Santa Claus's arrival.

February 10, 1931.—Visited. Both boys seem to be making a good adjustment. They are apparently well and happy.

March 17, 1931.—Visited. The foster-mother and her sons are fond of the boys. The children seem to feel entirely at home. They are supplied with toys and with proper recreation. John told the visitor of a picnic supper they had had recently in the park on a warm day. They are looking forward to excursions to the lake this summer.

John has good habits; he is clean about his person. He responds to reasoning and affection. He has gained several pounds since he was placed in this home (see medical record of recent examination). He attends the Ross School, grade 4B, and all reports from the teacher are good.

Harold is a well-behaved affectionate boy. He is an attractive little fellow and liked by everyone. He was found to be in good health. Harold attends the Ross School, grade 1A, and has a good school report. Both boys attend Sunday School regularly.

May 17, 1931.—Following is John's school report received from the Ross School.

Month ending April 24, 1931, 4B grade. 14 days absent. 1 day tardy. Deportment, good; Personal Appearance, good; Reading, G; Penmanship, G; English, G; Arithmetic, G; Spelling, G; Geography, G; Drawing, G; Music, G; History, G.

Following is Harold's school report received from the Ross School:

Month ending April, 1931. 2nd grade. 2 days absent; 1 time tardy. Deportment, good; Reading, A; Penmanship, A; English, A; Spelling, A.

June 1, 1931.—John continues to make a good adjustment. He has a temper which is easily aroused. However, he is learning to control it. He is also inclined to be impudent at times. The foster-mother punishes him by deprivation or by sending him to bed.

Harold is bright-looking, affectionate and happy. He shows evidence of good training.

September 10, 1931.—Visited. John is happy in this home and informed the visitor that he hopes to remain there. He has made a fair adjustment to the group but loses his temper occasionally in playing with other children. He is a contrast to his brother Harold, is quick in his movements and decision. John is gaining weight all the time, looks much better than formerly, and is proud of the fact that he is gaining. However, the foster-mother thinks he is in need of a tonsillectomy.

Harold has continued to get along well until recently when he took a dollar from the foster-mother's pocket-book. She had left the pocket-book on the table for an instant after paying a bill at the door, and had then gone to the basement. She later found that the dollar was missing and knew that Harold was about the house. She said nothing until later, when one of the other boys came in with a dollar bill which he said he found in the alley. Upon questioning Harold, the foster-mother finally got him to admit that he had taken the dollar and hidden it under a stone in the alley. She talked to the boy in an attempt to learn why he had taken the money. He could give no explanation and seemed to be sorry, so she did not punish him and it has not been repeated since. The boy is inclined to be "sneaky" about unimportant things. He is slow in everything that he does and is also sensitive. She thinks this trait is responsible for his sneakiness. There has been no difficulty in school; the boy passed his grade in the spring.

November 10, 1931.—The foster-mother reports that Harold has had no further trouble with stealing. She did not punish him, but talked to him about it. He continues to get along well in the home. She is attempting to change his attitude of destruction and believes that she has made some headway as she has gained the boy's confidence. The boy's toilet habits. are good, and there are no indications of masturbation. He has an excellent appetite and sleeps well.

The boy attends school regularly and is in grade 2A. He has no difficulty with his work. He attends Sunday School regularly and is to be in a Christmas play.

Harold has recently been examined by the school nurse, examination negative.

John continues to gain in weight, he is happier and responds better to affection and reasoning. He is learning to control his temper. John has learned to play like a normal boy of his age; he likes football particularly and is interested in aviation.

December 1, 1931.—School reports. Both boys had all excellent and good grades.

December 3, 1931.—Recently while in the Children's Agency office waiting for an escort, John was given a picture of his brothers and sisters, and his sisters' addresses. He was delighted and has written a letter.

The boys are very happy in the home. Harold often asks the foster-mother to adopt them.

February 25, 1932.—John came in from school and shook hands with the visitor. He is more easy in manner and converses well. He is more serious than Harold and is continually thinking of the future. He recently told the foster-mother that he would be glad when he could earn a living so that he could buy her things. He mentioned a new dress and also expressed a wish to have her dental work done. He often asks her to adopt him. John passed his grade in school; he is now in 5B. He belongs to the school chorus and sang a song for the visitor.

Harold is an attractive boy with brown hair and brown eyes. He is pleasant and very well liked by everybody. He skipped a grade in school and is very proud of it. He read for the visitor. He has recently learned the Twenty-third Psalm and has been given a Bible at Sunday School because of this.

SUMMARY OF RECORDS, FEBRUARY 25, 1932—JULY 7, 1935

Both boys have continued to live with Mrs. Hutchins. They seem to have found much security. John is described as a lovable, friendly, and easygoing boy, who is sensitive. He is doing good work in school. Harold is thought to be equally ambitious. He is dependable and affectionate and is especially devoted to the foster-mother. He often stays in to help her with the household tasks. John graduated from the eighth grade January 31, 1935.

JEAN AND CLARENCE ROBINSON

[The two separate records have been written up together here to save some repetition.]

March 12, 1930.—Jean and Clarence were committed to the Children's Agency and placed in the Receiving Home.

March 24, 1930.—Letters sent to State Department, inclosing history sheets.

July 17, 1930.—Letter sent to Child Guidance Clinic, inclosing psychiatric histories and requesting early appointments.

August 26, 1930.—Visitor attended a Staff Conference on Jean Robinson. Dr. Monroe, psychiatrist, stated that she tested in the average grouping in intelligence, and he thought that if placed in a stable environment away from her sisters, she might adjust well. She has become very dependent on her sisters at all times. She needs to learn to mingle with other children and to take her own part. If possible, it was advised that she be kept a while longer in the Receiving Home, where she would be with a large group of children.

August 29, 1930.—The following letter was received from the Child Guidance Clinic, giving a report of their examination of Jean.

Jean Robinson was referred to this clinic for occasional enuresis, extreme shyness, dependence upon her older sisters, and for study prior to making vocational placement plans for her. She was examined August 26, 1930.

Physical examination showed evidence of old otitis media but no perforation of left eardrum. There was a deep wheezing sound during the latter half of expiration over practically the entire chest. This may have been due to a slight cold. The upper side of the right chest lags and expands less than the left. One right post cervical lymph node was palpable and the knee jerks were slightly increased.

The psychological examination gave her a chronological age of five years, six months, a mental age of five years, eight months, and an Intelligence Quotient of 103 which places her in the average classification.

In the psychiatric examination it was noted that this child was abnormally shy. She also showed a slight but rather definite sullenness. It is believed that she has no particular attachment for either the mother or the father and no real desire to return to the home. She did, however, express her desire to return to her real home but expressed it in such a way that the examiner believes that this is merely imitation of the older sisters' desire or else the older sisters have coached her in this regard. She shows a peculiar degree of immaturity and dependency so often seen in children who have received too much supervision at the hands of older children. From time to time during the course of the day, the examiner noticed that the two older children were constantly supervising the activities of Jean and Clarence.

The following recommendations are made: (1) Re-examination of chest in three months. (2) Ordinary treatment of her cold. (3) Jean and Clarence should be placed together but separated from the older siblings, and their home should be carefully selected with a view towards its permanency. These children may readily develop marked feelings of insecurity due to their previous background, and, for this reason, each change of foster home may well prove quite detrimental to them. (4) In regard to enuresis, ordinary habit training, such as no water after supper, making her go to the toilet just before bed-time and requiring her to wash the sheets which she wets, will probably soon result in the cessation of her enuresis.

Also attended Staff Conference on Clarence. Dr. Monroe, psychiatrist, stated that owing to the lack of co-operation no adequate diagnosis could be made of Clarence. Psychological examination gave him an I.Q. of 51, but this cannot be thought to be reliable as the child was so seclusive that he refused to respond to most of the tests. It was felt that he will probably rate in the lower average grouping if tested later when his co-operation is secured. For this reason no definite plans can be made for him until further tests can be made. He should by all means be separated from his sisters and be placed in a group where he will have opportunity to mingle with other children and to develop self-reliance.

August 29, 1930.—A letter came from the Child Guidance Clinic, giving a report of their examination. They asked that Clarence be returned to the Clinic several months later for a check-up and that he and Jean be placed together if possible.

September 18, 1930.—Jean and Clarence were removed from the Receiving Home and placed with Mr. and Mrs. Neal Norton, R.F.D., Rockville, Illinois. Free home, foster-parents to furnish the clothing.

November 3, 1930.—Attempted to visit but found family had gone to Berlin, Wisconsin, to visit Mrs. Norton's mother for a week. The visitor talked with Mrs. Norton's brother-in-law, who stated that the family are fond of the two children and hope they can continue to have them in their home. At first Clarence was shy; he is not willing to play with the other children without being urged to do so. He is affectionate and occasionally, with great emotion, tells his foster-parents how much he loves them.

Jean's cold has finally disappeared. She has a good appetite and seems to be gaining.

November 10, 1930.—Letter to Mrs. Norton regarding a physical examination for Jean.

November 26, 1930.—A letter from Mrs. Norton said that the doctor had found no evidence of tuberculosis when he examined Jean.

December 18, 1930.—Visitor called at the foster-home. The family seem devoted to the children and would like to adopt them immediately. The visitor suggested that it might be wiser to wait for a time.

It took Jean several weeks to overcome her shyness in the home, but at present she is perfectly at ease. She seldom speaks of her older sisters. She seems to be gradually forgetting them. The foster-mother considers her well trained; she is capable of dressing herself without any assistance. The foster-mother is a very calm person and has a great deal of patience. For the first month Jean was in the home she continued to cough but for the last two months she has been much better. The foster-mother keeps her out of doors as much as possible. The visitor found her out sliding. She has splendid color, and her eyes are bright and sparkling, much more so than when placed; she also seems more active and peppy. Jean takes an afternoon nap of about three hours and goes to bed about eight o'clock. The foster-mother has not started her in Sunday School and will not do so until spring.

Clarence has splendid color and a very good appetite. Both he and Jean look as if they have gained since being placed. Clarence still is very shy. He must see a stranger three or four times before he is friendly with him. If the foster-mother leaves the home, he is quite upset. At first he was dependent upon someone to dress him; he would make no effort to assist himself at all. Gradually the mother has made him dress himself, and now he can do it with very little assistance. He can put on his overshoes. At first he continually asked for his sister Mary, but for weeks now has not mentioned her. He seems to have forgotten entirely that he has not always lived in this home. Once or twice he asked Mrs. Norton how he got into their home.

February 17, 1931.—Letter from Mrs. Norton asking for Clarence's birth date as they would like to celebrate it.

February 21, 1931.—Letter advising Mrs. Norton that Clarence was born September 29, 1926.

May 1, 1931.—The foster-mother has not been feeling well the last few months, and the family physician has advised the extraction of her teeth. Her mother and an unmarried sister are assisting with the housework.

They are all fond of the children. They consider Jean a very bright child. She is happy and always looking out for Clarence. Her cough has disappeared entirely.

Clarence is subborn sometimes, but these occasions seem to be disappearing. He is extremely shy.

Both children have gained in weight and have good color. They are attending the Methodist church at Rockville.

August 25, 1931.—Visitor called at the Norton home and found Mrs. Norton much improved in health. They are remodeling their home and are now making it modern.

Jean was wiping the dishes. Mrs. Norton says that Jean is always anxious to help her; she permits her to wipe the dishes and feed the chickens. Jean is gaining continuously, her face is round, and her body is well filled out. She has no sign of a cough and has splendid color. The foster-mother believes that she is a model child. She will enter the first grade next week.

Clarence is gradually overcoming his timidness and is more talkative. He is yet rather slow in movement and in play always follows Jean. Occasionally he loses his temper, but he does not hold a grudge.

Mrs. Norton has heard from Mary. She has begged to come to the home for a visit, warning Mrs. Norton not to tell the Children's Society about her letters. Mrs. Norton did not wish to answer this letter before discussing the matter with the worker.

February 12, 1932.—Jean is growing taller and is losing two of her first teeth. The foster-mother makes no complaint about the child's behavior. She believes her to be a good average child. She makes her bed and wipes the dishes.

Following are her grades for four months:

Deportment....	G	G	G	G	Arithmetic........	G		
Industry.......	VG*	VG	VG	VG	Language........	G	G	G	G
Reading........	G	G	VG	VG	Drawing........	G	G	G	G
Writing........			G	G	Phonics.........	G			G

* VG—very good.

Miss Sabin spoke highly of Jean. She is a very ambitious student, a most lovable child, and very easy to handle in the schoolroom.

The foster-mother states that Clarence's stubbornness is no problem at the present time. The visitor was able to carry on some conversation with him. He is a very polite, well-trained child.

[Report of this type made on all children leaving the Receiving Home.]

REPORT OF CHILD LEAVING RECEIVING HOME

Name: Clarence Robinson   Entered March 21, 1930

I. Behavior
  A. Stealing..............Never takes a toy that doesn't belong to him—wants his own unmolested.
  B. Lying. ....No.
  C. Truancy

II. Personality Traits
  A. Cheerful—Sulky........When with people he likes he carries a sunny face. He can be cross and pouty if a stranger talks with him.
  B. Shy—Aggressive.......Extremely shy when strangers are near.
  C. Affectionate..........Very affectionate.
  D. Impertinent..........No, but he can hold his own with the children.
  E. Good sense of humor....Moderate.
  F. Worrisome...........No.
  G. Temper tantrums......Yes, but not often now. When he first came to us he would lie on the floor and kick when it was nap time.
  H. Destructive..........He is getting to be quite well behaved and we can reason with him. He is not destructive with toys or his clothing.
  I. Imaginative..........No.
  J. Tendency to cry.......No.
  K. Energy well directed....Yes.

III. Interest
  A. Flitting—Persistent.....Persistent.
  B. Responds quickly—
      Slowly..............Quickly.
  C. Lack of interest.......Takes a keen interest in everything going on as long as no stranger appears.
  D. Daydreaming..........No.

IV. School
  A. Scholarship
  B. Special ability
  C. Conscientious
  D. Backward

V. Relationship with Other Children
  A. Plays in a group—
      By self.............He can amuse himself, and also plays nicely with the children.

B. Leader—Follower......Follower.
C. Bully
D. Tease
E. Cruel—Kind..........Kindhearted.
F. Quarrelsome...........No.
G. Selfish—
    Shares with others....Inclined to be selfish.
H. Associates.............Children all like him.

VI. Habits
A. Pride in personal ap-
    pearance...........Loves nice clothes, and keeps himself neat and orderly.
B. Ability to assume re-
    sponsibility.........His task is to put the high chairs around the table each meal, and he does it like a big boy. Occasionally he decides not to, but no one insists upon his doing it as it happens so seldom.
C. Care of personal pos-
    sessions.............He takes splendid care of his little treasures.
D. Attitude toward work
E. Food.................Has a good appetite and table manners are quite satisfactory.
F. Sleep................Sound sleeper
G. Enuresis.............Once in a great while he has an accident at night, but never soils his clothes.
H. Sex..................No. We thought he handled himself when first with us but since he is kept clean there's no evidence of masturbation.

VII. Control and Supervision.
Type Productive of Best
    Results...............The only trouble he has caused is his stubborn desire for one particular person to look after his wants. He responds to kindness.

VIII. Health..................Very good. He is to have a tonsillectomy.

IX. Remarks...............Learns his verses and prayers slowly. Days later we will hear him saying them to himself. When he first came in it took nearly the entire household to take a throat culture, and now he will let Mrs. Peters do anything. He took his tests and was vaccinated like a soldier. He is slower than most children of his age, but we feel this is due to his extreme bashfulness and sensitiveness. He has made such rapid strides that we feel he has mentality, but due to his early care it will take a long time before he will be up to par. His sisters made a baby of him, would not allow him to do a thing for himself. We wonder if he won't be much better off placed in a home away from them. One must live with Clarence to know his true worth.

SUMMARY OF CASES OF CLARENCE AND JEAN ROBINSON
FEBRUARY 12, 1932—JULY 18, 1935

Both children have remained in the Norton home on a free basis. The foster-parents are very fond of them and are planning to provide high-school and also college education for them if they want it.

Jean during this period is described as a quiet, obedient, easygoing child, unselfish, and willing to do anything for Clarence. According to the last school report available she had been promoted to the fifth grade, with no grade below 85.

Clarence is described as a self-willed, stubborn, and dictatorial boy. Though the foster-parents have found him more difficult to handle than Jean, they are very fond of him. According to the last school report he had been promoted to the third grade.

Both children seem to be popular with the neighborhood children and participate in the parties and recreation trips of the neighborhood.

Through the summer of 1933 the foster-mother occasionally heard from Mary and took the children to see her at one time.

JAMES ROBINSON

March 12, 1930.—James was committed to the Children's Agency on a temporary custody order, Fairfield County to pay board at the rate of $5.00 per week.

July 3, 1930.—James was removed from the boarding-home of Mrs. Mathias Grab, a temporary home, Vinton, Illinois, and placed with Mr. and Mrs. S. J. Gardner, Stanhope, Illinois. Free home.

July 9, 1930.—Letter received by the Children's Agency from the foster-mother:

Just a few lines to let you know we are getting along fine, with the "Little Bundle of Sunshine" you brought us last Thursday. Words cannot express our happiness; we both think he is just adorable (and of course he is), and his

Daddy says you wouldn't find another like him in a million. He is such a happy little fellow, one couldn't help but just love him.

I was so excited last Thursday evening, I didn't have sense enough to ask you to go home with us for dinner, and Stephen would have taken you to Clearfield; but I hope you will forgive me for my thoughtlessness, as I could think of nothing but the dear little boy you had just brought us.

If I wrote volumes it would all be how happy we are, with our wonderful boy, and since you know that, I may as well close with the hopes you will visit us often.

September 12, 1930.—After two attempts Mr. and Mrs. Gardner were found at home in the evening.

Mrs. Gardner has been helping her husband two or three days a week in the office since his office girl left a few weeks ago. Occasionally she takes James with her, building him a little fence in the corner of the office and heating his milk on an oil stove.

James drinks two quarts of goat's milk a day, and Mrs. Gardner wonders if he is gaining too rapidly. He eats vegetables and soups and oatmeal and he loves tomatoes.

He has beautiful dark eyes and curly hair, and the Gardner relatives whom they visited in Missouri, who do not know he is a foster-child, think he looks like Mr. Gardner. Mr. Gardner's mother though at first very doubtful as to their adopting a child, is now very fond of him, and takes care of him part of the time when Mrs. Gardner is working.

October 8, 1930.—The worker found James at home with the grandmother, who is a strong, nice-looking woman, and a personal friend of the Kents, with whom visitor stays. They say she is a very able and worthy woman. She took pride in exhibiting James's accomplishments. He tries to talk but when bashful whispers instead of speaking aloud. He goes around with a fly swatter and has great fun with his doll. He has walked about three months. The goat from which they get the milk for James took the blue ribbon at the Clark County Fair. He has two bottles before he goes to bed.

James had a rather serious cold which the doctor said might easily have developed into pneumonia. He still coughs a little.

He weighs twenty-eight pounds. He is quite bowlegged as a result of his weight and walking so early. He never did creep but began to walk at about eleven months. Mrs. Gardner does not think he is nearly so bowlegged, however, as he was a few months ago. He has been suffering from a severe cold and seems to catch cold very easily. Last week one night, Mrs. Gardner was up with him all night.

He makes almost no attempt to talk as yet, only saying a few words, such as "mamma," etc. He feeds himself with a spoon and drinks most of his milk out of a cup although he still uses the bottle when he goes to bed and takes tomato juice in a bottle. He has only eight teeth. He seems to understand almost anything he is told to do, knows how to turn on the radio and will do so when he is told, will get any toy that is mentioned, and point at objects that are named.

February 10, 1931.—Verified birth of James Robinson; James was born August 1, 1929, at St. Xavier's Hospital, Dalton, Illinois.

James is cuter than ever; his hair is getting curly and a boy's haircut makes him look quite a little older. His legs are much straighter, but he still wobbles when he walks. He wears four-year-old-size suits.

June 5, 1931.—James's sister, Rachel Robinson, was placed in the Gardner home on this date. The baby immediately took a liking to her and learned to say "sis" before she had been in the house twenty-four hours. He is somewhat jealous of her, however. He will come and climb into the foster-mother's lap whenever she shows any affection for the sister.

October 13, 1931.—In August the Gardners moved back to Manning, Illinois, largely because they thought that the Manning High School would be much better for Rachel than the Stanhope High School.

James, or Richard, as they call him now, weighs thirty-one pounds. He did weigh considerably more but lost it during the summer, when he had a serious attack of diarrhea which amounted almost to cholera infantum.

He is beginning to put sentences together now and talks quite plainly. He calls himself "Wee-wee." Now that Rachel is in school and the book-keeper has left the poultry house, Mrs. Gardner sometimes takes him to Stanhope with her for the day. He likes to play around the office, but is very mischievous and gets into things. Whenever he is scolded he will try to change the subject or remark that he is "helping daddy," making it difficult for them to punish him.

November 11, 1931.—This is certainly a beautiful baby with big brown eyes and rather light curly hair. The grandparents and the father, however, have recently insisted on a boy's haircut, and he does not look nearly so babyish as he did on the last visit. He has outgrown most of the clothes his foster-mother made for him during the summer; he seems to be stretching out now and not gaining much in weight. His legs are very much straighter; in fact they are hardly bowed at all.

He eats practically everything at the table, but it is a little hard to get him to take as much of the vegetables as they think he needs. He still drinks a great deal of milk. His teeth are straight and white and fully up to normal for his age.

The Gardner family certainly worship this baby and would be terribly broken up if he would have to be taken away from them. (Carbon copy to State Department.)

SUMMARY OF CASE OF JAMES ROBINSON, TO MAY 6, 1935

James has continued to live in the Gardner home, where he is much loved. He is an interesting, imaginative boy who gets a great deal of pleasure out of living. In the fall of 1934, he was started to school. He was getting along well at the time of last entry.

7. Barbara Ann Sobral

*(A Very Interesting Story of a Little Girl Who Had Been Given
Away by Her Mother but Was Finally Returned to Her)*

December 18, 1930.—Miss Saunders, of the Family Agency, telephoned the Children's Agency (Midland, Illinois), stating that she had received a letter from the Department of Public Welfare, Indianapolis, Indiana, asking that a visit be made to the home of Mrs. Manuel (Becky) Gay, relative to Barbara Sobral. Miss Saunders has forwarded the letter to the Children's Agency.

Letter addressed to the Family Agency of Midland, Illinois, from the Department of Public Welfare, Indianapolis, Indiana, *re*: Sobral, Joseph and Ann, and children, Barbara (six) and Juanita (three):

Mr. and Mrs. Joseph Sobral and their daughter are receiving temporary assistance from our Department because of Mr. Sobral's unemployment. Today Mr. and Mrs. Sobral called in our office and asked us to write to your organization regarding their daughter Barbara, age six years, who is at present with a Mrs. Becky (Manuel) Gay at 510 Lockwood Ave., Midland.

Mrs. Gay is the godmother of Barbara, and two years ago when the Sobrals went to Hartville, Illinois, to visit Mrs. Sobral's mother, Mrs. Ann Baumann, they stopped in Midland to visit Mrs. Gay. Mrs. Gay was very much taken with Barbara and offered to keep her temporarily. She has been with Mrs. Gay since that time. The Gays have grown extremely fond of the child and offered to adopt her. However, Mr. and Mrs. Sobral do not wish to have their child adopted, and are very desirous of having her home with them.

The Sobrals showed us a letter which they had received from Mrs. Gay in which she requests from $300 to $1,000 board bill before she will allow Barbara to return to her parents. It is of course impossible for the Sobrals to pay any money for Barbara's board since Mr. Sobral worked only three months last year and has been receiving relief for a long time in Indianapolis.

It would appear that Mrs. Gay is using the request for money in order to force the Sobrals to relinquish Barbara.

We should like to have you call on Mrs. Gay and try to convince her that she should return the child to her parents. If she is willing to do so, would you kindly inform us what plans you are able to make with Mrs. Gay.

Thank you for your co-operation.

Later.—The following letter was written by the Children's Agency to the Department of Public Welfare, Indianapolis, Indiana:

Your letter of December 10 written to Miss Saunders of the Family Agency has been referred to us.

I shall be very glad to have this investigation made as soon as possible and shall write you again concerning it.

December 29, 1930.—Visited Mrs. Gay at 510 Lockwood Avenue. Found that she had moved two weeks previous and had left no address.

Later.—Letter written by Children's Agency to the Department of Public Welfare, Indianapolis, Indiana:

I visited the address which you gave me for the Gays at 510 Lockwood Avenue but was told that they had moved about two weeks ago. No one was able to tell me where they had gone.

I called the City Water Department where Mr. Gay is listed as being employed and was told that they had no record of him during the past month. Mr. Gay is a laborer, and the City Water Department keeps no addresses on laborers. I am trying to get in touch with his foreman, however, to see if any information can be secured from him.

In the meantime, I thought perhaps you might be able to secure the Gays' new address for me. Possibly Mrs. Sobral has heard from Mrs. Gay. I shall try as hard as possible to locate them.

January 5, 1931.—Letter received by the Children's Agency from the Department of Public Welfare, Indianapolis, Indiana:

We wish to acknowledge your letter of December 29, and appreciate the efforts you have made in locating the Gay family. We advised the Sobrals of the fact that the Gays had moved.

Mrs. Sobral told us that the Gays were great friends of the Police Commissioner of Midland and she felt sure that the Commissioner could give some information regarding the whereabouts of Barbara. She also said that the Gays sometimes call Barbara, Ann. It might be possible that through the Board of Education you could trace Barbara. She might be known to them under the name of Ann Gay.

Thank you for your co-operation.

January 14, 1931.—Telephoned Miss Tanner, Board of Education. Found that Barbara was registered under the name of Ann and was attending the Winslow School. She had registered at the Central School in September, 1930, and her home address was then 515 West Madison Avenue. On November 19 she was transferred to the Winslow School, her address being 1410 West Maryland Avenue.

Later.—Telephoned Mr. Allen, principal of the Winslow School. He said that the school had no home address, as Ann apparently was unable to give it. She gave in a vague way the directions for reaching the home but said she did not know the house number. Mr. Allen said she did not appear to be in good health. Her teacher had suggested that she had heard rumors that her mother had a bad reputation and was running an unfavorable boarding-house.

January 15, 1931.—Visited Winslow School. Miss Morley, Ann's teacher, gave the child's birth date but she did not know her address. She said Ann is well behaved. She comes to school well dressed, but her complexion is sallow and the teacher suspects that her home is not what it should be. Miss Morley suggested that Miss Kelly, Ann's former teacher at the Central School, knew something of the family history.

Later.—Talked with Ann. She is a slight, apparently hyperactive child. She had on a pretty, bright-red flannel dress, attractively embroidered. She said she had come late to school that morning because her mother and daddy had overslept. She explained also that she had overslept because she did not get to bed when other children did as she wanted to stay up and watch the "horses go around." It was found that she meant the toy horses which are part of a slot machine equipment which the mother had in her house. Ann talked quickly and rather spontaneously. She was quite emphatic that Mrs. Gay is her real mother and that she had been kept by Mrs. Sobral for a short time while her own mother was not able to keep her. She dislikes Mrs. Sobral and says that she whipped her all the time. She told of once having been asked to wash Juanita's face. Juanita would not stay still, so she tied her. Mrs. Sobral whipped her, and Ann proceeded to tie her again and received another whipping. Another time Juanita was wearing a silk dress while Ann had to wear a pair of overalls. That made Ann angry and she took the silk dress off the other child, put it on herself, and dressed the other child in her overalls. Incident upon incident Ann related showing that her experience with Mrs. Sobral remained vividly in her mind and that these experiences were extremely unpleasant. She said she had been living with a Mrs. Gillis at 515 West Madison Avenue, whom she likes. Mrs. Gillis had kept her because her own mother had so many boarders. She said she loved her mother dearly and she liked her daddy, Mr. Gay, too. Sometimes they got after her when she peeped through keyholes. Also one time her daddy got after her because she came in through the front door. Apparently she is supposed to enter the house only through the rear entrance.

Later.—Visited Mrs. Howard Gillis, 515 West Madison Avenue, former boarding-mother. Mrs. Gillis is an elderly French woman. She was born and reared in Paris. While there she managed a dress shop but, when she came to America and was not able to speak good English, she was compelled to make a living in some other way. She began raising dogs and selling them. At the present time she has twenty-six Boston terriers. She has one which knows forty different tricks and she has him perform on the stage frequently. Mr. Gillis works at the Burkhart Clock Works. They have one son, who is married and living in Colorado. During the summer of 1929 Mrs. Gillis sold a dog to Mrs. Gay, alias Becky West. Later Mrs. Gay asked her to care for a little girl known as Ann Sobral. Mrs. Gillis missed her grandchild so much that she decided to take the child for the sake of companionship. Mrs. Gay paid her $5.00 a week and furnished the child's clothing. She said Mrs. Gay always paid the board and dressed the child beautifully.

Mrs. Gillis became so fond of the child that she wanted to adopt her. At first Mrs. Gay said Ann's mother was dead and then she said she was still living but she, Mrs. Gay, did not know her whereabouts. She said Mr. Sobral had legally adopted her but when Mrs. Gay's attorney, Allan Kerr, requested that Mr. Sobral show the adoption papers he was unable to do so. For a while Mrs. Gay said she would agree to allow Mrs. Gillis to adopt Ann but later she refused. Mrs. Gillis thinks Ann's real mother is Mrs. Gay, as the child resembles her strikingly, both in physical features and in action. Mrs. Gillis said Mrs. Gay had been a "sporting woman" for many years and it would not be "convenient" for her to admit that Ann is her own child. The maternity of the child probably will always be a question, although Mrs. Gillis suggested that Mr. Sobral at one time lived as Mrs. Gay's "man." She said the Sobrals have adopted another child, and she thinks they adopted these girls for white-slavery purposes as they run houses of prostitution also.

Mrs. Gillis had objected to keeping Ann as Mrs. Gay insisted upon taking her with her over the week ends. Mrs. Gillis was trying to teach Ann proper manners and she responded well, but it was all spoiled after the child had been with Mrs. Gay for a few days. Neither did she think that it was a fit place for a girl to visit. Ann had made several remarks indicating that she knew something about Mrs. Gay's means of livelihood. For example, one day when Mrs. Gillis was speaking of having but one pair of badly worn shoes, Ann had said, "Grandma, when I get big I'll buy lots of nice clothes for you." She went on to describe silk underwear, hosiery, dresses, etc. Also she said she would dress beautifully herself and have a big car and travel around the world. When Mrs. Gillis asked her how she could do all that on an ordinary girl's wages, Ann replied that she would do like her mother did, namely, "put a man to bed." She explained that she had peeked through the keyhole and had seen the happenings in her mother's place. Another time she said that her mother worked hard because she did not go to bed when other people did but instead she stood in the window. When Mrs. Gillis suggested that perhaps her mother was sick and that was why she stood in the window, Ann was quite emphatic that that was not the reason. And again, when Ann heard Mrs. Gillis explaining to a friend that the reason Ann's mother could not keep the child was because she had so many boarders, Ann interrupted and said that was not the truth—her mother had a lot of men around the house but they were not boarders as she had but three small rooms.

Mrs. Gillis said that the Manuel Gay, with whom "Becky" lives for the present, is a Mexican. He does not work but is supported by her. She even gives him a big car to drive. Ann is fond of him and he of her. He usually called for her in that car. Ann loves Mrs. Gay dearly, and Mrs. Gay is exceedingly fond of Ann.

Mrs. Gay had wanted Mrs. Gillis to lie about Ann's age as she did not want the child to have to begin school, since she thought then there would be too many questions asked. Mrs. Gillis thought there was a possibility that Ann might be a year older than Mrs. Gay said. Ann is said to have been baptized at St. Mary's Cathedral. Mrs. Gay does not belong to any church, but the Sobrals are Catholic; hence, she had Ann baptized in the Catholic faith. Mrs. Gillis also is a Catholic and has suggested to Mrs. Gay that she place Ann with the Catholic Sisters as then she would be certain to receive good care, but Mrs. Gay refused. Mrs. Gay is determined Ann shall never be taken from her.

Both Ann and Mrs. Gay had told Mrs. Gillis how cruel Mrs. Sobral had been to Ann. Ann had fairly shuddered when the Sobral name was mentioned although she liked Mr. Sobral fairly well.

Later.—Visited Detective Bureau. Found that Mrs. Gay is known to the Detective Bureau as Becky West. Her present address is 516 Lockwood Avenue. She is registered with the Bureau as running a house of prostitution.

Later.—Visited Mrs. Gay, 516 Lockwood Avenue. She told a long story of Ann's past history. Mrs. Gay is apparently a young woman. She has reddish-brown, bobbed hair, she is small and quite thin. She quite openly spoke of her "house" and her "girls." She said that under no circumstances would she think of allowing Ann to live with her as after all she still has a little respect. She was certain that Ann knew nothing of what went on in the house as she kept her in a rear downstairs room.

Later.—Visited Mrs. Jennie Found, 1410 West Maryland Avenue. Mrs. Found was a middle-aged woman. Her home was comfortably and gaudily furnished. She had kept Ann for a period of six weeks beginning November 19, 1930. Mrs. Found's sister is a clerk at the Reddings Store, where Mrs. Gay bought most of Ann's clothing, and it was through her that arrangements were made for Ann to be boarded with Mrs. Found. Mrs. Gay paid her $5.00 a week and furnished all the child's clothing. Mrs. Found refused to keep Ann longer because Mrs. Gay was slow in her board payments and would not keep Ann's clothing dry cleaned as she had promised to do. She was anxious to know if Ann was to be taken from her mother, as she would like to take the child into her home rather than have her placed in an institution. She thought Ann a well-behaved, sweet child. Mrs. Found is a Catholic. At first she pretended that she knew nothing of Mrs. Gay's social standing, but later it developed that she knew much more than she chose to reveal. No attempt was made to discuss Mrs. Gay with her, however.

Later.—Letter written by the Children's Agency to the Department of Public Welfare, Indianapolis, Indiana:

Mrs. Gay was finally located at 516 Lockwood Avenue under the alias of Becky West. She is conducting a house of ill-fame. Mr. Manuel Gay is living with her as her husband. She has been boarding Ann with private families who are known to be respectable in every way. For the past week, however, she has had Ann living with her while she is looking for another boarding-home.

Mrs. Gay tells us that Ann's real mother was a Bohemian girl who was employed in a house of ill-fame conducted by Mr. and Mrs. Sobral in South Bend, Illinois. This girl is said to have either died or disappeared, leaving Ann with the Sobrals. The Sobrals were ordered out of South Bend after Mr. Sobral had killed either the mayor or chief of police or some other important city official during a disturbance in the Sobral's house of prostitution. Mr. Sobral was ordered by the Court to return to his native country, Mexico, as he was not an American citizen but instead he went to Indianapolis. On their way to Indianapolis they visited with the Gays in Midland and left Ann with them, saying that they would come and get her in a week's time. Nothing was heard from the Sobrals for about eighteen months. Six months ago Mrs. Sobral came to Midland demanding that Ann be given over to her. Mrs. Gay had become fond of the child and, inasmuch as she had done so much more for her than the Sobrals had and the child herself disliked Mrs. Sobral, saying that she was cruel to her, Mrs. Gay refused to let them take her. She turned the matter over to her attorney, Mr. Allan Kerr. The Sobrals have said that they legally adopted Ann, but when Mrs. Gay's attorney asked that they submit their adoption papers as proof, they failed to do so. Mrs. Gay said that Ann was in a deplorable condition physically when the Sobrals left her in Midland. She had sores all over her body and was badly undernourished. She has seen that the child has had continuous medical attention, and the child now appears to be in good physical health. Mrs. Gay says she loves Ann as much as if she were her own child and she would die were Ann taken from her. She would under no circumstance consider allowing Ann to be taken to the Sobrals as she knows they are people of bad character and were extremely cruel to her. She says that they are at present engaged in bootlegging, going to Mexico for their liquors. She also says that the other child whom they now have is an adopted child. It was suggested that the Sobrals adopted these two girls with a view to white slavery when they became grown.

Interviews were had with the two boarding-mothers who have cared for Ann during the past two years. Both say that they have received a regular payment of $5.00 a week from Mrs. Gay for the child's care and that Mrs. Gay has also furnished Ann's clothing.

They say that Ann has always been very well dressed. The only source of difficulty in these placements apparently has been that Mrs. Gay has insisted upon keeping Ann with her over the week ends with the consequence that she was difficult to manage when she returned to the foster home.

Ann was seen alone at school. She is quite insistent that Mrs. Gay is her real mother and that Mrs. Sobral was but a woman who cared for her for a time when her own mother was financially not able to do so. She voluntarily related incidents portraying Mrs. Sobral's cruelty to her. She said she was beaten and that never would she consider going to the Sobrals who preferred Juanita to her. She liked Mr. Sobral but not his wife. She said she loves her mother, "Becky," dearly and never wanted to leave her and that her daddy, Mr. Gay, was good to her also. Ann attends school regularly and is considered a very bright, alert child in her school work. She was well dressed and appeared happy

It appears that there is a question of the Sobrals' legal right to this child and also of their moral fitness to care for her. It would be interesting to know their reaction to the story given by Mrs. Gay, and you probably can determine what kind of reputation they now have in Indianapolis. Even if the child is not sent to the Sobrals, it is probable that we shall take steps toward having her removed from Mrs. Gay's place of habitation.

We trust that the real truth can be deduced from the two stories given by the

Sobrals and Mrs. Gay with a view to making a permanent placement plan for Ann.

January 20, 1931.—Visited Father Macdonald, St. Mary's Cathedral. Ann's birth date had been given at the time of her baptism as March 10, 1924. She was baptized on April 9, 1929. Her place of nativity was given as Midland, Illinois, her father as Joseph Sobral, and the mother as Ann Baumann. Her sponsors were Mary Polowski and Manuel Gay. Ann's name was given as Barbara.

Later.—Visited County Court. Was unable to verify Ann's birth.

Later.—Talked with Mrs. Sylvester, probation officer. She said that Mrs. Colonel McLaren had reported the situation to her but she had done nothing about it because of lack of time. Mrs. McLaren had got all her information from Mrs. Gillis, Ann's former boarding-mother.

Letter written by Children's Agency to the County Clerk, South Bend, Illinois:

We are very anxious to verify the birth of Barbara Ann Sobral. There is considerable doubt in regard to this child's parentage and there probably will be some difficulty in locating her, but it is very important that we be able to determine her legal birth date. It is reported to us that she was born on March 10, 1924.

It is possible that she may be registered with "Sobral" as her surname or perhaps "Gay." Other possible surnames are Polowski and Baumann. The most likely, however, is Sobral. The father's first name is said to be Jose and the mother's either Ann, or Jennie, or Becky.

We shall be deeply grateful for whatever information you might furnish us regarding this child's birth date.

January 23, 1931.—Letter received from County Clerk, South Bend, Illinois:

I have carefully examined the record under the various surnames but found nothing. Evidently the birth certificate failed to reach this office.

January 28, 1931.—Letter written to the County Clerk, South Bend, Illinois:

We thank you kindly for attempting to verify Ann Sobral's birth date.

We are sorry that you were unable to locate it but we shall make further attempts to secure information about it.

February 3, 1931.—Letter received from the Department of Public Welfare, Indianapolis, Indiana:

We were greatly interested in your letter of January 15 regarding Joseph and Ann Sobral and the child Barbara. We recently interviewed Mrs. Sobral in the office of our director, Mr. Gilbert Frampton. We learned that Mr. Sobral is at present being held in our County Jail and that deportation proceedings are pending. Mrs. Sobral was told by the Immigration authorities that he would no doubt be deported to Mexico.

Mrs. Sobral first assumed a greatly surprised attitude that there should be the slightest doubt as to her or her husband's excellent character. Her attitude changed during the interview, and she finally told us the facts of the case quite frankly. She said she had lived in Hartville, Illinois, until she was fifteen years old, and that she married her husband in August of 1923 in Hartville. She said that she knew the mother of Barbara very slightly but that the latter had had many illegitimate children and before Barbara's birth asked Mrs. Sobral if she would consent to adopt the child. Mrs. Sobral said that the child was legally adopted in Harrison County, Hartville, Illinois, on July 26, 1926. She later brought in the adoption papers to prove this statement. The adoption was signed by Mr. Harvey Underwood, the County Clerk of Hartville, Illinois.

Regarding Juanita, the younger child, Mrs. Sobral first said that she had also legally adopted her. Later she said that the child was given to her by Mrs. Winn of the Children's Service of Bancroft, Illinois. She said that Mrs. Winn would be able to verify her statements regarding Juanita.

She admitted that her husband had been deported to Mexico and that the charges against him concerned the Mann Act, and that she, herself, had signed the complaint. However, she said that she did not know what she was signing and that later she made a statement setting forth that she signed the papers against her husband in ignorance of what their import was.

The adoption papers for Barbara give Barbara's parents' name as Steve and Julia Czarny. Barbara's name was formerly Jane and was changed to Barbara at the time of adoption.

Mrs. Sobral seems determined to get Barbara back into her custody. She has secured the services of an attorney, Mr. Thomas Richardson, 722 Fourth National Bank Building, Indianapolis, and it seems that Mr. Richardson is very much interested in the Sobral family.

We have not told Mrs. Sobral definitely that Barbara has been located or that she has been taken from the custody of the Gay family. We shall be interested to learn any further information you have secured and we shall also write you of any developments on the case in Indianapolis.

We wish to thank you for your splendid co-operation and assistance in this matter.

February 4, 1931.—Letter written to the County Clerk, Hartville, Illinois:

We are interested in verifying Ann Sobral's legal adoption, which is said to have occurred in Harrison County, Hartville, Illinois, on *July 26, 1926.* The adoption was said to be signed by a Mr. Harvey Underwood, County Clerk of Hartville, Illinois.

May we have a verification of this fact as soon as possible?

We thank you kindly for your co-operation.

P.S. Ann's name before adoption was said to be Jane Czarny, her parents being Steve and Julia Czarny.

February 6, 1931.—Letter received from County Clerk, Hartville, Illinois:

According to our records Jane Czarny was adopted by Joseph Sobral and Ann Sobral under date of July 16, 1926, said child to be thereafter known as Barbara Sobral.

This is shown in Adoption Record 54, page 241.

Later.—Visited Mrs. Gay, alias Becky West, 516 Lockwood Avenue. Mrs. Gay stated that she had placed Barbara with Mrs. Gillis, the former boarding-mother, the same day that the case-worker had visited previously. She is paying Mrs. Gillis $6.00 a week and furnishing Barbara's clothing.

Later.—Telephoned Mrs. Gillis, Barbara's boarding-mother. Found that Barbara is with her and is attending Central School regularly and also attending the First Baptist Sunday School. She said she expected to keep Barbara indefinitely, and the arrangement was that the Gays could come to visit but never could they take Barbara to their place of living. She said Barbara is pleasant and obedient and she means to teach the child good manners and morals.

February 7, 1931.—Letter written to the County Clerk, Hartville, Illinois:

We thank you kindly for your time and trouble in verifying the adoption of Jane Czarny, now Barbara Sobral.

Later.—Letter written to the Department of Public Welfare, Indianapolis, Indiana:

We were glad to receive the information contained in your letter of February 2, 1931, noting that Sobrals do have a legal right to Barbara.

Mrs. Gay has placed Barbara to board with a Mrs. Gillis, 515 West Madison Avenue. She is paying Mrs. Gillis $6.00 a week in addition to providing her clothing. This placement was made before our organization took any steps in suggesting that she be moved from the Gays. Hence, we have had nothing to do with the Sobral case beyond seeking information necessary for a reply to your letter.

In view of Mrs. Gay's bad reputation it is certain that a long time permanent plan has to be made for Barbara, and since the Sobrals' legal residence is in Indianapolis we shall consider it the responsibility of an Indianapolis agency to make that plan.

We assure you that we shall be glad to co-operate in whatever future plan you may make for the care of this child.

February 18, 1931.—Letter received from the Department of Public Welfare, Indianapolis, Indiana:

Mrs. Sobral plans to go to Midland in the near future to get Barbara, and we are wondering whether she will encounter any difficulty.

In correspondence with Mrs. Winn of the Children's Service of Bancroft, Illinois, we learn that Mrs. Winn had been in correspondence with the Children's Service of Indianapolis. However, our Children's Service has the case under the name of Juanita's parents and therefore was not registered in our Social Service Exchange on the Sobral case.

Any further plan concerning the advisability of allowing the Sobrals to adopt Juanita has been stopped, and we believe that Juanita will be returned to the Children's Service Society in Bancroft.

We have just learned from the Immigration authorities that Mr. Sobral has been ordered deported to Mexico for life. We are not sure just what Mrs. Sobral plans to do with Barbara, but she has expressed a desire to go to Hartville, Illinois, to the home of her parents.

February 20, 1931.—Air-mail letter received from the Department of Public Welfare, Indianapolis, Indiana:

Many startling facts regarding the Sobral case have been brought to light since we wrote to you February 16. Through the Immigration authorities we have learned that both Mr. and Mrs. Sobral have a long record of vice.

Mr. Sobral has been found guilty of fraudulent entry into this country and is to be deported to Mexico after serving four years on sentences given him previous to his last deportation from Kansas City, Missouri, July 28, 1928. He had been convicted in Kansas City for "Violation of prohibition and as the manager of a house of prostitution, and one who had been previously deported as a manager of a house of prostitution."

We also learned that Mrs. Sobral made a sworn statement before the United States Commissioner of Immigration, Mr. Frank Marshall, of Kansas City, Missouri, that she had prostituted for Joseph Sobral for two or three years before her marriage to him on August 24, 1922. She continued her life as a prostitute after her marriage. She had left her home when she was fifteen years of age and had gone to Chicago and lived with her sister, Elizabeth. She shortly afterward came to Indianapolis with a man by the name of O'Malley, to whom she was not married, and lived with him in a hotel for a short time. He paid her way back to Chicago, and directly afterward Mrs. Sobral met the man who is now her husband. This information was given by Mrs. Sobral in 1922, at the time her husband was under investigation for his later deportation to Mexico for violation of the Mann Act.

Mr. Sobral stated at that time that he was born in Orizaba, Mexico, April 28, 1892. He had never become a naturalized citizen of the United States. He was then living with his wife, Ann Sobral, age nineteen years, who was a prostitute, and Mr. Sobral was living on her earnings. He said he first entered the United States in July, 1909, through El Paso. He crossed without inspection. He later went to South Bend and then to Des Moines. In 1916 he was living in St. Louis. Prior to his marriage to Ann, whose maiden name was Baumann, he had lived three years with one woman and short periods with two other women, to whom he was not married.

Mr. Sobral had a record of eleven arrests prior to his arrest by the Immigration Department in 1922. In most instances he had been released because of insufficient evidence and in no case had he served time. There were four arrests for running disorderly places, one for rape, one for suspicion of violation of the Harrison Drug Act, four times on suspicion of robbery, and once for larceny.

We have been able to prove that the Sobrals came to Indianapolis in June, 1929. As they have been receiving aid from this Department intermittently since January, 1930, Mrs. Sobral has not been able to establish residence here. Her husband, of course, would not be able to establish residence any place in the United States, as you know.

During the time that Mr. Sobral was under investigation for deportation in 1928 he corresponded with the Immigration Department in Kansas City and gave 815 Seventh Street, South Bend, Illinois, as his address in February, 1928, and 1136 Oak Street, South Bend, June 6, 1928. Mr. Sobral was out under bond at that time.

The adoption papers of Barbara, which we have seen, are dated July 16, 1926, and they show that Mr. and Mrs. Sobral were then living at 815 Seventh Street, South Bend, Illinois. The parents of Barbara, Steve and Julia Czarny, resided at 1115 Oak Street in South Bend at the same time.

We found it rather difficult to get this information at the Immigration Office as no one is allowed to read their records, and we had to depend on one of the inspectors to give it to us. It was difficult for him to locate the information we wanted in the two very large files on the case, one of which was on the trial here in Indianapolis and the other consisted of copies of information on Mr. Sobral's previous record which was sent by the United States District Attorney's office of Midland, Illinois. Mr. Sobral was previously prosecuted in Midland, Illinois, and the inspector with whom we talked advised us to let you know that you can get complete information on these people from that office. Upon reading the records on this case for our benefit, the inspector discovered the Sobrals were married one month before the law was passed September 22, 1922, which protects the wives of deported aliens from deportation when they are citizens of this country in their own right. The old law holds good for those married before this law went into effect. Because of this as well as the discovery of Mrs. Sobral's sworn statement that she was a prostitute for many years, he decided to have her brought in by their officers for questioning with a view to her possible deportation. If she is detained here for investigation you will have plenty of time to make an adjustment in regard to Barbara.

In the light of the foregoing information we are confident you will feel as we do that every effort should be made to prevent Mrs. Sobral from securing the custody of Barbara. It would seem possible that the adoption might be set aside because of the illegal status of Mr. Sobral in this country, and the possible misrepresentations made at the time of the child's adoption. We are expecting the Children's Service of Bancroft, Illinois, to take the child Juanita at once.

It will give us pleasure to continue our co-operation on this case, and we shall notify you regarding the disposition made in regard to Mrs. Sobral.

Later.—Conference with Judge Arthur, County Court. When the Sobrals' situation was outlined to Judge Arthur, he stated that he did not think the adoption could be revoked and added that probably little co-operation would be available from Harrison County in working out a placement plan for the child, since she was living in Summit County.

February 23, 1931.—Letter written to the Children's Service, Bancroft, Illinois:

I believe that you are already acquainted with the Sobral case in regard to Juanita, a child whom the Sobrals received from you and later wanted to adopt. We understand that you are planning to stop adoption proceedings in this instance.

In view of the very unsatisfactory and complicated legal status of the Sobrals, it is obvious that a more permanent plan for the future care of Barbara, their other child, is necessary as well.

[There follows a brief family history, then the letter continues:]

In the light of the foregoing information we are confident that you will think it essential that some plan be made for Barbara away from the Sobrals. Would it not be possible that the adoption be set aside because of the illegal status of Mr. Sobral in this country, and the possible misrepresentations made at the time of the child's adoption, as apparently the Sobrals were in no respect fit guardians for the child? Barbara's only legal residence is apparently Harrison County; and since the adoption took place there, it seems it would be the responsibility of that County to have it revoked and to make some other arrangements for the child's care.

When the Sobrals were en route to Indianapolis from South Bend, they stopped in Midland for a few weeks' visit. At that time they left Barbara with a Mrs. Manuel Gay, alias Becky West, who is conducting a house of prostitution here and is supporting a Mexican by the name of Manuel Gay from her earnings. For a time Barbara lived here with the Gays and as a consequence has acquired a sophisticated attitude toward life and is quite cognizant of the manner in which the Gays and Sobrals make their livelihood; in fact, she has said to her present boarding-mother that she expected to earn a living in like manner some day herself.

Fearing that she would get into difficulty when Barbara entered school, Mrs. Gay has boarded her with an elderly woman in Midland, a woman apparently of good reputation, who is giving the child good physical care. Mrs. Gay is paying for her board. Although Mrs. Gay is fond of the child and wants to keep her, it is obvious that her fitness is quite as questionable as is the Sobrals.

Undoubtedly a plan should be started at once for the placement of Barbara, and we shall be glad to co-operate in any way in the plan that you deem advisable. Even if the adoption cannot be revoked, certainly the Sobrals could be declared unfit guardians by the Court and then Harrison County should make proper plans for her care.

February 27, 1931.—Letter received from the Children's Service, Bancroft, Illinois:

Your letter opens an entirely new light on the Sobral family. I cannot understand how this information escaped us when they applied for the little girl, Juanita. They were referred to us by a social worker in South Bend, Illinois, and some of their references were county officials in whom we had a great deal of confidence. Others who seemed to know them well also recommended them to us, but I confess that we were either very much deceived or very negligent in our investigation.

I thank you most sincerely for your summary of the case regarding Barbara Ann. I was under the impression that this child had been returned to her own mother, as Mrs. Sobral had told me before they left for Mexico that the mother of Barbara wished to have her back. You will be interested in knowing that the child, Juanita, who is a ward of Children's Service, has been removed from the Sobral home and returned to the Society. We had nothing to do with the placement of Barbara, but I am asking our worker to talk with the judge who granted the adoption to know whether or not this adoption could be set aside. I have a feeling that it will require a new petition declaring the child dependent in the county in which she now resides. This should not be difficult and with your history I am sure you could easily show that Barbara is a dependent child and the Sobrals unfit guardians.

However, I would have no authority to go into this case for the Illinois Children's Service and would suggest that the matter be taken up as a new case in your county.

We will try to locate the parents of Barbara in South Bend or some relatives in the old community although it was some years ago that the child was adopted.

March 2, 1931.—Letter received from the Department of Public Welfare, Indianapolis, Indiana:

We are enclosing a copy of our summary on the Sobral case, also a copy of a letter from the Children's Service of Bancroft, Illinois, for your record.

Miss Avison of the Illinois Children's Service told us that she would get in touch with you regarding this case and co-operate in any way possible in preventing Mrs. Sobral from gaining the custody of Barbara. It is possible she has already told you of our experience with regard to Juanita.

Since making our summary we have learned that Mrs. Sobral has had a hearing in the County Jail and is out on a $500 bond. Her attorney, Mr. Richardson, has been a very zealous worker in her defense. He enlisted the interest of the Mexican Consul in her regard, and through him had her bond reduced from $1,000 to $500.

From the Immigration Office we have learned that Mr. Richardson has promised to secure employment for Mrs. Sobral and he has stated that he has commenced divorce proceedings for her.

We shall be interested to learn what disposition has been made in regard to Barbara.

We surely appreciate your fine co-operation.

[The following summary of the case was inclosed in preceding letter:]

Through a letter written by Thomas Richardson, attorney, in the Fourth National Bank Building, referred to us by the Mayor's Office December 9, 1930, our Inter-City Bureau first came in contact with the case of Joseph and Ann Sobral. Mr. Richardson asked assistance for the Sobrals in securing the return to them of their adopted daughter Barbara, who was being held in Midland, Illinois, by people with whom they had left her a couple of years ago, pending the time when they would be settled and in a position to take her. It seems Mrs. Sobral had gone after the child about six months ago, and the family who have her insisted upon the payment of $300 to $1,000 before they would release her. As Mr. and Mrs. Sobral were unable to meet those financial demands, Mr. Richardson believed we would be in a position to have the child returned.

Through clearing the case in our Social Service Exchange we found the Sobral family were receiving aid from our South Side Office.

Through Mrs. Sobral we learned the Children's Service of Indianapolis was supervising a child who had been placed in the custody of Mr. and Mrs. Sobral by the Illinois Children's Service, with a view to her adoption. Mrs. Sobral had at first insisted she had adoption papers for Juanita and the case was well known to Mrs. Winn of the Children's Service, Bancroft, Illinois. We at once addressed an inquiry to this society, and their reply came to us simultaneously with Mrs. Sobral's confession that the child was not adopted.

The Children's Agency of Summit County in Midland, Illinois, to whom we wrote regarding Barbara, or Ann, as she was known there, wrote us January 15, 1931; a copy of their letter is attached to this summary.

From the record of the Children's Service of Indianapolis we found the case was known to them from April 3, 1930, and it had been registered under the name of Brink. The mother's name, Mildred Brink, and the child's name, Gertrude, were given on the application, and Mrs. Joseph "Sobral" was mentioned in the body of the application. As our case on the Sobral family went through Social Service Exchange under the names of Joseph and Ann Sobral, it can readily be understood why our two agencies did not get together on the case at an earlier date.

The Children's Service of Indianapolis had been asked by the Illinois Children's Service to supervise Juanita, who had been placed by them with the Sobral family a few years ago. These two societies had been reluctant to agree to conclude adoption proceedings, as the home conditions had never come up to the standards of their requirements. However, home conditions had very greatly improved recently, but when the County Agent and the Indianapolis Children's Service approved the adoption December 6, 1930, the Illinois Children's Service still hesitated to give the papers.

In the meantime it had come to light that Mr. Sobral was being held in the County Jail by the Indianapolis Immigration Department for fraudulent entry into the United States from Mexico. We also learned that he had been previously deported to Mexico for violation of the Mann Act, but he shortly afterward returned to this country and came to Indianapolis.

Mrs. Sobral brought the adoption papers for Barbara to our office.

Upon learning the status of Mr. Sobral's situation in Indianapolis we notified the Illinois Children's Service to send to Indianapolis for Juanita. We found the Indianapolis Children's Service had also sent the same request. They had previously received authority from the Illinois Children's Service to take Juanita into their custody pending the arrival of one of the workers from the Illinois Children's Service. Mrs. Sobral refused to give the child to them, and her attorney supported her in this decision. The Indianapolis Children's Service consulted Mr. Runyan of the Legal Aid Bureau, and they were advised the most expeditious way to handle the matter would be to have the Illinois Society send for the child.

Through Mr. A. J. Reid, United States Immigration Inspector, we secured information regarding both Mr. and Mrs. Sobral. From their record on Mr. Sobral's late trial in Indianapolis and his previous record, copies of which had been sent to them from the office of the United States District Attorney in Midland, Illinois, we secured the information which is embodied in our letter dated February 19, 1931, to the Children's Agency of Summit County, Midland, Illinois.

Upon examination of the records from the United States District Attorney's Office in Midland, which referred directly to Mrs. Sobral, Mr. Reid decided she was eligible for deportation. He later sent officers to her home and notified her to call in his office for an interview.

In the meantime Miss Avison of the Illinois Children's Service arrived in Indianapolis. In company with Mrs. Fisher of the Indianapolis Children's Service she called at the home of Mrs. Sobral, but they were unable to secure any information regarding her or Juanita. They were told Mrs. Sobral was no longer there. They later came to our office, and Mr. Frampton telephoned the Prosecuting Attorney's Office and also Judge Vincent of the Juvenile Court. It was decided the custody of Juanita could be gained through the filing of a neglect and dependency complaint by our Department. Judge Vincent stated that he would take care of it without delay.

Accordingly Miss Meyer, our court worker, accompanied Miss Avison and Mrs. Fisher to the Juvenile Court, and a complaint was filed by her. They secured writ and accompanied by a police officer, called at Mrs. Sobral's address. They were informed by other tenants there that Mrs. Sobral had left there early in the morning, February 20, and had taken the child with her. Her whereabouts were unknown. Miss Meyer and the other workers then went to the Immigration Office and were conferring with them on the case, when one of the tenants, who lived at the same address with Mrs. Sobral, came into the office and gave her new address, where she was in hiding. She was located there by Miss Meyer and an Immigration Officer; the writ was served, and the child taken to the Detention Home. Mrs. Sobral was taken to the County Jail, where she is being held by the Immigration Department.

On February 21, 1931, Judge Vincent sustained our Neglect and Dependency complaint and ordered the child returned to the jurisdiction of the Illinois Children's Service; she was later taken by Miss Avison to Chicago. It was learned that Mr. Sobral is to be returned to Kansas City, where he is to serve two suspended sentences of two years each before his deportation to Mexico.

[Copy of letter from Children's Service, Bancroft, Illinois, to Department of Public Welfare, Indianapolis, also inclosed in preceding letter:]

Your letter is quite surprising since we have been in touch with the Sobral family through the Indianapolis Children's Service.

The Sobral family at one time lived in South Bend, Illinois, and they were considered respectable Mexicans, conducting a legitimate business rooming-house for Mexican men. The family did not live at the place of business but had its own home in which a little girl had been placed by her mother. This is probably the child Barbara whom you mention. The younger child, Juanita, is a ward of the Illinois Children's Service whose nationality has been difficult to determine. There was a question of Negro blood, but after intensive investigation the mother of the child declared that the father was a Mexican. At the time of placement with Mr. and Mrs. Sobral they were considered respectable citizens of South Bend, and the man seemed to be a leader among the Mexican people as he was seemingly much better educated than those in his neighborhood.

A complaint was made against him for selling intoxicating liquors at his place of business, but he was not brought to trial on that charge. Instead there was found to be a flaw in his passport papers from Mexico, and for this reason he was deported from Harrison County, Illinois, to Mexico. I had never heard of any charge on the Mann Act. At that time we made as careful an investigation as we could and were assured even by county officials that the man was probably the victim of jealousy among his countrymen in the community because of his financial success.

The Sobrals were in Mexico about two years, during which time we were in as close touch as we could be by correspondence. They then returned to the

United States and settled in Indianapolis. We referred the case to the Indianapolis Children's Service, asking for supervision and reports. The Children's Service has been very co-operative; and although the reports at first were not very favorable, I believe they have honestly tried to give us the exact situation in the family. During all of this time Mr. and Mrs. Sobral have begged for permission to adopt Juanita. We have not felt justified in granting adoption until we could secure a favorable report from the Indianapolis Children's Service and your County Agent. This has recently come to us, and in November, 1930, Mrs. Ruth Fisher of the Indianapolis Children's Service advised us that the County Agent had approved adoption of our ward by these people. We have not, however, forwarded the necessary papers and are holding the matter for further information.

Your letter indicates that the child should probably be removed from this home. We await your advice and assure you that we are responsible for this child and wish to do what is right for her. I trust you will keep us informed.

March 7, 1931.—Letter written by Children's Agency of Midland to the Department of Public Welfare, Indianapolis, Indiana:

Thank you kindly for your summary of the Sobral case, and also the copy of a letter to your organization from the Children's Service, Bancroft, Illinois.

No definite step has as yet been taken on Barbara's behalf. We have written the Illinois Children's Service agent having Hartville, Illinois, in her territory, but we have not had a final word from her as yet. We shall try to hurry the matter as much as possible.

We shall be glad to inform you of the final disposition made regarding Barbara when that time arrives and, if any important move is made relative to the Sobrals in Indianapolis, we shall appreciate any such word from you.

March 8, 1931.—Clipping from newspaper, *Times*, March 8, 1931:

TWO ENGAGE IN BATTLE OVER CHILD

MEXICAN ON WAY TO PENITENTIARY AFTER FIGHT OVER CUSTODY OF GIRL HE CLAIMS HIS DAUGHTER

Jose Sobral, a native of old Mexico who was thrown out of the United States as an "undesirable" but who wouldn't stay put out, and Mrs. Becky Gay of 510 Lockwood Avenue, disagreed most violently Saturday as to the custody of a little seven year old girl. The woman came out victorious in this round while the man headed toward Leavenworth penitentiary as the guest of the government. Sobral startled federal court attachés Saturday by claiming that a child of his was being held here in a residence at 510 Lockwood Avenue for $1,000 ransom. This declaration came just after he had been sentenced to spend two years in the penitentiary for disregarding an order to "stay deported." The man, who speaks broken English, told federal officials that the Mexican revolt had forced him to take his family and leave Mexico in favor of the Texas border.

He came to Midland, he said, to regain custody of his child whom he had left here about a year ago. He was then en route to Indianapolis with his wife, he continued. Since then, Sobral declared, he has been unsuccessful in trying to regain possession of the child. Mrs. Gay, who lives at 510 Lockwood Avenue, admitted having custody of the child for the past year but declared Sobral's story is a tissue of lies and announced that she would keep possession of the girl—Ann Sobral—unless the child is legally taken from her. She claims the child is not the daughter of Mr. and Mrs. Sobral, as they are Mexicans while Ann is Bohemian. She admitted Ann was left in her custody more than a year ago. "The baby was sick at that time, broken out with a terrible rash, and it was necessary for me to put her under a physician's care," she said. "The baby was placed in the home of a respectable family on Madison Avenue in Midland, where I have been paying $7.50 each week during the past year for her board and room. While living there, the child has been attending school," Mrs. Gay told officials. Mrs. Gay told Chief of Police P. S. Kelly that when the alleged parents of the child did not reappear within a few months, she went to South Bend, Ill., where they had made their home, to make an investigation. Here, she said, she discovered that Sobral was not the father of the girl, and his wife was not the mother. Mrs. Gay, of German descent, is married to Manuel Gay, a Mexican. The woman told Chief Kelly that she had become tremendously fond of the little girl and would not give her up without a fight. She refused to give the name the child goes under at present or to reveal her address. "Sobral's friends might make an attempt to kidnap the girl," she pointed out. Mrs. Gay also explained to police officials that the girl had never been a visitor at the house on Lockwood Avenue. The woman agreed to accede to Sobral's request that he might see the girl once more before leaving for prison, if the police would furnish her with protection. Sobral, however, was removed to Leavenworth Saturday night before the child could be brought to the jail. After hearing Mrs. Gay's story, Chief Kelly referred the matter to the Child Welfare Bureau for investigation. Records show that Sobral was deported from the United States in 1906 but returned in 1928 and was convicted of conducting a house of ill fame in South Bend, Ill. He returned to Mexico again. The next year he was back in South Bend and was convicted on a liquor charge. Both sentences were suspended providing he would leave the country. Police also were told by Mrs. Gay that Sobral had approached her several months ago regarding the matter of returning the girl. At that time, she said, she went to county officials and following an investigation by the county court she was informed that she "might keep the child." Mrs. Gay has retained Allan Kerr, local attorney, to supervise her fight to retain possession of the little girl.

March 10, 1931.—Discussed Sobral case at Case Committee. It was suggested that the case be taken up with Miss Adams, Director of Child Welfare of the State Department, as she might be able to throw some light in regard to the relative legal responsibilities in this case of Harrison and Summit counties.

March 12, 1931.—Talked with United States Attorney. The United States Attorney reported that the Federal Court hearing held on March 7, 1931, had had no bearing on the legal status of Barbara. The newspaper's emphasis relative to Barbara's welfare was wholly erroneous as far as that Court hearing was concerned. The Federal Court had no jurisdiction regarding custody of the child as that was entirely up to the local courts. Mr. Sobral was arraigned before the Federal Court on that date and sentenced to two years at Leavenworth Penitentiary, which sentence was to be served preceding his deportation to Mexico. The reason that the hearing was held in Midland was because there is no Court held in South Bend and all federal matters concerning the geographical area are handled in Midland. It was therefore in Midland that Mr. Sobral was originally ordered deported to Mexico, and it was in violation of that Court order that he was again arraigned at this time after having been picked up by the Indianapolis Immigration authorities.

Mr. Sobral did enter a plea for clemency in Court on March 7, 1931, stating that he had a six-year-old child dependent upon him. He was told that the child would be cared for in some manner and that her care had nothing to do with his serving a sentence as he was in no way a fit legal guardian. The reason that Mrs. Gay appeared in Court was the fact that it was she who had reported to the authorities that Mr. Sobral had not gone to Mexico as he had been ordered to do by the Court and she was in Court as a witness.

Later.—Letter from the Children's Agency of Midland written to the Children's Service, Bancroft, Illinois:

Since receiving your letter of February 25 concerning Barbara Sobral we have been waiting anxiously for some word from the worker in Harrison County, but as yet have not heard from her. We are most anxious to have this case gone into there as soon as possible.

I feel very strongly that the child is a proper charge for Harrison County. She was merely left in Midland while the Sobrals were passing through here. At the time of her adoption and later, the Sobrals had a residence in Harrison County and have not been able to obtain a residence anywhere since then. The child, of course, cannot obtain a residence in her own right.

Will you take up the matter with your director again and see if she can get some action from the proper authorities in Harrison County? Thank you for any help that you may be able to give us.

March 12, 1931.—Conference with Miss Adams, Director Child Welfare, State Department. Told Miss Adams of the situation in the Sobral case. She did not think Harrison County would be willing to accept the child, and she said that the Juvenile Court law provides that a child can be declared dependent wherever he is found. It would, therefore, be possible to bring Barbara into the Summit County Juvenile Court and have her declared dependent. However, Miss Adams offered to write Judge Delaney of Harrison County and ask if he would be willing to accept Barbara.

Miss Adams said that the case of Barbara is a very good illustration of what can happen in an independent placement and asked that the Children's Agency give her a history so that the matter can be presented to the legislature when the new law on independent adoptions comes up.

March 17, 1931.—Letter written to Miss Adams, State Department.

I am enclosing the history of the adoption of Barbara Ann Sobral, the case I talked to you about the other day. This is a case, I believe, that you are interested in presenting to the legislature.

Today we received a letter from Mrs. Boyer, the worker in Harrison County. She said that she had talked to Judge Delaney about this case and he had advised the adoption matter of Barbara was closed and could not be reopened since the close of the term of Court in which it was docketed and disposed of. He also said that since Barbara was never declared dependent in Harrison County she was not a ward of the Court there and should be declared dependent wherever she happens to be. He holds that the case should be handled in Midland.

It looks as though Harrison County was unwilling to do anything in regard to this case, but I should be very glad for any assistance that you might be able to give us.

Letter received from the Illinois Children's Service worker in Harrison County:

I have just received a note from Mrs. Winn of the Bancroft office, asking that I answer your letter of the twelfth. Our Bancroft stenographer is ill. The history of the case, together with my more recent inquiries, is in Bancroft, left there about two weeks ago for Mrs. Winn's use in evaluating the case. I have never handled the Sobral case; Mrs. Winn has been doing so. However, I did verify the adoption of Barbara and learned that her true mother was a prostitute, who formerly lived in South Bend at the address given and later lived at Sheyboygan, Wisconsin. The petition for adoption gave street addresses in each place which I do not recall.

I visited Meredith Haines, South Bend, in charge of the Garfield Park Community House, who was reference for the Sobrals at the time of their application for the second child. She told me that Barbara's mother has a history of immorality, has only been married once, and now lives with that husband and their two daughters, both of whom are older than Barbara and are in the public school in the neighborhood. Mr. Czarny refused to accept the paternity of Barbara, and would not live with Mrs. Czarny if she kept Barbara, so Mr. and

Mrs. Czarny consented to the adoption of Barbara by the Sobrals, as evidenced by their written consent in the Adoption files of the County Clerk. Mrs. Czarny had an affair with some St. Louis man about this time and went with him to Wisconsin. Mr. Czarny took some legal action against the man and went to Wisconsin and brought his wife home. She has also given birth to a fourth child since Barbara's birth as a result of her philanderings and gave that child away too. The Czarnys live in a house two doors away from the Community House, the daughters enjoy the privileges of the Community House, and are on a par with the average girl in this foreign neighborhood. Mr. Czarny is a Macedonian and his wife a Hungarian. At the time of my neighborhood inquiry I thought it was not desirable to visit the Czarnys but if you wish I will do so.

I consulted with Judge Patrick A. Delaney, Juvenile Judge of the Harrison County Court. He advised that the Adoption matter of Barbara is closed and cannot be reopened since the close of the term of Court in which it was docketed and disposed of. The filing of a new dependency petition would be necessary for the removal of the child from the foster parents. Barbara was never declared dependent in Harrison County and therefore is not a ward of the Court here. The child should be declared dependent wherever she is, and this declaration of dependency can be made on any child at any time in any Juvenile Court. Children are declared dependent or delinquent legally after a residence of twenty-four hours, which is the time necessary for service of summons prior to hearing. He holds the case should be handled in Midland, since you have the evidence there which would be grounds for dependency.

March 21, 1931.—Conference with Mr. McFadden, Executive Secretary, Illinois Children's Service. Talked with Mr. McFadden about the Sobral case during the conference of the Child Welfare League of America in Chicago. Mr. McFadden was confident that Harrison County would not be willing to accept Barbara because the child had already been adopted and because the family had left Harrison County. He said that the Juvenile Court Law provided that the child could be declared dependent where the child was found and it would be within Judge Arthur's right to declare this child dependent. Told Mr. McFadden that there was a question as to whether Summit County should assume the support of this child when she really had no residence here.

Mr. McFadden said that he would be willing to have Barbara made a ward of the Illinois Children's Service if Children's Agency wished that and they would then assume her care.

March 24, 1931.—Discussed case at Case Committee meeting. Told Case Committee of the interview with Miss Adams and Mr. McFadden. The question was brought up as to whether the Children's Agency would be putting too much responsibility on the Illinois Children's Service by having Barbara made a ward of that organization. Mrs. Allen (board member) suggested that Mr. McFadden had been very co-operative in the past. Since Barbara will probably need boarding-home care for some little time before she is ready for a free-home placement, it was suggested by the Committee that it might be a good plan for the Children's Agency to assume the burden of the boarding-home care for Barbara and request the Illinois Children's Service to make a special effort to place her in a free home when the proper time came.

March 25, 1931.—Letter received from Mrs. Sobral, forwarded from Family Agency, Midland:

Am writing these few lines as I've got word from the Welfare Dept. here that you people are holding my baby that you people took away from Mrs. Manuel Gay, in Midland. I'm in a position that I can support my baby and am asking you to please write and leave me know when I'll be able to send her train fare to bring her.

Will appreciate your kindness very much for any information. The baby's name is Barbara Sobral.

April 11, 1931.—Talked with Judge Arthur, County Judge. Outlined to him the position of the Sobrals and Gays relative to the legal status of Barbara. Judge Arthur suggested that in as much as there was a probability of the Gays fighting for the legal right to Barbara that the Children's Agency talk with Mr. Palmer, Assistant States Attorney, to get his advice and promise that his office would assist in case a fight should occur in Court.

April 13, 1931.—Visited Mrs. Gillis, Barbara's boarding-mother.

Found that Barbara was home from school because of illness. She was prettily dressed in a bright pink silk dress and matching pink socks with a green border. She recognized the case-worker as the one who had talked with her at the school some months previous.

Mrs. Gillis said that the Gays had called for Barbara the previous day, saying that they wished to take her for a ride in the country. Barbara was not feeling well, but Mrs. Gillis thought the fresh air would be beneficial; hence, allowed her to go with them. Later it was found that Barbara had been taken to the Gays' home, which was absolutely contrary to the agreement made between Mrs. Gillis and Mrs. Gay at the time Barbara was last placed in the Gillis home. Barbara denied having been to the Gay home when asked directly by Mrs. Gillis, but the fact was divulged inadvertently by remarks made by the child. For example, she told of having been taken to the toilet and also having lain in her mother's bed because she was not feeling well. According to Mrs. Gillis, Barbara is a wholly different child whenever she returns from being with the Gays.

She is compelled to lie about so much that has been going on. She is fairly "stupid" on account of having to keep so much concealed from Mrs. Gillis. She is a polite, well-behaved child as long as she does not see the Gays too often. She is being taught to have as perfect manners as possible, and strangers comment on her politeness when they visit the Gillis home. Mrs. Gillis said that Barbara has a fund of knowledge relative to sex matters which comes to the surface now and again when playing with the neighbor girls. Frequently Mrs. Gillis hears comments made while the girls are playing together; on such occasions she immediately tells them that nice girls do not discuss such matters.

Later.—Talked with Miss Gorman, teacher at Central School. She reported that Barbara is doing failing work. She "shows off" continually. For instance, she will deliberately mispronounce a word and then look about the room to see how large an audience she has. Again she is frequently seen pulling up her bloomers as far as possible and then flicking her skirt so that the upper portion of her thigh becomes evident. The teacher considers her a very self-conscious child. She seems to be nervous, also, and has great difficulty in remaining quiet in her seat at any time. Barbara delights to talk to the teacher about her family affairs, and she has always given the teacher to understand that Mrs. Gay is her real mother and that Sobral is not her correct name. The teacher said that at the first of the year, Mrs. Gay represented herself at school as Mrs. Sobral.

Later.—Talked with Mr. Palmer, Assistant State's Attorney. After the Sobral case had been outlined to him, he suggested leaving the Gays out of the picture entirely as they had absolutely no legal right to the child. However, if they should appear in Court, he promised that his office would offer its assistance to the Children's Agency. He pointed out that Mrs. Gay was not even the child's custodian, but rather Mrs. Gillis. He suggested that a dependency petition be filed at once, and that Mr. and Mrs. Sobral be served a summons by publication.

Later.—Talked with Mrs. Sylvester, probation officer. She said that a petition could be filed at any time, and since the address of both Mr. and Mrs. Sobral is known, a summons could be served on them direct and service by publication thus eliminated.

April 14, 1931.—Mrs. Sylvester, probation officer, telephoned. She stated that Mrs. Gillis, boarding-mother, had telephoned her the night previous to say that the Gays had taken Barbara to their home for the evening and brought her back. She feared they might be contemplating kidnaping the child as they had spoken of selling their place of business and leaving Midland. She asked if she should allow Barbara to go to school, and Mrs. Sylvester advised that she do so. Mrs. Sylvester suggested that the Children's Agency file a petition as soon as possible.

Telephoned Mrs. Gillis, boarding-mother.

Mrs. Gillis explained that Barbara had not been taken to the Gay home, but rather Mrs. Gillis had telephoned Mrs. Gay to reprimand her for having taken Barbara to her home on Sunday contrary to their previous agreement. Later in the evening Mr. Gay came out to the Gillis home and scolded around considerably, saying that they had already filed adoption papers for Barbara and that soon she would be their child and they could do with her as they pleased. He said that Mr. Kerr is their attorney. Mrs. Gillis said also that an unknown man had phoned her the night previous to tell her that Barbara had been seen at Mrs. Gay's house on Sunday. He would not reveal his identity. Mrs. Gillis told the caseworker that she would be willing to testify in Court to any information she knew regarding the life of the Gays.

April 16, 1931.—Filed dependency petition in County Court.

Mrs. Gillis was in Mrs. Sylvester's office when the case-worker arrived. Barbara had been taken to St. Francis Hospital with a case of measles the night before. Mrs. Gillis had called Mrs. Sylvester, and Dr. Lindemann had come out to take the child to the hospital. Mrs. Gillis and the Gays accompanied Barbara to the hospital. Mrs. Gay was furious when she learned that Mrs. Gillis had notified the probation officer, as she said she preferred having her own doctor in attendance and she did not want to have anything to do with the Court officials. Mrs. Gillis appeared to be quite in favor of a dependency petition being filed and the consequent removal of Barbara from Midland. She said that when she had learned from the case-worker that Mrs. Gay was not Barbara's real mother, a different light was thrown on the entire situation, and she was very much opposed to Mrs. Gay's having Barbara under her supervision. When Mrs. Gillis told Mrs. Gay that she had found out Barbara was not her own child, Mrs. Gay became very angry. It was agreed that Mrs. Sylvester would notify the hospital authorities that no one should be allowed to remove Barbara from the hospital with the exception of Mrs. Sylvester. The Court hearing was set for April 27, 1931.

April 17, 1931.—Letter written to County Clerk, Hartville, Illinois:

We are very desirous of verifying the birth of Jane Czarny which is said to have occurred either in or near Hartville or South Bend, Illinois.

The birth dates suggested are *October 5, 1924,* or *March 10, 1924.*

Thank you kindly for your co-operation in this matter.

April 18, 1931.—Letter written to United States Commission of Immigration, Kansas City, Missouri:

The case of Barbara Ann Sobral, a six-year-old child, adopted by Jose and Ann Sobral in July, 1926, has come to the attention of our organization.

Mr. Sobral is now in Leavenworth Penitentiary, and Mrs. Sobral is under arrest in Indianapolis, subject to a possible deportation to Mexico. Barbara is now under the supervision of a woman who is the manager of a house of prostitution.

It is obvious that some more satisfactory plan should be made on behalf of this child. A dependency petition has been filed, alleging her adopted parents as unfit legal guardians and asking that the Court be made the child's guardian.

As a part of the evidence to be submitted showing the Sobrals to be unfit guardians, we are very desirous of getting certain facts direct from your office. For example, we understand that Mr. Sobral was deported to Mexico in 1922, there being numerous charges against him. May we have a list of those charges. and the date and immediate circumstances surrounding his consequent conviction? Then, too, Mrs. Sobral is said to have made a sworn statement at the time of Mr. Sobral's deportation in 1922, that she prostituted for Mr. Sobral both before and after their marriage. May we have a copy of that statement? If not, may we have a statement from you quoting the sum and substance of that legal document?

You may have other information in your office of which we do not know that would be of value to us at this time; if so we should appreciate your sending it to us.

The Sobral case is scheduled for a Court hearing on April 27; hence, we are anxious to have word from you just as soon as possible.

Thank you very kindly for your co-operation in this matter.

April 20, 1931.—Letter received from the County Clerk, Hartville, Illinois:

In reply will say that I examined years 1923–24 and 25. In 1925 I find one Sofia Czarny, born December 25, 1925.

Later.—Letter written to County Clerk, Hartville, Illinois:

I thank you very kindly for your attempt to verify the birth of Jane Czarny. I omitted, unintentionally, the names of this child's father and mother, which are Steve and Julia Czarny.

I doubt that this additional information will help you, however, as I note that you examined the years 1923–24–25 for the name Czarny.

April 21, 1931.—Mrs. Sylvester, probation officer, telephoned. She asked if the Children's Agency could have a boarding-home available for Barbara by Saturday, as she would be able to leave the hospital by that time. She was told that a home probably will be available, as a special effort will be made to make that possible. She said that she understood Mr. Kerr would not be taking the case for the Gays after his conversation with Mrs. Gillis, who told him of the dependency petition having been filed.

Later.—Talked with Mrs. Gillis, boarding-mother. She stated that Mr. Kerr, the attorney for the Gays, had telephoned her. He asked if she was still interested in adopting Barbara. She told him that she was not after having found that Mrs. Gay was not the child's real mother, for she knew that, were she to adopt Barbara, she would always be troubled by frequent contacts with Mrs. Gay and she thought that that would not be good for the child's well-being. Mrs. Gillis said she did not know whether or not Mr. Kerr would fight the case for the Gays.

Mrs. Gay owes Mrs. Gillis $19 board, and she thinks she probably will not get it. However, she has a fairly good supply of clothing for Barbara which had been bought by Mrs. Gay and she will keep that, if she is not paid the money. She will be willing to allow Barbara to take the clothing with her when she is placed in a home by the Children's Agency. She wanted to talk with the case-worker and asked if a visit could be made within a week. She also said that as a token of good luck she wanted to give Barbara a cross which she should wear throughout her life.

Read the United States Attorney's record. Found that at the time of Mr. Sobral's first conviction in Kansas City in 1922, Mrs. José Sobral and Mr. Werner Baumann, 1526 Carlyle Avenue, Hartville, Illinois, paid the $150 bond on Mr. Sobral's behalf. On April 7, 1931, a parole report made out by the United States Attorney in Midland to the warden of Leavenworth Penitentiary was as follows:

In 1922 subject was arrested by the Immigration authorities in South Bend on a charge of operating a house of prostitution. A hearing was had on this charge and following this hearing on December 19, 1922, he was ordered deported to Mexico. He was actually deported through the port of Rio, Texas, on January 2, 1923.

On February 16, 1925, the Immigration Officers found him back at South Bend again involved in the operation of a house of prostitution. He was arrested, and his return investigated. Investigation showed that he had stayed in Mexico only a few months, and had surreptitiously returned to the United States later in 1923. Following this investigation, an indictment was returned against him in Criminal No. 523, charging him with a violation of the Immigration Act in re-entering the United States after being deported. On May 15, 1928, he pleaded guilty to this charge and was sentenced to two years in the United States Penitentiary at Leavenworth. The Court suspended the sentence on condition that he return to Mexico by July 1, 1928, and remain out of the United States.

Several weeks ago our office learned that subject was back in the United States, living at Indianapolis, Indiana. We had him arrested, and had an investigation made. This investigstion revealed that he remained in Mexico less than six months after leaving on July 1, 1928, and returned to the United States the first part of 1929. The investigation showed that he had gotten back to the United States in some manner not yet satisfactorily explained, but possibly through the use of a forged passport. On returning to the United States he went to Indianapolis and has been there since, living there, so we understand, under an assumed name.

Subject was removed to our district, and on finding that he was back in the United States once more, Judge Rathbon ordered the mittimus issue committing him to the penitentiary on the sentence imposed upon him. When brought before Judge Rathbon, subject claimed that he returned to the United States only because he was forced to do so by the Rebellion of 1928, which drove the citizens of Laguna out of the city into the United States. He further claimed that he told the officials who he was, when he came, and that he got a legitimate passport. These statements of his as to how he got back into the United States do not correspond with what our investigations have developed, though it is possible that the officials of the Immigration Service at El Paso, Texas, made a mistake and allowed him to come in on payment of head tax. However, subject's explanation why he had to remain in the United States after the Mexican Rebellion was all over with, was practically impossible to believe. . . . .

Subject appears to be a habitual operator in various sorts of vice. He likewise is an alien who refuses to be permanently deported.

A summary of this report was also sent to the District Director, United States Department of Labor, Immigration Service, Kansas City, Missouri.

April 22, 1931.—Visited Mrs. Gillis. Told her that it would facilitate finding a suitable foster-home for Barbara if the case-worker had a picture to show. Mrs. Gillis gladly gave over a recent snapshot of Barbara. She said that Mrs. Gay had visited the day before and paid her $9.00 back board money; thus she still owes $10. When she made the $9.00 payment, she took Barbara's Sunday clothing, as she had understood from the nurses at St. Francis Hospital that Barbara was ready to go home any time and she wanted to have the clothing ready in which to take her home. Mrs. Gillis told her that she must not remove the child from the hospital without first getting permission from Mrs. Sylvester, probation officer, as the County was paying for the child's care there.

Mrs. Gillis said she was certainly glad that a home could be found for Barbara so that she would be entirely free from Mrs. Gay's influence. She thought she could have given Barbara a good home if Mrs. Gay did not visit, but it was impossible when the child spent part of the time with Mrs. Gay. Upon her return from trips with Mrs. Gay she would exhibit all sorts of new ideas. She was fond of dancing the hula-hula dance and turning somersaults. She liked to do anything which gave her an excuse to pull her bloomers up as far as possible. When she played with dolls she made a point of pulling up their clothes also.

Mrs. Sylvester, probation officer, telephoned. She wanted to know if a home could be ready for Barbara on the following day as she was ready to leave the hospital. She had telephoned the head Sister asking that they not allow Mrs. Gay to take the child. Told her that a home would be available if at all possible.

April 23, 1931.—Barbara transferred from St. Francis Hospital to the home of Mrs. A. T. Stanley, Elton, Illinois, at the regular boarding rate of $20 a month. (Inasmuch as Barbara herself prefers being called by her second name, Ann, and her foster-parents have been calling her by that name, from now on Barbara will be referred to in this record as Ann.)

RECORD OF ANN SOBRAL AT FIRST ADMISSION DATE
April 23, 1931

Physical health and habits.—Ann examined by Dr. Hudson, and her general condition was found to be normal. Her weight was normal. She had two carious teeth. There was a question as to whether or not her adenoids had been satisfactorily removed.

Education and mentality.—Ann was in the 1A grade at school and was doing poor work. She entered the first grade at Central School in September, 1930, at the age of six years and six months. She was irregular in attendance because of frequent minor illness. She was transferred from Central to Winslow School and back again to Central during the year and also missed one month's time because of measles. Her teachers consider her a little show-off and not at all interested in her school work.

Personality.—Ann is a slight, hyperactive child. She talks quickly and quite spontaneously. She has dark brown silky hair which waves slightly around her face. She expresses strong likes and dislikes for individuals, as, for example, she said she hated Mrs. Sobral and dearly loved Mrs. Gay. She portrays great heights of enthusiasm in both behavior and speech. She is exceedingly affectionate, bestowing hugs and kisses generously upon those to whom she takes a fancy. She obviously craves much special attention and is happy only when she is the center of attraction. She is sophisticated to the degree of a high-school student and speaks glibly of matters being discussed by adults within her hearing. She loves to dress up and wear pretty clothes. She has a tendency to be a bit saucy and even pert in her remarks.

Visited Mrs. Gillis, former foster-mother. Got some of Ann's clothing, as it was inadvisable to take her on a shopping tour immediately upon her dismissal from the hospital. Mrs. Gillis said she was extremely fond of Ann and wanted to keep in touch with her, even though she would not want to see the child again, because it would be too hard to say goodbye.

Ann seemed quite content in going to her new foster-home. She asked if her mama (Mrs. Gay) could come and see her at her new home but was satisfied with the explanation that she would be staying in her new home but a few days; hence, it would be unlikely that Mrs. Gay would visit her. When she came to the Stanley home she was delighted with the farm animals and went through the entire house on a tour of inspection. When she said quite frankly that she was hungry, Mrs. Stanley told her there was a hot dinner waiting. Ann did not appear at all lonesome or afraid to be left with the new foster-mother.

Letter received from the County Clerk, Hartville, Illinois:

Am unable to find any birth record of Jane Czarny, but according to our adoption records she was two years of age on the 10th day of March, 1926, which would mean this child was born March 10, 1924.

April 24, 1931.—Letter received from Kansas City Immigration Office:

In response to your inquiry regarding the records of Jose and Ann Sobral in connection with your proceedings to have the adopted American-born child of these people made a ward of the Court, the following record appears in our files:

Jose Sobral was born in Orizaba, Mexico, April 26, 1896; came to the United States in 1909 and again in 1911. On October 13, 1918, he was arrested because of suspected rape and, from that time up to September 8, 1922, he was arrested twelve times for robbery, larceny, poolroom keeping, suspicion of violating the Harrison Drug Act, et cetera, but was never convicted as he himself naïvely stated he was a "fixer" for Mexican cases. The woman's name was Ann Baumann. She was born at Hartville, Illinois, April 2, 1905. When this couple was arrested by the police at the Grady Hotel in this city, she was found to be afflicted with gonorrhoea and was sent to the House of the Good Shepherd by the Court until cured. At that time she testified against Jose Sobral, stating that she met this Sobral and went to live with him at 1215 Green Street, that he caused her and two other girls to go out and hustle for him; she said the money she made she gave to Sobral.

During the time she was living with him he took her and another girl to South Bend, Illinois, and each of these girls had intercourse with Mexicans who paid them $3.00 apiece, which money was given to Sobral. After she was cured of her venereal disease, she was paroled to her father in Hartville, Illinois.

Sobral went to Hartville, took the girl, and married her in August, 1922. After he married her he brought her back to the Grady Hotel in Kansas City and she got out on the street and hustled and turned the money over to Sobral.

Sobral was deported to Mexico on the charge that he had been found assisting a prostitute and had been found receiving benefit from the earnings of a prostitute, in December, 1922.

In May, 1928, he was arrested by this office and was sentenced on the charge of re-entering the United States after having been deported, to a term of two years in the United States Penitentiary at Leavenworth, by Judge Rathbon in the United States Court. He also pled guilty to possession and sales of liquor and was sentenced to two years in jail. These two sentences were suspended on condition that he immediately return to Mexico, never to re-enter the United States. He and his wife and, I believe, their adopted child, did leave the United States via automobile and returned to Mexico.

We were informed in January, 1931, that he was living in Indianapolis, Indiana, with this girl and we again had him arrested. He was returned to the jurisdiction of Judge Rathbon, who revoked his parole and sentenced him to the United States Penitentiary at Leavenworth. When he has finished serving his time he will again be deported to Mexico, but he may be again prosecuted before he is deported.

I do not know where Jose and Ann Sobral obtained this six-year-old child that they adopted in 1926, but they both claim that she was an American-born child. That is all our records show.

Later.—Letter written to Kansas City Immigration Office:

We thank you very kindly for your detailed report summarizing the record on Jose and Ann Sobral. We do appreciate your prompt and fine co-operation in this matter.

The Court hearing will be held on April 28, at which time this adopted child of the Sobrals will be made a ward of the Court and will be placed in a foster home

May we assure you again of our real appreciation of your assistance in this case.

Later.—Mrs. Sylvester, probation officer, telephoned. She reported that Mrs. Gay had left Ann's Sunday clothes with her, asking that they be delivered to the child. She had stated that she did not want the child to appear in Court in rags. She also left for Ann a picture of herself and Ann, taken the previous summer. She wants Ann to keep that picture for memory's sake.

Later.—Delivered clothes for Ann at Stanley home. Ann was joyful upon seeing her dress-up clothes again and proceeded to try on her hat and to show off her little silk dresses to the foster-mother. When the case-worker arrived, Ann was dressed in a Dutch costume, a white cap, white apron, white kerchief, and blue dress. The costume belongs to Mrs. Stanley's fifteen-year-old daughter, who used it at a masquerade. Ann was enthusiastic about tripping through the house all dressed up in that fashion. Mrs. Stanley said Ann had not been lonesome at all. She has a good appetite, but apparently her menu is very limited as there are a large number of foods with which she is not at all acquainted. She is quite agreeable to trying a little of each new food, however, and Mrs. Stanley hopes that she will gain in weight while at her home.

Mrs. Stanley is obviously fond of Ann, remarking on her dainty and refined manner. She reminds her much of her own daughter. Mrs. Stanley's daughter arrived home while the case-worker was there and was immediately induced by Ann to read a book to her. Mrs. Stanley said that Ann knows nothing of the rudiments of the Catholic religion, but she is planning to teach them to her.

Later.—Mrs. Sylvester, probation officer, telephoned. The Court hearing will have to be delayed until May 1, 1931, at least, as the summons to Mr. and Mrs. Sobral has not yet been returned.

Later.—Telephoned Mrs. Stanley, foster-mother. Told her of the postponed Court hearing. She said she was glad to be able to keep Ann a little longer.

Later.—Mrs. Gillis, former foster-mother, telephoned. She wanted to know when the Court hearing would be and also inquired about Ann. She was pleased to hear that the child seemed to be happy and contented in her new home.

Later.—Mrs. Gay telephoned. She seemed to be under the impression that she was telephoning a children's institution. She inquired as to Ann's health and was told that the child was wholly well and quite happy. She said she wished she had placed her in a Home long ago, that is, at the time the case-worker had suggested it to her, and then she would not have gotten into so much trouble. She seemed to blame Mrs. Gillis for much of the disturbance. An attempt was made to explain that Mrs. Gillis was not responsible but that the Sobrals had shown themselves wholly unfit to be the legal guardians of a child. Mrs. Gay said that when Mr. Sobral passed through Midland en route to Leavenworth Penitentiary he had begged her to get him out on parole, promising he would then give her Ann. She told him there was nothing she could do to help him. Mrs. Gay said she had sold her former place of business and was living in a three-room house at 412 South Fourth Street. She hopes to adopt Ann as she has a good home for her. Mr. Gay is working every day for a contractor who lives at 807 West Oak Street.

April 29, 1931.—Mrs. Sylvester, probation officer, telephoned. She said that the summons to Mrs. Sobral had been returned but she had received word from Leavenworth Penitentiary that Mr. Sobral could not be found.

Later.—Telephoned United States Attorney's Office. Was told that that office does not have a record of the number which had been given Mr. Sobral upon admission to the penitentiary but they have a record showing that he was sent there on April 8, 1931. He was escorted by a marshal. His real name is Jose Sobral but he used as an alias first name, Joseph. It was suggested that when a letter is written to the Warden at Leavenworth it be explained that Mr. Sobral is there serving a sentence which had been imposed upon him in 1928.

Later.—Telephoned Mrs. Sylvester, probation officer. Gave her the details regarding Mr. Sobral's sentence to Leavenworth and suggested that they be included in a letter written to the Warden, as it would hurry matters to have the summons served on him in person rather than wait for another twenty days, which would be necessary if he were served by publication.

April 30, 1931.—Mrs. Gay in office. She said she had talked with her attorney, Mr. Kerr, and he had told her that he saw no reason why she could not visit Ann in her present boarding-home and that she should go over to the Children's Agency office and ask for permission to do so. She said she had some toys for the child and she craved seeing her once again, even if it were but at a distance.

Mrs. Gay explained that when Ann was first placed with her by the Sobrals she would have been quite willing to give her back at the end of a month as she was not then attached to the child, but during the past year and a half she has learned to care very much for Ann and she cannot bear the thought of being separated from her. She said she would be willing to do anything to get the child. She had thought of taking Ann from Mrs. Gillis' home and going to Pennsylvania with her, but Mr. Kerr had warned her against this as she does not have any legal right to the child. Mrs. Gay said she has given up her past occupation and for three weeks has been living in a three-room house, for which she pays $15 a month rent. Mr. Gay is not able to get work every day but he works whenever it is possible. She said he helped a contractor in building houses, digging sewers, etc.

Mrs. Gay was born in Germany. Her mother died when she was a mere child. She has three married sisters, each of whom has a family, and a father living in Pennsylvania. Her family knows nothing of the way in which she makes a living in Midland. When asked how she got started in that kind of life, she merely shrugged her shoulders and said she did not know. She has lived in Midland ten years and has been engaged in her present occupation for seven years. She said she married Mr. Gay because he was the only man with whom she came in contact who offered her marriage and begged her to leave the House. After her marriage she quit for a few months but drifted back again, as she did not have the pretty things that she had been accustomed to previous to her marriage. She said Mrs. Gillis seems to want to blame Mr. Gay for her type of livelihood, but that is absolutely wrong, as she herself is wholly responsible. She does not take part in the activity herself but keeps girls in the House for that purpose. She had such a small place that she was allowed to have only three girls and recently she had but two girls working for her.

When Mrs. Sobral asked to leave Ann with her, she said she was afraid to take the child as the law would make trouble for her having a child in such a House. She was compelled to keep Ann there for several months as she was in such a terrible physical condition that she knew no strangers would be willing to take her into their home. She never allowed Ann in the same room with any of her girls and did not allow her to eat out of the same dishes or to use the same toilet, as she realized the danger of possible disease infection. She said that Ann never did see a girl in bed. She and Mr. Gay took Ann back to visit Mrs. Gay's relatives in Pennsylvania on Decoration Day, 1930, and at this time Mrs. Gay told her folks that Ann was her own adopted child. She said if only she could get the child now she would leave Midland and go back to live near her sisters. Mr. Gay used to work in a tinshop in Pennsylvania, and she thought probably he could get a similar job if they returned to Pennsylvania at the present time. She said she had not visited Ann oftener at the Gillis home because she realized that was a respectable neighborhood and for Mrs. Gillis' sake she did not want to be seen going there too frequently.

About three months ago Mrs. Sobral came to Midland asking for Ann. She had insisted on Mrs. Gay's taking her to see the child between 9:00 and 11:00 P.M., whereupon Mrs. Gay told her that Ann was with decent folks and they were in bed at that hour, adding that "they are not like you and I." Mrs. Sobral became angry and went to Mr. Cooley, lawyer, trying to get him to assist her in seeing the child; but Mr. Cooley had agreed with Mrs. Gay in that that was no hour to disturb decent people.

Mrs. Gay was told that she must get permission to see Ann from Mrs. Sylvester, probation officer, but she was urged also that she not insist upon seeing her for a while, as it would make it more difficult for the child to remain satisfied in her new foster-home.

May 1, 1931.—Mrs. Stanley, boarding-mother, in office. Mrs. Stanley had come into town to do some shopping and she thought the case-worker would be interested in seeing Ann, hence she brought her into the office. The case-worker was not in.

Mrs. Sylvester, probation officer, telephoned. She said that Mr. Kerr had telephoned her asking that Mrs. Gay be allowed to go out and see Ann. When Mrs. Sylvester told him she did not think this could be arranged, he wondered if the child could be brought in so that Mrs. Gay could see her here. Mrs. Sylvester had said she would have to consult Children's Agency, whereupon Mr. Kerr got rather "uppity" and said that inasmuch as Mrs. Gay had supported the child for three years he thought she should be allowed to have some contact with her. Mrs. Sylvester suggested that it might be well to be frank and tell Mr. Kerr that according to present plans, Mrs. Gay is not considered to have any standing in the case whatsoever. She suggested that case-worker see Mr. Kerr and talk the matter over with him.

May 2, 1931.—Conference with Mr. Kerr, attorney for Mrs. Gay. He was cordial in his manner. He was careful not to commit himself in any way. He asked what future plans the Children's Agency had in mind for Ann. He did make the statement, however, that Mrs. Gay was not the woman to care for the child and that he would not have the audacity to go into Court asking that Ann be given to her. Apparently the Children's Agency's plans met with his approval. He wanted to make sure that he would be notified if any new developments occurred in the Sobral case.

May 8, 1931.—Mrs. Stanley, boarding-mother, in office with Ann. As soon as Ann entered the office she asked to see "Miss Tomlin." On being asked why she wanted to see Miss Tomlinson, she replied, "I want to ask her if I can't stay here always." She also began telling about the baby goslings, chickens, and kittens on the farm.

Later while Ann was talking with Miss Tomlinson, Mrs. Stanley said that the child seems to like the farm. She has Ann play in the side yard a great deal where she can watch her. She and Albert, another boarding-child, play house together. She has her little table in the yard and gathers bouquets for it. She and Albert get along very well. Albert seems to look upon her as a baby sister.

Ann is very good to mind. Mrs. Stanley said she was allowing her to eat anything she wants. She thinks since the child has just come from the hospital this will be good for her.

Told Mrs. Stanley that Ann probably knows a great deal more than the average child of her age and asked if she had seen any evidence of this. Mrs. Stanley said she had seen none, whatsoever, that to her Ann appeared to be a very innocent child.

She has not said anything to Ann about staying with her, but Ann has been anxious to see Miss Tomlinson to ask if she might continue to stay there.

Later.—Talked with Mrs. Sylvester, probation officer. She said that the notice of the Court hearing has been served on Mr. Sobral. She has set the hearing for ten-thirty, May 15. She does not intend to notify either Mr. Kerr or Mrs. Gay of the hearing.

Later.—Mrs. Gillis, former boarding-mother, telephoned. She had visited Mrs. Gay at her new address, and Mrs. Gay had said she was going to prove in Court that she was Ann's real mother and thus she would be fighting for her own flesh and blood. Mrs. Gay intends to fight the case to the finish.

May 9, 1931.—Letter written to the Children's Service, Hartville:

Since our last communication several new developments have occurred in the Sobral case, and it appears to be necessary for us to ask your assistance again.

A dependency petition has been filed on behalf of Barbara, and the Court hearing is to be held on May 15. A summons has been served on both Mr. and Mrs. Sobral. Mr. Sobral is now in Leavenworth Penitentiary, and Mrs. Sobral is said to be getting a divorce from Mr. Sobral.

The woman with whom the Sobrals left Barbara when they passed through Midland en route to Indianapolis is a Mrs. Manuel Gay. She is the manager of a house of prostitution here. She is living with a Mexican by the name of Manuel Gay, to whom she says she is married. Her trade name is Becky West, and she says her maiden name is Mary Polowski.

Mrs. Gay is determined to get possession of Barbara, as she appears to be fond of the child. She has employed an attorney and says she will fight the case to the bitter end. Her most recent plea is that Barbara is her own child and thus she is fighting for her own flesh and blood. She purposes to prove this in Court. On the surface that seems to be an absurd assertion for her to make in view of the few scattered bits of information we have about the Czarny family.

May we ask, however, that you visit Mrs. Czarny and learn the details surrounding the birth of Barbara which can be used as proof in Court, showing that she is absolutely this child's mother? What is the name of the doctor who attended the mother at Barbara's birth? Was the child born at home or in the hospital? What is the name of the father of the child? Were there any witnesses present at the birth other than the doctor? How much did the baby weigh at birth? Was it a normal delivery? What was the term of pregnancy? Does she remember the exact birth date of the child? How old was the child when she was given to the Sobrals? Did Mrs. Czarny ever know the woman who now calls herself Mrs. Gay?

We will leave it to your own good judgment to decide how much should be told Mrs. Czarny about the Sobrals' present condition. Of course, it would be inadvisable to divulge any information regarding Barbara's whereabouts.

We should appreciate as early a reply as possible in view of the fact that the Court hearing occurs next Friday. We thank you kindly for your prompt attention in this matter.

Later.—Mrs. Sylvester, probation officer, telephoned. She said that Judge Arthur has received a letter from Mr. Sobral, asking that Ann be given either to his wife or to his wife's father.

May 11, 1931.—Procured a copy of the letter written to Judge Arthur by Mr. Sobral:

I am writing you in regards to a summons which I received here demanding my presence in Midland, Ill., on May 15. I am informed I can not be there.

Am writing you in regards to the matter, which I trust you will look after. as I and family were on our way from Mexico to Indianapolis, Indiana, we, stopped at 516 Lockwood, at Becky Gay's residence. While there she asked me to let her take my daughter to the church and have her baptised so she would be the child's Godmother. I let her do it. My daughter's name is Barbara Sobral. After that she wanted me to leave her there until my wife and I got settled down; then she said we could come and get her. She also said the child's clothes and board would not cost us anything. I would not consent to this; so Becky gave me several drinks until I became intoxicated, then I told her she could keep my daughter until we were settled down, which we did in Indianapolis, Indiana.

After four months I sent my wife to Midland to get my child, and Becky Gay would not let my wife have her. Nor see her until she gave her the sum of One Thousand Dollars ($1,000) so my wife did not have money to look after the matter with so she came back to Indianapolis. Sometime afterwards we received three letters demanding money for our child, two in English asking One Thousand Dollars. One the third said if we would send Three Hundred Dollars we could have our child if we would pay the rest of the amount of One Thousand Dollars in payments. This has been going on for a year or more as sickness and scarce employment has kept me from getting any money to spare.

Trusting you will look after this matter for me as I do not want my child in the kind of a place as this said woman is operating as I am sure she is sellings alcoholic drinks and running a house of illfame. I do not know who this said Party Ester Tomlinson is. My child was left in the care of Becky Gay.

If my child can be taken away from her I want my wife to have her or my fatherinlaw, Mr. Werner Baumann, 1526 Carlyle Avenue, Hartville, Illinois. I wrote Becky Gay about a month ago about this matter but received no answer. Trusting to hear from you soon.

May 12, 1931.—Discussed at Case Committee meeting the advisability of allowing Ann to remain in her present foster-home, where a twelve-year-old boy was being boarded. The dangers of this situation were recognized, but it was also felt that this home seemed to be particularly well fitted to Ann and Mrs. Stanley could probably be depended upon to give careful supervision. It was decided that the matter should be gone into carefully with Mrs. Stanley, and if she were willing to keep Ann always with her and never allow her to be alone with Albert, it could be tried.

Later.—Miss Saunders, Family Agency, telephoned. She said a letter had been received from the Assistant Warden at Leavenworth Penitentiary, giving Mr. Sobral's version of his rights to Ann. Miss Saunders will give the letter to the Children's Agency.

Later.—Called at Family Agency for the letter from the Assistant Warden, Leavenworth Penitentiary:

A summons has been issued against Joseph Sobral by the Summit County Court at Midland, upon the petition of Esther Tomlinson, presumably for the custody of Barbara Ann Sobral, daughter of Joseph and Ann Sobral, and hearing set for May 15, 1931.

According to Joseph Sobral, at present an inmate of this institution, this child was left with Becky Gay, 516 Lockwood Avenue, Midland, Ill. He believes that this woman and Esther Tomlinson are one and the same party. He states that the child was left with this party after much persuasion on her part and with the understanding that it was only a temporary arrangement. He and his wife were on their way to Indianapolis from Mexico, where inmate had previously been deported. Subsequent to their arrival in Indianapolis, inmate states he sent his wife to Becky Gay at Midland with the intention of bringing the child back to Indianapolis, but Becky Gay refused to give up the child except upon condition that the Sobrals pay her a stipulated sum. Mrs. Sobral returned to Indianapolis without the child. Subsequently letters were received from Becky Gay stating she would relinquish custody of the child for $1,000, of which $300 could be paid at once and the balance in instalments. This amount Sobral refused to pay. He states that his wife, Mrs. Ann Sobral, now residing at 4856 Clark Street, Indianapolis, is in possession of letters to this effect. According to his statements the child is now with Becky Gay or Esther Tomlinson as the case may be. He adds that she is running a house of ill repute, or at any rate is dispensing illicit liquor, and that it is no place for the child. They do not wish to lose control or custody of the child and ask that the pending proceedings be stayed.

Inmate's wife is believed to be working as Ann Baumann for the Ford Motor Company, West La Salle Street, Indianapolis. She can be reached at 4856 Clark Street as above.

This inmate was interviewed about May 1, by Miss Maxine Dawson, Supervisor, Social Service, Bureau of Prisons, Washington, D.C., upon her recent visit to this institution, and it was her intention to investigate the case upon her return to Washington. At that time the summons had not been served upon Sobral. It is doubtful if Miss Dawson has yet arrived in Washington, and as the case requires immediate attention if the hearing which is scheduled for May 15 is to be stopped or postponed, may I ask that you endeavor to stay the hearing until the case can be more thoroughly investigated.

I am forwarding a copy of this letter to Miss Dawson in Washington, as it may be you will desire to communicate with her provided you are able to have the hearing set for some future date.

Letter written in answer to letter from Assistant Warden, Leavenworth Penitentiary:

Your letter of May 11 addressed to Miss Saunders, Family Agency, of this city has been turned over to our organization as we are handling the Sobral case, since we are the children's agency for Summit County.

Before going further into an explanation of the case, may I bring to your attention that the said "Esther Tomlinson" is a social case-worker for the Children's Agency and thus has no connection with the said "Becky Gay."

The Sobral case first came to our attention when a letter was received from the Department of Public Welfare, Indianapolis, Indiana, asking that an attempt be made to persuade Mrs. Becky Gay to return Barbara Ann Sobral to her parents in Indianapolis. In trying to locate Mrs. Gay and the child a detailed investigation was made. After an extensive correspondence between our organization and the agencies in Indianapolis, Kansas City, and South Bend, Illinois, we have found the following information relative to the Sobrals.

[Quotations from the letter written by District Director of Immigration, Kansas City District, received April 24, 1931, and from the letter from the Department of Public Welfare, Indianapolis, Indiana, received March 2, 1931, giving the history and record of the Sobrals are omitted.]

We have considerably more information on this case but this briefly gives a picture of the situation. Barbara, as you no doubt already know, is an adopted child of the Sobrals. Quoting from a certified letter dated February 2, 1931, from the County Clerk, Harrison County, Ill.: "According to our records Jane Czarny was adopted by Joseph Sobral and Ann Sobral under date of July 16, 1926, said child to be hereafter known as Barbara Sobral. This is shown in Adoption Record 54, page 241."

It is obvious that the Sobrals are not a fit influence for the rearing of this child and knowing that Mrs. Gay is a woman of very poor reputation, being a manager of a house of ill-fame in Midland, we were desirous of removing Barbara from these influences as quickly as possible.

We have placed Barbara in one of our approved private boarding-homes, and she is making an excellent adjustment there. She is so happy and satisfied that she begs us repeatedly that she may remain there always. We hope eventually to find a good adoptive home for Barbara as she is an attractive child and if placed in a good environment at this early age, she may develop into a fine, decent, young woman.

Trusting that this letter will serve to explain to you our position in this case, and assuring you that we will be glad to give you any further information you desire, we wish to remain

May 13, 1931.—Visited Mrs. Stanley, boarding-mother, with Superintendent of Children's Agency. Discussed with Mrs. Stanley the possibility of allowing Ann to remain in her home, stressing the point that the closest supervision would be necessary, as ordinarily the Children's Agency was opposed to placing children of opposite sex of approximately the same age in the same foster-home. Mrs. Stanley promised that close supervision would be possible and that she would take Ann with her whenever she left home and leave Albert Reese, the other child being boarded in the Stanley home by the Children's Agency, with Mr. Stanley. Mrs. Stanley was told that Ann has considerable knowledge of the "goings-on" at Mrs. Gay's home. Mrs. Stanley said she had never seen any indication of ultra-sophistication on the part of Ann. Mrs. Stanley has become fond of Ann and wants to keep her. Ann and Albert play together without any trouble, and Mrs. Stanley always watches them carefully.

Ann has asked Mrs. Stanley's permission to call her mother. It was explained that Ann has no mother of her own, and Mrs. Stanley said she would be willing to allow Ann to call her mother if she asked to do so. The Reese children have never called her mother because they have their own mother; hence, they are accustomed to calling her "Mrs. Stanley."

Ann was enthusiastic about showing the case-worker all the new stock which had been born since her arrival at the Stanley home, such as goslings, chickens, pigs, and colts. Mrs. Stanley promised to bring Ann into Midland for the Court hearing.

May 15, 1931.—*Hearing.* Ann declared a dependent ward of the County Court, and Mrs. Sylvester, probation officer, made legal guardian with power to consent to adoption, the County to pay the Children's Agency at the rate of fifty cents a day for her care.

Mrs. Stanley brought Ann in for the hearing. Ann was prettily clad in a pink silk dress and wore short pink silk socks, clothing which had been purchased for her by Mrs. Gay.

Later.—Mrs. Gay in office. She had a telegram with her which was signed by her sister, Hazel Draper, from Pennsylvania, stating that she would be willing to take Ann for adoption. Mrs. Gay said she had sold all her property and intended to leave for Pennsylvania if she could take the child with her. The case-worker was not in, and she was advised to return the following morning, which she did not do.

Later.—Visited Mrs. Gillis, former foster-mother. Delivered the handbag which she had loaned at the time of Ann's transfer from the hospital to her new foster-home. Mrs. Gillis gave the case worker a large doll which had belonged to Ann and also a nickel and three pennies which Ann had saved.

May 16, 1931.—Mrs. Gillis telephoned. She said she had visited Mrs. Gay at the address of 412 South Fourth Street. She found no one at home but was told by neighbors that Mrs. Gay had returned to her former address of 516 Lockwood Avenue about a week previous. She has apparently gone back to her former occupation. Mrs. Gillis said she had met Mrs. Gay's sister from Pennsylvania during one of her visits to Midland. She is older and more coarse-looking than Mrs. Gay and is in the same business as Mrs. Gay. She has a little girl of her own.

May 18, 1931.—Letter received from the Assistant Warden, Leavenworth Penitentiary:

I wish to thank you heartily for your enlightening report on the Sobral case. I sincerely regret having had to accept the inference of Mr. Sobral which inadvertently linked your name with that of Becky Gay. However, it was felt that the case warranted immediate action if the statements made by Sobral were to any extent reliable.

Your interest in the case and the action taken are indeed commendable in view of the facts set forth in your letter. I am sure that Miss Maxine Dawson, Supervisor, Social Service at Washington, referred to in my letter to Miss Saunders, will be pleased to learn of the outcome of the case. A copy of your letter is being forwarded to her today. If she desires additional data from you she will undoubtedly get in touch with you. In so far as Sobral is interested as to what is being done, I shall advise him accordingly.

May 19, 1931.—Visited Mrs. Stanley, foster-mother. Found that Mrs. Stanley and Ann had gone in to Elton, Illinois, and were unavoidably detained there because Mrs. Stanley's car had broken down. It had been the purpose of the case-worker to bring Ann into Midland for a physical examination. Word was left with Mr. Stanley, asking that Mrs. Stanley bring Ann to Midland some time during the week.

Later.—Visited Dr. McCluggage. Found that on April 22, 1929, Dr. McCluggage had treated Ann for eczema and impetigo. He had prescribed a salve of ammoniated mercury. On July 28, 1930, Ann had been brought to him with a severe cough. The diagnosis was coryza and infected tonsils. On July 29, 1930, a tonsillectomy was performed by Dr. McCluggage at St. Francis Hospital.

Dr. McCluggage has been treating Mrs. Gay for several years. In December, 1923, she was found to have a four plus Wassermann. Dr. McCluggage has no record of a Wassermann having been taken since that time. He has taken vaginal smears every month in accordance with the police regulations, and her smears have always been negative. Manuel Gay has been coming to Dr. McCluggage for G. C. treatments, although it has been several months since his last treatment. Mrs. Gay had come to Dr. McCluggage's office a few weeks previous, asking him to swear that Ann was her own child. He told her that his two brief contacts with the child were not sufficient for him to make any such assertion. Dr. McCluggage was told briefly that Ann was the adopted child of a couple who were of the same caliber as the Gays and that the child had been placed under the guardianship of the Court so that Mrs. Gay no longer was in touch with her.

May 25, 1931.—Mrs. Gay in office. Mrs. Gay said she had been sent to the Children's Agency office by Mrs. Sylvester, probation officer, to whom she had already shown a telegram supposedly from Mrs. Gay's sister, a Mrs. Hazel Draper, 2618 Dearborn Street, Johnsonburg, Pennsylvania. In that telegram Mrs. Draper expressed her willingness to take Barbara for legal adoption.

Mrs. Gay said her sister is a good, respectable woman, who is married and has three children of her own. Mrs. Gay's father, Mr. Joe Polowski, is living in Johnsonburg also. Mrs. Gay said she came to the United States when she was twelve years old. She went to school in the United States for a couple of weeks only and then went to work in a glass factory in Johnsonburg. She described herself then as a "foreign lady."

It was pointed out to Mrs. Gay that if Barbara were placed with her sister it would mean exactly the same thing as if she were placed with Mrs. Gay herself, and even though she thought she had sworn off from her past life, she was not a fit influence for a child. She insisted, however, that she would fight the case. She said she was planning to visit in Pennsylvania over Decoration Day and she wished she could take Ann with her. She was told that this would be impossible, and it was suggested, if she had sold all her property in Midland as she said she had done, she could just as well move to Pennsylvania permanently at the present time since Mr. Gay did not have steady work in Midland anyway. Mrs. Gay said she had not moved back to 516 Lockwood Avenue as had been the report but that she was living with a Mrs. Dick Barney at 2015 South Tenth.

May 26, 1931.—Letter written to the Assistant Warden, Leavenworth Penitentiary:

We are in receipt of your letter of the 16th and are glad that our explanation was adequate in making clear our interest in the Sobral case.

We were pleased to note also that prisoners' stories are really listened to by the prison officials, as I think it is the popular idea that this is not true in prisons.

We shall be glad to give Miss Dawson any further information she may desire.

May 27, 1931.—Talked with Mrs. Sylvester, probation officer. Told her that Mrs. Gay had come to the office asking that her sister's home be investigated and that Children's Agency thought this should not be done as it would only give false hopes to Mrs. Gay. Told Mrs. Sylvester that it was thought that Mrs. Gay should be definitely given to understand that she could have no more contact with Ann. Mrs. Sylvester said she would try to do this.

May 28, 1931.—Letter received from Mrs. Sobral:

Am writing you these few lines in regards to my Baby. Its true that I received summons from court but was unable to appear, but now Miss Tomlinson I will appreciate your kindness very much if you would be able to give me some information about the Baby, I am in a position to take good care of the Baby as I work every day at the Ford Motor Co. and the people I live with would take very good care of the Baby for me. Its true that Im separated from my husband but I feel that I should have the Baby.

Dont you think so Miss Tomlinson?

I would like to write you a long letter but I think I better wait until I hear from you and about Barbara.

May 29, 1931.—Letter written to Mrs. Sobral:

In reply to your letter of May 23 I wish to state that Barbara has been made a ward of the Summit County Court of Illinois and that the Probation Officer of that Court is now her legal guardian.

Barbara has thus been removed from the custody of Mrs. Manuel Gay and will not be given into her custody again.

May I suggest, moreover, that you do not plan to have the child with you any more either, as we think that she would not get the proper care under your supervision? We are well acquainted with the kind of life you lived previous to your marriage to Mr. Sobral and also all about the life you and he lived in South Bend and Hartville. You will recall that all such details were made known through an investigation made by the Kansas City Immigration Office at the time of Mr. Sobral's deportation. We have had other sources of information as well.

No doubt you have become fond of this child, but if you are sincerely interested in Barbara's welfare, you will realize that it is to her benefit that she be placed in a good respectable family where she can be reared amidst all good influences. At the present time Barbara is with a private family and appears happy and contented.

Trusting that you will appreciate our viewpoint in this matter and that you will realize that the Court now has full legal authority over Barbara, we wish to remain

June 1, 1931.—Telephoned Mrs. Gillis, former boarding-mother. Asked her whether or not she would be willing to give the Children's Agency the clothing that Mrs. Gay had bought for Ann. She seemed to be unwilling to do so, explaining that she had a family in the neighborhood whom she was helping and she had given part of the clothing to one of the little girls in that family, as the mother had died and the father was unsteadily employed. She said she also has a niece whom she helps at times and since Mrs. Gay owes her $10 she thought she would have the right to dispose of the clothing to these families in whom she is particularly interested. She was told that the Children's Agency was quite willing to have her do as she pleased about it and merely wanted to know definitely what disposal was made of them before making additional purchases for Ann.

June 10, 1931.—Visited Mrs. Stanley, foster-mother. Ann and Albert Reese were stemming gooseberries and were racing with each other, the winner having been promised by Mrs. Stanley the largest piece of gooseberry pie. Ann thus far was ahead of Albert. Ann was her usual excitable, demonstrative self. She appeared happy and dashed here and there showing the case-worker animals around the farm. She insisted on cutting a bouquet of roses to give to the case-worker.

Mrs. Stanley said that she has some difficulty in insisting on Ann obeying her, as Ann becomes saucy at times but never has actually refused to obey. Ann never speaks of being lonesome for anyone. Mrs. Stanley has fixed over a couple of old dresses which belonged to her own daughter so that Ann can wear them about the house; hence, it is unnecessary to buy any additional clothing until the opening of school in the fall. Ann enjoys running about the yard barefooted.

June 11, 1931.—Letter received from the Children's Service, Hartville, Illinois:

About a month ago I endeavored to see Mrs. Czarny, real mother of Barbara. I was unable to locate her in the neighborhood. Yesterday I was successful in finding Steve Czarny, father of Barbara, at home. He advised me that Barbara's own mother gave birth to Barbara at their home March 10, 1924. Mrs.

Czarny deserted her husband and children four different times. She deserted him again when Barbara was about one and one-half years old. Mr. Czarny had been ill for about eighteen months with an eye infection and could not care for the baby. He is not sure that he is the real father, and the Sobrals desired to take the child, so he gave her into their hands. He advised me that Mrs. Czarny was attended by a midwife named Veronica Jelinek and directed me to her. He knows no one by the name of Manuel Gay, Becky West, or Mary Polowski.

He would not consent to the return of Barbara into his own home though he is very fond of his two daughters ten and eleven years of age. If Barbara were returned he would break up his home. He suspects that Arthur Watkins, whereabouts unknown, is the real father of Barbara.

I visited Mrs. Veronica Jelinek, 1516 West Lincoln Street, midwife. From her certificate stub I obtained information that she attended at the birth of Jane Czarny, 1236 Green Street, who was born March 10, 1924, at 8 P.M. Father's name, Steve Czarny, age twenty-eight, laborer. Mother's name, Julia Prokes, age twenty, Hungarian. Certificate delivered December 18, 1924. Mrs. Jelinek has attended Mrs. Czarny at her four confinements. The last baby was born in 1928, and Mrs. Czarny confessed Mr. Czarny was not the real father of the child.

I also visited Harrison County Clerk and found the registration of birth as reported by Mrs. Jelinek, but the spelling had been changed to Jane Karny. Their file number is 30838.

June 12, 1931.—Mrs. Stanley in office with Ann. Mrs. Stanley had brought Ann to town to be taken to the dentist. An appointment was made for her that morning

June 13, 1931.—Letter written to the Children's Service, Hartville, Illinois:

We do appreciate your detailed report on your visit to the Czarny home.

Barbara is making a splendid adjustment in her new foster home and the Court hearing went off smoothly.

Thank you again kindly for your assistance in this case.

July 8, 1931.—Visited the foster-home. Found that Mrs. Stanley and Ann had gone to town. Mr. Stanley said that Ann was getting along as well as usual.

July 10, 1931.—Mrs. Stanley telephoned. Dr. Rupp had examined Ann's teeth but had not done anything. He said the teeth were decayed but did not think it worth while to fill them as she would lose them soon.

July 16, 1931.—Visited Mrs. Stanley, foster-mother. Ann came rushing toward the case-worker in her usual demonstrative fashion. She seemed happy and began bringing several new playthings which she had acquired, including several dolls and some books. Mrs. Stanley said she was eating much better as she now eats everything except oranges, bananas, and pop. Ann said she had become ill because of eating too much of these.

Mrs. Stanley had taught her several prayers, and Ann offered to say them all for the case-worker, which she did in an exceedingly rapid manner. Mrs. Stanley was also teaching Ann the ABC's and some simple problems in arithmetic. Ann was unable to write anything at all except her name. Mrs. Stanley was hopeful that she might be able to handle the second-grade work rather than start in the first grade again and thus lose an entire year. She expected to talk with the local school teacher and get some hints regarding subject matter which Ann could be taught during the summer time. Fifteen minutes a day were spent on Ann's school work.

August 3, 1931.—Talked with Mrs. Sylvester, probation officer. Mrs. Gillis, former boarding-mother, had recently telephoned Mrs. Sylvester, asking about Ann. She said that Mrs. Gay had told her that she had placed Ann with her sister, who was going to adopt her. Mrs. Gay had said that when she got Ann from the boarding-home she was so under-nourished and weak she could scarcely walk.

Told Mrs. Sylvester Ann seemed to be getting along very well in her boarding-home.

Later.—Met Ann and Mrs. Stanley on the street. As soon as Ann saw the case-worker she rushed up and bestowed a very wet kiss on her cheek. She then began to tell what they had had for dinner, having apparently eaten downtown, and said she had gotten two new dresses, pointing to the one she had on as one of them.

August 6, 1931.—Mrs. Gay in office. Mrs. Gay said she would like to buy some clothing for Ann as she would soon be starting to school. Not knowing the exact size, she offered to leave money for a pair of shoes. After a conference with the Superintendent, it was decided that it would be inadvisable for this organization to accept any money from Mrs. Gay, as it was possible she had some ulterior motive in mind; hence, Mrs. Gay was told that inasmuch as she could not be given permission to see the child, it was better that she did not buy clothing for the child either. She asked if it would be all right to bring Ann's old clothing to the office and she was given permission to do that.

August 7, 1931.—Mrs. Gay in office. The case-worker was not in, but Mrs. Gay left a large box of clothing for Ann. Most of the clothing was new. A list of the clothing was as follows: four new print dresses, two new slips, three new bloomers, four new handkerchiefs, three new pairs half-socks, one pair of new slippers, one old suit of underwear, one old dress and bloomers to match, two old balls, one old doll, one bag of candy, one bag of "jacks," and two paper-doll cut-out books.

August 11, 1931.—Post card from Ann.

August 12, 1931.—Visited Mrs. Stanley, foster-mother. Delivered the new clothing to Ann, and she went into great ecstasy as the package was unwrapped before her eyes. She recognized certain old belongings of hers and was told that they had come from Mrs. Gay but she did not ask who had bought the rest of the clothing for her, and nothing was said of the source. The shoes were too small for her and so the case-worker decided to attempt their exchange. Ann exclaimed over the fact that the doll included in the package made her seventh doll.

Mrs. Stanley said that Ann had had a grand time visiting at Sandy Beach over the week end and they were planning to go again the following week end. Ann went bathing and she was permitted to dance with Mrs. Stanley's five-year-old nephew while the adults danced together.

August 27, 1931.—Mrs. Stanley, foster-mother, in office with Ann. She said she would take Ann's shoes and have them changed for a larger size. Mrs. Stanley was on her way to the State Fair. Ann was the usual happy, demonstrative child.

September 1, 1931.—Visited Mrs. Stanley. Mrs. Stanley was not home, but Mr. Stanley talked with the case-worker about Ann's school work. She is trying to do the second-grade work, and the teacher thinks, with help at home, she can carry the work. He said that his wife had been calling neighbors in order to get secondhand books for Ann and Albert Reese. On Ann's first day at school she said she did not like it but after that first day she became enthusiastic, stating that she preferred the country school to the city school.

September 14, 1931.—Mrs. Stanley in office. Mrs. Stanley said that Ann is to have her first communion in a few weeks and that she will provide all the necessary white communion clothes. Ann has to be helped a lot with school work, as she seems to have little or no background in any of the studies. She thinks that Ann will be able to hold her own in the second grade, however, with plenty of help at home.

October 6, 1931.—Mrs. Stanley, foster-mother, in office. She brought in a winter coat of Ann's which needed cleaning badly and said that she could get it cleaned for forty cents. Consent for this was given.

Ann is getting along splendidly. Her school work seems to be going very well, except that she is having difficulty with reading. Mrs. Stanley had coached her in spelling and writing during the summer but hardly knew how to do it in reading as Ann did not seem to be able to read at all.

When questioned as to whether the children were ever alone after school, Mrs. Stanley said she is always particular to be at home by the time school is out. Today she does not have to be back, however, as she has a friend visiting her who is at home.

Ann does not mention Becky West any more. One day when they were out riding and were near her former boarding-home, Ann had said, "That's where I used to live." No one replied, and Ann did not say anything further about it.

October 6, 1931.—Visited the Stanleys. Mrs. Stanley was not at home, but talked with Mr. Stanley. Suggested to him that it would be better if his wife had the two foster-children come home for a hot lunch at noon. He agreed that he thought that would be much the better idea, as he himself had always had a hot noon-day meal when he went to school. Mr. Stanley said it is a pity that they do not have another girl about Ann's age so that she could have a play companion. The neighbor children live too far distant for her to play with them.

October 7, 1931.—See clipping from *Illinois News*. (The said Manuel Gray was Manuel Gay, the husband of Becky West, the woman with whom the Sobrals had left Ann at one time.)

SHOOTS MAN CONVERSING WITH HIS WIFE

MANUEL GRAY WOUNDED BY JOHN CUTLER AT THE NORTH STATION
MAY NOT RECOVER

Manuel Gray, 516 Lockwood Avenue, was shot and perhaps fatally wounded early last night by John "Bull" Cutler, 718 South Seventh Street. The shooting took place at the east entrance of the North Railroad Station about 8 o'clock. Cutler was arrested by police at the scene of the shooting and was held pending further investigation of the affair. Cutler's wife, Fern, who was talking to Gray at the time of the shooting, also was arrested, but after being questioned by authorities, was released. Gray, who is employed as a laborer on the clearing of land for Eagle Lake, was reported in a critical condition at St. Francis Hospital at an early hour this (Wednesday) morning. The bullet, a .38 calibre slug, entered Gray's throat and lodged in the spinal cord near the base of the skull. Assistant State's Attorney James Farney, who arrived at the scene of the shooting before the police, took charge of the investigation and ordered Cutler, his wife, and Mrs. John Farba and Mrs. Pauline Leek arrested.

Mrs. Leek, who lives at 325 South Fifth Street, and Mrs. Farba, who gave her address as 2015 Lamont Avenue, were with Cutler's wife at the time of the shooting, having walked from the former's home to the railroad station. Cutler admitted the shooting when questioned by Farney and police. He told authorities that Gray had been going out with his wife; and when he found the couple together, Gray threatened him, and attempted to draw a revolver. "I was watching my wife tonight and saw her with the other two women walking south on Fifth Street about 7:45 o'clock. After getting in the downtown district the three went to the railroad station. After remaining inside for a few minutes I noticed them go out the east door to the sidewalk," Cutler told authorities. "They were outside only a few minutes when I saw Gray coming from the north to meet them. My wife called to him, and the three women went over to meet him. I was furious and went through the station to the place where the four were standing. Gray reached for his gun, and at the same instant I pulled mine, and fired." Cutler told authorities that he remained on the scene until police arrived and arrested him. Mrs. Cutler, when questioned by Farney, said that she had not been living with her husband for about four months. She denied going out with Gray, authorities said. "I've seen him on the street and talked to him, but as for going out with him . . . . No!" the woman declared. "My husband told me many times that he was going to kill Gray if he ever caught me with him, and when I saw Manuel tonight I knew that something was going to happen when John came," Mrs. Cutler in her statement to police said. Gray was questioned at the hospital by Farney and in a statement said that, while he had a revolver, he did not attempt to draw it. Police told of taking the weapon out of Gray's pocket while he was lying on the walk near the station. Gray also told Farney that he had never been out with Cutler's wife. "I've seen her on the street, but I've never been out with her," the wounded man declared. Mrs. Leek and Mrs. Farba when questioned told about the shooting and both admitted to police that they ran as soon as Cutler walked up to where his wife and Gray were standing at the station. Lee Downing, station porter at the North Railroad station, told police that he took the revolver from Cutler after the shooting and held him until police arrived.

October 8, 1931.—Clipping from *Illinois News:*

MAN SHOT BY WOMAN'S IRATE HUSBAND DIES

MANUEL GRAY SUCCUMBS WHILE JOHN CUTLER, ASSAILANT, IS HELD BY POLICE

Manuel Gray died at St. Francis Hospital about 5:15 P.M. Wednesday as result of a gunshot wound inflicted Tuesday evening by John Cutler. Cutler was formally charged with murder in a warrant issued through the state's attorney's office last night. He is being held in the city prison without bond. Gray was fatally wounded by Cutler about 8 P.M. Tuesday while standing near the east entrance to the North depot. He was conversing with Cutler's wife, Fern, and two of the latter's women friends at the time the shot was fired. Coroner Norman Osborne conducted an inquest into Gray's death at 2:30 P.M. today. Mrs. Cutler and her friends, Mrs. John Farba and Mrs. Leek, are expected to testify that they did not see Gray draw his revolver from his pocket when accosted by Cutler. Following the shooting Tuesday evening, Cutler waited at the North station until police arrived and then surrendered. He admitted the shooting, police reported. Mrs. Cutler and her two friends were detained for questioning after the shooting fray but later were released. Alleged relationship between Mrs. Cutler and Gray is believed to have been the motive for Cutler's act. Mrs. Cutler has denied her husband's accusations, and Gray, questioned at the hospital by Assistant State's Attorney James Farney, said he "had never gone out with Mrs. Cutler, and had only a speaking acquaintance with her."

October 13, 1931.—Mrs. Stanley, foster-mother, in office. Mrs. Stanley got an order for some heavy underwear, dresses, nightgown, and hose. She said that Ann is still poor in her reading but that she is being helped at home. Mrs. Stanley has been allowing Ann to take her lunch to school as she has no girl to play with at home and Mrs. Stanley thinks that playing with girls about her own age is a valuable experience. The case-worker agreed that was true but that this experience should be made possible some other way rather than necessitating her having to eat a cold lunch daily when a hot one is so easily accessible.

November 2, 1931.—Visited Ann at school. Ann was playing hilariously with the other children during the recess period. She exuberantly told the case-worker of the stars that she had been receiving for good work at school. According to the teacher Ann's main difficulty is in reading; she does not recognize syllables in words. The teacher thought Ann was improving, although it seems difficult for her to concentrate long enough to get the benefit of help which the teacher might be willing to give her. The teacher thinks Ann is a sweet child and said she acts fairly well with the other children, although she has a habit of wanting to boss them a little too much.

November 30, 1931.—Mrs. Stanley in office. She wanted to know what plans had been made for the children's Christmas and she was told nothing definite had been decided as yet but that word would be sent her as soon as a decision had been made. She said Ann complained about being cold, and Mrs. Stanley thought she ought to be wearing shoes rather than slippers.

Mrs. Stanley said that Ann had her first communion on October 4, 1931, at Our Lady of Sorrows Church, Father Huffman, Elton, Illinois.

December 23, 1931.—Mrs. Gay in office. She left a doll for Ann's Christmas present. She also wanted the size of Ann's shoes, saying that she would buy a pair for her. The regular case-worker was not in; and Mrs. Gay said she would return the following day, which she did not do, however.

December 24, 1931.—Christmas card received from Ann.

January 11, 1932.—Visited Mrs. Stanley, foster-mother. Procured material for a social history for the Child Guidance Clinic.

I. IDENTIFYING INFORMATION

Name—Ann Sobral. Address—Mrs. A. T. Stanley, Elton, Illinois.

Age—7 yrs. 10 mos. Birthplace—South Bend, Illinois. Birthday—3-10-24.

Color—White. School grade—2nd.

Name of father—unknown.

Name of mother—Julia Czarny, South Bend, Illinois.

Name of siblings: Unknown. (It is reported that there are three half-sisters.)

Name of person referring: Children's Agency.

II. IMMEDIATE REASON FOR REQUESTING EXAMINATION

Patient is legally eligible for adoption but before an adoptive home is found it is desired that more specific knowledge be gotten relative to patient's mental and personality status.

III. PERSONAL HISTORY

Behavior.—When patient was first placed in the present foster home, she took a brooch belonging to the foster mother and lost it. The foster mother explained to her that everything about the house belonged to her and that patient must never take anything without first asking the foster mother. Since then patient had shown no tendency toward taking anything not her own. No problems of truancy, lying, or sex have been evident.

Control and supervision.—Whenever any form of discipline seems necessary, foster mother deprives patient of something of which she is especially fond, such as candy or ice cream when they go to town. No corporal punishment has ever been deemed necessary. Patient reacts quickly and deeply to any correction: the slightest sign of disapproval on the part of the foster mother is sufficient to modify patient's behavior.

Outstanding personality traits.—Patient is of a naturally cheerful and enthusiastic temperament. She is active and "always on the go." Her energy is well directed rather than that resultant from a nervousness. She is neat about her appearance. She adores pretty clothes and raves about the most insignificant new article bought for her.

Patient is exceedingly demonstrative in her affection. If anyone pays any special attention to her, she is ready to throw her arms about that person's neck and bestow kisses, even at the first meeting. Patient became happily adjusted immediately upon placement in the Children's Agency's foster home.

Patient is overjoyed whenever she is praised. She likes to have people compliment her on her prettiness and her pretty clothes. Patient plays well with the other children. She is more of a leader than a follower, as she is very outspoken and does not hesitate to make suggestions regarding what she wants done.

Developmental history.—Nothing is known of this phase of patient's life.

Habits and hygiene.—Patient retires at about 8:00 P.M. and rises at 7:30 or 8:00 A.M. She sleeps alone and sleeps quietly.

Patient has a hearty appetite. At first there was some difficulty in getting her to eat a variety of foods but now she eats a little of everything placed before her. She has good table manners.

When patient first came to the foster home she wet the bed almost every night but now she does this only occasionally, approximately once a month. Although patient is allowed to drink all the milk she wants for supper, she is not permitted to drink any water after 4:00 P.M.

Sex.—While patient was being boarded in a private home selected by a Mrs. Gay, a family friend, there were some reports indicating an irregular sex interest on the part of patient. Patient revealed in her conversation with the foster mother an extensive fund of sex knowledge from her contacts with Mrs. Gay, who is a prostitute by trade. The foster mother would hear sex matters discussed (in patient's conversation when playing with other little girls). One time she found that a neighbor girl had taken down her bloomers and was exhibiting herself to patient. Patient was at that time fond of dancing the hula-hula dance and turning somersaults. When she played with dolls she made a point of pulling up their clothes as far as possible. This sex interest seems to have disappeared since coming to her present foster home, probably largely because there has been no influence that would keep such ideas present in her mind. Her playmates are new, and she no longer is in contact with Mrs. Gay. Patient was cognizant of what occurred at Mrs. Gay's place of business. For instance, she told the former foster mother that she was going to have beautiful clothes and ride around in a big car like Mrs. Gay and in order to have these luxuries she would do as Mrs. Mrs. Gay, namely, "put a man to bed." She explained that she had peeked through the keyhole and seen what went on in Mrs. Gay's place.

Medical history.—Patient had eczema and impetigo at six years and measles at seven years. When given a complete medical examination on 5-22-31, her general condition was found to be normal. Patient's teeth were cared for in June, 1931.

Interests and recreation.—Patient has no special abilities in handwork. She is fond of music. She enjoys listening to the radio and then goes about the house singing the songs which she has heard. She has sung in special church programs, and the director says she has the best voice and the best musical appreciation of any one in the group.

She enjoys playing with dolls and with live animals, especially puppies. Her quick and whole-hearted adjustment in her present foster home was due in part to her enthusiastic interest in the farm animals, which was an entirely new experience for her. She is taken to see a movie on the average of once a month. She also attends community programs sponsored by the church and school in the rural district in which she is now living.

Her most intimate playmate is a twelve-year-old boy who is being boarded in the same foster home. Her other playmate is the foster mother's five-year-old nephew, who visits the foster home almost daily. This little boy and patient enjoy "playing school" with patient as the teacher.

School.—Patient was in the first grade three semesters and did not pass in the spring of 1931. However, she had been so irregular in her attendance on account of her changing family status, and she seemed so alert and quick of comprehension, that in September, 1931, the teacher was asked to allow her to try second-grade work. The teacher agreed to this plan and she is carrying the second-grade work in fine order, being among the best in the class.

IV. HOME AND NEIGHBORHOOD

(Here was included a brief report on the child's family and background history.)

V. SOURCES OF INFORMATION

Mrs. A. T. Stanley, foster mother, Elton, Illinois.

Miss Sarah Shuman, teacher.

Children's Agency case record.

January 16, 1932.—Ann given physical examination by Drs. Miller and Sawyer.

January 21, 1932.—Ann examined at Child Guidance Clinic. Report secured:

Dr. Miller reports that physical examination, including blood Wassermann, is negative except for one carious tooth and enlarged anterior cervical lymph nodes, which are probably secondary to the carious tooth. She should consult a dentist for treatment of the carious tooth.

Psychological examination gives her a mental age of eight years nine months upon the Stanford-Binet scale, which, with her chronological age of seven years ten months, gives her an intelligence quotient of 112, a superior rating. In the examination she was alert, spontaneous, and responsive. Her reading was not quite up to the level of her general ability.

In the psychiatric examination patient was frank, open, and responsive to the examiner. She seems to be a rather normal child. Her vivid imagination made somewhat easier the investigation of her fantasy life, and there seemed to be little evidence of any preoccupation with sexual memories related to the previous unwholesome environment. Her memories of this period also seem centered more particularly about the presents given her by Mr. and Mrs. Gay than by any preoccupation with sexual observations she might have had the opportunity to make.

We see no evidence to indicate any influences resulting from her previous environment which would interfere with her making a good adjustment in an adoptive home, though it is impossible, of course, to predict what latent impressions the sexual awakening at the time of puberty might call forth in activity. A good home environment, however, during the next few years will undoubtedly do very much to fortify her already rather good adjustment.

ROBERT M. THORPE, M.D., *Psychiatrist*

Assets and liabilities were listed as follows:

ASSETS

1. Patient's happy and affectionate personality.
2. Patient's apparent physical well-being.
3. Patient's apparent readiness to forget her past unwholesome experiences.

LIABILITIES

1. Mother's history of immoral living.
2. Paternal history unknown.

January 26, 1932.—Mrs. Gillis, former foster-mother, telephoned. She inquired after Ann's welfare and was told that Ann was well physically, seemed happy in her home, and was doing satisfactory school work. Mrs. Gillis said she hoped that some day she would be able to see Ann again.

January 28, 1932.—Conference with Miss Tate and staff, Illinois Children's Service. The possibility of a free home for Ann was discussed, and the task of attempting to find a home for her was given to Miss Cooley of the Southern District.

January 29, 1932.—Letter written to the Children's Service, Hartville, Illinois:

You will recall our correspondence relative to the Sobral case in June, 1931, at which time you visited the Garfield Park Community House, South Bend, Illinois, near the home of Barbara's own mother, Mrs. Steve Czarny.

In your letter of June 10, 1931, you told of a visit to the Czarny home, at which time you talked with Mr. Czarny when his wife was not at home. You procured some very valuable information at that time, but we are anxious to know a few more facts as the time has arrived when we want to place Barbara in an adoptive home.

We know practically nothing of the maternal and paternal family history. May we ask that you interview Mrs. Czarny with a view to learning as much as possible about her own family history and that of Barbara's father. What was the mother's maiden name? The date and place of her birth? Will you describe her appearance (build, coloring, refined, or ordinary)? What education does she have? How does she impress you in regard to intelligence? What kind of work has she ever done? What was her father's occupation? What kind of early childhood did she have (happy, hard-working, strict discipline, numerous siblings)?

Whom does Mrs. Czarny claim as the father of Barbara? Does she say it is Arthur Watkins, whom Mr. Czarny suspects? What does she know of that man's early family history? What was his nationality? Was he foreign born? What was his occupation and education? What does she know of his character?

We will be glad to get any information available, especially any items which have a favorable tone to them as little Barbara's past contacts are far from being in her favor when an adoptive home is to be considered. Thank you most kindly for your co-operation.

February 9, 1932.—A letter and package of family photographs were sent from the Children's Service, Hartville, Illinois:

Some time ago Mrs. Steve Czarny, mother of Barbara Sobral, came to my office asking that the visitor confer with her through a neighbor when in South Bend. Today I visited the mother, first going to 1521 Locust Street, the home of Frank and Flora Radl, who in an exceedingly friendly way promised to go two blocks to get the mother to confer with visitor at the George Bartak home, 1614 Locust Street, because in the Radl home a male cousin of Mr. Czarny also lives. In a remarkably short time Mrs. Czarny came to see me.

Mrs. Czarny is a very pleasant, refined woman with strong affections and a kind heart. Her maternal instincts are strong. She is quite an attractive woman, about five feet tall, weighs one hundred and seventy-five pounds, has blue eyes and medium-light hair. She was dressed very neatly and in good taste.

I confess she impressed me most sympathetically as a very much injured woman, although there was no objectionable bitterness, rather a natural regret because of everything that has happened. She would do anything to obtain the return of Barbara to her home and suffers much because she cannot have her and her other baby with her.

Mrs. Czarny is confident that she is the only bad one in the maternal grandparents' family and still says she is not naturally bad, although because of her strong affections she has always appealed to men. She vows that her husband is the father of Barbara, although out of jealousy and suspicion he will not accept the paternity. He is a hard-working, thrifty man, and as she states, has love for no one but himself, although she is aware he is very fond of her and would do anything possible for her and their two daughters, Emily Czarny, who will be twelve on June 2, and Mary, who will be eleven on June 28. The husband talks too much so that many times she has had to leave the house to get away from him. He has also been a hard-drinking man. He has been out of full-time employment for months but draws an occasional day's pay as core-maker with Young Radiator Company near by.

Mrs. Czarny will be twenty-eight on September 5 and Mr. Czarny was thirty-six on November 8. Both were born in the old country. Mrs. Czarny gave birth to all four children before she was twenty years old. She was married by a Justice of the Peace at Valley View, Indiana, having eloped to get married.

Mr. and Mrs. Czarny have never agreed religiously. He is Greek Orthodox and she is Roman Catholic. Emily and Mary consequently are receiving no church religious instruction. They do attend sometimes the neighborhood Sunday School at the Garfield Park Community Center.

Mrs. Czarny tells about living at 1732 Grove Avenue, South Bend, in two rooms. There were three men roomers, the husband's nephew, Arthur Watkins, and the minister who baptized her babies, with them. The pastor was particularly her friend and objected to Mr. Czarny's treatment of her and his whiskey-making, in which he still engages. Mrs. Czarny was not well at this time. Her husband was employed, and Arthur Watkins became her friend and helper. It was this man with whom she ran away to Wisconsin, taking with her her three children, Emily, Mary, and Barbara and she become pregnant the fourth time by him. Before the birth of these last two children the husband urged a miscarriage which she refused. He took Federal Court action at Kansas City against Arthur Watkins and went to Indianapolis and brought Mrs. Czarny home after she had been away from him for fifteen days. She stated her last baby was given away when she was two weeks old—that her husband could never look at her and wanted her consent to take the child along the railroad track and leave her.

He never treated Barbara well, and as she hoped to have Barbara near her, she gave her to the Sobrals, who were their neighbors. She is confident that Barbara will remember her, as she always chose to go with Mrs. Czarny even though she had learned to accept the Sobrals as parents. She said she has hated her husband for years and has never been able to forget his abuse. He still deceives her and did not tell her of visitor's visit to him previously until one night when he was drunk. She states she has left him eight times, ran away from him twice, has always wanted her children with her, and has made an effort to bring this about.

She wished particularly to request that Barbara be placed with her sister, Mrs. Frank (Mary) Kriz, 722 Union Avenue, South Bend, Illinois, who has two children, a girl who will be fifteen on August 6 and a boy who was thirteen on January 2. These children receive regular religious church instruction and attend St. Cecelia's Catholic School. The family own two properties and have slight indebtedness on the one in which they now live. Mrs. Czarny had the statement from Mr. and Mrs. Kriz that they will provide a home for Barbara and feels secure in the fact that Mr. Czarny will not interfere with this placement as he will have nothing to do with the child and Mrs. Czarny has learned to bear her suppressed mother-love burdens without his co-operation.

Barbara's half-sister, Rosabelle Vance, who was given to Mr. and Mrs. Jack Vance, 2425 Seventh Street, Marion, when she was two weeks old is not interfered with in the foster parents' home although Mrs. Czarny sees the child occasionally. Mrs. Czarny had pictures of Barbara and Rosabelle when they were nine months old. She had their pictures which she greatly treasured but because she kept them about the house Mr. Czarny destroyed them. She now has a small album of her treasures secretly kept in the Bartak home and tore from the album photographs which I am sending you under registered mail, separate cover, that you may better understand the family. Mrs. Czarny is glad to pass these to you in the hope that it will give an opportunity to have Barbara near her.

The supplementary sheet enclosed gives you something of the history revealed in the pictures.

I am advised that Dr. Hubsch of South Bend operated on Mrs. Czarny for

CHILD WELFARE CASE RECORDS

gallstones and might be used as a desirable reference. Mrs. Czarny's maiden name was Prokes. Barbara is said to resemble Mrs. Czarny and the Kriz children.

I visited Mrs. Meredith Haines, social worker, Garfield Park Community House, who speaks very highly of the Kriz family, stating she has never heard of any family disturbance there. The children attend church and school regularly and both Mr. and Mrs. Kriz are thrifty, hard-working people. She would recommend the home for Barbara. She thinks very highly of Mrs. Czarny and can understand why the Czarny children attend church irregularly at the Community House. She is confident that Mr. Czarny is bootlegging; and whenever the neighborhood people bootleg, they limit the contacts of the children with the Community House lest the children give out incriminating information.

I have not considered it my province to make an investigation of the Kriz home or references to verify Mrs. Czarny's story. She is more than willing for me to go into a thorough investigation, and I shall be pleased to co-operate with you further by making these inquiries if you so desire. At any rate I should greatly appreciate an early return of the pictures and a report which will give us information regarding the possibility of placing Barbara or what other disposition has been made.

PHOTOGRAPHS

1. Picture of Barbara's maternal grandmother with Mrs. Czarny on her lap, and aunt, Mrs. Kriz, standing. They are in Hungarian national costume and were photographed in Europe.

2. Picture of Mrs. Czarny and Mrs. Kriz when they were nine years and sixteen years old.

3. Picture of Mrs. Czarny when she was twelve years old. She matured early. States that she married early as was the custom of her people.

4. Picture of Mrs. Czarny when she was fourteen years of age and pregnant with her first child.

5. Picture of Mr. and Mrs. Czarny and their children, Emily and Mary. Barbara is said to resemble Emily.

6. Barbara's sisters, Emily and Mary.

7. Picture of Emily and Mary, flower girls at a wedding. Mrs. Czarny made apologies for their tight dresses which photographed noticeably.

8. Picture of Mrs. Czarny and Mrs. Kriz; the latter is seven and a half years older, and, as you note, some taller.

9. Mrs. Kriz in national costume.

10. Picture of maternal grandparents' graves at Maple Grove Cemetery near South Bend. Maternal grandmother died of cancer; maternal grandfather in an automobile accident. The children in the cemetery picture are Mrs. Kriz's two children.

11. Most recent picture of Mrs. Czarny but hardly does her justice.

Later.—Letter written in reply to letter from the worker of the Children's Service, Hartville:

We were very much interested in the detailed account of your interview with Mrs. Czarny and also the pictures, which helped tremendously in portraying Barbara's family background. Your impression of Mrs. Czarny certainly throws a different light on her character from that which we got from your previous correspondence. It is too bad that she was not seen before, isn't it, as perhaps then the Kriz home could have been investigated a year ago with a view to Barbara's possible placement. We shall take good care of these pictures and shall return them to you in the near future.

It was most interesting to learn that there is a possibility for Barbara's placement in the home of a responsible relative. Yes, we should appreciate your co-operation in making an investigation of the Kriz home. In view of the very unreliable information that was procured from references in South Bend, including county officials in whom a great amount of confidence was had, at the time of Gertrude Brink's placement in the Sobral home, it is hoped that as thorough an investigation will be made as possible at this time. You may recall that that child was removed from the Sobral home by the Children's Service about a year ago when they discovered the true status of the Sobral family.

In considering the Kriz home, we must face the fact that Barbara will definitely be placed in close contact with her own immediate family as well. What will be the influence of her father's attitude toward her paternity in his actions toward her? Is he likely to "throw that up" to her in later life? What contacts does he have with the Kriz family?

Barbara is an attractive child. She is very demonstrative in her affections. She responds generously to any show of affection toward her. She is a happy, light-hearted little girl and is doing excellent work in school.

Please know that we are sincerely appreciative of all that you can do in determining the acceptability of the Kriz home.

February 12, 1932.—The following letter was received from the Children's Service, Hartville:

I have your letter of the 9th inst. and will investigate thoroughly the Frank and Mary Kriz home as we are well aware of the many complicated features in the placement of Barbara in the environment proposed.

I am enclosing the original letter received from Barbara's mother last week, which shows the refinement of the mother. The letter advises the return of the photographs to a neighbor, but if you will kindly send them directly to me we will take care of the proper delivery.

As a part of our investigation we desire to make inquiry into the Federal records that are said to be on file in the Kansas City Federal Court unless you have already taken steps through other sources. In that event, will you kindly send us a copy of your information together with any other additional information you think will be helpful.

Copy of letter from Ann's mother to Children's Service, Hartville:

I talked this matter over with my sister, Mary Kriz, and she has decided to take my daughter, Barbara Sobral.

If it will not inconvenience you, she would like to have you come to her in regard to this either Saturday afternoon or Sunday of this week.

Her address is 722 Union Avenue, South Bend, Illinois. Please go direct to her home as she is very anxious to talk things over.

When you send the photographs back please address the package as follows:

Mrs. George Bartak,
1614 Locust Street,
South Bend, Illinois

because she is to hold them for me. My name doesn't need to be on the package.

Thanking you for your past kindness for everything, I remain

February 13, 1932.—Valentine card received from Ann.

February 15, 1932.—Letter written to Children's Service, Hartville:

Thanking you for your letter of February 11, may we state that we have absolutely no information relative to the Czarnys except that contained in the letters which we received from you. Thus, we know nothing of the Kansas City Federal Court records.

We have a record of the Sobrals from the Federal Court records but nothing relative to their adoption of Barbara or of their relationship with the Czarnys.

We do appreciate the close co-operation which you are making available to us in this case.

February 18, 1932.—Mrs. Stanley in office. She got an order for dresses, bloomers, and hose for Ann. She said that Ann was getting along well both at home and at school. She was told of the possibility of Ann's own aunt giving her a home. Mrs. Stanley showed a snapshot of Ann taken on the day that she had her first communion. Ann was prettily clad in a white dress and was wearing a white veil. Mrs. Stanley said that Ann loves pretty clothes.

March 4, 1932.—Mrs. Stanley and Ann in office. Mrs. Stanley came in to get an order for some clothing. Ann had a bag of candy and was effervescing in enthusiasm as usual. She was doing well in school. She told jubilantly about a little black-and-white chick which she had. She is gaining some in weight but her gain is slow.

March 23, 1932.—Letter written to Children's Service, Hartville, Illinois:

It is some time since we last heard from you, and we are anxious to have a report on your investigation of the Kriz home just as soon as possible.

We are finding it necessary to make certain changes in our boarding-home program and would like to know what plans we can count on for Barbara's future.

We are gratefully appreciative of your co-operation.

April 7, 1932.—Mrs. Stanley in office. She said Ann is doing good work in school. The teacher had said she was the best pupil in her class. Ann is bothered with constipation and she has to take cathartics frequently. The cathartic used is aromatic cascara. It was suggested that she bring Ann to the doctor on Saturday, as he could give her some recommendations in regard to diet and also recommend a specific type of cathartic that he prefers to be used.

Later.—Letter received from Children's Service, Hartville, Illinois:

Enclosed find report on the proposed foster home for Barbara Sobral.

Mrs. Winn, my supervisor, and I have gone into the matter very thoroughly and anticipated all the complications in the course of our inquiry with references. We are satisfied to have the child placed in our territory and, of course, will be willing to handle the situation for you pending the proposed adoption. Everyone is confident that the Kriz family will be able to control the situation, and Mr. Czarny knows of the proposed plan and has assured us that since it is their affair he will not bother himself about the child. There is every evidence that Barbara will be loved by everyone else. Who can say but that she may win a place with Mr. Czarny, too, although there is no evidence that there will be frequent contact with him.

Kindly advise us what decision you reach in the matter and what you will expect of us in the further handling of the case. The foster parents are ready to receive the child at any time you may designate.

REPORT ON PROPOSED FOSTER HOME

This is the home of Frank and Mary Kriz, 722 Union Avenue, South Bend, Harrison County, Illinois, who formerly lived at 1238 Green Street, and have been in the county twenty-five years.

The members of the family are Frank Kriz, a Hungarian of forty-two years, who was born in Kalocsa, Hungary; his wife, Mary Prokes Kriz, thirty-five, born in Kiskunhalas, Hungary; Mary Elizabeth Kriz, born August 6, 1916, in South Bend, Illinois, and now in ninth grade at high school; and Alfred Kriz, born January 2, 1919, in South Bend, and in 7A at St. Cecelia's School. The parents were married August 22, 1914, at St. Cecelia's Catholic Church, South Bend, by Father A. F. Schwartz, priest. Mr. Kriz's parents are both dead, his mother having died when he was twelve years old. He has one brother living now, Alfred Kriz, in Kalocsa, Hungary. A sister died in childhood, and a brother Julius was killed in the World War. Mrs. Kriz's parents are also dead. Her brother, Sandor Prokes, and his wife, Mary, are living at 1238 Green Street, South Bend; and her sister, Julia Czarny, at 1115 Oak Street, South Bend.

MR. KRIZ

Health.—Good.

Personality.—He is 5 ft. 7 in. tall, weighs 155 pounds, has heavy, dark curly hair and clear skin, and is neat in appearance. He has a pleasant disposition, a keen mind, and refined manners. He went through eighth grade in the old country and completed the advanced course in English at Garfield Community House High School. He is honest and his habits are good; he occasionally takes a glass of beer but touches no other liquor and prefers milk and cream. He does not use tobacco and is not profane.

Church.—He is a faithful member of St. Cecelia's Catholic Church and attends regularly.

Social life.—He is a member of Vehovay Lodge at Garfield Park Community House. He sometimes takes part in friendly games of cards with men in the stores near by.

Employment.—For eighteen years prior to June, 1931, he was foreman for the King Tool and Die Company in the pattern department, earning from $90 to $110 every two weeks. Since June 8, 1931, he has been with the Willoughby Malleable Iron Company working regularly and earning forty cents an hour, which averages $21.90 a week.

Property.—Mr. and Mrs. Kriz own real estate valued at $12,000 at 722 Union Avenue. It is insured for $5,000 in Vehovay Aid Association of Pittsburgh, Pa.

MRS. KRIZ

Health.—Good.

Personality.—She is 5 ft. 6 in. tall, weight 174-184 pounds, and she has blue eyes and dark brown hair. She came to the United States when she was ten years old. She attended school twenty-four months in the old country and six months in South Bend. When she was thirteen years of age she started to work. She is honest and her habits are good; however, she is more careless in her speech than her husband.

Church.—Although she is a member of St. Cecelia's Catholic Church she attends irregularly.

Social life.—Vehovay Lodge.

Employment.—Worked for two years, eight months at Ajax Rubber Works and three years and a half at Hamilton Beach Manufacturing Company. Has been employed regularly by Willoughby Malleable Iron Company since June, 1931, forty-five cents an hour, $18.45 a week. She will stop work if Ann is placed in the home. Has $150 saved for her needs already.

Property.—Real estate at 1238 Green Street is clear and is valued at $4,700, insured for $2,200 with Hungarian Vehovay Aid Association, Pittsburgh, Pa. She also owns an extra lot on which the family intends to build eventually.

Parents' attitude toward children.—There is a wholesome parental attitude, affectionate, considerate, and inspirational. They think children should have what they need for proper nourishment, education, and clean amusement, and spend money willingly for these things. They try to interest their children in the best. Her husband likes to play with children and has the ability to get things done through creating interest and giving encouragement. She keeps children busy at worth-while pleasures and tasks. Her own daughter studies music.

Underlying motive for taking child.—The child being considered belongs to this family, who have always wished that she had been placed with relatives. They will care for her as for their own child.

Influence and standing in community.—Mr. Kriz is a man of high intelligence and moral standards, a man of position and influence for good. Mrs. Kriz is a thrifty, industrious woman of good reputation. Although less a leader than her husband, she makes a devoted wife and mother and favors the best. They have two well-trained children of their own.

Home.—The house is a frame building valued at $7,000, which the family owns. The yard is 100 by 125 ft. There are five rooms with bath, furnace heat, lighted by electricity. Three rooms are used as bedrooms; the parents have one, and Alfred and Mary Elizabeth each have one. The family sometimes keeps chickens; they will raise some for their own use this summer. They own a 1929 Nash Sedan.

The house is modern, in good condition, comfortably furnished, furnishings showing good care, housekeeping good. Attention to convenience and usefulness is everywhere evident. The family use their high basement for a summer kitchen and dining-room, and throughout the house everything is neat. The yard shows the best of care with grass, shrubs, and attention to landscaping. There is a double concrete garage.

The family owns a radio, phonograph, and walnut piano. They take the *South Bend Record*, a paper issued twice a week, a Hungarian newspaper, and the *Kansas City Sunday Post Dispatch*.

The house is next door to a Baptist church; the street is wide and unpaved. It is in a neighborhood of good, well-kept workingmen's homes on the main street in this prosperous foreign-residence section, near large industrial plants.

Plans for foster child.—She will be expected to perform duties in keeping with her age. Their own son and daughter are very helpful and assist happily and well in work about the house. Child will sleep in her own bed in the cross-ventilated bedroom with Mary Elizabeth Kriz. She will attend Catholic school ten blocks from home, which is in session ten months in the year. There is school bus service. She will be sent to high school if she shows desire and ability to do so. Her companions will be the children of the foster parents, relatives, and others in the neighborhood who will be carefully chosen. The husband, wife, son, daughter, and the two nieces, Emily and Mary Czarny, were all interviewed and are all longing for the child.

References.—Physician, Dr. L. F. Rolf

Minister, Father Hunt, Assistant to Father Schwartz, St. Cecelia's Catholic

Church, 1316 Indiana Avenue, South Bend, recommends family without reservations as respected, fine, churchgoing people; strong parents with well-brought up children. They would be responsible and devoted in their obligations to anyone. He referred visitor to Mrs. Frank Jelinek as reference, as an active high-type Hungarian woman.

F. R. Herbst, Grocer: The family are honest customers and good citizens. He would think child very fortunate to be offered such a home. The Krizes have a happy home life and have reared their own children so they are good, ambitious, and well behaved.

Mrs. Meredith Haines, Social Worker, Garfield Park Community House, South Bend: She has never heard of a family disturbance in this home. Children attend church and school regularly. Both parents are thrifty, hard-working people. She recommends home for Barbara.

Mrs. Frank Jelinek, 942 Union Avenue: Both Mr. and Mrs. Kriz are fine people and have raised their own children so they are well thought of. She believes they would do by the foster child all they would do for their own and protect the child from abuse by others. She knows the Czarny children are well behaved. There is no doubt but that child will be loved by both families except perhaps for Mr. Czarny, but the Krizes will prevent him from interfering.

General impressions and recommendations.—The Kriz home is a wholesome, thrifty home with industry, ambition, and spiritual ideals. Although it is only about two blocks from Czarny home, Mr. Czarny visits the Kriz home only about once a year as he is not liked by maternal relatives. The Czarny daughters, Mary and Emily, ten and eleven years of age, remember and love Barbara and enjoy the Kriz home atmosphere, escaping their own home. The Krizes give every assurance that Barbara will not be interfered with by Mr. Czarny. They are already planning for religious training, looking forward to confirmation and a large party to celebrate in accordance with custom.

Type of child recommended for this home.—Barbara Sobral (adoptive name of Jane Czarny). Barbara was given to the Sobrals by her mother without knowledge of maternal relatives. Maternal grandmother would have taken child, and maternal aunt, Mrs. Kriz, now wants the privilege, believing child should be with own blood relatives. Mr. Czarny who refuses to accept paternity of Barbara has promised not to interfere with the placement.

April 12, 1932.—Discussed at Case Committee meeting. The plan of placing Ann with her maternal aunt, Mrs. Kriz, at South Bend was discussed fully by the Case Committee, and it was decided by the Committee that this plan should be tried.

Later.—Letter written to the Children's Service, Hartville, Illinois:

Thank you kindly for your splendid, detailed report on the investigation of the Kriz home.

The Sobral case was discussed at the Case Committee Meeting today and it was decided that we would allow the placement of Barbara in the home of her maternal aunt, Mrs. Frank Kriz, upon your recommendation. We, of course, would want you to supervise this placement over a period of a year until the child is legally adopted by the Krizes.

We shall be driving to South Bend with Barbara this coming Sunday, April 17. We shall probably arrive about 2:00 P.M. If it is satisfactory with you we shall take her direct to her aunt's home.

We are mailing under separate cover the pictures which you sent us some-time ago.

Unless we hear from you to the contrary we shall bring Barbara Ann to the Kriz home at the appointed time, and we thank you again very kindly for your excellent co-operation in this case.

Later.—Letter written to Mrs. Stanley, foster-mother:

We have received word to the effect that one of Ann's aunts is interested in taking the child into her home to be legally adopted later. This aunt's home has been carefully investigated and it has been found to be a very good one. As I have mentioned previously, we are always pleased to be able to place children with their own relatives whenever possible.

Ann's stay with you during the past year has undoubtedly been of great benefit to her, and we sincerely appreciate the time and energy you have ex-pended on this child's behalf.

Will you please bring Ann into Midland this coming Saturday morning, April 16? Please have all her clothing packed and ready to go with her. Also, arrange to get a signed school transfer, indicating specifically the grade in which she is now placed. In telling Ann of her change in homes, you may simply say that she has an aunt who loves her dearly and would like to have her come and stay with her. This aunt has a fifteen-year-old girl and a thirteen-year-old boy, who remember Ann and are anxious to have her come and make her home with them.

I hope you will be able to be at our office with Ann this coming Saturday morning at about 10:30.

April 14, 1932.—Letter received from the worker of the Children's Service, Hartville, Illinois:

I will visit the Kriz family tomorrow and advise them of your plans to trans-fer Barbara to their home as given in your letter of the 12th last.

When you are driving through Hartville en route to South Bend, I shall be pleased to have you stop at my home, 216 Oakdale Avenue. You will drive right past my residence on State Highway No. 4, also known as No. 6. It may be that I can also drive in my coupé to South Bend with you should that be agreeable to us both at that time. However, I shall be glad to confer with you. No doubt time is also a valued possession with you.

April 16, 1932.—Letter received from Mrs. Stanley:

Your letter of the 12th inst. received, and as you requested I shall try to be at your office with Ann at 10:30 Sat. April 16.

With a heavy heart

Later.—Ann brought to the Children's Agency by Mrs. Stanley.

There was an abundance of tears on the part of both the foster-parents and Ann as the moment of parting arrived. The foster-parents said they had become so fond of Ann that they would even be willing to give her a free home with the possibility of adoption in the near future. It was pointed out to them that it was the ideal situation for Ann to be able to return to her own relatives when there was a good home available for her.

Ann was taken to the Children's Home and allowed to remain there overnight.

April 17, 1932.—Ann transferred from the home of Mrs. A. T. Stanley, Elton, to the home of her maternal aunt, Mrs. Frank Kriz, 722 Union Avenue, South Bend, Illinois.

On the trip to South Bend, Ann asked several questions relating to her people. She was surprised to learn that her real mother was still alive as she was under the impression that she was dead. After being told that she had been in this world but eight years, she wondered how she could have been with so many different people during that short period of time and why her mother had given her to the Sobrals. She was told that her mother had two other little girls and she was having a difficult time in taking care of all of them and Mrs. Sobral did not have a little girl of her own and had offered to take care of her.

Ann was given a warm welcome upon her arrival at her aunt's home. Her own mother and her two sisters were there, in addition to the aunt and uncle and their two children. Ann resembles her relatives strikingly. Her two sisters placed their arms about her, and she was quite pleased with the enthusiastic display of affection shown her. She seemed quite content to remain with them when the case-worker left.

May 2, 1932.—Letter and report from the Children's Service, Hartville, Illinois.

Attached find short report on follow-up visit after recent placement of child in the Frank and Mary Kriz' home, 722 Union Avenue, South Bend, Illinois.

Although I did not see the foster parents I am confident that the adjustment is being made as rapidly as we could expect and that the child is receiving much interest and devotion.

The foster mother had not stopped her work but gets home about five-thirty. The children get home at four-thirty and the sixteen-year-old foster sister has been assuming the responsibility of care for the home until the parents return from their employment. The house is very well cared for and when I warned the mother that we do not wish a child of such young age to be neglected because of lack of adult care, she stated that should any question be raised she would be glad any day to come to the house to be with the child. However, she could not see but that the present arrangement should satisfy everyone, and I am inclined to believe that ample consideration is given to the child's needs without requiring this at present.

REPORT OF CHILDREN'S SERVICE

April 17, 1932.—Barbara transferred from Children's Agency of Summit County to foster home, Mr. and Mrs. Frank (Mary) Kriz, 722 Union Avenue, South Bend, Illinois, by Midland visitor, Esther Tomlinson.

Miss Tomlinson also stopped at the visitor's residence, Hartville, and explained that the Children's Agency would like supervision by Children's Service for one year with regular quarterly reports.

The child expressed a dislike for the Sobral family, seemed much fonder of Mr. Sobral than Mrs. Sobral. She expressed real affection for the boarding-mother, Mrs. Stanley. She is bright, active, happy, but has sensed that her own relatives had abandoned her.

Visitor explained that she would be told by her new foster parents who her real mother is. The whole community understands the family relationship as well as the child's half-sisters; and visitor is of opinion, because of the intense affection expressed, that the child will not want for devotion once she gets adjusted to the situation.

April 27, 1932.—Visited foster home; nobody at home. However, mother saw visitor drive by and came to foster parents' home. Mother has purchased all the clothing which the child thus far has had provided for her and believes she will be able to continue this. On last Saturday she took Ann to town, purchased a new spring coat, light blue taffeta dress, yellow georgette dress, hat, white leather slippers, and two other dresses which friends had given money for.

Last Sunday was foster mother's birthday and she had a party. She also had one for Ann, who is now known as Jane Kriz. Fifteen children were present. There was a special birthday cake with eight candles and a figure eight on it to celebrate the child's birthday of last month. She calls foster mother "Aunt Mary mother" and calls her mother "mother." One day when she was coming home from Catholic School which she attends with her foster brother, they walked by the mother's home. Father was near the gate and asked her her name as she passed by. She told him "Jane Kriz." He asked her a second time, and she rather emphatically repeated the name. One time when the foster parents took Jane to her mother's home and the half-sisters were going away with them, father was present and as the child left, none of them was saying goodbye, so he asked Jane if she would say goodbye to him. She said yes and returned to him shaking hands as he wished. He intended at that time to transfer a twenty-five-cent piece from his hand to hers; it, however, fell on the floor and she quite innocently picked it up and gave it to him. The father then said it was for her, and she thanked him and took it. Jane senses a dislike or restraint and after that when she went by the house and one of the children wanted to go in, she said, "Don't go in there because my mother and sisters like me but my father does not," and did not wish to visit. She, however, is exceedingly fond of the foster parents and they are equally fond of her. There is no jealousy among the children of attention shown Jane, and they are delighted with her; they say she is sweet and bright. Mother gave visitor a package of fancy cakes left over from the parties.

April 30, 1932.—Letter written to Children's Agency, inclosing a copy of report.

August 3, 1932.—Letter and report received from Children's Service, Hartville, Illinois:

Enclosed find report of recent visit to the foster home of Barbara Sobral. It appears that Barbara, who is called Jane Kriz, is adjusting well in this home.

REPORT

Visited foster home July 26, 1932. Saw Barbara, who is called Jane, foster brother, and foster sister. All were happy, and visitor is repeatedly surprised at the good nature and fine sense of responsibility they feel toward each other and the housekeeping. Foster parents are still employed away from home and were absent at the time of visitor's call.

Jane expressed herself naturally and pleasantly as being exceedingly happy that she is with foster parents, although asked visitor to say "Hy" to Miss Tomlinson of Midland, and wished she might have a confirmation picture from the boarding-home in Midland as she could not find it just before she was transferred to Harrison County. Jane is somewhat heavier than when placed, but she did not know her exact weight. She has a good healthy color. She was wearing a dark blue china silk dress, and her hair was well trimmed and combed.

The foster sister, who is a little mother, almost sixteen years of age, states that Jane minds well and they have never been happier than they have been the past four months since Jane has been with them.

Jane attends church regularly with the family. She also attends Catholic parochial school.

She spends her leisure time sometimes at the near-by recreation center. She has been with the family on two Mississippi River boat excursions this summer. She likes to sew and is generally helpful, although visitor could see that she did not have too heavy a responsibility.

Jane in a natural way tried to explain that some times they have to leave the dishes when they go to school until they get home in the afternoon as they do not have time to do them. The foster mother always prepares the breakfast, and it is all that the children can do to get up, get dressed, eat their breakfast, and get away to school in the morning, but they always clean up the dining-room before the evening meal. The house and yard are always immaculate, showing considerable care and artistic taste.

Visited mother, Mrs. Julia Czarny, who stated she is well satisfied with the arrangement for Jane in her foster home. Father accepts the child as he would any friend. When she comes near by, he has given no trouble. However, father's liquor manufacturing was interfered with by a county raid two weeks ago when they found whiskey and mash on the ground. He was arrested and is out on bonds, which were met by foster parents. He is now refraining from further participation in the traffic.

Later.—Letter written by Children's Agency of Midland to Children's Service, Hartville, Illinois:

We thank you kindly for your report on your visit to Jane Kriz's foster home. We are happy to hear how contented she seems to be. Please tell her that we often think about her and miss seeing her cheery face in our office because she always seemed so happy when she was in Midland.

I shall speak to Jane's former foster-mother, asking that she send her one of the confirmation pictures.

August 9, 1932.—Mrs. Stanley, former foster-mother, in the office of Children's Agency. Mrs. Stanley said that her husband was planning to drive to Bancroft the following week and he would like to visit Ann in her new home if that would be satisfactory with the Children's Agency and with her foster-parents. Mrs. Stanley was told that a report had been received telling of Ann's happy adjustment and that the foster-parents had told the case-worker at the time that Ann was placed that there would be absolutely no objection to her foster-parents visiting or writing her. Mrs. Stanley said that her husband would be delighted to learn that he could see her again as he had been so lonesome for her.

SUMMARY FROM APRIL, 1932, TO MAY, 1936

Ann remained in the home of her aunt and uncle, Mr. and Mrs. Kriz, but her interest in her mother's family increased rapidly. She frequently asked the mother why she could not live with them. The mother furnished her clothes, and was very affectionate with the child.

When work became very irregular in September, 1933, for Mr. and Mrs. Kriz, it was decided that Ann should go to live with her mother. This was agreeable to the father as the mother had threatened to leave him because of his drinking. He, being very fond of the mother, was anxious to keep her and willing to take Ann in order to hold the mother. During the first months the placement seemed most satisfactory. Ann was extremely happy and well liked by her half-sisters. The father's work was very irregular, but the mother was not discouraged and tried to manage on whatever he was able to earn.

Through 1934 the situation gradually changed. Poor economic conditions discouraged the father, and he started drinking again. When drunk he was very disagreeable about Ann. The mother had him arrested and moved with the three children into two rooms in a double house belonging to Mrs. Kriz. Since that time the mother has been able to get some housework and has also had some help from the Public Relief Agency. She is an excellent housekeeper, and the rooms are always clean and attractive. The three girls are about the same size and are most companionable. Ann does well at school and is liked by the teacher and the children. Ann is an alert, attractive child. All three girls are well dressed, quiet, and well behaved. The mother seems to manage them very well.

The mother has again had contact with her youngest child, whom she gave in adoption. This child enjoys visiting her mother and her sisters. The four children seem to be fond of each other, and the mother is hoping that eventually she may have all of them.

The mother is an interesting, colorful person. She stands out in her community as the undisputed leader. The activities of the Hungarian Catholic church and the Hungarian Home are to a great extent dependent upon her. She is peculiarly resourceful in assisting her neighbors and others in need in the community.

CASE RECORDS OF CHILDREN PLACED IN FOSTER-HOMES BECAUSE OF SPECIAL PROBLEMS

1. Emily Novelli

(The Placement of a Little Child Who Presented Serious Feeding Problems)

INFANT WELFARE SOCIETY RECORD

January 13, 1932.—The following letter was written to the superintendent of the Children's Shelter by the nutritionist, Roosevelt Infant Welfare Station:

I am writing concerning Emily Novelli, about whom I talked with you over the telephone this afternoon. Emily was born December 26, 1929, and is the youngest of three children in an Italian Catholic home. The parents are Dominic and Mary Novelli of 1728 Lindon Avenue, and the other children are Teresa, born in 1923, and Angeline, born in 1925.

Emily is two years old and weighs eighteen pounds and twelve ounces. Six months ago she weighed eighteen pounds and four ounces, which makes a total gain of eight ounces in six months. Her physical condition is, of course, very poor, due mainly to lack of training. Her mother speaks Italian only, but her father speaks English and seems very co-operative. He has been worried about the child and states he will do anything we recommend. He seems to think, as I do, that if the mother were once shown what can be accomplished by proper training, she would accept our advice. She dislikes hearing the child cry and so gives in to her on all occasions. She says Emily cares only for cake, so she gives her cake.

The child's physical condition is so poor that she is likely to die from malnutrition if she is left in the home, and I feel very strongly that, after a period with you, she will not return to the same situation, as the mother does not lack intelligence and only needs to be convinced. I hope to assist in placing this child with you for a time.

Clearance with Social Service Exchange shows the following agencies registered on the case: February 27, 1920, Central Charity Bureau; April 13, 1931, Infant Welfare Society.

January 25, 1932.—Letter written to the superintendent of the Children's Shelter by the nutritionist, Roosevelt Infant Welfare:

In accordance with our telephone conversation of January twentieth, I am sending you one of our feeding rules for children from two to six years old. This gives all the necessary information, I believe, but I should like to talk with the person at whose home you arrange to place Emily Novelli, in order to discuss our recommendations in greater detail.

CHILDREN'S SHELTER RECORD

Admission.—Emily Novelli was admitted to the Children's Shelter on January 19, 1932.

Appearance.—The day Emily was admitted to the Children's Shelter she was an extremely pale, sickly-looking child. She had a most unhappy expression, and there were large blue circles under her eyes. She is very small boned and thin and finds it difficult to walk, as her legs do not seem strong enough to hold her up. She has small, even features, rather small brown eyes, and a head of heavy black hair.

Placement.—Emily remained in the Children's Shelter for ten days, pending her placement in a foster-home. She was then placed in the home of Mrs. Louise Irwin, 4520 Erie Street. There were no other children in the home at the time. On February 20, 1932, a seven-year-old girl was also placed there. Florence, the seven-year-old, is an average, active, wide-awake girl. Mrs. Irwin, the foster-mother, is a widow. There was a twenty-six-year-old son in the home. Emily was readmitted to the Children's Shelter on May 16, 1932, as the Irwins were spoiling her with too much attention, and she was becoming dependent and inclined to "show off." She remained in the nursery school in the Children's Shelter until June 2, 1932. At this time she was placed in the home of Mrs. Maranger, 10025 South Lawrence Avenue, as it was necessary to close the nursery. Mrs. Maranger is a calm, even-tempered, extremely intelligent graduate nurse who has had experience in dealing with children's feeding problems. Mrs. Maranger is quite a superior person; and the household, which consists of Mr. and Mrs. Maranger and one child, a girl of eight, is a happy wholesome, congenial one.

ADJUSTMENT IN THE CHILDREN'S SHELTER, JANUARY 19–29, 1932

Emily was very unhappy in the nursery group. There were fourteen other children, ranging in age from fourteen months to four years. She became fatigued with the routine and activity of the group. She did not play with the other children or enjoy them; she stayed by herself, oftentimes whining and crying in an undertone. She did not play with toys for any length of time. She did not make up with any members of the nursery-school staff. It was quite evident that she was unhappy.

ADJUSTMENT IN MRS. IRWIN'S HOME, JANUARY 29–MAY 16, 1932

Emily became very happy and was an active little girl while in Mrs. Irwin's home. She ran about freely and would dance when the radio was turned on. She loved accordion music. When she first went to the home she cried when anyone talked to her, but she became very friendly. It was noted that as she stayed on in the foster-home she became almost aggressive and wanted to "show off." The foster-mother was so fond of the child that she was not firm with her, and as a result Emily became spoiled. She wanted attention all the time. If she were crossed, she cried and stamped her feet. However, she did eat much better and learned to eat vegetables and fruit. She understood everything that was said to her and mimicked adults. She enjoyed playing out of doors. She liked to play with pots and kettles. She was also very fond of an old doll, which she put to bed and fed in a most motherly fashion. She became very affectionate, so much so that she wanted the foster-mother to hold her whenever she sat down. It was quite evident that Emily would not learn to help herself and develop as she should if she were to remain in a home where she was pampered.

Emily, therefore, was readmitted to the Children's Shelter on May 16, 1932.

May 20, 1932.—Letter written to Miss Frizzell of the Infant Welfare Society by the case-worker at the Children's Shelter:

You will be interested to know that Emily is now back in the Children's Shelter. We will make every effort possible to educate Mrs. Novelli in child training, and are assuming that the Infant Welfare is continuing its interest in the Novelli family and also making every effort to help the parents so that Emily may be returned to her home. I do not believe that the Children's Shelter can continue a care program unless the Infant Welfare co-operates so that Emily can return to a better home than the one she left.

May I hear from you if there is any question?

ADJUSTMENT IN THE NURSERY GROUP IN CHILDREN'S SHELTER
MAY 16–JUNE 2, 1932

Emily changed a great deal since her first stay in the nursery group. She seemed eager to play with other children. She was suggestible and copied the behavior of other children in so far as her play activities and eating habits were concerned. She fed herself and wanted to be the center of attention and sometimes cried and whimpered in an effort to gain attention. She smiled and was friendly with the members of the staff. Her toilet habits were excellent.

Emily was placed in the home of Mrs. Maranger on June 2, 1932.

June 3, 1932.—Letter written to Mr. and Mrs. Novelli by the case-worker at the Children's Shelter:

I am enclosing a visiting permit for Emily. She was placed in the home of a graduate nurse, a Mrs. Maranger, at 10025 South Lawrence Avenue. It will be possible for you to visit her on Tuesday afternoons once a week. She awakens from her nap at two-thirty and therefore would be ready to see you about three o'clock. I am sure that you will be delighted with the place, and we are, of course, anxious to have Emily gain weight. There is a doctor living in the Maranger home, so that she has medical service near at hand. Emily is, of course, under our care. If you have any question regarding the boarding-home, kindly get in touch with me.

ADJUSTMENT IN MRS. MARANGER'S HOME, JUNE 2–OCTOBER 2, 1932

Personality traits.—Emily, as a rule, was a happy child. She was, however, inclined to become sulky and morose suddenly. One time when worker was visiting, Mr. Maranger came home and greeted Mrs. Maranger. Emily became angry because he had intruded, and she started to cry and pout. She was not demonstrative and never became enthusiastic over any activity or person. At times she was irritable, and it was evident that she wanted to be left alone. She was inclined to be whiny at times and sounded like a little puppy dog whimpering. She was easily upset by new experiences. She was destructive with her toys. Emily continued to be an affectionate child. She overcame her tendency to "show off" and her desire to be the center of attention.

Difficulties.—Emily had temper spells, at which times she rolled on the floor and screamed. These spells occurred when she could not do as she wished; for example, if a child refused to give her a toy, she would lie on the floor and sometimes scream as long as five minutes at a time. She also held her breath. These temper spells occurred less frequently when she learned she did not gain her point and she was ignored completely. She has been known to scream when the foster-mother gave attention to another person.

Control.—It was found that by ignoring Emily the temper spells decreased. The tendency to whine and whimper decreased also when she was ignored. An effort was made to surround her with a very happy atmosphere and to talk to her in a pleasant tone. With this treatment her tendency to whine disappeared, and she became more pleasant. She was made to do things for herself, not helped, and was ignored when she tried to "show off." Her general disposition was much calmer and pleasanter at the time she was dismissed.

Relationship with children and adults.—Emily enjoyed being with other children, whom she imitated; however she was selfish with her playthings and found it difficult to share. As soon as a child picked up one of her playthings, she would immediately want the same toy but she did learn to give and take a little before she left the foster-home. She often tried to act like Joan, Mrs. Maranger's eight-year-old child. One day Joan had her legs crossed and was sitting in a relaxed fashion in a chair reading. Emily got a large picture-book, climbed on a chair, crossed her legs in the same way, and pretended she was reading too. Emily understood what was said to her. She made little effort to talk and instead made motions with her hands. An effort was made to make it necessary for the child to talk before she received what she wanted.

Relationship with Emily's family.—Mr. and Mrs. Novelli visited Emily on an average of twice a month, and both seemed extremely fond of her. Mr. Novelli is the more intelligent of the two. He is a mild, earnest-mannered person, who seems to feel full responsibility for his family. He takes a most protective attitude toward his wife, who is like a small child and seems helpless and bewildered. Mrs. Novelli can speak no English, so that Mr. Novelli has to explain everything in Italian. Both Mr. and Mrs. Novelli are always neatly dressed in clean, old clothing. The foster-mother made an effort to explain the feeding and sleeping schedule to the parents.

Personal habits and hygiene.—Emily was a restless sleeper. She used to roll herself to sleep; that is, she would go from one side to the other for a half-hour at a time. When she first went to the foster-home she cried and moaned at night. She often would lie on the floor and rock herself.

Her toilet habits were excellent.

Emily was inclined to get dirty quickly; if there was any mud or dirt, she always found it. She liked pretty clothes and loved to be dressed up. She was quite vain and used to look at herself in the mirror. Emily learned to dress herself, but did so very slowly. She could not, of course, lace her shoes.

Though Emily was seen by the pediatrician at the Children's Shelter twice a month, she did not gain as had been hoped. She was an extremely poor eater. She picked at her food and did not relish it. She wanted to be fed, rather than feed herself. An effort was made to let her go without food if she refused to feed herself, but it was found that she would go without food for two meals rather than make the effort. It was possible to make her eat when she was given small servings and told that if she did not eat her vegetables she could not have her dessert, for she liked sweets.

She played with her food and hammered the dishes and table with her spoon. She never asked for food between meals, nor did she seem happy when mealtime came around. However, her feeding habits did improve, and she ate better in the Maranger home. The foster-mother thought Emily might eat if she ate with the family and saw them eating; however, she became distracted and also wanted the food the family had. Consequently, she was given a little table where she sat by herself and always ate before the family.

Interest and recreation.—Emily would run about in a carefree manner, usually with no apparent objective. She had a large play pen in the back yard, in which she kept all her toys. She had several dolls, a doll buggy, kitchen cabinet, tin dishes, and several old pans and covers. She loved to play with the dolls and would cover and uncover them again and again. She was quite self-sufficient and could entertain herself by the hour. She liked to play in the sand and would fill a pail, dump it, and then fill it. She loved to play with the dog. She would chase him, and he seemed to understand as he was very playful. The dog and Emily would run about the back yard, the dog barking and Emily laughing and screaming. Emily liked to look at pictures for a short time but, as her muscular control was poor, at first she did not cut them out. She improved greatly in this respect though and learned to turn somersaults, go to bed and get up, and to get on and off a chair by herself. When first placed she used to fall in running, but this tendency disappeared.

Disposition.—In order to help work out a satisfactory permanent plan for Emily, she was referred by the Infant Welfare to the Child Guidance Clinic for study and recommendations. She was examined on September 12, 1932. After this a conference was held, attended by the psychiatrist, Dr. James, and the psychologist, Miss Green, of the Clinic; Miss Frizzell and Miss Chase of Infant Welfare; and Miss Boyd, the case-worker from the Children's Shelter.

October 17, 1932.—Letter received by the case-worker at the Shelter from the Child Guidance Clinic:

We are enclosing a copy of the Case Summary of Emily Novelli, who was examined at out Clinic September 12, 1932, having been referred by the Infant Welfare Society. This summary includes a discussion of the findings and a summary of the case. It also includes the recommendations as formulated by the staff conference. We were very glad that you were able to attend this conference, as your report contributed a great deal to our understanding of the case.

We shall be glad to keep in touch with this child through the Infant Welfare Society from time to time and shall arrange for psychiatric interviews between the parents and our psychiatrist as the need arises. We wish to thank you again for your excellent report.

CHILD GUIDANCE CLINIC CASE SUMMARY
OF EMILY NOVELLI

I. *Initial statement of problems*

    A. An undersized, pale child of two years, nine months, referred to the Clinic by the Infant Welfare Society in September, 1932, because of severe feeding difficulty.

    B. *Brief history of onset and development of problem.*—The feeding difficulty has been present ever since the child began to take solid food; that is, when she was about a year old. She has been very badly undernourished since the Infant Welfare Society has known her, since she was a year and a half old. The child was placed in the Lakeside Sanitarium by the Infant Welfare Society and later in two foster homes by the Children's Shelter. The problem has improved somewhat since she was placed by Children's Shelter eight months ago. At present she eats very small quantities and plays with her food. Actual food dislike consists of liver, apricots, and puddings.

II. *Family background*

The father, Dominic, was born in 1876 in Italy. He completed the eighth grade. He came to the United States in 1903, but has returned three times for short visits. He has been in Chicago since 1917. He speaks very little English. He is a laborer by trade, but has been unemployed for two years. His health is very good. He is much interested in the children. He has been married twice, his first wife having died in 1918, leaving him with three children. He married his present wife in 1920, after having sent her money to come over to this country.

The mother, Mary, was born in 1890 in Italy. She has very little education, and is considered very nervous and queer. She has a severe temper and is very impatient with children. Recently she had a gynecological operation at Research Hospital and has had some psychiatric treatment.

Siblings.—Theresa, nine years, a peculiar child; Angeline, seven years, also a peculiar child; Emily, patient.

All children have been severe feeding problems. The children by the father's first marriage live in the neighborhood and come to see the family frequently.

III. *Developmental and health history*

Pre-natal: Labor and delivery normal.

Eating: Severe feeding problem.

Sleeping: Restless.

Speech: Retarded and infantile.

IV. *Findings of clinic examination*

Physical.—Underweight and small for her age. Findings of old rickets. Under constant supervision of Infant Welfare Society. She has gained since being placed in foster homes. Her diet at home has been inadequate and too highly seasoned.

Psychological.—C.A., 2–9; M.A., 2–2. Good co-operation and attention. Motor co-ordination poor. Speech development poor.

Personality and behavior.—An affectionate, happy child. Tendency to overactivity; continually occupied. Tendency to temper tantrums disappeared in foster home; however tendency to whine has continued. Poor speech development. Rather infantile behavior and general development below average for age.

Outstanding environmental factors.—Child living in foster home. Poor economic status of family receiving aid from Emergency Relief. Lack of adjustment to American standards; Italian spoken in home. Lack of understanding in preparation of child's food.

Mother's difficult personality—impatient and poor methods of handling children. Mother's poor health.

Father fond of child and willing to co-operate; quite intelligent in co-operation.

Two older siblings "peculiar personalities"; have been severe feeding problems.

Lack of proper play equipment and play space at home.

V. *Discussion of findings*

The child's feeding difficulty apparently has originated from the fact that she has had no regular habit training at all. She has been allowed to have her own way from the beginning. She has never been given the right food at home, but has eaten with the family and received highly seasoned food. The mother has appeared absolutely inadequate in handling the child. No consistent method has been carried out. The mother is probably markedly lacking in intelligence and in ability to carry out recommendations. The father, however, seems anxious to co-operate and appears to have adequate intelligence.

The fact that the patient has improved since being removed from the home would seem to indicate that the difficulty was due to the way she has been handled, and indicates that she is capable of improving in this respect. However, the problem is still present, and the child is a very poor eater.

The present foster home does not seem adequate, although the child has improved in many ways. The foster parents consider the child "peculiar." Also, it is not possible for the Children's Shelter to continue paying the $7.50 a week for the child, and other arrangements will have to be made. There are three possibilities of placing the child: (1) a small institution such as Harris Orphanage; (2) another foster home; (3) own home with attendance at nursery school.

Although there are many disadvantages in returning the child to her home, there also seem to be some things in favor of it. The family is now more interested in better diet and would probably co-operate better than formerly, especially if the child were home on a more or less probationary status. Arrangements can probably be made for the child to enter Roosevelt Nursery School. The Infant Welfare Society will continue very active supervision of this child. If the child does not progress when she is at home, she can be removed to an institution, such as the Harris Orphanage. The advantage of nursery school is very important, since the child's best progress was made when she was in the Children's Shelter, where she was with other children her own age.

VI. *General objectives of treatment*
   1. To help the child develop better feeding habits and to improve her whole physical condition and development.
   2. To get the parents to have a more intelligent understanding of the fundamental principles of child training and to obtain their co-operation in providing proper environment for the child in regard to feeding and general management.

VII. *Recommendations as formulated by staff conference*
   1. The child will return home for a probationary period, under the continued active supervision of the Infant Welfare Society.
   2. The Infant Welfare Society will apply at once for the child's admission to the Roosevelt Nursery School. She will not return home until she can immediately start going to nursery school.
   3. Dr. James will talk to both Mr. and Mrs. Novelli before the child returns home, discussing with them general methods of child training, especially in regard to feeding.
   4. Miss Boyd, Children's Shelter, and Miss Chase, Infant Welfare Society, will in two months' time carefully discuss the progress that Emily seems to be making in the home and in nursery school. If it seems best for the child, she will at that time or later be removed from the home and placed in the Harris Orphanage.
   5. Dr. James, Child Guidance Clinic psychiatrist, will have interviews with the mother and father as the situation would seem to warrant.

   Type of service from Child Guidance Clinic.—Co-operative.

October 3, 1932.—Emily was dismissed to go to her parents.

SUMMARY, OCTOBER 3, 1932—FEBRUARY 23, 1935

During this time Emily was very closely supervised in her own home by the nurse from the Infant Welfare. The nurse tried to insist on better food habits and adequate sleep. She also stressed the importance of nursery-school attendance. Very little was accomplished with the parents. Again the psychiatrist at the Child Guidance Clinic was asked for help.

The parents were taken in to have a conference with him. After a time the father confided in the nurse that the mother "talked crazy" and was very difficult in the home, that she drank considerably. They were able to get her into Psychopathic Hospital, but the doctors there reported her behavior as normal and returned her to her home. She refused to have Emily go to the Harris Orphanage.

Soon, however, the mother became so difficult that the father had her committed to the State Hospital. During the six months when the mother was away, a relative came in and cooked for the family. The mother returned home after a six months' hospitalization, insisting that she felt very well. She was as unco-operative as before regarding Emily, and the case was closed in February, 1935.

2. David Ford

(The Successful Foster-Home Placement of a Mentally Defective Boy)

September 13, 1930.—The Juvenile Court referred the child, David Ford, to the Children's Agency for placement because he was constantly truant from home. The Child Guidance Clinic believed that he might be benefited by foster-home placement.

The family (Negro) consists of stepfather, Jim Shearer, age thirty-eight; mother, Hazel Shearer, age twenty-seven years; Genevieve, sister, age nine; and David, age eight years.

Henry Ames, the alleged father of the children, is thought to be dead. He would be thirty-eight years old if alive, according to the mother. He was born in Cambridge, Alabama. He came of farm people and was working on a farm near the one where mother worked when she met him. Mother knows very little of father. She knows that he came from a large family and did not have very much education. He was a thin, active man who seemed to be very strong. Mother had five children by him, two of whom were twins.

Hazel Ford Shearer, mother, was born in Daggert, Alabama, January 11, 1903. Her people were farmers also, and she worked in the fields from the time she was large enough to the time she came to Chicago four years ago. Mother and a brother of hers were illegitimate children of her mother and a Mr. Ford of whom mother knows very little. The maternal grandmother later married Joe Gibbons, by whom she had eight children. She and maternal stepfather did not get along very well and about seven years ago they separated. Maternal grandmother came to Chicago to live. Mother went as far as the fifth grade in school in Alabama.

The mother met the alleged father when a very young girl and became pregnant by him when she was seventeen years old. She lived with him "off and on" for the next three or four years, having four pregnancies during this time. Genevieve and David are the only two living children. She came to Chicago to join the maternal grandmother and a maternal uncle four years ago and lived with the grandmother. The marriage to stepfather took place on July 13, 1929. She had one miscarriage after coming to Chicago. She will not give the name of the man in this case. Mother has worked irregularly at various laundries, but is not working at present.

Mother is genuinely interested in the children, but seems to feel that she is not able to manage them. It seems that David is an irritating factor in the home, and the mother fears that he may be the cause of her losing her husband. The stepfather is evidently the only security she has known and she does not want to run any chance of losing him.

Jim Shearer, the stepfather, was born in Georgia. His father was a farmer. He has three sisters and a brother living in Georgia. His father and mother are living also. He has had no formal education and has been employed for over a year as a laborer by the Rogers Foundry at Forty-first and Elm streets. When working regularly he earned between $20 and $30 a week. At present he is earning only $12 a week working two or three days.

The stepfather seems to want to do the right thing for David but cannot understand him and feels that his behavior is due to ingratitude. He states that he has done all he can for David and cannot understand his behavior.

Genevieve (sister) is nine years old. She was the first of mother's children and was born in Daggert, Alabama, April 15, 1921. Genevieve is in the subnormal room at the Adams School. About a year ago she gave trouble in school by screaming out suddenly for no apparent reason. The school asked for an examination by the Child Study Department of the Board of Education, and she was found to have an I.Q. of 68. It was recommended that she be placed in a special room with special attention given to nutrition.

David was born in Daggert, Alabama, May 27, 1922. His mother was eighteen years old and in good health at the time of his birth. She worked in the fields during most of the pregnancy. The birth was normal. David began walking and talking at the age of one year, five months, but did not talk enough to be understood until the age of two. He still has a speech defect. He had measles as a small child and at the age of seven years had pneumonia. Since then he has been retarded in school and falls asleep in school and at home.

David started in the Penn School in kindergarten when he was five years old. The family moved in March of that year, and he was transferred to the Adams School. He was promoted to the first grade and was getting along very well until he had pneumonia. Before he recovered, his family moved again, and David then went to the Lee School. They moved again March 10 of this year and he was again transferred to the Adams School, where he was placed in a special room in June, 1930.

David was examined by the Child Study Department of the Board of Education on May 22, 1930. He is listed with them under the name of David Ames Shearer. He was then in the first grade and was referred by the Adams School because of irregular attendance, unfavorable home conditions, and transfers. The examination shows David with a chronological age of eight years, a mental age of five years, two months, with an I.Q. of 65. Recommendations were: tonsillectomy and placement in a special division.

David goes away from home without reason according to the mother and is returned or picked up by the police and placed in the Detention Home. When asked why he ran away he answers, "Just because." Although the mother reported to the Juvenile Court that David stole from home and from the neighbors, when asked about this at the Child Guidance Clinic she denied that he stole from neighbors and said he had stolen from her only once when she left some change lying about the house. David does protective lying.

The mother states that David has always had quite a temper. When he was a baby if anyone tried to play with him, he screamed at the top of his voice. He has temper tantrums in school now. The last time the mother had to go to school about this, some child had taken his pencil and paper and he began screaming and fighting.

The mother stated at the Child Guidance Clinic that David does not have any special friend; that he prefers playing alone. The Juvenile Court record reported that he plays with a group of boys who loiter around the River Road district and who are constantly getting into mischief and running away from home. The mother for a time whipped David; but his teacher suggested that this was not helping, and she began locking him in his room to punish him. He usually fell asleep during this isolation. The family live in a small dirty four-room apartment in a very undesirable residential section near River Road. This neighborhood is thickly populated by Negroes from the South who have not become accustomed to the northern modes of living. There are few facilities for recreation, and houses of prostitution are in the immediate neighborhood. There is much street-walking among the prostitutes. There is a great deal of poverty in the district (Juvenile Court Record).

The Juvenile Court has known the family since July 8, 1930, when David was picked up by an officer and placed in the Detention Home. When his truancies continued and the Court realized that some plan must be made, they asked for an examination by the Child Guidance Clinic.

The Child Guidance Clinic examined David at the suggestion of the Juvenile Court, August 4, 1930. The following recommendations were made:

1. Removal from home
2. Placement, if possible through Children's Agency, in a foster-home
3. Tonsillectomy
4. Patient not to attend school until mental age becomes six years
5. Commitment to a feeble-minded institution if foster-home placement is impossible.

The Case Committee (of Children's Agency) decided that David should be accepted for placement and that case work should be done with the family with the view of returning David to them at some later date. It was decided that David should be sent to school.

October 6, 1930.—David Ford was committed to the Children's Agency with the usual order on the County for $25 per month, and he was placed in the Children's Shelter until arrangements could be made for foster-home placement.

October 9, 1930.—David was placed in the home of Lester and Maude Williams, Cicero, Illinois, rate of board $20 per month.

On the way to the new foster-home and during the purchase of clothing David maintained a listless and noninterested attitude. He spoke infrequently, and his responses were limited to monosyllables and motions of the head. He showed no interest in the home to which he was going. He had taken a few toys in a small box, and these trinkets apparently occupied his mind. On the train and in the taxi he sat quietly and expressed his desire only for something to eat.

This calm ended, however, when the home had been reached and the visitor was on the point of leaving. He screamed and cried, and the combined efforts of the visitor and both foster-parents were of no avail. The apparent object of this outburst was the desire to be returned to the Children's Shelter, to which he is evidently attached. Finally, he became composed and went to sleep from sheer exhaustion.

Mrs. Williams, the foster-mother, was kindly in her greetings and sympathetic but firm in her handling of the situation. Later she reported by telephone that the boy was reasonably happy and had so far given no further trouble.

October 14, 1930.—Mrs. Sutton, the principal of the Adams School, promises to send the Child Study record to the Cooke School.

Mrs. Tollman, principal of the Cooke School, says the boy has been in school only one day and they have been unable to determine his grade placement.

Mrs. Ball, teacher, says that David is not able to do the second-grade work. She is testing him on a 1A scale.

October 20, 1930.—Mrs. Maude Williams, foster-mother, at home, finds David very retiring and lacking in aggressiveness. He refuses to play with any of the children except a neighbor girl upon whom he wishes to shower his toys. He has been very obedient but usually wants his own way and, if refused, he sulks and does not listen to reason.

October 24, 1930.—See copy of Decree of Commitment filed. See copy of History Sheet received from Juvenile Court filed.

November 7, 1930.—See copy of History Sheet on child sent to Children's Division of the State Department of Public Welfare.

Mr. Williams, foster-father, at home, says he regards David as a "fine lad." He has no complaint to make of his conduct. At first he was a habitual enuretic, but the foster-parents have had a fair degree of success by waking him before they retire. The foster-father understands that David has not had great success in school and is trying to help him with the essentials of reading and numbers. David had no knowledge at all of the alphabet and could not count to five in order. The foster-father thinks that this is due to poor school training and not to David's native capacity. The boy plays about the house and in the yard and was fond of the horse until the horse became ill and David thought he was dead.

Mrs. Williams, the foster-mother, found that David was very hungry at first and apparently could not be satisfied. She fed him all he wanted, and his appetite gradually became normal; but he still eats heartily.

He retires early, usually about seven o'clock, sleeps soundly, and awakens at about seven in the morning. It was at first hard to establish regular hours.

January 2, 1931.—See letter from Juvenile Court asking that Genevieve, sister of David, be considered for placement.

January 6, 1931.—Mrs. Hazel Shearer was located at 2231 South Maple Street. She told visitor that she is quite concerned about Genevieve but is helpless. She inferred that the stepfather beat Genevieve, that she knew about it but could do nothing about it. She was anxious that Genevieve be placed in a good home.

The stepfather has very little work now, and the mother has no work at all. They are living in a four-room apartment with another couple. This apartment is much cleaner than the other and much better lighted and ventilated. The mother stated that the landlord at 2226 South Maple Street made them move because they could not pay their rent.

The mother asked for David's address, saying that she is very anxious to visit him. She would also like to know where Genevieve is placed so she can visit her. She was given a Children's Agency card and was told that she might call the office during the week and learn where Genevieve is to be placed.

January 8, 1931.—Case Committee chairman agreed to accept Genevieve for placement.

January 9, 1931.—Mrs. Tollman, the principal of Cooke School, finds that David is having a most difficult time in school. He is now in the 1B class and even there seems to make no progress. He sits listless for hours and is not able to give attention to his work. The teacher classes him as "stubborn" and finds him a very disturbing child in the room. When he does not wish to do a certain thing he will lie on the floor, roll from side to side, and scream. This conduct completely demoralizes the classroom, and the teachers therefore do not want him in their rooms. Mrs. Tollman, principal, punished David by putting him for a few hours in a dark closet. David's screaming so disturbed the school program that she felt obliged to send him to bring in the foster-parents. Instead of going home David wandered about the neighborhood until the foster-mother was advised by the neighbors.

Mrs. Williams, foster-mother, at home, thinks that David needs a physical examination. He is quite "absent-minded." He will begin a task and forget what he started out to do before the task has been accomplished. Sometimes he is quite apt but what he learns today he forgets tomorrow.

January 12, 1931.—Genevieve Ford (sister) committed to the Children's Agency by order of Court and placed temporarily in the Detention Home.

January 15, 1931.—The Case Committee recommended that the Children's Agency carry out the recommendations of the Child Guidance Clinic and remove David from school until he has attained a mental age commensurate with school age. It was further recommended that a home be found suitable for the placement of both children. It was considered advisable to allow David to remain in the Cooke School until this change could be effective.

January 20, 1931. Periodic summary.—David has grown heavier and taller since he was placed in this home last September. His eyes appear brighter, and he is quicker both in his movements and in his speech, although he is still far from prompt in his responses. He has spent much time out of doors daily and has more color in his cheeks.

Mrs. Hughes, teacher, states that she has been able to get David to read fairly well, but he does not remember what he learns. He has also improved in number work. In spite of these achievements, he is still very disturbing, cries, and makes catcalls incessantly. This conduct at first made him interesting to other children, but it annoys them now and disturbs the order of the classroom. He was to appear in the Easter and graduation exercises of the school but because of his conduct he was denied participation in both.

David spends a great deal of time playing alone. Whenever he is thrown in contact with other children, there is friction; immediately he begins fighting. He still has an almost uncontrollable temper and often gets into difficulties by bothering other children. He apparently cannot keep his mind on whatever he is doing and frequently falls asleep when performing a given task. He does not recognize the exercises in a reading-book which he has just completed. If he is sent on an errand, he must be followed up to make sure that he carries it through.

David harbors many fancied or real grievances against his family. He insists that they were cruel to him and stubbornly resists any plan to be placed with his sister, Genevieve. He insists that he does not want to be with her, and any talk about it always meets with defiance and tears.

Although David has made little visible mental improvement, he seems to be happy and satisfied here. He returns from school, changes his clothing, plays a bit, then eats a hearty dinner. After this meal he reads for a time, usually falling asleep about 7:00 P.M. He is always in bed about eight o'clock and sleeps eleven or twelve hours. In spite of his difficulties at school he is fairly well behaved at home. Although the foster-parents are positive in their discipline, they understand David and do not irritate him. The foster-mother thinks that the tantrums which David displays are injurious to his health as he is always left weak and nervous.

February 4, 1931.—Genevieve was placed in the home of Mrs. Bernice Foot, 1245 South Balboa Avenue, rate of board $20 a month.

November 10, 1931. Periodic summary.—Although the physical aspects of the foster-home are not the best that the Agency has to offer, the choice of this home for David, especially at the present time, seems to have been a happy one. Simple fare, simple daily routine, and simple social contacts offer him the protection and security that his mentality particularly demands. A more complex home situation would in all probability lead to endless conflict. The foster-parents themselves do not demand too much of him and indeed seem to understand his problems much better than do his teachers who still seem to expect normal performance of him. The foster-parents have tried very hard to help David to make a satisfactory school adjustment.

During the summer months, Mr. Williams, foster-father, cultivated a small farm where David spent most of his time. He seemed very happy and interested in this work.

In accordance with the recommendations of our Case Committee, plans were made to place David and his sister, Genevieve, in the same foster-home. In order to break down David's resistance to such a plan it was finally decided that Mrs. Bernice Foot, foster-mother, would take Genevieve to visit David occasionally and, after a satisfactory contact had been made, would invite David to spend a day with Genevieve in Mrs. Foot's home. When they came to visit, David recognized his sister and immediately ran into the back yard. After a great deal of persuasion he came inside and spoke briefly with Genevieve and her foster-mother. He became gradually more cordial, but did not invite them to visit again. Mrs. Foot, who had once entertained the idea of having both the children in her own home, after seeing their reactions toward each other, felt that they were not ready to be together. This opinion was further strengthened by the fact that Genevieve herself was at the time causing endless trouble by her own temper and was a little later given up by Mrs. Foot. In view of this rather positive demonstration of what had been considered as probably an imagined opposition, it is felt that the safest plan for the present is an extension of the present arrangement.

Although David's conduct during the last school year was far from satisfactory, his grades were commensurate with his ability. A report for the semester ended June, 1931, reads: Deportment, P; Arithmetic, F; Drawing, F; Reading, F; Writing, E; Phonics, F; and Music, F.[1] He was transferred to the second grade under Miss James and came into immediate conflict with her because of his stubbornness and unwillingness to be crossed.

[1] F = Fair, P = Poor, and E = Excellent.

David had a general routine examination at Harper Hospital in September. He was found to weigh sixty-eight pounds, which is ten pounds overweight. His tonsils were removed, and his health has been generally good.

April 18, 1932.—David has continued throughout the winter to improve in his behavior at home as well as at school. Mr. and Mrs. Williams seem to grow more and more attached to him and fondly refer to him as "Dave." David busies himself about the house and goes about his work and play as if totally unaware of anyone else. He is apparently happy here and never fails to be upset by a trip into the city. On one occasion while the visitor was calling, he sat silently in a corner for a long time and then began to tell how much progress he was making in school. He then brought out a few crude toys which he was constructing.

Recently while calling in the city with his foster-parents, David was sent to see his grandmother, who lived near the persons visited. When he arrived at the home of his grandmother, he refused to have anything to do with her and stood silent for a few moments and left. When Mrs. Williams heard of his conduct, she accompanied him back to the home, but on the way met an uncle of David's who greeted him cordially. This uncle David apparently recognized but had little to say to him. Mrs. Williams then explained David's conduct at the home of his grandmother, whereupon the uncle replied, "Even a dog remembers when he has been mistreated."

Mrs. Tollman, the principal, states that David is gradually causing less trouble in school and his school work has shown a gradual improvement. She thinks that he understands his work better. He himself says that the work is not so hard as it used to be.

He has found companionship in two convalescent boys residing in the home of Mrs. Miles, about a half-mile away. David likes to visit these boys as the Miles have a rather large barnyard of animals and poultry.

With the children of the neighborhood David is also more friendly and is much more popular as he grows out of his antagonistic spirit toward them.

Mrs. Williams finds it difficult to regulate David's diet as he is very fond of meat. If permitted, he will make an entire meal of meat and will appear dull and sluggish long after. He does not care for sweets, however, except fruit preserves. In general he has a very good appetite.

SUMMARY OF RECORD TO MAY 20, 1935

The foster-father died March 18, 1933, and David was a great comfort to the foster-mother. Mrs. Williams remarried October 5, 1933, but her husband died about ten months later. Through all this trouble the foster-mother said many times that she could not have gotten along without David. The Agency made plans for him to go to camp, but she did not want him to go because she needed his help and company.

He did not progress at school, and it was finally decided that he should be taken from school as it was believed his poor adjustment there was making everything difficult for him. The plan of the Agency at the time of the last entry was to attempt to get him into a small garage where he could learn about machinery and automobiles. It was also believed that he would eventually enjoy work on a big farm if it were ever considered wise to separate him from the foster-mother.

3. Bernie Baker

*(The Placement of a Seriously Neglected Negro Boy Who Had
Developed Behavior Problems)*

This case was referred to the Children's Agency (Chicago) on March 13, 1930, by the Juvenile Court. The foster-parents, an elderly couple, with whom the boy is now living, refuse to take the boy back into their home because of incorrigibility. The superintendent of the Chicago Parental School declares that he can no longer remain there.

The family consists of the father, Peter (died in St. Paul, Minnesota, 1916); mother, Mable, age forty-eight; children: Bernie, fifteen; Mrs. Marie Louise Mandel, thirty-three; John Baker, twenty-eight; Mrs. Beulah Corbett, twenty-five; Frank Baker, twenty-three; and Sadie Mabel Baker, seventeen.

Foster-parents are Mr. and Mrs. Sid Graber.

Peter Baker is alleged to have deserted and died in St. Paul, Minnesota, about 1916.

Mable Baker was born in Gadson, Virginia, in 1885. Little is known of her early history. There is evidence, however, that she learned to sew and cook and became an expert in these lines in spite of her reputed laziness. She claims to have married Peter Baker and moved to Harrisfield, Pennsylvania, although there is no record of the marriage. Here she worked in private families as a maid.

Mr. and Mrs. Baker had domestic difficulties from the very beginning and finally in 1909 they were separated. The children recall her as quarrelsome, lazy, and slovenly, and she made no attempt to care for them. It was her custom to leave them and be away for weeks at a time, "to hunt work," she said, but in reality to have a good time. The Associated

Charities of Harrisfield record her as begging from door to door during this time.

Several attempts were made to secure aid from the maternal grandparents, but they refused because of the acknowledged illegitimacy of Marie and John and the probable illegitimacy of Beulah and Frank. Although the mother consistently refused to live with the father, they maintained some sort of relationship. Finally she went to live again with Mr. Baker in St. Paul, where he had settled with his parents. This reconciliation did not last, and she returned to Harrisfield and secured a position for herself.

Nothing more was heard of her until 1917. She was still in Harrisfield and interested in a Royce Fillman, who was a married man but who had promised to marry her. She took him to court but did not make a good case, as it was found that she had had an illegitimate child two years earlier (December 10, 1914) presumably by this same man. This child is Bernie. Mother gave the child to Mrs. Mary Sabin, mother of Mrs. Graber, then living in Harrisfield, and disappeared.

About two years later the Juvenile Court declared the children dependent. Bernie was to be placed, but his mother returned and took him to South Carolina. She then moved to Gadson and then to Harrisfield. In 1927 she sent Bernie to Mr. and Mrs. Graber and again disappeared.

In 1928 she telephoned Mrs. Graber to learn how Bernie was getting along but stated that she is no longer interested in him. She has not been seen since but has been heard of in and about Chicago.

Marie Louise was born in 1897 in Gadson, Virginia. She was married in Harrisfield and moved to Chicago, where she lives at 4400 Wentworth Avenue.

Beulah was born in Harrisfield in 1905. She was a ward of Harrisfield Juvenile Court when she married Mr. Corbett, a railroad porter, and came to live with her sister, Mrs. Mandel.

Sadie Mabel, born in 1913, is also a ward of the Juvenile Court of Harrisfield. She is in the Davis Home for Girls in Harrisfield.

Bernie was born in Harrisfield, December 10, 1914.

Bernie stayed with his mother until he was six months old and was then given by her to Mr. and Mrs. Sid Graber, who were living in Harrisfield. He stayed with these people until he was three, then went to Gadson with his mother.

In March, 1925, Mrs. Marie Mandel, sister, asked the Chicago Juvenile Court to have him placed as she was going to a sanitarium. She said he had been in the city since 1924. He was placed in the Chicago Parental School in May, 1925. A letter in 1925 from the superintendent of the Chicago Parental School asked to have him removed as space was needed.

There followed lengthy correspondence by the Juvenile Court with the Associated Charities and with the Department of Public Welfare of Harrisfield, Pennsylvania, as to whether he was the legal responsibility of Illinois or Pennsylvania. Although the Department of Public Welfare of Pennsylvania disclaimed responsibility in January, 1926, the boy was returned to Harrisfield in June of that year. Early in 1927 Mrs. Baker sent the boy again to Chicago with a telegram to Mr. and Mrs. Graber to meet him at the station.

In March, 1929, Sid Graber, 1632 Parkway Avenue, complained to the court of the boy's conduct. He began being truant from school and on March 15, 1929, was placed in the Juvenile Detention Home by the truant officer.

He was placed in the Franklin Special School but made a poor adjustment and was brought again to the police at the Warren Avenue Station by Mrs. Graber, who stated that although the boy had done well at the Coles School he apparently could not adjust at the Franklin. He was then committed to the Chicago Parental School, where he is now. The principal of the Parental School has written the court that no one has visited Bernie in the four months he has been there, that he has become restless, and probably should be cared for in some institution for dependent children.

Bernie does not care much for games. He would like to be a truck driver when he is old enough. During tests he appeared indifferent and the probability is that he is "naturally lazy," not caring for vigorous exercise, and that he has not found any occupation which is particularly interesting.

He was in fourth grade before going to the Franklin School; his behavior is reported as disobedient and defiant; he steals and is a truant.

TREATMENT BY OTHER AGENCIES

Associated Charities of Harrisfield had contact with the family from 1907 until 1927.

The Juvenile Court of Harrisfield had registered on the family.

The Municipal Tuberculosis Sanitarium of Chicago, Wentworth Dispensary, examined mother in 1924.

The Juvenile Court of Chicago first knew the family in March, 1925, when Mrs. Marie Mandel asked to have Bernie placed as she was going to a sanitarium.

The Child Study Department of the Chicago Board of Education examined Bernie at Franklin School, October 11, 1929. They recommended that he be committed to Chicago Parental School to break up bad habits. Later he should be given a chance to do shopwork of different kinds in the hope that he might become interested.

REPORT FROM FRANKLIN SPECIAL SCHOOL

Name.—Bernie Graber (Bernie Baker).
Address.—1632 Parkway, 1st front.
Age.—14 years, 10 months.
Born.—12-10-14. *Sex.*—Male. *Color.*—Black.
Place of birth.—Harrisfield, Pennsylvania.

A. *Personal history*
   a) Behavior
     1. Truant from home and school.
     2. Stealing.
     3. Boy is disobedient, defiant and a general trouble maker.

(History of behavior and school are both incomplete and somewhat vague due to the incomplete social history.)

Examined by Illinois Society for the Prevention of Blindness, May 28, 1928, and refracted. (Is not wearing glasses now.)

   b) School
     1. (Johnson). 1 yr. 1B.
     2. (Harrisfield, Pa.). 6 mo.
     3. (Adams). 6 mo. 2B.
     4. (Kramer). 4 mo. 3B.
     5. Lee. 1927–28. 3B. Conduct—Poor.
          1928–Feb., 1929. 4B–4A. Conduct—Poor.
          28 days absent in 7 mo.
          Transferred Sept. 4, 1928, to Ingrahm School—out of the district.
     6. Ingraham. Sept.,1929–Feb.,1929. 4B. Conduct—Poor. Ability—Poor.
          Demoted 4A–4B.
          Very fond of reading—very poor in arith.
          Transferred 2-7-29 to Coles—"Constantly impertinent to teachers, boastfully defiant, habitually tardy, trouble maker."
     7. Coles. Feb., 1929—Sept. 16, 1929. Special Center for Boys.
          Attention—Fair. Application—Fair. Conduct—Bad.
          Ability—Reading—Good.
               Numbers—Good.
               Handwork—Fair.
          "Above average in school work—very zealous at times."

The following report was given by one of the teachers of the Special Center who has a reputation for being most sympathetic and understanding—the classroom teacher's report was not available: "Bernie Graber was an incorrigible truant. His attendance was terrible. He left school several times whenever he so desired providing the opportunity presented itself. He is a proven thief as he has taken things in school which were later found on his person. We were able in at least a half-dozen occasions to trace the stolen property to him and he admitted his guilt. He is a constant agitator in the room and his personal conduct has been terrible. I have had him in my room many times because his conduct was bad. I believe he has ability but the trend of his mind is pointed in the wrong direction."

Examined at Child Study—see report.

    8. Franklin. Sept. 16, 1929.

             Days absent—11.

             In Detention Home October 18, 1929, to October 28, 1929.

Was in Parental School May 14, 1925, to December 29, 1925.

B. *Social history*

    a) *Family*

Bernie Graber was given by his mother to Mrs. Mary Sabin when he was an infant. He lived with her until he was about four years old. At that time the mother sent him to a friend in South Carolina for two years. From there he went with his mother back to Harrisfield for five years. During this time Mrs. Sabin came to Chicago to live with her daughter, Mrs. Mary Graber. Without warning, Mrs. Baker sent a telegram to Mrs. Graber, "Meet Bernie at Union Station at 8:00 P.M." He was eleven years old at this time. Mrs. Graber met him and took him to her home. The next day Mr. Graber took him with him on the truck. He got off when Mr. Graber was busy, wandered around, was lost, and taken to the Detention Home, where he remained for two weeks before they located him. He has since made his home with them.

The family report that he has stolen money from them, lies about anything, says "it is too hard to be good." He had come home very late—11:00–1:00— but had never stayed away from home overnight until October 10, 1929. He had not returned when the Visiting Teacher was in the home October 16, 1929, except for a few minutes while both Mr. and Mrs. Graber were at work and at which time they feel sure he stole fifty cents from the grandmother.

He was taken to the Detention Home October 18, 1929, to October 28, 1929. This is the fifth time he has been in the Detention Home. Mrs. Lemon is the Juvenile Court officer.

The family report that his own mother, three sisters and one brother are living on the South Side; that the mother has telephoned to them, but they do not know where she lives and know that she does not care for the boy.

On October 9, 1929, he and Jimmie ——— were flipping trucks, and Bernie was slightly injured. Jimmie was sent to the hospital because of injuries.

b) Economic status

Mr. Graber is a truck driver for the Forge Metal Company, earning $42.50 per week. He states that he has had this job for twenty years. Mrs. Graber does housework about two days a week. Buddie, the oldest child, eighteen, works at a chicken house, earns $15 a week.

They are buying a three-flat building and occupy the first flat (seven rooms). The home is very neat and comfortable, and both Mr. and Mrs. Graber seem to be ambitious for their children, who attend the Ingraham School. Mr. Graber says that he had a $25 Christmas Savings Account for his own children and also for Bernie.

c) Household

Sid Graber—Father	Edith—7
Mary—Mother	Bennie—5
Buddie—18	Bernie Baker—14
Bessie—11	Mary Sabin—Grandmother

d) Both Mr. and Mrs. Graber say that they have felt sorry for the boy and have wished to give him a home but they have been unable to cope with him and are very much discouraged.

REPORT OF EXAMINATION OF CHILD STUDY DEPARTMENT OF CHICAGO SCHOOLS, FEBRUARY, 1929

To..

Child's name: Bernie Graber (col.) Age...................Grade...............................

Parent or Guardian...Address ....

School—Coles

Mental.—According to the Stanford-Binet test, the subject's mental ability is average (or slightly below), his chronological age being twelve years four months, his mental age eleven years, and his I.Q. 89. He would have rated higher but for his profound ignorance of school subjects. He is not used to thinking with numbers, and his word knowledge is exceedingly limited. His reasoning was good on the induction test—where the learning materials were objective. He quickly understands what is said to him. No adult could have given better interpretation of the fables than he did. His co-operation was good, although he did not hurt himself trying; he took the test casually; interested in the different stunts we tried but seemingly unconcerned when he failed.

School attainments.—His present ability in arithmetic and spelling is 3B, and in reading 4A.

Home situation.—The guardian did not accompany him so that little could be learned except that Bernie is an orphan, who knows nothing whatever about his parents.

School situation.—Retarded, a truant, and a conduct problem. Subject said he spent one week this term in a Detention Home. The truant officer reports that his conduct is exceedingly bad; he goes to other schoolrooms, bolts through the door, and creates havoc. Bernie himself says that he has "yelled" or talked aloud and thrown books. He did not say this boastfully but admitted it unashamedly when questioned.

The teacher reports that he is a habitual truant and arrives late every day that he comes. He is very defiant in class. He seems to lose his temper and "go slightly insane" upon being teased, she says.

School history.—He was transferred from Ingraham to Coles Special Center for boys January 24, 1929, for these reasons:

1. Constantly impertinent to teachers
2. Boastfully defiant
3. Habitually tardy
4. Trouble maker

Diagnosis.—A boy with plenty of native ability who for some reason did not learn during his early school life. Then finding himself retarded and considered a failure, he began to compensate by truancy and bad conduct. He is an active and healthy boy. His behavior gives him the esteem of a certain group of boys. He is a potential criminal.

Recommended.—(1) Remedial teaching, particularly in arithmetic. (2) An attempt at sympathetic understanding on the part of the teachers. Get him interested in some activity at which he can excel. Praise him plentifully for it and so lead on to further accomplishments.

Note.—We want to stress the fact that this boy is not really subnormal.

Case Committee of Children's Agency recommend foster-home placement for Bernie.

April 22, 1930.—Committed to the Children's Agency with an order on the County for $25 per month.

Bernie Baker was placed in the home of Mrs. Loretta Smith, 3216 St. James Avenue, rate of board $20 per month.

May 13, 1930.—See copy of History Sheet received from the Juvenile Court filed. See copy of Decree of Commitment filed.

May 26, 1930.—Bernie is adjusting well and his teacher reports progress; she believes he will be able to make the next grade with his class

May 27, 1930.—Bernie, on the telephone, tried to pretend to the secretary of Children's Agency that he was an official of the Wilson School and inquired if Bernie's (his own) record was satisfactory. When he was told that his voice was recognized he said he was anxious about the report and wanted to know if it was satisfactory. (See School Report filed.)

June 1, 1930.—See copy of Report on Child Placing Fund Case filed.

June 14, 1930.—Bernie was taken to the Scholastic Track Meet and he seemed to enjoy it very much.

June 25, 1930.—Bernie was promoted to 6B grade.

July 18, 1930.—Bernie left for the Y.M.C.A. Camp for four weeks. See letter received by Agency from Bernie:

DEAR SIRS:

Mr. Ebersole, I am writing regarding an order which I placed in on the 19th of July. It was supposed to have been sent on the 22 of July to Camp Roosevelt RFD No. 7, Downey, Michigan.

Please rush the order as I don't expect to remain up here much longer.

Yours truly,

August 18, 1930.—For good behavior and excellence in leadership Bernie was given an extra two weeks' outing by the "Y" Camp Director free of charge.

September 6, 1930.—Bernie placed in the home of Mrs. Susie Evans, 5465 Ames Avenue, rate of board $20 per month.

September 9, 1930.—Bernie, in office, wanted to transfer to McCullough School. He is pleased with his new foster-home and desires to remain.

Mrs. Evans, the foster-mother, at home, had talk with Bernie and visitor in order that "we may all understand one another." She asked that if anything displeases Bernie he be gentleman enough to discuss his difficulties either with her or with the visitor and pleaded with him not to run away or hide his grievances.

Bernie in turn expressed his appreciation of the foster-parents and insisted that he felt at home and likes Mr. and Mrs. Evans very much.

October 3, 1930.—Mrs. Susie Evans, foster-mother, on the telephone said that Bernie is getting along very well and seems very pleased with the home.

October 4, 1930.—Bernie, in the office, states that he is happy with Mrs. Evans. Foster-parents allow him to use the car occasionally.

October 30, 1930.—Mrs. Porter, the principal of the McCullough School, after reading school record of past two months is favorably impressed with Bernie's adjustment in school and in the community.

He has been present every day and tardy only once since September 1. He was given a G in deportment, but most of his teachers feel that since he has given absolutely no trouble and is making every effort to please he probably merited an E.

Mrs. Louisa Gray, teacher of 6B at McCullough School, is very much pleased with Bernie's attitude and his commendable attempts at co-operation. He is still rather dull and slow at response but is making such an effort toward progress that she feels that he should be encouraged. He is still very poor in reading and spelling but is being drilled in these subjects and has shown marked improvement.

Mr. and Mrs. Evans are very much interested in the boy; they make frequent visits to the school in his behalf. Mr. Evans is enthusiastic and genuine in his concern for the welfare of the boy. He also is coaching him at home.

November 1, 1930.—Mr. Evans, foster-father, telephoned that Bernie has an eruption of the skin.

Later.—Bernie, in office, for haircut and shoe repairs.

November 6, 1930.—Mrs. Evans, foster-mother, at home, feels that, although Bernie tries hard to please, he lacks a sense of responsibility and does his chores poorly or not at all. He has only a few routine tasks to perform in the afternoon, and inspection proves that frequently these tasks have been neglected for a week. In the face of all evidence to the contrary Bernie insists that he has performed his duties. Mr. and Mrs. Evans now have him perform these duties before school and have had a little better success. He informs the foster-mother that he is thirteen although his court record shows sixteen years.

He plays little with the children of the neighborhood, but likes to sit among older people who call at the house. He is very pleasant about doing his home work, and Mr. Evans often helps him with it at night.

Bernie attends church regularly. He is Catholic and is devoted to that church; he can usually be appealed to through his religious principles.

When he first came he would refuse more food, then later while clearing the table he would remove the remainder and eat it. When asked if he had removed it he would deny it. Now, however, he is more frank and shows greater confidence in his foster-parents.

He is still secretive about the money which he earns at odd jobs and hides it away, later trying to secure additional funds from the foster-mother, who is trying to encourage him to depend upon himself for his spending change.

Mr. and Mrs. Evans allow Bernie to attend selected movies, and these never fail to impress him deeply. He saw "When Africa Speaks" at a loop theatre and spent days discussing it with them. He is not careful of the selection of books and prefers the detective and adventure stories. He is interested in boxing and does it at school.

November 13, 1930.—Mrs. Evans, foster-mother, telephoned that Bernie had had a "run-in" with the police squad and since then has been unruly. The foster-parents took a scout knife from him, and he insists that they give it back to him. Unless his attitude changes, the foster-mother is afraid she will have to give him up.

November 14, 1930.—Mrs. Evans, foster-mother, at home, says that she had several days ago sent Bernie to the store and that on the way he encountered the squad who had ordered his hands up. The boy was slow to respond, and one of the squad men slapped his face. The boy returned home in a sullen mood and spent the rest of the evening sulking but did not give any explanation. Later Mr. Evans saw Bernie in the basement cleaning and tampering with an old gun which the foster-father had thrown away. Sensing a change in the boy's attitude, he requested him to put away the gun which he did, but left it in the top of the tool chest. The foster-parents then cautioned the boy that with his disposition and quick temper he should not keep any weapons which might cause him trouble. The matter was then dropped.

The next day Bernie told Mrs. Evans of the incident with the police. Recalling the actions of the boy since this occurrence, Mrs. Evans talked with him concerning the matter and expressed indignation that the police had done such a thing.

This conversation was overheard by Mrs. Sumner, a roomer in the home, and later in Mrs. Evans' absence, seeing the boy sharpen a scout knife, she demanded that he give her the knife. He refused saying he would place the knife where he usually kept it in a drawer. When the boy left the house, Mrs. Sumner took the knife from the drawer and gave it to the foster-mother for safekeeping. The boy missed the knife from its usual place and demanded that Mrs. Sumner return it. When Mrs. Sumner disclaimed any knowledge of the knife Bernie approached her room door saying, "Mrs. Sumner, I warn you that you must give me my knife." Mrs. Sumner then stepped to the door and slapped him. Since that time the boy has avenged himself by singing taunting songs, making faces, and generally annoying the household.

Bernie insists that his playing with the gun and sharpening the knife were merely coincidental. He was contemplating a scout meeting when he sharpened the knife and had no malicious intentions. He resents Mrs. Sumner's interference because he feels that she had no right to share in his discipline. Mr. and Mrs. Evans he recognizes as his foster-parents and tries to comply with their wishes, but Mrs. Sumner's attitude and personality conflict with his own. She has made fun of his religion and called him "mocking names." He feels that he can get along as well in the home as formerly if Mrs. Sumner is not permitted to bother him.

The foster-parents agreed with the visitor that the best solution to the situation and the ultimate readjustment of the boy depend upon the understanding of his personality and Mrs. Sumner's refraining from interference in the boy's affairs.

November 15, 1930.—Bernie, at home, says that he is quite satisfied to let the matter drop and is making an effort to show his best side. He wants to secure a transfer to the Morgan School as he feels he is not given credit for his efforts at McCullough. Although the teachers all give him credit for improvement in his weakest subjects, spelling and reading, he has not improved greatly since September but still receives a P on his report card. He promised to remain at McCullough until February, when the visitor would try to arrange for his transfer to another school, preferably a junior high school

November 29, 1930.—Mr. Evans, the foster-father, telephoned that he will keep the boy no longer as he is beyond his control.

December 1, 1930.—Mrs. Evans, at home, says that on Saturday she sent Bernie to the Atlantic and Pacific store around the corner and he did not return for a long time. The foster-father had gone all over the neighborhood looking for him. When he did return he was vague in his accounts of his whereabouts but finally admitted that he did not go and come home as he was told. The foster-mother then began to scold him, and he responded with sullenness and lack of interest. He was then told that since the foster-parents had not succeeded with him as they had hoped, they would have to give him up. Mr. Evans had then called the office to have the boy removed. As the replacement could not be made until two days later (it being late Saturday evening), Mrs. Evans told the boy that he could remain in the house under exactly the same privileges that he had enjoyed before but foster-mother would exercise no control over him. Bernie then went outside and remained until nine-thirty, when the foster-mother was to leave for a formal dance. After her departure Mrs. Sumner reported that he went into the kitchen and turned on the gas to kill her. (The boy points out that he could not have had such intention as he himself was in the house.) He then turned on the radio loudly and sang rowdy songs, dancing about wildly. After some time at this he went to bed. The next morning (Sunday) he went to church as usual, returned, and spent a normal day.

Bernie expressed his real regard for Mr. and Mrs. Evans and, although admitting his bad behavior, insisted that it was all directed toward Mrs. Sumner, whom he decidedly despises.

Later.—Bernie was placed in Juvenile Detention Home temporarily with the privilege of attending school daily at the McCullough School.

The boy consented readily to the arrangement and cheerfully made the trip to the Juvenile Detention Home.

December 11, 1930.—Bernie was placed with Mrs. Helen Benson, 6345

Pine Street, rate of board $25 per month. (To be paid from Children's Agency. County not to be billed.)

December 12, 1930.—Mrs. Susie Evans, former foster-mother, telephoned that a neighbor had called with her little boy to get a sled which the little boy accused Bernie of taking from the basement when he left the Evans home the previous Saturday. Mrs. Evans insists that Bernie was in the basement of her home working on a sled a few days before his removal. She had seen no sled in his possession before this incident.

December 13, 1930.—Bernie, in the office, explained that he had had the sled before he left the home of Mrs. Smith. He had moved it when he left and it had been in the boy's basement for the time intervening. The paint was not new as visitor might observe.

December 26, 1930.—Mrs. Benson, the foster-mother, at home, states that the boy gives her no trouble and is quite easily controlled. He enjoys sleeping and retires early preferring to remain late in bed but is not permitted to do so by the foster-mother, who encourages him to get up and find something to occupy himself during the holidays. He spends most of his spare time skating on the Washington Park Lagoon. He also spends time seeking odd jobs as delivery boy for near-by merchants. She is trying to develop in him a spirit of self-reliance and independence, feeling that he is approaching the age when he will be self-supporting. He seems to understand this and at least gives the impression of trying to provide some things for himself.

December 30, 1930.—Bernie, in the office, says that the sled was given to him by a person who lived in the building in which he had lived formerly. There was a large spot of grease on the top of the sled which Bernie painted over so as not to soil his clothing. The Caney boy, he claims, confided to him that he had lost his sled and that his mother would probably punish him for it. He offered to bring the sled into the office for inspection.

Later Mr. Brown, the former janitor at 3216 St. James, called at the office to explain that he was present when the sled was given to Bernie by some tenants who were moving and whom the boy had helped with packing.

January 10, 1931.—Mrs. Benson, the foster-mother, at home, says that Bernie got a transfer to the Walker School January 5, and seems to be quite satisfied there. He is still expecting a promotion in February.

January 28, 1931.—Mrs. McManus, the teacher of the 5A room at the Walker School, states that Bernie is not able to do 5A work and that she does not understand upon what basis the 6B classification at the

McCullough was made. He was tried in 6B for two weeks but was a total failure and is barely able to maintain himself in 5A. He is expected to repeat the grade as his foundation is very poor.

It would seem that the assistance of Mr. Evans, the former foster-father, helped Bernie very much. Mrs. Helen Benson, the foster-mother, says that Bernie applies himself diligently to his studies at night. He is ambitious and anxious to succeed but seems to be quite resentful of his poor foundation.

PERIODIC SUMMARY, MAY 26, 1931

Except for a few minor difficulties Bernie has adjusted well in this foster-home. He has made himself quite a part of the household and seems to regard the foster-mother as a person whose insight is incredible. Having reared several other boys, she understands Bernie so well that her sympathies for him have been aroused. She finds him careless and forgetful but she is ever patient, and bit by bit he has improved his behavior. He cannot concentrate and is likely to forget a thing as soon as he is told. He is, however, anxious to please the foster-mother and the Agency and is quite proud of his achievements.

Scholastically Bernie has made wonderful improvement, and his effort has been doubled. His teacher reports him as obedient and enterprising. Bernie proudly exhibits two report cards showing excellent conduct, good academic work, and a decided improvement in arithmetic. A roomer in the foster-home, a Mr. Denton, is very patient in helping Bernie and often gets down on the floor to assist him.

The boy is very devoted to his church and is a constant attendant. He took his first communion several weeks ago and now wears a pin which designates this fact. The foster-mother has found that an appeal to his religious sense never fails. The habitual lying has persisted, but little by little he has ceased to lie to the foster-mother. After he had been caught several times by her he seemed to feel that it was useless.

Bernie has a job on a vegetable wagon, earning seventy-five cents a week. This money he uses for spending change. He is very pleased that he has a job and always presents less of a problem when he has something to do. He looks forward each week to the succeeding Saturday when he can go on the wagon. The employer has promised him a regular position for the summer if he does not find something better.

Bernie was committed a little over a year ago. In that time his appearance has changed considerably. He is now several inches taller, has grown much heavier, and he has a more cheerful expression as contrasted with the sad, woebegone expression of last year. He is very proud of his clothing and keeps it in good condition. He is fond of all kinds of amusements and has developed a taste for better books. A great deal of the time which was formerly spent in reading trashy literature is now spent on school work and the remainder is devoted to adventure stories of the better type.

Seldom does Bernie speak about himself or his past life. In a former foster-home he used to make up fanciful tales about himself and his family, but recently he has spoken little about himself. Once he mentioned his sister, Mrs. Mandel, but never followed out the conversation. He does, however, speak of his institutional placements and gives proper credit to each for whatever it contributed toward his personality. He seems to realize that he is rapidly approaching young manhood and its responsibilities but does not appear entirely capable of adjusting himself to this. He is, however, making strides, and it is hoped that he will gradually make the transition without too great an emotional upset. The Agency has to some extent eased that anxiety and insecurity which he felt for some time, and which probably put him into an explosive frame of mind capable of blowing up with the slightest friction. A new feeling of security has been a prominent factor in the boy's adjustment.

PERIODIC SUMMARY OF DEVELOPMENTS, OCTOBER 29, 1931

During the summer, Wilbur Clayton, a ward of the Children's Agency, was placed in the home with Bernie, who enthusiastically undertook to help the Agency and the foster-mother to bring about improvement in Wilbur's conduct and personality. Bernie's own experience and personal insight were two of the greatest assets in this case. Besides, the task seemed to appeal to him, and it was felt that the assumption of this responsibility would have a wholesome effect upon Bernie himself. In consideration of Bernie's history of improvement, if he should have someone who would look upon him somewhat as a big brother, the relationship might develop beneficially for both.

The plan worked well. Bernie shouldered the new responsibility gallantly, and Wilbur accepted his leadership graciously. Bernie was careful and painstaking in his care for Wilbur. As an example, he did not care to go to the Y.M.C.A. Camp himself but fell in at once to prepare Wilbur. He packed his things, aroused him early, and at six-thirty appeared at the door of the Y.M.C.A., leading Wilbur and carrying his knapsack.

Since Wilbur's return and throughout his stay in the home, Bernie has been his constant companion and adviser, never failing to give him counsel and instruction wherever he can.

Later another ward, Phillip Ford, was placed in the home temporarily. He, however, showed such preference for the home that he was permitted to remain longer than was at first intended. The foster-mother sensed trouble immediately. Phillip did not fit into such a simple scheme of things, and his restlessness and constant raging against authority soon had its effect on the other boys. Bernie became less congenial, less co-operative, and even less truthful. The removal of this boy, Phillip, improved the situation at once, the effects of his stay passed over, and Bernie gradually fell into a more desirable mode of living.

Within the last three weeks the first ward that the Children's Agency placed in the home of Mrs. Benson (1926), who was at that time employed by them, returned voluntarily to the home, and Mrs. Benson accommodated him with room and board. This boy's name is George Miles, and he is twenty-one years of age. He had, since leaving the home, secured a very well-paid position in the offices of Jones Brothers, Wholesale. Since this young man's return to the home, Bernie has imitated all his better characteristics, his manner, his taste in dress, etc. This has made for Bernie an increasing pride in his appearance and greater care for his person.

Bernie is increasingly more polite. The foster-mother recalls an incident which occurred when he first came to the home which illustrates this. Mrs. Benson had made a practice of taking Bernie about wherever she went. One night, when on the way home from a political meeting, Bernie walked boldly and defiantly between a man and a woman who were walking along Garfield Boulevard. The man ignored the incident and merely expressed himself with a frown of disapproval. Mrs. Benson, however, rebuked Bernie. He at once assumed an air of hostility and loudly proclaimed, "They were nobody; why should I step aside for them. I am not obligated to anyone." These remarks made the foster-mother so annoyed that she promptly took him by the arm and marched him home. Once there, she told him in no uncertain terms how unbecoming his conduct had been and told him never to repeat it under these or any other circumstances. Bernie "swelled up to burst," according to the foster-mother, but gradually regained his calm and the incident has not been repeated.

Only once since has Bernie forgotten himself so far as to have to be reprimanded, but in this instance his apology was immediate and genuine.

Near the end of the past school year, Bernie's record was one of constant effort and improvement. His teacher characterized him as obedient and enterprising. He presented two excellent report cards showing creditable conduct and decided improvement in his weakest subject, arithmetic. He was promoted to 6B grade and was very proud of his achievement. His present teacher, Miss Norris (Room 301), finds him very easy to handle and anxious to learn. She has agreed to give her co-operation in helping Bernie over his difficulties. His attendance has been perfect.

The school dentist has recommended that Bernie have several fillings. An exposed nerve requires the attention of a skilled private physician. Upon recommendation of the Municipal Tuberculosis Sanitarium, Harper Hospital has undertaken to do this work.

February 16, 1932.—Regular visits have been made to the foster-home, and the foster-parents have made every effort to help Bernie become a more self-reliant and dependable person. The foster-mother continues to put him gradually more and more on his own. The foster-parents are not demonstrative but show in many ways that they do have the boy's interests at heart, and Bernie has not failed to appreciate this attitude.

Bernie has not accustomed himself to lavish affection, and the type of interest which the foster-parents show appeals to the boy more than a superficial overwhelming type could possibly do. Recognition is made of the fact that Bernie is growing up, and the discipline and control are governed accordingly. Advice and reason have been employed in general; and, whenever these methods are not effective, Mr. Benson makes the boy sit down and discusses the situation quite firmly and frankly with him. Bernie has to listen though he may not express agreement.

Bernie still presents some difficulties. It is apparent that the boy's adjustment has become more satisfactory. He has a tendency however for trying to put things over cleverly and with the least amount of effort. With this is a tendency toward petty lying and exaggeration. This behavior is probably a compensation for a feeling of inferiority in grade placement. Bernie is always anxious to appear in authority. He will tell you that the teacher has left him in charge when in reality she has left no one in charge; he will telephone the office and state that he is Mr. Benson speaking in order to secure greater recognition.

It has been found that to give Bernie a little responsibility is very satisfying to him but to give him too much causes shirking on his part. He has taken pride in caring for Wilbur and feels himself partly responsible for Wilbur's failures.

Miss Norris, the teacher of Room 301, states that Bernie has been doing passing work but she cannot commend his effort. She thinks that Bernie does not apply himself to his utmost. At the blackboard his work is good while at the desk it is mediocre and careless. Miss Norris feels that he neglects his seat work because there is less open competition and less possibility to show off. She complains also that Bernie is frequently dictatorial and self-assertive in the passing of the lines.

His school work has improved greatly especially in arithmetic, and he was promoted to 6A. Miss Norris did not give him a double promotion because she feels that his efforts did not justify it. Her co-operation was again solicited. She promised to watch the boy carefully and give him some special recognition to substitute for his own unacceptable efforts.

July 7, 1932.—The foster-mother telephoned the office that Bernie was determined to leave that day. There had been trouble between them for several months, but she had not told the worker. The boy had taken his clothes to another foster-home that morning and wished to stay there. That transfer was made, and Bernie was left in the Adams foster-home consisting of the foster-parents and their foster-sons, twelve, thirteen, and fourteen years old, also wards of the Children's Agency.

Good reports came from the home regarding Bernie. The foster-mother has given him a great deal of freedom, but when she wishes to discipline him he is obedient. There has been no lying or stealing in this home.

Bernie is taking treatments for gonorrhea. The visitor had a talk with him about the manner of contracting the disease, and the boy was very grateful for sex information as he had never been given such instruction.

February 21, 1933.—The police picked up Bernie for burglarizing a locker in the basement of an apartment. He was found before he had taken anything. He told the visitor that a man in a Buick car who looked Mexican had asked if he wanted to earn some money and had told him to break into a trunk in the locker and get a package of papers. The man gave him $10 and promised more when he delivered the papers. Bernie thought it was an easy way to earn money and did not think of the consequences. The police had taken his $10; he had learned his lesson and would not do it again. He was told to report to the Big Brothers every Saturday morning.

June 18, 1933.—Bernie went on a three weeks' cruise with the Boy Scouts.

For a year Bernie continued to make a satisfactory adjustment in his foster-home. Both foster-parents liked him and felt that he was a good influence on the younger boys in the home.

In May, 1932, an attempt to get a school report was unsuccessful. The report blank was returned stating that the boy was not enrolled. This was thought to be a mistake, however, as the foster-father had been to the school twice during the semester and had been given satisfactory reports each time. Also there was a report card showing satisfactory work. In June Bernie told the visitor that he had been promoted and would enter high school next fall.

The following fall the visitor went to the high school where he was told that they had no record of Bernie but that the boy would be going to another high school from that address. Confronted with this, Bernie said he had given an old address but that he had later inadvertently given the correct one and they had just arranged a transfer. He wants a part-time job which will allow him to continue to go to school or a full-time job which will enable him to support himself.

Later the other high school was visited for a report on Bernie's progress but they had no record of such a boy either. Bernie then admitted that he had not attended high school. He thought he was too old to go to school but thought the visitor would be disappointed so he had lied to him about it.

About the beginning of 1934 the attitude of the foster-parents changed regarding Bernie. They feel that they can no longer trust him and ask that he be removed from the home. He continues to be a well-mannered, well-behaved boy but Mrs. Adams has reason to suspect that he has been buying and selling stolen bicycles. She hasn't proof but the boy's activities are very suspicious and he should be moved so he won't contaminate the other boys.

April 11, 1934.—Bernie was discharged from the care of the Children's Agency. He has wanted to be independent of the Agency for some time. Attempts were made to secure work but unsuccessfully until he said a man in Detroit had arranged to give him work driving a truck. He would not give the name or address of the man but it was finally decided to let him go.

May 7, 1934.—Bernie in office. He is working as truck driver evidently for a bootlegger, taking cans of hard liquor from Detroit to places near Chicago. The boy forces the saloon-keepers to buy his product rather than legal liquor; he carries a gun and is told to use it if anyone bothers him or the truck. The visitor talked to him of the dangers involved but he said he couldn't get anything else and he was tired of living on charity. He would do something else when he had an opportunity. His whole attitude seems against law enforcement and he thinks anything to make money is all right. Later that same day he visited his former foster-home and stole two shirts and a pair of trousers from one of the boys there.

December 6, 1934.—An entry states that nothing further has been heard of the boy.

4. Nancy Saylor

(The Placement of a Child with Hysterical Paralysis)

Date of application to Children's Agency.—January 26, 1932.

Applicant.—Miss Skinner, Child Guidance Clinic.

Child.—Nancy Saylor.

Birth date.—December 10, 1919, Chicago, Illinois.

Reason for application.—Child has hysterical paralysis. There is danger of her becoming an emotional cripple unless she is helped. Prognosis is good if given immediate treatment. Psychiatrist says she should not be at home.

Present situation.—Nancy is placed as an emergency measure in Mrs. Windslow's home at 342 Virginia Avenue, which was recommended by the Children's Aid. That agency will not accept the case but is willing to let this home be used for Nancy temporarily. Board is being paid by the social worker at the University Hospital. Mrs. Saylor and her older daughter Jane are living at 7421 Eighteenth Street. Mr. Saylor is in New York City, looking for work. Mrs. Saylor is trying to get work. Andrew, her son, is at Shadyhill Home for Children.

Family history.—See copy of reports of December 16, 1931, and January 6, 1932, to Child Guidance Clinic from Miss Brooks, social worker at University Hospital. See also copy of report of January 22, 1932, to Miss Brooks from Child Guidance Clinic.

MISS BROOKS'S REPORT OF DECEMBER 16, 1931

Identifying information.—Saylor, Andrew, father, born Baton Rouge, Louisiana. Lydia (Bane), mother, born Richmond, Virginia. Jane, sister, seventeen years. Andrew, Jr., brother, fourteen years. Nancy, patient, born Chicago, December 10, 1919.

Address.—7421 18th Street—telephone National 0846.

Previous address.—534 Park Road.

Referred to.—Social Service, April 21, 1931, by Dr. Swanson for transfer from the University Hospital to the Shadyhill Home for Children.

Medical statement.—Patient had had diagnosis of hyperthyroidism and enlargement of the heart in the Pediatric Department. Orthopedic diagnosis at time of referral: Strained foot.

Relationships with hospital.—Andrew was a patient in the University Hospital with osteomyelitis involving frontal sinus and hip joint. The family had been difficult to deal with and had demanded special privileges. There had been friction with the Admitting Office because their scale of living was so obviously not adjusted to their statement of finances. Nancy had been a clinic and house patient at the University Hospital. The mother had tried to insist on hospital admission when it was not needed, so that a special order was given that she should not be admitted to the hospital. The recommendation to the Shadyhill Home was largely because of the home conditions. The parents did learn not to ask for special privileges, but there has always been friction with the nursing staff. They resented being referred to a social worker, and their attitude has been one of suspicion and superiority that has only occasionally given way to a real desire for help.

Family: Grandparents.—The maternal grandmother was a convert to Catholicism. She apparently exerted a strong influence over her children. Mr. Saylor has never spoken of his family.

Parents.—Mr. Saylor is a salesman who has apparently made a success in the cosmetics line. His wife says he has earned $24,000 a year. His last steady work was with Madame Zurich, Inc. A year and a half ago he lost that work and since then he has been out of work most of the time. He has recently found work selling toilet goods, but is not on a salary basis. Mr. Saylor likes to give the impression of being a successful business man and is most anxious to keep up appearances. He is emotional and irritable when opposed. He has been so discouraged over his lack of work that he has talked about suicide. He is over-solicitous about his children's health, and feels that his wife is not careful enough with them. He likes to spend money when he has it. His account of business affairs shows him ready to borrow money without much prospect of repaying it, and not too scrupulous. One project he was enthusiastic about was getting in touch with widows in small cities persuading them to invest money in starting small toilet goods shops. Mr. Saylor was thirty-five when he married. He complains about his wife's extravagance but seems sincerely fond of her.

Mrs. Saylor is an impetuous, headstrong woman, who makes a very good appearance, but who has a most irritating manner. She is self-conscious and seems to feel that the most important thing in life is to appear to be prosperous. She is devoted to her children but is overindulgent. She has had voice-training and hopes to earn money singing over the radio or in concerts. She has tried selling real estate and has talked about other attempts in business dealings—none of which has turned out well. She has not been willing to face the fact that she has no money and goes to bed prostrated when a crisis comes. She seems to despise her husband because of his inability to support her and particularly because he has been willing to ask help of a social agency. Mrs. Saylor says that she was very young when she married Mr. Saylor and that she has been thoroughly unhappy with him. She says he "has no respect for women" and that she has never been able to have a home as she has had to move from place to place as his work changed. Mr. Saylor accuses her of extravagance, spending money on clothing that should be used for living expenses. He says she has women friends who encourage her in this and that she is out of the house so much that the children have been neglected.

Jane, seventeen, is an attractive girl with a downright, unaffected manner. Several weeks ago she told her parents that she "had no respect for either of them" and shortly afterward left home without their knowledge and went to a maternal aunt in the South. Mrs. Saylor is well satisfied with this arrangement, as she says her sister has a comfortable home and good standards of living.

Andrew is a precocious, attractive boy, badly crippled with osteomyelitis. He has a long convalescence ahead with a guarded prognosis so far as regaining the use of his leg is concerned. After several months in the University Hospital here, he was transferred to Shadyhill Home for Children in Glen Ridge and is still there. He is making a good adjustment there and doing well in his school work. He is devoted to his parents and was worried a great deal about the family finances, writing letters to encourage his father that were far beyond his age.

Nancy is not an especially attractive child; she seems to have had less attention from the family than either of the other two children. She likes to be the center of attention and makes the most of every opportunity to draw attention to herself. Although she says she likes to be at home, she has seemed to prefer to be in a hospital. At Shadyhill Home she was given crutches when she first came, and was with difficulty persuaded to give them up. She did not fit into the group easily and gave the impression of being rather stupid. Her family wrote her while she was there, telling her to demand good care, as they were paying for it, although she was a free patient. She was unwilling to do the foot exercises shown her, and her discharge from Shadyhill Home was recommended on the ground that the association with orthopedic cases was tending to make her exaggerate her own symptoms. Her parents refused then to consider any further care, and she went back to school this fall, apparently in good condition though still complaining about her feet. At this last admission her exaggeration of symptoms and her desire for attention and sympathy have been more marked than ever.

Living conditions.—The family has lived in apartment hotels recently as they have no furniture. Several years ago in Detroit they left their furniture in the care of an acquaintance, who disposed of it and kept the money. Last May they were evicted for non-payment of rent and moved into one room in another apartment hotel. The whole family has lived in this one room, though Mr. Saylor has been away most of the time and has sometimes gotten an extra room when he was in town. They have just taken a two-room apartment in this same hotel, so that, with Jane gone, Nancy has a room to herself.

Finances.—In May they were entirely out of money, having borrowed everywhere they could. A neighbor was bringing them food. The morning they were to be evicted they went most unwillingly to the Family Welfare Agency. They were given $10 with which to move and were asked to come back—but never did. Since then, Mr. Saylor has had just enough work so that they have lived off his expense allowance. Mrs. Saylor has had new clothes this fall, and her demand for the money for clothes rather than meeting other bills brought the family friction to a crisis.

Religion.—Mrs. Saylor is Catholic, brought up by her mother who was a convert. Mr. Saylor is Protestant, with no particular church connection, and the children have none. This has caused a great deal of friction.

Present situation.—Nancy has been fitted with corrective shoes and is at home. She spends a good deal of her time in bed, reading and playing with her doll. She walks about the apartment by holding on to the furniture. She interrupts any conversation with remarks about her symptoms, such as numbness and pains in various places. She is doing some school work, which her teacher sent to her.

Attitude toward the Child Guidance Clinic.—Mr. Saylor welcomed the clinic and wanted Mrs. Saylor to make the contact as he blames Mrs. Saylor for Nancy's state of mind. Mrs. Saylor remarked that this contact was "another blot on my family," but seemed pleased at the prospect of an interested listener to her troubles and agreed to keep the appointment. She later said she felt all Nancy's difficulties were due to approaching puberty, and said she needed no treatment.

We shall be very grateful to have this case taken over for study and treatment.

MISS BROOKS'S REPORT OF JANUARY 6, 1932

Supplementing my report of December 16 regarding Nancy Saylor, I wish to report that Nancy was readmitted to the University Hospital here December 21, 1931, following a report that an osteopath called in by the family had pronounced her paralyzed. The orthopedic and neurological services had found no pathology to account for the patient's symptoms and have made a diagnosis of hysteria. Nancy's home situation is so bad that it seemed unwise to send her back while waiting for the parent's new appointment with the Child Guidance Clinic, so we have held her here, giving her no treatment except occupational therapy. She is required to dress each day, and each day walks a few steps with the nurses' help. She works happily in the Occupational Therapy Shop and helps herself get from wheel chair to work table. She is today working on a table loom and will be promoted to a foot loom as rapidly as possible. Mrs. Saylor is being told that we are keeping Nancy here only pending your advice, hoping that it will help make her keep this second appointment. We do not feel that staying here is accomplishing anything except protecting the child from unwise treatment at home.

Mrs. Saylor has told me the story of what she considers the beginning of Nancy's paralysis. The parents had gone out to spend the evening with a friend of Mrs. Saylor's, of whom Mr. Saylor disapproved. Some liquor was served, and Mr. Saylor took offense at the conversation and left in "a huff." That night he and Mrs. Saylor had a violent quarrel; Mrs. Saylor was screaming, and Mr. Saylor was telling Nancy to call the police to take her mother out. Nancy was also screaming, and her father struck her across the face to make her quiet.

It is interesting that on Christmas Eve after this quarrel the parents went together to Shadyhill Home, where Andrew was taking part in the play which the children were giving. They sat across the aisle from me on the trip and relaxed against each other with their hands interlocked, getting obvious rest and comfort in each other's presence.

Mr. Saylor has lost his job and, I think, has gone to New York. How he gets the money to travel is something the family have not explained.

We are, of course, anxious to discharge Nancy from our ward and are waiting word from you.

CHILD GUIDANCE CLINIC REPORT OF JANUARY 22, 1932

You will probably want a report of our discussion of the case of Nancy Saylor.

No physical examination was made as we believed that nothing could be added to the work already done at University Hospital.

Nancy was given a Stanford-Binet Test (January 20, 1932), which indicated that her intelligence is average and that she is capable of doing work in 6A or possibly in 7B with some training in arithmetic.

Our psychiatrist was impressed with Nancy's maladjustment of personality and felt that the paralysis is only one symptom of a much larger and more important difficulty. There was a marked flirtatious and erotic interest coupled with a strong desire to retain the prerogatives of childhood. There was probably a marked attachment to the father and a correspondingly intense antagonism toward the mother. In a single interview it was impossible to make more than a hurried survey of the main personality deviations. However, the psychiatrist plans to devote considerable time to intensive psychotherapy in Nancy's case. Our Social Service Department has agreed to take this case for intensive service and to attempt a foster-home placement and follow-up care. Through them we shall arrange for interviews with the patient, her sister, father, and mother.

January 26, 1932.—The case was discussed by the Application Committee (Children's Agency). Committee agreed to accept Nancy for care in our hospital January 30, 1932, since a place has to be found for her by that time. The Committee did not think it was wise to place Nancy immediately in a foster-home, as was requested, until we knew more about the child and her family.

January 27, 1932.—Read record at Child Guidance Clinic and talked with Dr. Watson and Miss Skinner, social worker. They approve of the plan suggested by the Committee at the Children's Agency. Dr. Watson recommended that we be very firm with Mrs. Saylor if she gives any orders and simply tell her unless she wants to co-operate with us she can take Nancy home. He doubts if she would go this far because he doesn't believe she really wants Nancy at home.

Dr. Watson plans to work intensively with Nancy. There are several possibilities that may account for her condition—imitation of her brother, of whom she is very fond, and fear because there is a great deal of talk about paralysis in her home because several relatives died of it.

Miss Skinner said Nancy had been improving at Shadyhill Home until after her mother's visit when she told her not to try to walk because she would injure herself.

SUMMARY OF CHILD GUIDANCE CLINIC RECORD

January 8, 1932.—Mrs. Saylor came in after several delays in obtaining a history date agreeable to either parent.

Relation between parents.—Mrs. Saylor described Mr. Saylor as being irritable and quick to criticize. She said he made statements which cut like a knife. When he is away there is perfect harmony. When he is home they have "pitched battles." Mr. Saylor is staid and straight-laced and he nags constantly at his wife and children. Mrs. Saylor said she almost always refuses to go out with him because he humiliates her so. He is very jealous of her for no reason and he is madly in love with her. She said, "You would think he would get tired of the same face across the breakfast table for eighteen years." Mrs. Saylor said she had been absolutely faithful to him up to now but couldn't say for the future. Her friends are unconventional according to her husband's standards. The women drink and smoke and one married couple maintain separate apartments. Mrs. Saylor said she holds her head high when she has only a nickel, but Mr. Saylor slinks down when he is down and out. Mrs. Saylor is making the most of her freedom and is training her voice. Mr. Saylor is demonstrative like Nancy, but she is not.

Relation between father and children.—Mrs. Saylor said the three children are "mad about their father." She doesn't know why, except for the fact that "he is crazy about them."

Family history.—Mr. Saylor is fifty-five. He is a southerner. Mrs. Saylor knows little about his family, but he was somewhere near the end of many siblings. Two of his brothers and sisters died from paralysis in middle age. Mrs. Saylor thinks he will die young although he seems to be in excellent health. He fears for his longevity and hints of high blood pressure. He has been successful in business.

Mrs. Saylor is forty, the youngest of nine children. She is also a southerner. She admitted that she was a great social success. She attended finishing school.

Her parents died in their sixties from vague illnesses. There is no history of mental or physical difficulties in the siblings. Mrs. Saylor spoke proudly of one brother who almost became managing editor of a Hearst paper, but periodic drinking kept him from getting this position. Her mother was a "woman before her time," gifted in every intellectual and artistic field and a wonderful mother to her children.

Mrs. Saylor said neither she nor Mr. Saylor keep up any family connections.

In giving information about the children's medical history, Mrs. Saylor was very vague. She could not remember when they walked or talked. She remembered they all developed "very rapidly." She said their childish illnesses were so mild she couldn't remember them. She said all her children are aggressive.

Record contained report of family's contact with Family Welfare Agency:

May 23, 1931.—Referred by Miss Brooks. Mr. Saylor was unemployed and without prospects of getting a job. Mrs. Saylor was working for the McNulty Real Estate Company on a commission basis, but she had earned only $40 in several months. They owed $250 for two and one-half month's rent. Other expenses were being met by loans from relatives and friends. They were expecting immediate eviction. They were given money for food and a furnished room.

July 1, 1931.—Family Welfare Agency attempted to get in touch with Mr. and Mrs. Saylor at Miss Brooks's request, but they did not respond.

January 28, 1932.—Read record at the University Hospital. Miss Brooks has known the Saylor family since the spring of 1931. They were known to the hospital six months previous to this time.

Miss Brooks believes that Mrs. Saylor brought Nancy to the University Hospital to get her out of the way. Her pride would let Nancy go to a hospital but not to a social agency. After Nancy was dismissed to Shadyhill Home, Miss Brooks tried to persuade Mr. and Mrs. Saylor to place her with a normal group of children but they would not accept such a plan. They do not want to accept any kind of social service.

This fall when Nancy came to the hospital she complained of pain in her feet; and although there was no evidence of anything wrong, it is impossible to prove that she did not have pain. Nancy did not try to help herself while in the hospital but was trying to do what her family wanted and make herself eligible for hospital care.

Mrs. Saylor in particular is the "sporty-type, cocktail-drinking kind." She does feel a certain responsibility for her children but wants Nancy out of the home so she can have a career. She would like to go on the stage. Mr. Saylor believes that plenty of money will solve all problems. Miss Brooks thinks Mr. Saylor is more co-operative than Mrs. Saylor.

January 30, 1932.—Nancy was admitted to the Children's Agency. Her legs were perfectly stiff, and the taxi driver had to carry her to the hospital. Miss Skinner accompanied Nancy.

February 10, 1932.—Called at the Child Guidance Clinic at Dr. Watson's request. He was pleased with Nancy's adjustment.

February 11, 1932.—Talked with Nancy today. She showed worker the three letters which she had received from her father, mother, and brother. Mr. Saylor's letter was written from the Hotel Stratford, New York City. His letter was written in rather a religious vein. He said he was praying for her to get better and told her to try to get well. He wrote, "God bless you and the people caring for you." He said he was working some and hoped to be able to get back and care for his family.

Andrew's letter expressed genuine concern about Nancy. He said he thought of her and worried about her a great deal and told her she was a brave girl. While worker was reading this Nancy said, "I just love my brother. I believe I love him better than anyone in the world, even better than mother and father."

Mrs. Saylor's letter was just a hastily penciled note. It began, "Dear Baby," and asked Nancy's forgiveness for not visiting. She said it was such a long trip to the Children's Agency Hospital. She said, "There is no news except I love you—that's no news, is it? Love and love and more love. Mother."

Nancy said the whole family with the exception of her father are interested in art. "He just sits around and smokes." Her mother has a contralto voice and sings over the radio under the name of Dorothy Parker. Andrew and Jane draw. "Andrew does architectural drawings, but sister and I take to life."

She is very anxious to go to Rose Cottage because the girls talk so nicely about it.[1] It sounds like such a homelike place. Nancy showed worker how well she is using her legs now. She tried to stand up without crutches but was pretty shaky. She was pleased when the worker told her she was going to get her regular shoes from her home because the doctor didn't think she needed the orthopedic shoes any longer.

February 13, 1932.—Visited Mrs. Saylor at her apartment in the Savoy Hotel. Although Mrs. Saylor was expecting the worker at ten, when she arrived at eleven-thirty, Mrs. Saylor was wearing a short polka-dotted nightgown, flannel robe, and mules. Her hair was beautifully done and her face was made up. The room was in great disorder. She asked worker

---

[1] [The Agency has two cottages where children may live in small groups.]

to excuse her appearance, saying the telephone had been ringing the entire morning so she hadn't a minute to do her work. Jane was in bed. About twelve o'clock the maid came in and put the room in order.

Mrs. Saylor greeted worker with, "Isn't Nancy a darling *baby*?" She talked for several minutes about Nancy's wonderful disposition. She said Nancy had never been spanked or scolded. Mrs. Saylor spoke of her distress at having her family scattered, in very exaggerated terms.

Mrs. Saylor said Nancy's illness started about one and a half years ago when she probably stubbed her toe. Andrew was so ill then that Nancy's continual complaint, "My foot hurts," was so annoying that Mrs. Saylor paid no attention to her at first. She said she just sort of brushed Nancy aside like she would a buzzing mosquito. One day she complained more than usual, and Mrs. Saylor looked at her foot and noticed two toes badly swollen. She had her soak her foot in hot water and gave her the best of care.

Shortly after this, Nancy became thoroughly drenched one night on her way home from the movies. After this she complained of a pain in her head, then her leg, and hip. When it got no better after treatment at home, Mrs. Saylor took her to the University Hospital. They found nothing wrong with her foot, to Mrs. Saylor's great disgust, but did find a small goiter, which they treated. After she was home about two months, her toes swelled again. Mrs. Saylor took Nancy back to the hospital. At this time they sent her to Shadyhill Home. Nancy loved it there.

It was a terrible disappointment to her that on the day Andrew went to Shadyhill Home, Nancy left. This was the one chance she had to see him in a year. Mrs. Saylor said she had never seen "such beautiful love as has always existed between Nancy and Andrew. When just little tots there was such a sweet relationship" between them.

After Nancy returned home from Shadyhill Home, she continued to complain of pain, although she learned to walk fairly well. In November she again had trouble and returned to the hospital. This time they stretched the tendons. Nancy complained that the clamp was so tight that the back of her heel was cut. When she came home after this she was in "pitiable" shape. She hobbled around as though she had no joints— like a person crippled with "epilepsy." She was returned to the hospital helpless in just a short time. Mrs. Saylor went into detail in telling why it is so ridiculous to think Nancy's condition is due to hysteria. Nancy was never a child to complain, so she knows she must have pain. It is just bravado when she makes light of her pain and when she seems contented away from home. Mrs. Saylor said Nancy has always had a lovely home.

She wanted to make it clear that the family had been used to better things. She is pleasantly surprised with the Children's Agency, but it is hard to have to place Nancy in a charitable institution.

Mrs. Saylor said her husband has been very unlucky in recent years in getting into concerns "starting on a shoestring" and then failing. At present he has no prospect of work. Mrs. Saylor expects to start training February 15 as saleslady for the Patsy Corset Company. She said she does not know whether or not she can do the work as she has never had to work in her life. She mentioned a sister-in-law who works at Rothstein's, in the toilet-goods counter, who says that a great deal of this kind of goods is being sold even in times of depression.

Mrs. Saylor is singing over the radio on Thursday from three to three-fifteen. She brought out several of Jane's drawings—nudes of Nancy and several nudes of Jane's girl friends and a sketch of Mr. Saylor sitting in a big chair smoking. The pictures showed talent. She also showed a picture of a ship which Andrew had drawn which was well done. Mrs. Saylor told the worker that she has three wonderfully talented children.

She would like very much to return to New York if Mr. Saylor could get work there. They went to Albany from Detroit to live when Nancy was three years old. They came back to Chicago about five years ago.

March 2, 1932.—Nancy received a post card from her father today, mailed from Miami, Florida.

March 15, 1932.—Visited. Mrs. Saylor was at work, but Jane was at home. Jane said her mother does not get home until nearly seven o'clock at night. It is very hard on her because she has never been used to work. She was raised in "the lap of luxury." Jane believes it is a question when the family will ever get together again. She said, "It is just awful to want things you can't have, not that we were ever rich but we certainly lived very comfortably." She said her mother is making just enough money to get by on. Jane is impatient to get to work. She wants to have a studio as soon as she finishes high school. She thinks it is really a good time for a new artist to get started in a time of depression. They have to accept less for their work, and people will hire them whereas if money were plentiful they would employ artists with a reputation. Jane said she is about disgusted with high school, for the senior year is entirely review.

Jane spoke of Nancy as that "poor baby." She does, however, accept the fact that her paralysis was due to hysteria. Jane said she would never cease to be grateful to the University Hospital for the care they had given Nancy and Andrew. Jane said as sort of an afterthought, "Mother and father are too."

Talked to Jane about placing Nancy in Rose Cottage. She thought it would be fine for Nancy to go there.

March 20, 1932.—Nancy was placed in Rose Cottage.

March 25, 1932.—Mrs. Saylor telephoned to get permission to take "her *baby*" home for Easter. She had talked with the nurse before and was quite impatient when told that the children were not allowed to stay out overnight. The worker told her that Nancy could leave immediately after breakfast and suggested that she could go home alone and save her the long trip about which she complained. Mrs. Saylor was aghast at the mere thought. She said she still worries about Jane when she is out alone and she is eighteen. She said she is the baby of her family and is treated as such to this day.

She accepted the fact very well that she could not receive any special favors about visiting and said she would take Nancy out for the day.

April 5, 1932.—See following letter to Mrs. Saylor:

Mrs. Dunkel happened to mention that Nancy did not get back to the cottage Easter Sunday until after eight o'clock. I think I probably forgot to mention when I talked with you over the telephone that we do expect all of the children in at seven. With a group of children such as ours, we have found that it works out best for the interests of all to have pretty definite rules about visiting and the hours for the children to return if they have been away for the day. I know you understand the problems we have in caring for groups of children and will co-operate with us in helping Nancy observe our regulations.

I presume Nancy has told you about the art class she is attending at the Women's Club. She seemed to enjoy her first class very much, and I think it will be good for her to have this outside interest.

April 19, 1932.—See following letter to Mr. Saylor:

I understand that you visited Nancy recently at Rose Cottage. I should like very much to see you and have an opportunity to discuss Nancy's problems with you. I am sorry that I was not able to see you before we admitted Nancy because we always like to talk with both parents before we accept children for care.

I expect to be in the office all day Thursday and should like to have you come there then if possible. It will be best if you telephone and make an appointment if you plan to come any other day.

April 20, 1932.—Mrs. Saylor left a message for the social worker to call immediately. The worker did not get in until six hours after the message was left. When she telephoned, Mrs. Saylor was entirely over her anger.

First of all she mentioned the letter to Mr. Saylor and asked why the worker wanted to see him. She seemed satisfied with the explanation given. She then told how busy he is when in town but said she would let the worker know when he is returning to Chicago. Mr. Saylor is a high-class salesman and is known all over the United States. He worked for Doans' Cosmetics Company for about ten years, and then his brother persuaded him to become an automobile salesman. This was the year of the war, and since then things have been pretty hard.

Mrs. Saylor said there are two things she insists upon: one that Nancy receives medical attention and the other that she not be allowed to run around the streets alone.

She thinks that anyone should be able to see that one of Nancy's hips is much larger than the other. She is convinced that Nancy had infantile paralysis and that she will be a cripple for the rest of her life unless something is done for her. When Mrs. Saylor was told that Nancy is quite contented, she said, "That's just the trouble, her father thinks she is being weaned away."

Mrs. Saylor thinks it isn't safe to allow the children to make trips around the city alone. The worker explained that they were never allowed to go alone except to places which they knew well and that we could not refuse to allow Nancy to go alone when we allowed other girls her age to go. Mrs. Saylor said that, even though Jane is eighteen, she is never allowed to go out alone unless she knows exactly where she is going.

April 30, 1932.—Mr. Saylor telephoned and talked to the superintendent. He asked that Nancy be allowed to spend the day at her home Sunday though she was at home only two Sundays ago, and the Children's Agency's rules are that children may visit at home only every third Sunday. He said he was rarely at home and wanted to spend the day with her. He was granted the privilege with the request that he be careful not to ask that too many exceptions be made for Nancy. Mr. Saylor asked if the superintendent did not think Nancy would be better off at home. When it was suggested that he come to the Children's Agency to discuss the question, he was very angry and said he guessed we wanted to put him "through a civil service examination." He says he can't bring himself to face those from whom he "accepts charity." However, he would like to meet the Children's Agency workers as he thinks they "have been kind to Nancy." But he would not say specifically when, if ever, he could come to the office.

June 4, 1932.—Mrs. Saylor telephoned to say she wished to ask for a special privilege. Andrew is to be home Sunday, and she would like to have Nancy home for the day. She wants this to be a surprise for Nancy.

When told that we had heard she was planning to take Nancy home after school was out, Mrs. Saylor said, "Yes, it won't be long until I have my little girl with me again. I talked to Miss Skinner recently, and she said Dr. Watson had discharged Nancy as there was absolutely nothing wrong with her." The worker told Mrs. Saylor that we should like to see her and Mr. Saylor before Nancy went home. Mrs. Saylor said they would be glad to see us if that were possible. Mr. Saylor is in and out of the city, and she will have to stay at home every minute to look after Andrew. He is to be at home for a month. He is not quite right mentally, and the hospital agreed to let him stay at home for a month's vacation. Mrs. Saylor gave up her work long ago. She said she would have had Nancy at home much earlier if she had not thought it would be a shame to make her change schools again. When it was suggested that the social worker could call on her, she said that would be "lovely."

Telephoned Dr. Watson. He is very much opposed to having Nancy go home as he is afraid that all the good that has been done will be undone. He said he was amazed at the change in the child. There was no truth in Mrs. Saylor's statement that the Child Guidance Clinic had discharged Nancy.

Miss Brooks had notified him about Andrew's being at home for a month, and the Saylors know that Nancy could not possibly stay at home while he is there. The state of his health makes it absolutely necessary that he have a separate bed and they have only one bedroom.

Dr. Watson has talked with Mr. Saylor over the telephone and he feels that he is certainly a poorly adjusted individual. Dr. Watson has an appointment with Mrs. Saylor for sometime during the latter part of June and he believes that he will talk plainly to her about her own problems and about the effect she has on Nancy. He says he may make her very angry so she will have nothing more to do with the Child Guidance Clinic or she may possibly accept his advice. Dr. Watson said Mrs. Saylor is rather confused in her feelings toward him. She professes to dislike him very much but she has a great deal of respect for him. So far Dr. Watson has had pretty good success in being rather "rough" with Mr. and Mrs. Saylor and when they have said they were going to take Nancy home he has told them to go ahead. Then they have backed down and expressed their appreciation for all that has been done for Nancy.

Dr. Watson agrees that it is better for him to talk plainly to Mr. and Mrs. Saylor about their effect on Nancy's behavior than it is for the Children's Agency to say anything to antagonize them. If Nancy does go home and her problems develop again, they may come back to the Agency.

Unless something in particular occurs, Dr. Watson advises that we let things "ride along" until he sees Mrs. Saylor.

June 6, 1932.—The following letter was received by the Children's Agency from the Child Guidance Clinic:

This is to notify you that our social service department is discontinuing active work with Nancy Saylor. Our psychiatrist, Dr. Watson, will be very glad to co-operate with you further if you so desire.

We feel that your staff members have done an unusual piece of work in bringing about Nancy's present adjustment and are sorry to learn that Mrs. Saylor is planning to take the child home. We shall be interested in any future developments, and should new problems arise we shall be ready to consider again becoming active.

June 14, 1932.—Telephoned Miss Brooks. She made no definite statement to Mrs. Saylor that she could not take Nancy home while Andrew is at home. The Saylors have taken a larger apartment in the same hotel and can probably manage because Mr. Saylor is away so much. Miss Brooks said that she has not visited Andrew, and the visiting nurse whom they sent in was practically "high-hatted" out of the hotel. They told her they did not need her services.

Visited. Found Mr. and Mrs. Saylor and Andrew at home. Mrs. Saylor was playing solitaire, and Andrew was sitting on the davenport apparently doing nothing. Mr. Saylor immediately entered upon a long dissertation on Andrew's illness and described in detail every operation he has had and those still to be done. He called the worker's attention to the depression in his forehead and said the throbbing of his brain could be seen. Mr. Saylor talked about staphylococcus and streptococcus infections and used many scientific terms. He said he had made a study of these things, when he was selling biologicals. Every attempt to change the subject failed, and Mr. Saylor returned to the subject of his children's illnesses until he had said all he cared to say. Andrew looked very uncomfortable during this reference to his ailments. Mr. Saylor said Andrew had been getting despondent over his future and had recently told him that he could jump out of the hotel window or could cut his wrist with his boy-scout knife. During the discussion of physical ills Mr. Saylor mentioned that he thought Andrew was all right mentally.

He then started on Nancy. He believes she is too smart. She always had mature ideas and could always discuss subjects like a grown person. Mrs. Saylor went over in detail for the third time the various steps in Nancy's illness. When she told about her goiter she remembered that her thyroid is very bad again. Her eyes were bulging and glassy and her throat swollen when she saw her last Sunday. She said, "Isn't that so, Andrew?" "I did not notice her throat, but I guess her eyes were big." Mr. Saylor said they must get treatment for her immediately. She gained several pounds when previously treated for goiter.

Both Mr. and Mrs. Saylor spoke of Nancy's hips not being even. Mr. Saylor is certain she had infantile paralysis. He had her stand "naked in the sunlight" and made her stand in various positions and there was no way she could stand that one hip was not higher than the other. Mrs. Saylor is certain that Nancy deliberately makes them appear the same at times. She has learned to "almost throw her hips out of joint and compensate for the shortness by throwing the upper part of the well leg outward."

Mr. Saylor is going to have Nancy play tennis when she gets home because he thinks this will be very good for her. He told Mrs. Saylor to get Nancy a complete outfit.

Mrs. Saylor is through with the Child Guidance Clinic and has told Dr. Watson so. She can't understand a person like him because he permitted her to insult him without getting angry, when she compared him to a doctor who had treated her kidneys when she had a streptococcus throat because he believes in treating heads when the trouble is in a toe. She said Dr. Watson told her that she would have a chronic invalid on her hands if she took Nancy home and that Jane was one of the most maladjusted girls he had ever seen and would end up in an insane asylum. Mrs. Saylor said she wondered how he could say such a thing when Jane had made 118 on a test given her at the Clinic. Mrs. Saylor thoroughly enjoyed telling of the answers she made to the doctor's statements. Mr. Saylor interrupted to say that he even asked Mrs. Saylor if her sexual relations with her husband were happy. He thinks all psychiatrists are interested in doing is to "dig up filth" and believes they are in the same mental state as the people whom they treat else they would not be in such business. Mr. Saylor thinks a normal person wouldn't dare suppose that he could tell just why a person acts in a certain way. According to him, all psychiatrists have superiority complexes.

After he was through discussing his children's illnesses and the medical profession, Mr. Saylor began on business conditions and his own job. He went back over all his reverses and explained how unfortunate he was in getting with companies with inadequate financial backing. At present he is with a firm which sells a line of French cosmetics, which has plenty of money, but he is working for a small salary. However, they are greatly pleased with his work and have already suggested a week's vacation with pay although he has been with them only nine weeks. So far Mr. Saylor has sold a great deal more than was expected of him but he is afraid the 10 per cent tax which will be put on the goods after June 21 will greatly affect his sales.

Mrs. Saylor plans to take Nancy home just as soon as school is out. She said Nancy called her today and said she could hardly wait to get home and asked Mrs. Saylor to come for her at one o'clock Friday as school closes at twelve. Mrs. Saylor said that Dr. Watson told her that Nancy said she did not want to go home. Mrs. Saylor asked Miss Skinner, and she told her Nancy could hardly wait to get home. Nancy told Mrs. Saylor about being punished for burning the toast and answering back. Mrs. Saylor said she felt that Nancy was given too much work to do especially with her active thyroid. Once Nancy had to wipe up the kitchen floor alone. Mr. Saylor didn't think that was so much work and that she would have tasks if she were at home. Both Mr. and Mrs. Saylor expressed their appreciation for all that had been done for Nancy and they apparently feel very friendly toward the Children's Agency in spite of some disagreements.

Mrs. Saylor assured the worker that she has ample room for Nancy and is especially anxious to have her at home while Andrew is there. They have a bedroom, an in-a-door bed, a davenport, and a day bed.

When camp was suggested for Nancy, both Mr. and Mrs. Saylor were very much interested.

Today Mr. Saylor did far more talking than Mrs. Saylor. She laughed at many of the things he said, and there was no suggestion that they were not in perfect agreement until Jane was mentioned. Mr. Saylor said she was boy crazy. Mrs. Saylor immediately reprimanded him, but he went right on insisting that Jane was crazy about boys. Finally the argument ended in a bet of dinner and a movie if they found that Jane had gone out with a boy this afternoon. Although the argument ended as rather a joke, Mrs. Saylor was plainly annoyed.

June 17, 1932.—The worker was able to talk with Dr. Watson today after many attempts. He was told of the visit with Mr. and Mrs. Saylor. He said he had accomplished nothing with Mrs. Saylor and that he was not going to have any more contact with her. Dr. Watson said if it would help our relationship with the Saylors to agree with them that he had been of no help to feel perfectly free to do so. He thoroughly approved of the plan to send Nancy to camp.

Nancy was dismissed from the Children's Agency.

June 24, 1932.—Telephoned Mrs. Saylor to tell her that Nancy could go to camp on July 13 and that the social worker would call on her before that time to give her instructions about the time of leaving, etc. Mrs. Saylor said she would be glad to see the worker at any time.

July 7, 1932.—Visited. Nancy was sitting in the hotel lobby in her bathing suit. She said her mother would be down. Mrs. Saylor explained that she had company and that her place is so small it didn't accommodate many people. Andrew is still at home, and the doctors are willing that he stay as long as he gets along well. Mrs. Saylor does not want him to be put in a cast during the summer if it can be avoided. Mrs. Saylor expressed her appreciation for our making it possible to send Nancy to camp.

July 13-27, 1932.—Nancy at Holiday Camp.

September 7, 1932.—Visited to see if Nancy had her school transfer. Mrs. Saylor was greatly distressed because the Children's Agency was mentioned on the transfer. Nancy will enter Roosevelt Junior High. Mrs. Saylor associates with her principal in a social way and will be humiliated when she finds out about Nancy's placement at the Children's Agency. Mrs. Saylor said she hadn't said anything to Nancy about it and added that she didn't believe Nancy would mind as much as she does. She said, "It is funny about Nancy, she has always had a faculty for picking up the 'ornriest kids,' janitors' daughters and foreigners. Of course, it is sweet of her to want to associate with them. I suppose she knows it would be hard for them to make friends. Nancy is so different from Jane." Nancy has recently renewed her acquaintance with a girl friend she had before she went to the Children's Agency, and Mrs. Saylor is so glad because Nancy has been all alone. She has really been pathetic because she has had no friends. In Mr. Saylor's work he always associates with the highest class, and so she couldn't allow Nancy to pick up with just anyone. Mrs. Saylor talked about "people of our standing" and then explained that she didn't mean financial standing but people with ancestry and a family tree. She and Mr. Saylor are English on both sides.

Mrs. Saylor believes it is ridiculous to say that God created all men equal. "If He had He would have made everyone white." She knows that there are people who aren't as good as she is. The Negroes should be segregated, Civil War or no Civil War. Even the Negroes recognize that. Her colored cook whom she brought north with her once told her about seeing a dirty black wench walking with a white man; she recognized that this man was just as low as the Negro.

Mr. Saylor lost his job two weeks ago and is leaving for Boston tonight. He may go into business with his brother in Boston.

Mrs. Saylor is looking for work. She thinks of working for the Civic

Improvement Society, which is working for separate schools for the colored people, separate banks, etc. She said the worker would be shocked if she knew the number of Negroes at Arlington High School.

Jane can find no work.

Andrew is still at home. He has had three operations on his shoulder this summer, and in a short time will begin having the plastic surgery done.

Nancy had a fine time at camp. She said Harriett, her friend at camp, was a nice little girl but not quite her kind.

When the worker left Mrs. Saylor said, "Now, you'll come to see us again, won't you?"

The following is the chronological health record kept by the Children's Agency nurse:

HEALTH HISTORY OF NANCY SAYLOR

Mrs. Saylor could not remember very much about Nancy's development. See summary of Child Guidance Agency.

Information obtained from Miss Brooks, University Hospital:

8–25–30.—First contact. Surgical out-patient department—left Morton's metatarsalgia.

1–3–31 to 2–3–31.—University Hospital—questions of toxic goitre—slightly hypertrofied heart—slight mitral insufficiency.

4–21–31 to 4–23–31.—Orthopedic Hospital for isolation period prior to admission to Shadyhill Home.

11–12–31 to 12–6–31.—Orthopedic Hospital—question of short tendon, given physiotherapy.

12–21–31 to 1–20–32.—Nancy brought to University Hospital helpless.

January 22, 1932.—See report from Child Guidance Clinic. (In Child Guidance Clinic record there was a notation about Nancy's comment that at home nothing seemed real, even her mother. Nancy said her mother visited her newly made up, with a new set of eyelashes. Mrs. Saylor laughed when Nancy said this and asked her if she wanted a fat old mother.)

See social worker's interview with Mrs. Saylor, February 13, 1932.

January 30, 1932.—Nancy was brought to the Children's Agency by Miss Skinner of the Child Guidance Clinic. The taxi driver had to carry her.

NURSE'S REPORT ON NANCY DURING HER STAY AT CHILDREN'S AGENCY HOSPITAL JANUARY 30–MARCH 20, 1932

January 30, 1932.—Physical examination by Dr. M. Luthy. No findings.

Nancy stated that she could bend her knees at night, and in the daytime they straightened out. She asked for a bedpan and was told that we had none but she could walk to the bathroom. She waited quite a while and then hopped to bathroom, holding on to the nurse.

February 2, 1932.—At night she decided she could not walk to the bathroom and demanded a bedpan. Night nurse said there was none and anyway Miss Mann, nurse, wanted her to walk. Nancy said, "Never mind, Miss Mann is not home." When told she was, Nancy got up and in a rather hurt tone of voice said this was all the "bunk" anyway. She has not refused to go to bathroom since.

February 3, 1932.—Sat in chair to have hair cut.

February 4, 1932.—Walked to bathroom. Tub bath—cried a few big tears and said she was in pain. Miss Mann said she did not wonder that anyone could be uncomfortable who twisted herself all out of shape as Nancy did. She was left alone in the tub for a few minutes. When it came time to get out she said she could not get out but Miss Mann said she did not know what they would do; maybe she would have to sleep there as she could not lift her out and she was alone. Nancy managed to get up and out of the tub. She made herself stiff at first and then when no attention was paid to her, got out very nicely. She was all right until after 7:00 P.M. when the night nurse came on duty and she thought Miss Mann was off duty; then she began making a fuss about the terrible pain in her hip from lying in that hard tub. Miss Mann went in, told her to stop trying to twist her hip and spine out of shape, and immediately she stopped and went to sleep.

February 5, 1932.—Nancy was moved to the big dormitory where she has to walk about forty feet each way to the bathroom. She is walking with one crutch, holding on to another child but holding her left leg stiff and her foot out of shape. She gets no attention regarding her physical condition. Nancy sleeps with her chin almost on her knees, her appetite is excellent, she seems happy, and is apparently enjoying it here. She is not being entertained.

February 8, 1932.—Walks to the bathroom with two crutches, but is making considerable fuss about it.

February 9, 1932.—The superintendent told Nancy that she must go to the dining-room for meals, as the hospital staff were too busy to wait on people who were not very ill. She was offered help in dressing but she refused it. She went to the dining-room with two crutches, and goes through many unnecessary motions to attract attention. Other children very kindly offered their help.

February 11, 1932.—Nancy said she might as well make her bed if she had to be up to go down to meals. She asked for work and listed the clothes of a new child admitted. She makes health posters for the hospital.

February 12, 1932.—Tub bath. Not much fuss, but complained about pain; stopped when no one paid any attention. Miss Mann was ill in bed. Nancy came in on her crutches, looked rather pained, and went out.

February 20, 1932.—Miss Mann returned from the hospital, and again Nancy came in and looked her over but offered no comment of any kind. She has been eating her meals in the dining-room.

February 22, 1932.—Nancy has been complaining of earache. She wants medicine in her ears and a hot-water bottle. Mrs. Clarke, matron, suggested she see Miss Mann first. On examination, the eardrum was found to be normal, no inflammation either in canal or drum. Miss Mann said she did not wish to hear any more regarding earache; later Nancy mentioned it again to Mrs. Clarke, who again suggested seeing Miss Mann. Nancy's reply was, "Oh, she said there was not much wrong with my ear." The earache was not mentioned again. The first day Miss Mann was on duty, Nancy came to the desk, stood and looked at her several minutes, then said, "Well, now that you have been in bed a week and are so weak, you can appreciate how I feel." Miss Mann, without looking up from her desk, said, "But I did not know you had been ill." Nancy, "Everybody said I was in a pitiful state." Miss Mann, "Yes, undoubtedly very pitiful when a well, healthy girl of twelve goes to bed." Nancy, with some tears and a little show of temper, "Oh, how you talk to me."

Nancy has a tendency to sulk; she does not enjoy sulking or a display of temper as she is completely ignored at such times. When left alone in a room by herself with the door shut, she soon comes out smiling. It is quite probable that this temper would become much worse if anyone paid any attention to it.

February 25, 1932.—Miss Mann told Nancy that she would have to get along with only one crutch. Nancy cried and said, "You are so mean to me; you think it is all imagination and I am really sick. I have so much pain," but she gave up the crutch.

February 26, 1932.—Nancy asked Mrs. Clarke for a crutch. Mrs. Clarke said she could not give it to her without Miss Mann's permission. Nancy asked Mrs. Clarke to ask Miss Mann for it. Later when Nancy saw Miss Mann, she began crying and begging to use a second crutch. She did not make any effort to take the crutch although it was right beside her. Several times during the next day she asked for her crutch and walked very stiff, not bringing her foot down flat at all.

February 28, 1932.—About this time Nancy became very interested in Rebecca Kendall, a four-year-old child who had been brought in from a boarding-home with an earache. Of her own accord, she took over almost all the care of Rebecca, making her bed, and after a day or so, even wanted to bathe her. She was allowed to do this and when seen in the bathroom she was laughing and acting quite normal as she was bathing Rebecca. After this she took more interest in other young children in the hospital and without being asked to do so, took it upon herself to see that they had their hands and faces washed for meals and their hair combed.

March 2, 1932.—Mrs. Clarke told Nancy that Miss Mann intended taking her other crutch away on Thursday, the following day, and asked Nancy to surprise her and put it away without being told to. A few hours later Nancy was in the bathroom washing Rebecca when she called to Mrs. Clarke and told her there was a present on her bed for her, her crutch. She walked then holding on to the wall and one of the other children.

March 5, 1932.—Walking without holding to objects to assist her.

March 7, 1932.—Miss Mann told Nancy that as soon as she walked without crutches she might go downtown with her.

March 8, 1932.—Took Nancy downtown. The streetcar was crowded so she had to stand up all the way. She stood with both feet flat on the floor, hips level, semed to enjoy looking around the stores. She was sent home alone on the streetcar; she came home very happy, "thrilled" she said.

March 10, 1932.—Took Nancy to Rose Cottage to visit. She seemed very happy at the prospect of going there both to visit and to live. She stayed for dinner in the evening. When driving home, she said, "Oh, Miss Mann, you don't know how happy you have made me. I must admit I almost hated you, but I love you now." She talked about how happy she was all the way in.

March 11, 1932.—Nancy fell on the cement walk while playing with a child's scooter, striking her head. She came in with one of the children and went to bed. Later when Miss Mann called her for supper she seemed dazed and said she had a headache and did not want any supper. She was given a glass of milk, which she refused because of nausea. Later the children who had been playing with her told how she had fallen. When questioned, Nancy said she did not remember playing with a scooter and had no idea how she got home to bed. Miss Mann called Dr. M. Luthy, who said Nancy had a very slight brain concussion from the bump. To remain in bed, with ice cap, head elevated, liquid diet for forty-eight hours. Nancy complained of dull headache. Her eyes react to light normally, no symptoms of skull fracture, pulse remains about 92–104. Nancy has been running a temperature of 99–99.4 daily in the afternoons.

Dr. Luthy looked up record at University Hospital, found that she had been running some temperature while a patient there. No cause for temperature found.

March 13, 1932.—Miss Mann visited Andrew at Shadyhill. A sweet boy who would be very good-looking if it were not for the terrible scar following a sinus operation—a place on his forehead extending down over the bridge of his nose, in all about two inches long and one inch wide, also sunken down into his face about one-quarter of an inch. His left leg was in extension. He inquired about Nancy, seemed genuinely glad to hear she was so well, and sent his love to her. Jane was visiting him at the time and from all appearances is a sweet, charming young girl who showed rather good sense from the way she talked about her sister and brother. She was very anxious to have Nancy back in school.

March 15, 1932.—Nancy still had a slight headache until Monday afternoon. Her mother wished to see her during the week and said she could not come on Sunday as she had to go to see Andrew. Mrs. Saylor asked permission to visit Nancy after work some evening. She was told that visiting hours in the hospital were from 3:00 to 5:00 but was given permission to come from 6:30–7:00 P.M. the following Thursday.

March 17, 1932.—Nancy was improved. No headache, got up this afternoon. Her mother came at exactly 6:30, embraced Nancy, hugging and kissing her several times, then took her in the dormitory, holding her in her lap, talking to her, calling her "Darling baby" (she always talks of Nancy as her "baby"), kissing her several times on her mouth while she talked to her and continually rocking.

She stayed between fifteen and twenty minutes and then said she was very tired and must go home. She thanked Miss Mann several times for what she had done for Nancy and hoped some day she might be able to repay in some measure. She said she had never seen Nancy look so well. She seemed more friendly than at previous visits.

March 18, 1932.—Nancy got a bag of pecans from her father (sent from Florida), and made some fudge using some of the pecans.

March 19, 1932.—Nancy has been helping to get her things packed to go to the cottage. She continually says she does not want to go now. It is possible that she doesn't want to go to school. She has not been in school for such a long time and is such a tall child, she may dread being in school with smaller children. Another supposition is that she has not been very happy in other places she has been and is very happy here and is sure of this and not sure of her happiness in the cottage.

Examination by Dr. Luthy—no findings.

March 20, 1932.—Nancy went for a walk this morning. In the afternoon her mother telephoned, saying she would not be able to come to see Nancy today. She talked to Miss Mann regarding Nancy's condition; asked if we were sure Nancy was well. She was afraid that we were making a grave mistake in sending the child to the cottage. She is not willing to accept any diagnosis of hysteria regarding Nancy's condition and is quite certain that the hip is "out of the socket." Miss Mann explained to her that if a bone were out of the socket it would be extremely painful. Mrs. Saylor says she knows Nancy's hips are far from level when she stands. Miss Mann explained that when Nancy stood with one foot flat on the floor and only the toes touching of the other foot, naturally one hip would be higher than the other. When she stands with both feet flat on the floor, her hips are level. There have been no complaints as to pain or real discomfort. During the afternoon Nancy walked about three blocks to a show in the neighborhood and came home elated because she had met Dr. Luthy and he was surprised to see her walking so well.

In the evening Miss Mann took her to Rose Cottage. Nancy was rather reluctant to go. When she got there, she cried when Miss Mann left and asked if she would still keep her "case" now that she was at the cottage, because when she "left the University Hospital they dropped her case." Miss Mann said she did not have "cases" but she would continue to be her friend as before.

Regarding Nancy's condition when placed March 20, 1932, she still runs afternoon temperature of 99–99.4, positive Von Pirquet, pulse 84–92. Weight ninety-five pounds. Temperature will be taken daily in the afternoon; she will be weighed monthly. Her appetite is excellent, she is always hungry. Sleep—good, about ten to eleven hours. Active in play, always kind to others, even those she does not like very well. She is always well mannered, never impudent. She obeys quite well, shows good executive ability, works quietly, is capable, always asks the other children to do things in a very quiet tone, and they always do what she asks. She is not quarrelsome. She is not very neat about her care of clothing, leaves things lying around; she is clean about her person and likes to look nice.

She talked a great deal about her mother, her wonderful voice and the places she has sung, how beautiful she is, and how many men always admire her mother wherever she goes; always speaks of her mother as a very small woman, although she is a fairly large well-built woman, good-looking, well dressed, good appearance. Nancy scarcely ever speaks of her father, only mentions him when she gets a postal card from him.

March 20, 1932.—Nancy placed in the cottage at 421 Mount Pleasant Avenue.

March 21, 1932.—There was a very bad snowstorm today. Mrs. Dunkel packed a lunch for all the children at Rose Cottage so they would not have to walk home for lunch. Since this would be Nancy's first day at school, she suggested that Nancy wait but she didn't wish to do so.

At noon Nancy and Maxine Allen walked home in the snow for a pencil for Nancy.

March 30, 1932.—The superintendent visited Rose Cottage today; and when she left, Nancy asked if she might walk to the corner with her. Nancy talked about art very seriously.

She said she loved being at Rose Cottage but that the group didn't afford her very much inspiration for her art work. The children are very much too well fed and well dressed to be good subjects for drawings. Nancy said unlike most children she is able to express herself in art. She would like to take drawing lessons but doesn't want to begin by drawing lines and circles. She wants to study from life.

April 2, 1932.—Nancy was enrolled in the art class at the Women's Club. Miss Larabee is the instructor. The class meets from nine-thirty to twelve on Saturday mornings. Nancy will make the trip by herself. The carfare and twenty cents are furnished by the Children's Agency, five cents from Nancy's allowance. At the first lesson Nancy made a bust of a man. She said the teacher rejected some but accepted hers.

April 20, 1932.—Talked to Aunt Elizabeth (matron). Nancy went home on her first Sunday at the cottage, and got back about nine in the evening. On the following Sunday Mrs. Saylor came to visit, and was very considerate and pleasant. On the following Sunday, the tenth, Mr. and Mrs. Saylor visited Nancy and everything was pleasant. On April 17, Mr. and Mrs. Saylor again visited. Nancy had been ill with a stomach upset and was upstairs in bed. Her parents visited her there. Mr. Saylor called Aunt Elizabeth and asked if she had ever seen Nancy undressed. He asked her to come up and made Nancy stand before the window. He called attention to Nancy's hip, insisting that one hip was higher than the other. He said, "I don't want my daughter to be crippled in mind and body." Nancy said, "But I get good grades in school, Father." Mr. Saylor ordered Aunt Elizabeth to see that a weight is put on Nancy's foot, but was told he should consult the Children's Agency nurse or superintendent regarding the matter. He also asked for a camera to take Nancy's picture nude and said he would have one taken later to show the family doctor. He then said he would prefer to have Nancy home. Nancy said quite clearly to them in Aunt Elizabeth's presence that she did not want to go home. She said, "It isn't that I don't love you but I can't live at home. There is no order there."

Later Nancy told Aunt Elizabeth confidentially that her father and mother quarreled; her father never makes enough money to satisfy the mother. She thought they would quarrel when they got home as she noted several remarks that made her know they were angry at each other. She repeated that she loved them but did not want to go home.

On Monday, April 18, Nancy fell in gym class and hurt her arm. She was sent home and the arm was bandaged. Later the nurse asked that Nancy come in to the Children's Agency after school the following day. Nancy did not want to come before as she was to meet her mother downtown after school on Tuesday to buy a gift for her brother. She met her mother as planned. About 7:00 P.M. the mother telephoned Aunt Elizabeth, furious because she thought Nancy's arm had been neglected. She would not bring Nancy to the Children's Agency hospital as she was "too tired," so Aunt Elizabeth had to get help in the cottage and go fifty-four blocks to escort the child to the Children's Agency. When she met Mrs. Saylor, Mrs. Saylor said before Nancy that she had talked to her doctor and he had said that Nancy's mind was "only half-developed."

Later.—Mrs. Saylor telephoned the Children's Agency nurse and complained bitterly because Nancy is not getting proper care.

Later.—Talked to the nurse, Miss Mann. She reported Nancy had an X-ray at St. Martin's (Nancy had objected to returning to the University Hospital). She wanted to go to St. Martin's like the children at the Children's Agency. She has a slight "green stick" fracture. She can go to school tomorrow. On the way to St. Martin's, Nancy told Mrs. Clarke that she did not want her mother to take her to "her own doctor" because they would make her go to a hospital and she did not want to do it.

April 26, 1932.—Nancy came in today because of an infected toe. She made light of her ailment.

April 30, 1932.—Nancy went to see Dr. Watson at the Child Guidance Clinic by appointment.

May 1, 1932.—Nancy was at home all day. She got back to the cottage at seven-thirty, one-half hour late. Mr. Saylor brought her. After a day at home Nancy lapses into baby talk for a day or two. She seemed sad and somewhat upset.

June 8, 1932.—When the superintendent visited Rose Cottage, Nancy asked in a very important tone to talk to her alone. She complained in a whining voice that Aunt Ida, assistant cottage mother, was very cruel to her. That morning she was helping make the toast and allowed it to burn in the oven. Aunt Ida called her stupid for doing this. Nancy resented this and refused to do any of her work all morning, and talked back to Aunt Ida. When Aunt Elizabeth, cottage mother, came home at noon she told Nancy that she would have to wash all the dishes after supper by herself as punishment for her refusal to work in the morning. This Nancy considered too much of a punishment. The superintendent told Nancy that she should not complain over such small things. She asked Nancy if she were never rude to Aunt Ida and Aunt Elizabeth. Nancy admitted at once that she was often rude and that she should accept occasional scoldings from them without whining even though they might seem too severe.[2] Nancy cried and said she would be careful after this not to complain unless she actually had something worth complaining about. She went in to do the dishes as she had been asked to do.

June 12, 1932.—Nancy Saylor in hospital for two days with cold and headache. She said she was going home as soon as school is out. When she left for the cottage, she said goodbye and said when she left here, she knew she would never see us again. Her mother would never let her visit. She seemed unhappy about going home.

June 17, 1932.—Nancy was dismissed from the Children's Agency.

[2] [Superintendent explained that though she was always ready to listen to the children and wanted them to be happy, she did not approve of complaining over trifles.]

INDEX

INDEX